# CONTESTING ECONOMIC AND SOCIAL RIGHTS IN IRELAND

Why do states opt to constitutionally entrench economic and social rights? Why do societies demand them? These are the central puzzles of *Contesting Economic and Social Rights in Ireland.* While most studies of socio-economic rights focus on legal or normative argumentation, Thomas Murray proposes that questions of rights and redistribution necessitate the analysis of power and freedom in society. He illustrates the politics of socio-economic rights through an in-depth case study of the evolution of socio-economic rights conflicts, discourses, and constitutionalism in Ireland. Murray draws on new archival, case-law, and statistical research to reconstruct socio-economic rights discourses from across Irish society, to demonstrate the tension between state and civil society discourses, and to trace an untold history of their contested development over time. From the mid-nineteenth to the early twenty-first century, Ireland's conservative and nationalist constitutional projects have tended to dominate or incorporate social democratic and radical ones, albeit in a process continually contested at critical junctures. The rich and diverse history of people's struggles for justice 'from below' – from organic courts in days of popular militancy to unemployed marches, from housing action protestors to striking workers – provides an alternative, oppositional perspective on constitutionalism from which to recuperate and assess the possibilities and limits of advocating economic and social rights today.

THOMAS MURRAY is Lecturer in Equality Studies at the School of Social Policy, Social Work, and Social Justice, University College Dublin, Ireland. He is a former visiting researcher at the Institute of Social Sciences and Humanities, Benemérita Universidad Autónoma de Puebla, Mexico.

# CONTESTING ECONOMIC AND SOCIAL RIGHTS IN IRELAND

## Constitution, State, and Society, 1848–2016

*Thomas Murray*
*University College Dublin*

CAMBRIDGE
UNIVERSITY PRESS

**CAMBRIDGE**
**UNIVERSITY PRESS**

University Printing House, Cambridge CB2 8BS, United Kingdom

Cambridge University Press is part of the University of Cambridge.

It furthers the University's mission by disseminating knowledge in the pursuit of education, learning and research at the highest international levels of excellence.

www.cambridge.org
Information on this title: www.cambridge.org/9781107155350



First published 2016

*A catalogue record for this publication is available from the British Library*

ISBN 9781107155350 Hardback

Additional resources for this publication at www.cambridge.org/

*For my grandmothers,*
*Kathleen Holohan and Theresa Murray*

# CONTENTS

*Acknowledgments* *page* viii

Introduction: The Politics of Economic and Social Rights 1

1 Constitution 'from Below' in Ireland: 1848–1922 48

2 'Not Alone Personal Liberty but Economic Freedom': Socio-economic Rights in the Making of the 1922 Irish Free State Constitution 84

3 'Highly Dangerous'? Socio-economic Rights in the Making of the 1937 Irish Constitution 112

4 Contesting the Irish Constitution and the World-System: 1945–2008 160

5 The Polarities of Justice and Legal Business 187

6 Contesting Property Rights 209

7 Contesting Trade Union Rights 230

8 Contesting Family, Education, and Welfare Rights 245

9 Reproducing the Value-Consensus State 271

10 Constitution 'from Below' in Ireland: 1945–2008 293

Conclusion: Contesting Economic and Social Rights Today 326

*Bibliography* 354
*Index* 381

# ACKNOWLEDGMENTS

I first thought about writing this book in Santa Clara, Cuba, began researching it in Dublin, Ireland, and more or less concluded it in the mountains of Chiapas, Mexico. Throughout my travels, many generous people have provided me with help, advice, and encouragement. They are all, of course, innocent of the results. I would like to thank, first and foremost, Graham Finlay, my doctoral advisor at University College Dublin, for his extraordinary dedication, wise counsel, and good humour. He continues to be a terrific source of encouragement, philosophy, and insight. Sincere thanks also to John Coakley, John O'Dowd, Bryan Fanning, Thomas Mohr, and Robert Fine, who each took an active, enthusiastic interest in my work. They helpfully critiqued this book's earliest, roughest drafts and provided much needed advice besides.

My research simply would not have been possible without the dedicated staff of UCD Library and Archives, Pearse Street Public Library, the National Library of Ireland, the National Archives of Ireland, and the New York Public Library. They were unfailing in their courtesy and helpfulness. I should also like to acknowledge the UCD School of Politics and International Relations (SPIRe), the UCD Graduate Research and Innovation Fund, and the Irish Research Council for their financial support during my doctoral studies.

Thank you to Finola O'Sullivan and the publishing team at Cambridge University Press for their advice, patience, and practical support. Thanks, in particular, to the anonymous reviewers whose invaluable advice helped the book's final revisions a great deal.

Beyond the immediate writing process, this book and its author have been shaped by many kind words of friendship and wisdom. I have been fortunate to enjoy the company of outstanding colleagues at UCD SPIRe, UCD School of History and Archives, UCD Centre for Adult Education, the Institute of Public Administration, and now the UCD School of Social Policy, Social Work, and Social Justice. Thank you, in particular, to John Baker, Tom Garvin, Niamh Hardiman, Iseult Honohan, Attracta Ingram, Michael Laffan, Conor McCabe, Michael Mulreany, Conor Mulvagh, Michelle Norris, Andy Storey, Ben Tonra, and Judy Walsh. A special word of thanks to John Heffernan, who first introduced me to Karl Marx, judicial vampires, and the Paris Commune as an undergraduate; something clearly resonated. Thanks also to all of my own students down through the years, some of whom may be surprised to discover that our classroom discussions were often seedbeds for the ideas presented here.

A wider, almost invisible community of active scholars and scholar-activists influenced the book's ideas and arguments. In particular, I received many helpful comments and suggestions from participants at numerous conferences, seminars, and workshops, including the Political Studies Association of Ireland, the European Consortium of Political Research, the Irish Jurisprudence Society, the DCU Centre for Socio-Legal Studies, the Irish Centre for the History of Labour and Class, the World-Ecology Network, the Left Forum, and Historical Materialism as well as the Dublin Anarchist Bookfair. Special thanks to Paul Bowman, Donal Coffey, Laurence Cox, Sharae Deckard, Brian Fagan, Andrew Flood, Tom Hickey, Mark Hoskins, Gregor Kerr, Farah Mokhtareizadeh, Gary Murphy, Aileen O'Carroll, Sinéad Pembroke, Seán Prior, John Roche, Dermot Sreenan, Gerry Whyte, and Joel Kupferman.

The Institute of Social Sciences and Humanities, Benemérita Universidad Autónoma de Puebla, Mexico, provided a fresh, volcanic environment for making final manuscript revisions. Thanks to each member of its committed community of staff and students. Heartfelt thanks, in particular, to Edith Gonzálaz, Sagrario da Saude, Dawn Paley, Daniele Empoli, Hierson Rojas, and John Holloway for coffee, conversation, and much laughter while I finished the book. I also learned a great deal at the Zapatista community of Oventic, Chiapas. Thanks to Natalio, Paloma, Stephanie, and Efraín for sharing their community with me, as well as to Nancy and Liam for creating a home away from home in San Cristóbal de las Casas.

Thanks to all my friends, including Colm, Francis, Jamie, Marty, Michael Sharkey, Niamh, Gauri, Peter, Colin, Matthew, Rachel, Robbie, Robert, Michael Timmons, Adam, and Sef.

Finally, much love and thanks to my family, in particular, to my always amazing sisters, Theresa and Debbie, and to my always supportive parents, Sheila and Joe. *Contesting Economic and Social*

*Rights in Ireland* is dedicated to their mothers – Kathleen and Theresa – strong, loving, and inspiring women who lived through many of the changes described in these pages. Finally, to Sharae, *grá geal mo chroí*, thank you.

# INTRODUCTION: THE POLITICS OF ECONOMIC AND SOCIAL RIGHTS

*There is no more potent tool for rupture than the reconstruction of genesis: by bringing back into view the conflicts and confrontations of the early beginnings and therefore all the discarded possibles, it retrieves the possibility that things could have been (and still could be) otherwise. And through such a practical utopia, it questions the 'possible' which among all others, was actualised.*

– Pierre Bourdieu[1]

*Constitutional problems are not primarily problems of law, but of power.*

– Ferdinand Lasalle[2]

IRELAND'S MULTITUDES were unexpected.[3] On 1 November 2014, more than 150,000 people filled and made lively the country's rain-drenched streets and city centres. From Dublin to Galway and Cork to Donegal, some one hundred protest groups gathered in their communities to demonstrate their opposition to Irish Water, a water-metering utility introduced after the financial crisis of 2008 as part of Ireland's bailout programme. Over the preceding year, the initial actions of community groups physically preventing the installation of water meters had grown into a countrywide celebration of civil disobedience and mass refusal to pay water charges. People had had enough. 'Austerity has gone too far' was the most cited reason given for protesting. Other reasons given were 'to stop the future privatisation of water', to abolish

[1] Pierre Bourdieu, 1994, 'Rethinking the State: Genesis and Structure of the Bureaucratic Field' in *Sociological Theory*, 12 (1), pp. 1–18, p. 4.

[2] Ferdinand Lassalle, 1976 [1862], *What is a Constitution?* Barcelona: Editorial Ariel, p. 5.

[3] 'Ireland' is generally used throughout this book to refer to the twenty-six counties of the Republic of Ireland. Depending on the political context, this territory has also been designated the Irish Free State, Eire, the Irish Republic, and Ireland. See John Coakley, 2009, '"Irish Republic," "Eire," or "Ireland"? The Contested Name of John Bull's Other Island' in *Political Quarterly*, 80 (1), pp. 49–58.

water charges and to oppose the 'bank bailouts/debt'. Water, some demonstrators claimed, was 'not for profit' but 'a human right'.[4]

Certain organisations sought to give formal expression to talk of human rights on the streets. On May Day, 2015, the 'Right2Water' campaign announced its 'Policy Principles for a Progressive Irish Government'.[5] The campaign advocated the constitutional recognition of rights to water and to housing, accompanied by rights to jobs and decent work, to health, to debt justice, to education, and to democratic reform.[6] Similarly, the previous year, the government-appointed Constitutional Convention voted by a majority of more than 80 per cent to create constitutional rights to health, housing, and adequate living standards, including those rights listed in the International Covenant for Economic, Social, and Cultural Rights (ICESCR).[7] Both the 'Right2Water' campaign and the Constitutional Convention suggest wider support for socio-economic rights. According to one recent poll, more than 70 per cent of the Irish public believes that the Constitution should be amended to protect additional rights such as those to health and social security.[8]

The Irish government, responding to these mass mobilisations and to organisations' claims for economic and social rights, has maintained the state's traditional stance as to their legally binding status. This position has involved rhetorical support for socio-economic rights at a domestic level and, internationally, becoming party to the ICESCR.[9] However,

[4] Rory Hearne, 2015, 'The Irish water war, austerity, and the "Risen people": An analysis of participant opinions, social and political impacts, and transformative potential of the Irish anti-water-charges movement', pp. 2, 15. Available at: www.maynoothuniversity.ie/sites/default/files/assets/document/TheIrishWaterwar_0.pdf.

[5] The Right2Water campaign is an umbrella group of the trade unions UNITE, MANDATE, the Communication Workers Union, the Civil and Public Services Union, and OPATSI. It is an important element of a much broader, decentralised community movement that includes anti-austerity groups, opposition and left political parties, and independent TDs (Teachtaí Dála, Irish: Dáil deputies or members of parliament).

[6] These rights are considered necessary for creating a fair and democratic society today and, intriguingly, for realising the historic promises of the 1867 and the 1916 Proclamations of the Irish Republic. Available at: www.mandate.ie/Documents/111930_12796_R2W-Unions_Policies_A5.pdf.

[7] The one hundred-member Convention comprised of a chairman, twenty-nine parliamentary members of the Oireachtas, four representatives from Northern Ireland's political parties, and sixty-six randomly selected citizens. Its remit concerned a narrow range of provisions but a concerted civil society effort by a range of non-governmental organisations (NGOs) facilitated its considering the inclusion of socio-economic rights on its agenda. See www.constitution.ie.

[8] Amnesty International Ireland, 2014, *Bringing ESC Rights Home*. Dublin: Amnesty Publications, p. 7.

[9] Ireland signed the ICESCR in 1989, and further signed up to introducing a complaints mechanism in 2012. However, in the absence of sufficient political will, the state has yet to give

the Irish state has also consistently opposed basing legislative or administrative provisions explicitly on the recognition of specific socio-economic rights as international human rights, and further opposed the provision of effective means of redress to individuals or groups alleging violations of those rights.[10] Historically, various Irish governments have further opposed the constitutional entrenchment of socio-economic rights. In June 2015, the Irish government effectively reaffirmed this position in its submission to the United Nations Committee for Economic, Social, and Cultural Rights.[11]

The contemporary water struggle in Ireland illustrates how diverse groups across the political spectrum can use the discourse of universal human rights ideologically, which is to say in a manner that promotes particular forms of politics in order to advance particular interests and values. For the state, its commitment to socio-economic rights is compatible with continuing austerity policies in pursuit of economic growth and with vetoing a referendum to constitutionalise socio-economic rights. Conversely, trade unions and NGOs demand such rights be realised more immediately through state intervention and constitutional entrenchment. Rupturing this traditional left-right debate on the role of the state, many of Ireland's water protestors took the law into their own hands, taking direct action to prevent the installation of water meters, and to uphold their claimed human rights. Invoking a discourse of universal norms then are quite distinct political actors with quite distinct interests articulating different visions of socio-economic rights and of the means needed to realise them.

The 'essentially contested' nature of socio-economic rights raises challenging questions about their usefulness to political projects for human emancipation, questions closely linked to the nature of power and freedom in contemporary society.[12] This book proposes a critical interrogation of the politics of constitutionalising economic and social

domestic legal effect to the range of rights committed to under international law, or to fund effective complaints and monitoring systems. See Noeline Blackwell, 'Government only paying lip service to economic right to housing', in *Irish Times*, 10 December 2015.

[10] As of July 2015, 164 states were parties to the ICESCR. See UN Treaty Collection, 2014. Available at: https://treaties.un.org/Pages/ViewDetails.aspx?src=TREATY&mtdsg_no=IV-3&chapter=4&lang=en. See also Henry Steiner, Philip Alston, and Ryan Goodman (eds.), 2008, *International Human Rights in Context*, Oxford: Oxford University Press, p. 264.

[11] I return to the politics of socio-economic rights in contemporary Ireland in the concluding chapter.

[12] W. B. Gallie, 1955–6, 'Essentially Contested Concepts' in *Proceedings of the Aristotelian Society, New Series*, Vol. 56, pp. 167–98; see also Steven Lukes, 2005, *Power: a radical view*. London: Macmillan.

rights, focusing primarily on the contested role of socio-economic rights in the emergence, making, and development of the 1937 Constitution of Ireland. I aim to demonstrate whose rights were secured and to account for why this was this case. The book's purpose, in effect, is to tell the largely untold story of the 1937 Irish Constitution as a site of social conflict, paying particular attention to the contestation of socio-economic rights 'from below'.[13] The analysis then is not about whether constitutions should include economic and social rights so much as it is the broader ethico-political relations implicated in their consideration and contestation.[14]

The politics of constitutionalising socio-economic rights, I suggest, may be most fruitfully understood as a world-systemic politics.[15] On this account, the presence, effectiveness, and role of socio-economic rights in a state's constitutional order will vary primarily according to its core or peripheral position in the 'historical capitalist world-system' and the local balance of contending 'anti-systemic forces'.[16] Constitutional transformations in Ireland, from the nineteenth to the early twenty-first century, have involved important conflicts over socio-economic rights and their realisation. Associated debates in state and society have ranged from the meaning of economic sovereignty to the ownership of natural resources, from control of the credit system to the provision of

[13] Boaventura de Sousa Santos and César A. Rodríguez-Garavito, 2005, *Law and Globalization from Below: Towards a Cosmopolitan Legality*. Cambridge: Cambridge Studies in Law and Society. Balakrishnan Rajagopal, 2003, *International Law from Below: Development, Social Movements and Third World Resistance*. Cambridge: Cambridge University Press.

[14] Considering people's socio-economic rights claims as 'ethico-political' draws attention to an epistemology of power as hegemony, one in which politics is not prioritised over economics, and both are never privileged over understanding moral, intellectual, or everyday life. See Richard Howson, 'From ethico-political hegemony to Post-Marxism' in Marcus E. Green (ed.), 2011, *Rethinking Gramsci*. London: Routledge, pp. 167–76, p. 170.

[15] World-systems analysis is an interdisciplinary approach to understanding the emergence of the modern world. Inquiry typically concentrates on world-systems rather than nation-states, emphasises the need to consider historical processes over long periods of time, and synthesises bodies of knowledge traditionally viewed as distinct disciplines, including history, economics, political science, sociology, and law. Within this approach, the world-system of historical capitalism is generally understood as forming a social reality comprised of interconnected nations, firms, households, classes, and identity groups of all kinds, connected through two key, contested processes: the evolving transnational division and integration of labour and processes of state formation and decline. See Immanuel Wallerstein, 2004, *World-Systems Analysis: An Introduction*. Durham, NC: Duke University Press.

[16] On the Marxian idea of the law crystallising contending social forces, see Robert Fine, 1995, *Democracy and the Rule of Law*. London: Pluto. On the historical capitalist world-system and anti-systemic movements, see Giovanni Arrighi, Terence Hopkins, and Immanuel Wallerstein, 2011, *Anti-Systemic Movements*. New York: Verso; Giovanni Arrighi, 1994, *The Long Twentieth Century: Money, Power and the Origins of Our Times*. London: Verso.

health, housing, and education. Thus far, conservative and nationalist constitutional projects have tended to either dominate or incorporate social democratic and radical ones, albeit in a process continually contested at critical junctures by civil society and by the organised left, both old and new.[17] The rich and diverse history of people's struggles for justice 'from below' provides an alternative, oppositional perspective on constitutional development from which to assess and recuperate the possibilities and limits of advocating socio-economic rights today.

The present chapter seeks to ground these aims and arguments more substantively. I outline the strengths and limitations of the existing literature on the politics of constitutionalising economic and social rights before justifying the use of world-systems analysis as well as the selection of the Irish case-study. The closing sections detail the merits of critical discourse analysis as a means of revealing the relationship between particular statist and revolutionary discourses on rights and the general, contested development of the historical capitalist world-system. In tracing this relationship, I draw on a rich tradition of critical social theory of law, from Karl Marx through Antonio Gramsci to Pierre Bourdieu, and a wide range of primary and secondary sources to construct a new account of socio-economic rights and constitution-making in Ireland. First, however, I outline precisely why this kind of analysis is important, now more than ever.

## SOCIO-ECONOMIC RIGHTS IN CRISIS: TOWARDS DAVOS OR PORTO ALEGRE?

Neoliberal capitalism staggers on.[18] The contemporary period of political and economic malaise is not a passing, momentary difficulty in an essentially equilibrated capitalist system but rather a pronounced structural crisis of world-systemic proportions, characterised by simultaneous, linked crises of ecology, capitalism, and democracy. Politically, what is currently at stake is the successor system to a capitalist

[17] 'Civil society' is understood critically here to mean those contested, changing spaces of human interaction, association, and community formation in which competing norms and organisations emerge, develop, and reshape society. Civil society is distinct from and presents an implicit challenge to both state and capital, suggesting a potentiality for the greater diffusion of power in society. See Paul Ginsborg, 2005, *The Politics of Everyday Life: Making Choices, Changing Lives*. Cambridge: Yale University Press.

[18] Gérard Duménil and Dominque Lévy, 2010, *The Crisis of Neoliberalism*. Cambridge: Harvard University Press. David Harvey, 2007, *A Brief History of Neoliberalism*. Oxford: Oxford University Press.

world-economy in terminal decline.[19] Immanuel Wallerstein has identified two opposing, diffuse groups in this struggle over the world-system's future development trajectory.[20] Proponents of the 'spirit of Davos' want a different system, one that is no longer capitalist but still retains three of its worst features: hierarchy, exploitation, and polarisation. A pronounced and increasing concentration of wealth and power in the capitalist world-economy underpins this convergence of interests.[21] Today, the world's richest 85 people control more wealth than the poorest 3.5 billion.[22]

The remarkable consistency of approach to crisis resolution adopted by governments in the Global North is a function of this spirit. Responding to the credit crunch of 2007–8, governments and technocrats had states assume responsibility for spectacular levels of debt created by private banking institutions. While the question of who must pay for the crisis lingers, those most directly responsible, 'the party of Wall Street', soon emerged larger and emboldened.[23] Meanwhile, under the banners of 'national competitiveness' and 'economic necessity', ensuing economic stagnation provided opportunities to press for the further neoliberalisation of our societies. The 'tough decisions' determined by these 'realities' will result in the further erosion of working conditions and living standards; the further undermining of the welfare state; and the further enclosure and privatisation of existing bio-environmental and intellectual commons.[24] 'Social Europe', as the

[19] Rumours of capitalism's demise have often been exaggerated. To be clear, however, this is an argument concerning its medium-term prospects to the mid-twenty-first century, based primarily on the historic development of the capitalist world-system and the ongoing instability prompted by the signal crisis of the US-led cycle of accumulation from the 1970s onwards. Immanuel Wallerstein, 2011, 'Structural Crisis in the World-System: Where Do We Go from Here?' in *Monthly Review*, 62 (10), pp. 1–7. See also Henrik Braconier, Giuseppe Nicoletti, and Ben Westmore, 2014, 'Policy Challenges for the Next 50 Years', *OECD Economic Policy Papers*, No. 9, Paris: OECD Publishing; Paul Mason, 2015, *Postcapitalism*. London: Allen Lane.

[20] Immanuel Wallerstein, 2014, 'Anti-Systemic Movements, Yesterday and Today' in *Journal of World-Systems Research*, 20 (2), pp. 158–72, p. 171.

[21] Some 0.15 per cent of the world's population (10.9 million people), mostly white, male, and concentrated in core regions of North America, Europe, and Japan, effectively control two-thirds of the world's GDP; 0.001 per cent (73,000 people or so), control one-fifth, some $15.4 trillion. See www.tni.org/report/state-corporate-power-2012. See also Chrystia Freeland, 2013, *Plutocrats: the rise of the new global super-rich*. London: Penguin.

[22] Ricardo Fuentes-Nieva and Nicholas Galasso, 2014, *Working for the Few*. London: Oxfam Publications. Available at: www.oxfam.org/en/policy/working-for-the-few-economic-inequality.

[23] David Harvey, 2011, 'Rebels on the Street: The Party of Wall Street Meets its Nemesis', 28 October 2011. Available at: www.versobooks.com/blogs/777-david-harvey-the-party-of-wall-street-meets-its-nemesis.

[24] David Harvey, 2012, *Rebel Cities*. London: Verso; 2010, *The Enigma of Capital*. London: Profile. On 'tough' decision-making, see Tony Judt, 2010, *Ill Fares the Land: A Treatise on our present*

president of the European Central Bank announced in 2012, is 'already gone'.[25]

Conversely, proponents of the 'spirit of Porto Alegre' want a system that has not existed before, 'one that is relatively democratic and relatively egalitarian'.[26] The uprising of the Ejército Zapatista de Libéración Nacional (EZLN) in January 1994 marked the beginning of a world left counteroffensive against the relatively short-lived successes of the world right between the 1970s and 1994. The EZLN paved the way for successful alter-globalisation protests at Seattle in 1999, for the formation of the World Social Forum in Porto Alegre in 2001, and for the emergence of what is now known as the Global Justice Movement.[27] Similarly, across Europe and North America in 2011, by pitching tents at Wall Street and associated sites of financial power, Occupy, the Indignados, and associated movements of the city squares succeeded in placing not simply inequality but capitalism – the unnamed name for the dominant force of social organisation – as a focus of public debate.[28] Simultaneously, these groups raised important questions about contemporary societies' minimalist structures of public participation and provided a canvass for the presentation of all manner of grievances and struggles.[29] Calls for economic and social rights have featured consistently amidst diverse civil society and scholarly responses to these tumultuous events.[30]

'Economic and social rights' are understood here to mean people's ethico-political claims to a better way of life, the understanding, expression, contestation, institutionalisation, and realisation of which have

*discontents*. London: Allen Lane; Mark Fisher, 2009, *Capitalist Realism: Is there no alternative?* London: Zero Books.

[25] 'Q&A: ECB President Mario Draghi' in *Wall Street Journal*, 23 February 2012. Available at: http://blogs.wsj.com/eurocrisis/2012/02/23/qa-ecb-president-mario-draghi/.

[26] Wallerstein, 2011, 'Structural Crisis in the World-System', pp. 1–2.

[27] See Immanuel Wallerstein, 2014, 'The Neo-Zapatistas: Twenty Years After'. Available at: http://iwallerstein.com/neozapatistas-twenty-years/.

[28] Richard Wolff, 'Occupy Wall Street ends capitalism's alibi' in the *Guardian*, 4 October 2011. Available at: www.guardian.co.uk/commentisfree/cifamerica/2011/oct/04/occupy-wall-street-new-york.

[29] David Graeber, 2013, *The Democracy Project: a history, a crisis, a movement*. London: Allen Lane; Federico Campagna and Emanuele Campiglio, 2012, *What We Are Fighting For: a radical collective manifesto*. London: Pluto.

[30] In the United States, Columbia University Seminar on Full Employment, Social Welfare, and Equity, 'A New Bill of Rights for the 21st century'. 18.10.2013; in Ireland, Amnesty Ireland Conference, 'Human Rights, Human Dignity: Health and Housing in Ireland'. 21.10.2008; and in Switzerland, COHRE, 2003, Litigating economic, social, and cultural rights: achievements, challenges, and strategies. Geneva, Switzerland: Centre on Housing Rights and Evictions. On the recent intensification of socio-economic rights contestations, see Katharine Young, 2012, *Constituting Economic and Social Rights*. Oxford: Oxford University Press, p. 12.

all changed dramatically over time. This is a broader interpretation than that adopted by many legal scholars and sociologists who usually define social and economic rights as normative and legal claims to specific material resources, notably social security, work, leisure, health, housing, education, water, and food.[31] In this regard, these accounts typically follow the work of British sociologist Thomas Marshall, whose classic categorisation distinguished the emergence of social rights in the twentieth century from the development of civil and political rights, including property rights, in the eighteenth and nineteenth centuries, respectively.[32] In contrast, the politics of economic and social rights, at least as envisaged here, considers both formal and popular rights discourses as well as the historically emergent social relations out of which they arise and to which they refer.[33]

In defence of considering socio-economic rights as contingent historical phenomena with fluid meanings rather than historical or cultural universals, it should be noted that adopting too rigid a definition risks side-lining subaltern usages. Not infrequently, popular discourses challenge or ignore established, often state-centric or formal concepts and understandings. Similarly, our accepting Marshall's 'generations of rights' thesis *a priori* risks naturalising a hierarchy of rights, making the constitutionalisation of property rights or the discarding of welfare rights appear more inevitable than might actually have been the case.[34] Recognition of the porosity of socio-economic rights discourse leaves open to inquiry the respective importance of various rights in any given historical moment.[35] Finally, narrow understandings of socio-economic rights typically concentrate on questions of distribution, downplaying the social processes or power relations that make redistribution necessary. In particular, a broad understanding of social and economic rights facilitates a closer examination of the tensions amongst property rights, production, and rights to resource (re)allocation.

31 On the flexibility of socio-economic rights discourse, see Tom Campbell, 2006, *Rights: A Critical Introduction*. London: Routledge, p. xiiii, 159–63; see also Asborn Eide, 2001, *Economic, Social, and Cultural rights: a textbook*, London: M. Nijhoff; P. R. Ghandhi, 2000, *Blackstone's International Human Rights Documents*. London: Blackstone.

32 T. H. Marshall, 1950, *Citizenship and Social Class*. Cambridge: Cambridge University Press.

33 On this approach, we can best appreciate what socio-economic rights actually mean by comparing and contrasting our uses of them now with other earlier uses or their progenitors. Gallie, 1955–6, 'Essentially Contested Concepts'; see also, Campbell, 2006, *Rights*, p. xvii.

34 Irish constitution-makers in the 1920s used the term 'economic rights' to refer to both property and welfare rights, suggesting a greater degree of equivalence than might otherwise be assumed.

35 Additionally, in single-country case studies, definitions of socio-economic rights tend to vary according to local usage. See Malcolm Langford, 'The Justiciability of Social Rights: From Practice to Theory' in Malcolm Langford (ed.), 2008, *Social Rights Jurisprudence: emerging trends in international and comparative law*. Cambridge: Cambridge University Press, pp. 3–45, p. 3.

Where demands for socio-economic rights are mobilised and seriously considered, resulting political and academic debates tend to take place within certain coordinates. One key locus of discussion concerns what should be designated, claimed, and upheld as a socio-economic right, if indeed anything should at all.[36] Advocates forward the state's protection of citizens' minimal living standards as a means of ensuring peoples' well-being, social cohesion, and civic participation. They also emphasise the interdependence and indivisibility of all human rights: socio-economic rights are thus considered necessary to the enjoyment of civil and political rights, and vice versa.[37] Traditionally, those opposed to recognising socio-economic rights tend to argue that the state should restrict itself to enforcing 'negative' rights of non-interference such as the individual's right to property or to freedom of speech and association. On this view, 'positive' rights to welfare provision amount to so many state distortions of otherwise equilibrated markets and, moreover, threaten to diminish individual liberty and initiative.[38]

A related point of debate concerns how socio-economic rights, if accepted, can be given content and used to defend or improve living standards in practice. Approaches here include national, regional, and international monitoring through domestic legislatures and courts as well as inter-state commissions, courts, and organisations.[39] Among the most important institutions involved in the resurgence of socio-economic rights from the late 1980s onwards has been the United Nations Committee on Economic, Social, and Cultural Rights.[40] Following the pioneering jurisprudence of the South African Constitutional Court in the 1990s, one approach, that of explicitly stating socio-economic rights in the state's basic law or constitution and

[36] See Steiner, Alston, and Goodman (eds.), 2008, *International Human Rights in Context*, pp. 263–94.

[37] Rosalind Dixon, 2007, 'Creating dialogue about socio-economic rights' in *International Journal of Constitutional Law*, 5 (3), pp. 391–418. See also Amartya Sen, 1999, *Development as Freedom*. New York: Random House.

[38] F. B. Cross, 2001, 'The Error of Positive Rights' in *UCLA Law Review*, 48 (4), pp. 857–924; Cass Sunstein, 1993, 'Against Positive Rights' in *East European Constitutional Review*, 2 (1), ff. 35; Robert Dahl, 1957, 'Decision-making in a Democracy: Supreme Court as national policy-maker' in *Journal of Public Law*, 6 (2), pp. 279–95.

[39] Examples of regional procedural mechanisms include the Inter-American Commission on Human Rights or the European Committee of Social Rights. See also Steiner, Alston, and Goodman (eds.), 2008, *International Human Rights in Context*, pp. 295–374.

[40] Malcolm Langford and Jeff A. King, 'Committee on Economic, Social, and Cultural Rights: Past, Present, and Future' in Malcolm Langford (ed.), 2008, *Social Rights Jurisprudence: emerging trends in international and comparative law*. Cambridge: Cambridge University Press, pp. 477–516, p. 477.

providing judicial enforcement mechanisms, has become particularly prominent.[41]

The particular debate on the justiciability of socio-economic rights reflects an influential, schismatic understanding of human rights, dividing 'negative' civil and political rights from 'positive' claims to redistribution or socio-economic redress.[42] Proponents claim that elected parliaments frequently marginalise the poor and that constitutional guarantees of minimal living standards are necessary to ensure their political influence and fairer resource re-allocation in future.[43] National judiciaries can gain competencies either in directly re-allocating resources or in engaging in 'constitutional dialogue' with the executive in order to ensure that decision-making concerning core rights and living standards is robustly and publically justified.[44] On this view, judicial interpretations of economic and social rights can transform existing administrative practices and political norms.[45]

Conversely, opponents argue that budgets and associated decision-making on socio-economic rights standards are the preserve of democratically elected and accountable parliaments and governments. Reforms that might concentrate more power in the hands of unelected and therefore unaccountable judiciaries ought therefore to be opposed.[46] On this view, the turn towards judicial review procedures favours those with sufficient resources to pursue a litigation strategy and empowers a legal intelligentsia at the expense of other political fora.[47] Moreover, concentrating on judicial review and even winning

41 While the focus of this book concerns the politics of constitutionalising socio-economic rights in one country, it is important to acknowledge the diversity of movements and groups seeking to advance or claim socio-economic internationally and through various mechanisms. In particular, international developments, notably those within the UN or various constitutional courts, can interact in important ways with developments within states to build support for making socio-economic rights justiciable. See Philip Alston, 'Foreword' in Langford (ed.), 2012, *Social Rights Jurisprudence*, Cambridge: Cambridge University Press, pp. ix–xiv, pp. ix, xii.

42 See Isaiah Berlin, 1958, *Two Concepts of Liberty*. Oxford: Clarendon Press.

43 William Forbath, 2012, 'Workers' Rights and the Distributive Constitution' in *Dissent*, Spring, pp. 58–65. See also William Forbarth with Joseph Fishkin, 2014, 'The Anti-Oligarchy Constitution' in *Boston University Law Review*, 94, ff. 669.

44 Varun Gauri and Daniel Brinks (eds.), 2010, *Courting Social Justice: Judicial Enforcement of Social and Economic Rights in the Developing World*. Cambridge: Cambridge University Press.

45 Danie Brand, 'Introduction' in Danie Brand and Christof Heyns (eds.), 2005, *Socio-Economic Rights in South Africa*. Pretoria: Pretoria University Law Press, pp. 1–56. On the merits of constitutional dialogue and processes of value-based, deliberative problem solving, see Young, 2012, *Constituting Economic and Social Rights*.

46 Ran Hirschl, 2007, *Towards Juristocracy: the origins and consequences of the new constitutionalism*, Cambridge: Harvard University Press; 2004, 'The Political Origins of the New Constitutionalism' in *Indiana Journal of Global Legal Studies*, 11, pp. 71–108.

47 See Duncan Kennedy, 1998, A *Critique of Adjudication: fin de siécle*. Harvard: Harvard University Press.

socio-economic rights-claims on an individual, case-by-case basis risks diverting attention from underlying social conditions and majoritarian political arenas, whether parliament or civil society.[48]

In the battle between the spirits of Davos and Porto Alegre, then, the discourse of socio-economic rights appears strangely compatible with both. In terms of the latter, 'courts have ordered the reconnection of water supplies, the halting of forced evictions, the provision of medical treatments, the reinstatement of social security benefits, the enrolment of poor children and minorities in schools, and the development and improvement of State programmes to address homelessness, endemic diseases, and starvation'.[49] Moreover, the discourse of socio-economic rights still appears useful to those who would politicise economic decision-making in order to make it more democratic and more egalitarian. Proponents argue for contemporary movements' resuscitation of earlier socio-economic rights projects, such as Franklin D. Roosevelt's 'second bill of rights' in the United States, or highlight recent experiments in popular constitution-making, notably in Bolivia, Ecuador, and Iceland, which have linked material rights to well-being with opposition to neoliberalism, ecological sustainability, decommodification, and direct democracy.[50]

At the same time, however, socio-economic rights discourses both re-emerged with and featured in the 'new right' or neoliberal rhetoric of both Ronald Reagan and Margaret Thatcher who envisaged retaining

48 For a critique of judicial review and argument in favour of reformed institutions, see Richard Bellamy, 2007, *Political Constitutionalism: A Republican Defence of the Constitutionality of Democracy*. Cambridge: Cambridge University Press. For discussion of the potential demobilising effects of litigation strategies on social movements, see Tshepo Madlingozi, 'Post-Apartheid Social Movements and Legal Mobilisation' in M. Langford, B. Cousins, J. Dugard, and T. Madlingozi (eds.), 2013, *Socio-economic Rights in South Africa: Symbol or Substance?* Cambridge: Cambridge University Press.

49 The fact that there are now some two thousand judicial and quasi-judicial decisions from twenty-nine national and international jurisdictions on such rights is non-trivial. See Malcolm Langford, 'The Justiciability of Social Rights: From Practice to Theory' in Malcolm Langford (ed.), 2008, *Social Rights Jurisprudence: emerging trends in international and comparative law*. Cambridge: Cambridge University Press, pp. 3–45, p. 3.

50 In a wartime State of the Union address, Roosevelt proposed a right to employment, with a living wage; farmers' rights to a fair income; freedom from unfair competition and monopolies; a right to food, clothing, and leisure; a right to housing; a right to medical care; a right to social security and a right to education. On liberal and Marxist arguments for their revitalisation, see Sunstein (2004, *The Second Bill of Rights)* and Harvey (2010, *The Enigma of Capital*, pp. 253–9; 2007, *A Brief History of Neoliberalism*, p. 294), respectively. On recent, popular constitution-making experiments, see Phoebe King, 'Neo-Bolivarian Constitutional Design' and Anne Meuwese, 'Popular Constitution-Making in Iceland' in Denis Galligan and Mila Versteeg, 2013, *Social and Political Foundations of Constitutions*. Cambridge: Cambridge University Press, pp. 366–97 and 469–96.

a minimum social safety net, sufficient to enable equal opportunity to participate in the market.[51] In practice, the constitutional recognition of socio-economic rights in countries such as India and South Africa appears to have neither impeded their neoliberal economic development, nor lessened rapidly widening social inequality.[52] Conversely, the welfare provisions that now exist to varying degrees in contemporary states 'emerged as a result of an emphasis on public goods, the general welfare and the common good, not as an expression of rights'.[53] Notably, Sweden, Finland, and Denmark have long adhered to a robust welfare regime while being less than enthusiastic about judicial review and constitutional rights. Socio-economic rights thus appear 'quite negligible' factors in terms of ensuring human development.[54] The crucial difference between these competing conceptions of socio-economic rights centres on political agency, specifically the means or process by which such rights are realised as well as the ultimate horizon or vision of society envisaged by those who demand them. This vital point requires unpacking.

Ambiguities in the theory and practice of socio-economic rights relate to a wider tendency of human rights discourse and activism towards the suppression or dissimulation of the political. Marx's critique of rights is vital here, reminding us that rights discourses covertly accept a division characteristic of capitalist society between the state (enforcing rights) and civil society (comprised of atomised, individual rights-bearers).[55] Conceiving of the world in terms of 'rights' potentially imposes limitations on making collective demands against systemic

[51] Cass Sunstein, 2005, 'Why does the American Constitution lack Social and Economic Guarantees?' in *Syracuse Law Review*, 56, pp. 1–25. On the *de facto* harmonisation of socio-economic rights standards with neoliberal globalisation, see Paul O'Connell, 2011, 'The Death of Socio-Economic Rights' in *Modern Law Review*, 74 (4), pp. 532–54.

[52] Balakrishnan Rajagapol, 'Socio-economic rights and the Indian Supreme Court' in Steiner, Alston, and Goodman (eds.), 2008, *International Human Rights in Context*, pp. 326–7. See also D. M. Davis, 2006. 'Adjudicating the socio-economic rights in the South African constitution: towards "deference lite"?' in *South African Journal on Human Rights*, 22, pp. 301–27; Paul O'Connell, 2011, 'The Death of Socio-Economic Rights' in *Modern Law Review*, 74 (4), pp. 532–54.

[53] Campbell, 2006, *Rights*, p. 9.

[54] Ran Hirschl and Evan Rosevear, 'Constitutional Law Meets Comparative Politics: Socio-economic Rights and Political Realities' in Tom Campbell, K. D. Ewing, and Adam Tomkins (eds.), 2011, *The Legal Protection of Human Rights: Sceptical Essays*. Oxford: Oxford University Press, pp. 207–28, pp. 213, 223. See also Marius Pieterse, 2007, 'Eating Socioeconomic Rights: The Usefulness of Rights Talk in Alleviating Social Hardship Revisited' in *Human Rights Quarterly*, 29: 3, pp. 796–822.

[55] Karl Marx, 'On the Jewish Question' in O'Malley, Joseph (ed.), 1994, *Marx's Early Political Writings*, pp. 28–56. See also Robert Fine, 1995, *Democracy and the Rule of Law*. London: Pluto; Tom

problems (such as unemployment) or on imagining radical transformation (such as the decentralised worker control of production).[56] Socio-economic rights discourses, by depicting 'the poor' or 'socially excluded' as minoritarian categories, emerge as claims to state protections against the apparently arbitrary nature of poverty.[57] A more robust challenging of the state's actual relationship to 'poverty' and 'social exclusion' is discomforting for those actors and NGOs dependent on the state for funding or for ameliorating particular social conditions, always in the short term.[58]

The politics of constitutionalising economic and social rights is thus far from straightforward but rather continually poses important, contested ethico-political decisions. There is always a danger here of merely treating the symptoms of social problems (unequal distribution) rather than their source (the process by which unequal distributions are produced).[59] A similar health warning attaches to proponents of any political project that would dissimulate power relations, thereby reproducing existing structures of authority and domination or replacing them with new ones. Recognising this, I suggest, it is important to reconfigure the coordinates of the debate on constitutionalising socio-economic rights, that of the legitimacy of their entrenchment or judicial recognition, towards a clear-sighted, critical analysis of the broader ethico-political processes and relations out of which these decisions arise and to which they refer.

## THE POLITICS OF CONSTITUTIONALISING ECONOMIC AND SOCIAL RIGHTS

> No mere declaration of rights can suffice; institutions are required to make the rights effective.
>
> – Karl Polanyi[60]

Campbell, 1983, *The Left and Rights: A Conceptual Analysis of the Idea of Socialist Rights*. London: Routledge and Kegan Paul; and Hugh Collins, 1982, *Marxism and Law*, Oxford: Oxford University Press.

56 Duncan Kennedy, 1982, 'Legal Education as Training for Hierarchy' in *Journal of Legal Education*, 32, pp. 591–615, p. 598.

57 Duncan Kennedy, 'Three Globalisations of Law and Legal Thought: 1850–2000' in David Trubek and Alvaro Santos, 2006, *The New Law and Economic Development: a Critical Appraisal*, pp. 19–73, p. 67.

58 Harvey, 2010, *The Enigma of Capital*, p. 253. See also INCITE! Women of Colour against Violence, 2009, *The Revolution Will Not Be Funded*. Cambridge, MA: South End Press.

59 Karl Marx, 'Critique of the Gotha Programme' in Terrell Carver (ed.), 1996, *Marx's Later Political Writings*. Cambridge: Cambridge University Press, p. 215.

60 Karl Polanyi, 1944, *The Great Transformation: The Political and Economic Origins of Our Time*. Boston: Beacon Press, p. 76.

> Constitutions written at the great turning-points of history always embody decisions about the future structure of society. Furthermore, a constitution is more than its legal text; it is also a myth demanding loyalty to an externally valid value system.
>
> – Franz Neumann[61]

The historical origins of both society and state recognition of economic and social rights are diffuse, with diverse roots in the world's major religions, philosophical traditions, and political programmes.[62] The most prominent constitutional precedents include the Constitution of Mexico (1917), the first and subsequent Soviet Constitutions in Russia, and the Constitution of the Weimar Republic (1919). Indicative of a wider process of increased state and society recognition, socio-economic rights featured prominently alongside civil-political rights in the 1948 Universal Declaration of Human Rights. Thereafter, the emergence of socio-economic rights co-evolved with the rapid diffusion of higher law constitutionalism and judicial review in the second half of the twentieth century.[63] A dramatic increase in the number of social and economic rights expressly protected in constitutional texts has since occurred, beginning with a set of postcolonial constitutions in the 1960s, and sharply increasing after the collapse of the Soviet Union in 1990.[64] Over the same period, the debate on their substantive recognition became synonymous with the political and ideological divisions of the Cold War era and, from the 1970s onwards, between the Global North and South. In this respect, the constitutional courts of India and, in particular, South Africa featured most prominently among the world's providers of ground-breaking socio-economic rights case-law.[65]

Today, some three-quarters of the world's written constitutions refer to a right to education, nearly half to a right to health care, and most also include a more generic protection of the 'right to life' or of 'human dignity'.[66] Judicial interventions on behalf of socio-economic rights have also come to occupy an important role in the politics of

61 Franz Neumann, 1966 [1942], *Behemoth: the structure and practice of national socialism*. New York: Oxford University Press, p. 17.

62 Steiner, Alston, and Goodman, 2008, *International Human Rights in Context*, p. 269.

63 Alec Stone Sweet, 'Constitutions, Rights, and Judicial Power' in Daniele Caramani (ed.), 2011, *Comparative Politics*. Oxford: Oxford University Press, pp. 218–39, p. 233.

64 David Law and Mila Versteeg. 2011. 'The Evolution and Ideology of Global Constitutionalism'. *California Law Review* 99(5): 1163–257.

65 See Philip Alston, 'Foreword' in Langford (ed.), 2012, *Social Rights Jurisprudence*. Cambridge: Cambridge University Press, pp. ix–xiv, pp. ix.

66 V. Gauri and D. Brinks (eds.), 2010, *Courting Social Justice*, p. 1.

welfare.[67] Comparative studies suggest that poor countries and countries with socialist traditions tend to have on average higher constitutional commitments to socio-economic rights.[68] Unsurprisingly, then, Latin American constitutions include more economic and social rights, and more justiciable economic and social rights, than any other region of the world. Amidst the wider literatures of comparative constitutional law and political science, however, works specifically addressing why states constitutionally entrench socio-economic rights occupy a remarkably short shelf space.[69] We might usefully divide these works according to their falling along a schematic spectrum between 'formalist' and 'instrumentalist' approaches to jurisprudential or socio-legal inquiry.[70]

Towards the formalist pole are those who consider constitutional law to be autonomous from the social world and who look primarily to comparative constitutional law in order to identify and elaborate legal principles through formal reasoning.[71] While this tends to be the 'professional ideology' of legal practitioners, both conservative and liberal political commentators more generally tend to accord the law primacy to other social phenomena.[72] Jurisprudential analyses of this sort

[67] 'In one Brazilian state alone, Rio Grande do Sul, right to health cases grew from 1,126 in 2002 to 17,025 in 2009; that same year the highest non-constitutional court in Brazil heard nearly six thousand such cases, resulting in large percentages of state medication budgets being allocated by courts. The Indonesian Constitutional Court issued a series of opinions from 2004–2006 that doubled budget allocations to the education sector – redirecting about 5 per cent of the entire national budget. In 2004 the South African Constitutional Court required a recalcitrant Mbeki government to launch a major program to prevent the transmission of HIV from mothers to infants, likely averting tens of thousands of HIV infections. In India, the courts have issued numerous consequential rulings on the constitutional rights to health care, education, housing, the environment, nutrition, and labour. Even in Russia people turn to the courts by the hundreds of thousands in efforts to secure pensions'. Daniel M. Brinks and Varun Gauri, 2014, 'The Law's Majestic Equality? The Distributive Impact of Judicializing Social and Economic Rights' in *American Political Science Association*, 12 (2), pp. 375–93, p. 377.

[68] Avi Ben-Bassat and Momi Dahan, 2008, 'Social Rights in the Constitution and in Practice' in *Journal of Comparative Economics*, 36 (1), pp. 103–19. Courtney Jung and Evan Rosevear, 2011, *Economic and Social Rights in Developing Country Constitutions: preliminary report on the TIESR data set.* Toronto Initiative on Economic and Social Rights.

[69] Mark Tushnet, 2009, *Weak Courts, Strong Rights: Judicial Review and Social Welfare Rights in Comparative Constitutional Law*. Princeton: Princeton University Press, pp. 3–17; see also Hirschl and Rosevear, 'Constitutional Law Meets Comparative Politics: Socio-economic Rights and Political Realities', p. 207.

[70] Pierre Bourdieu, 1987, 'The Force of Law: Toward a Sociology of the Juridical Field' in *Hastings Law Journal*, Vol. 38, pp. 805–53.

[71] Hans Kelsen's 'pure formalism', which identifies in the law a self-contained universe of norms, is a paradigmatic example. See Kelsen, 1967, *Pure Theory of Law*. Berkeley: University of California Press.

[72] Friedrich Hayek, 1990, *The Constitution of Liberty*. London: Routledge. H. L. A. Hart, 1997, *The Concept of Law*. Oxford: Oxford University Press.

make up the majority of recently published research on constitutions.[73] Providing or denying formal legal or normative justification for the constitutional recognition of socio-economic rights – rather than explaining why recognition occurs or linking it to wider socio-political transformation – is the primary concern of this cosmopolitan literature.[74] Implicitly, by focussing on the necessity of alternative modes of legal reasoning, constituent assemblies and constitutional courts emerge as the primary arenas where the entrenchment of socio-economic rights is made possible.

Towards the instrumentalist pole, conversely, are those who view constitutional law as registering and reproducing wider societal dynamics, whether those are prevailing values, interests, or institutional arrangements. We might characterise these approaches as 'cultural contextualist' (or 'expressivist'), 'materialist contextualist', and 'functionalist', respectively. Cultural contextualists concentrate on establishing whether constitutionalising or 'inventing' socio-economic rights is congruent with a society's wider norms.[75] Cass Sunstein, for example, has demonstrated not only the deep normative roots of the New Dealers' 'Second Bill of Rights' in American political culture but also how the Supreme Court's later rejection of those norms registered a growing cultural conservativism in the 1970s.[76] Similarly, for Paulo Wright-Carozza, the 1917 Mexican constitution, including its socio-economic rights provisions, served as a model to other Latin American countries because it 'tapped into the broadly shared understandings of human dignity and society'.[77]

'Functionalist' accounts emphasise the relationship between constitutions, state-building, and state legitimacy, underlining the domestic

[73] Alec Stone Sweet, 2011, 'Constitutions, Rights, and Judicial Power', p. 218.

[74] On the normative tension between values of democracy and distributive justice, see Cecil Fabre, 2000, *Social Rights under the Constitution: government and the decent life*. Oxford: Oxford University Press. See also Sandra Fredman, 2008, *Human Rights Transformed? Positive Rights and Positive Duties*. Oxford: Oxford University Press; Henry Shue, 1996, *Basic Rights: Subsistence, Affluence, and US Foreign Policy*. Princeton: Princeton University Press. In the Irish context, Gerry Whyte has provided a *tour de force* elaboration of potential legal-normative bases for reading socio-economic rights into the Irish Constitution. Whyte, 2002, *Social Inclusion and the Legal System: Public Interest Law in Ireland*, Dublin: Institute of Public Administration. See also Aoife Nolan, 'Ireland' in Malcolm Langford (ed.), 2012, *Social Rights Jurisprudence: emerging trends in international and comparative law*. Cambridge: Cambridge University Press, pp. 295–322.

[75] Lynn Hunt, 2007, *Inventing Human Rights: a history*. London: Norton.

[76] Sunstein, 2004, *The Second Bill of Rights*. New York: Basic.

[77] Paulo W. Carozza, 2003, 'From Conquest to Constitutions: Retrieving a Latin American Tradition of the Idea of Human Rights' in *Human Rights Quarterly*, 25 (2), pp. 281–314, p. 311.

and international necessity of written constitutions expressing legal-rational principles for the stable, predictable control of authority. These accounts draw particular attention to how constitutions emerge from and relate to a wider, often pre-existing institutional context.[78] In terms of socio-economic rights, there would appear to be a higher level of entrenchment in French civil law jurisdictions, notably in Spain, Portugal, and Latin American countries, than in English common law countries.[79] More particularly, socio-economic rights' constitutional entrenchment will typically follow, not precede, a state's more gradual development of statutory welfare codes.[80] Notably, the Constitution of the Weimar Republic recognised economic and social rights, but only after World War I had made a capital-labour compromise a necessary and institutional reality.[81] Similarly, the turn towards public interest litigation to constitutionalise socio-economic rights from the 1970s onwards resulted from minoritarian groups' attempts to circumvent 'blocked' parliamentary and corporatist institutions.[82] Recent work on socio-economic rights has synthesised formalist analyses of legal norms with contextualist accounts of culture and institutions.[83]

Finally, interest-based accounts of socio-economic rights entrenchment emphasise the wider social relations or constellations of power that determine constitutional development. Analyses in this genre characteristically underline the relationship between constitutionalism and anti-majoritarian politics, specifically the defence of the rights of propertied minorities from mob-rule or, in the precise meaning the Greeks attributed to the term, 'democracy'. Charles Beard's 'economic interpretation' of the US Constitution remains the classic work in

78 Those in power often turn to constitutions, courts, and judicial review as a means of insuring their policy priorities against those political uncertainties inherent in constitutional design or in changing social and electoral contexts. Tom Ginsburg, 2003, *Judicial Review in New Democracies: Constitutional Courts in Asian Cases*. Cambridge: Cambridge University Press, p. 18; see also the discussion on 'constitution-as-function' in Zachary Elkins, Tom Ginsburg, and James Melton, 2009, *The Endurance of National Constitutions*. Cambridge: Cambridge University Press, pp. 38–47.

79 Ben-Bassat and Dahan, 2008, 'Social Rights in the Constitution and in Practice'.

80 Mary Ann Glendon, 1992, 'Rights in Twentieth-Century Constitutions' in *University of Chicago Law Review*, Vol. 59, pp. 519–38.

81 Chris Thornhill, 2013, *A Sociology of Constitutions*. Cambridge: Cambridge University Press, pp. 275–326.

82 Kennedy, 2006, 'Three Globalisations of Law and Legal Thought: 1850–2000', pp. 66–7. See also Cappelletti, Mauro (ed.), 1981, *Access to Justice and the Welfare State*. Florence: European University Institute.

83 See Young, 2012, *Constituting Economic and Social Rights*.

this genre, although his findings have been improved upon.[84] Similar dynamics applied in situations of postcolonial constitution-making. In newly decolonised Ghana (1957), Nigeria (1959), and Kenya (1960), political elites promoted the constitutional entrenchment of rights as devices for protecting established interests from majoritarian politics.[85] Seen from this perspective, then, Western states began to recognise economic and social rights primarily as part of national elites' conservative strategy to counter the growing popularity of socialist ideas arising out of the Russian Revolution.[86] While social rights, as Thomas Marshall observed, accompanied the gradual growth of income equality and enlargement of citizenship status, the aim of such rights remained that of 'class-abatement'.[87]

This collective body of scholarship may nevertheless be challenged on the grounds of its theoretical approaches and assumptions. Formalist and culturalist accounts often accord the law primacy to other social phenomena. Hence, when the crucial tension between established rights to property and claimed rights to resource reallocation is examined, the violent, 'de-sacralised' power relations and implications of property rights regimes are more often hidden or assumed than explicitly examined.[88] Closely related to liberalism more generally, these perspectives tend to assume the state is a neutral site through which the conflict of competing interests can be resolved fairly and to reduce the political to that which takes place through the state. Conversely, in dismissing as 'ideological' or 'epiphenomenal' the structure of constitutional forms, functionalist, and interest-based accounts risk emptying their analyses of the specific role of the legal field in the reproduction of those power relations that they claim to reveal.[89]

[84] Charles Beard, 1921 [1913], *An Economic Interpretation of the Constitution of the United States*. New York: Macmillan. See Graeber, 2013, *The Democracy Project*, pp. 150–83.

[85] Hirschl, 2007, *Towards Juristocracy*, p. 4; Julian Go, 2003, 'A Globalizing Constitutionalism? Views from the Postcolony, 1945–2000' in *International Sociology*, 18:1, pp. 71–95.

[86] J. T. Shotwell, 1933, 'The International Labor Organisation as an Alternative to Violent Revolution' in *The Annals of the American Academy of Political and Social Science*, 166, pp. 18–25. See also Eric Hobsbawm, 1992, *Nations and Nationalism since 1780: Programme, Myth, Reality*. Cambridge: Cambridge University Press, pp. 101–63.

[87] '[C]lass-abatement in this form was not an attack on the class system. On the contrary, it aimed, often quite consciously, at making the class system less vulnerable to attack by alleviating its less defensible consequences'. Marshall, 1950, *Citizenship and Social Class*. Cambridge: Cambridge University Press, pp. 32–3.

[88] Rosa Congost, 2003, 'Property Rights and Historical Analysis' in *Past and Present*, 181 (Nov.), pp. 73–106.

[89] Bourdieu, 1987, 'The Force of Law', pp. 805–53.

The recent postmodern turn in socio-legal analysis, away from Marxist and Weberian foundational theories towards law's 'formative contexts', has prompted a much closer consideration of the symbolic systems or discourses implicated in the reproduction of law and legality.[90] In the Marxist theoretical canon, in particular, the 'relative autonomy' of the law, a partial response to the problematic 'base-superstructure' metaphor, has consistently been acknowledged to be among its most unsatisfactory elements.[91] Politically, this position is associated with privileging the urban proletariat as the revolutionary subject, thereby occasioning problematic blind spots regarding the intersection of class with gender, race, postcoloniality, sexual orientation, or multiple 'other' identities.[92] Marx's positioning of the state as the primary mechanism for bringing about revolutionary transformation has also been challenged, notably by recent scholarship concerning the micro-politics of discipline, surveillance, and liberation.[93]

Ultimately, these competing approaches share a central point of contention: the law's autonomy within society. This theoretical debate, Pierre Bourdieu suggested, cannot be resolved *a priori*. In place of the false dichotomy suggested by formalist and instrumentalist accounts, the law's autonomy must itself be interrogated in terms of its emergence from particular 'historical conditions' and previous social struggles.[94] This evaluation of the significance of examining the particular historic development of constitutional discourses presupposes a certain conception of the problem of ideology – in the present instance, competing 'socio-economic rights' ideologies, a certain conception of the relationship between theory and history as well as a certain conception of emancipatory social transformation. These theoretical assumptions and their methodological implications need to be spelled out before we examine

90 Roberto Unger, 1996, 'Legal Analysis as Institutional Imagination' in *Modern Law Review*, Vol. 59, (1), pp. 1–23, p. 20. Kennedy, 2006, 'Three Globalisations of Law and Legal Thought: 1850–2000', pp. 66–7, 71. See also David Harvey, 1989, *The Conditions of Postmodernity*. Oxford: Blackwell.

91 Karl Marx, 'Preface to "A Contribution to the Critique of Political Economy"' in Terrell Carver (ed.), 1996, *Marx's Later Political Writings*. Cambridge: Cambridge University Press. Fine, 1985, *Democracy and the Rule of Law*.

92 Catharine A. MacKinnon, 1982, 'Feminism, Marxism, Method, and the State: An Agenda for Theory' in *Signs*, Vol. 7, No. 3, pp. 515–44.

93 Balakrishnan Rajagopal, 2003, 'International Law and Social Movements: challenges of theorising resistance' in *Colombia Journal of Transnational Law*, 41:2, pp. 397–433, pp. 413–5; on new ways of rethinking Marx and liberation, see John Holloway, 2010, *Crack Capitalism*. London: Pluto Press.

94 Bourdieu, 1987, 'The Force of Law', p. 815.

the concrete politics of constitution-making and rights contestation in Ireland.

## CO-CONSTITUTIVE TRANSFORMATION: THE DIALECTIC OF LAW, SOCIETY, AND HISTORY

The politics of constitutionalising socio-economic rights is, as I suggested at the outset, most usefully understood as a 'world-systemic' politics. In this dialectical mode of inquiry, constitutions and economic rights are accorded neither primacy nor 'epiphenomenality'; their development is accounted for in neither formalist nor instrumentalist terms. A world-systems analysis seeks to integrate the insights of formalist, cultural contextualist, institutionalist, and interest-based accounts and to account for the development of constitutional forms in terms of their forming part of 'a rich totality of many determinations and relations'.[95] Specifically, it is considered possible to acknowledge the production of constitutional norms, rights, and discourses as part and parcel of the transformation of a symbolic order, while nevertheless insisting on understanding these developments within an overall frame of historical materialist inquiry (emphasising money power and capital circulation) and class politics.[96] More precisely, the presence, justiciability, and ultimate effectiveness of socio-economic rights in a state's constitutional order will vary primarily according to its core or peripheral position in the 'historical capitalist world-system' and the domestic balance of contending 'anti-systemic forces'.[97]

Responding to the strengths and limitations of formalist and instrumentalist inquiries outlined earlier, the present study attempts to synthesise these perspectives within an overall frame of a reconstructed world-systems analysis, the better to analyse and understand the values, ideas, institutions, interests, and social relations operative in the social phenomenon of economic rights contestation and entrenchment. In place of a reductive economism or statism, however, this work is animated by an attempt to pursue a rigorously dialectical mode of thought and analysis. Somewhat alien to the cause–effect model typically forwarded in the social sciences, this form of analysis emphasises

[95] Karl Marx, [1857], '"Introduction" to the Grundrisse' in Carver, 1996, *Marx's Later Political Writings*, p. 146.
[96] See Harvey, 1989, *The Conditions of Postmodernity*, p. 355.
[97] See next section. See also Arrighi, Hopkins, and Wallerstein, 2011, *Anti-Systemic Movements*, p. 30.

a logic of process or change, outlining the relation-based nature of 'human society or social humanity', as well as the incessant flux or movement of these structured relations.[98] Social transformation is understood as a subjective movement, or 'sensible human activity, practice' as Marx puts it, in which material conditions (natural and social) are constraints that delimit a range of possibilities for human action.[99]

Dialectical inquiry, then, must first consider the 'given' nature of the lens through which we view the social world. Marx's discussion on 'the method of political economy' is precisely relevant here. Categories of investigation tend to be given in a particular society and, hence, social inquiry 'does not *really* begin *scientifically* where it is first talked about *as such*'.[100] This problem is potentially acute when studying law or constitution-making as a social phenomenon. As Bourdieu puts it, since the self-evidence or common-sense of 'the field of law' comes without saying, it also goes without saying. Those social agents most directly responsible for the reproduction of the legal field come to reproduce practices and discourses tending towards the deep sedimentation of orthodoxies, relations of power and domination resistant to recognition or conscious articulation and, as such, to change.[101] In general, therefore, critical inquiry aims to deconstruct given categories of experience of 'socio-economic rights' contestation, legal or otherwise, in order to reformulate that experience according to a more holistic analysis of law as practice, as sensible human activity.

More particularly, this commitment to dialectical inquiry has important implications for how one might theorise the relationship between law and society as well as for our approach to the analysis of historically specific matrices of constitutional law and socio-economic rights. In terms of the former, the claim that legal institutions and ideas have 'a dynamic, or dialectical, or constitutive relationship' to social and economic activity is of such long-standing as to be almost axiomatic.[102] Here too, Marx provides a useful, albeit incomplete, critique of the role of law in society.[103] In early societies based on petty commodity

[98] See Bertell Ollmann, 2000, 'What Is Political Science? What Should It Be?' in *New Political Science*, 22: 4, pp. 553–62, p. 559.
[99] Karl Marx, 1992, *The German Ideology, including Theses on Feuerbach*. New York: Prometheus Books. See also Peter Osborne, 2005, *How to Read Marx*. London: Granta Books, pp. 27, 43.
[100] Marx, '"Introduction" to the *Grundrisse*' in Carver, 1996, *Marx's Later Political Writings*, p. 152.
[101] Bourdieu, 1987, 'The Force of Law', p. 848.
[102] See Kennedy, 2006, 'Three Globalisations of Law and Legal Thought: 1850–2000', pp. 19–20.
[103] Fine, 1984, *Democracy and the Rule of Law*, pp. 100–7.

production, he suggested, the juridical relation, taking the form of the contract, was co-constitutive of the economic relation. With the generalisation of commodity production, however, the level of coercion required to enforce rights to property and exchange increased; proprietors thus established a force greater than their own capacities to do so, the state. With the onset of capitalist relations of production, the 'wage-contract' between labour and capital took on the appearance of a simple exchange in form. Freely agreed to in theory, however, the contract concealed coercive social relations, capital's extraction of surplus-value from labour, in practice.[104]

Thus, law mystified social relations between people, making them appear in the form of private relations between people and things, that is to say, as rights of property. Marx's critique, then, moves beyond simply revealing exploitative social relations and the role of the state in ensuring their reproduction but further suggests legal mystification as generative of a potent synthesis of both coercion and consent. In capitalist societies, workers, as guardians of a property (labour-power), are offered 'a wide field of choice, of arbitrary will, hence of formal freedom'.[105] Through the state, moreover, the organised working class could assert their 'rights as free labourers' against the rights of capitalists as free owners of private property. Importantly, at this point of regulating relations between people, the law's independence stands out firmly. Later generations of Marxist scholars, notably Wolf Heydebrand, have emphasised how this 'objectivity' is facilitated by institutional developments, notably the specialisation of the functions of apprehension, adjudication, and punishment in the police, courts, and penal system, respectively. Courts are central to the legitimation of public authority yet access is largely mediated by the private sale of legal services, prompting a recurring contradiction between their functioning as sites of legal business and of justice.[106] Nevertheless, this range of freedom, albeit limited, transforms ideologies centred on the sanctity of 'rights' into viable means of persuasion.

This critique directly informs Marx's aforementioned rejection of 'rights' consciousness but it also introduces the possibility, largely unexplored by Marx, of considering seriously the politics of law and rights

104 See in particular Marx's criticism of Jeremy Bentham's 'classic' conception of the contract as the expression of both employers' and workers' autonomous 'free will'. Karl Marx, 2003 [1887], *Capital I: A Critique of Political Economy*, p. 172.

105 Fine, 1984, *Democracy and the Rule of Law*, p. 120.

106 Wolf Heydebrand, 1977, 'Organizational Contradictions in Public Bureaucracies: Toward a Marxian Theory of Organizations' in *The Sociological Quarterly*, Vol. 18 (1), pp. 83–107, p. 97.

as experienced by dominated groups. By problematising the relationship between law and mass consciousness, Antonio Gramsci provides an important contribution here.[107] This relationship is one of 'hegemony', through which class domination is not always exercised by coercion but by securing political legitimacy and the active consent of the governed. Crucially, for Gramsci, the law's inherent contradictions, such as those between proclaimed norms and substantive inequality or injustice, generated 'contradictory consciousness' and the possibility of a 'good' as opposed to 'common' sense of law and justice amidst the dominated class. The law, therefore, cannot be reduced to an economic base but rather provides a terrain of struggle between contending class forces. Any particular, historically achieved matrix of law and rights thus reflects a crystallisation of the balance of power, coercive and consensual, between contending class forces.

In the present analysis, I use the term 'constitution from below' to denote the social phenomenon whereby participants in a conflict claim 'socio-economic rights' outside of the law's formal norms, institutions, and processes. In practice, this might involve people reading economic demands or 'natural rights' into the state constitution or drawing attention to the gap between the document's expressed ideals and existing state practices or even actively constituting collective senses, spaces, and practices of justice through direct actions such as boycotting, squatting, or striking. The recuperation of lived experiences of rights contestation challenges the extent to which established Marxian socio-legal analysis may privilege theory over the popular experience of history as life. With decidedly ethico-political implications, it provides an approach to inquiry more sympathetic to including and understanding the diverse voices of gender, race, postcoloniality, and sexual orientation amongst all kinds of 'others'.[108] It also challenges us to think critically about politics, often in ways that do not privilege the state and the winning of state power as the primary, even exclusive mechanism for emancipatory social transformation.[109] This reorientation further offers hope of overcoming the tendency of left-wing projects of social

[107] Duncan Kennedy, 1982, 'Antonio Gramsci and the Legal System', *Vol. VI, ALSA Forum No. 1, 1979*, p. 36. Rajagopal, 2003, 'International Law and Social Movements', pp. 426–30. See also Eric Hobsbawm, 2011, *How to Change the World: Reflections on Marx and Marxism*. New Haven: Yale University Press. pp. 314–34.

[108] Unger, 1996, 'Legal Analysis as Institutional Imagination', p. 20; MacKinnon, 1982, 'Feminism, Marxism, Method, and the State', pp. 515–44. See also Harvey, 1989, *The Conditions of Postmodernity*.

[109] Rajagopal, 2003, *International Law from Below*.

transformation to accentuate categorisations of domination to the detriment of ways of talking about liberation.[110]

The autonomist Marxist, Antonio Negri, provides a succinct, provocative summary of the overall theorisation of the relationship between law and emancipation forwarded here.[111] Instead of the notion of 'the people' found in the bourgeois constitution, in which the many are subsumed under the unity of the state, a subsuming that conceals, misrecognises, and therefore helps to reproduce the interests of the dominant, Negri offers the concept of 'proletarian constitution'.[112] He is concerned precisely with those involved in collective resistance, with those asserting an alternative to the valorisation processes commanded by the State ('the exclusive representative of collective capital'), with those asserting 'the time of life'. It is constructed along two paths. The first affirms a separation from/antagonism against the State; the second is that which takes place within and from within this separation. Proletarian constitution thus 'sinks its base in the autonomous expression of values: self-valorisation, auto-determination, community . . . [I]t is eminently practical determined liberation'.[113]

Viewed in this way, the recent wave of movements in the world's city squares, cresting in late 2011 and early 2012, 'give new meanings to freedom, our relation to the common, and a series of central political arrangements, which far exceed the bounds of the current republican constitutions . . . They are foundational principles that we already take to be inalienable rights, like those that were heralded in the course of the eighteenth-century revolutions'.[114] These movements, having inspired 'a revolution at the level of common sense', provide an alternative understanding of freedom, democracy, and emancipation from which to view the development and significance of earlier constitutional forms.[115] However, the extent to which theorisations of law, rights, and society can shed light on the concrete histories of a particular matrix of socio-economic rights is far from straightforward.[116] In this

[110] Holloway, 2010, *Crack Capitalism*.

[111] Antonio Negri, 2003, *Time for Revolution*. London: Continuum.

[112] The class content of 'proletarian' is not simply ready-made, to be read off a catalogue of empirical differences such as occupation or income; rather class distinctions are always an effect of struggle, of collective resistance to power. See Matteo Mandarini, 'Translator's Introduction' in Negri, 2003, *Time for Revolution*, p. 6.

[113] Negri, 2003, *Time for Revolution*, p. 124.

[114] Michael Hardt and Antonio Negri, 2012, 'Take Up the Baton' in *Jacobin Magazine*, 5. Available at: www.jacobinmag.com/2012/05/take-up-the-baton/.

[115] See Graeber, 2013, *The Democracy Project*.

[116] See E. P. Thompson, 1981, *Whigs and Hunters: the origin of the Black Act*. London: Breviary.

regard, the key contribution of world-systems analysis, the approach adopted here, is to bridge this division of theory and history by positioning the 'historical capitalist world-system' as the primary unit of analysis.

## CONSTITUTIONS AND SOCIO-ECONOMIC RIGHTS IN THE HISTORICAL CAPITALIST WORLD-SYSTEM

The world's earliest written constitutions, such as those documented by Aristotle in Greece in the fourth century BC, typically delineated the distribution of authority within a political community. Although potentially misleading as a guide to actual practice, this 'power map' broadly set out the formal rules, functions, and institutions of government.[117] In some cases, more explicitly normative constitutions further enunciated the political community's assumed collective aims or values. In seventh-century Japan, for example, Prince Shōtoku's 'Seventeen-Article Constitution' outlined the Buddhist and Confucian virtues required of the Emperor's subjects and officials for the good running of the state. From the late eighteenth century onwards, however, as the Age of Revolutions swept Europe and the Americas, the modern state constitution was re-imagined to act as a limit to the arbitrary power of government, particularly to separate the functions of government from private influence.[118] The goal, as A. V. Dicey put it, was to substitute 'a government of laws' for 'a government of men', thereby ensuring, in an instructive choice of words, 'equality before the law, or the equal subjection of all classes to the ordinary law of the land'.[119] Constitutionalism, as Carl Friedrich later claimed, would provide 'a system of effective, regularised restraints upon government action'.[120] Among the most important of such restraints was the explicit statement of constitutional rights.

In the modern era of state constitutionalism, from the late eighteenth century to the present, new constitutions have typically been created in the wake of exceptional circumstances or crises, their framers generally

117 I. Duchacek, 1973, *Power Maps: The Comparative Politics of Constitutions*. California: University of California Press; Giovanni Sartori, 1994, *Comparative Constitutional Engineering: An Inquiry into Structures, Incentives, and Outcomes*. Basingstoke: Macmillan.

118 Thornhill, 2013, *A Sociology of Constitutions*, p. 196. See also Immanuel Wallerstein, 1989, 'The French Revolution as a World-Historical Event' in *Social Research*, 56:1, pp. 33–52.

119 Alfred Venn Dicey, 2005 [1885], *An Introduction to the Study of the Law of the Constitution*. London: Elibron, p. 198.

120 Carl Friedrich, 1937, *Constitutional Government and Politics*. New York: Harper.

seeking to endow a newly emergent regime with authority.[121] Seven 'waves' of modern constitution-making, Jon Elster suggests, occurred in the wake of major socio-political upheavals, including (1) the late eighteenth-century constitutions of the post-revolutionary United States, Poland, and France; (2) the 1848 revolutionary constitutions of Europe; (3) the post–World War I constitutions of 'new' European nation-states; (4) the post–World War II constitutions of Japan, Germany, and Italy; (5) the post-decolonisation constitutions of Africa, Asia, and South America; (6) the mid-1970s constitutions of newly democratised Southern Europe; and (7) the post-1989 constitutions of post-communist Central and Eastern Europe.[122] Albeit minimally elaborated, Elster's thesis of constitutional waves is nevertheless richly suggestive and merits development.

Drawing on the theorisation of law and society outlined in the previous section, I suggest that the various constitutional forms and particular rights matrices emergent in each 'wave' crystallised the shifting balance of systemic and anti-systemic relations in the historical capitalist world-system (see Table I.1). There are good *prima facie* reasons for thinking so. The crisis events for each of Elster's constitutional 'waves' correspond in remarkable ways with significant turning points in the contested formation of the world-system. Examined more closely, the qualitative nature of each wave's constitutional forms, expressing nationalist, liberal, social democratic, or social revolutionary ideologies to varying degrees, also correspond with the demands of contemporary popular anti-systemic movements in core or peripheral regions. Potentially accounting for these changes, Duncan Kennedy has forwarded an important periodisation (and geographical understanding) of three overlapping 'globalisations' of 'classic' (1850–1930), 'social' (1900 to c. 1970), and 'neoformal' (c. 1945 onwards) law and legal thought.[123] However, world-systems analysis, by foregrounding the contested development of cycles of accumulation in the historical capitalist world-system, not only incorporates the transnational nature of various nation-states' constitutional transformations but more usefully

[121] Constitutions are thus often short-lived experiments, with only half enduring beyond nineteen years. Zachary Elkins, Tom Ginsburg, and James Melton, 2009, *The Endurance of National Constitutions*. Cambridge: Cambridge University Press.

[122] Jon Elster, 1995, 'Forces and Mechanisms in the Constitution-Making Process' in *Duke Law Journal*, Vol. 45, No. 2, pp. 364–96, p. 368.

[123] Each globalisation provided a broadly shared conceptual or justificatory vocabulary of socio-legal change, not a one-size-fits-all model of law reform. Kennedy, 2006, 'Three Globalisations of Law and Legal Thought: 1850–2000', pp. 22–3.

TABLE I.1 Constitutional waves in the historical capitalist world-system

| Legal thought | Crisis | Constitutional waves |
|---|---|---|
| Classic (1848–1930) | '1789' | Various US states, the United States, Poland, and France |
| | '1848' | Europe: France, Germany, Italy (regions) |
| Social (1900–1970) | '1917' | Post–World War I 'new' European states<br>Post–World War II Japan, Germany, and Italy |
| Neoformal (1945–) | '1968' | De-colonisation:Africa, Asia, and South America<br>Liberal Democratisation: Greece, Spain, and Portugal |
| Neoliberal (1989–) | '1989' | Neo-Liberal Democratisation:<br>Central and Eastern Europe; South Africa<br>Afghanistan and Iraq; attempted EU constitution |

*Sources*: Elster, 1995, 'Forces and Mechanisms in the Constitution-Making Process'; Kennedy, 2006, 'Three Globalisations of Law and Legal Thought: 1850–2000'; Arrighi, Hopkins, and Wallerstein, 2011, *Anti-Systemic Movements*.

accounts for the timing of such transitions in legal institutions and ideas. This critical summation requires unpacking.

The world-system of historical capitalism, as outlined in the work of Giovanni Arrighi, Terrence Hopkins, and Immanuel Wallerstein, combined two key, mutually reinforcing processes: the creation of an economic world-system and the formation of an inter-state world-system.[124] The former process involved the development of an inter-regional division of labour along a continuum of 'core', 'semi-peripheral', and 'peripheral' locales, with high-skilled, capital-intensive accumulation taking place towards the former pole and low-skilled, labour-intensive production, notably resource extraction, taking place towards the latter. Concomitantly, the inter-state system's emergence was central to providing security of labour-power, property, and trade as well as opening up new markets, colonies, and ecologies to exploitation.

[124] Arrighi, Hopkins, and Wallerstein, 2011, *Anti-Systemic Movements*.

Historically, throughout the long nineteenth century, the world-systemic core lay in Europe, underpinned by free trade and an inter-state system dominated by a number of 'Great Powers', including France, Germany, and, pre-eminently, the British Empire. World War I marked a decisive moment of rupture, signalling the decline of the British Empire's hegemony. Following World War II, the United States emerged as the leading capitalist core. During a new cycle of 'free enterprise' accumulation, multinational corporations spearheaded growing international trade and the US acted as 'hegemon' in the inter-state system.[125] This process produced a number of crucial antagonisms and corresponding anti-systemic movements, which may be divided, for analytical purposes only, into 'social' and 'national' popular tendencies.[126]

'Social' antagonisms emerged between landed and landless in predominantly agrarian, peripheral societies and between capital and wage-labour in predominantly industrial, core societies.[127] Strong, surprisingly pre-industrial community ties and shared class interests nourished the grand movements of 'proletarian socialism' between the European Revolutions of 1848 and the end of the Spanish Civil War in 1939.[128] Concomitantly, a series of 'national' antagonisms emerged in the course of inter-state formations and contestations, principally between national bourgeoisies and imperial metropoles. Over the late nineteenth and early twentieth centuries, political elites' concessions to popular, organised social and national movements (or 'parties') underpinned the emergence of the modern nation-state, combining mass electoral democracy with putative labour and welfare reforms. Colonial administration was typically bureaucratic and extremely centralised, 'designed for control, maintenance of order and downward transmission of policies formulated elsewhere'.[129]

Modern constitutions, from the late eighteenth century onwards, broadly sought to establish a formal realm for the state as separate from

125 Arrighi, 1994, *The Long Twentieth Century*.

126 Arrighi, Hopkins, and Wallerstein, *Anti-Systemic Movements*, pp. 30–3.

127 Within world-systems analyses, 'social' antagonisms are understood to encompass capital-labour dynamics as well as contending status-groups or 'other' identities based on gender, race, ethnicity, religion, and sexual preference amongst others. See Wallerstein, 2004, *World-Systems Analysis*, p. 36.

128 Murray Bookchin, 1997, *The Spanish anarchists: the heroic years, 1868–1936*. New York: Free Life Editions, pp. 6–8.

129 Stewart MacPherson and James Midgley, 1987, *Comparative Social Policy and the Third World*. Brighton: Wheatsheaf, p. 9. On postcolonial influence in the Irish case, see Mel Cousins, 2005, *Explaining the Irish Welfare State*. New York: Mellen Press, pp. 7–8.

arbitrary or private influence.[130] The subsequent development of the economic/inter-state world-system and associated antagonisms, however, occasioned important variations on this basic constitutional form. An era of 'classic' constitutionalism coincided with the rapid development of the British Free Trade cycle of accumulation from the mid-nineteenth century onwards. Constitutions created in the wake of the 1848 Revolutions strongly evidenced a contemporary tension between 'national' and 'social' antagonisms in their formation. Classic constitutionalism registered wider nationalist influences in claiming an organic unity between the state's fundamental law and the nation's essence or *geist*. Constitutional projects were explicitly identified with nation-state building by the independence movements of the Habsburg, Ottoman, French, and British Empires as well as by unification advocates in Italy and Germany.[131]

At the same time, in terms of social antagonisms, the widespread emergence of new forms of labour, factory workers in newly industrialising cores, and farm workers in cash-cropping peripheries, stimulated the development of particular legal forms, notably the prioritisation of contract law as well as of the individual as the central juristic subject.[132] Constitutions thus registered the primacy of private over public law and, insofar as 'economic rights' were concerned, of property and contract. The democratic component of 'national sovereignty' and 'basic rights' forwarded in these constitutional projects was thus strictly limited.[133] The French Constituent Assembly of 1848 most clearly illustrated these limitations.[134] Initial drafts fused material rights to employment and decent living conditions with classic, liberal rights of property, free belief, education, and equality of access to public office. With the 'party of order's' brutal suppression of the Parisian workers' revolt, however, the balance of class forces soon dictated the former, 'social' constitutional forms' eradication.[135]

130 'The true function of constitutionalism was to protect the bourgeoisie from the princes, who rejected the revolutionary slogans, and from the masses, who accepted them'. L. C. B. Seaman, 1964, *From Vienna to Versailles*, London: Routledge, p. 39.

131 See Thornhill, 2013, *A Sociology of Constitutions*, p. 250.

132 Kennedy, 2006, 'Three Globalisations of Law and Legal Thought', p. 36. See also Eric Wolf, 2010, *Europe and the People without History*. Berkeley: University of California Press.

133 See Thornhill, 2013, *A Sociology of Constitutions*, p. 250.

134 See Alexis de Toqueville, 1995 [1893], *Recollections: The French Revolution of 1848*. London: Transaction Publishers; Karl Marx, 'The Eighteenth Brumaire of Louis Napoleon' in Carver (ed.), 1996, *Marx's Later Political Writings*.

135 The militant *ouvriers* of 1848 had two historic demands, the right to form associations and the 'right to work', or rather the right to the means of life until employment could be found. The

Social constitutionalism emerged pronouncedly in the early twentieth century, coinciding with the accentuation of a series of systemic and anti-systemic antagonisms as well as the rapid development of state capacities. Proponents of social legal thought redefined law as a purposive activity, thereby providing a justificatory vocabulary for state intervention to meet societal needs and to respond to collective, interdependent problems, including war, mass unemployment, urbanisation and slum living conditions, as well as financial regulation. These problems became acute in the wake of the Wall Street Crash of 1929 and the Great Depression of the 1930s. Politically, the overarching goal was to limit polarisation in society by ensuring social mobility and, in doing so, to limit the appeal of revolutionary groups, particularly in the wake of the unexpected Bolshevik victory in Russia in 1917. Public law now came to increasingly regulate and delimit private law. Both international and domestic law regimes now provided for social and economic rights.

Hence, in addition to retaining much of the earlier classic constitutionalism's emphasis on 'national sovereignty', constitutions formed in the period of world war (1914–18) and revolutionary upheaval (1917–23), notably those of Mexico (1917) and Weimar Germany (1919), strongly reflected the newly emergent logics of social constitutionalism. In core countries, reflecting the growing strength of organised labour and the need for nation-building projects to incorporate these movements, socio-economic rights took the form of legalising universal social insurance and entitlements based on need. The German Constitution articulated *Wohlfahrtstaat* principles, including socio-economic rights, and, significantly, allocated constitutional rights not as universal rights of citizens but as particular rights of productive groups or classes.[136] In peripheral countries, such as Mexico, socio-economic rights took the form of labour and land reforms. Importantly, both constitutions retained classic constitutional rights, including guarantees of the rights of property and free contract.

latter demand left open the question as to what institutional form this inalienable right would take. Of the resulting proposals, Louis Blanc's ideas for 'social workshops', oriented toward cooperative production for human needs not profit, proved most popular. Murray Bookchin, 1998, *The Third Revolution: Popular Movements in the Revolutionary Era, Volume Two*. London: Cassell, p. 107. See also Priscilla Robertson, 1952, *Revolutions of 1848*. Princeton: Princeton University Press.

136 It further outlined co-determination procedures in the workplace and provided for the nationalisation of key industries. Thornhill, 2013, *A Sociology of Constitutions*, p. 287.

The post–World War II era occasioned the globalisation of a third, hybrid mode of law and legal thought, 'public law neoformalism'. For three decades, the cores of the now US-led capitalist world-system witnessed unprecedented levels of economic and social development, a phenomenon commonly attributed to 'embedded liberalism' or diverse forms of state intervention to ensure full employment, growth, and citizens' welfare, founded on a class compromise between capital and organised labour.[137] In both cores and peripheries, political elites faced with conflicting pressures of tradition and of modernisation – in both market and family law – shifted resulting disputes away from the domain of electoral politics and turned to the judiciary to resolve them instead.[138] Concomitant 'rights revolutions' witnessed a pronounced shift in the nature of constitutional courts' caseloads (away from traditional business and property disputes towards civil, political, and socio-economic rights conflicts) and a marked increase in the power of constitutional courts.

Perhaps the foremost example of judicial activism in the 1950s and 1960s is provided by the United States, where the Warren and Burger Supreme Courts introduced significant precedents concerning race and gender equality as well as criminal due process and electoral fairness. Public law neoformalism provided a justificatory discourse for this disruptive mode of juridical activity, enabling actors to invoke 'supposedly transcendent but also positively enacted values in constitutions or treaties', whether classic or social norms, to justify changing the status quo.[139] The European Court of Justice, for example, has been neoformalist in its interpretation of the canonical 'freedoms' of goods and persons in a single market, 'pushing the project further and faster than the Member States had been prepared to go on their own'.[140]

The US-led cycle of accumulation underwent a profound crisis in the mid-1970s, concluding capitalism's golden age and inaugurating the contemporary neoliberal era. The term 'neoliberalism' designates the politico-economic response to this crisis of elites (financiers, owners and managers of corporations, politicians, and bureaucrats),

137 Harvey, 2005, A *Brief History of Neoliberalism*, p. 10.
138 Kennedy, 2006, 'Three Globalisations of Law and Legal Thought', p. 70.
139 Kennedy, 2006, 'Three Globalisations of Law and Legal Thought', p. 64.
140 Alex Sweet Stone, 2010, 'The European Court of Justice and the judicialization of EU governance' in *Living Reviews in European Governance*, Vol. 5, (2), p. 5. Gustav Peebles, 1997, '"A Very Eden of the Innate Rights of Man"? A Marxist Look at the European Union Treaties and Case Law' in *Law & Social Inquiry*, Vol. 22 (3), pp. 581–618.

specifically their attempts to remove capital from the constraints of 'embedded liberalism' through the introduction of labour market flexibility, the deregulation of financial operations and the privatisation of state assets and services. The essence of neoliberalism is, as Pierre Bourdieu put it, 'a programme for destroying collective structures which may impede the pure market logic'.[141] Constitutionalism has traditionally played a prominent role in the thought of 'free market' advocates such as Frederick Hayek or Milton Friedman. Their proposed 'dethronement of politics' involved the substitution of general constitutional rules for the state's discretionary authority, prohibiting government from dirigiste or redistributive interventions that might stultify the spontaneous order of a market economy.[142]

The recent prominence of specifically 'neoliberal constitutionalism' within the broader 'neoformal' mode of law and legal thought is thus unsurprising. In the post-1989 era of globalisation and widening inequality, a robust, anti-majoritarian logic of property rights entrenchment, redefining the public sphere in more privatised and more commodified ways, has accompanied the expansion and deepening of international trade and investment rules.[143] This logic has shaped the legal infrastructure of the World Trade Organization (WTO), European Union (EU), and North American Free Trade Agreement (NAFTA) as well as a range of national constitutions, notably those recently created in Central and Eastern Europe and the Middle East but also, through judicial activism, those of much older standing.[144]

This account of neoformal, at times neoliberal, constitutionalism provides a context for understanding recent developments in constitutionalising social and economic rights. The results have been

[141] Pierre Bourdieu, 1998, 'Utopia of Endless Exploitation: The Essence of Neoliberalism' available at: http://mondediplo.com/998/12/08bourdieu.

[142] Rachel Turner, 2008, *Neo-Liberal Ideology: History, Concepts, and Policies*. Edinburgh: Edinburgh University Press, pp. 167–92. See also Perry Anderson, 2007, 'Depicting Europe' in *London Review of Books*, Vol. 29 (18), pp. 13–21; Richard Bellamy, 1994, 'Dethroning politics: Liberalism, constitutionalism, and democracy in the thought of F. A. Hayek' in *British Journal of Political Science*, 24: 3, pp. 419–32.

[143] Stephen Gill, 1995, 'Globalization, Market Civilization, and Disciplinary Neoliberalism' in *Millennium*, 24, pp. 399–412; Gustav Peebles, 1997, '"A Very Eden of the Innate Rights of Man"? The European Union Treaties and Case Law' in *Law and Social Inquiry*, 22 (3), pp. 581–618; David Schneiderman, 2000, 'Investment Rules and the New Constitutionalism' in *Law and Social Inquiry*, 25 (3), pp. 757–87.

[144] Klaus Von Beyme, 'Constitutional Engineering in Central and Eastern Europe' in Stephen Whyte, Judy Batt, and Paul Lewis, 2003, *Developments in Central and East European Politics*. Durham: Duke University Press; Neil Walker, 'The Shifting Foundations of the European Union Constitution' in Galligan, Denis and Mila Versteeg, 2013, *Social and Political Foundations of Constitutions*. Cambridge: Cambridge University Press, pp. 637–60.

ambiguous in both theory and practice. In India, the Supreme Court has been praised for its expansive interpretation of the Constitution's Directive Principles while at the same time criticised for its role in supporting state-led development of damming and industrialisation projects resulting in much human suffering and ecological devastation.[145] Similarly, in South Africa, the 1996 Constitution included social and economic rights while the courts won international acclaim for their development of jurisprudence in this area. Nevertheless, the practical implications of socio-economic rights for those homeless or in need of health care have been negligible in many cases.[146] South Africa remains among the most neoliberal and unequal of countries in the world. The contemporary era of neoformal law and legal thought has produced a series of *ad hoc* compromises on socio-economic rights in the world's constitutions and courts rather than their clear-cut development or neoliberal roll-back.[147]

## IRISH CONSTITUTIONALISM AND THE WORLD-SYSTEM

Faced with understanding the often complex ethico-political processes at stake in the constitutionalisation of socio-economic rights, world-systems analysis does not provide a reductive, determinist account but rather seeks to give a fuller, more critical expression to emergent intellectual trajectories in the contemporary field of comparative constitutional scholarship. Traditionally, constitutional studies tended to utilise the single-country case study to the detriment of wider comparison.[148] Nevertheless, comparative constitutional studies are currently undergoing something of a renaissance.[149] Increasingly, scholars are diversifying beyond the US constitution and utilising multiple case studies. Similarly, in socio-economic rights scholarship, researchers

145 'Report of the Special Rapporteur on the Right to Food, Jean Ziegler, Mission to India' and 'Rajagopol, Socio-Economic Rights and the Indian Supreme Court' in Steiner, Alston, and Goodman (eds.), 2008, *International Human Rights in Context*. pp. 324–6, 326–7.

146 Mark Tushnet, 2009, *Weak Courts, Strong Rights: Judicial Review and Social Welfare Rights in Comparative Constitutional Law*, Princeton: Princeton University Press, pp. 227–64; Mark Kende, 2003, 'The South African Court's Embrace of Socio-Economic Rights: A Comparative Perspective' in *Chapman Law Review*, Vol. 6, pp. 137–60. See also Brinks and Gauri, 2010, *Courting Social Justice*; Malcolm Langford, 2009, *Social Rights Jurisprudence: Emerging Trends in International and Comparative Law*. Cambridge: Cambridge University Press.

147 Kennedy, 2006, 'Three Globalisations of Law and Legal Thought', p. 63.

148 Tushnet, 2009, *Weak Courts, Strong Rights*, pp. 3–17.

149 Ran Hirschl, 2011, 'The Continued Renaissance of Comparative Constitutional Law' in *Tulsa Law Review*, 45, pp. 771–80.

are moving beyond the analysis of case-law in the Indian and South African constitutional courts to incorporate the jurisprudence of national courts in Latin America, Asia, and some Western states.[150] New technologies, in particular, have allowed for the compilation of 'big data' as the basis for large-n comparative studies.[151] The problem with both single and multiple case-study approaches, however, is that the hermetic isolation of nation-states remains assumed, more or less implicitly. Problematically, scholars tend to attribute to internal dynamics changes happening in strictly analogous ways in other jurisdictions.[152]

In recent years, however, an alternative wave of 'global' accounts, a world literature of constitutional development has begun to emerge, characterised by its proponents' common tendency to account for commonalities among diverse constitutions, at least in part, in terms of the transnational migration of constitutional ideas.[153] Again, these analyses fall unevenly along the formalist-instrumentalist continuum. Hence, common constitutional forms, including shared forms of socio-economic rights entrenchment, owe to transnational conditions of social and political upheaval;[154] to global capitalism's neoliberal discipline and anti-majoritarian stability;[155] to universaling rationalisation;[156] to the increased salience of cosmopolitan norms;[157] or to cosmopolitan framers' or judges' 'constitutional borrowing'.[158]

Recent scholarship has critically challenged and developed these analyses by further incorporating the role of global-local social movements in the contestation and development of law.[159] It highlights the

150 Philip Alston, 'Foreword' in Langford (ed.), 2012, *Social Rights Jurisprudence*, p. x; Katharine Young's recent research, for example, draws on South Africa and the United States as primary comparators but further analyses Colombia, Ghana, India, and the United Kingdom among others. Young, 2012, *Constituting Economic and Social Rights*.

151 See the Comparative Constitutions (http://comparativeconstitutionsproject.org) and Constitute (www.constituteproject.org/#) projects as well as the Toronto Initiative for Economic and Social Rights (www.tiesr.org).

152 Kennedy, 2006, 'Three Globalisations of Law and Legal Thought', p. 25.

153 Tushnet, 2009, *Weak Courts, Strong Rights*, pp. 3–17.

154 Elster, 1995, 'Forces and Mechanisms in the Constitution-Making Process', pp. 364–96.

155 Gill, 1995, 'Globalization, Market Civilization, and Disciplinary Neoliberalism'; Hirschl, 2007, *Towards Juristocracy*.

156 Kennedy, 2006, 'Three Globalisations of Law and Legal Thought'; Thornhill, 2013, *A Sociology of Constitutions*.

157 Held, David, 'Democracy, the Nation-State and the Global System' in David Held (ed.), 1991, *Political Theory Today*, Stanford: Stanford University Press, pp. 197–235.

158 Elkins, Ginsburg, and Melton, 2009, *The Endurance of National Constitutions*.

159 Rajagopal, 2003, *International Law from Below*. Santos and Rodriguez, 2005, *Law and Globalisation from Below*.

danger that a world-systems analysis of the 'globalisation' of constitutional forms in the abstract risks speaking past concrete practices and subaltern cultures of contestation and resistance.[160] The necessity of analysing these discrete, at times almost silent practices speaks to the necessity of a detailed analysis of the contested globalisation of socio-economic rights in a single country case-study. Primarily for this reason, while much consideration is given to analogous and contemporaneous developments in other jurisdictions, the scope of this work is geographically limited to the contestation and crystallisation of constitutional forms in the Republic of Ireland only.

Analysis of the 1937 Constitution of Ireland makes for a particularly interesting comparative case-study. This constitution-making moment blends a mix of socio-legal cultures – including a common law tradition in the Atlantic English-speaking orbit; a wider European or continental law tradition mediated by its legal intelligentsia and by the dominant position of the Catholic Church; and a postcolonial heritage suggesting commonalities with the experience of states in today's Global South.[161] The British state's legacy was most obviously enduring. Gaelic Ireland had been re-created as an English-speaking country, subject to laws modelled substantially on those of England, in the seventeenth and eighteenth centuries.[162] Economic peripheralisation, particularly the prominence of agriculture, heavily influenced future economic strategies and social policy development. State interventions in the late nineteenth century to promote small-scale family farming, primarily via land redistribution, both anticipated and ensured the centrality of the family in subsequent social policy.[163]

Welfare state development in the Irish Free State was also heavily influenced by the centralised nature of inherited colonial welfare institutions and by the policy stance of its core planning institution, the Department of Finance.[164] For much of the twentieth century, Ireland's borders also remained subject to political conflict and dispute, an unusual phenomenon for most states and one that helps account for

[160] See Robert Allen, 2004, *No Global: the people of Ireland versus the multinationals*. London: Pluto Press.

[161] Terrence McDonough (ed.), 2005, *Was Ireland a Colony? Economics, Politics, and Culture in Nineteenth-Century Ireland*. Dublin: Irish Academic Press.

[162] Tom Garvin, 1996, *1922: The Birth of Irish Democracy*. Dublin: Gill and MacMillan, p. 195.

[163] See Tony Fahey, 2002, 'Catholicism and Industrial Society in Ireland' in J. H. Goldthorpe and C. T. Whelan (eds.) *The development of Industrial Society in Ireland*. Oxford: Oxford University Press, pp. 241–63.

[164] Cousins, 2005, *Explaining the Irish Welfare State*, p. 12.

the comparative resilience of nationalist politics.[165] The Irish experience of independent statehood anticipated later waves of decolonisation in Africa, Asia, and Latin America in which various nationalist political parties incorporated social movements before adopting former colonisers' governance apparatuses and economic ideologies upon gaining statehood.[166]

Ireland is, however, a somewhat odd comparative case, demonstrating a number of historically specific or distinguishing features.[167] Although poorest among the Western nations, the country enjoyed a comparatively higher level of economic development and social stability than the world-system's colonised peripheries. In part, Ireland's stability owed to mass emigration, a recurring and, for some, useful 'safety valve'.[168] The contested nature of British rule in Ireland also produced important, strategic interventions. Relative to other agrarian peripheries, Ireland also had higher levels of mass education for younger people, a function of British educational and Anglicisation policies.[169] State-sponsored land purchase created a sizeable native class of owner-occupiers prior to independence, a social stratum common to other Western electoral democracies and a bulwark to radical social transformation.[170]

Irish civil society also had comparatively longer experience of electoral, mass party politics.[171] The movement for Catholic Emancipation in the 1820s was arguably the first mass democratic mobilisation

[165] John Coakley, 'Society and Political Culture' in John Coakley and Michael Gallagher (eds.), 2010, *Politics in the Republic of Ireland*, London: PSAI Press/Routledge, pp. 37–71, pp. 40–50.

[166] Franz Fanon, 2001, *The Wretched of the Earth*. London: Penguin; see also Go, 2003, 'A Globalizing Constitutionalism? Views from the Postcolony, 1945–2000'.

[167] On the difficulty of categorising Ireland in either European or 'Third World' historiography, see Joe Lee, 1989, *Ireland, 1912–1985*. Cambridge: Cambridge University Press, pp. xiii–xiv. The difficulty stems in part from the manner in which comparative studies often use modernisation theories uncritically, overlooking core-periphery relations and selecting core-centric variables to the exclusion of important variables in peripheral contexts concerning political independence, economic dependence, and religion. See Mel Cousins, 2005, *Explaining the Irish Welfare State*. New York: Mellen Press, p. 11. For an overview of the debate in Irish historiography and literary studies, see Barbara Bush, 2014, *Imperialism and Postcolonialism* New York: Routledge, pp. 62–76.

[168] The view that emigration countered revolution was extolled by the Department of Finance. Lee, 1989, *Ireland, 1912–1985*, pp. 227, 278.

[169] John Coakley, 'Society and Political Culture' in John Coakley and Michael Gallagher (eds.), 2010, *Politics in the Republic of Ireland*, London: PSAI Press/Routledge, pp. 37–71, p. 42.

[170] Garvin, 1996, *1922*, pp. 24, 191.

[171] Electoral democracy has often proved more difficult to establish in poor countries. Seymour Martin Lipset, 1960, *Political Man*. London: Heinemann. See also Garvin, 1996, p. 190.

in Europe.[172] Catholic identity became interwoven with national identity while the Catholic Church exercised a central role in popular culture. This was also unusual. Unlike in Africa, Asia, Latin America, or in continental Europe, the Catholic hierarchy was not popularly identified with the old regime or ruling class but rather formed an intermediary between that class, its state, and the majority Catholic population.[173] Until relatively recent times, Ireland witnessed comparatively higher levels of Catholic affiliation, a sociological fact that reinforced the hierarchy's unusually robust position of moral, political, and supernatural authority.[174]

Hybrid case-studies of the Irish sort are potentially useful because they allow us to generate insights for – or test low-level hypotheses applicable to – a wide range of locales. In the present inquiry into socio-economic rights entrenchment, the Irish Free State Constitution (1922) belongs to the same inter-war 'wave' of constitution-making which occasioned the very earliest constitutional entrenchments of these rights, including Mexico (1917), Soviet Russia (1918), and Weimar Germany (1919).[175] Similarly, Bunreacht na hÉireann (Irish: Constitution of Ireland) (1937) was made in the context of the Great Depression when, internationally, the state's 'social' interventions in the 'classic' liberal market and legal regimes, of the kind expressed in the US New Deal and ultimately FDR's 'Second Bill of Rights', were greatly expanding.[176]

172 Jim Smyth, 'Moving the Immovable: the civil rights movement in Northern Ireland' in Linda Connolly and Niamh Hourigan (eds.), 2006, *Social Movements and Ireland*. Manchester: Manchester University Press. pp. 106–23, p. 120.

173 See John Coakley, 'Society and Political Culture' in John Coakley and Michael Gallagher (eds.), 2010, *Politics in the Republic of Ireland*, London: PSAI Press/Routledge, pp. 37–71, p. 45. See also Walter Korpi, 1992, *Welfare State Development in Europe since 1930: Ireland in Comparative Perspective*. Dublin: Economic and Social Research Institute.

174 Tom Inglis, 1998, *Moral monopoly: the rise and fall of the Catholic Church in modern Ireland*. Dublin: University College Dublin Press, pp. 247–8. See also Ruth Fletcher, 2001, 'Post-Colonial Fragments: Representations of Abortion in Irish Law and Politics' in *Journal of Law and Society*, 28 (4), pp. 568–89.

175 Elster, 1995, 'Forces and Mechanisms in the Constitution-Making Process'.

176 The US Supreme Court only engaged partially with socio-economic rights discourses, even during its most activist phases. However, from the 1970s onwards, a series of important cases and jurisprudence concerning education rights emerged at state level. See Cass Sunstein, 2004, The Second Bill of Rights: FDR's Unfinished Revolution and why it is needed now more than ever. New York: Basic Books; Christopher Berry and Charles Wysong, 2012, 'Making Courts Matter: Politics and the Implementation of State Supreme Court Decisions' in *The University of Chicago Law Review* 79(1): pp. 1–29; Steiner, Alston, and Goodman, 2008, *International Human Rights in Context*, pp. 347–51.

Over the intervening decades, dramatic social transformation occurred, including in the nature and role of the constitution, the welfare state, and associated public interest litigation. Notably, during the 1990s and 2000s, as socio-economic rights' constitutional recognition strengthened internationally, oppressed and electorally insignificant groups, including Travellers, asylum seekers, children, the homeless, and the disabled, combined constitutional litigation strategies with civil society activism to claim rights to housing, education, and dignity.[177] Nevertheless, throughout this long period of social transformation, Ireland's constitution-makers', judges' and governments' recognition of socio-economic rights remained strictly limited. Clarifying the Irish state's exceptionalism or opposition with regard to socio-economic rights entrenchment – why it did not happen here – is a useful step towards identifying what the constraints on entrenchment are more generally.

Within Irish constitutional studies, however, the role of socio-economic rights has yet to be fully explored or accounted for. The first wave of Irish constitutional studies, led by Brian Farrell, Basil Chubb, Alan Ward, and John Kelly, primarily concentrated on the Irish 'state tradition' as a liberal legacy of British rule as well as on the nationalist or confessional aspects of the 1922 and 1937 constitutions.[178] While recent scholarship, notably by Gerard Hogan and Bill Kissane, has usefully contextualised Irish constitutionalism within wider European and Transatlantic traditions of constitution-making, the focus of this research continues to centre on the shifting intersection of liberal institutions and norms with nationalist and Catholic

[177] Travellers form an ethnic and indigenous minority in Ireland with a distinctive culture, of which nomadism is an important part, and who, as individuals and as a community of some 25,000 people, experience high levels of prejudice and state discrimination. See Joint Committee on Justice, Defence, and Equality, 2014, The Report on the Recognition of Traveller Ethnicity, Dublin: Official Publications Office.

[178] Brian Farrell, 1970–1, 'The Drafting of the Irish Free State Constitution: I, II, III and IV' in *Irish Jurist*, 5/6, pp. 115, 343, 111, and 345; Brian Farrell (ed.), 1988, *De Valera's Constitution and Ours*, Dublin: Gill and Macmillan; Basil Chubb, 1991, *The Politics of the Irish Constitution*, Dublin: Institute of Public Administration; Basil Chubb, 1978, *The Constitution and Constitutional Change in Ireland*, Dublin: Institute of Public Administration; John Kelly, 1967 (2nd edition), *Fundamental Rights in the Irish Law and Constitution*, Dublin: Allen Figgis and Co.; John Kelly, 'The Constitution: Law and Manifesto' in Frank Litton (ed.), 1988, *The Constitution of Ireland 1937–1987*, Dublin: Institute of Public Administration; John Kelly, 2003 (4th edition), Gerard Hogan and Gerry Whyte, 2003, *J. M. Kelly: The Irish Constitution*. Dublin: LexisNexis Butterworths; Alan Ward, 1994, *The Irish Constitutional Tradition: Representative Government in Modern Ireland*. Dublin: Catholic University of America Press.

ones.[179] In comparative constitutional studies, similarly, the Irish case is most readily forwarded as an example of a socio-legal order deeply expressive of and divided by questions of national identity and values.[180] Sociologists have also forcefully critiqued the white, patriarchal, and settled (as opposed to Traveller) norms reproduced in the 1937 Constitution in the course of Irish nation-building.[181] Conflicts over socio-economic rights, however, have yet to be specifically explored or fully accounted for.

Constitution-makers' rejection of socio-economic rights provisions tends to be mentioned in passing only, perhaps as having 'attracted little attention'.[182] Similarly, the significance of these decisions and the politics underpinning them are usually unmentioned or simply dismissed in cultural terms as egalitarian naïvéte falling foul of framers' 'innate conservatism'.[183] In terms of the subsequent usage and development of the 1937 Constitution, Chubb's thesis on the 'normative force' of the Irish constitutional tradition, a basic law gradually adjusting to changing societal norms, remains the standard explanatory account of change.[184] Subsequent politicians' and judges' opposition to recognising economic and social rights is thus deemed to stem from common law traditions of judicial deference to property rights and to the principle of the separation of powers. However, we do not explain anything with an appeal to tradition; rather we must ask why tradition persists.[185] Culture, ideas, norms, and values clearly matter here. Yet constitutions, to paraphrase Franz Neumann, do not simply demand loyalty to an

179 Gerard Hogan, 2005, 'De Valera, the Constitution and the Historians' in *Irish Jurist*, 40 (2), pp. 293–320; Gerard Hogan, 2012, *The Origins of the Irish Constitution: 1928–41*, Dublin: RIA; Bill Kissane, 2011, *New Beginnings: Constitutionalism and Democracy in Modern Ireland*, Dublin: University College Dublin Press.

180 Hanna Lerner, 2011, *Making Constitutions in Deeply Divided Societies*. Cambridge: Cambridge University Press, pp. 152–192, 48; Tushnet, 2009, *Weak Courts, Strong Rights*, p. 12.

181 Ronit Lentin, 1998, '"Irishness", the 1937 Constitution and Citizenship: a Gender and Ethnicity View', *Irish Journal of Sociology*, 8(1), pp. 5–24; Fletcher, 2001, 'Post-Colonial Fragments: Representations of Abortion in Irish Law and Politics'.

182 Dermot Keogh and Andrew McCarthy, 2009, *The Making of the Irish Constitution*. Cork: Mercier Press, p. 180.

183 Brian Farrell, 'From First Dáil through Irish Free State' in Brian Farrell (ed.), 1988, *De Valera's Constitution and Ours*, p. 18; see also Kissane, 2011, *New Beginnings*, p. 37.

184 Chubb, 1991, *The Politics of the Irish Constitution*, p. 117; Kissane, 2011, New Beginnings, p. xii; see also Thomas Murray, 2013, 'Where we are: review of Bill Kissane's *New Beginnings*' in *Dublin Review of Books*. Available at: www.drb.ie/essays/where-we-are.

185 C. Wright Mills, 1959, *The Sociological Imagination*. New York: Oxford University Press, p. 154.

externally valid value system; they also embody decisions about the future structure of society.[186]

Scholarship on the Irish Constitution has yet to consider seriously how constitutionalism intersects with economic institutions or development, narrowly or broadly understood. Nor has attention to the normative force of the Irish Constitution necessarily resulted in scholars' engagement with popular, non-elite values and ideas concerning constitutionalism. Social movement analysis, a recent addition to Irish political research, is remarkably overlooked.[187] The papers of the makers of the 1922 and 1937 constitutions, available at University College Dublin Archives, the National Archives, and the National Library, the reports of associated 'constituent assembly' debates, as well as subsequent case-law and conflicts have not been fully explored for these conflicts and linkages. The conspicuous absence of critical sociological research in this regard presumably owes something to its absence in Irish legal studies more generally.[188] The analytic approach taken here has been to begin with a historically specific constitutional order, to analyse the processes involved in its formation, contestation, and use and to contextualise these within the dynamics of the historical capitalist world-system.

If we wish to look beyond the fetish of the final constitutional form, inquiry into the politics of constitutionalising 'socio-economic rights' must begin with the labour process involved in constitution-making and constitutional development. The texts generated in the course of these activities provide evidence of instances when 'socio-economic rights' were open to question and interpretation by all manner of social agents, of relatively fluid moments of formulation prior to the crystallisation of a particular constitutional form. The critical discourse analysis

186 Neumann, 1966, *Behemoth*, p. 17.

187 See Linda Connolly and Niamh Hourigan, 'Introduction' in Linda Connolly and Niamh Hourigan (eds.), 2006, *Social Movements and Ireland*. Manchester: Manchester University Press. pp. 1–10, p. 4. Overlooking social movement critiques, norms and discourse facilitates the identification of 'democratic politics' with electoral-representative or liberal democracy. Notwithstanding claims of scientific objectivity, this is a deeply ideological position, one that overlooks both the limitations of liberalism as well as the availability of alternative conceptions and criteria of democracy. On the critique of liberal political science, see Bertell Ollmann, 2000, 'What Is Political Science? What Should It Be?' in *New Political Science*, 22: 4, pp. 553–62. On the variety of models of democracy, see Ricardo Blaug and David Schwarzmantel (eds.), 2004, *Democracy: a reader*. New York: Columbia University Press.

188 Chapter 9, exploring the conditions for legal cultural production in Ireland, accounts for this absence or, rather, blindness. See Nial Osborough, 1976, 'Irish Legal Scholarship' in *Irish Jurist*, 11 (1), pp. 1–2; David G. Morgan, 1985, 'Review' in *Irish Jurist*, 20 (2), pp. 445–50.

of these texts brings back into view all the conflicts and discarded possibles of the Irish Constitution's early beginnings. In doing so, it clearly demonstrates the structures of power – institutional and interest-based as well as normative and discursive – that supported the discarding of socio-economic rights provisions and benefitted from the defence of the status quo. At the same time, the broadening of our conception of power and 'the political', beyond class and the state, to include discourse has important implications for how we might understand and therefore identify ideology.

## CRITICAL DISCOURSE ANALYSIS

Dialectical inquiry has been likened to opening a series of inward-looking windows in a circular room, with each successive viewpoint providing a different perspective on the whole room: only by collating these distinct perspectives and considering how they relate to one another does the whole really begin to make sense.[189] Similarly, if the foregoing theoretical sections outlined a series of potential windows on the politics of constitution-making and socio-economic rights contestation in Ireland, this section will discuss how to open them. Simply stated, the basic methodological premise here is that texts are important elements of social events which, through critical discourse analysis, can open windows of understanding on often complex phenomena.[190] An important political struggle attaches to the imposition of dominant systems of classification. For Bourdieu, language constitutes a dividing line between misrecognition and consciousness: 'words wreak havoc when they find a name for what had up to then been lived namelessly'.[191] Critically contextualising socio-economic rights discourses specifically suggests a dialectical motion between the texts generated in the course of constitution-making in Ireland and an overall world-systems analysis of the contested social conditions out of which they arose and to which they referred.

In the present analysis, a number of existing formalist and instrumentalist studies of the Irish Constitution delineate the contours of the

189 Bertell Ollman, 2003, *Dance of the Dialectic: Steps in Marx's Method*. Urbana: University of Illinois.

190 Norman Fairclough, 2003, *Analysing Discourse: Textual Analysis for Social Research*, London: Routledge. p. 223.

191 Bourdieu (citing Jean Paul Sartre), 'Structures, Habitus, Power: Basis for a Theory of Symbolic Power' in Dirks, N. B., Eley, G., and Ortner, S. B. (eds.), 1994, *Culture/Power/History: a reader in contemporary social theory*. Princeton: Princeton University Press. pp. 155–99, p. 177.

field of socio-economic rights contestation. While numerous accounts delineate the development of Ireland's political institutions and welfare infrastructure, the limitations of existing sociological research on the Irish judiciary and legal system necessitated original research. Examining the formal structures of the legal field and its growing business, quantitatively and qualitatively, necessitated analysis of statutes establishing the courts and compiling statistics, provided in the *Irish Statistical Abstracts* or *Courts Service Reports*, on its caseload. The field's sociological contours emerged from the study and compilation of biographical data on the judiciary, through class, educational, and professional formation, available in memoirs as well as secondary sources such as the *Dictionary of Irish Biography* and the *Irish Times*, the national paper of record.[192] A detailed examination of contributions to the *Irish Jurist* law journal from its inception in 1935 to the present day complemented this institutional study with cultural analysis of a shifting 'battle of ideas' concerning socio-economic rights and constitutionalism more generally.[193]

The texts generated in the course of constitution-making and subsequent legal conflicts form the primary data of this analysis. These materials vary according to the nature of the contestation under study, presenting moments when socio-economic rights were open to formulation, question, and interpretation by all manner of social agents. In terms of Irish state constitution-making in 1922 and 1937, these texts include the drafting committee's drafts, papers, and correspondence, as well as the parliamentary reports of the subsequent constituent assembly debates that make reference to 'socio-economic rights' broadly understood. Thereafter, given that the 1937 constitution's socio-economic provisions have featured in hundreds of cases, I selected particular socio-economic rights contestations for critical discourse analysis on the basis of jurists' identification of the case as significant or 'leading'. The Supreme Court lists a series of 'important judgments' while wider legal professional estimations of importance may be gauged from majority or consensus opinion in authoritative book and journal publications on constitutional law, notably John Kelly's *The*

192 J. McGuire and James Quinn, 2009, *The Dictionary of Irish Biography*. Cambridge: Cambridge University Press.

193 *The Irish Jurist* journal functioned as a proxy for wider legal professional and academic opinion in Ireland, providing an important context for understanding contemporary case-law and its significance to practitioners and to civil society. On intellectual and cultural battles in twentieth-century Ireland, see Bryan Fanning, 2008, *The Quest for Modern Ireland: The Battle of Ideas, 1912–86*, Dublin: Irish Academic Press.

*Irish Constitution* and *The Irish Jurist*.[194] However, while this analysis begins with 'leading' texts from the state's archives and case-law, predominantly expressing political, administrative, and legal professional opinion, it does not end there.

Constitution-making in Ireland has tended to be a top-down exercise in consolidating state institutions and making representative democracy more manageable.[195] Subsequent scholarly accounts risk reproducing this perspective if they privilege state archives and expert legal knowledge over understanding civil society and social relations. The approach taken here has been to recuperate examples of socio-economic rights contestation 'from below', instances where people attempted to articulate alternative socio-economic rights discourses to those within the established constitutional order. Commitments to tracing these subterranean rights discourses however raise important challenges. In the absence of an archive for 'the people', I have concentrated on analysing the rights discourses of constitutions produced by both parliamentary and popular groups during the same period that the 1922 and 1937 constitutions were being created. Thereafter, I examine five moments of 'socio-economic rights' contestation concerning unemployment (1950s), housing action (1960s), children's rights (1970s), rent restrictions (1980s), and trade union empowerment (1980s), episodes in which the constitution's rights provisions were invoked and, once again, which contemporary jurists or scholars indicated as significant.

In terms of source material, I have relied here on participant accounts, biographies, and interviews provided in the literature and newspapers of those people, communities, trade unions, NGOs, and political movements involved in order to reconstruct the ethico-political practices and socio-economic rights discourses involved. These practices and discourses often emerged from the activities of comparatively small groups. They are not forwarded here as necessarily representative of wider public opinion, or even of their authors' imagined communities or bases of support. Nevertheless, while the analysis of these experiences falls far short of a 'people's history' of the constitution, it does form an important counterpoint to the discourses presented in orthodox case-law and further identifies a wider terrain of

[194] Available at: www.supremecourt.ie/supremecourt/sclibrary3.nsf/pagecurrent/9FA0AA8E8D261FC48025765C0042F6B3?opendocument&l=en.

[195] Kissane, 2011, *New Beginnings*, pp. 145–8.

debate about justice and socio-economic rights than the study of case-law alone would suggest.

Once identified, all socio-legal texts were subject to a three-stage critical discourse analysis.[196] Stage one involved identifying actors' propositional statements, concerning the extent, likely causes or probable future of 'socio-economic rights', and normative resolutions, concerning what, if anything, ought to be done and who, if anybody, is responsible for doing it. Stage two involved assessing the texts' 'dialogicality', determining the author's inclusion or exclusion of 'other' voices and the fairness of their representation. During stage three, these findings were collated, compared, and contextualised. What is acutely important throughout is identifying how actors invoke universals and particulars: 'ideology' rests on the power to project particular interests as universal ones, causing them to be misrecognised as such.[197] It follows that actors' assumptions cannot be deemed ideological on textual evidence alone, but only after determining their relationship to power in society.[198]

Contextualising the discursive construction of socio-economic rights and associated (potentially ideological) assumptions posits a critical movement between the texts generated in the course of socio-economic rights contestation and the world-systems analysis of the social and economic conditions out of which they arise and to which they refer. To a limited though important degree, the earlier theorisation of classic, social, and neoformal legal discourses in the world-system provided a useful conceptual apparatus for questioning, contextualising, and understanding the politics of socio-economic rights contestation in Ireland generally. However, appearances notwithstanding, discourse analysis is not a linear procedure; the data do not simply populate *a priori*, literature-derived categories.[199] The actual research process entailed a

[196] I coded the texts manually with highlighter pens, handwritten notes, and annotations. See Fairclough, 2003, *Analysing Discourse*, pp. 42–59.

[197] See Loïc Wacquant, 2005, *Pierre Bourdieu and democratic politics*. Cambridge: Polity, p. 178.

[198] Fairclough, 2003, *Analysing Discourse*, p. 223. Any analysis of ideologies as simply 'legitimating discourses' which fails to take corresponding institutions into account probably contributes to the efficacy of those same ideologies. Bourdieu, 1994, 'Structures, Habitus, Power: Basis for a Theory of Symbolic Power', p. 184.

[199] 'Of course the mode of presentation must differ in form from that of inquiry. The latter has to appropriate the material in detail, to analyse its different forms of development, to trace out their inner connection. Only after this work is done, can the actual movement be adequately described. If this is done successfully . . . then it may appear as if we had before us a mere a priori construction'. Marx, 2003, *Capital I*, p. 28. See also Matthew Clarke, 2008, *Language Teacher Identities: Co-constructing Discourse and Community*. Toronto: Multilingual Matters, pp. 66–7.

cyclical moving between data, wider literatures, and the research questions, leading to a gradual refinement and clarification of the key discursive themes structuring the data. Through this iterative process, I developed a deeper understanding of the ideological 'value-consensus' underpinning social agents' discourses.

The relationship between 'discourse' and 'ideology' requires clarification at this point. Discourse may be defined simply as a way of talking about a certain set of objects in the world; hence, socio-economic rights discourse is simply a way of talking about socio-economic rights in the world. Yet, as Raymond Williams has emphasised, discourse is also 'integrative', providing people with shared meanings or interpretive horizons, including those concerning power and authority.[200] We might distinguish 'discourse' from 'ideology', however, if we clarify that the latter involves a particular 'containment' of shared and integrative meanings for the purpose of advancing particular or class interests.[201]

This raises an important question as to what extent both proponents and critics of socio-economic rights are ideologically driven, bringing to bear a 'strategy of containment' in defining the terms of the politics of socio-economic rights and thereby dissimulating relations of power. In the Irish case of contesting socio-economic rights, constitution-makers, political actors, and judges have usually adopted a 'value-consensus' discourse, tending to absent social processes, power relations, and conflict and to present the state as a consensual, value-neutral framework in which competing interests can be resolved.[202] Conversely, political actors attempting to articulate socio-economic rights from below have often relied on a more oppositional understanding of the state, considering it in terms of unequal power relations and depicting it as being

[200] Raymond Williams, 1977, *Marxism and Literature*. London: Oxford University Press; see also Arif Dirlik, 1993, *Anarchism in the Chinese Revolution*. Berkeley: University of California Press, pp. 32–46.

[201] Fredric Jameson, 1981, *The Political Unconscious: Narrative as a Socially Symbolic Act*. Ithaca: Cornell University Press, pp. 52–3.

[202] On the value-consensus state, see Patrick Hillyard, 1972, 'Public Attitudes towards the Police in a medium-sized town in Northern Ireland', in the *Irish Jurist*, 7 (1), pp. 62–76, p.71; see also Bourdieu, 1987, 'The Force of Law', p. 814. While adopting a pluralist conception of democracy, the American political scientist Robert Dahl underlined the degree of consensus required to underwrite any political decision-making: 'In a sense, what we ordinarily describe as democratic "politics" is merely the chaff. It is the surface manifestation, representing superficial conflicts. Prior to politics, beneath it, enveloping it, restricting it, conditioning it, is the underlying consensus on policy that usually exists in the society among a predominant portion of the politically active members'. Dahl, 1956, *Preface to Democratic Theory*. Chicago: University of Chicago Press, p. 132.

controlled by (or representing the interests of) society's dominant group or class.

In sum, as the following analysis of archives, case-law, and popular protest suggests, the politics of socio-economic rights should be understood alongside the broader ethico-political processes and relations out of which such contestations arise and to which they refer. The overall argument runs as follows. Chapter 1 examines popular, civil society attempts at constitution-making in Ireland in the decades preceding state-initiated constitution-making projects, with a particular emphasis on the period of revolutionary upheaval between 1917 and 1923. Chapters 2 and 3 present the results of a critical discourse analysis of the 1922 and 1937 constitution drafting processes, respectively, situating these findings in a comparative, world-systems analysis. Successive Irish constitutions' strictly limited form of socio-economic rights entrenchment, I suggest, owed primarily to political decision-makers' consistent privileging of classic nationalist constitutionalism over more social democratic alternatives. Their choices and influential positions, in turn, were strictly conditioned by the Irish Free State's semi-peripheral status and, in particular, by the manner in which this status, culturally and structurally, favoured popular, anti-systemic mobilisation along 'national' rather than 'social' lines.

The second half of the book analyses the emergence of contemporary socio-economic rights discourses in Ireland. Chapter 4 traces the politics of constitutional change in Ireland and the world-system between 1945 and 2008. Chapter 5 examines the changing nature of the Irish legal field and its implications for how the 1937 Constitution was contested in the courts and for the particular forms of rights that judges subsequently discovered and guaranteed. Chapters 6, 7, and 8 present a critical analysis of Irish judges' socio-economic rights discourses, arising in twenty-three leading cases involving property, trade union, as well as family, education, and welfare rights conflicts, respectively. In general, the courts functioned as sites for the contestation and liberalisation of 'Catholic social' constitutionalism in family law and the robust defence of classic rights of property and contract. The Irish Supreme Court's rejection of an expansive socio-economic rights constitutionalism in the early 2000s must be understood in terms of this definite historical trajectory. Chapter 9 examines the ideology of the value-consensus state underpinning these institutions, decisions, and discourses, including its social and legal-cultural origins.

Finally, Chapter 10 analyses the experiences and discourses of those who challenged state policy or judicial decision-making on socio-economic rights and, in doing so, created alternative, participatory spaces of justice. Ideologically, this form of politics adhered to a different mode of thinking, against and beyond the value-consensus state. Subaltern forms of socio-economic rights advocacy involved, to varying degrees, an oppositional sense of the state as reflecting the interests of a dominant group or class and a rejection of the notion that the Constitution and the courts are somehow 'above politics'. The resulting political dynamic was not one of petitioning the state for a right so much as making that right a reality by acting and living as if it already existed. Simultaneously, this politics of solidarity involved a rejection of the majoritarian/minoritarian dichotomy involved in conventional rights struggles, and a revitalisation of the old labour motto, 'an injury to one is an injury to all'.[203] In today's pressing circumstances, the critical recuperation of these memories, contestations, and ideas is vital.

203 'An injury to one is an injury to all' is a slogan first made popular by the Industrial Workers of the World (IWW). In the early twentieth century, the IWW counted the labour organisers James Connolly and Jim Larkin among its members and Ireland's increasingly syndicalist labour movement adopted the slogan wholeheartedly. See William Dudley Haywood, 1929, *The Autobiography of Big Bill Haywood*. New York: International Publishers, p. 186.

CHAPTER ONE

# CONSTITUTION 'FROM BELOW' IN IRELAND: 1848–1922

> *The principle I state and mean to stand upon is this: that the entire ownership of Ireland, moral and material, up to the sun and down to the centre, is vested of right in the people of Ireland; that they, and none but they, are the landowners and lawmakers of this island . . . Let laws and institutions say what they will, this fact will be stronger than all laws and prevail against them, the fact that those who own your lands will make your laws and command your liberties and your lives.*
>
> – James Fintan Lalor, 1848[1]

> *That the first and last principle of the Irish Citizen Army is the avowal that the ownership of Ireland, moral and material, is vested of right in the people of Ireland.*
>
> – Constitution of the Irish Citizen Army, 1914[2]

A decade of popular militancy immediately preceded and decisively shaped the formation of the Irish Free State and the drafting of the Irish Free State Constitution in 1922. What has been termed the 'Irish Revolution' (1913–23) adhered to the conservative postcolonial trajectory outlined and critiqued by the Afro-Caribbean psychiatrist and theorist Franz Fanon, in which a nationalist party gradually substituted itself for a mass anticolonial and social movement.[3] The Sinn Féin party effectively reasserted the principle that the masses are incapable of governing themselves, notwithstanding ample evidence to the contrary in the form of self-governing communities, arbitration courts, and soviets. This had important implications, most notably in terms of the 'detached complicity' between nation-building elites and the established market

[1] Cited Leo Kohn, 1932, *The Constitution of the Irish Free State*. London: G. Allen and Unwin Ltd, p. 26.

[2] 'Constitution of the Irish Citizen Army' in D. J. Hickey and J. E. Doherty, 2003, *A New Dictionary of Irish History*. Dublin: Gill and MacMillan, p. 221.

[3] On the argument that nationalism is an insufficient response to colonialism see Fanon, 2001, *The Wretched of the Earth*. London: Penguin; see also Balakrishnan Rajagopal, 2003, 'International Law and Social Movements: challenges of theorising resistance' in *Colombia Journal of Transnational Law*, 41:2, pp. 397–433, pp. 423–6.

economy.[4] Sinn Féin's leadership did not view the classic laws of market, property, and contract as problematic per se, rather their having being formerly skewed against 'the Irish people'. Thus, its constitutionalism envisaged the silent reproduction of market law and the strident defence of an Irish nationalist, often specifically Catholic, culture. This national constitutionalism, as was common in many postcolonial jurisdictions, was most clearly expressed in family law, notably resulting in a remarkably enduring defence of patriarchal relations.[5]

Popular militancy in Ireland, notably between 1917 and 1923, occurred alongside a global wave of worker militancy in the aftermath of the Russian Revolution of 1917. The nationalist movement's waging a guerrilla campaign against British rule occurred alongside Sinn Féin's creation of a state within a state while broad swathes of civil society boycotted established institutions and disrupted existing patterns of domination. Trade union militancy escalated, resulting in numerous general and local strikes as well as a number of worker soviets. With the retreat of law enforcement in 1919, farmers and labourers engaged in midnight campaigns of intimidation, cattle-driving, and assault in order to expropriate and redistribute land. Concomitantly, a network of popularly elected, local arbitration courts sprung up, notably to decide the terms of land redistribution. Sinn Féin sought to restrain agrarian agitation or class conflict, notably through a more formal 'Dáil Court' structure, oriented towards the preservation of property rights. This politics of justice 'from below' from mid-1920 onwards anticipated the conservative, contested reformation of the former judicial system in the Irish Free State as well as the role socio-economic rights would play in the making of the 1922 constitution.

In critically assessing the socio-economic rights discourses of this formative period, both Fanon's writings as well as contemporary actors remind us to pay attention to the perspectives of non-party actors within the mass movement.[6] The various social agents involved in these intersecting anti-colonial, agrarian, and social conflicts created a diversity of manifestoes, programmes, and constitutions, many of which articulated contending 'socio-economic rights' discourses. These

4 Sinn Féin (Irish: Ourselves). Fanon, 2001, *The Wretched of the Earth*, p. 65.
5 See Kennedy, 2006, 'Three Globalisations of Law and Legal Thought', pp. 30–1.
6 'The people's effort can be seen only by knowing something of their lives and their relationship to our underground government and armed resistance. We who fought effected a small part of the total energy induced . . . ' Ernie O'Malley, 2008 [1936], *On Another Man's Wound*. Dublin: Anvil Books, p. 21.

included the Constitution of the Irish Citizen Army (1913), the Proclamation of the Irish Republic (1916), the Sinn Féin Manifesto (1918), as well as the Dáil Constitution and Democratic Programme (1919). Different social groups coincided on attempting to appropriate 'socio-economic rights' discourse, to rearrange its terms in keeping with their priorities and interests and, in doing so, to silence those elements of the discourse inimical to those interests. What 'the ownership of Ireland' would mean in practice was a particularly sharp locus of conflict amongst socialist revolutionaries, agrarian agitators, property owners, clergy, soldiers, and nationalist party politicians. Future constitution-makers would reference these revolutionary-era texts and discourses as well as the more specific terms of sovereignty, nationalism, socialism, distributivism, and natural law theory animating them.

The latter half of this chapter analyses the emergence of Ireland's anticolonial movement, its relationship to economic conditions and social struggles and, in particular, its implications for the creation of alternative sites of justice and the articulation of alternative concepts of socio-economic rights. I wish to begin however by situating these formative struggles and discourses within a longer historical, world-systemic context. Ireland's legal institutions and ideas had a dialectical, or co-constitutive, relationship to its incorporation into the historical capitalist world-system and to concomitant socio-political struggles over what was a complex colonising process.[7] Existing medieval institutions came to be appropriated by a Protestant landlord caste in the seventeenth and eighteenth centuries before wholesale land transfers to a Catholic owner-occupier class in the late nineteenth century preceded their appropriation of the legal field in the twentieth. Significantly, albeit less observably, the close-knit communities of Irish peasant society often found formal law and property rights to be irrelevant.[8] A diverse range of customary dispute-resolution practices existed on the rundales and ranches and it was through these sites of justice that the mass agrarian conflicts of the nineteenth century were conducted. Long before the 'Irish Revolution' then, Irish people had popular experience creating alternative sites and practices of conflict resolution as well as distinguishing between law and justice.

[7] Eamonn Slater and Terrence McDonough, 2008, 'Marx on Nineteenth-Century Colonial Ireland: Analysing Colonialism beyond Dependency Theory' in *NIRSA Working Paper Series*, 36, pp. 1–35.

[8] Éanna Hickey, 1999, *Irish Law and Lawyers in Modern Folk Tradition*. Dublin: Four Courts, pp. 8, 150.

## REVOLUTION AND RIGHTS IN IRELAND AND THE HISTORICAL CAPITALIST WORLD-SYSTEM

Emerging in sixteenth-century Europe, the capitalist world-system gradually incorporated Ireland as a semi-periphery within Britain's regional economy.[9] In economic terms, the process aided England's drive toward hegemony and led to Irish industrialisation, especially in linen production, but at the cost of eliminating indigenous wool production and thereby limiting capacities for future industrialisation. It transformed the countryside, occasioning land clearances and tenant farming while also creating conditions for mass emigration and periodic famine. Politically, incorporation into the world-system initially occasioned a range of colonising strategies, including genocide, plantation, Anglicisation, and enforcing religious conformity, but ultimately came to be mediated by a new ethno-class division in which land ownership became the salient basis of inequality.[10] The late seventeenth-century settlement imposed by England established a propertied Protestant minority as rulers, with core support, over the mainly unpropertied Catholic majority, among whom the folk memory of illegitimate land confiscations remained potent.

During the 1800s, Ireland was even more effectively incorporated into the newly hegemonic British Empire's free trade cycle of accumulation. Following customs and monetary union in 1825, the Irish pound was tied to sterling and almost free trade conditions followed.[11] The country's proto-industries collapsed in the ensuing competition with rapidly industrialising rivals; the economy shifted to the export of food and primary commodities such as wool and leather. Between 1816 and 1920, as rising demand in Britain's cities raised beef prices by more than 300 per cent, Irish agricultural production correspondingly

[9] Denis O'Hearn, 2001, *The Atlantic Economy: Britain, the US, and Ireland*. Manchester: Manchester University Press. While Ireland would normally be classed as a 'semi-periphery' within world-systems analyses, the word 'periphery' is sometimes used here to better emphasise peripheralisation as an evolving, relational process rather than a fixed status.

[10] The European wars of religion following the Protestant Reformation coincided with the English conquest of Ireland. The ensuing persecution of Catholicism transformed the priest into the personification of political and religious resistance to English rule. This synthesis was, for a time, to become basic to Irish nationalism. Seán Ó'Faoláin, 1980, *The Irish*. New York: Penguin, pp. 105, 119.

[11] The gold standard secured cattle exports as well as the Irish banks' investing grazier/merchant proceeds in the City of London, with associated implications for Dublin Castle's pursuing balanced budgets and parsimony in public expenditure. See Conor McCabe, 2011, *Sins of the Father: Tracing the decisions that shaped the Irish economy*. Dublin: History Press. See also Raymond Crotty, 1986, *Ireland in Crisis: A study in capitalist colonial underdevelopment*. Dingle: Brandon Press.

shifted from labour-intensive tillage to livestock rearing. During the period 1825–70, cattle exports jumped from 76,000 to 451,000 per year, sheep exports from 50,000 to 681,000. By the 1910s, no less than 97 per cent of Irish exports went to Britain.[12]

By the early 1900s, Southern Irish industry remained comparatively small-scale – only 130 companies employed more than one hundred employees – and predominantly centred on agricultural processing, brewing, and distilling. Farming accounted for more than half of the population's direct employment and, indirectly, provided the main source of income for Irish towns' and cities' tertiary services. Incorporation into the world-system occasioned an internal peripheralisation as the densely populated, small farm and rundale (common field) plains of Connacht and the western seaboard counties came to provide labour and young livestock for the larger, exporting ranches of Munster and Leinster in the south and east. The Irish banking cartel reinvested the proceeds of the graziers' cattle-trade in the city of London, thereby severely limiting domestic capacities for investment or diversification in both industry and agriculture.

The acceleration of world-systemic incorporation processes, notably land clearance and de-industrialisation, accentuated associated conditions of mass unemployment, emigration, and at times starvation. During the nadir of the Great Hunger (1845–52), more than one million people died from starvation and disease and a further one million emigrated. Ireland's experience of the golden age of liberal capitalism thus anticipated the late nineteenth-century imperial-peripheral famines of India, China, Brazil, Ethiopia, Korea, Vietnam, the Philippines, and New Caledonia, during which some thirty to sixty million people died.[13] Long term, the population of the island of Ireland declined from eight million in 1800 to four million in 1900, a figure that remained unchanged until the late twentieth century.[14] Among European experiences of industrialisation, moreover, the Irish 'flight from the land' (or the export of cheap labour-power to the world-system's

[12] See O'Hearn, 2001, *The Atlantic Economy*, pp. xi, 104, and 114.

[13] See Mike Davis, 2000, *Late Victorian Holocausts: El Nino Famines and the Making of the Third World*. London: Verso.

[14] On the uniqueness of Ireland's population implosion among Western nations, see Lars Mjoset, 1992, *The Irish Economy in Comparative Institutional Perspective*. Dublin: National Economic and Social Council, pp. 62–7. Today, the population of the island of Ireland is approximately 6.5 million, comprising 4.6 million in the Republic of Ireland and 1.8 million in Northern Ireland.

cores) was unique insofar as those fleeing did not go to native cities but rather foreign ones.[15]

Throughout the nineteenth century, the development of core-periphery relations was the subject of intense contestation. Politically, the caste-like quality of landlordism, both in terms of class relations and religious distinctions, was already well established. The landlords and their agents emerged as a powerful and relatively autonomous part of the colonising regime, protecting their interests from tenants (and the landless) primarily through their control of the colonial administration at Dublin Castle as well as their ambiguous political allies at Westminster.[16] Correspondingly, the mass of the working population consisted of agrarian farmers and landless labourers.

The emergent, indigenous capitalist class tended to be rooted in medium- and small-scale enterprise servicing the wider British regional economy. By the early 1900s, the country's major property interests, including banks, graziers, railway companies, breweries, and dairies as well as a newly emerged middle stratum of 'native' owners of small business and medium-sized farms, supported reproducing, deepening, and accelerating these core-periphery linkages. Again, these groups found support in Dublin Castle, notably in its adherence to low taxation and expenditure in order to maintain the integrity of the Irish currency on the gold standard, thereby securing financier/grazier exports of livestock and capital to the City of London. Contesting this class's dominance, an urban, politically organised working class had emerged by the early twentieth century.

In Ireland, as in other (semi-)peripheries, 'anti-systemic' conflict combined both 'social' and 'national' movements, with the latter proving dominant. Not atypically in predominantly agrarian colonies, secret society traditions surfaced whenever inhabitants required physical force to intimidate landlords or their agents into lowering rents, tithes, or other exactions as well as stopping evictions.[17] Secret societies such as the Whiteboys, Defenders, Hearts of Oak, Ribbonmen, and Thrashers tended to remain diffuse in the countryside and organised around local, short-term aims. In contrast, 'national' advocates in urban areas adopted rigid, centralised organisational forms and advocated long-term goals, chiefly Irish variations on the republican and nationalist

15 Evanne Kilmurray, 1988, *Fight, Starve, or Emigrate*. Dublin: Larkin Unemployed Centre, p. 8.

16 Slater and McDonough, 2008, 'Marx on Nineteenth Century Colonial Ireland', p. 18.

17 For a detailed case-study of a landlord's assassination in Co. Roscommon during the Famine, see Peter Duffy, 2007, *The Killing of Major Denis Mahon*. London: Harper.

ideologies then flourishing in the wake of the 1789 French Revolution and the 1848 European Revolutions.[18]

Republicanism in Ireland incorporated radical democratic, secular, and levelling aims. Inspired by the French Revolution and by Tom Paine's defence of its achievements in *The Rights of Man*, the Constitution of the Society of United Irishmen (1797) stated its first aim as 'forwarding a brotherhood of affection and a communion of rights and a union of power among Irish men of every religious persuasion'.[19] In the popular imagination, republicanism came to be associated with labourer and tenant interests in lowering rents, ending tithes, and land redistribution.[20] Again, in the 1840s, the romantic nationalist 'Young Ireland' movement contained articulate intellectuals, notably James Fintan Lalor, who advocated a general rent strike in order to compel land redistribution to the native peasantry.[21] The nationalist movement as a whole, however, tended to emphasise unity around an Irish identity (Gaelic, Catholic, and peasant) that was nostalgic, conservative, and estranging to many Protestants, particularly in the northeast.[22] Social tensions surfaced periodically, but unity in the face of the external enemy countered the articulation of workers', women's, or others' specific interests.

After the Famine and the failed 1848 Rebellion, Irish republicans such as the Irish Republican Brotherhood (IRB; or Fenians) adopted clandestine, militant means to advance their goal of independent statehood for Ireland, at times identifying this goal with a radical social

[18] The French Revolution redounded throughout the capitalist world-system, and changed people's basic conceptions of what politics was about. Over the following century, at least three previously fringe ideas became mainstream: that social change is normal and desirable; that the proper institution to manage the course of social change is the state; and that states receive their legitimacy from an entity known as 'the people'. Immanuel Wallerstein, 1989, 'The French Revolution as a World-Historical Event' in *Social Research*, 56:1, pp. 33–52.

[19] Note that a majoritarian understanding of rights, based on collective solidarity, is advanced here. Without 'brotherhood', 'communion', and 'union', 'every reform of Parliament must be partial, not National . . . and insufficient for the freedom and happiness of this country'. 'Constitution of the Society of United Irishmen of the City of Dublin' in Richard Musgrave, 1802, *Memoirs of the Different Rebellions in Ireland*. Dublin: Parchbank. pp. 231–4, p. 232. Paine's manifesto appeared in Dublin in March 1791, and in eight months it sold 40,000 copies, twice the sales in England. Peter Linebaugh, 2003, 'On the Bicentennial of the Hanging of Thomas Russell'. Available at: www.counterpunch.org/2003/10/21/on-the-bicentennial-of-the-hanging-of-thomas-russell/. See also Ó'Faoláin, 1980, *The Irish*, p. 91.

[20] Nancy Curtin, 1994, *The United Irishmen: Popular Politics in Ulster and Dublin, 1791–1798*. Oxford: Oxford University Press, pp. 119–20.

[21] F. S. L. Lyons, 1973, *Ireland since the Famine*. Collins: Glasgow, pp. 108–9.

[22] Andrew Flood, 2010, 'How not to make a revolution: Young Ireland, the Chartists, and 1848'. Available at: www.anarchism.pageabode.com/andrewnflood/revolution-young-ireland-1848.

programme capable of generating agrarian and working-class support.[23] The Fenian insurrection of 1867, quickly repressed, identified the necessity of a radical mass movement for future republican success.[24] The Proclamation of the Irish Republic (1867) declared the organisation's aims as 'founding a Republic based on universal suffrage, which shall secure to all the intrinsic value of their labour', arguing that '[t]he soil of Ireland, at present in the possession of an oligarchy, belongs to us, the Irish people, and to us it must be restored'.[25] In late nineteenth-century conditions of economic recession, as landlord-tenant conflict on a mass scale escalated, the IRB proved central to landless labourers' and tenants' organising in the Irish National Land League and waging 'land wars', periods of mass direct action against rents and evictions and for land ownership and redistribution. While harbouring radical elements, the Land League and its successor organisations were supported mainly by farmers having usufruct of at least some land, as distinct from the landless.[26]

Over the same period, 'constitutional nationalists', so-called because of their adherence to representative politics in the British parliament, represented a small though growing male, property-owning franchise. The blocked political system administered from London fostered a credibility crisis for the conventional channels for participation in Ireland.[27] Constitutionalists could parley militant forms of resistance to secure concessions on national independence (or 'Home Rule') in the course of negotiations with the metropole. Of the most consequential of these reforms, Daniel O'Connell's securing of Catholic enfranchisement proved essential to the creation of a nationalist, mass party tradition in Ireland.[28] Moreover, between 1880 and 1910, the Irish Parliamentary Party, a disciplined, electoral machine of the

[23] Owen McGee, 2005, *The IRB: The Irish Republican Brotherhood from The Land League to Sinn Féin*. Dublin: Four Courts Press.

[24] On the parallels between Fenian insurrectionary methods and contemporary forms of political violence in Europe, particularly the transition from Blanquism to guerrilla campaigns in Italy, see Niall Whelehan, 2012, *The Dynamiters: Irish Nationalism and Political Violence in the Wider World*. Cambridge: Cambridge University Press, p. 8, pp. 61–2.

[25] 1867 Proclamation cited in Alan O'Day, 1998, *Irish Home Rule, 1867–1921*. Manchester: Manchester University Press, p. 8; for a critique of republican constitutionalism, see Tom Garvin, 2008, 'An Irish Republican Tradition?' in Iseult Honohan (ed.), *Republicanism in Ireland: Confronting Theories and Traditions*. Manchester: Manchester University Press, pp. 23–30.

[26] It was, as Tom Garvin put it, 'a movement dominated by a nascent rural petite bourgeoisie'. 1986, 'The Anatomy of a Nationalist Revolution: Ireland, 1858–1928' in *Comparative Studies in Society and History*, 28 (3), pp. 468–501, p. 479.

[27] Jim Smyth, 'Moving the Immovable', p. 120.

[28] Garvin, 1996, *1922*, p. 190.

Anglo-Irish and Catholic nationalist gentry under the leadership of Charles Stewart Parnell and later John Redmond, negotiated successive Liberal and Conservative governments' regulation and subsequent abolition of the established Anglo-Irish landlord caste.

Anti-systemic struggles and mass mobilisations prompted strategic efforts by the British state and Dublin Castle aimed at Anglicisation, pacification, control, and peripheral reconstitution.[29] A national system of primary education was introduced in 1831 while a Poor Law system, based solely on 'indoor relief' in a network of workhouses, followed in 1838. Land transfer and redistribution, however, paralleling the experience of British India, functioned as perhaps the single most important form of intervention.[30] At the turn of the twentieth century, under the auspices of the Irish Land Commission and Congested Districts Board occurred the wholesale transfer of landlord estates to a newly dominant stratum of 'native' small- and medium-sized owner-occupier farmers. A large 'coolie' class of labourers, however, remained landless and impoverished. The expansion of the Poor Law to include medical treatment, the introduction of old age pensions, and the development of insurance schemes against unemployment and illness marked Ireland's welfare state as advanced in European terms but very narrowly focussed.[31] Social policy interventions thereafter typically concentrated not on distributive (social welfare) or consumption-based (education, health, and housing) policies but on production (land redistribution).[32]

The Catholic Church played an important role both in the development of welfare institutions and in the wider process of conservative pacification. Unlike in continental Europe and the Spanish or Portuguese colonies, the Church in Ireland was not popularly identified

[29] While the 1848 Revolutions unleashed social and national unrest across Europe, no major upheaval hit Great Britain, notwithstanding the presence of well-organised radical forces. The British Tories had discovered 'enlightened conservativism', the granting of minor concessions repeatedly over time to convince sufficient numbers that substantive change was occurring. It proved to be a more effective means of quelling revolt than physical repression. Immanuel Wallerstein, 2014, 'Anti-systemic Movements, yesterday and today' in *Journal of World-Systems Research*, 20: 2, pp. 158–72, p. 159.

[30] Kennedy, 2006, 'Three Globalisations of Law and Legal Thought', p. 36.

[31] Ireland's highly agrarian workforce combined with Church and medical profession opposition to free GP schemes ensured coverage for unemployment and sickness insurance was below average. Mel Cousins, 2005, *Explaining the Irish Welfare State*. New York: Mellen Press, pp. 22–4.

[32] Cousins, 2005, *Explaining the Irish Welfare State*, p. 24. See also Michelle Norris and Tony Fahey, 2011, 'From Asset Based Welfare to Welfare Housing? The Changing Function of Social Housing in Ireland' in *Housing Studies*, 26 (3), pp. 459–69, pp. 460–4.

with the ruling class. On the contrary, it mediated social relations among landlord, tenant, and labourer and asserted its authority to negotiate with the colonial administration on behalf of the native population, some 95 per cent of whom were Catholic. Founded in 1795, the Catholic seminary at Maynooth, Co. Kildare attracted early on clericalist refugees from the French Revolution who advanced a remarkably conservative theology of obedience to the throne.[33] Late nineteenth-century Irish Catholicism was further distinguished from Southern European Catholicism in its deeply conservative ultramontanism, or deference to papal-episcopal authority ahead of secular alternatives.[34]

The growth of secular national and social movements after 1848 prompted Pope Leo XIII's *Rerum Novarum* (1870), a conciliatory encyclical decrying the harsh conditions of industrial work, exhorting owner-worker cooperation as part of the natural order of things and, in the meantime, advocating Christian resignation and respect for public order for the working class.[35] In contrast, outside of the north-eastern counties, which were predominantly Protestant and unionist, organised Catholicism in Ireland was comparatively unchallenged. The Catholic hierarchy's strict policing of the population's sexuality, in particular, existed in a direct affinity with the emerging property regime that demanded consolidation and singular inheritance (primogeniture); 'illegitimate' relationships could spawn confusion over succession rights and rights to land, with potentially disastrous consequences for the preservation of family property.[36]

Politically, the Church's hierarchy, typically drawn from the more affluent farming strata, aligned itself with constitutional nationalism, providing a reservoir of organised labour-power to its advancement. The Church functioned as a conservative bulwark against the articulation of class conflict, opposed militant struggle, and pronounced

[33] Ó'Faoláin, 1980, *The Irish*, p. 105.

[34] See Roy Foster, 1988, *Modern Ireland: 1600–1972*. London: Penguin, pp. 386–7.

[35] The encyclical's chief architect was Luigi Taparelli D'Azeglio, an Italian Jesuit central to the Thomist revival of the nineteenth century. Responding to the industrial revolution as well as the social revolutions of 1848, Taparelli saw in subjective Cartesian thinking the roots of the surrounding conflict between capitalism and socialism. Heralding Thomas Aquinas as the only means to true metaphysics, he advocated 'social justice', thereby coining the phrase, as well as the principle of subsidiarity, according to which each level of society, recognising their respective rights and duties, are to cooperate rationally rather than resort to competition or conflict. See John Moloney, 1991, *The Worker Question: a new historical perspective on 'Rerum Novarum'*. Dublin: Gill and MacMillan.

[36] Hickey, 1999, *Irish Law and Lawyers in Modern Folk Tradition*, p. 141.

anathemas on all oath-bound, secret societies. Parenthetically, the IRB demanded the separation of church and state in its 1867 proclamation.[37] For supporting constitutional nationalists, the bishops expected deference to their 'moral monopoly' and, in particular, control over the material means of producing that monopoly among the poor, specifically education, health, and charitable services.[38] For the recently created petite bourgeoisie of owner-occupiers, leaving such services under church control was not merely pious; it also ensured minimising taxation for state provision. By the early 1900s, a conservative alliance had formed between the two groups, one that would have important implications for the later development of Irish constitutionalism and socio-economic rights. Within this wider terrain of social and political struggle, the Irish legal field formed an important, evolving site of contestation.

## LAND, LAW, AND JUSTICE FROM BELOW

> 'Ireland is the only geographical district in Europe diminishing in wealth and population. The population of Ireland is now less than it was in 1805; I believe the rental to be less than it was in 1805. Every county town in Ireland except Belfast and Cork has gone down; county society is vanishing out of Ireland; the ruins of castles and abbeys are everywhere to be seen. There are few gentlemen's houses. Institution after institution is disappearing. As property vanishes, those who live by the litigation concerning that property also disappear'.
>
> – Barrister Denis Caulfield Heron, 1868[39]

> 'We watched the judge at the Assizes clothed in scarlet and ermine. He sat erect in his carriage, guarded by cavalry with drawn swords. The escort was a result of the land war; their white spotless bridles had a metal core in memory of the slashing pikes of the '98 rebels'.
>
> – IRA veteran Ernie O'Malley, 1936[40]

[37] Charles Kickham's *Knocknagow*, a novel set in mid-nineteenth-century Tipperary, depicts the subtle class divisions and ties of mutual aid in a preindustrial, agrarian society. Priests play a central role here in maintaining social peace, interceding with landlords on their parishioners' behalf and enjoining charity for the needy. Conversely, the book's republican veterans of 1798 advance alternative, militant norms to counter evictions: 'I say 'tis justice in the eye uv God', said old Phil Morris, 'to punish the bloody tyrants-the robbers and murdherers that rob the people uv their little spots, an' turn 'em out to perish'. Kickham, 1988 [1870], *Knocknagow: or the homes of Tipperary*. Dublin: Anna Livia Press, pp. 69–70, 222.

[38] Tom Inglis, 1998, *Moral monopoly: the rise and fall of the Catholic Church in modern Ireland*. Dublin: University College Dublin Press, p. 57.

[39] Kenneth Ferguson, 2005, *King's Inns barristers, 1868–2004*. Dublin: Honorable Society of King's Inns, p. 117.

[40] O'Malley, 2008 [1936], *On Another Man's Wound*, p. 21.

At least superficially, the law signalled England's success in assimilating Ireland.[41] The inherited courts system, medieval in origin, centred on the imposing Four Courts at Inns Quay in Dublin city and, through regular assizes and quarter sessions, borough, sheriffs', church, and manorial courts, reached deep into the country's localities.[42] The most important local jurisdictional courts were composed of 'Justices of the Peace' who heard less serious criminal matters, hosting preliminary hearings to the Assizes or Petty Sessions in addition to sitting four times a year in Quarter Sessions. These judges could compel persons 'not of good fame' to be of good behaviour or to 'keep the peace' by threatening committal to prison for refusal.[43] To ensure uniformity in the administration of justice, an appeal process existed from all Irish courts to the House of Lords. Irish justices also advised the civil government in administrative matters, serving on both the Privy Council and on a range of boards and commissions for charities, hospitals, mental asylums, and industrial schools.

Legal business, for barristers, consisted of litigation and title work, such as the drafting of companies' memoranda and articles of association. Solicitors, the 'lower branch' of the legal profession, were directly involved in commercial activity, taking positions as company directors or agents for landlords, banks, insurance companies, or moneylenders.[44] Land and property relations featured prominently. For barristers, a significant amount of legal work consisted, 'on the Common Law side, of actions by absentee landlords to eject their tenants and, on the

[41] Gaelic Ireland's Brehon law system was purposely eclipsed following the Norman invasions of 1171, and then almost totally replaced by English law in the seventeenth century as the Crown established control over Ireland. Elizabethan England's jurists drew on these precedents to develop legal justifications for later imperialist adventures, including the doctrine of 'discovery'. Colonisers used these doctrines to override indigenous legal regimes around the world, most notably in North America. By the end of the nineteenth century, a two-tier system of dominant (metropolitan) law and servient (indigenous) law operated in many of Great Britain's colonial possessions. Hans S. Pawlisch, 1985, *Sir John Davies and the Conquest of Ireland: A Study in Legal Imperialism*. Cambridge: Cambridge University Press. See also Robert Miller, Jacinta Ruru, Larissa Behrendt, and Tracey Lindberg, 2010, *Discovering Indigenous Lands: the doctrine of discovery in the English Colonies*. Oxford: Oxford University Press.

[42] The Four Courts housed the Chancery Court and the three common law courts of King's Bench, Common Pleas, and Exchequer. The chancery heard land and succession claims while the common law courts dealt primarily with commercial matters such as contracts and claims for damages. R. B. McDowell, 1957, 'The Irish Courts of Law, 1801–1914' in *Irish Historical Studies*, 10 (40), pp. 363–91, p. 363. See also T. C. Barnard, 1993, 'Lawyers and the Law in Later Seventeenth-Century Ireland' in *Irish Historical Studies*, 28 (111), pp. 256–82.

[43] V. T. H. Delany, 1975, *The Administration of Justice in Ireland*. Dublin: Institute of Public Administration, p. 33.

[44] Daire Hogan, 1986, *The Legal Profession in Ireland: 1789–1922*. Dublin: Law Society, p. 9.

Chancery side, of suits by mortgagees to compel the absentees to pay their debts'.[45] Solicitors held a state-guaranteed monopoly in the preparation of property deeds and also succeeded in having their remuneration for conveyancing determined not by the length of the property deed but by the value of the land (*ad valorem*).[46] The Land Acts and the operations of the Land Commission also created new business, both in tenant purchases and in fair rent adjudications. The fortunes of the Irish legal profession were tied to the fortunes of the grazier economy and of the Anglo-Irish landlord caste in particular. As the *Irish Law Times* lamented, 'If the land question is settled in the next score of years or so, the legal business of the country will become further depressed'.[47]

As the market economy expanded and intensified, successive government reforms rationalised the courts' basis of authority and, with the coming of the railways, ensured its diffusion into the localities. From the mid-nineteenth century, Dublin Castle introduced paid 'Resident Magistrates' and appointed judges exclusively from among members of the Irish bar.[48] Similarly, lower court judges were no longer local amateurs, often land- or business-owners with vested interests in the cases put before them, but selected according to professional qualification.[49] The Supreme Court of Judicature (Ireland) Act 1877, the centrepiece of reform, introduced the unified 'legal year' – based on the Christian/farming calendar of Michaelmas, Hilary, Easter, and Trinity – and also fused the several courts of common law and equity into one unified court system for 'the more convenient dispatch of business'.[50] In the early twentieth century, government reforms reorganised the law courts' upper tier into a Supreme Court and High Court and expanded the courts' administrative network of registrars, receivers, and taxing masters.[51]

45 John Atkinson, Q. C. quoted in Hogan, 1986, *The Legal Profession in Ireland: 1789–1922*, p. 84.

46 Hogan, 1986, *The Legal Profession in Ireland: 1789–1922*, p. 118.

47 Cited in Ferguson, 2005, *King's Inns Barristers*, pp. 74, 117.

48 Hogan, 1986, *The Legal Profession in Ireland: 1789–1922*, pp. 1–2.

49 McDonnell, 'The Irish courts of law, 1801–1914', p. 371.

50 The Supreme Court of Judicature Act provided that the separate courts of chancery, queen's bench, common pleas, exchequer, probate, matrimonial causes, the landed estates court, and admiralty were to be fused into one supreme court that would administer law and equity concurrently. McDowell, 1957, 'The Irish Courts of Law, 1801–1914', p. 370.

51 Lawrence McBride, 1991, *The Greening of Dublin Castle*. Washington, DC: Catholic University of America Press, pp. 28, 37. The Supreme Court was divided in turn into a Court of Appeal and the Lords Justice of Appeal. The High Court of Justice was further divided into six parts – Chancery, Queen's Bench, Exchequer, Probate and Matrimony, Admiralty, and Bankruptcy.

In this newly emerging market for legal services, legal professional organisations such as the Bar Council and the Law Society acted successfully to entrench their monopoly privileges, such as maintaining barristers' exclusive right of audience in the upper courts as well as setting fees, both directly and by controlling the supply of practitioners through the King's Inns. Incomes at the Irish Bar and Bench typically amounted to £3,000–£5,000 a year.[52] Classic legal theorists' proposition that the law was accessible only to those professionals capable of 'scientific' legal reasoning found ready adherents. As two Irish barristers explained in a mid-nineteenth-century pamphlet, '[s]o long as the law remains as we have shown it must remain – a science of great difficulty – so long a successful lawyer must be in receipt of a large income'.[53]

The Anglo-Irish landlord caste – conservative, Protestant, and Trinity College-educated men – dominated entry to the legal profession and appointment to the bench well into the twentieth century. Judges' and land commissioners' fathers were typically landlords, lawyers, ministers, or businessmen.[54] Class privilege was simultaneously an issue of religious exclusivity. Catholic lawyers who refused to conform were traditionally excluded from the higher ranks of the legal profession.[55] By the late nineteenth century, only 1,200 of the 5,000 justices of the peace, 150 of the 400 practising barristers and 3 of the 21 justices of the superior courts were Catholic.[56] Personal ties of blood and marriage further combined with the effects of professional training and etiquette to reinforce a gendered, class-determined 'distance' from the majority population.[57]

From the late nineteenth century onwards, the nascent petite bourgeoisie of small- and medium-sized owner-occupiers, overwhelmingly

The Land Commission was also attached to the High Court. This tier comprised of some seventeen judges, three land commissioners, and the Lord Chancellor, also a member of the executive at Dublin Castle.

52 McBride, 1991, *The Greening of Dublin Castle*, p. 35.

53 Hogan, 1986, *The Legal Profession in Ireland: 1789–1922*, p. 83.

54 F. E. Ball, 1921, *The Judges in Ireland, 1221–1921, Vol. 2*, London: John Murray, pp. 331–87. In 1886, for example, out of 5,000 justices of the peace, some 2,700 were landed proprietors while only 350 were farmers. McDowell, 1957, 'The Irish Courts of Law, 1801–1914', p. 372.

55 Colum Kenny, 1987, 'The exclusion of catholics from the legal profession in Ireland, 1537–1829' in *Irish Historical Studies*, 25 (100), pp. 337–57, p. 337.

56 McBride, 1991, *The Greening of Dublin Castle*, pp. 31, 36–7. See also McDowell, 1957, 'The Irish Courts of Law, 1801–1914', p. 372; Ferguson, 2005, *King's Inns Barristers*, p. 51.

57 Judicial memoirs such as Maurice Healy's emphasise the importance of 'old boys' networks as well as collective wining and dining in local hostelries on judicial circuits or the King's Inns for the formation of legal professionals' *esprit de corps*. Healy, 1939, *The Old Munster Circuit*. London: M. Joseph Ltd.

Catholic, challenged Unionist-Liberal party patronage and religious discrimination in the legal field through the Irish Parliamentary Party.[58] The subsequent opening up to competition of legal-administrative positions ensured that, at least for the Catholic petty bourgeoisie, the race for respectability would centre on the school, competitive examinations, and professional appointment. By the 1910s, Catholic men filled the courts' administrative offices while 2,400 of the 6,000 justices of the peace and 8 of the 18 justices of the superior courts were also Catholic.[59] Even then, however, the French sociologist Louis Paul-Dubois could still characterise the Irish courts as part of the 'English oligarchy'.[60]

The legal profession's fate was closely tied to that of the state; the final prerequisite for advancement was political experience. Of those appointed to the Irish bench between 1801 and 1914, more than half had sat in the House of Commons and nearly three-quarters had been law officers or advisors to the Chief Secretary of Dublin Castle.[61] Until 1906, all but one of the Irish justices were members of the Kildare Street Club, the country's most exclusive social organisation and synonymous with unionism.[62] While the Law Library included practitioners of moderate nationalist views, it remained predominantly conservative and unionist. At the outbreak of World War I, all parliamentary factions at the bar united in support of the British Empire.[63] Similarly, in terms of legal culture and jurisprudence, although Ireland witnessed 'the first adventure of the common law', both unionist and nationalist practitioners looked to Westminster where the intellectual workshops of that law remained firmly based.[64]

58 The legal profession was well represented in the Irish Parliamentary Party. Among its 103 MPs in the 1910–18 parliament, there were 11 solicitors and 20 barristers, including the party leader, John Redmond, his brother, William, and other prominent members such as A. M. Sullivan and Tim Healy. Ferguson, 2005, *King's Inns Barristers*, p. 71. Hogan, 1986, *The Legal Profession in Ireland: 1789–1922*, p. 146.

59 McBride, 1991, *The Greening of Dublin Castle*, pp. 31, 36–7. See also, McDowell, 1957, 'The Irish Courts of Law, 1801–1914', p. 372.

60 L. Paul Dubois, 1908, *L'Irlande Contemporaine*. Dublin: Maunsel, p. 189.

61 This includes those appointed, after 1877, to the high court and the court of appeal. McDowell, 1957, 'The Irish Courts of Law, 1801–1914', p. 366. McBride, 1991, *The Greening of Dublin Castle*, pp. 8–10.

62 McBride, 1991, *The Greening of Dublin Castle*, p. 34. The Irish Bench, one judge later observed, 'was reserved as payment for political industry, sometimes it was blood-silver for a nationalist Judas'. Hugh Kennedy, cited in Gerard Hogan, 1987, 'The Supreme Court and the Single European Act' in *Irish Jurist*, 22 (1), pp. 55–70, p. 70.

63 Ferguson, 2005, *King's Inns Barristers*, p. 78.

64 Nial Osborough, 1996, 'Letters to Ireland' in *Irish Jurist*, 31 (1), pp. 226–54, p. 252.

The King's Inns and Law Society prioritised practitioner-oriented instruction and mock trials as well as the study of 'books of authority' (Coke's *Institutes*, Bracton's *De Legibus*, Littleton's *Tenures*, Foster's *Crown Law* and Blackstone's *Commentaries*) but stifled the introduction of continental alternatives.[65] Irish legal education typically produced no more than a 'mere mechanical collector of cases'.[66] Legal cultural dependency ensured adherence to the British legal tradition with its emphasis on the common law, judicial precedent, and parliamentary sovereignty.[67] Politically, the doctrine of parliamentary sovereignty was of some importance to unionist ideologies. A. V. Dicey attacked Gladstone's first Government of Ireland Bill (1886) on the grounds that British subjects did not require the protection of a written constitution or guarantees of individual liberty but enjoyed personal liberty and rights as free subjects of the crown, limited only to the extent that they themselves had determined through their elected representatives.[68] For Anglo-Irish judges and practitioners, similarly, deference to parliament was accepted practice and declarations of fundamental rights the objects of abiding suspicion.[69]

This developing legal field formed an important, albeit uneven site for contesting core-peripheral and social relations. Ireland's semi-peripheralisation took classic legal form. In terms of family law, classic legal thought rationalised the practice of legal non-intervention in the household on the basis that state intervention would corrupt or destroy the distinct 'sphere' of the family, thereby rendering many of the formal rights of wives and children unenforceable.[70] By the early twentieth century, the *Irish Citizen*, a paper of the emergent feminist movement, routinely highlighted male domination of the law and legal institutions. Elizabeth Priestly-McCracken of the Irish women's suffrage movement claimed that the privacy of the home reinforced women's economic dependence on men and often compelled women to keep domestic violence and marital rape silent and hidden: 'The legal

65 See Delany, 1975, *The Administration of Justice in Ireland*, p. 16.
66 Mark O'Shaughnessy, 1872, 'On Legal Education in Ireland' in *Journal of the Statistical and Social Inquiry Society of Ireland*, Vol. VI, Part XLII, pp. 124–66.
67 See John McEldowney, 2004, 'Challenges in Legal Bibliography' in *Irish Jurist*, 39 (1), pp. 215–42.
68 See Hugh Tulloch, 1980, 'A. V. Dicey and the Irish Question: 1870–1922' in *Irish Jurist*, 15, pp.137–65.
69 John Kelly cited in Hogan and Whyte, 2003, *J. M. Kelly: The Irish Constitution*, p. i.
70 Duncan Kennedy, 2006, 'Three Globalisations of Law and Legal Thought', p. 34.

profession were completely on the side of men and offered no help to women who complained of brutality. The legal profession contributed to the view that it is a man's prerogative to beat his wife'.[71]

In terms of market law, the post-Famine shift to land-intensive livestock production determined significant transformations in the established property rights regime. Writing in the mid-nineteenth century, Irish jurists such as William Hancock, William Ferguson, and Andrew Vance justified the transformation of 'backward', 'feudal' property relations as a natural development of free market principles and a bulwark to 'those communist doctrines respecting the organisation of labour, which are alike destructive of wealth, morality, and social order . . .'[72] With the passing of Deasy's Act (1860), the reclassification of feudal 'tenure' agreements to market 'contracts' facilitated a rapid increase in tenant evictions in the course of grazier-led consolidation.[73] The now geographically extensive, professional court network was central to this process. Through it, Dublin Castle could prosecute those suspected of agrarian militancy while landlords, with the aid of groups such as the Property Defence Association, could pursue debt-incumbent tenants, resulting in thousands of 'sheriffs' sales' of the tenants' goods, usually livestock.[74]

Irish tenants, deprived of their time-honoured rights in the soil, now sought to reassert customary claims over improved dwellings, buildings, and fences as well as traditional ideas of the 'irremovable tenant', heresies to the law of contract.[75] The Irish Land League and Irish Parliamentary Party fought for and secured government recognition of these customary rights by the 1880s before turning towards increased land transfer and redistribution in subsequent years.[76] Remarkably, the

71 Louise Ryan, 'An analysis of the Irish suffrage movement using new social movement theory' in Linda Connolly and Niamh Hourigan (eds.), 2006, *Social Movements and Ireland*. Manchester: Manchester University Press. pp. 40–57, p. 50.

72 W. N. Hancock, 1850, *Impediments to the Prosperity of Ireland*. London: Simms and McIntyre, p. 32.

73 Landlord and Tenant Law Amendment Act (Ireland) 1860.

74 Adam Pole, 2005, 'Sheriffs' Sales during the Land War, 1879–82' in *Irish Historical Studies*, 34 (136), pp. 386–402, p. 401.

75 Congost, 2003, 'Property Rights and Historical Analysis', pp. 103–4.

76 The Land Act (1870) acknowledged the tenants' customary right to compensation for improvements and for disturbance. The Land Law (Ireland) Act (1881) reinstated the customary position of land being held by tenure not contract, specifically a statutory tenure whereby a tenant could enjoy the possession of his holding at a 'fair rent' – fixed on a judicial basis through the newly established Irish Land Commission courts – for a statutory period of fifteen years.

Land League's ambivalent slogan – 'The Land of Ireland for the People of Ireland' – reflected the ideological parameters of classic legal thought. The formulation derived directly from the writings of the mid-nineteenth-century Young Ireland movement.[77]

In the course of the Famine, radicals within Young Ireland proposed the creation of a peasant proprietorship, the destruction of landlordism to be achieved through a general strike on rents. Ideologically, James Fintan Lalor was not opposed to private property rights in land but rather held that such rights were conditional, not absolute. In classic legal fashion, Lalor traced the beginnings of society to a social contract and maintained that in English law the land was handed over by the people to the king, who, in turn, granted it to the landlords. He denied, however, that the rule of the monarch in Ireland was based on any such contract but proclaimed the land of Ireland to belong to the people of Ireland, 'not in a communistic sense but in the same way as by legal fiction the land of England belongs to the Crown'.[78] This classic national jurisprudence, however, hints at alternative, 'communistic' understandings of land ownership and suggests the much more pronounced bifurcation between law and justice reproduced amongst the majority population.

In the eyes of the majority labourer and tenant population, the administration of justice was a projection of the colonisers' power and prestige. The Anglo-Irish bench, a later judge would recall, was 'an enemy institution in the eyes of the people'.[79] The consequence of the absence of consent to, or general acceptance of, the Crown courts was predictable: each conviction was portrayed as inevitable, each acquittal as being despite, not because of, a system of alien law.[80] In particular, the majority population, as evidenced by later submissions to the Irish Folklore Commission, strongly identified with a belief that separate laws existed for rich and poor. Even in disputes where the law was favourable, recourse to the courts was costly and, by implication, unavailable; while paupers' procedures existed on paper, their use was virtually unheard

[77] Lyons, 1973, *Ireland since the Famine*, pp. 108–9.

[78] Thus, limiting the landlords' power over tenants was justifiable on the grounds that their tenure was given by the people, who would not give them power to oppress themselves. Thomas P. O'Neill, 1955, 'The Irish Land Question, 1830–1850' in *Studies*, 44 (175), pp. 325–36, p. 333.

[79] Hugh Kennedy cited in Hogan, 1987, 'The Supreme Court and the Single European Act', p. 70.

[80] John MacMenamin, 2008, 'Review: Foxton, Revolutionary Lawyers' in *Irish Jurist* 43(1), pp. 137–9.

of.[81] In popular folk belief, securing justice often necessitated a labourer or tenant finding someone influential, like a 'good' landlord, to take up their case for them.[82] In these circumstances, the common law court emerged as one doubtful site of justice amongst multiple others.

Arbitration was the most common form of dispute resolution. On the rundales of Connacht or the 'souming' commons of Ulster, where farmers' flocks mingled on common grazing grounds or mountainsides, disputes frequently arose over the ownership of livestock. Parties to local arbitration were expected to make their case themselves in public, as opposed to hiring an advocate. These open-ended, customary procedures contrasted with the common law courts' use of restrictive rules of evidence which, by permitting only proximate events to be mentioned in argument, tended to violate the complex social fabric of local relationships. Although the Catholic parish priest may also have been called upon to intervene, the extent to which religious discipline was imposed in arbitration proceedings correlated with what the community deemed to be reasonable. Those who refused to accept the decision of an arbitration would be boycotted, a communal sanction.[83]

As the tenant right movement escalated from the 1860s onwards and as successive Liberal and Conservative governments conceded land reform, the bifurcation between these alternative modes of justice and the common law courts emerged in ever sharper relief.[84] The attempted liberalisation of landlords' property rights occasioned an increase in evictions, infringing on popular understandings of justice that rent-paying tenants had a perpetual right to use the soil. Far from a process of gentlemanly agreement then, the subsequent negotiating of 'fair' rents or land purchase approximated that which was acceptable to a region's tenants, a situation resolved not in the Land Courts but through running battles between agitators and the police.[85]

The basis for the government's coercive response to popular disorder was well established. Between 1800 and 1845, no fewer than thirty-five coercion acts were passed or renewed, introducing restrictions on the

[81] T. Molony, 1931, 'Legal Aid for Poor Persons' in *Journal of the Statistical and Social Inquiry Society of Ireland*, Vol. 17, p. 16; Claire Carney, 1979, 'The Growth of Legal Aid in the Republic of Ireland' in *Irish Jurist*, 14 (1), pp. 61–82, pp. 66, 72.

[82] Hickey, 1999, *Irish Law and Lawyers in Modern Folk Tradition*, p. 46.

[83] Hickey, 1999, *Irish Law and Lawyers in Modern Folk Tradition*, pp. 133, 156.

[84] See Heather Laird, 2005, *Subversive law in Ireland, 1879–1920: From 'unwritten law' to the Dáil courts*. Dublin: Four Courts Press.

[85] Terence Dooley, 2004, *The Land for the People: The Land Question in Independent Ireland*, Dublin: University College Dublin Press, p. 9.

carrying of arms, increasing the powers of magistrates and police officers in 'proclaimed' districts and imposing financial penalties on 'disturbed' areas. (Whether Westminster or Dublin Castle actually observed the common law in Ireland was therefore doubtful).[86] In 1871, the government introduced detention without trial for persons suspected of membership of agrarian secret societies. Internment was reintroduced in 1881 under 'protection of person and property' legislation as a weapon against the Land League. People suspected of 'threatening order' were prosecuted under Coercion Acts through the courts. While effective against localised disorder and secret societies, however, such measures were largely ineffectual against mass political activity.[87]

Tenants and labourers responded to rack-renting landlords and legal prosecutions by shunning, intimidating, and making fun of all those involved in the common law process, including barristers and process-servers as well as bailiffs and 'grippers', responsible for the seizure of goods for the non-payment of rent and for the carrying out of eviction orders.[88] Pageantry (or 'wren-boys') accompanied anti-eviction activity.[89] John Millington Synge's *The Aran Islands* (1907) documents how local islanders responded to attempts to levy 'distress' on debt-defaulters:

> Till this year no-one on the island would consent to act as bailiff, so that it was impossible to identify the cattle of the defaulters. Now, however, a man of the name of Patrick has sold his honour, and the effort of concealment is practically futile. This falling away from the ancient loyalty of the island has caused intense indignation ... [On the day that Patrick commenced his duties, the entire population came out to jeer and abuse him. There, in front of her friends and neighbours, Patrick's mother solemnly cursed him aloud].[90]

Popular practices of boycotting and informal arbitration declined according to the receding strength of the tenant right movement, resurfacing during the 'ranch wars' of the early 1900s and, most notably, during the crucial moment of anti-systemic rupture and popular militancy that preceded Irish independence.

86 Virginia Crossman, 1991, 'Emergency Legislation and Agrarian Disorder in Ireland, 1821–41' in *Irish Historical Studies*, 27 (108), pp. 309–23.
87 Crossman, 1991, 'Emergency Legislation and Agrarian Disorder in Ireland, 1821–41', p. 323.
88 See Hogan, 1986, *The Legal Profession in Ireland: 1789–1922*, pp. 3, 9.
89 Laird, 2005, *Subversive law in Ireland, 1879–1920*, pp. 60–1.
90 J. M. Synge, 1979 [1907], *The Aran Islands*, p. 88. See also Hickey, 1999, *Irish Law and Lawyers in Modern Folk Tradition*, p. 86.

## WORLD REVOLUTION AND SOCIO-ECONOMIC RIGHTS IN IRELAND: '1917'

The world-revolutionary moment of '1917' marked a decisive moment of transformation in the historical capitalist world-system, signalling the decline of the British Empire and the emergence of the United States as the new capitalist hegemon. During World War I (1914–18), national political elites throughout Europe had secured popular mobilisation for their respective war efforts on the promise of political and social reform, notably an extended franchise and proto-welfare state measures.[91] Wartime upheavals, defeats, and defections, however, sparked a worldwide wave of labour mobilisations and popular militancy, the most important feature of which was the unanticipated victory of the Bolshevik Revolution in Russia. The six-year period between 1917 and 1923 occasioned a global wave of working class unrest and militancy, involving general strikes in the US and Europe, as well as worker uprisings in Austria, Hungary, Germany, Italy, and Spain.[92] Concomitantly, the war weakened or destroyed the multinational European empires, replacing them with a patchwork of nation-states carved out from their territory. In this moment of anti-systemic rupture, the victorious Allied powers played the Wilsonian card of national self-determination and social reform against the Bolshevik card of international revolution.[93]

Questions of national self-determination and social reform loomed large in Ireland during the years immediately preceding the rupture of '1917'. In terms of the latter, the Dublin Lock-Out (1913–14) clearly marked the balance of capital-labour forces prior to the war. The Lock-Out was the culmination of a protracted struggle between organised labour and the Dublin Employers' Federation, a group of more than three hundred employers led by William Martin Murphy. Living conditions for labourers and their families had been dire for generations with most living in overcrowded, three-room dwellings in the countryside, or slum tenements in the cities. Diseases such as tuberculosis, influenza, and rickets were rampant.[94] Jim Larkin and James Connolly founded the Irish Transport and General Workers Union (ITGWU) in these circumstances with the international-syndicalist vision of

91 Eric Hobsbawm, 1994, *Age of Extremes: The Short Twentieth Century, 1914–1991*. London: Michael Joseph, pp. 85–109.
92 Pierre Broué, 2005 [1971], *The German Revolution: 1917–23*. Leiden: Brill.
93 Hobsbawm, 1992, *Nations and Nationalism since 1780*, pp. 101–63.
94 Terrence Brown, 2004, *Ireland: a social and cultural history, 1922–2002*. London: Harper, p. 15.

forming 'one big union' to overthrow capitalism and build a workers' commonwealth.[95]

Following a series of successful sympathetic strikes, the Employers' Federation, with the support of Dublin Castle, responded to a strike on the Dublin Tramways by locking out more than 20,000 unionised workers. Dublin's tenements slowly starved. While Larkin sought to build solidarity with British trade unions, the Irish Citizen Army (ICA), perhaps the world's first workers' militia, formed to protect workers from the Dublin Metropolitan Police and employers' hired union-breakers.[96] Meanwhile, the Catholic hierarchy and lay organisations physically opposed philanthropic actions to provide foster homes for strikers' children in Protestant England, advocating charitable relief instead. Significantly, the alarming escalation in working-class organisation induced a minority of employers and Jesuits to propose not just charitable relief but 'social rights' as necessary to preserve Dublin's workers from godless, un-Irish ideas of communism.[97] Ultimately, the Lock-Out resulted in a decisive albeit costly victory for the city's major employers, leaving a bitter, enduring legacy.

On the question of national self-determination, a civil conflict along Nationalist-Unionist lines appeared likely over the same period. Anticipating the passing of a Home Rule bill for Ireland, some half a million unionists, concentrated in northeast Ulster, had signed a Solemn League and Covenant, pledging resistance. The situation escalated in 1913 with the formation and arming of the Ulster Volunteer Force and the subsequent counterformation of the nationalist Irish Volunteers, supported politically by John Redmond's Irish Parliamentary Party and heavily infiltrated by the IRB. Cumann na mBan, a women's paramilitary organisation, formed as an auxiliary to the Irish Volunteers.[98] To the relief of Dublin Castle, the outbreak of World War I diffused these tensions as Westminster suspended Home Rule for the war's duration.

95 Padraig Mannion (ed.), 2013, *Lock-Out Centenary*. Dublin: Dun Laoghaire Commemorative Committee; see also Stoneybatter and Smithfield People's History Project (SSPHP), 2014, *The Irish Citizen Army in Stoneybatter, Smithfield and the Markets*. Dublin: SSPHP.

96 'Irish Citizen Army' in D. J. Hickey and J. E. Doherty, 2003, *A New Dictionary of Irish History*. Dublin: Gill and MacMillan, pp. 221–2. See also Seán O'Casey, 1919, *The Story of the Irish Citizen Army*. Dublin: Maunsel.

97 Finín O'Dricoll, 'Social Catholicism in Independent Ireland: The Challenge to the Fiscal System' in Mike Cronin and John Regan (eds.), 2000, *Ireland: The Politics of Independence, 1922–49*. Dublin: Macmillan, p. 134; see also James Connolly's critique of Catholic, natural rights discourse in 'Labour, Nationality and Religion' in Donal Nevin (ed.), 2011, *Writings of James Connolly: Collected Works*. Dublin: SIPTU, pp. 121–70, esp. pp. 138–48.

98 Cumann na mBan (Irish: Women's Council).

Irish nationalists split. The Irish Parliamentary Party urged enlistment. Some 170,000 southern Irishmen did so, many of them economically conscripted from Dublin's tenements. Some 8,000 Irish Volunteers, however, refused. Presented with an opportunity to strike, the military council of the IRB now co-opted the Irish Citizen Army and strategically manoeuvred the remaining Irish Volunteers, renamed as the Irish Republican Army (IRA), into an insurrection. During the Easter Rising of 1916 some 1,200 soldiers, predominantly workers and small farmers, forcefully occupied sites throughout Dublin, including the Four Courts and Law Library.[99] Sporadic clashes with the Royal Irish Constabulary also occurred throughout the country. Patrick Pearse, nominal commander-in-chief, proclaimed the foundation of an Irish Republic on behalf of an Irish provisional government, establishing its headquarters in the General Post Office.[100]

The Proclamation of the Irish Republic (1916) featured prominently in later constitution-making moments and socio-economic rights contestations.[101] The Proclamation reiterated 'the right of the people of Ireland to the ownership of Ireland', a purposely ambiguous fusion of national and social aspiration.[102] It also featured a definite 'social' content:

> The Republic guarantees religious and civil liberty, equal rights and equal opportunities to all its citizens, and declares its resolve to pursue the happiness and prosperity of the whole nation and of all its parts, cherishing all the children of the nation equally, and oblivious of the differences carefully fostered by an alien government, which have divided a minority from the majority in the past.[103]

[99] Hogan, 1986, *The Legal Profession in Ireland: 1789–1922*, p. 145. Stein Larsen and Oliver Snoddy, 1973, '1916 – A Workingmen's Revolution? An analysis of those who made the 1916 revolution in Ireland' in *Social Studies*, 2 (4), pp. 377–98.

[100] McBride, 1991, *The Greening of Dublin Castle*, p. 208.

[101] See D. J. Hickey and J. E. Doherty, 2003, *A New Dictionary of Irish History*. Dublin: Gill and MacMillan, p. 134.

[102] The social vision of the 1916 leadership, as Declan Kiberd has noted, was couched in the language of nationalist revival. Hence, Pearse argued that liberal, child-centred methods of education approximated a return to old Gaelic systems of fosterage while Connolly suggested that a welfare, socialist state would revive old Irish forms of landholding, albeit with popular government rather than a chieftain holding wealth in the name of the people. 'Patrick Pearse: Irish Modernist' in Róisín Higgins and Regina Ní Chollatáin (eds.), 2009, *The Life and After-Life of Patrick Pearse*, Dublin: Irish Academic Press, pp. 65–80, p. 67.

[103] The phrase refers to political and religious differences as well as visions of a more materially egalitarian society. On its fruitful mis-remembering, see John O'Dowd, 2011, 'Remembering the Constitution: The Easter Proclamation and Constitutionalism in Independent Ireland', *IBIS Working Paper Series*, 104, pp. 1–18. Available at: www.ucd.ie/ibis/filestore/wp2011/104_odowd.pdf.

That the Proclamation was addressed to 'Irishmen and Irishwomen' was a significant acknowledgment of women's political rights, reflecting the involvement of Cumann na mBan at a time when they were denied a vote in parliamentary elections. While the German legal scholar Leo Kohn suggested that the Proclamation envisaged 'economic democracy', the relative strength of the Irish Citizen Army to the IRB and Irish Volunteers in fact ensured the exclusion of revolutionary socialist aims such as democratic control of production, distribution, and exchange.[104] Moreover, the Proclamation's reference to 'Most High God' indicates the text's simultaneous classic or 'national' discourse, and further distinguishes Irish republicanism from Europe's secular equivalents.[105]

Occurring in the midst of World War I, the Easter Rising elicited a response commensurate to a perceived act of treason in wartime, or to a perceived instance of emergency coercion in times of rebellion. Martial law was declared in Dublin as the British army fought the rebels to a ceasefire and then executed the leadership. As the Royal Irish Constabulary interned and deported some 3,400 suspected revolutionaries, popular opinion began to shift against the status quo. A heretofore marginal nationalist party, Sinn Féin, claimed the 1916 Proclamation as its own. The party, led by the most senior surviving member of the IRA Éamon de Valera, sought the immediate establishment of the Irish Republic by abstaining from Westminster and forming a constituent assembly in Dublin. Subordinate to the Empire's war effort, Dublin Castle invoked nineteenth-century coercive legislation to proclaim the Irish Volunteers, the Irish Citizen Army, Cumann na mBan, and Sinn Féin 'dangerous associations'. By 1918, mounting British losses in France also raised the prospect of conscription in Ireland, prompting a mass anti-conscription movement. Some two million people signed a pledge of resistance and on 23 April, the trade unions organised a one-day general strike in protest.[106]

Meanwhile, questions of social reform remained unresolved. The immediate postwar period occasioned social polarisation, economic recession, rising unemployment, and a sharp decline in the living conditions of the working class.[107] Graziers, dairies, railway owners, and

104 See Kohn, 1932, *The Constitution of the Irish Free State*, pp. 26, 33.

105 The reference to 'the dead generations' from which Ireland received 'her old tradition of nationhood' may be viewed similarly.

106 McBride, 1991, *The Greening of Dublin Castle*, p. 242; see also Hogan, 1986, *The Legal Profession in Ireland: 1789–1922*, p. 243.

107 Diarmaid Ferriter, 2005, *The Transformation of Ireland*. London: Profile Books, p. 210.

financiers thrived in the agricultural boom brought about by wartime demand. Conversely, the wages of urban workers and rural labourers lagged behind rising prices.[108] Land reform over the past half-century had offered nothing to thousands of landless labourers and, in many cases, offered so little to tenants that 'land hunger' spiked after 1917.[109] Moreover, emigration, a traditional safety valve for popular discontent, was not possible in wartime.[110] During the ensuing military conflicts in Ireland, Dublin Castle ceased to maintain public services. Existing welfare structures, including hospitals, orphanages, and other forms of public charity, collapsed. The American Committee for Relief in Ireland secured Westminster's approval to distribute civilian aid through the Irish White Cross, a non-political, non-sectarian organisation led by Quakers.[111] Notwithstanding their efforts, dire living conditions persisted. In these circumstances, the 1918 flu pandemic killed some 20,000 people in Ireland, about eight times as many fatalities as brought about by the national conflict.[112]

Ensuing popular militancy in Ireland formed part of the '1917' rupture within the historical capitalist world-system. 'National' and 'social' anti-systemic struggles overlapped: a rapid escalation in labour and agrarian militancy coincided with the Irish Republican Army's pursuit of an anticolonial struggle through force of arms. Organised labour was notably resurgent. Between August 1918 and August 1923, there were five general strikes, and eighteen local strikes, twelve of these in 1919. Trade union membership rose dramatically, from 100,000 in 1916 to 255,000 in 1920.[113] The ITGWU was central to promoting

108 O'Hearn, 2001, *The Atlantic Economy*, p. 113; Crotty, 1986, *Ireland in Crisis*, p. 73. The Irish banks' liquid balances in London increased as exports prospered, with domestic savings rising fourfold between 1900 and 1920. Pádraig McGowan, 1990, *Money and Banking in Ireland*. Dublin: Institute of Public Administration, p. 41.

109 The crucial dynamic was securing sufficient land to earn a livelihood, usually more than 25 acres. See Dooley, 2004, *The Land for the People*, pp. 41–2. While the banks raised interest rates and the British Treasury ceased advancements for land purchase, the Congested Districts Board postponed the acquisition of estates and consequently failed to release enough land to satisfy demand. Instead, the Board rented out land it had already acquired and graziers let conacre at exorbitant rates, leading to widespread accusations of profiteering. Mary Kotsonouris, 1994, *Retreat from Revolution: The Dáil Courts, 1920–24*. Dublin: Irish Academic Press, p. 19.

110 Louis Cullen, 1987, *An economic history of Ireland since 1660*. London: Batsford, p. 172.

111 D. H. Akenson and J. F. Fallin, 1970a, 'The Irish Civil War and the Drafting of the Free State Constitution' in *Eire Ireland* (5), pp. 16–20; James Douglas, 1998, *Memoirs of Senator James G. Douglas (1887–1954)*, pp. 61–78.

112 Ruth Barrington, 1987, *Health, Medicine and Politics in Ireland 1900–1970*, Dublin: Institute of Public Administration, pp. 123–32.

113 Ferriter, 2005, *The Transformation of Ireland*, pp. 210–1.

workers' direct actions. Irish dockers and railway workers, mirroring their British counterparts' refusal to handle goods for the White Army deployed against the Russian Revolution, refused to handle weapons for the British military, a factor crucial to the IRA's success. Workers also took over the running of more than eighty workplaces and established soviets at the Cleeves factory in Limerick, at the foundry in Drogheda, Co. Louth, and in the coal mines of Arigna, Co. Roscommon and Castlecomer, Co. Kilkenny.[114]

From 1919 onwards, as the IRA forced the retreat of law enforcement to cities, rural communities created a network of local militias and arbitration courts. Communities boycotted the established legal system and gathered in public halls, schools, and farmhouses to elect lay arbitrators to settle disputes, including conflicts over rents and land. All involved risked imprisonment or worse.[115] In these circumstances, small farmers and landless labourers, concentrated in Connacht and along the Western seaboard, revived traditional campaigns of intimidation to secure land from the grazier class. Localised rent strikes escalated into widespread cattle-driving and land-grabbing. Kevin O'Shiel, a Sinn Féin lawyer, observed how landlords 'had their fields cleared, their cattle and sheep driven along the hard roads of Connacht for miles until they died of exhaustion and hunger and the value of all was disastrously diminished'.[116] For the first time in Ireland, landlords were forcibly ousted from their homes. Between 1920 and 1923, some 300 burnings of 'big houses' occurred.[117] In the absence of police, graziers in the Irish Farmers' Union favoured the creation of a 'White Army' to combat 'agrarian Bolshevism'.[118] As Sinn Féin TD Erskine Childers put it, 'There was a moment when it seemed that nothing could prevent wholesale expropriation'.[119]

Those people involved in agrarian agitation, diffuse and dispersed, did not produce programmatic declarations concerning 'socio-economic rights' so much as revive long-standing, communal norms of cooperation, arbitration, and justice.[120] Conversely, the revolutionary

[114] Kostick, 2009, *Revolution in Ireland*, pp. 5, 148.
[115] Kotsonouris, 1994, *Retreat from Revolution*, p. 46; O'Malley, 1936, *On Another Man's Wound*, p. 185.
[116] Kevin O'Shiel, 'Memories of my Lifetime' in the *Irish Times*, 22 November 1966.
[117] Dooley, 2004, *The Land for the People*, p. 42.
[118] Lee, 1989, *Ireland: 1912–1985*, p. 181.
[119] See Dooley, 2004, *The Land for the People*, p. 46.
[120] In an age before mechanisation the help of neighbours or the 'meitheal' (a group of workers providing free labour in return for similar assistance at a later date) were essential to small

currents within the organised labour movement explicitly articulated 'rights'. Crucially, however, they directed these claims to the movement itself rather than to the state. The Constitution of the Irish Citizen Army (1914), re-appropriating James Fintan Lalor's earlier linking of national and social demands, declared that 'the ownership of Ireland, moral and material, is vested of right in the people of Ireland'.[121] Internationalist in vision, the constitution further declared a commitment to 'support the rights and liberties of the democracies of all nations', 'the democracy' here not being a form of state but rather an emancipatory potential, the revolutionary proletariat.[122] Mirroring the dominance of anarcho-syndicalism in the self-consciously internationalist workers' movement of the early twentieth century, the key mechanism for achieving the ICA's vision was compulsory trade union membership as a prelude to collective industrial action.[123] Within the wider labour movement, elements remained sceptical of representative politics. The ITGWU explicitly praised the early Soviet model of direct democracy as representing 'a higher form of political development than the Constituent Assembly'.[124]

Antisystemic 'social' and 'national' forces enjoyed an uneasy coexistence in the course of Ireland's long '1917'. Sinn Féin, buoyed by three by-election victories, sought to secure an authoritative position within the broader social movements. The party leadership, thoroughly infiltrated by the IRB, were acutely conscious of the potential for class conflict and determined to ignore or suppress clashes which might distract from the 'foreign enemy'. From its founding, the party spoke in terms of 'an abstract Ireland and a monolithic Irish people' in all areas of policy and while denouncing imperialism, would not associate itself with class war.[125] Sinn Féin swiftly co-opted the support of trade

farmers working the land. Cormac Ó Comhraí, 2013, *Revolution in Connacht*. Cork: Mercier Press, p. 8.

121 'Irish Citizen Army' in D. J. Hickey and J. E. Doherty, 2003, *A New Dictionary of Irish History*. Dublin: Gill and MacMillan, pp. 221–2. See also Seán O'Casey, 1919, *The Story of the Irish Citizen Army*. Dublin: Maunsel.

122 Richard McAleavey, 2014, 'Whatever happened to the Irish democracy?' In: *Cunning Hired Knaves*. Available at: https://hiredknaves.wordpress.com/2014/03/21/whatever-happened-to-the-irish-democracy/.

123 Anarcho-syndicalism provided 'the main vehicle of global opposition to industrial capitalism, autocracy, latifundism, and imperialism'. Benedict Anderson, 2006, *Under Three Flags: anarchism and the anti-colonial imagination*. London: Verso, pp. 2, 54; see also Dirlik, 1993, *Anarchism in the Chinese Revolution*.

124 *Voice of Labour*, 20 January 1918; Dublin City Library and Archives.

125 Michael Laffan, 1999, *The Resurrection of Ireland: the Sinn Féin party, 1916–1923*, Cambridge: Cambridge University Press, p. 253.

unions and their associated party organisation. The Labour party, now led by Thomas Johnson and William O'Brien, did not contest the 1918 general election (or the 1921 election after that), acquiescing in Sinn Féin's demand for a national plebiscite on leaving the Empire.[126] In a landslide victory, Sinn Féin won seventy-three seats, the Unionist party twenty-six, and the Irish Parliamentary Party six. Sinn Féin's elected candidates subsequently abstained from Westminster and met in Dublin to form Dáil Éireann, an underground, illegal yet Westminster-styled parliament.[127]

Popular militancy prompted Sinn Féin to articulate socio-economic rights. The party's 1918 election manifesto contained a 'Catholic social' discourse, subsuming class differences into the nation and its harmonious social order. In contrast to the 1916 Proclamation's declaration of 'the right of the people of Ireland to the ownership of Ireland', Sinn Féin's manifesto, genuflecting to the Catholic hierarchy, declared that the nation's right to sovereignty rested 'upon immutable natural law'.[128] According to Alfred O'Rahilly, a Corkonian academic and Sinn Féin propagandist, the Irish 'nation' constituted a 'mystical body' or 'corporate personality' that possessed a 'natural right' to independence '*ex natura rei*' ('in the nature of things').[129] Moreover, in contrast to the ICA constitution, where power resided in organised labour and popular assemblies, the new parliament and constituent assembly would act as 'the supreme national authority to speak and act in the name of the Irish people, and to develop Ireland's social, political and industrial life, for the welfare of the whole people of Ireland'.[130] Escalating popular militancy, however, compelled Sinn Féin to issue a stronger statement of socio-economic rights.

126 Conor Kostick, 2009, *Revolution in Ireland: popular militancy, 1917–1923*, Cork: Cork University Press, pp. 38–9, 126.

127 Kissane, 2011, *New Beginnings*, p. 20.

128 A fundamental concept of medieval western political philosophy, natural law was believed to represent the natural order of things established by God as the creator of the universe. The resulting norms for governing human conduct legitimated claims for restitution against wrongdoing. These claims, or natural rights, were universal in scope. See Campbell, 2006, *Rights*, pp. 5–6.

129 Propaganda for the Sinn Féin movement featured natural law discourse of this sort. Sinn Féin's commitment to defend the Irish Republic and Dáil by physical force if necessary was therefore justified by the just war theory of Thomas Aquinas. See Alfred O'Rahilly, 1921, 'The Sovereignty of the People' in *Studies*, Vol. X (37), pp. 39–56, p. 46.

130 Aodh de Blacam, 1921, *What Sinn Féin Stands For*. Dublin: Sinn Féin.

The 1919 'Democratic Programme' of the First Dáil declared all rights of private property to be subordinated to the public welfare.[131] Drafted by Labour leader Tom Johnson and sharply edited by Sinn Féin's Seán T. O'Kelly, the programme reproduced the ideas of Patrick Pearse and James Connolly in its claim that 'the nation's sovereignty extends not only to all its citizens, but to all its natural possessions, the national wealth and wealth-producing processes'. The Government of the Republic further assured Irish citizens of opportunities to serve the public welfare and in return to receive 'an adequate share of the produce of the Nation's labour'. It would further ensure 'that no child shall suffer hunger or cold from lack of food, clothing, or shelter', provide 'the means and facilities requisite for their proper education and training as Citizens of a Free and Gaelic Ireland', make available 'a sympathetic native scheme for the care of the Nation's aged and infirm' and 'take such measures as will safeguard the health of the people'.[132]

In contrast to organised labour, decentralised articulations of class conflict continued to prove more difficult for the IRB, Sinn Féin and Dáil Éireann to incorporate. Agrarian conflict, in particular, threatened to split the IRA's rank and file.[133] The IRA's support for the Dáil could not be relied upon. Within the inter-state system, Sinn Féin's credibility as a party of government was at stake, upon which depended international recognition of the Irish Republic as well as funding, both international and domestic, for arms and the war effort. Among the most important strategies in keeping the national movement 'unriven by class warfare' was the Sinn Féin party's incorporation of the popular court system.[134]

## FROM POPULAR TO PARTY COURTS: THE RESURGENCE OF CLASSIC LEGAL THOUGHT

During the period 1917 to 1923, the established legal apparatus broke down and an alternative, popular court network emerged only to be

131 'Democratic Programme' in *Dáil Debates*, 21 January 1919; available at: http://oireachtasdebates.oireachtas.ie/debates%20authoring/debateswebpack.nsf/takes/dail1919012100016?opendocument.

132 The majority of Sinn Féin representatives, being absent from the First Dáil, were largely unaware of the Democratic Programme: it was adopted for 'essentially propagandist reasons' and never implemented. Farrell, 1988, 'From First Dáil through Irish Free State', p. 21.

133 Ó Comhraí, 2013, *Revolution in Connacht*, pp. 62–5.

134 James Casey, 1970, 'Republican Courts in Ireland 1919–1922' in *Irish Jurist*, 5 (2), pp. 321–42, p. 342.

subsumed to the nationalist party and ultimately replaced by the former legal system in the Irish Free State. Sinn Féin, motivated by a desire to prioritise 'national' over 'social' conflict and to retain centralised political control, played a crucial role in ensuring this outcome. By 1919, antagonism towards the existing legal apparatus was pervasive: Dublin Castle was held responsible for martial law, mass arrests, suppressing newspapers, public meetings and, in proclaimed districts, even fairs and markets. The IRA declared attendance at British courts to be an act of treason to the Irish Republic and imposed cordons around towns prior to court meetings. The wider hostility of the local population, refusing lodgings to assize judges, was also significant to their undermining.[135] With the exception of the Four Courts which continued to function, the IRA's burning of the Customs House and Companies Registration Office in May 1921 effectively brought the established courts to a halt.

A popular courts network evolved organically in these circumstances. Following customary procedures of dispute resolution and earlier precedents such as the Land Courts set up by the National League in the 1880s, communities elected local arbitration courts in Counties Mayo, Sligo, Roscommon, Kildare, and Galway.[136] (The preponderance of such courts established in the west is a good indicator of the level of agrarian conflict requiring resolution). Among their central tasks was to decide upon cases in which tenants' right to purchase holdings was at stake.[137] Courts were held in all sorts of places, from public halls or schools in towns to creameries, farmhouses, and barns in the countryside.[138] Litigants, after signing a pledge to abide by its findings, entered the court to have their case heard by three arbitrators, elected by a local convention composed of representatives of Sinn Féin, the Volunteers, Trades Councils, and Cumann na mBan. The vast majority of arbitrators were laypeople and unremunerated. All involved ran significant risks of imprisonment and possibly worse.

The courts, according to one reporter, operated 'in a common sense way, relying not upon a complete and formal code of legal precedent, but upon considerations of equity and of the normal law as generally understood'. There was 'no pomp or ceremony of any kind . . .'[139]

135 O'Malley, 1936 [2008], *On Another Man's Wound*, p. 185.
136 Hogan, 1986, *The Legal Profession in Ireland: 1789–1922*, p. 150.
137 Dooley, 2004, *The Land for the People*, 41.
138 Davitt cited in Kotsonouris, 1994, *Retreat from Revolution*, p. 46.
139 *News Bulletin*, June 1920 cited in Dooley, 2004, *The Land for the People*, p. 48.

As Ernie O'Malley observed: 'Parish and District Courts settled cases quickly on their merits; there was no forensic eloquence; common sense and good will replaced involuntary legal formulae. Justice was elemental, strict, but impartial and human; costs were low'.[140] Again following customary norms, the courts relied primarily upon moral rather than physical coercion: 'Sentences varied from fines and a shake-hands to parading culprits outside chapel gates on Sunday with their offences and sentences tied around their necks on cardboard, or banishment from Ireland. Sentences were read at chapel gates or posted up'.[141]

From mid-1920 onwards, Sinn Féin attempted to establish authority over these courts as a means of restraining agrarian conflict and land redistribution. After a series of agrarian outrages, a deputation of Connacht landlords called on the Minister for Home Affairs Arthur Griffith to establish 'independent' land courts. Directly following the Connacht landlords' request, the first court under the direct authority of Dáil Éireann sat at Ballinrobe, Co. Mayo on 17 May 1920.[142] The following month, the Dáil decreed that the Courts of the Republic would not hear land claims until the end of the war. According to Griffith, 'people who were putting forward these claims were not nationalists at all. They were merely out to create a state of anarchy which ought to be put a stop to'.[143]

Sinn Féin's putting a stop to 'anarchy' proved difficult however. When the Ballinrobe judgment went against the claimants, some of them continued to occupy the farm, a tactic repeated by other unsuccessful claimants in the area. Subsequently, an IRA unit rounded up the rebels and detained them on an island in Lough Corrib until they agreed to unequivocal obedience to the orders of the court. Throughout the war, the willingness of IRA units to conduct such operations remained far from certain.[144] In some cases, their capacity to do so was further limited. Throughout early 1922, for example, the Limerick Workers' Housing Association prevented the IRA from carrying out decrees for repossession in the city.[145] To further diffuse tensions on the land, the Dáil introduced a 'National Land Bank' to finance land purchases agreed to by the new land courts. Importantly, however, the

140 O'Malley, 1936 [2008], *On Another Man's Wound*, p. 186.

141 O'Malley, 1936 [2008], *On Another Man's Wound*, p. 186.

142 O'Shiel, 'Memories of my Lifetime' in the *Irish Times*, 22 November 1966.

143 'Decrees; Claims to Land' in *Dáil Éireann Debates*, Vol. 1, 29 June 1920. Available at:http://historical-debates.oireachtas.ie/D/DT/D.F.C.192006290071.html.

144 Kotsonouris, 1994, *Retreat from Revolution*, p. 25.

145 Kotsonouris, 1994, *Retreat from Revolution*, p. 77.

bank was never sufficiently capitalised to supplant the Land Commission and functioned primarily as a useful propaganda vehicle for Sinn Féin, persuading agitators that the law-abiding would receive land in due course.[146]

From the mid-1920 onwards, the new 'Dáil Courts' (or 'Sinn Féin Courts') replaced local arbitration with a formal, hierarchical court structure, incorporating a right of appeal from 'parish' and 'district' courts to 'high' and 'supreme' courts in Dublin. There was a greater emphasis on professional status, from the ten paid party organisers responsible for the courts' administration to the new district and superior court judges, all of whom had to be lawyers. The new tier of professional judges comprised of typically young, privileged men, trained in the classic legal system and Catholic nationalist in outlook. While allowing the citation of Brehon, Roman, French, and other law codes in court then, they generally applied the law of the courts they replaced, specifically the law as it existed on 21 January 1919, marking the first day of the First Dáil. By 1921, as the boycott of the former legal system continued, more than nine hundred parish courts and seventy district courts were operating. People had every reason to believe that the Dáil Courts, popular emblems of the new Irish Republic, would continue.

Paul Vignoles, a court organiser in Donegal, observed that his contemporaries recognised 'the Republican Courts as being the first courts established by them'.[147] The Dáil Courts' use of the Irish language, Brehon law codes, and nationalist symbolism was important to sustaining their wider legitimacy, particularly given the alienation of the majority population from the former legal system. The Dáil courts, however, received the most fulsome praise from landowners, many of them unionist, whose lands were now freed of trespassers or whose stolen property was recovered. Landlords in Dublin similarly approached the Dáil Ministry with requests for arbitration in disputes over rent increases. (Wary of the new judges' sympathies, the tenants of the Artisan Dwelling Company chose instead to collect money for an appeal to the House of Lords).[148] The new Dáil Courts were essential to Sinn Féin's effort both to become and to portray itself as a responsible government in waiting. Their creation also illustrated the party's commitment to enforcing the existing, classic laws of market, property, and

146 McBride, 1991, *The Greening of Dublin Castle*, p. 277. See also F. G. Hall, 1949, *History of the Bank of Ireland*; Finín O'Dricoll, 'Social Catholicism in Independent Ireland', p. 123.

147 Letter, 27.07.1922, *Kennedy Papers*, UCDA P4/1067.

148 Kotsonouris, 1994, *Retreat from Revolution*, p. 18.

contract, provided they were no longer skewed against 'the Irish people'. Tellingly, property-owners' now looked to Dublin instead of Westminster to report expropriation.[149]

In these circumstances, 'classic' legal forms and discourses – notwithstanding social democratic and radical alternatives – remained dominant. In Westminster, escalating popular militancy compelled the Liberal-Conservative government to negotiate with Sinn Féin as a reasonable alternative to 'anarchy', particularly once the IRA and British Army had fought to a standstill and truce by mid-1921.[150] British-Irish government negotiations positioned predominantly 'national' as opposed to 'social' political representatives (primarily Michael Collins and Arthur Griffith) and jurists (notably Robert Barton, Eamon Duggan, George Gavan Duffy, and Hugh Kennedy) as mediators between Dublin and London.[151]

The resulting Anglo-Irish Treaty (1921) denoted sovereignty in classic legal terms, resurrecting a state-form with a monopoly on the right to command in its territory. While the 'Empire' was now designated a 'Commonwealth of Nations' for the first time, altering the imperial status quo in Canada, Australia, New Zealand, and South Africa, the Treaty stopped short of British recognition of Irish sovereignty.[152] Instead, it designated the new 'Irish Free State' a self-governing dominion within the Commonwealth, subject to certain reservations providing for the option of partitioning the six 'northern' counties of Ireland as well as for the retention of monarchical legal forms, strategic naval ports, and national debt payments. The Treaty would have superior legal status to any future Irish Free State constitution.

Whereas the proto-constitutional discourses of the preceding decade contained a remarkable social content, the Treaty envisaged the reproduction of pre-existing, classic rights of private property and free trade, remaining silent on issues such as the completion of land purchase or the redistribution of large untenanted estates.[153] Instead of economic re-organisation, the ownership of Ireland was understood by party elites almost exclusively in terms of state-formation and the defence of a unique nationalist culture and identity. Irish nation-building, as in

149 See Casey, 1970, 'Republican Courts in Ireland 1919–1922', p. 321.

150 Between 1919 and mid-1921, the war between the IRA and the British Army resulted in the death of some 2,000 people on the island of Ireland, 750 of whom were civilians.

151 D. W. Harkness, 1969, *The Restless Dominion: The Irish Free State and the British Commonwealth of Nations, 1921–31*. London: Macmillan.

152 Lerner, 2011: *Making Constitutions in Deeply Divided Societies*, p. 169.

153 Dooley, 2004, *The Land for the People*, p. 42.

multiple postcolonial countries, prioritised the articulation of a distinctive, 'native' family law regime, centred on the Catholic Church hierarchy's 'moral monopoly' and remarkably defensive of patriarchal social relations.[154] Welfare provision would remain predominantly voluntary and charitable as opposed to public or rights-based.

The Irish Free State would adopt a conservative governance apparatus, incorporating executive dominance over parliament, a bicameral legislature with an upper and lower house, and a written constitution setting out entrenched rights for minorities. Eerily, a generation earlier, the unionist legal scholar, A. V. Dicey had proposed precisely this institutional arrangement as best able to defend propertied elites from mass electoral democracy.[155] Similarly, and notwithstanding their popularity, Griffith and Collins assured Prime Minister Lloyd George that the 'Dáil Courts' would be wound down.[156] The Courts of Justice Act (1924) broadly re-established the former legal apparatus.[157] Assessing their significance, Darrell Figgis, a Sinn Féin judge and subsequent constitution-maker, observed that the Dáil Courts primarily kept 'the national demand for freedom . . . clear from . . . the snares of a class war'. They 'constituted the only practical form of justice or means of controlling cattle-driving and otherwise limiting anarchy'.[158]

## CONCLUSION

Popular rights discourses had roots in both past and contemporary international struggles. In the wake of the French Revolution of 1789, the Society of United Irishmen advocated a 'communion of rights', linking rights to solidarity and collective action. After Europe's springtime of nations of 1848, 'the right of the people of Ireland to the ownership of Ireland', an ambiguous fusion of both national and social anti-systemic goals, animated the radical outlook of diverse social movements, insurrectionists, and thinkers, from the Young Ireland rebellion

154 Inglis, 1998, *Moral Monopoly*, p. 57. See also Fletcher, 2001, 'Post-Colonial Fragments: Representations of Abortion in Irish Law and Politics'; Kennedy, 2006, 'Three Globalisations of Law and Legal Thought: 1850–2000', pp. 30–1; 50–4; Partha Chatterjee, 1994, *The Nation and its Fragments: Colonial and Postcolonial Histories*, Princeton: Princeton University Press.

155 See Hugh Tulloch, 1980, 'A. V. Dicey and the Irish Question: 1870–1922' in *Irish Jurist*, 15, pp. 137–65.

156 Kotsonouris, 1994, *Retreat from Revolution*, p. 23.

157 A right of appeal to the Privy Council was also provided for in the Constitution of the Irish Free State until its abolition in 1933.

158 Darrell Figgis, 1927, *Recollections of the Irish War* cited in Casey, 1970, 'Republican Courts in Ireland 1919–1922', p. 322. Hogan, 1986, *The Legal Profession in Ireland: 1789–1922*, p. 152.

through the Land Wars to the Dublin Lock-Out and the Easter Rising. In the aftermath of the Russian Revolution of 1917, popular militancy in Ireland occurred alongside a global wave of worker militancy. Throughout, different social groups coincided on attempting to appropriate socio-economic rights discourse, to rearrange its terms in keeping with their priorities and interests and, in doing so, to silence those elements of the discourse inimical to those interests.

Importantly, in terms of the means to be adopted to realise those rights in practice, the direct democratic and syndicalist nature of the Irish Citizen Army's internationalist vision opposed the representative democratic means and nationalist vision advanced by the Sinn Féin mass party. Sinn Féin effectively reasserted the principle that the masses are incapable of governing themselves, notwithstanding ample evidence to the contrary in the form of self-governing communities, arbitration courts, and soviets. This had important implications, most notably in terms of the 'detached complicity' between nation-building elites and the established market economy.[159] In particular, the mass party's decision to centralise and dis-empower the popular courts network brought to an end a radical democratic experiment in which agrarian, communal norms nourished a modern revolutionary movement.

Throughout 1922, popular dis-empowerment gathered pace. The making of the Irish Free State Constitution occurred as a split in the national movement over the Treaty crystallised into a civil war. As during the war of independence, the 'national' question remained simultaneously a social one. The civil war reopened fissures in the penumbra of 'law and order', republicans occupied the Four Courts and incidents of agrarian agitation and working class militancy increased. The experience of recent mass struggles and the development of the civil war loomed large in constitution-makers' decision-making. Both classic and social constitution-makers recognised popular mobilisations as anti-systemic threats. 'The recent revival of cattle-driving', as one framer put it, 'indicates the enormity of a problem which the Irish State cannot long defer without danger to itself'.[160] Certain constitutional provisions, another hoped, would have a 'chilling' effect on revolutionary movements.[161] Economic and social rights discourses, as elsewhere, now emerged, partly as a remedy to perceived social injustice, partly

[159] Fanon, 2001, *The Wretched of the Earth*, p. 65. [160] France, UCDA P4/320.
[161] Kennedy, UCDA P4/336; 342.

as an analgesic response to the more radical-democratic demands of organised communities and workplaces.

Constitution-makers and the Constituent Assembly would look to international constitutions as well as earlier, proto-constitutional texts, particularly the 1916 Proclamation and the 1919 Democratic Programme, to propose egalitarian provisions, notably concerning land redistribution, education, welfare provision, and children's rights. The fate of these proposals was decisively shaped by the emergent balance of core-peripheral and social relations. In the course of the mass popular struggle in Ireland, the preponderance of the anticolonial mass party and the centralisation of power it entailed – first as Sinn Féin, then as Provisional Government – ultimately ensured a 'classic', national constitution. The combined forces of state formation and of ruling class consolidation ensured the repression of republican then popular militancy, the reproduction of semi-peripheral economic processes and the predominance of classic national constitutional forms over social democratic and radical-democratic alternatives. The Irish Free State and its Constitution would thus encode many of the myths presupposed by an 'Irish Ireland'. This outcome was far from inevitable but rather represented the crystallisation of a lengthy drafting process, the critical analysis of which reveals the force, contestation, and defence of the historical capitalist world-system, always hiding in plain sight.

**CHAPTER TWO**

# 'NOT ALONE PERSONAL LIBERTY BUT ECONOMIC FREEDOM': SOCIO-ECONOMIC RIGHTS IN THE MAKING OF THE 1922 IRISH FREE STATE CONSTITUTION

*The most glaring inequalities in wealth which are found in the world today result from the fact that an individual purchases a piece of land that has great strategic value, and in course of years becomes extremely wealthy through no effort of his own but merely from the value given to that land by the community at large . . . I therefore urge a Constitutional provision which would give the right to an All-Ireland parliament adequate powers to deal with the unearned increment.*

– Clement France[1]

*I do believe that we have the opportunity of creating a truly Irish Ireland in the Constitution and for this end we must all work.*

– Hugh Kennedy[2]

Ireland was not alone in experiencing a surge in popular militancy and self-organisation.[3] In February 1919 in the city of Seattle, Washington, more than sixty-five thousand workers engaged in a five-day general strike, shutting down the city in order to force an end to wartime wage controls. Government and employers united in using the strike to launch a series of red scare panics throughout the United States. Meanwhile, workers divided in support of the Industrial Workers of the World, with its One Big Union policy as a prelude to worker control of society, and the American Federation of Labour, which aimed at securing remedial legislation instead. Clement J. France, a legal counsel at the Port of Seattle and a third-party, Farmer-Labour politician, sided with the latter set of aims, running unsuccessfully

[1] 'Document 24', *Kennedy Papers*, UCDA P4/320.
[2] 'Letter to Capt. R. J. Boyd, 26.06.1922', *Kennedy Papers*, UCDA P4/318.
[3] This chapter develops ideas first explored in Thomas Murray, 2015, 'Socio-economic Rights versus Social Revolution? Constitution Making in Germany, Mexico, and Ireland, 1917–23' in *Social and Legal Studies*, 24 (4), pp. 487–508.

for the US Senate in 1920.[4] The following year, France was selected as a Quaker representative of the American Committee of Relief in Ireland, distributing aid to civilians through the Irish White Cross as military violence closed existing welfare infrastructure. Given the IWC's success and non-partisanship, the Provisional Government invited a number of its members, including France, to join a committee tasked with drafting a constitution for the Irish Free State.

France's experiences in Seattle neatly encapsulate what Duncan Kennedy has described as the 'globalisation of social legal thought', a transformation in modes of legal argument arising in response to the problems of industrial-urban capitalism in the late nineteenth century, as working-class organisations in Europe and North America confronted government and employers with collective demands for improved working and living conditions. The *langue* of the 'social', Kennedy argues, provided jurists with a conceptual vocabulary, modes of reasoning, and characteristic arguments with which to critique the classic legal thought associated with the defence of the *laissez-faire* state.[5] Instead, the law required rethinking as a purposive instrument, to be designed for the social or common good, howsoever defined. Politically then, this broad 'legal consciousness' encompassed a wide range of positions from liberalism to social democracy, from Catholic corporatism to Italian fascism, but excluded advocates of the classic liberal market as well as proponents of revolutionary class struggle. To varying degrees, both classic and social modes of argument featured in the wave of constitution-making which occasioned the very earliest constitutional entrenchments of social and economic rights, notably Mexico (1917) and Weimar Germany (1919).[6]

The Irish Free State Constitution (1922) belongs to the same inter-war wave of constitution-making, occurring in similar circumstances of

[4] The Port of Seattle was a Municipal Corporation charged with the development and administration of the largest port on the Pacific Coast. France was also a member of the Council of the National Municipal League of America, an organisation formed to improve Municipal Government in the United States and to advocate the breaking up of monopolies and the public ownership of utilities. Founded in 1918, the Farmer-Labour party was a left-wing, third-party movement in the United States that aimed at farm labourer and urban worker 'social' protections and government ownership of certain industries. The Democrats co-opted the party in 1944. C. J. France, 'Comments on the Foregoing Article' in *Studies*, Vol. 12, No. 47 (Sep. 1923), pp. 356–60, p. 356. See also 'The 1919 Shipyard Strike and the General Strike' in *Online Encyclopedia of Washington State History* available at: www.historylink.org.

[5] Kennedy, 2006, 'Three Globalisations of Law and Legal Thought', p. 38.

[6] Jon Elster, 'Forces and Mechanisms in the Constitution-Making Process', p. 368. See also Agnes Headlam-Morley, 1929, *The New Democratic Constitutions of Europe*. London: Oxford University Press.

wartime and revolutionary upheaval. The drafters of 1922, Leo Kohn would later observe, 'mocked the time-honoured empiricism of the British constitution by the enunciation of basic principles': they 'postulated fundamental rights'.[7] Their choice of 'fundamental rights' was far from inevitable but rather the product of lengthy, at times acrimonious, debates in which 'economic rights' and 'economic sovereignty' featured prominently. The committee, critics, and constituent assembly deeply considered transformative socio-economic provisions, some of which they considered absolutely essential to the new constitution. These included proposals concerning the public ownership of natural resources, the regulation of rapidly rising land values, universal education, and children's welfare. The final draft, however, was limited to two programmatic declarations only, one specifying a right to education and the other Irish Free State ownership of resources vested in the previous state.

Clarifying Irish exceptionalism with regard to Mexico and Germany – or why it didn't happen here – appears a useful step towards identifying what the particular constraints on socio-economic rights entrenchment were. The 1922 Constitution's strictly limited form of socio-economic rights entrenchment, I suggest, owed to political decision-makers' consistent privileging of classic nationalist constitutionalism over social democratic or radical alternatives. Their choices and influential positions, in turn, were strictly conditioned (though not determined) by the Irish Free State's economic peripheralisation and, in particular, by the manner in which this process, culturally and structurally, favoured popular, anti-systemic mobilisation along 'national' rather than 'social' lines. A Hobbesian politics of securing the state for the Provisional Government permeated the constitution-making process. In justifying the Free State's use of repression against republican and social agitation, Hugh Kennedy, the government's senior legal advisor, argued that disorder would have to be overcome by 'utterly ruthless action', similar to that used by the Reichswehr-Freikorps in crushing the Spartacist uprising in Weimar Germany.[8]

A critical discourse analysis reveals the distinct tension in the constitution-making process between slavish adherence to the established apparatus of governance and introducing fundamentally new features, such as socio-economic rights or initiative and referendum

[7] Kohn, 1932, *The Constitution of the Irish Free State*, p. 81.
[8] Garvin, 1996, *1922*, p. 162.

procedures. Substantive adherence to classic legal institutions and ideas was broadly accepted in pursuit of a distinctive, 'national' constitution. Importantly, over the course of their deliberations, the drafting committee canvassed a wide range of international experiments in constitutional engineering. However, both the British state and the Free State Provisional Government made a number of concerted interventions to diminish egalitarian proposals, primarily in order to secure support from those groups who benefitted from the reproduction of economic peripheralisation. The Provisional Government further sought to secure the blessing of the Catholic Church's hierarchy. Meanwhile, universalising, value-consensus discourses of 'Irish Ireland' and Catholicism operated to reproduce those particular power relations which they helped to conceal.

## THE SOCIAL ORIGINS OF CONSTITUTIONALISM IN THE IRISH FREE STATE

The 1922 Irish Free State Constitution was shaped by the power of those groups dominant in the immediate aftermath of the Irish war of independence (1919–21). Directly, its making owed to the Anglo-Irish Treaty (1921) concluded between British and Irish government representatives. Anglo-Irish talks would continue throughout 1922. On the Irish side, political debate and division appeared to centre precisely on this classic, national question of state sovereignty. The Irish Republican Army (IRA) split in two as did Dáil Éireann, the underground parliament comprised exclusively of members of the Irish nationalist Sinn Féin party. Pro-treaty Sinn Féin accepted the Treaty as a pragmatic political compromise in circumstances of comparative military disadvantage, a position which enjoyed the support of the majority of the IRA leadership as well as a slender parliamentary majority. Throughout 1922, this latter group fulfilled the role of 'Provisional Government' newly established under the Treaty. Anti-treatyites in the IRA's rank and file rejected the Treaty as an abandonment of the 'Irish Republic' which had been both fought for in 1916 and popularly voted for in the 1918 general election. Anti-treaty Sinn Féin left the Dáil in protest to mobilise wider opinion against the Treaty and the Provisional Government.

Intra-nationalist divisions over Irish sovereignty crystallised in a brief, violent civil war (1922–3). On 10 April, the anti-treaty IRA occupied the Four Courts, interrupting the Provisional Government's assessment of the newly created draft constitution. In this tense atmosphere, Collins and de Valera, pro- and anti-treaty Sinn Féin leaders respectively, agreed a pact to fight the forthcoming general election jointly, such that sitting parliamentary members would not be opposed by the opposing faction and would form a coalition government afterwards. (Neither saw anything wrong in denying the wider population, especially in areas with uncontested seats, a chance to accept or reject the treaty itself). The agreement gave the Provisional Government time to draft the constitution on the proviso that it would be submitted to the electorate prior to the election.[9]

Immediately before the election-day of 16 June, however, Collins repudiated the terms of the pact, urged voters to vote for stability and had the Dublin newspapers publish the draft constitution on the morning of the election itself. While the return of unopposed candidates makes the results difficult to interpret, there was a turnout of 62.5 per cent of a total electorate of some 1.4 million with some 75 per cent voting for pro-treaty parties.[10] Both Labour and the Farmer's Party were pro-treaty; official neutrality on the part of the Irish Labour Party and Trade Union Congress masked a tendency to support the Provisional Government.[11] The Third Dáil (or provisional parliament under the Treaty) comprised of fifty-eight pro-treaty Sinn Féin TDs, seventeen Labour, seven Farmer's Party, and ten Independents; the thirty-six anti-treaty Sinn Féin TDs refused to take their seats.

The British Cabinet, suspecting the Provisional Government of colluding with anti-treaty Sinn Féin-IRA in order to force further concessions, now demanded that the Provisional Government assert its authority over the anti-treaty IRA stationed in the Four Courts and threatened to use British troops to do so. When the republican garrison kidnapped a general of the newly formed National Army, Collins bombarded the anti-treatyites into surrender. Conflict continued in Dublin until July while the anti-treaty IRA's presence in the South or 'Munster Republic' was effectively ended once the National Army landed troops and heavy armour in September 1922. The civil war resulted in the loss of some 1,500 lives, the internment of some 11,000 anti-treatyites and, ultimately, the conservative entrenchment of the Irish Free State.

9 Akenson and Fallin, 1970, 'The Irish Civil War and the Drafting of the Free State Constitution: III', p. 10.
10 Ferriter, 2005, *The Transformation of Ireland*, p. 254.
11 Kostick, 2009, *Revolution in Ireland*, p. 187

Throughout 1922 and 1923, class relations, without overlapping directly with national divisions, were simultaneously at stake in the civil war. Indeed, initially, the Provisional Government spent more time dealing with threatened strikes, soviets, and agrarian agitation than with issues such as the partition of Ireland or discontent from republicans.[12] Agrarian radicalism subsided, however, as the Provisional Government offered land redistribution through the Land Commission, strictly on condition of good behaviour. Opposition to the Treaty strongly correlated with poorer areas of high emigration and agrarian radicalism.[13] The majority of anti-treatyite Sinn Féin and IRA leaders, however, were reluctant to identify the holy work of republicanism with vulgar material concerns. Only when the Provisional Government had effectively ended the civil war as a military contest in September 1922 did they seek to broaden their appeal by adopting a social rhetoric. From Dublin's Mountjoy prison, Liam Mellows now publically advocated 'the putting into operation of the democratic programme adopted by Dáil Eireann when first established'.[14]

Wider popular support for the anti-treatyite position, so essential to the IRA's provisioning and success during the independence conflict, was less forthcoming. Pro-Treaty Sinn Féin was joined by the country's major property interests, including the banks, graziers, creameries, and railway owners, who pressed for a speedy re-imposition of 'constitutional government'.[15] The Catholic Church also supported it, fearful of rising lawlessness and the threat of 'military dictatorship' posed by the anti-treaty IRA.[16] The victory of the Irish Free State in Munster occasioned a widely heard Bishop's Pastoral, in which the hierarchy condemned those responsible for 'the seizing of public and private property', as well as anti-treaty forces, denying them moral sanction or the rites of confession or communion. The Farmers' Party was much more forthright about its opposition to labour, with one TD claiming in the Constituent Assembly debates that 'there were not enough lampposts in Ireland to hang agitators from Liberty Hall'.[17] Notwithstanding these strange bedfellows, the Labour Party and Irish Trade Union Congress

12 Kostick, 2009, *Revolution in Ireland*, pp. 5, 148.

13 Peter Pyne, 1970, 'The Third Sinn Féin party, 1923–1926', in *Economic and Social Review*, 1 (1), pp. 29–50, 229–57.

14 'Liam Mellows', *The Times*, 21 September 1922. See also Ó Comhraí, 2013, *Revolution in Connacht*, p. 146.

15 Kostick, 2009, *Revolution in Ireland*, p. 180.

16 Harty to O'Rahilly, 23.03.1922, *O'Rahilly Papers*, UCDA P 178/24.

17 *Dáil Debates*, Vol. I. 19 September 1922.

broadly supported the institutions of the Irish Free State. Labour was, however, non-committal about the new constitution.[18]

The civil war provided the Provisional Government with a pretext to enact a series of 'special powers' and 'public safety' resolutions, targeted not just at ensuring the military defeat of the anti-treaty IRA but also at curtailing agrarian agitators and striking workers. Irish Free State soldiers and police engaged in a brutal clampdown on strikes, including firing shots at unarmed protestors in the course of breaking up a postal workers' strike in Dublin and several more organised against wage cuts throughout 1923. Ongoing land seizures proved particularly ungovernable. Patrick Hogan, Minister for Agriculture, established a Special Infantry Corps in 1923 to restrain agrarian disorder. In March, in Runnamoat, Co. Roscommon, men, women, and children rushed at the corps to prevent it from impounding their livestock. The soldiers fired shots in the air, dispersed the crowd, and rounded up the stock for sale in Dublin. Thereafter, the Enforcement of Law (Occasional Powers) Act granted bailiffs increased powers, such that landlords now returned to the courts to have their rents paid.[19]

The ensuing state-building process precluded those direct democratic forms of politics that had so recently animated Irish civil society. In fact, pro-Treaty Sinn Féin broadly though not uncritically adhered to Westminster's established model of government, law, and administration.[20] This would entail party dominance over the executive and executive dominance over parliament, resurrecting the former legal system to replace popular arbitration courts and, following the example of the British Treasury, maintaining Department of Finance control within the civil service. The Department was central to reestablishing the nineteenth-century Gladstonian fiscal doctrine necessary to Ireland's semi-peripheral development, dictating parsimony in state expenditure on welfare and industry so as to maintain the integrity of Irish currency and the cattle trade, thereby protecting the financier-grazier mode of accumulation.

The Provisional Government looked to the Catholic Church to legitimate its contested authority. Contrary to portrayals of the 1922

[18] After attending a Labour party meeting on the constitution, James Douglas wrote to Hugh Kennedy: 'They were not hostile but I don't think they really know where they are'. If the constitution were easily amended, he thought, the party 'would not feel obliged to protest'. Correspondence 28 September 1922, *Kennedy Papers*, UCDA P4/315/48. See also Ferriter, 2005, *The Transformation of Ireland*, p. 256.

[19] Dooley, 2004, *The Land for the People*, p. 51.

[20] On attempted experimentation, see Kissane, 2011, *New Beginnings*, pp. 8–15.

Constitution as more secular than its successor, the Provisional Government frequently consulted the hierarchy in private during the preparation of the new constitution.[21] Archbishop O'Donnell, for instance, opposed an article declaring freedom of conscience and profession of religion to be 'inviolable rights of every citizen' on the basis that it 'hit off the limits of the toleration extended to error by the Church'; a saving clause – 'without prejudice to public order or morality' was subsequently added.[22] The bishops, then, expected deference to its 'moral monopoly' and, in particular, control over the means of reproducing that monopoly, specifically education, health, and associated welfare services.[23] In the circumstances, constitution-making presented the Provisional Government with an opportunity to pursue a robust exercise in 'institutional self-dealing'.[24] The shifting balance of core-periphery and capital-labour relations nevertheless prompted a compelling battle of socio-economic rights discourses.

## CLASSIC, SOCIAL, AND CATHOLIC SOCIAL CONSTITUTIONALISM

The drafting of the 1922 Irish Free State Constitution involved four phases.[25] First, from January to March, the Provisional Government appointed an eight-man committee to draft a new constitution. During the second phase, in April and May, the government reviewed the committee's three draft constitutions before selecting a definitive version. Phase three, in June, involved further Anglo-Irish negotiations. The constitution became public only on the day of elections for the Third Dáil, nominally a Constituent Assembly. Interrupted by the outbreak of civil war, the final phase of drafting, from mid-September onwards, involved the parliamentary discussion and executive amendment of the final draft. The Dáil enacted The Constitution of the Irish Free State (Saorstát Éireann) Act 1922 on 25 October; the British parliament enacted The Irish Free State Constitution Act 1922 on 5 December,

21 Patrick Murray, 2000, *Oracles of God: the Roman Catholic Church and Irish politics 1922–37*, Dublin: University College Dublin Press, p. 60.

22 Bishop of Dromore to Kennedy, September 1922, *Kennedy Papers*, UCDA P4/349.

23 Inglis, 1998, *Moral monopoly*, p. 57.

24 Justin Blount, Zachary Elkins, and Tom Ginsburg, 'Does the Process of Constitution-Making Matter?' in Tom Ginsburg (ed.), 2012, *Comparative Constitutional Design*, Cambridge: Cambridge University Press, pp. 31–68, pp. 44–50.

25 See Kissane, 2011, *New Beginnings*, pp. 28–56; Akenson and Fallin, 1970, 'The Irish Civil War and the Drafting of the Free State Constitution'; Farrell, 1970–1, 'The Drafting of the Irish Free State Constitution: I, II, III, and IV'.

TABLE 2.1 Timeline of the 1922 constitution-making process

| | |
|---|---|
| Anglo-Irish Treaty signed | 6 December 1921 |
| Drafting committee first meet | 24 January 1922 |
| Drafts A, B, and C produced | March 1922 |
| O'Brien critique | April 1922 |
| *Anti-Treatyites occupy Four Courts* | *10 April 1922* |
| Provisional government examines Draft B | 1 May 1922 |
| British government examines draft constitution | 1 June 1922 |
| Draft Constitution made public | 16 June 1922 |
| Election | |
| *Civil War begins* | *28 June 1922* |
| Dáil constituent assembly begins | 18 September 1922 |
| Dáil enacts | 25 October 1922 |
| Constitution of the Irish Free State (Saorstát Éireann) Act 1922 | |
| British parliament enacts | 5 December 1922 |
| The Irish Free State Constitution Act 1922 | |
| Royal Proclamation of IFS and Constitution | 6 December 1922 |
| *Anti-Treatyite 'Dump Arms' order* | *24 May 1923* |

and the next day, following a royal proclamation, both the Irish Free State and its Constitution officially came into existence (Table 2.1).

The government-appointed drafting committee was comprised of Hugh Kennedy and John O'Byrne (senior legal advisors to the Provisional Government), James McNeill (ex-colonial administrator and director of Sinn Féin's National Land Bank), James Douglas (outfitter business owner), Darrell Figgis (writer and propagandist), and Clement France (labour lawyer). Two academics, James Murnaghan (Professor of Roman Law and Jurisprudence at University College Dublin) and Alfred O'Rahilly (Professor of Mathematical Physics at University College Cork), also accepted invitations to join. The Labour party was unrepresented but supportive, 'naively hoping' that the document would reflect the 1919 Democratic Programme.[26] While the Provisional Government considered appointing Catholic clergy, the hierarchy believed, correctly as it turned out, that it could have its priorities realised more effectively through informal, private consultations

[26] Kissane, 2011, *New Beginnings*, p. 29.

instead.[27] Throughout, the Provisional Government relied significantly on the opinion of those trained in the established legal-administrative system, notably Kennedy who featured prominently in ongoing Anglo-Irish negotiations. Douglas, Figgis, France, and McNeill, active in relief distribution through the Irish White Cross, appear to have been further valued for their non-partisanship.

Classic legal discourses framed the drafting committee's debates. The drafters' *modus operandi*, meeting each day at 8 A.M. in Dublin's exclusive Shelbourne Hotel, suggested that they approached constitution-making as a classic, legal-scientific project, at once rational, objective and, in a curious sense, apolitical. Adhering to a science of government was not surprising given the framework imposed by the Anglo-Irish Treaty on their deliberations but this tendency was particularly true of legal-administrative professionals such as Kennedy, O'Byrne, McNeill, and France.[28] This approach initially involved the men in considering a range of Commonwealth, American, and international analyses of law, history, and political science. Similarly, discussions on the design of society and government involved their examining census figures relating to population and employment.[29] Most remarkably, the group compiled a series of easy-to-reference booklets detailing how all manner of provisions, ranging from executive functions to the control of absinthe, appeared in various constitutions around the world.[30]

In terms of institutional design, the drafters canvassed alternatives to the established Westminster model of parliamentary sovereignty yet broadly adhered to the Whitehall system of administration, the latter centralising power in the treasury (or Department of Finance).[31]

[27] When his initial attempts to organise 'a Committee of Bishops to examine the Constitution from the Catholic standpoint' failed, O'Rahilly was consoled by Archbishop Byrne who was certain that consultation could be 'obtained quite as well privately and informally as if any committee were put together'. Throughout the process, O'Rahilly maintained a constant exchange of correspondence with the Catholic hierarchy. See O'Rahilly Correspondence, 02.02.1922, *O'Rahilly Papers*, UCDA P178/10.

[28] On constraints, see Lee, 1989, *Ireland: 1912–1985*, p. 59.

[29] Both R. J. P. Mortished, secretary to the committee, and Figgis used this data to produce proposals on functional representation, an emergent form of social legal thought. See UCDA P4/320.

[30] Later published as Select Constitutions of the World, the volume referenced Yugoslavia, Poland, Austria, Estonia, Czechoslovakia, Germany, the Soviet Union, Mexico, Denmark, Australia, France, Switzerland, Canada, Belgium, Norway, Sweden, and the United States. Kissane, 2011, *New Beginnings*, p. 31.

[31] The Irish system of financial controls was based on Hilton Young's *The System of National Finance* which also underpinned the British system. The committee set out these principles in

The committee disagreed, however, about the future executive's precise powers – a disagreement centred on how to incorporate anti-treaty Sinn Féin – and ultimately divided to produce three draft constitutions.[32] Reformers also advocated 'popular sovereignty' as a corrective to the concentration of executive power in the Westminster model.[33] France outlined the manner in which the referendum and the initiative (whereby a petition of a certain number of voters could be used to call a public vote) operated in Washington State.[34] Kennedy was convinced that these mechanisms would give strength to the law ('the people being directly behind it'), counteract the influence of wealth by making corruption almost impossible and, importantly, have 'a sobering effect on revolutionary movements'.[35] That the majority believed economic and social rights should be left to a future national parliament may be inferred from their support for a 'Progressive Economic Policy' that both Sinn Féin (pro- and anti-treaty) and Labour could support.[36]

At the same time, culturally, the committee was deeply concerned with accomplishing an 'Irish Ireland policy'.[37] Its members broadly shared the classic premise that a state's system of law either reflected or should reflect the underlying normative order in a nation's history, identity, or *geist*, and that it was the 'scientific' task of national jurists to elaborate positive legal rules on the premise of this coherence.[38] In this sense, 'the people' authored every constitution made in this period, a task which conveniently did not necessitate their physical presence at jurists' deliberations. The committee agreed that, notwithstanding the limitations of dominion status or the 'artificial' fostering of the 'English Common Law', it was up to 'the national genius of the Irish people' to 'work out their destiny'.[39] Creating a distinctive, 'national' constitution ensured the committee discussed reviving both the Irish language and the medieval Brehon laws of Gaelic Ireland.

Some members, notably Kennedy and O'Rahilly, understood 'Irish Ireland' in specifically religious terms and emphasised (Irish/Catholic)

Articles 36, 37, 54, and 61 where they attracted little controversy. See Ronan Fanning, 1978, *The Irish Department of Finance: 1922–58*. Dublin: Institute of Public Administration, pp. 26, 52–3.

32 UCDA P4/ 307. 33 Kennedy, UCDA P4/336; 342.

34 *Kennedy Papers*, UCDA P4/336. 35 *Kennedy Papers*, UCDA P4/342.

36 UCDA P4/320. 37 *Kennedy Papers*, UCDA P4/307.

38 Kennedy, 2006, 'Three Globalisations of Law and Legal Thought', pp. 26, 29.

39 UCDA P4/352; UCDA P4/308; 320; 1252. Even Clement France, a relative newcomer, regarded it as 'needless' to emphasise the history of the 'native' people's dispossession to an 'alien race'. 'Document 24' in *Kennedy Papers*, UCDA P4/320.

natural law theory as a counterweight to (English/Protestant) legal positivism.[40] Catholic political theory along these lines posed a specific 'theological difficulty' for forms of social constitutionalism seeking to regulate private property rights.[41] Long into the twentieth century, conservative Catholic jurists distinguished the natural, God-given rights of man, which included the right to own property, from merely temporal, material rights to welfare being established in liberal, social democratic, and communist states.[42] Proponents of secular or social democratic forms of socio-economic rights had to contend with the committee's ideological adherence to both classic and Catholic legal discourses. Clement France, in particular, felt compelled to argue repeatedly that his proposals were not 'incompatible with the individualistic conception of the social order'.[43]

Social constitutional discourses nonetheless featured prominently in the committee's debates. From the outset, the committee claimed the constitution would 'afford an instrument whereby the national genius of the Irish people may work out their destiny to secure, *not alone personal liberty, but economic freedom*, and thereby attain happiness and prosperity for all'.[44] In one of the very earliest draft constitutions, we find a 'Fundamental Rights' section consisting of a 'social' declaration of national sovereignty, a list of 'Personal Rights' (primarily civil and political rights concerning liberty of person and dwelling, religious freedom, assembly, and free speech), and, importantly, a heading, 'Economic Rights', the spaces beneath left blank.[45] Filling these spaces, the committee agreed, was vital. Drafters involved in the Irish White Cross had recently witnessed 'appalling poverty . . . in every city and hamlet in Ireland'. Poverty, France argued, 'can only be rectified by taking a bold stand on . . . basic principles of natural right and justice'. At the same time, as civil war loomed, disaffected labourers and rural agitation posed an existential challenge: 'The recent revival of cattle-driving indicates the enormity of a problem which the Irish State cannot long defer without danger to itself'.[46]

Social constitutional discourses took two primary forms, 'liberal-social' and 'Catholic-social'. In terms of the former, Clement France

[40] See Kohn, 1932, *The Constitution of the Irish Free State*, p. 81.
[41] See Archbishop Harty's letter to O'Rahilly, UCDA P178/24.
[42] Denis O'Keefe, 1941, 'Catholic Political Theory' in *Studies*, Vol. 30 (4), pp. 481–88. See also Fanning, 2008, *The Quest for Modern Ireland*.
[43] UCDA P4/320. [44] UCDA P4/308; 320 [my italics]. [45] UCDA P4/306.
[46] UCDA P4/320.

argued for constitutional provisions to re-direct the Free State's economic development, transforming its semi-peripheral development trajectory. Hence, state ownership and development of natural resources as well as strategic public utilities, such as harbours and 'aerodromes', were vital to Ireland's becoming 'a great commercial and trading nation'.[47] To permit their control in private hands, France claimed, 'would be subversive of the welfare of the general public':

> In fact, the history of countries with Republican institutions, notably the American Republic, has proven that democracy and freedom cannot be obtained by reserving political liberty alone. The persons who control and own the great Natural Resources of the Country also control the freedom and well-being of the people . . . The result has been in America that notwithstanding a Republican and Democratic Government, an economic autocracy has developed which controls the Government of the Country and the personal liberties of the people almost as effectively as was ever done by an absolute monarchy.[48]

Constitutionalising norms of public ownership, he suggested, was necessary to 'stem the tide of pressure . . . to give away a birthright for a temporary advantage'.[49]

France's most provocative constitutional proposal challenged the cornerstone of the financier-grazier structure of accumulation: private ownership in land. Citing the example of New York's Astor family, he argued that 'the most glaring inequalities in wealth which are found in the world today result from the fact that an individual purchases a piece of land that has great strategic value, and in course of years becomes extremely wealthy through no effort of his own but merely from the value given to that land by the community at large'. To rectify this perceived failure of classic legal thought, France suggested constitutionalising land value tax reforms similar to those proposed by the political economist Henry George.[50] The state would nationalise all large farm holdings, divide them into economic holdings, and lease them back to farmers on condition that they engaged in agricultural production. This would counter labour-extensive grazier production, assuage the land

[47] France, 'Document 24', *Thomas Johnson Papers*, National Library of Ireland (NLI), Ms 17,136; see also UCDA P4/320.

[48] UCDA P4/308; 325; 339.

[49] NLI Ms 17,136; UCDA P4/320.

[50] See Henry George, 2009 [1881], *Progress and Poverty*. Cambridge: Cambridge University Press. On George's important links to Michael Davitt and the Land League, see also Anna George de Mille, 1944, 'Henry George: The Fight for Irish Freedom', in *The American Journal of Economics and Sociology*, 3: 2, pp. 251–72.

hungry, and ensure that any increase in land values – the 'unearned increment' – would become a public asset.[51] In a telling reflection on the Irish banking cartel's interests in the cattle trade and land speculation, France forwarded a plan for a $25 million industrial finance corporation to stimulate indigenous manufacturing.[52]

Alternatively, O'Rahilly articulated a 'Catholic-social' constitutionalism. His 'draft C' advocated employer-worker cooperation and harmony between classes through creating vocational negotiating institutions and guaranteeing both the rights and duties of property-owners.[53] Instead of state regulation or progressive taxation, the Catholic intellectual trusted to landowners' sense of duty to the community to provide employment or, in hard times, charity. O'Rahilly's education proposals further illustrated the doctrinal and institutional limits to Catholic social constitutionalism. Borrowing from the Polish Constitution, he proposed constitutionalising educational grants for adults as well as 'exceptional and needy children'.[54] After private consultation with the hierarchy, however, O'Rahilly excluded public provision in subsequent drafts, reduced the state's role to one of supervision only, and clearly articulated the hierarchy's preferred line of parental responsibility for children's rights and education.[55] Instead, the committee, universally recognising reform as 'controversial',[56] drafted to maintain existing educational practice: 'All citizens of Saorstat Éireann have the right to free elementary education'.[57]

The wider committee, to varying degrees, supported social rights proposals. They featured in each of the draft constitutions presented to the Provisional Government in March. Most notably, and notwithstanding queries that it committed the state to 'socialistic government',[58] the opening declaration of national and economic sovereignty directly

51 NLI Ms 17,136; UCDA P4/320.

52 See Farrell, 1970, 'The Drafting of the Irish Free State Constitution', p. 352.

53 After *Rerum Novarum* (1891), Catholic political theorists across Europe acknowledged social justice concerns though struggled to reconcile themselves to liberal democracy or to radical-popular alternatives. In Ireland, where it enjoyed a comparatively unchallenged hegemony, the Catholic Church generally resisted state-led redistribution or welfare provision as encroaching on its sphere of material and moral influence. Intellectuals such as O'Rahilly frequently adopted the new social rhetoric only to find the hierarchy opposed to its practical application. On the distinction between Catholic theology and Catholic culture in twentieth-century Ireland, see Enda McDonagh, 1987, 'Philosophical-Theological Reflections on the Constitution' in Litton, Frank (ed.), *The Constitution of Ireland 1937–1987*. Dublin: Institute of Public Administration, pp. 192–205.

54 UCDA P4/309; 328. 55 UCDA P4/333. 56 UCDA P4/339.

57 UCDA P4/306; 307. More republican invocations of education as 'a primary duty of citizenship' remained pencilled annotations only. See UCDA P4/326.

58 UCDA P4/332.

**Box 2.1 Economic Sovereignty Provision, March 1922**

**Article 1:**
The nation's sovereignty extends not only to all the men and women of the nation, but to all the material possessions of the nation, the nation's soil and all its resources and all the wealth and wealth-producing processes within the nation. All right to private property is subordinated to the public right and welfare of the nation. It is the duty of every man and woman to give allegiance and service to the commonwealth, and it is the duty of the nation to ensure that every citizen shall have the opportunity to spend his or her strength and faculties in the service of the people. In return for willing service it is the right of every citizen to an adequate share of the produce of the nation's labour.

invoked the 1916 Proclamation of the Irish Republic and the 1919 Democratic Programme (Box 2.1).[59] This article – 'the Pearse statement', according to Kennedy[60] – included the subordination of all right to private property to 'the public right and welfare of the nation' as well as 'the right of every citizen to an adequate share of the produce of the nation's labour'. Moreover, in addition to a right to primary education, the committee listed the natural resources to be reserved in the Irish Free State, albeit in the 'classic' sense of securing the state's title to certain classes of property customarily reserved in the Crown.[61] The committee considered these socio-economic provisions 'essential to the Constitution'.[62] During the following months, however, reflecting the repression of popular militancy and increased security of the state and the financier-grazier class, a pronounced reassertion of classic constitutional discourses occurred.

## 'THE FULL VALUE OF DOMINION POTENTIAL'

Nothing so foreshadowed the redistributive proposals' fate as the Provisional Government's immediate delivering of them to an economist for costing. George O'Brien, Professor of National Economy at University College Dublin, articulated a classic laissez-faire response.

[59] UCDA P4/331; 339. [60] UCDA P4/363. [61] UCDA P4/308; 325.
[62] UCDA P4/339.

Generally, he was sceptical toward public law, preferring the Westminster parliamentary sovereignty model which the constitution 'should fetter as little as possible'.[63] He attacked, in particular, the drafts' declaration of 'economic sovereignty' and education rights provisions.[64] The subordination of private property rights to the nation's public right and welfare was deemed 'wide and liable to misconstruction': 'it ought to be made quite clear that no expropriation can take place except for pressing necessity, after full inquiry, and with full compensation'. He denied the citizen's right to an 'adequate share' of the nation's wealth: 'I do not know what the last sentence of the present article means'. The drafting committee contested these critiques. Figgis argued that O'Brien's concerns had not been realised in Switzerland where similar provisions operated: 'To lay down as a constitutional stipulation that all expropriation requires compensation would impose an impossible limitation on legislation'.[65] The social and economic rights provisions, Douglas claimed, were 'a good general statement of democratic principle'.[66]

The Provisional Government consulted the Catholic hierarchy extensively and privately about the constitution's education provision.[67] Figgis conceded that parental obligations concerning children's education, was a matter for legislation: 'Details of such a controversial kind must be avoided in a Constitution'.[68] Laissez-faire opposition to state expenditure and Catholic ideology concerning the family sustained one another. O'Brien dismissed education rights as liable to entail state expenditure and advocated reducing the state's role to a supervisory one only: 'the fact should be emphasised that the State's duty to provide education for children only arises on the failure or incapacity of the parents' doing so'.[69] If a compromise had to be made, the cost-free Catholic social constitution, suggested by O'Rahilly, was preferable.

The Provisional Government, notwithstanding the drafting committee's appeals, broadly adopted O'Brien's preference for a classic constitution, shorn of socio-economic rights. This position coincided with

[63] *Kennedy Papers*, UCDA P4/339. Similarly both Tim Healy, Sinn Féin barrister and 'father' of the Irish Bar, and the Dáil Cabinet would have preferred a shorter document than the draft presented, 'one which will not require explanation and defence'. Minister Patrick Hogan cited in *Kennedy Papers*, UCDA P4/339.

[64] UCDA P4/339. [65] UCDA P4/339. [66] UCDA P4/339.

[67] Minutes of Provisional Government meetings, 10 April 1922 to 24 May 1922; Farrell, 1970–1, 'The Drafting of the Irish Free State Constitution', pp. 130, 351; see also Bishop of Dromore to Kennedy, September 1922, *Kennedy Papers*, UCDA P4/349.

[68] UCDA P4/339. [69] UCDA P4/339.

**Box 2.2 Economic Sovereignty Provision, May 1922**

**Article 1:**
The Nation's sovereignty extends not only to all the men and women of the Nation, but to all the material possessions of the nation, the Nation's soil and all its resources and all the wealth and wealth-producing processes within the Nation; and all right to private property is subordinated to the public right and welfare of the Nation.

**Article 2:**
It is the duty of every man and woman to give allegiance and service to the commonwealth, and it is the duty of the Nation to insure that every citizen shall have opportunity to spend his or her strength and faculties in the service of the people.

defending established institutions and core-periphery linkages, notably the Department of Finance's commitment to fiscal austerity and the gold standard, the financier-grazier interest in maintaining the market in land as well as the Catholic Church's interest in maintaining control over welfare provision. The domestic balance of class forces underpinned these institutions' survival. In particular, the Provisional Government appears to have been persuaded by the argument that land reforms would generate hostility among existing owner-occupiers. If the state captured the 'unearned increment', Archbishop Harty warned O'Rahilly, 'the farming element of the community would rise in opposition to the Constitution which would be looked on as confiscating the farmers' property . . . The Treaty cannot afford to encounter such opposition at the present time'.[70] O'Brien echoed the archbishop. Declaring rights to shares in the nation's wealth, he argued, were 'highly controversial' and 'might frighten a certain section of the electorate'.[71]

Ongoing Anglo-Irish negotiations ensured that the articles declaring economic sovereignty (Box 2.2) were minimised further (Box 2.3).[72]

[70] UCDA P178/24. [71] UCDA P4/339.
[72] Kissane, 2011, *New Beginnings*, p. 37; Lerner, 2011, *Making Constitutions in Deeply Divided Societies*, p. 169; Thomas Mohr, 2008, 'British Involvement in the Creation of the Constitution of the Irish Free State' in *Dublin University Law Journal*, 30, pp. 166–86.

**Box 2.3 Sovereignty Provision, September 1922**

**Article 1:**
The Irish Free State (otherwise hereinafter called or sometimes called Saorstát Eireann) is a co-equal member of the Community of Nations forming the British Commonwealth of Nations.

**Article 2:**
All powers of government and all authority, legislative, executive, and judicial, in Ireland are derived from the people of Ireland, and the same shall be exercised in the Irish Free State (Saorstát Eireann) through the organisations established by or under, and in accord with, this Constitution.

While the hostility of British negotiators to sovereignty declarations owed to their attempts to preserve the imperial status quo in the Commonwealth, there was simultaneously a class dynamic at play here. The 1922 Constitution, in allowing for a judicial appeal to the Privy Council of the House of Lords, both ensured the constitution conformed to the Treaty and safeguarded extensive British property rights in Ireland.[73] Moreover, Austen Chamberlain, Lord Privy Seal, objected to the 'Soviet character' of Articles 1 and 2.[74] They were, suggested Lord Hewart, 'of communistic tendency'.[75] The Provisional Government had instructed the Irish negotiators, Hugh Kennedy among them, to concentrate on national sovereignty issues or, as Collins put it, on getting 'the full value of the dominion potential'.[76] Hence, when the British Law Officers demanded the offending articles' removal, they acquiesced. Kennedy's decision reflected both his particular commitments to classic constitutionalism – the second article was, he wrote, 'an unnecessary declaration'[77] – as well as the more general attitude of the Provisional Government towards social constitutionalism.

During the 'Constituent Assembly' debates that autumn, the Labour party, involved for the first time, attempted to resuscitate the socio-economic rights provisions. Labour's arguments, emphasising the rights

[73] Kissane, 2011, *New Beginnings*, p. 47.
[74] Mohr, 2008, 'British Involvement in the Creation of the Constitution of the Irish Free State', pp. 172–3.
[75] UCDA P4/362. [76] UCDA P4/363. [77] UCDA P4/363.

and duties of property in an otherwise harmonious national community, more closely resembled O'Rahilly's Catholic social proposals than France's liberal-social interventions.[78] Tom Johnson thus assured the Provisional Government that 'economic sovereignty' would not mean the nationalisation of land but simply the view that property was held in trust for the public welfare.[79] Constitutional safeguards would similarly prevent the Dáil's 'handing over' the nation's natural resources 'to any foreign capitalistic or other corporations' and ensure that 'the interests of the Nation as a whole' were served in their exploitation.[80] Citizens had a duty to work for the welfare of the community and, in return, the state had a duty to provide the citizen with 'an opportunity to gain his [sic] livelihood by economic labour' or with provision for 'his' support.[81]

Labour's affinity to Catholic social ideology was most readily apparent in their education rights proposals. T. J. O'Connell, returning to the 1919 Democratic Programme, proposed:

> The rights of the children to food, clothing, shelter and education sufficient for their proper physical welfare and training as citizens of Saorstat Eireann is guaranteed. It is the duty of all citizens to ensure that their children and wards receive adequate education. To this end provision shall be made by the State for the free education of the young up to an age to be prescribed by law. School attendance shall be compulsory. Provision shall be made by the State so that secondary and higher educational institutions shall be readily accessible in the case of persons with small means. All schools and educational establishments, public and private, shall be controlled by the State within limits to be determined by law.[82]

O'Connell tempered any perception of challenging church control in education, however, by reaffirming the hierarchy's position on parental responsibility. Hence, it was 'of course' the duty of parents to educate their children; Labour was merely proposing that the state had a duty to enable every parent to do so.[83]

The Provisional Government, by now assured of military victory in the civil war and preparing to repress residual agrarian and labour militancy, reasserted the classic priorities of state power ('law and

78 See UCDA P4/341. 79 *Dáil Debates*, Vol. 1, Col. 494–5, 708; 20 September 1922.
80 *Dáil Debates*, Vol. 1. Col. 1659; 18 October 1922; *Dáil Debates*, Vol. 1. Col. 70; 25 September 1922.
81 See Johnson, *Dáil Debates*, Vol. 1. Col. 755, 26 September 1922.
82 *Kennedy Papers*, UCDA P4/341. 83 *Dáil Debates*, Vol. 1. Col. 697; 25 September 1922.

order') and of economic necessity ('national economy'). It rejected all proposals for economic and social rights. W. T. Cosgrave claimed the principle of economic sovereignty was unnecessary window-dressing, 'something to show the people outside what strong people we have here'.[84] Echoing the British Law Officers, Kevin O'Higgins similarly declared it would be unwise 'to embody in the constitution what certainly looks very much like a Communistic doctrine'.[85] For Ernest Blythe, providing every citizen with an opportunity to gain his livelihood was moreover 'a rather tall order': 'the whole thing might be uneconomic'.[86] Similarly, Labour's proposed socio-economic rights of the child were deemed to involve 'a very large amount of controversial matter which could not be admitted into the Constitution'.[87] It was not necessary, O'Higgins claimed, to set out 'all the most modern and up-to-date amplifications of those rights. A certain amount can be safely left to legislation hereafter . . . '[88] By the end of the constituent assembly debates, the economic and social rights proposals were roundly defeated, typically by a two-to-one majority according to the number of seats occupied by the pro-treaty Sinn Féin and Labour parties.

After all the possibilities of socio-economic rights raised throughout the drafting process, the 1922 Irish Free State Constitution featured two 'programmatic declarations' only (Box 2.4). Article 10 no longer associated education with citizenship duties or welfare provision and, by omission, registered the continuation of clerical control in practice. Article 11, concerning the vesting of 'lands and waters, mines and minerals' in the Free State, sanctioned the maintenance of existing forms of tenure and left the precise terms of these property relations to future parliamentary discretion. Although the article left open the possibility of a 'progressive nationalisation of natural resources', the balance of competing social forces in the 1920s dictated that successive governments would instead reproduce classic free market norms and core-periphery linkages.[89] Having detailed the Irish constitution-making process, it is now possible to locate it in a more comparative,

[84] Dáil Debates, Vol. 1. Col. 707; 21 September 1922.
[85] Dáil Debates, Vol. 1. Col. 707; 25 September 1922.
[86] Dáil Debates, Vol. 1. Col. 757–8; 26 September 1922. Blythe also feared that the national ownership of natural resources 'might compel the State actually to work the resources itself, which, of course, we would not want to tie ourselves to'. Dáil Debates, Vol. 1. Col. 708; 25 September 1922.
[87] See UCDA P4/340. [88] *Dáil Debates*, Vol. 1. Col. 698/ 754–5; 25 September 1922.
[89] Kohn, 1932, *The Constitution of the Irish Free State*, p. 174.

**Box 2.4 Articles 10 and 11, 1922 Irish Free State Constitution**

**Article 10:**
All citizens of the Irish Free State (Saorstát Eireann) have the right to free elementary education.

**Article 11:**
All the lands and waters, mines and minerals, within the territory of the Irish Free State (Saorstát Eireann) hitherto vested in the State, or any department thereof, or held for the public use or benefit, and also all the natural resources of the same territory (including the air and all forms of potential energy), and also all royalties and franchises within that territory shall, from and after the date of the coming into operation of this Constitution, belong to the Irish Free State (Saorstát Eireann), subject to any trusts, grants, leases or concessions then existing in respect thereof, or any valid private interest therein, and shall be controlled and administered by the Oireachtas, in accordance with such regulations and provisions as shall be from time to time approved by legislation, but may in the public interest be from time to time granted by way of lease or license to be worked or enjoyed under the authority and subject to the control of the Oireachtas: Provided that no such lease or license may be made for a term exceeding ninety-nine years, beginning from the date thereof, and no such lease or licence may be renewable by the terms thereof.

*Source:* Kohn, 1932, The Constitution of the Irish Free State, pp. 389–418.

world-systems analysis and to clarify the more specific and special constraints on socio-economic rights entrenchment.

## QUERÉTARO, WEIMAR, AND DUBLIN: WORLD-SYSTEMS PERSPECTIVES

The 'Great War' (1914–18) and Russian-Internationalist Revolution (1917–23), as noted in the previous chapter, marked a decisive moment of transformation in the historical capitalist world-system, stimulating both the rapid development of state capacities and the emergence of a remarkable social constitutionalism. Earlier constitutional waves, notably following the 1798 and 1848 Revolutions, accompanied the development of centralised state power and classic legal rights, both capable of withstanding local or private interests to ensure the rule of law over the rule of men. In the course of '1917', a wider wave of constitution-making registered and reproduced emergent configurations of power, notably the development of state capacities in wartime to direct economic production and states' mobilisation of national populations on the basis of democratic and 'social' reform.[90] Working class or popular militancy dramatically increased pressures for social constitutionalism in the world's cores and peripheries.

In core regions, reflecting the growing strength of organised labour and the need for nation-building projects to incorporate these movements, socio-economic rights took the form of legalising universal social insurance and entitlements based on need. The Weimar Constitution (1919) presents a paradigmatic case. In Germany, an uprising of the German Workers' and Soldiers' Councils concluded German participation in World War I, brought an end to the Hohenzollern monarchy, and resulted in the election of the Social Democrats to government. The balance of class forces, indicated by the wartime incorporation of labour into collective bargaining and by the defeat of the Spartacist uprising by the Social Democrats and Freikorps, crystallised in the provisions of the Weimar Constitution. In the Constituent Assembly debates, animated by a shared desire to end reactionary Prussian influence, Germany's late-imperial liberals such as Hugo Preuss and Max Weber coincided with social democrats such as Hugo Sinzheimer on the creation of a *Volkstaat*, or 'people's state', combining political and welfare reforms as part of securing popular support for a federal nation-state.[91] The result was a 'pronounced material constitution', combining guarantees of property and free contract (Article 152–3) with social provisions for state ownership of industry (Article 153.2), trade union recognition and co-determination as well as universal welfare entitlements (or *Wohlfahrtsstaat* principles), allocated as rights not of citizens but of productive groups or classes.[92]

[90] Reforms included extending the franchise, granting full legislative powers to elected parliaments, proto-welfare state measures, and increasing via corporatist mechanisms the decision-making role of hitherto excluded social groups such as trade unions. See Kennedy, 2006, 'Three Globalisations of Law and Legal Thought', p. 46.

[91] P. M. R. Stirk, 2002, 'Hugo Preuss, German political thought and the Weimar constitution' in *History of Political Thought* 23:3, pp. 497–516.

[92] Thornhill, 2013, *A Sociology of Constitutions*, p. 287.

In peripheral regions, social constitution-making concentrated on entrenching labour and land reforms. In Mexico, a complex revolutionary period brought an end to Porfirio Diaz's autocratic regime, previously supported by the Catholic Church as well as US and British capital and military power. The Querétaro Constitutional Congress of 1917 registered the victory of the 'Constitutional Army', an amalgam of conservatives, liberals, and Catholic reformers, most notably José Natividad Macías.[93] Concomitantly, the Congress represented the exclusion of the much more radical, revolutionary possibility of indigenous land collectivisation forwarded by Emiliano Zapata in the Plan of Ayala. The 'social liberalism' of the ensuing Mexican Constitution (1917) thus guaranteed the classic rights of property while simultaneously providing for free, mandatory education (Article 3), land reform and redistribution (Article 27) as well as 'labour and social welfare' (Article 123), including workers' health and safety, rights to organise and to strike, and the establishment of pension, unemployment, and accident insurance.[94] Importantly, as in Weimar, the Mexican constitution still retained classic constitutional rights, including guarantees of the rights of property and free contract.

Constitution-making occurred within specific deliberative coordinates, including the polarity between direct democratic forms of popular self-organisation and representative democratic forms such as the party and constituent assembly, as well as, within the latter debates, the tensions between classic and social forms of constitutionalism. Within the popular constitutional discourses of the period, 'economic rights' signified a radical horizon, looking to 'the democracy', not the state, for their realisation. The Constitution of the Irish Citizen Army, for example, explicitly linked the realisation of 'the right of the people of Ireland to the ownership of Ireland' to the proletariat's collective control of production and direct democratic participation. Concomitantly, in the West of Ireland, those involved in agrarian agitation resurrected traditional practices of popular arbitration and land expropriation. This upsurge in popular, collective self-organisation and direct action in Ireland not only occurred alongside revolutionary movements such as the Spartacists in Germany or the Zapata-led

93 Paulo Wright-Carozza, 2003, ' From Conquest to Constitutions: Retrieving a Latin American Tradition of the Idea of Human Rights', p. 307.

94 Wright-Carozza, 2003, 'From Conquest to Constitutions', p. 303; F. Y. Ramos, 1967, 'The Social Rights Enshrined in the Mexican Constitution of 1917' in *International Labour Review* 96 (6), pp. 590–9.

indigenous movement in Mexico, but more fundamentally invoked communal, surprisingly pre-industrial norms of justice, similar to those that animated proletarian movements in Europe and North America between 1848 and 1939.[95]

In these circumstances, classic and social forms of constitutionalism emerged as intersecting forms of ideological containment for representative political parties. While the dominant legal discourse of the period was classic, in Mexico and Weimar Germany, popular militancy prompted constitution-makers' further inclusion of social and economic rights provisions. Similarly, in the Irish case, popular militancy compelled Sinn Féin to accept social legal discourses, initially in the form of Catholic social thought but later, as the popular conflicts deepened, more explicitly in terms of an interventionist state in welfare and land redistribution, such as the 1919 Democratic Programme outlined. The spectre of revolutionary movements or 'anarchy' further compelled Irish constitution-makers in 1922 to return to the 1919 Programme's economic sovereignty and socio-economic rights proposals. Hence, in Dublin as in Weimar, the constitution-making process canvassed the possibility of entrenching state-ownership and universal entitlements. These included Clement France's proposals to introduce state ownership of natural resources as well as Alfred O'Rahilly's and T. J. O'Connell's promotion of distributive welfare arrangements, notably socio-economic rights for children. At the same time, in Dublin as in Querétaro, constitution-makers considered major agrarian reforms, the most prominent of which in the Irish case was France's proposal to capture the unearned increment as a means of transforming the country's financier/grazier-led economy.

The social constitutionalism at stake in the 1922 Irish Free State Constitution thus appears as a potential hybrid of both core and peripheral discourses. Ultimately, however, the constitution-makers settled on a much more classic form of nationalist constitution, centred on securing the state's monopoly on the right to command within its territory. The 1922 Irish Constitution largely provided for the reproduction of the institutions of the former regime, notably its parliamentary, administrative, and legal systems as well as the Irish Land Commission. The Provisional Government accepted classic laissez-faire norms and rejected the possibility of any state intervention that might tax or otherwise threaten established property-holders or deny the Catholic

[95] See Bookchin, 1997, *The Spanish anarchists: the heroic years, 1868–1936*, pp. 6–8.

Church's control over welfare provision. Irish exceptionalism with regard to socio-economic rights cannot be understood without reference to the balance of core-peripheral and social relations in the historical capitalist world-system.

The manner of Ireland's semi-peripheral, postcolonial incorporation into the world-system structured the possibilities of political responses to that incorporation. In contrast to Germany, organised labour in Ireland was incorporated into an anticolonial movement, partly on the basis of the trade union movement's and Labour party's ties to Sinn Féin and partly on the basis of a promised Democratic Programme of social reforms. In contrast to Mexico, 'agrarian Bolshevism' in Ireland was attenuated by the fact that the Irish Land Commission was already firmly established as a model of social intervention and regime stability; as a consequence, land ownership was less concentrated and plans for collectivisation less forthcoming. Moreover, since the Catholic Church in Ireland was not popularly identified with the colonising regime, as was the case in Mexico, its role in education and welfare provision was not explicitly challenged by secular or feminist currents.[96]

Women's liberation, advanced through Cumann na mBan, the Irish Women's Franchise League, and the Irish Women's Workers' Union, similarly came to be overshadowed by and subordinated to Sinn Féin.[97] The 'national question' notably dominated debate on women's rights in the making of the 1922 Irish Free State Constitution. While equal suffrage had been achieved, the constitution's equality guarantee did not prevent subsequent legislation that openly discriminated against women in the Irish Free State, including laws on entry to the civil service, eligibility for jury service, citizenship, and conditions of employment.[98] Conversely, in Germany, women's participation and autonomy had been central to the anti-systemic movements of the revolutionary period and to the associated advance of both gender equality and socio-economic rights.[99] The crucial conservative victory came in 1919–20 with Sinn Féin's incorporation of popular labour and agrarian

[96] See Anna Macias, 1980, 'Women and the Mexican Revolution, 1910–1920' in *The Americas*, 37 (1), pp. 53–82.

[97] Ferriter, 2005, The Transformation of Ireland, p. 218; Ryan, 2006, 'An analysis of the Irish suffrage movement using new social movement theory'.

[98] Thomas Mohr, 2008, 'The Rights of Women under the Constitution of the Irish Free State' in *Irish Jurist*, 41 (1), pp. 20–59.

[99] Article 109 of the German Constitution notably established formal legal equality: 'All Germans are equal before the law. Men and women have fundamentally the same civic rights and duties'. Weimar Germany also removed barriers to women's entry into the professions and public service. Nevertheless, there remained a 'yawning gap between normative constitutional

struggles into the nationalist mass party on the promise of the Democratic Programme and through the restructuring of the popular arbitration courts.

Popular militancy in these circumstances effectively won Sinn Féin a seat at the negotiating table with the British Empire. Certainly, British participants in Anglo-Irish negotiations expressed hostility to 'communistic' socio-economic provisions. More important for the fate of these proposals, however, was the detached complicity between the established political economy and the nationalist, mass party form. The centralisation of power in nationalist elites – first as Sinn Féin, then as Provisional Government – facilitated the silent reproduction of market law and the strident defence of an Irish nationalist, Catholic, and patriarchal culture. The 'national' constitution thereby privileged financier-graziers interests, maintaining the established political economy of the cattle trade with Britain and capital investment in the City of London, and ensured the Catholic hierarchy's control over social reproduction and the state's minimal welfare effort. Constitution-makers' classic and social discourses approximated an ideological containment of agrarian and labour movements' directly democratic ideals and, in legitimating the state, served to justify these movements' physical repression and defeat.

## CONCLUSION

Controversy, etymologically speaking, comes from the Latin *controversus*, meaning 'turned in an opposite direction'. Throughout the constitution-making process, the word appears repeatedly in connection with suggested economic and social rights provisions. These included proposals to transform Ireland's semi-peripheral economy and to promote more distributive welfare arrangements, notably for children. Certain interests, however, were not for turning. Drafted in private, what was an ostensibly objective blueprint for 'the Irish People' quickly became subject to the influence of those whose interests counted. Throughout the process, but particularly once its authority was secure, the Provisional Government deemed 'controversial' and rejected the possibility of any state intervention that might tax or

commitments and the discrimination of everyday life'. See Ute Frevert, 1989, *Women in German History: From Bourgeois Emancipation to Sexual Liberation*. New York: St. Martin's Press, pp. 215–6.

otherwise threaten established property-holders or deny the Catholic Church's control over welfare provision. Given the industrial school system's legacy of child abuse or the ongoing role of land speculation in exacerbating social inequality, the dismissal of T. J. O'Connell's proposals with respect to the rights of the child and Clement France's with respect to the unearned increment represent particularly stunning examples of constitutional roads not taken.

Facilitating this outcome, the 'Irish Ireland' of classic legal discourse approximated an official truth produced by collective euphemisation.[100] Constitution-makers deployed this discourse ideologically to justify the reproduction of the law of the market, as well as associated grazier, property, and minimalist welfare regimes. Varieties of 'social' legal discourse broadly presupposed the national economy's market integration, even as it attempted to salve its worst effects.[101] Hence, France's proposals were for state-led intervention to break up banking and grazier monopolies in order to extend property rights to small holders and commercial industries. 'If adopted', he argued, they 'would give the first chance that has ever yet been offered for free play of individual effort, for free and unfettered competition between man and man'.[102] Similarly, George O'Brien, a jurist in the classic mode, could endorse Alfred O'Rahilly's proposals to guarantee property rights, to pay full compensation to expropriated landowners and to minimise state involvement in welfare provision. This exchange, in particular, anticipated an enduring alliance between Catholic social proponents and market liberals in the ensuing decades.[103] Similar cost-free Catholic social discourses would receive a much more robust articulation in the 1937 Irish Constitution than they had in 1922.

Ideologically, if classic legal discourse was premised on the existence of a normative order (the nation), so too were liberal-social (society) and Catholic-social (spiritual community) discourses. Whether classic or social, jurists conceived of classes as discrete 'elements' within the unified body or normative order of 'Irish Ireland'. To varying degrees, class divisions, like the property rights that supported them, were considered natural, immutable, and incapable of change. In presupposing this value-consensus order, in which the state is deemed to be a neutral arbiter in conflicts between competing interests or elements,

[100] See Pierre Bourdieu, 1994, 'Structures, Habitus, Power: Basis for a Theory of Symbolic Power'.
[101] Kennedy, 2006, 'Three Globalisations of Law and Legal Thought', p. 38.
[102] 'Document 24' in *Kennedy Papers*, UCDA P4/320.
[103] See Fanning, 2008, *The Quest for Modern Ireland*.

all of these discourses imposed important limitations on social agents' conceptions of freedom, equality, and political transformation. They notably excluded the possibility of direct as opposed to representative democracy or of common ownership as opposed to social democracy. To recognise these ideological limitations is to acknowledge an aporia, a space for society which is against and beyond the value-consensus state, and to acknowledge the radically different meanings of 'economic sovereignty' and 'economic rights' that animated popular democratic forms and discourses during the preceding years of mass mobilisation and militancy.[104] Revitalised trade union, republican, communist, and women's movements re-emerged in 1930s Ireland, creating new constitutions and articulating new socio-economic rights discourses.

[104] See Negri, 2003, *Time for Revolution*, pp. 123–4.

CHAPTER THREE

# 'HIGHLY DANGEROUS'? SOCIO-ECONOMIC RIGHTS IN THE MAKING OF THE 1937 IRISH CONSTITUTION

> *Article IX. The Government will take measures . . . to secure that the issue of credit, which at the present day 'supplies as it were the life blood of the entire economic body' should not fall directly or indirectly under the control of foreign or international financiers, nor be abused in the interests of private individuals or syndicates to the injury of the common good.*
>
> – Edward Cahill to Éamon de Valera[1]

> *'Community effort'. This is Karl Marx terminology.*
>
> – John Charles McQuaid to de Valera[2]

Bunreacht na hÉireann (1937) was created at a time of international upheaval and pronounced ideological contestation.[3] The Great Depression of the 1930s had occasioned a pronounced transformation of the historical capitalist world-system, notably ending the hegemonic roles of both the British Empire and the City of London.[4] The decade was characterised by the gradual dismantling of multilateral trade in favour of economic self-sufficiency, by the collapse of the League of Nations in favour of autarkist empires and, above all, by mass unemployment.[5] Classic economic liberalism was dead, and would remain so for half a century. Among liberal democracies, various forms of state or 'social' control of capital emerged instead, typified by France's Matignon Agreements or by the New Deal in the US. Social democracy formed an often unsympathetic alternative to the social revolution

1 *De Valera Papers*, UCDA, P150/2393. 2 *De Valera Papers*, UCDA P150/2411.

3 This chapter develops ideas first explored in Thomas Murray, 2015, 'Socio-Economic Rights and the Making of the 1937 Irish Constitution' in *Irish Political Studies*. Available at: http://dx.doi.org/10.1080/07907184.2015.1095738.

4 Arrighi, 1994, *The Long Twentieth Century*, pp. 277–85.

5 Hobsbawm, 1991, *Nations and Nationalism since 1780*, p. 132; see also Hobsbawm, 1994, *Age of Extremes*, pp. 85–109.

and radical democracy attempted in Republican Spain and Anarchist Barcelona.[6]

There were more authoritarian alternatives.[7] In Italy and Germany, fascist parties introduced a highly coercive system of corporate societal management, achieving full employment while preserving the classic freedoms of capital (free investment, free accumulation, free exchange of contract, and free selection of markets).[8] Similarly, authoritarian nationalists in Poland, Austria, Hungary, and Portugal selectively invoked Catholic corporatism to justify curtailing organised labour. Concomitantly, in Russia, Joseph Stalin's Communist Party introduced a series of Five-Year Plans, using a centrally planned economy to achieve rapid industrialisation and increased military capacity.

In contrast to wider European experiences, the Irish Free State's social conflicts were not of a scale or nature to threaten the state's continued existence as a representative democracy.[9] In both parliament and civil society, the national anti-systemic movement remained in the ascendant, its party leadership largely committed to renegotiating sovereignty with Westminster while preserving existing institutions of government and administration in Dublin. After the civil war, anti-treatyite Sinn Féin entered government as Fianna Fáil in the 1930s, promising a rejection of the Anglo-Irish Treaty together with a timely social programme of self-sufficiency, land redistribution, employment, and improved welfare. Prioritising core-peripheral over social conflict, nationalist co-option drew sustenance from the cohesion and conservatism of Ireland's property-owning agrarian society as well as the role of the Catholic Church, uniquely in Europe, in dominating the public sphere. Nevertheless, Ireland's state and civil society constitution-makers were faced with an uncertain future, a fact that heightened ideological volatility and class tensions.

The Great Depression notably accentuated social polarisation. Associated conflicts included a mass boycott of land annuities to Great Britain, agrarian agitation over land redistribution, campaigns against

6 Bookchin, 1997, *The Spanish anarchists*; Julián Casanova, 2010, *The Spanish Republic and Civil War*. Cambridge: Cambridge University Press.

7 Michael Oakeshott, 1950, *The Social and Political Doctrines of Contemporary Europe*. New York: Cambridge University Press; Gregory Luebbert, 1991, *Liberalism, Fascism, or Social Democracy*. Oxford: Oxford University Press.

8 Thornhill, 2013, *A Sociology of Constitutions*, p. 323; Neumann, 1966, *Behemoth*.

9 Brian Girvin, 2002, *From Union to Union: Nationalism, Democracy and Religion in Ireland*. Dublin: Gill and Macmillan, p. 77; Luebbert, 1991, *Liberalism, Fascism, or Social Democracy*, p. 451; Casanova, 2010, *The Spanish Republic and Civil War*, p. 35.

slum landlordism and major strikes in transport and building, the largest since the foundation of the state. The Spanish Civil War also prompted rival mobilisations of both left- and right-wing political groups and ideologies, with communist, republican, and feminist groups mobilising on the left, fascist and authoritarian nationalists on the right. All groups created programmes and constitutions that reflected the increased prominence of state intervention in the economy. These included the 'red republican' Constitution of Saor Eire (1931), the Army Comrades Association or 'Blueshirt' Constitution (1932), the IRA's Constitution and Governmental Programme for the Republic of Ireland (1933), the Programme of the Republican Congress (1934), as well as the Labour Party constitution, 'Worker's Republic' (1936).

In these circumstances, the politics of 'social' constitutionalism and socio-economic rights conjured up dramatically different political visions of the future. In civil society, conservatives and authoritarians generally saw Catholic social corporatism as a means of curtailing or reconciling labour and agrarian agitators through various combinations of coercion and reform. Conversely, 'red' republicans, communists as well as a number of trade unionists and feminists explicitly envisaged the state's enforcement of socio-economic rights as part of challenging the structure of Irish society, specifically the nexus of church, state, and capital. Faced with such mobilisations and ideological challenges, the state's constitution-makers' shared concern for social cohesion was the principal motivation *both* for *including* some gesture towards socio-economic rights in the 1937 Irish Constitution as well as for *excluding* substantive, legally binding commitments.

Though with important, locally determined Irish characteristics, the makers of Bunreacht na hÉireann adhered to a contemporary, global politics of 'class-abatement' in which political elites forwarded 'social legal thought', including socio-economic rights, in an attempt to make the class system less vulnerable to attack by alleviating its less defensible consequences.[10] Proposals concerning social credit, land redistribution, education, and welfare rights of various hues featured throughout the drafting. Deliberations over the precise wording of the document's socio-economic rights provisions reflected a series of recurring tensions between Fianna Fáil Taoiseach Éamon de Valera, who advanced a set of limited socio-economic reforms, civil servants such as

[10] Marshall, 1950, *Citizenship and Social Class*, pp. 32–3.

James MacElligott, who defended administrative norms of parliamentary sovereignty and of minimising social expenditure and clericalists such as John Charles McQuaid, who were keen to mould society according to papal encyclicals in theory but reluctant to cede authority in practice. Ultimately, the 1937 Irish Constitution entrenched a minimal set of socio-economic rights, primarily those concerning property, education, and child welfare provision, and advanced several, non-binding 'Directive Principles of Social Policy'.

The 1937 Irish Constitution cannot be located neatly within a particular 'wave' of constitution-making.[11] However, it did reflect wider European debates and discourses concerning the emerging 'social' state.[12] The balance of contending core-peripheral and social relations crystallised in a hybrid, semi-peripheral constitutional form. A classic constitution, the 1937 Irish Constitution emphasised the articulation of national sovereignty while conservatively maintaining pre-existing state and market institutions. At the same time, however, constitution-makers incorporated a Catholic form of social discourse, although disagreeing on whether it should take precedence over inherited institutions and norms. Ultimately, the constitution's social entrenchment was extensive in the field of family law yet strictly limited in terms of socio-economic rights entrenchment. Rightly recognised as retaining an electoral-democratic form of government, this form of constitutionalism also retained Ireland's peripheral agrarian political economy and associated class and gender hierarchies. In doing so, it further ensured the state's comparatively minimal welfare effort and its outsourcing to the Catholic Church in the years ahead.

## THE SOCIAL ORIGINS OF CONSTITUTIONALISM IN 1930S IRELAND

Socio-economic rights' entrenchment in 1930s Ireland was intimately connected to contemporary social struggles, notably those that concerned land, credit, labour, and living standards. Throughout the 1920s and 1930s, the balance of core-peripheral and social relations ensured

[11] For some comparative political scientists, the 1937 Irish Constitution arrived promptly on schedule, replacing the 1922 Irish Free State Constitution after fifteen years, the average lifespan of a constitution. Elkins, Ginsburg, and Melton, 2009, *The Endurance of National Constitutions*.

[12] Notably, if the term 'state' is virtually absent in the 1922 Irish Free State Constitution, it occurs more than twenty times in its successor. Kissane, 2011, *New Beginnings*, p. 88.

a conservative outcome to the Irish revolution, including the partition of the island and the reproduction of inherited peripheral-agrarian economic linkages. The Anglo-Irish Treaty (1921) demarcated national sovereignty and continued to structure core-peripheral relations. A number of significant changes, however, both precipitated and crystallised in the making of the 1937 Irish Constitution. Imperial decline combined with peripheral assertiveness, notably on the part of Canada, South Africa, and the Irish Free State, prompted the Statute of Westminster (1931), establishing legislative equality between the UK and the self-governing Dominions of the British Empire. Fianna Fáil, elected to government from 1932 onwards, used these developments to overturn the Treaty settlement. The party removed the oath of fidelity from the 1922 Irish Free State Constitution, abolished the right of appeal to the Judicial Committee of the Privy Council, boycotted the office of the Governor General and, following King Edward's abdication in 1936, unilaterally declared 'external association' between the Irish Free State and the United Kingdom.[13]

Inter-state relations developed alongside inter-economic conflicts. Throughout the 1920s, successive Cumman na nGaedheal governments ensured that the Free State remained tied to the sterling area's free trade conditions and its currency anchored to the gold standard.[14] This supported the graziers' cattle trade to the UK and the Irish banking cartel's investment of the proceeds of that trade in the City of London.[15] Conversely, Fianna Fáil linked its republicanism to social radicalism and proposed improving living standards through protected national economic development and redistributive measures. After the Wall Street Crash, Britain's introduction of protectionist measures left Ireland as virtually the only free trade economy in Western Europe.[16] Fianna Fáil's autarkist proposals thus coincided with international trends towards increased state intervention. There were ramifications for Westminster-Dublin relations. The Irish government ceased paying land annuities owed to Britain for loans provided under the Land Acts, payments agreed as part of the Treaty. British sanctions against

13 See Hogan, 2012, *The Origins of the Irish Constitution: 1928–41*; Kissane, 2011, *New Beginnings*.
14 Mary Daly, 1992, *Industrial Development and Irish National Identity, 1922–1939*. New York: Syracuse University Press, p. 32.
15 O'Hearn, 2001, *The Atlantic Economy*, p. 113.
16 Cormac Ó'Gráda, 1997, *Rocky Road: the Irish economy since the 1920s*. Manchester: Manchester University Press, p. 143; Fanning, 1978, *The Irish Department of Finance*, p. 210.

Irish exports preceded retaliatory Irish levies on British imports in the ensuing Anglo-Irish Economic War (1932–8).

The 1937 Irish Constitution was further shaped by the power of those groups dominant within Irish society in the course of the Great Depression, a period of attempted economic transformation, social polarisation, class conflict and conservative repression. Society in the new Irish Free State remained divided according to a peripheral-agrarian class structure. Of a population of approximately three million people, two thirds lived in rural towns and communities. A majority, some 56 per cent of all adult males, depended on agriculture for their livelihoods.[17] The dominant social group comprised of those graziers or livestock exporters on large holdings in excess of 100 acres, concentrated in the East and South of the country. The vast majority of farmers were smallholders, dependent on neighbours for sharing farm implements and reliant on family, particularly women and children, for labour. Some 80 per cent of Irish farms depended on family labour in contrast to 33 per cent in Britain.[18]

The Irish Free State's institutions were designed to support this peripheral-agrarian economy and its beneficiaries. In order to secure livestock and dairy exports, Cumann na nGaedheal established mechanisms to maintain parity between sterling and the new Saorstát punt (or Irish pound).[19] The Irish banking cartel continued to operate in the sterling area much the same as before, dictating the terms of state supervision and siphoning domestic deposits into the City of London's more lucrative markets. The retained Whitehall model of administration ensured decision-making remained concentrated in government ministers and their respective departments, chiefly the Department of Finance. Adhering to membership of the sterling area, the Department of Finance continued to advocate for Gladstonian fiscal doctrine, maintaining the integrity of the 'new' Irish currency through parsimony in public expenditure.[20] A recession in agriculture in the late 1920s prompted the government to pursue balanced budgets with zeal, justifying cuts to welfare as proof that the new nation-state could manage its own affairs.

[17] Coakley and Gallagher, 2010, *Politics in the Republic of Ireland*, p. 435.
[18] Dooley, 2004, *The Land for the People*, pp. 117, 206.
[19] See Fanning, 1978, *The Irish Department of Finance*, pp. 177, 209.
[20] O'Driscoll, 2000, 'Social Catholicism in Independent Ireland', p. 127.

State support for financier-grazier interests in livestock and dairying had ramifications for land redistribution, an abiding source of social conflict. By defending a classic free market in land, Cumman na nGaedheal ensured that a growing number of farmers could increase their acreage by buying out their neighbours.[21] The reformed Irish Land Commission proved slow to redistribute large farmers' land to relieve congestion, concentrating instead on facilitating existing tenants' ownership. The banking cartel's restrictive lending policies further hindered land redistribution. The Commission frequently overlooked small farmers or landless labourers, unable to access the credit necessary to demonstrate their application's viability, in favour of shopkeepers, teachers, and clergy.[22] Irish land holdings remained disproportionately concentrated in the hands of a few and tendencies towards larger farms, land speculation, and rural population decline persisted. The reproduction of the labour-extensive grazier cycle sustained high levels of unemployment and emigration. Between 1921 and 1931, some 33,000 people emigrated annually. Emigration abated briefly during the Great Depression, falling to only 7,000 emigrants in 1932, but resumed as before when conditions abroad improved from 1936 onwards.[23]

The politics of the 1920s and 1930s, both in parliament and civil society, centred on contesting or defending these core-peripheral and social relations (inclusive of capital-labour, gender, ethnic, and 'other' identity relations). In the electoral arena, Cumman na nGaedheal and Fianna Fáil, the two largest parties of the period, shared nationalist aims centred on the island's political reunification and independence from the United Kingdom as well as the restoration of the Irish language. The continued salience of intra-nationalist divisions or 'civil war politics' owed in part to the class coalitions represented by the two parties. Cumman na nGaedheal, a cadre party, drew support from established elites who benefitted from preserving the peripheral-agrarian status quo, notably the country's banks, graziers, dairy owners, and transport companies as well as the national press and Catholic hierarchy.[24] Conversely, Fianna Fáil, a mass party committed to national self-sufficiency,

21 Brendan Edgeworth, 2007, 'Rural Radicalism Restrained: The Irish Land Commission and the Courts (1933–1939)' in *Irish Jurist*, Vol. 42 (1), pp. 1–28, p. 15.

22 Dooley, *The Land for the People*, pp. 73, 81.

23 Emmett O'Connor, 2011, *A Labour History of Ireland, 1824–2000*. Dublin: University College Dublin Press, p. 144; Ó'Gráda, 1997, A Rocky Road, p. 155.

24 Patrick Hogan, Minister for Agriculture, explicitly identified grazier interests with those of the nation and invoked *laissez-faire* doctrine to justify keeping farmers' costs low and minimising local taxation. Ó'Gráda, 1997, *A Rocky Road*, pp. 67, 156.

appealed to a diverse cohort of class fractions, including indigenous employers, small farmers, landless labourers, organised labour, and the unemployed.[25] Fianna Fáil's growing support among workers and trade unions was a telling indictment of the Labour party's conservative policies. The nationalist party mobilised this national-popular base successfully to return to government in successive elections between 1932 and 1948.

Successive Fianna Fáil governments, adhering to international autarkist trends, attempted to create a new structure of capital accumulation, national self-sufficiency, as a means of ending subordination to Britain.[26] The party deepened protectionist tariffs, accelerated import substitution industrialisation, and reconfigured the land ownership regime. A new licensing system prevented companies setting up in Ireland behind tariff barriers and promoted easy access to state officials to encourage private investment in manufacturing. However, if this was not forthcoming, Fianna Fáil increased state involvement.[27] Manufacturing employment rose from 62,608 (1932) to 101,004 (1939).[28] The party enforced improved conditions of employment, set limits for working hours, provided for the enforcement of collective bargaining agreements, and introduced minimum rates of pay for farm labourers.[29] Fianna Fáil also introduced a series of welfare budgetary measures, notably pensions for widows, orphans, and army veterans, as well as significantly increased health and housing provision.[30]

In agriculture, the Anglo-Irish Economic War (1932–8) prompted dramatic falls in livestock exports and intensified the state's shift towards self-sufficiency.[31] The switch from livestock to labour-intensive tillage, in particular, involved accelerating land redistribution to small farmers via the Irish Land Commission. The 1933 Land Act increased the commission's powers of acquisition. In theory, any large farm not providing employment or food for the community could be deemed inimical to 'the common good' and hence subject to the commission. Some 450,000 acres were subdivided and redistributed to labourers and

[25] Irish owners of small- to medium-sized firms, faced with increased competition in areas such as textiles and footwear, had long advocated state protectionism. Trade unions also supported protection as a path to state-led industrial development. See Richard Dunphy, 1995, *The Making of Fianna Fáil Power in Ireland: 1923–1948*. Oxford: Clarendon Press.

[26] O'Hearn, 2001, *The Atlantic Economy*, p. 115.

[27] Kieran Allen, 1997, *Fianna Fáil and Irish Labour*. London: Pluto Press, p. 40.

[28] Ó'Gráda, 1997, *A Rocky Road*, p. 153 [29] Allen, 1997, *Fianna Fáil and Irish Labour*, p. 48.

[30] Cousins, 2005, *Explaining the Irish Welfare State*, p. 26.

[31] Brown, 2004, *Ireland: A Social and Cultural History*, p. 131.

smallholders, the rate of redistribution being particularly high in the period between 1934 and 1937.[32] For their part, landowners successfully challenged the Land Commission in the courts where judges consistently interpreted the land legislation restrictively, thereby delaying compulsory resumptions and restraining 'rural radicalism'.[33]

Ideologically, Fianna Fáil's social reorientation of the Irish Free State cohered with a broader globalisation of social legal thought during the Great Depression. Specifically, Fianna Fáil coincided with the Labour party and Trade Union Congress (TUC) in justifying reforms by invoking contemporary Catholic social thought. In advance of the 1932 election, the Fianna Fáil leadership took particular care not to be identified with the anti-clerical 'communism' of the Republican left. 'Fianna Fáil policy', Seán T. O'Kelly argued, 'was the policy of Pope Pius XI'.[34] The Irish Trade Union Congress's president similarly argued that the social question could only be resolved 'on the lines adumbrated by Pope Leo XIII and by Pope Pius XI in the encyclicals'.[35] The hierarchy did not leave such professions of faith to chance. In February 1936, Bishop Kinane and bishops-elect Michael Browne and Cornelius Lucey held an investigation into the Labour party's new constitution, misleadingly titled 'Worker's Republic'. Labour party leader William Norton conceded several changes to establish its conformity with Catholic social principles.[36]

Ireland's reception of Catholic social thought differed from Europe's Catholic South insofar as the Catholic hierarchy did not face ideological competitors of comparable strength.[37] In increasingly polarised societies such as Italy, Spain, Portugal, and Hungary, Pope Leo XIII's *Quadrageissmo Anno* (1931), articulating a fuller expression of 'social justice', functioned to maintain working-class support from authoritarian and socialist movements.[38] In contrast, the Catholic hierarchy

[32] Dooley, 2004, *The Land for the People*, p. 203.

[33] *Estate of Rafferty* v. *Irish Land Commission* (1935) and *Potterton* v. *Irish Land Commission* (1935), *Estate of Peter C. Alley* v. *Irish Land Commission* (1936). See Edgeworth, 2007, 'Rural Radicalism Restrained', pp. 10–11.

[34] Murray, 2000, *Oracles of God*, p. 260.

[35] Allen, 1997, *Fianna Fáil and Irish Labour*, p. 57.

[36] Niamh Puirséil, 2007, *The Irish Labour Party, 1922–73*. Dublin: University College Dublin Press, p. 56.

[37] Jeffrey Prager, 1986, *Building Democracy in Ireland*. Cambridge: Cambridge University Press.

[38] In this articulation of social justice, free enterprise and private property should be retained but the proper ordering of economic life could not be left to market forces. Drawing on the medieval writings of Thomas Aquinas, the encyclical envisaged society as an ordered harmony of 'naturally' existing upper, middle, and lower classes. These divisions could be minimised however by ascribing decision-making power to vocational councils, drawn from economic sectors and cutting across class structures. See Moloney, 1991, *The Worker Question*.

in Ireland enjoyed popular deference to its authority. Post-1922, the position of the Catholic Church in the Irish Free State was bolstered by legislation – notably concerning divorce, contraception, abortion, adoption, and state censorship – and popularly confirmed during the Eucharist Congress (1932) which saw up to a quarter of the population attend mass in Dublin's Phoenix Park. In these circumstances, Irish political decision-makers, including the Catholic hierarchy, could adopt the rhetoric of Catholic social harmony without seeing the need either to justify it or to implement it in practice. For Catholic intellectuals anticipating constitutional change, *Quadrageissmo Anno* (1931) provided a basis to critique English-speaking, materialist philosophies of life, encompassing both liberal democratic and socialist conceptions of the good life.

The Catholic Church broadly helped legitimate the Irish Free State, though remained sceptical about the merits of electoral democracy until after World War II. A number of Catholic bishops and intellectuals not infrequently advocated 'natural law' as a desirable alternative to liberalism, offering the authoritarian 'Estado Novo' of Portugal's António Salazar as a model for emulation. In 1936, they presented their ideas to the Taoiseach and several senior civil servants at the Jesuit summer school, 'The Constitutional problem from the Catholic point of view'. Contributor Cornelius Lucey argued against 'the modern prejudice in favour of democracy' and held that government, as supreme guardian of 'natural law', had to be capable of curtailing the rights of 'inferior society' so as to ensure its observance.[39] Similarly, Edward Cahill, author of *The Framework of a Christian State* and de Valera's correspondent within the Jesuit Order, proposed that the new constitution 'should mark a definite break with the Liberal and non-Christian type of State'. Instead, Cahill suggested government be composed of rural, Parochial Councils to be elected by the family patriarch only.[40]

There existed wider and robust ideological opposition to imagining a welfare state replacing the responsibilities of family and church. God-given, natural rights of property and family were understood to trump those socio-economic rights merely created by the state.[41] When the

[39] Michael Browne further observed that since the people designated a ruler, 'who thereupon has the authority of natural law', it would be contrary to the encyclicals of Leo XIII and Pius X to imagine that the people governed by mandate or retained authority in the interim. Cited in Keogh and McCarthy, 2009, *The Making of the Irish Constitution*, p. 103.

[40] *De Valera Papers*, UCDA P150/2393; Edward Cahill, 1932, *The Framework of a Christian State*. Dublin: Gill and Son.

[41] Fanning, 2008, *The Quest for Modern Ireland*, p. 70.

Jesuit journal *Studies* hosted a symposium on constitutional reform in 1933, Michael Tierney rejected Tom Paine's 'The Rights of Man' for its 'Jacobin deification of the State' and advocated natural law as a path to a minimal State.[42] John Horgan argued for a constitution that recognised the natural rights of the family as the keystone of society. The Church commonly utilised the family's natural rights to defend its moral monopoly because it was through the family, particularly through the mother, that it reached into the home to supervise child-rearing and, in particular, educational formation.[43] Most forms of state as opposed to voluntary welfare provision met with episcopal reproach. In late 1935, when the state provided limited school meals in Belmullet, Co. Mayo, the local Canon Hegarty claimed that the queuing up of children to avail of the scheme was 'engendering Communism'.[44]

Compounding these ideological limits, a series of systemic or institutional relationships exhausted Fianna Fáil's social reorientation of the state. First, the government's Commission on Banking, Currency, and Credit (1934–8) parked the question of credit system reform for a generation while the Irish banking cartel continued unperturbed. The Irish Banks' Standing Committee attacked the government's welfare spending and land division policies, which, they argued, had ensured the loss of land as a security for credit and had destroyed its 'free market'.[45] Second, rhetorical hostility towards graziers concealed the state's continued dependence on the cattle trade to Britain, particularly as large farmers opted to live on credit and capital rather than switch to tillage.[46] By 1937, the UK still accounted for more than 90 per cent of Irish Free State exports.[47] Third, reducing land annuities and redistributing land were temporary remedies for agrarian hardship. Without credit, small holdings were undercapitalised, unsustainable, and soon sold back to larger farmers to fund rural emigration.[48] Official unemployment

[42] Fanning, 2008, *The Quest for Modern Ireland*, pp. 101–4.

[43] Inglis, 1998, *Moral Monopoly*, pp. 248–9.

[44] Murray, 2000, *Oracles of God*, p. 347.

[45] Fanning, 1978, *The Irish Department of Finance*, p. 270. Daly, 1997, *The Buffer State*, p. 245.

[46] Lee, 1989, *Ireland, 1912–1985*, p. 187.

[47] Erhard Rumpf and A. C. Hepburn, 1977, *Nationalism and Socialism in Twentieth-Century Ireland*. New York: Barnes and Noble, pp. 114, 117.

[48] The holdings created through the Land Commission were less than the 32.5 acres considered necessary to set up an economically viable farm. Those smallholders who did not sell and emigrate remained dependent on incorporation as calf breeders into the graziers' livestock production line. Dooley, 2004, *The Land for the People*, pp. 73, 81, 91; McCabe, 2011, *Sins of the Father*, p. 79; Edgeworth, 2007, 'Rural Radicalism Restrained', p. 15.

levels averaged at some 96,000 annually throughout the 1930s, peaking at 145,000 in 1936.[49]

Concomitantly, the state's expanding welfare effort generated opposition within the civil service. Austerity hawks in the Department of Finance, supported publically by the Irish Banks' Standing Committee, fought a rear-guard action against increased social expenditure. Diminishing agricultural returns occasioned by the switch from livestock to tillage ensured their voices returned to prominence in 1935.[50] Welfare provision remained means-tested and dependent on market or charitable institutions. Housing policy prioritised private home ownership, leaving slum landlordism unchallenged. The Catholic Church filled the space left vacant by the state, its moral monopoly dependent, at least in part, on controlling education, health, and charity services. The consequences of classic, laissez-faire policies, notwithstanding their Catholic social modification, were predictable and often devastating.

Living standards were sharply polarised. A quarter of the population lived in 'bad housing', accommodation with more than two people per room.[51] Professional slum landlords in Cork, Limerick, Waterford, and Dublin provided the worst examples. Dublin City's 6,300 tenements housed more than 111,000 people by 1939.[52] Health services were poorly funded and subject to means-testing. Infant and maternal mortality rates as well as the prevalence of diseases such as tuberculosis, influenza, and rickets remained comparatively higher in Ireland than in other European countries.[53] Education for the vast majority began and ended with the 'national' or primary school system, characterised by a lack of facilities and, again, Church control. Access to secondary education was limited to some 12,000 students while university education remained the privilege of some 5,000 students.[54] The

[49] Ó Gráda, 1997, *A Rocky Road*, p. 155. [50] Daly, 1997, *The Buffer State*, pp. 154–63.

[51] In the mid-1920s, some 37 per cent of the population lived in bad housing conditions, officially classed as houses with more than two people per room. Daly, 1981, *Social and Economic History of Ireland since 1800*, p. 191.

[52] Richard Mulcahy, Minister for Local Government, placed responsibility for working-class housing with local authorities (unable to borrow sufficient capital for housing schemes or slum clearance) while, through loans and grants, the government subsidised private home ownership for farmers and the urban middle class. Daly, 1997, *The Buffer State*, p. 221.

[53] Out of every 1,000 children born, 70 would die before their first birthday. Health inspectors in Irish schools found that the majority of children examined were 'verminous' while some 8.5 per cent were suffering from malnutrition. Diseases such as tuberculosis (TB), influenza, and rickets remained prevalent. Annually, some 5,000 people died of TB. Barrington, 1987, *Health, Medicine and Politics in Ireland*, pp. 129, 132.

[54] Daly, 1981, *Social and Economic History of Ireland since 1800*, pp. 181, 187–9.

Irish Free State also increased reliance upon church-controlled, cost-effective industrial and reformatory schools for working-class children, even as such schools were being closed in Britain.[55]

The prospects for constitutionalising socio-economic rights were hardly auspicious. In contrast to European countries where cross-class coalitions invoked norms of justice, citizenship, and solidarity to advocate for universal social rights, Ireland's public-private welfare provision more closely adhered to Victorian values of charity and state paternalism.[56] Nevertheless, Fianna Fáil's limited social reorientation of the state either aggravated large grazier land-owners or disappointed popular expectations. Between 1932 and 1935 in particular, popular discontent and class conflict found extra-parliamentary channels of expression and organisation, often replaying intra-nationalist, civil war hostilities in the process. From within and in response to social conflicts over land, credit, labour, and living standards, a variety of ideologies, constitutional forms, and socio-economic rights discourses emerged.

## SOCIAL CONSTITUTIONS OF THE RIGHT AND LEFT

To the left of the political spectrum, Saor Éire (1931) and the Republican Congress (1934) represented important though short-lived articulations of a socially radical or 'red' republicanism. Thanks partly to the efforts of organisers such as Peadar O'Donnell, Frank Ryan, and George Gilmore, the anti-Treaty IRA, comprising some 300 officers and 3,500 rank-and-file members, shifted leftward. The organisation promised increased land redistribution to land-hungry farmers and labourers and also played a key role in organising opposition to land annuities among all farmers.[57] Its successful annuities boycott in Donegal was subsequently emulated by non-payment committees across Ireland, before being adopted and moderated by Fianna Fáil. Garda Commissioner Eoin O'Duffy warned of a 'red terror' emerging in the countryside.[58] Meanwhile, in the cities, the IRA supported campaigns for improved working-class accommodation, including the Irish Women Workers' Union campaign against slum landlordism in Dublin's inner city. *An Phoblacht*, the republican newspaper, called for direct action: 'Take over

55 Ferriter, 2005, *The Transformation of Ireland*, p. 324.
56 Cousins, 2005, *Explaining the Irish Welfare State*, pp. 12–15.
57 Murray, 2000, *Oracles of God*, p. 317.
58 Donal Ó Drisceoil, 2009, 'When Dev defaulted: the land annuities dispute, 1926–38' in *History Ireland*. Available at www.historyireland.com//volumes/?id=115131.

the half-empty houses of the well-to-do and the half-occupied public buildings and let the worse-housed of the workers move into them until decent accommodation has been built for them. If the workers must live six to a room, why not make the parasite class live likewise?'[59]

The Constitution of Saor Éire (1931) proposed to 'break the connection with England and secure for the Republic of Ireland free expression of its National Sovereignty'. Achieving an independent Republic necessitated social revolution, which in turn necessitated a series of radical state inventions. The Constitution's socio-economic provisions proposed 'to abolish, without compensation, landlordism in land, fisheries and minerals; [t]o create a State monopoly in banking and credits; [t]o make the national wealth and credit available for the creation and fullest development of essential industries and mineral resources, through Industrial Workers' Co-operative, under State direction and management, workers to regulate internal working conditions'.[60] Similarly, the Republican Congress (1934), a subsequent socialist-republican movement comprised of delegates from the Communist Party of Ireland, the Irish Citizen Army, trade unions, as well as tenant, worker, and unemployed organisations, argued for a workers' republic. In the Athlone Manifesto, Congress declared: 'We believe that a Republic or a united Ireland will never be achieved except through a struggle which uproots capitalism on its way'.[61] It proposed land redistribution, a minimum wage for farm workers, and a united, militant trade union movement. It also advocated equal pay for women.[62]

Ideologically, these constitutions drew on a rich legacy of social radicalism, incorporating both James Connolly's vision for a workers' republic and Patrick Pearse's writings in which a nation's sovereignty extended to all its material possessions and trumped rights of private property.[63] In contrast to earlier republican writings, however, these constitutions emphasised material-class interests as opposed to the predominantly spiritual-national concerns of traditional republicanism. A class analysis also informed the red republicans' rejection of the Irish Free State and their proposal 'to vest all political power within the

59 'Get out of the Slums' cited in Murray, 2000, *Oracles of God*, p. 322.
60 Murray, 2000, *Oracles of God*, p. 318; Tim Coogan, 2002, *The IRA*, Palgrave: New York, p. 58.
61 'Republican Congress' in D. J. Hickey and J. E. Doherty, 2003, *A New Dictionary of Irish History*. Dublin: Gill and MacMillan, p. 416.
62 O'Connor, 2011, *A Labour history of Ireland*, pp. 134–8.
63 See Kissane, 2011, *New Beginnings*, pp. 21–5.

Republic in the working-class and working farmers'. Changed republican thinking owed to the anti-treaty IRA's failure to mobilise popular support during the Irish civil war and to the heightened possibility for popular radicalisation in the changed social and political circumstances of the 1930s. The Bolshevik seizure of state power in the 1917 Russian Revolution, as propagated by the Soviet Union and its supporters in the Communist Party of Ireland, also provided a model for revolution.

Republican leaders, notably Mary MacSwiney, J. J. O'Kelly, and Moss Twomey, as well as a majority of the membership dissociated themselves from left-wing formations and ideas. They presented the IRA as a body of sound Catholics and justified more moderate state inventions in terms of Catholic social thought. The IRA's Constitution and Governmental Programme for the Republic of Ireland (1933) proposed that the nation's soil, rivers, lakes, and waterways were to be 'the property of the people'.[64] The State would not control but rather encourage the cooperative organisation of agriculture; it would not monopolise but rather direct industry, distribution, and exchange, including credit and banking. The IRA Constitution also invoked the state's responsibility for adequate housing. The document, in effect, returned to conventional republican invocations of national as opposed to class interests. It sought to justify a Catholic social vision 'in which the greater part of citizens own land and capital in small quantities'.[65]

Responding to the IRA Constitution, the Catholic hierarchy reproached the republicans for failing to safeguard the absolute right of the individual to private property. According to Bishop Jeremiah Kinane of Waterford, private property rights were 'given to man by God's natural law' and not, as the IRA programme implied, derived from the State.[66] Tellingly, when Moss Twomey responded to the Bishop, he argued that the IRA's preferred social system conformed to Catholic social teaching. In support of the constitution's proposals to break the Irish banking cartel, he cited Pope Leo XIII's condemnation of the concentration of accumulated wealth in the hands of a few, specifically their 'immense power and despotic economic domination'. The Bishops' anxiety for the rights of property-owners, Twomey concluded, contrasted with the absence of any expression of concern for the vast majority of people who 'are propertyless and have no assured means, or

[64] Óglaigh na hÉireann, 'Constitution and Governmental Programme for the Republic of Ireland', 03.1933. See *Coyle O'Donnell Papers* UCDA, P61/11 (I).

[65] See Michael Price, *An Phoblacht*, 7.2.31. Murray, 2000: 339–41.

[66] Murray, 2000, *Oracles of God*, p. 339.

access to the means, of earning a livelihood; they either starve or exist on doles or charity'.[67]

Meanwhile, to the right of the political spectrum, agrarian militancy and land redistribution provoked large farmers into support for the National Guard, a conservative ex-army comrades association founded to defend Cumman na nGaedheal meetings from IRA intimidation. The National Guard or 'Blueshirts' grew to more than 30,000 members at its peak. Its leadership adopted elements of European fascism such as anti-communism, the right-arm salute, uniformed marches, and public rallies.[68] Following its proscription in 1933, Cumman na nGaedheal, electorally defeated and demoralised, united with the National Guard to form Fine Gael under ex-Garda Commissioner Eoin O'Duffy. The alliance fragmented, however, when Blueshirt activities shifted from being anti-republican to being anti-state, including street violence against republicans, withholding local authority rates and land annuities as well as disrupting communications. Fine Gael reverted to Cumman na nGaedheal type – 'respectable, pious, and churlish within the Oireachtas, and virtually invisible outside it' – while its manifesto, though Catholic corporatist, emphasised electoral-democratic aims and methods.[69]

The Constitution of the Army Comrades Association (1932) was a synthesis of Catholicism, anti-communism, nationalism, and economic and social corporatism.[70] In prioritising authoritarian leadership and militant anti-communism, O'Duffy looked to Benito Mussolini's *Carta del Lavoro* (1927), which adopted the rhetoric of corporate constitutionalism for a 'harmoniously unitary state' while, in practice, prohibiting independent trade unions and insisting that the industrialists and business class retained a veto over bargaining. On this interpretation, economic rights or 'rights of social ownership' provided a pretext for the curtailment of the labour movement and for private interests to secure access to state resources.[71] The ACA constitution was similarly selective in its reading of the corporatist elements of the Catholic social,

67 Murray, 2000, *Oracles of God*, p. 341.

68 There is little scholarly consensus on the Blueshirts. While the leadership was fascist, the rank-and-file may have been more motivated by old civil war nemeses. See Mike Cronin, 1997, *The Blueshirts and Irish Politics*, Dublin: Four Courts Press; Andrew Orridge, 1983, 'The Blueshirts and the "Economic War"' in *Political Studies*, 31 (3), pp. 351–69; Dooley, 2004, *The Land for the People*, p. 104.

69 O'Halpin, 1999, *Defending Ireland*, p. 120.

70 Draft suggestions for an ACA constitution, August, 1932. Richard Mulcahy Papers, UCDA, P7C/44 (1). See also O'Halpin, 1999, *Defending Ireland*, p. 115.

71 See Thornhill, 2013, *A Sociology of Constitutions*, p. 316.

emphasising Catholic, 'national' interests and banning trade unions' right to strike in favour of 'social harmony' in industry.[72] This right-wing form of Catholic social discourse aligned with employer and grazier interests.

Ireland's social conflicts, in contrast to wider European experiences in the 1930s, were not of a scale or nature to threaten the state's continued existence as a representative democracy. Popular protest was more often directed toward reform not social revolution or fascist reaction.[73] There were a number of important factors operative here. The state's institutions retained a degree of autonomy from organised economic interests or parties. Crucially, Fianna Fáil's refusal to purge the army or police of pro-treaty opponents was rewarded with obedience to government throughout the 1930s.[74] The state also retained popular legitimacy. Adhering to Sinn Féin's trajectory in the revolutionary period, civil society energies came to be incorporated into a mass party.[75] Fianna Fáil's national and social appeal combined with its extensive branch organisation to incorporate heretofore marginalised groups into a cross-class, electoral, and constitutional politics.[76] Radical left-wing, republican, or fascist groups had little response to the state's social concessions to organised farmers and workers.

The Catholic hierarchy roundly condemned communists and republicans involved in the various agrarian and urban agitations of the 1930s stating that Catholics could not belong to such 'sinful and irreligious' organisations.[77] The Catholic hierarchy was anxious to protect both its spiritual and temporal resources. Archdeacon William Byrne, the Principal of Waterford CBS, dismissed the republican activist Frank Edwards from his teaching post because he had participated in a campaign against local slum landlords. Although Byrne justified his dismissal on the grounds that 'people were attempting to set up in Ireland a state of affairs after the model of Moscow', he was also a trustee of the slum property at the centre of the dispute.[78]

[72] Allen, 1997, *Fianna Fáil and Irish Labour*, p. 57.

[73] Girvin, 2002, *From Union to Union*, p. 77.

[74] O'Halpin, 1999, *Defending Ireland*.

[75] The success of the left-republican land annuity boycott campaign, for example, prompted Fianna Fáil to include non-payment of annuities to Britain in its 1932 election manifesto. In government, however, de Valera retained annuities, now at a reduced rate, for the Irish Free State. Ferriter, 2005, *The Transformation of Ireland*, p. 416.

[76] Dunphy, 1995, *The Making of Fianna Fáil Power in Ireland: 1923–1948*.

[77] 'Saor Éire' in D. J. Hickey and J. E. Doherty, 2003, *A New Dictionary of Irish History*. Dublin: Gill and MacMillan, p. 429.

[78] David Smith, 2002, 'Frank Edwards: The man that fought the Bishop' in *Journal of the Waterford Archaeological and Historical Society*, No. 58.

Assured of their comparative isolation, successive governments resorted to emergency powers legislation and military tribunals to censor and suppress both left- and right-wing manifestations of class politics. In 1931, Cumann na nGaedheal inserted Article 2A into the 1922 Irish Free State Constitution, which provided for military tribunals to try certain scheduled offences, including the membership of 'unlawful' organisations such as the IRA and Saor Eire.[79] Fianna Fáil initially reversed this legislation in 1932 only to reappoint the military tribunals the following year in order to restrain the Blueshirts. From 1934, these tribunals also began to convict IRA members before de Valera similarly invoked Article 2A to declare the organisation illegal in 1936.[80] By 1935, after two years of gun battles in the streets of Cork and Dublin and guerrilla skirmishes in the countryside, confrontations between the IRA-radical Left alliance and the Blueshirts had ceased.

The ideological battles between left and right, however, continued. In the summer of 1936, the outbreak of the Spanish Civil War mobilised a pronounced 'red' scare led by the Catholic hierarchy and press.[81] The Irish Christian Front, formed by Dublin businessman and Fine Gael TD Paddy Belton, organised mass demonstrations in support of General Franco, the largest of which attracted some 100,000 people out on the streets of Dublin. Ireland's right- and left-wing radicals now emigrated to fight on opposing sides in Spain. Wary of the Catholic hierarchy and Fine Gael's accusations of communism, Fianna Fáil, Labour, and the TUC expressed sympathy for Spain's Catholics but avoided advocating either a Francoist or Republican position.

Moreover, the period between 1935 and 1937 was one of heightened trade union militancy. In 1935, some 2,800 workers, members of the ATGWU and ITGWU, engaged in strike action for improved pay and conditions on Dublin Tramways. The IRA's involvement, opening fire on strike-breaking army lorries, directly prompted its repression.[82] Two

[79] On 20 October 1931, the government declared twelve organisations 'unlawful': Saor Eire, the IRA, Fianna Eireann, Cumann na mBan, the Friends of Soviet Russia, the Irish Labour Defence League, the Workers' Defence Corps, the Women Prisoners' Defence League, the Workers' Revolutionary Party, the Irish Tribute League, the Irish Working Farmers' Committee, and the Workers' Research Bureau. Many of these had been involved in strike activities or the annuity campaign. Bill Kissane, 2004, 'Defending Democracy? The Legislative Response to Political Extremism in the Irish Free State, 1922–39' in *Irish Historical Studies*, Vol. 34 (134), pp. 156–74, p. 163.

[80] Article 2A formed the basis for the Offences against the State Act (1940).

[81] R. A. Stradling, 'Battleground of Reputations: Ireland and the Spanish Civil War' in Paul Preston and Ann MacKenzie (eds.), 1996, *The Republic Besieged: Civil War in Spain 1936–39*, Edinburgh: Edinburgh University Press, pp. 107–34.

[82] O'Halpin, 1999, *Defending Ireland*, p. 124.

years later, a builders' strike involved some 11,000 workers in fifteen unions throughout Ireland.[83] Mark Daly of the Dublin Trades Council claimed that Fianna Fáil's house-building programme owed not to government generosity but to builders' low wages.[84] The strike was the largest since the foundation of the state and lasted from April to October 1937, the period in which the Bunreacht was finalised and voted on. Faced with an uncertain future, the mere potential for class conflict that these struggles in the 1930s presented was sufficient to influence the makers of the 1937 Constitution's economic and social provisions.

## 'THE WEAKER SECTIONS' IN THE 1937 IRISH CONSTITUTION

In the making of the 1937 Irish Constitution, drafters' fears of class conflict motivated debates on socio-economic rights. The provisions ultimately adopted were far from an inevitable selection. Constitution-makers discussed property rights, land redistribution, and financial regulation as well as education, labour, and general living standards. The primary contributors in these particular debates were Taoiseach Éamon de Valera, James MacElligott, Secretary of the Department of Finance, and John Charles McQuaid, a priest of the Holy Ghost Order influenced by an austere, anti-Modernist French Catholicism. In general, their deliberations reflected a series of recurring tensions between de Valera, who advanced a set of limited socio-economic reforms, notably around land redistribution; clericalists who advocated for Catholic social interventions in family law while locating responsibility for welfare primarily with Church and family; and civil servants, often classic, laissez-faire advocates, who defended parliamentary sovereignty and minimising social expenditure.

The drafting process occurred over some three years. Throughout, government ministers generally deferred to de Valera in what they perceived to be his project.[85] In May 1934, de Valera convened a special Constitution Review Committee to review the 1922 Irish Free State Constitution. The Committee, led by John Hearne of the Department of External Affairs, also comprised of senior civil servants such as Philip O'Donoghue, Stephen Roche, and Michael McDunphy. It

[83] Ferriter, 2005, *The Transformation of Ireland*, p. 373.
[84] 'Building Trade Strike' in *Irish Times*, 14 May 1937.
[85] Ronan Fanning, 1988, 'Mr. de Valera drafts a constitution' in Farrell, Brian (ed.), *De Valera's Constitution and Ours*, Dublin: Gill and Macmillan, p. 38.

generally recommended continuity in government and administration. The Executive Council formally authorised the creation of a new constitution in June 1936. Thereafter, advocates for a Catholic social constitutionalism were plentiful. In September, de Valera requested and received 'Suggestions for a Catholic Constitution' from the Jesuit Order, specifically Patrick Bartley, John McErlean, Joseph Canavan, and Edward Coyne as well as Edward Cahill, who also provided 'Supplementary Suggestions'. De Valera corresponded frequently with his friend and advisor, the Holy Ghost Father John Charles McQuaid.[86] In October 1936, the Executive Council, the Fianna Fáil party executive as well as the civil service, notably Maurice Moynihan and J. J. MacElligott, received official drafts of the new constitution.

Towards the conclusion of the drafting process, MacElligott articulated a classic, laissez-faire critique of the draft constitution's socio-economic provisions, accepting their inclusion not as 'rights' but as 'principles' only. McQuaid broadly supported this limited form of recognition. It subsequently proved enduring. In the spring and summer of 1937, de Valera engaged in both parliamentary and wider public debates to advocate the new constitution. Fine Gael used the opportunity to question the powers of the Land Commission while the Labour party proposed several socio-economic rights provisions. Reminiscent of the Constituent Assembly in 1922, the government rejected these initiatives. Dáil Éireann enacted the Constitution of Ireland Bill (1937) on 15 June; the public narrowly approved the constitution by plebiscite on 1 July; and the 1937 Irish Constitution came into force on 29 December 1937 (Table 3.1). The specific drafting of the Irish Constitution's socio-economic provisions, the meaning of contributors' shifting nuances, and discourse over time, now merits closer attention.

From the outset, the bureaucracy's preference for a classic, laissez-faire constitutionalism, maintaining the inherited structures of government and administration, was readily apparent. When considering a list of fundamental articles to be retained from the 1922 Irish Free State Constitution, the 1934 Constitution Review Committee regarded the right to education (Article 10) as a matter for ordinary legislation rather

[86] The influence of various Jesuit or clericalist contributors on the wording of the constitution's socio-economic provisions is debated. Recent historical research suggests that McQuaid's role, particularly regarding the defence of private property and Church control of education, was pronounced, while Cahill's contributions were generally marginal. See Keogh and McCarthy, 2009, *The Making of the Irish Constitution*, p. 117. McQuaid became the Catholic Archbishop of Dublin in 1940, ruling as a Renaissance-era prelate over a 'dreary Eden' until 1972. See John Cooney, 2003, *John Charles McQuaid: Ruler of Catholic Ireland*. Dublin: O'Brien Press.

TABLE 3.1 Timeline of the 1937 constitution-making process

| The 1937 Constitution-making Process | |
|---|---|
| General Elections; Fianna Fáil governments formed | 1932/1933 |
| Civil Service Constitution Committee meets | 28 May – 3 July 1934 |
| Executive Council authorises de Valera to prepare draftKing Edward notified of intended bill | 5 June 1936 |
| Jesuit Order's 'Suggestions for a Catholic Constitution' | 24 September – October 1936 |
| First Draft given to Executive Council | 20 October 1936 |
| Edward Cahill's 'Supplementary Suggestions' | 13 November 1936 |
| John Charles McQuaid correspondence | November 1936 – June 1937 |
| First Official Draft Circulated to Executive Council/Civil Service | 16 March 1937 |
| Civil Service (Department of Finance) reaction-'Suggested Method of Dealing with Certain Directive Principles' | March – April 1937 |
| Dáil Debates– Labour party proposals | April 1937 |
| Dáil enacts Constitution Bill | 15 June 1937 |
| Plebiscite on 1937 Constitution | 1 July 1937 |
| General Election | |
| Constitution comes into force | 29 December 1937 |

than a 'fundamental' provision.[87] According to the Minister for Education, Thomas Derrig, the right to free education was too open to interpretation. It 'could be construed to put an obligation on the State not only to pay the teachers but also to build, equip and maintain schools, and provide free books and requisites for the schoolchildren'.[88] Derrig similarly questioned whether 'a small number of children . . . living on an island, or at a long distance from a National School, could successfully claim the right to be transported daily to a National School; or to have a School established for their own use'. The Committee's report subsequently excluded the right to education from its list of fundamental articles for retention in the new constitution, an absence foreshadowing the Department of Finance's later contributions.

[87] Keogh and McCarthy, 2009, *The Making of the Irish Constitution*, p. 70.

[88] Report of 1934 Constitution Committee, Appendix G: Extract from letter from the Department of Education (July 1934). *De Valera Papers*, UCDA P150/2365. Parenthetically, Derrig's reference to islanders indicates how the state typically provided symbolic recognition to the Irish language more readily than material supports to Gaeltachtaí, the predominantly Irish-speaking communities of the western seaboard.

De Valera's earliest drafts, composed between July 1934 and June 1936, similarly underline the continued salience of classic constitutionalism and its premise of a necessary coherence between law-making and the nation.[89] Initial versions of the preamble, for example, refer to 'the Irish people' and their dependence on 'Almighty God'. At this point, de Valera regarded as 'natural' the right to private property.[90] However, these drafts also make clear that from quite early in the drafting process the Taoiseach wanted Catholic social discourse to feature in the new constitution. Rejecting the review committee's recommendation, de Valera reintroduced the right to free elementary education. He also elaborated its centrality to citizenship, referring to both 'the cult of moral and civic virtue, as well as the development of the physical and intellectual faculties'.[91] Moreover, shortly after the government formally authorised the making of a new constitution, de Valera invited the Jesuit Order to submit a number of draft articles for consideration.

Specific proposals for a Catholic social constitutionalism now emerged. In common with international forms of social legal thought, the Jesuit committee advocated the creation of a property-owning, middle class as a form of social stability, thereby preserving both the Catholic family unit and the nation's agrarian social structure.[92] A Catholic Constitution, they suggested, would guarantee the right to private property while ensuring that the state could intervene so that 'neither the acquisition nor accumulation of private property, especially in land, takes place in such a way as to injure the common good'.[93] The committee underlined the point in an accompanying provision: 'It shall be the aim of the State to promote a wide distribution of private property, especially in land'. Similarly, Edward Cahill's 'Supplementary Suggestions', forwarded to de Valera a month later, advocated 'an ever

89 *De Valera Papers*, UCDA P150/2370.

90 Partial Drafts dated March/April 1936. *De Valera Papers*, UCDA P150/2371.

91 Partial Drafts dated March/April 1936. *De Valera Papers*, UCDA P150/2371. The classical republican emphasis on education for citizenship and 'civic virtue' received an echo in the Irish nationalist movement and featured in the Democratic Programme as well as the education provisions suggested by members of the 1922 drafting committee and, in the Dáil Constitutent Assembly, by the Labour party.

92 Bartley, McErlean, Canavan, Coyne, and Cahill canvassed a number of Catholic sources, including the 'social' encyclicals Rerum Novarum and Quadragesimo Anno, as well as the Canon Law and the Code of Social Principles from the Catholic School of Social Science in Malines, Belgium. *De Valera Papers*, UCDA P150/2393. De Valera also read Cahill's *Framework of a Christian State*. See Keogh and McCarthy, 2009, *The Making of the Irish Constitution*, p. 109; Kissane, 2011, *New Beginnings*, p. 58.

93 Jesuit Submission, *De Valera Papers*, UCDA P150/2393.

widening distribution of private property [so as] to enable and induce as many as possible to become owners'.[94] De Valera also returned to Alfred O'Rahilly's draft constitution produced in 1922.

In Irish Catholic social discourse, the natural family unit featured centrally in a properly ordered society. The Jesuit committee emphasised the family as 'indispensable to the continuous strength and well-being of the Nation'. In this context, their constitutional provisions included the 'natural right and duty' of parents to provide for their children's education. In practice, as outlined earlier, the natural rights of the family and of parents signified and envisaged clerical control of education. Cahill's 'Supplementary Suggestions' outlined a more detailed social reorganisation to accommodate family life. He included constitutional provisions guaranteeing a 'family wage' for agricultural and industrial employees, fair conditions of work and 'a due participation in the fruits of industry' as well as ensuring the use of natural resources for the common good and the introduction of a 'social credit' system.[95]

Incorporating these Catholic social proposals, de Valera clearly envisaged constitutionalising social policies premised on moderate state intervention to preserve private property, the family and, by extension, the nation. Drafts dating from the autumn of 1936 recognise private ownership ('one of the fundamental principles of ordered society') and the family ('the source of the preservation and increase of the race, the basis of moral education and social discipline and harmony, and the sure foundation of ordered society').[96] In effect, de Valera gave Fianna Fáil's recently enacted housing and Land Commission programmes constitutional form:

> Art. X 'The Family': It is the duty of the State to promote suitable housing schemes for the purposes of providing proper homes at reasonable rents for families in congested areas.
>
> Art. XXVIII 'Private Property': The ownership and cultivation of the land being one of the principal features of the national life, the exercise by the State of its right to the compulsory purchase of rural property for general utility purposes shall be subordinated to the principle that the

[94] *De Valera Papers*, UCDA P150/2393. [95] *De Valera Papers*, UCDA P150/2393.

[96] Draft B (14.10.36), VIII. Constitutional Guarantees, Art. XXVIII 'Private Property'. Draft A (14.10.36), VIII. Constitutional Guarantees, Art. 62. *De Valera Papers*, UCDA P150/2373. On the racial dynamics operative here, notably the exclusion of Travellers and migrants from 'Irishness', see Ronit Lentin, 1998, '"Irishness", the 1937 Constitution and Citizenship: a Gender and Ethnicity View', *Irish Journal of Sociology*, 8(1), pp. 5–24.

> agrarian structure of E[ire] . . . ought to be based on agricultural holdings capable of normal productivity and privately owned.[97]

In the first single draft of the new constitution, presented to the Executive Council on 20 October 1936, de Valera distinguished between 'Constitutional Guarantees' (Articles 32–38) and 'Economic Life' (Articles 39–43). Significantly, he maintained the justiciability of both.[98]

Education, however, proved a partial exception to the rule of Catholic social entrenchment, a potential source of church-state disagreement. Article 38.1 re-stated that '[a]ll citizens have the right to free elementary education'. Supplementary provisions, however, stated that the purpose of primary schooling was 'the formation of character, the cult of moral and civic virtue, as well as the development of the physical and intellectual faculties', again suggesting its centrality to citizenship and the state. Secular education was not envisaged: religion was to be compulsory and under the control of the particular Church to which the pupils concerned belonged. The important point, however, was that Church control was 'without prejudice to the supreme right of control reserved to the State educational authorities'. De Valera, it appears, considered retaining a civic right to education in the constitution, at least initially.

The 'ordered society' that de Valera envisaged advanced a rural, agrarian idyll of small farming households, opposed to urban industrialisation and to collective ownership.[99] 'The State', Article 34.5 declared, 'shall encourage early marriage and foster the production of large families by appropriate grants of remission of taxation in respect of children, by the promotion of saving and thrift schemes and by facilitating the provision of housing accommodation on reasonable terms'. The 'Economic Life' articles similarly reproduced the Catholic social vision of diffuse rural land ownership, promoting 'the maximum number of economic holdings privately owned' and further stipulating their

[97] Draft B (14.10.36), VIII. Constitutional Guarantees, Art. X 'The Family', Section 6 and Art. XXVIII 'Private Property'. *De Valera Papers*, UCDA P150/2373.

[98] The former section, as in earlier drafts, recognised the 'natural' right to private ownership as 'a basic principle of ordered human society' and the family as 'the basis of moral education and social discipline and harmony, and the sure foundation of ordered society'. *De Valera Papers*, UCDA P150/2373. Keogh and McCarthy also date a longer, more substantial draft to around the same time (late 1936). *De Valera Papers*, UCDA P150/2385. See Keogh and McCarthy, 2009, *The Making of the Irish Constitution*, p. 81.

[99] On 'ruritania', see Ernest Gellner, 1983, *Nations and Nationalism*. Ithaca: Cornell University Press.

productive use and 'husbandry' for 'the benefit of the community'.[100] The latter stipulation reflected decision-makers' fear of 'idleness' and corresponding desire to ensure a work ethic among land recipients.[101] De Valera also included more specifically vocationalist directives, declaring it to be 'the aim of social legislation to promote the association of employees with employers in the management and control of industry . . . and to facilitate the formation and function of professional guilds'.

The potentially redistributive implications of a Catholic social constitution attracted criticism. John Charles McQuaid, now entering into frequent correspondence with de Valera, articulated a more conservative, austere wording of the constitution's social and economic provisions, emphasising the right to private ownership as 'absolutely necessary'. After correspondence with McQuaid, de Valera changed the wording of the existing provision to emphasise personal responsibility. Thus, the State was 'to favour and where necessary supplement private economic initiative' while pledging itself 'to safeguard with special care the economic rights of the less favoured classes of Society'.[102] McQuaid further emphasised the scholastic distinction between mental and manual labour in a supplementary provision. The resulting 'just distribution of material resources', he claimed, aimed at 'aiding all the citizens to attain that higher level of prosperity and culture which is more consonant with human dignity'.[103]

The wording of the family rights provision and the gendering of the 1937 Irish Constitution owed much to McQuaid's interventions. Early drafts of the family rights provisions had been premised on the patriarchal assumption that man was, as Edward Cahill put it, 'ordained to be the breadwinner of the household'.[104] McQuaid now underlined the explicitly gendered nature of the constitution by introducing a further

[100] Article 40 provided that: 'The ownership, distribution and use of the land are under the special control of the State, and such control and supervision shall be exercised so as to promote the maximum number of economic holdings privately owned, the relief of congestion, and the establishment of working farmers on the land . . . It is hereby declared to the duty of landowners to work their holdings in accordance with proper methods of husbandry so as to maintain and develop the productivity of the soil to their advantage and for the benefit of the community'.

[101] See also Edward Cahill's provisions against idleness. *De Valera Papers*, UCDA P150/2393.

[102] *De Valera Papers*, UCDA P150/2387.

[103] 'The State, while acknowledging that work of body and mind is an honourable means of virtuous and creditable living, shall aim, by this just distribution of material resources, at aiding all the citizens to attain that higher level of prosperity and culture which is more consonant with human dignity'. McQuaid to de Valera, 16.01.37. *De Valera Papers*, UCDA P150/2395.

[104] *De Valera Papers*, UCDA P150/2393.

recognition that 'by her life within the home, woman gives to the State support with which the common good can be achieved'.[105] The constitution would continue to identify 'woman' with the private sphere, and further refer to the rights of the citizen and, by implication, the public sphere as 'his'. Similarly, these drafts' recognition of the family as 'the natural, primary and fundamental unit of society . . . possessing inalienable and imprescriptible rights, antecedent and superior to all positive laws', proved enduring.[106]

Meanwhile, de Valera's drafts ceased to refer to citizenship education – 'the culture of moral and civic virtue' – and indeed, for a brief period, ceased to refer to education as a 'right' altogether.[107] Church, not state, control over education was envisaged:

> In all schools and educational establishments for the instruction of young persons who have not reached the age of eighteen years, the teaching of religion is compulsory for all pupils. The direction and control of such teaching is the province of the particular Church or religious communion to which the pupils concerned belong, ~~without prejudice to the supreme right of control reserved to the State educational authorities~~'.[108]

McQuaid's preferred formulation was adopted. Hence, the state would respect the natural right and duty of the parents to provide, 'according to their means', for their children's education; state educational authorities should merely ensure that 'a certain minimum education, intellectual and moral, physical and social' was met.[109]

At this point, de Valera appears to have experienced some doubts about the existing social and economic rights provisions. A late draft constitution dated 15 March littered the article with annotations, brackets, question-marks, and crossings out.[110] The property provisions are circled, question-marked, and given the intriguing gloss: '*live his own life in his own way*'. For a brief instant, the 'natural' right to property becomes a '*temporal*' one only. Similarly, de Valera completely overturned the sense of Article 41.9: 'The State shall favour and where necessary ~~supplement private economic initiative~~ *control profit*'. Indicating a heretofore unexpected source of inspiration, the annotation

[105] *De Valera Papers*, UCDA P150/2387. [106] *De Valera Papers*, UCDA P150/2387.
[107] 11.01.1937. *De Valera Papers*, UCDA P150/2387.
[108] *De Valera Papers*, UCDA P150/2387.
[109] *De Valera Papers*, UCDA P150/2387 (2). 03.02.1937. *De Valera Papers*, UCDA P150/2387 (2).
[110] Draft Constitution dated 15.03.1937. *De Valera Papers*, UCDA P150/2401.

'Am[erican] Trust Laws' appears alongside a provision on the restraint of monopolies.[111] Together, these draft provisions suggest that de Valera considered, albeit briefly, a social constitutionalism based in Anglo-American positive law rather than Catholic natural law.

De Valera also questioned giving legal effect to the draft constitution's social and economic rights provisions. Annotations to the educational provisions – [*have right to*] and '*too great a responsibility?*' – suggest de Valera's unwillingness to impose constitutional obligations on the state. Similarly, Article 40 now replaced the word 'shall' with 'may' or 'endeavour to' in respect of several state duties to provide various forms of material welfare. The following day, the first official draft of the constitution was circulated to the Executive Council and to the secretaries of the various government departments.[112] The printed text, however, did not reveal de Valera's scribbled misgivings on either the Catholic social nature of the constitution or the justiciability of socio-economic rights.

The bureaucracy's preference for a laissez-faire constitutionalism stood in sharp contrast to these Catholic social proposals. A sole exception to the rule of ministerial and administrative deference to de Valera, J. J. MacElligott of the Department of Finance produced a detailed, thirty-nine-page commentary on the constitution. Similar to George O'Brien's critique of the Irish Free State Constitution in 1922, MacElligott derided the proposed socio-economic rights provisions at considerable length, claiming they were 'not of a kind usually enshrined in a Constitution' and 'mostly unnecessary'.[113] Fianna Fáil's recent welfare measures, which had introduced state pensions for the old, the blind, army veterans, widows, and orphans, had already 'given effect to the ideals underlying the provisions . . . and there was nothing to stop further legislative progress in the same direction'. Other provisions were vague, particularly those demanding the imbuing of public institutions with 'social justice', and, in the case of land redistribution, contrary to government policy: '[W]e do not settle "as many families as

[111] Building on Progressive Era legislation against monopolies, the recent Robinson–Patman Act (1936) introduced fixed minimum pricing to protect small businesses from chain stores. Such legislation was in keeping with the social legal thought advanced by Clement France in the making of the 1922 Irish Free State Constitution as well as by Franklin Roosevelt in his Second Bill of Rights. See Sunstein, 2004, *The Second Bill of Rights*.

[112] Keogh and McCarthy, 2009, *The Making of the Irish Constitution*, p. 123.

[113] *Department of Taoiseach Papers*, NAI S9715B. See also Keogh and McCarthy, 2007, *The Making of the Irish Constitution 1937*, p. 126.

practicable" on the land. "Five acres and a cow" would suffice if that were the policy. We create economic holdings of twenty-five acres.[114] MacElligott recommended minimising compulsory demands on public expenditure and, to that end, using the word 'may' and not 'shall' when formulating the socio-economic provisions.

The right to education provision exercised similar concerns. Echoing the 1934 Review Committee's concerns, Seán T. O'Kelly, Minister of the Department of Local Government and Health, feared that the wording might demand 'the full cost of erection of schools'.[115] There was 'some doubt', MacElligott agreed, as to whether the right to education committed the state 'to the provision of school books and other school requisites free to pupils of public primary schools . . . perhaps an amendment is necessary'.[116] Thomas Derrig, Minister for Education, queried whether the constitution might affect the running of industrial schools insofar as poverty, now apparently rendered unconstitutional, was a formal reason for a child's committal under existing legislation.[117] The point was 'a small one', he conceded, but legal advisers might consider it further. Derrig also wrote to de Valera to argue that the concept of 'state schools' be retained in the constitution, claiming that the Catholic hierarchy's attitude was 'narrower than the official Catholic position as defined in the 1929 Encyclical [*Divini Illius Magistri*]'.[118] Indicative of the pervasive culture amongst state office-holders then, even those ministers who questioned the bishops felt compelled to do so using papal encyclicals.

Contributors' debates on socio-economic rights reflected fears of class conflict and a need to transform both potential and actual social unrest into what contemporary Catholic theorists described as 'ordered tranquillity'.[119] McQuaid cautioned de Valera that the most potent form of social agitation was the unsettled strike: 'You will have noted that last year we had the Train strike and this year we are to be given a

[114] Comment on Article 41.7.2. *NAI Department of Taoiseach Papers*, S9715B.
[115] 22.03.1937. *NAI Department of Taoiseach Papers*, S9715B.
[116] *Department of Taoiseach Papers*, NAI S9715B.
[117] Between 1926 and 1951, the average number of people confined in either industrial schools, Magdalene laundries, mother-and-baby homes, or mental institutions was 31,500, or 1 per cent of the population. A similar proportion, one out of every hundred children, was also incarcerated. See Eoin O'Sullivan and Ian O'Donnell, 2012, *Coercive Confinement in Ireland: Patients, prisoners and penitents*. Manchester: Manchester University Press.
[118] Letter to de Valera from Tomás Derrig, 12.04.1937, *NAI Department of Taoiseach Papers*, S 9748. See also Keogh and McCarthy, 2009, *The Making of the Irish Constitution 1937*, p. 137.
[119] *De Valera Papers*, UCDA P150/2377.

huge Building strike. We are thus being kept in a state of social unrest with intervals of quiet'. If the state could manage such strikes through an 'Arbitration Board', he suggested, a 'great deal of the venom of Communism could be neutralised'.[120] 'Distributive justice', he advised, 'is especially the virtue looked for in rulers'.[121] Similarly, Cahill feared 'the want of due reverence for law and the suspicious attitude towards the legitimate civil authority which unfortunately are too prevalent amongst our people'. Constitutionalising socio-economic provisions such as land redistribution and credit reform was, as he put it, necessary 'to keep in check the activities of agitators who would sow disunion or discontent with the object of fermenting a destructive and unchristian class war'.[122]

Clericalists' desire for social order was equalled only by civil servants'. However, while agreeing on the necessity of social cohesion, MacElligott disagreed that constitutionalising socio-economic rights would secure this aim and might instead provide 'a breeding ground for discontent' and so prove 'highly dangerous'.[123] Notwithstanding the present capacities of the Land Commission, a constitutional right to land or housing might backfire 'when the present amount of land available for distribution is exhausted' and agitators demand the 'compulsory subdivision of the holdings already distributed'. Similarly, constitutional provisions for bank regulation or 'social credit' would hand agitators 'a weapon of attack on the Banks, the Agricultural Credit Corporation, the Industrial Credit Company, or against any large joint-stock concern'. On this view, socio-economic provisions constituted 'an unnecessarily powerful instrument of agitation'. In the wrong hands, MacElligott claimed, constitutional rights could be 'worked up to lead people astray'.

Following MacElligott's intervention, the civil servants circulated a 'Suggested Method of Dealing with Certain Directive Principles' which introduced the principle of judicial non-cognisance to the constitution.[124] Only now were provisions for social credit, land redistribution, and other rights to welfare reformulated as non-binding

[120] Correspondence from McQuaid to de Valera, 16 February; 8 March 1937. *De Valera Papers*, UCDA P150/2395.
[121] *De Valera Papers*, UCDA P150/2411. [122] *De Valera Papers*, UCDA P150/2393.
[123] *NAI Department of Taoiseach Papers*, S9715B.
[124] 'Suggested Method of Dealing with Certain Directive Principles'. Department of Finance to de Valera, 02.04.1937. *De Valera Papers*, UCDA P150/2416.

'directive principles' in Article 45. The Department of Finance segregated the constitution's 'personal rights' provisions, which entailed a legal remedy in the courts, from its 'guiding principles', which did not. The term 'personal rights' was not to be used in the latter instance so as 'to prevent confusion, as a "right" implies legal redress'. McQuaid agreed. 'Fundamental Guarantees and Principles of Social Policy', he suggested, would omit 'the noxious word "rights" which the lawyers say bespeaks legal redress'.[125] When the Department sketched out a probable result of this segregation, every socio-economic provision, including the property and education provisions, was listed as a guiding 'principle'.[126]

The draft constitution nevertheless entrenched socio-economic rights articles concerning property and education. Here too, McQuaid's interventions were significant. He insisted that the 1937 Constitution recognise the natural right of private property as 'absolutely necessary', lamenting the trend in England and France 'to admit the right of private property, but by methods of cooperative organisation and planned economy to deny the private control of property, which is to abolish the right of private property with increasing effectiveness'.[127] Arthur Matheson, the parliamentary draftsman, redrafted the property provisions accordingly (Box 3.1).[128] De Valera also adopted McQuaid's preferred formulations in relation to the family and to education in which church not state control was envisaged.[129]

The 1937 Constitution's socio-economic provisions thus safeguarded private property rights as well as the Irish Land Commission's limited work of redistribution. Moreover, the Department of Finance achieved its preference for minimal state spending while the Catholic Church had its control over the state's welfare institutions acknowledged as legitimate. Up to this point, the Constitution had been drafted in relative secrecy. Through the spring and summer of 1937, however, de Valera had to justify Bunreacht na hÉireann to a wider public in order to secure its popular acceptance. The Constitution's approval by referendum would depend on the upcoming election campaign as well as access to and control of the mass media. Earlier decisions would now

125 *De Valera Papers*, UCDA P150/2395; also P150/2407.
126 Civil Service Document, *De Valera Papers*, UCDA P150/2416.
127 See McQuaid on Private Property. *De Valera Papers*, UCDA P150/2411.
128 Matheson to O'Donoghue, 16.04.1937. *De Valera Papers*, UCDA P150/2411.
129 *De Valera Papers*. UCDA P150/2387.

**Box 3.1 Draft Property Provisions, May, 1937**

**Property Rights**

1.1 The State acknowledges that man, in virtue of his rational being, has the natural right, antecedent to positive law, to the private ownership of external goods.

1.2 The State recognises that the exercise of this natural right is not only allowable, but is, for social needs (*reasons*), absolutely necessary, and therefore guarantees to pass no law attempting to abolish the right of private ownership or the general right to transfer, bequeath, and inherit property.

2.1. The State recognises however that the exercise of the rights mentioned in the foregoing provisions of this Article ought, in civilised society, to be regulated by the principles of social justice.

2.2. The State, accordingly, may as occasion requires delimit by law the exercise of the said rights with a view to reconciling their exercise with the exigencies of the common good.

come under scrutiny in parliamentary debates and provoke small but determined civil society mobilisations.

## THE SOCIO-ECONOMIC PROVISIONS' RECEPTION IN PARLIAMENT AND CIVIL SOCIETY

> Are we to understand that their import is purely negative, that they are to bar the way against Communism but otherwise to leave things as they are?
>
> – Alfred O'Rahilly on the Directive Principles[130]

> [T]hese clauses are based on a fascist and slave conception of woman as being a non-adult person who is very weak and whose place is in the home. Ireland's fight for freedom would not have been so successful if Irish women had obeyed these clauses.
>
> – Betty Archdale, Six Point Group to de Valera[131]

130 Alfred O'Rahilly, 1937, *Thoughts on the Constitution*. Dublin: Browne and Nolan, p. 69.
131 Letter to de Valera, 14.06.1937. *Department of Taoiseach Papers*, NAI S9880.

During the parliamentary debates, Fine Gael and Labour concentrated their criticism of the draft constitution on the new office of president. Both parties remained largely silent on the constitution's Catholic social rights provisions, not wishing to risk a pre-election dispute with the Catholic hierarchy.[132] Fine Gael's John Costello worried that the Directive Principles could be 'moulded to the idea and theories of the socialists and even of the Communists'.[133] He sought, unsuccessfully, to challenge the powers of the Irish Land Commission, claiming that de Valera wanted 'to make civil servants judges', to set up a 'bureaucracy *in excelsis*' and, in so doing, to confer dictatorial powers on the president.[134] Seán MacEntee, Minister for Finance, and Philip O'Donoghue informed de Valera that Costello's amendment would encourage 'technical objections' to the Land Commission's powers to resume and acquire holdings, a welcome development for Costello's fellow lawyers but not for wider society.[135] The constitution remained unchanged.

The Labour party, as during the making of the 1922 Irish Free State Constitution, found itself trusting to the parliamentary power of suggestion. William Norton drew on Alfred O'Rahilly's draft constitution to advocate a series of Catholic social provisions:

> Article 40. 126. At the end of section 6 to add the following: – 'IV. In the interest of the community restrictions may be imposed by law on the formation and conduct of profit-making enterprises or associations'. (*NO . . . Where does this lead?*)
>
> Article 42. 130. In section 4 after the word 'education', line 1, to insert the words 'including school books, requisites and a free meal during school hours for each child attending school'. (*NO*)
>
> Article 45. 139. At the end of the Article to add a new section as follows: – 'The State shall endeavour to ensure that every section of the community engaged in wealth producing operations will have an influence in directing the policy and tendency of the enterprise'. (*NO – should be admitted to a knowledge of the direction of the enterprise*).[136]

132 Dermot Keogh, 1988, 'The Constitutional Revolution' in Litton, F (ed.), *The Constitution of Ireland 1937–1987*, Dublin: Institute of Public Administration, p. 63.

133 *Irish Independent*, 6 May 1937. See also Kissane, 2011, *New Beginnings*, p. 82.

134 John Costello, *Dáil Debates*, Vol. 67, 305–6, 12.05.1937.

135 Letters from Seán MacEntee, Philip O'Donoghue, and Revenue Commission to de Valera, 08.06.37, *De Valera Papers*, UCDA P150/ 2441.

136 '*Bunreacht na hÉireann (Dreacht)*'. *De Valera Papers*, UCDA P150/2441.

De Valera's annotations, outlined here, indicate his continued adherence to a restricted form of Catholic social constitutionalism, one that preserved the priorities of private ownership, the Catholic Church, and the Department of Finance.

Norton, again echoing debates in 1922, proposed an amendment to the property rights provision so as to capture for 'the community' the unearned increment in rising land values: 'Article 43. 131. "Laws shall be enacted to provide that increase in the value of land arising though community effort without expenditure by the owner of labour or capital shall accrue to the community"'.[137] McQuaid dismissed the proposal:

> No. 110/131: 'Community effort'. This is Karl Marx terminology. The doctrine on which the proposal is based seems to be Henry George's. That all the interest should accrue to the community seems scarcely just, for it takes no account of the foresight and initiative of the owner. That such revenues should be very heavily taxed seems quite just. It must be said that the amendment does not exclude compensation.[138]

In fact, Norton had looked once more to Alfred O'Rahilly, not Karl Marx or Henry George, for the wording of his proposed amendment.[139] That McQuaid dismissed it again suggests that his version of Catholic social constitutionalism was more conservative, particularly where private property was at stake.

Article 45, outlining the 'Directive Principles of Social Policy', continued to restrict the judiciary's capacity to provide a legal remedy in the event of their breach. The parliamentary debates, however, gave McQuaid and de Valera an opportunity to expunge their residual vocabulary of class politics. Heretofore, both men tended to write freely of 'the different classes and sections of the people', emphasising 'the people' and their organic unity in 'the body politics', 'the nation', or 'the community as a whole'.[140] Now, references to 'class' suggesting contending material interests were expunged. '[A]fter "workers"', McQuaid wrote of one article, 'I should insert, 'men and women', to make it complete and to stress the aspect of human persons'. When Labour's

137 '*Bunreacht na hÉireann (Dreacht)*'. *De Valera Papers*, UCDA P150/2441.

138 McQuaid on Private Property. *De Valera Papers*, UCDA P150/2411.

139 O'Rahilly's Draft C, Economic Life: Article 64 (3). *De Valera Papers*, UCDA P4/333.

140 *De Valera Papers*, UCDA P150/2393. See also McQuaid to de Valera, 16.01.37. *De Valera Papers*, UCDA P150/2395.

William Norton suggested that the State recognise the rights of its 'citizens' to 'work' de Valera reworded the proposed amendment to designate the right of 'men and women' to 'an adequate means of livelihood' – *IN PRINCIPLE*'.[141] The State was to pledge itself to safeguard the socio-economic rights of the community's 'poorer sections' and no longer those of its 'less favoured classes'.

In place of a class discourse then, McQuaid and de Valera substituted a discourse of poverty, charity, and state paternalism. A later draft involved an enduring change: 'The State pledges itself to safeguard with especial care the economic ~~rights~~ (*interests*) of the (poorer) *weaker* sections of the community . . . '.[142] This charitable approach, minimising state obligations on the basis of rights or justice, influenced minor changes of wording:

> *Draft D*: 46.2. iii. That there ~~shall~~ *may* be established on the land in economic security as many families as in the circumstances shall *be* ~~be just and~~ practicable.
>
> Draft E: 46.2.i. That the citizens ~~who are willing~~ may through their occupations find the means ~~of adequately meeting their own and~~ *of making reasonable provision for* their domestic needs.

To resolve any lingering doubts, de Valera made clear his intention that the constitution's rights provisions would primarily be a set of 'headlines to the legislature' and that it was up to the legislature to determine how to secure these ideals. Similarly, the Directive Principles would merely act as a 'constant reminder to the legislature of the direction in which it should work'.[143] On 14 June 1937, Dáil Éireann approved the amended draft Bunreacht na hÉireann by a vote of 62 votes to 48. Popular endorsement, however, was far from a foregone conclusion. Outside parliament, Fine Gael's W. T. Cosgrave suggested the Bunreacht had been 'received generally with indifference'.[144] Those involved in the left-wing agitations and upheavals of the 1930s, however, roundly criticised the draft constitution.

141 De Valera subsequently proposed an amendment to Article 45.2.1 so that after the word 'citizens' would be inserted 'all of whom, men and women equally, have the right to an adequate means of livelihood'. '*Bunreacht na hÉireann (Dreacht)*'. *De Valera Papers*, UCDA P150/2441.

142 Article 45.4.1. *De Valera Papers*, UCDA P150/2441.

143 *See Dáil Debates*, Vol. 67, Col. 1747, 1784–6; Vol. 68. Col. 216–7. 05.1937; *Dáil Debates*, Vol. 67, Col. 69, 05.1937.

144 *De Valera Papers*, UCDA P150/2441.

## Box 3.2 DIRECTIVE PRINCIPLES OF SOCIAL POLICY

**Article 45**

The principles of social policy set forth in this article are intended for the general guidance of the Oireachtas. The application of those principles in the making of laws shall be the care of the Oireachtas exclusively, and shall not be cognisable by any court under any of the provisions of this constitution.

1 The State shall strive to promote the welfare of the whole people by securing and protecting as effectively as it may a social order in which justice and charity shall inform all the institutions of the national life.

2 The State shall, in particular, direct its policy towards securing:-

i That the citizens (all of whom, men and women equally, have the right to an adequate means of livelihood) may through their occupations find the means of making reasonable provision for their domestic needs.

ii That the ownership and control of the material resources of the community may be so distributed amongst private individuals and the various classes as best to subserve the common good.

iii That, especially, the operation of free competition shall not be allowed so to develop as to result in the concentration of the ownership or control of essential commodities in a few individuals to the common detriment.

iv That in what pertains to the control of credit the constant and predominant aim shall be the welfare of the people as a whole.

v That there may be established on the land in economic security as many families as in the circumstances shall be practicable.

3 1° The State shall favour and, where necessary, supplement private initiative in industry and commerce.

2° The State shall endeavour to secure that private enterprise shall be so conducted as to ensure reasonable efficiency in the production and distribution of goods and as to protect the public against unjust exploitation.

4 1° The State pledges itself to safeguard with especial care the economic interests of the weaker sections of the community, and, where

necessary, to contribute to the support of the infirm, the widow, the orphan, and the aged.
2° The State shall endeavour to ensure that the strength and health of workers, men and women, and the tender age of children shall not be abused and that citizens shall not be forced by economic necessity to enter avocations unsuited to their sex, age or strength.

Feminists claimed that a number of articles threatened their rights as citizens and as workers, notably Article 41.2 which equated womanhood with motherhood and specified a woman's 'life within the home'.[145] The Women Graduates' Association, the Joint Committee of Women's Societies and Social Workers, together with the Irish Women Workers' Union mobilised a two-month campaign seeking the provisions' amendment or deletion.[146] Hannah Sheehy Skeffington objected to the replacement of the 1916 'model of equal citizenship' by a 'fascist model'.[147] Similarly, Louie Bennett of the IWWU wrote to de Valera to claim that the gendered provisions 'opens the door to Fascist legislation'.[148] De Valera's subsequent meeting with protestors resulted in a partial concession: the deletion of the phrase 'inadequate strength' in Article 45.4 (which claimed to protect women and children from unsuitable 'avocations' on such grounds).[149] The Constitution, however, retained Article 41.2 and continued to distinguish between men and women, identifying the public sphere with the former, the private sphere with the latter.

On the Republican Left, the *Irish Democrat* carried a critique of the draft constitution, summarising its import under the title 'No Republic, No King – But Capital!' Peadar O'Donnell and Frank Ryan of the Republican Congress condemned the constitution's declaring

145 Feminists had recently opposed legislation that restricted women's right to work and to earn equal pay. Supported by Fianna Fáil and Labour, the new laws aimed at reducing unemployment among men and at preventing non-unionised women being used as cheap labour. Mary McAuliffe, 2011, 'The Irish Woman Worker and the Conditions of Employment Act, 1936: Responses from the Irish Free State Women Senators', *Saothar*, Vol. 36, pp. 37–46.

146 See the IWWU's letter to de Valera in *Irish Times*, 13 May 1937. Yvonne Scannell, 1988, 'Role of Women' in Farrell, B., *De Valera's Constitution and Ours*, p. 126. Maria Luddy, 2005, 'A "Sinister and Retrogressive" Proposal: Irish women's opposition to the 1937 draft constitution' in *Transactions of the Royal Historical Society*, 15, pp. 175–95.

147 *Irish Independent*, 07.05.1937.

148 Karen Offen, 2000, *European Feminisms 1700–1950*. Stanford: Stanford University Press, p. 319.

149 UCDA P150/2387; see also Gerard Hogan, 'De Valera, the Constitution and the Historians' in *Irish Jurist*, 2005, 40 (1), pp. 293–320, pp. 310–6.

capitalism 'as something ordained by Providence forever, amen! Private property is declared sacred – a 'natural right' overriding all law. What does this mean if not that the despoiled and dispossessed masses, without property . . . are forever to remain despoiled and dispossessed . . . Poverty is sacred; having no property is sacred; wage slavery is sacred; the Poor Law is sacred'.[150] The Republican Congress also opposed the Catholic Church's new position as a 'State or semi-State church', violating republican principles and offending Protestant opinion throughout the island of Ireland. For O'Donnell, 'the Roman Catholic Bishops of the South' now occupied a privileged position as 'the watchdogs of the private property classes'.[151] Finally, the red republicans critiqued the constitution's 'stone-age conception of womanhood', supporting Sheehy Skeffington's claim that the steady erosion of the legal and practical status of women in the Irish Free State was now being given constitutional sanction, with 'the implication that God sanctioned them too'.[152]

Advocates of Catholic social constitutionalism also expressed disappointment. Alfred O'Rahilly thought the draft constitution merely mopped up the 'effete symbols of British imperialism' without sufficiently advancing new vocational institutions. While the constitution embodied 'Catholic social principles', its provisions contained far too much 'may' and not nearly enough 'shall': ' . . . if you seriously believe in this ideal, why not proclaim it in stentorian tones that will be heard by our bureaucrats? They will not be blown out of their nests by such feeble bleating'.[153] Similarly, B. B. Waters, a letter-writer to the *Irish Times*, observed that 'Article 45 does not contain a single mandatory clause to empower the State to make the economic reconstruction necessary to give effect to the social principles contained therein'. This was so even though 'the Holy Father is not afraid of mandatory clauses'. The natural rights of the family, Waters concluded, remained 'exposed to the alien jurisprudence imposed upon us by England' and the priority it accorded to the right of private property. 'On this principle', he warned, 'took place the evictions of last century'.[154]

De Valera's national radio broadcasts in support of the new constitution appealed to Catholic theodicy and to Irish nationalism. He

150 *Irish Democrat*. 8.05.37.
151 *Irish Democrat*, 22.5.37; see also Murray, 2000, *Oracles of God*, p. 329.
152 Irish Democrat. 8.05.37. See also Lawrence White, 2005, 'Peadar O'Donnell, 'Real Republicanism' and the Bell' in *Culture in the Republic*, Dublin: Ireland Institute, pp. 80–99, pp. 84–6.
153 Alfred O'Rahilly, 1937, *Thoughts on the Constitution*, p. 69.
154 B. B. Waters, 'Letter to the Editor' in *Irish Times*, 22 May 1937.

developed classic constitutional themes, assuming a fundamental coherence between law-making and the essentialist race or nation. 'There is a stage in the life of every community', he claimed, 'in which its customs as well as its philosophy of life naturally pass into its laws'.[155] Bunreacht na hÉireann was of 'the people', 'a code of their own making cast in the mould of their own history'.[156] It was a 'Christian constitution', containing more than mere 'legal machinery' but also 'a statement of some at least of the God-given rights of the individual both as a human being and as a member of society'.[157] Socialist and fascist governments in Europe had made a 'monstrous idol of the State'. In contrast, the new constitution of Ireland recognised 'the simple but fundamental fact that man is created for a supernatural end'. The 'whole philosophy of the Irish people', de Valera clarified in a later newspaper interview, was opposed to Communism: 'Tyranny, squalor and misery are the hotbed on which Communism grows and by removing these causes you prevent Communism from taking root and growing. That is what we are doing here'.[158]

Notwithstanding this rhetoric of Olympian detachment, de Valera's decision to hold the plebiscite for the constitution and the general election on the same day was a calculated one. Fianna Fáil had raised radical expectations in opposition but by 1937, after some five years in office, the Land Commission's rate of land redistribution was stalling, unemployment remained high, and the status quo ante of fiscal orthodoxy loomed large.[159] Instead of promised self-sufficiency, large sections of the population were newly dependent on clientelist relations with Fianna Fáil *cumainn* and parliamentary deputies to secure state supports for business or welfare.[160] The persistence of small but vocal republican, communist, and feminist groups as well as recent strikes by transport and construction workers further attested to anger at living standards and working conditions. The Bunreacht provided the Fianna Fáil party with an extra plank in its electoral platform. Albeit more significant than a 'flag-waving stunt', the Constitution reminded voters that their grievances were primarily national and, in the context of

[155] 'Broadcast, 15.06.1937', *De Valera Papers*, UCDA P150/2444.
[156] *De Valera Papers*, UCDA P150/2441. De Valera criticised the 1922 Irish Free State Constitution as fettered to the Anglo-Irish Treaty, failing to protect natural rights and divorced from 'the convictions, the beliefs and the spiritual character' of the Irish people. 'Broadcast, 30.04.1937', *De Valera Papers*, UCDA P150/2431.
[157] 'Broadcast, 15.06.1937', *De Valera Papers*, UCDA P150/2444.
[158] De Valera Papers, UCDA P150/2440.
[159] O'Connor, 2011, *A Labour history of Ireland*, p. 144. Lee, 1989, *Ireland: 1912–85*, p. 186.
[160] Dunphy, 1995, *The Making of Fianna Fáil Power in Ireland: 1923–1948*, p. 252.

the ongoing Anglo-Irish Economic War, owed primarily to perfidious Albion.[161]

Censorship and intra-nationalist divisions appear to have defined the subsequent plebiscite. In the preceding months, the media divided according to civil war party loyalties. The *Irish Press* and *Irish News* lauded the draft constitution; the *Irish Independent*, *Irish Times*, and *Telegraph* condemned it. The newspapers of left-wing and republican groups remained subject to censorship while feminist protests were also subject to a mainstream media blackout.[162] Ultimately, of the total electorate of some 1.8 million, 1.4 million people (or 76 per cent) voted. Some 134,157 votes were spoiled. The draft constitution was approved by a margin of 685,105 votes to 526,945.[163] Support and opposition closely reflected party loyalties, with both Fine Gael and Labour opposed. Only five constituencies rejected the Constitution and in all five Fianna Fáil were in the minority.[164] The endorsement helped de Valera achieve a 'new beginning' of a remarkably conservative kind, repudiating the Treaty settlement unilaterally and introducing new values, including popular sovereignty, natural law, and Catholic social concepts, while retaining the pre-existing 'state tradition' of heavily centralised executive authority within electoral-democratic institutions.[165]

Whether the 1937 Irish Constitution's social and economic provisions motivated popular decision-making is difficult to estimate. Contemporary commentators suggest that Catholic theodicy as a mass phenomenon, reinforced by censorship, left little space in the public sphere for mobilising social-material as opposed to national-spiritual concerns. Instead, to vote for the constitution was to endorse what the *Irish Press* described as 'hallowed traditions': the institution of the family, the indissolubility of marriage and, naturally, the right of private ownership.[166] 'The rural population of Ireland', Cahill later observed, 'are wonderfully responsive to religious motives and the religious appeal'.[167] Or as novelist Kate O'Brien wrote, 'Ireland, newly

[161] *De Valera Papers*, UCDA P150/2433. See the opinion of Professor Robert W. Binkley, Western Reserve University, May, 1937, *The Cleveland Ohio News*. See also Lee, 1989, *Ireland: 1912–85*, p. 202.

[162] Offen, 2000, *European Feminisms 1700–1950*, p. 319.

[163] 'Referendum Results: 1937–2009'. Department of the Environment, Community and Local Government. Available at: www.environ.ie/en/LocalGovernment/Voting/Referenda/PublicationsDocuments/FileDownLoad,1894,en.pdf.

[164] Keogh and McCarthy, 2009, *The Making of the 1937 Irish Constitution*, p. 210.

[165] Bill Kissane, 2011, *New Beginnings*, pp. 140–3.

[166] *Irish Press*, 16.06.37.

[167] *De Valera Papers*, UCDA P150/2393.

patrolled by the Church, would be unlikely to vote against the Holy Trinity'.[168] In the coming years, anti-systemic politics would continue to generate cracks and fissures in this Catholic social consensus. Fianna Fáil's appeal lessened significantly, particularly among small farmers in the west of Ireland. Nevertheless, the trajectory of groups moving from social protest into electoral politics was now firmly established. Clann na Talmhan (Irish: 'family of the land'), a new agrarian party promising land reclamation, progressive taxation, and social democratic reforms, emerged shortly after.[169]

## THE 1937 IRISH CONSTITUTION IN THE WORLD-SYSTEM

Bunreacht na hÉireann was created in a period of international upheaval, liberal democratic collapse, and intense ideological contestation. Responding to the Great Depression and to the existence of the Soviet Union but further conditioned by the local balance of anti-systemic relations, various nationalist 'middle ways' between laissez-faire capitalism and state socialism emerged. Associated forms of social constitutionalism could thus be progressive or authoritarian in either market or family law.[170] In terms of the latter, social jurists in both core and peripheral regions advocated decriminalising non-marital sex, permitting divorce by mutual consent, legalising the sale of contraceptives, destigmatising illegitimacy, and legalising abortion. Traditionalist opponents, emphasising the centrality of the family to the strength of the nation, extended beyond the Catholic Church to include conservative Protestant sects in the North Atlantic, and the Greek Orthodox Church in Europe, as well as advocates of Confucian or Shinto 'family values' in East Asia, or the conservative 'ulema' in the Middle East. The entrenchment of Catholic norms in the 1937 Irish Constitution merits consideration in this wider context.[171]

The most detailed elaboration of social and economic rights occurred 'outside' the historical capitalist world-system. In Russia, during a period of pronounced state terror directed against workers, peasants, and members of the Bolshevik party, the Constitution of the USSR (1936) or 'Stalin's Constitution' provided for a centralised planned

168 Cited in Ferriter, 2005, *The Transformation of Ireland*, p. 370.
169 Dooley, 2004, *The Land for the People*, p. 207.
170 Kennedy, 2006, 'Three Globalisations of Law and Legal Thought', pp. 46–56.
171 See Hogan, 2005, 'De Valera, the Constitution and the Historians'.

economy and further consolidated authority in the Communist Party (Article 126) and the Soviet bureaucracy. A section on the 'Basic Rights and Duties of Citizens' outlined a series of civil-political and socio-economic rights, including the right to work (Article 118); the right to rest (Article 119); the right to material security (Article 120); the right to education (Article 121); equal rights without distinction according to gender (Article 122) or nationality or race (Article 123); separation of church and state (Article 124) as well as freedom of speech, press, assembly, and street demonstrations (Article 125).[172] In reality, Stalin's Constitution was both paper tiger and propaganda exercise, retaining the old Tsarist heritage of centralised authority in the Communist Party while attempting to gain international recognition for the USSR as a non-aggressor.

Within the capitalist-world-system, the most authoritarian usage of social legal thought occurred in Germany and Italy where fascist parties introduced a highly coercive system of corporate societal management but protected free investment, free accumulation, free exchange of contract, and free selection of markets.[173] In Italy, Mussolini's Carta del Lavoro (1927) adopted the rhetoric of corporate constitutionalism for a 'harmoniously unitary state' while, in practice, prohibiting independent trade unions and ensuring industrialists retained a veto over bargaining. In Germany, the Nazi Law for the Organisation of Labour (1934) introduced a highly authoritarian corporatist arrangement in which trade unions were proscribed, obedience to a factory leader stipulated, and judicial powers granted to sanction professional misdemeanours. In both countries, material rights or 'rights of social ownership' provided a pretext for the curtailment of the labour movement and for private capitalist interests to secure access to the state and its resources.[174]

In core regions where liberal democracy still held sway, social recalibrations of the classic liberal market framework occurred, primarily in response to the flare-up of trade unionism, violent strikes, mass demonstrations, and 'red' agitation that swept the American and European continents in the 1930s.[175] In the UK, a Conservative-dominated

[172] Oakeshott, 1950, *The Social and Political Doctrines of Contemporary Europe*, pp. 156–9; see also Leon Trotsky, 1937, *The Revolution Betrayed*, New York: Doubleday & Doren Company, pp. 37–8.

[173] Thornhill, 2013, *A Sociology of Constitutions*, p. 323.

[174] Thornhill, 2013, *A Sociology of Constitutions*, pp. 314–16, 326; Neumann, 1966, *Behemoth*, pp. 41–5.

[175] Murray Bookchin, 2015, *The Next Revolution*. London: Verso, pp. 152–3.

'National Government' pursued limited policies of tariffs and house building.[176] In France, the Matignon Agreements provided for collective bargaining and increased unionisation. Increased state intervention occurred in the emergent hegemon. In the US, corporatism, in the form of labour/management councils in industry with power to make legally binding regulations, formed the centrepiece of the Democrats' 'New Deal' programme. Franklin Roosevelt later sought to entrench economic and social rights in the US Constitution but his 'Second Bill of Rights' fell afoul of Dixiecrat opposition to welfare state expansion.[177]

Developments in the English-speaking cores influenced the Irish constitution-makers' consideration of socio-economic rights. De Valera was prepared to countenance pragmatic state intervention such as tariffs or house-building programmes to a much greater degree than either laissez-faire civil servants or Ruritanian clericalists. Similarly, he adhered to the Westminster model of parliamentary sovereignty by leaving social interventions to ordinary legislation. There were important differences. In its lack of an industrial bourgeoisie, the Irish Free State resembled those peripheral regions where the 'spirit of enterprise' was instead a characteristic of states governed by national-popular *caudillos*.[178] Peron's Argentina, Vargas' Brazil, and Cardenas' Mexico adopted import substitution industrialisation, land redistribution, and welfare reforms at a similar time to de Valera's Ireland. Culturally, transformation was justified similarly in terms of a return to more traditional forms of social organisation.[179] The Latin American comparison, however, is somewhat superficial in material terms. Located within the Atlantic economy and inherited representative democratic institutions, Irish welfare state expansion and expenditure, though not as generous as the UK, was at about average European levels in this period.[180]

Comparisons with Europe's semi-peripheries are perhaps more instructive. The Irish Free State's peripheral-agrarian class structure resembled contemporary smaller Eastern European countries.[181]

176 Kennedy, 2006, 'Three Globalisations of Law and Legal Thought', p. 42.
177 Sunstein, 2004, *The Second Bill of Rights;* on how race and class divisions prevented a distributive constitution, see Forbath, 2012, 'Workers' Rights and the Distributive Constitution', p. 60.
178 Eduardo Galeano, 1997, *Open Veins of Latin America*. New York: Monthly Review Press, pp. 210–11.
179 Cousins, 2005, *Explaining the Irish Welfare State*, p. 90.
180 Cousins, 2005, *Explaining the Irish Welfare State*, pp. 26–8.
181 See Luebbert, 1991, *Liberalism, Fascism, or Social Democracy*, p. 99.

Nationalists here tended to invoke a corporatist form of social constitutionalism to justify more authoritarian government.[182] In Poland, Pilsudski replaced the 1921 Constitution, which had included liberal and social security rights, with a presidential constitution (1935), placing parliament under his authority and introducing new powers of emergency decree. In Austria, the 1934 Constitution was 'highly reactionary', strategically diminishing parliamentary pluralism and trade union capacities while dividing power among private elites by sectoral estate. In Portugal too, Salazar sought to develop a corporatist state via military junta.[183] Under the 1933 Constitution, the state was obliged to maintain 'equilibrium' between capital and labour in a 'national corporate economy' (Article 34). This was to be achieved by prohibiting strikes (Article 39) and privileging capital in labour disputes. In the Irish Free State, Catholic social proponents frequently looked to all three constitutions for inspiration.[184]

Spain, another semi-periphery, oscillated between both radical-democratic and authoritarian forms of social constitutionalism in rapid succession. The Constitution of the Second Republic (1931) declared that Spain was a 'democratic republic of workers of all classes', proclaimed universal suffrage and gender equality, guaranteed an extensive list of civil-political rights, and further included a Weimar-style 'social' constitutionalism.[185] The Constitution thus authorised state expropriation of private property for the national economy (Article 44) and anticipated new legislation for economic redistribution and increased worker control in industry and collective bargaining (Article 46). Subsequent constitutional amendments barred the Catholic Church and Jesuit Order from welfare provision. Religious orders were forbidden to hold property 'beyond that necessary to their maintenance' and clergymen were prohibited from teaching in state schools.[186] Reports of clerical dispossession in Spain not only prompted the red scares of 1930s

[182] On Polish and Austrian Constitutions, see Thornhill, 2013, *A Sociology of Constitutions*, pp. 301–3.

[183] Thornhill, 2013, *A Sociology of Constitutions*, p. 317.

[184] See the Jesuits' 'Suggestions for a Catholic Constitution' or McQuaid's correspondence, which also resembled Catholic reactionary thought in mid-1930s France. *De Valera Papers*, UCDA P150/2393/5.

[185] Thornhill, 2013, *A Sociology of Constitutions*, p. 319.

[186] Murray Bookchin, 2005, *The Third Revolution: Popular Movements in the Revolutionary Era*. New York: Continuum, pp. 133–5. After the Civil War, Franco introduced a highly selective social corporatist framework, restoring the balance of industrial power to employers and devolving responsibility for welfare provision to the Catholic Church. Thornhill, 2013, *A Sociology of Constitutions*, p. 320.

Ireland but also influenced the remarkable protection of Church property in the 1937 Constitution.[187]

Viewed in this comparative context, Bunreacht na hÉireann emerges as a conservative and electoral-democratic instrument. It is, first and foremost, an example of classic constitutionalism, aligning in a long tradition of core and peripheral elites negotiating 'sovereignty' throughout the nineteenth and early twentieth centuries. De Valera, consolidated at the head of a nationalist mass party, correctly believed a unilateral renegotiation of sovereignty was possible in the changed circumstances of the 1930s. The new constitution redefined the territory of the new state of 'Eire' to include the island of Ireland and secured its legitimacy on the basis of 'popular' rather than 'parliamentary' sovereignty. Thereafter, however, constitutional innovations were strictly limited. Centralised authority would remain in the executive and the representative political party at the expense of local government or more direct forms of popular autonomy. The Constitution's list of civil-political rights and its providing for the pre-existing laws of the market further indicate its debt to earlier waves of classic constitution-making.

Social legal thought, previously advanced by Clement France and by Alfred O'Rahilly in 1922, also influenced constitution-making in 1937. Proponents of Catholic social constitutionalism, the form of social constitutionalism most forcefully articulated throughout, did not succeed in introducing fundamental changes to the state's institutions such as vocational councils or social credit institutions.[188] Instead, in terms of entrenching socio-economic rights, the state devised a mechanism for their rhetorical recognition in the form of 'Directive Principles'. However, Catholic social contributors succeeded insofar as the Constitution protected the role of the Catholic Church in various institutions of care and social reproduction, from the family to wider forms of charity, education, and health provision, as well as in the regulation of public discourse and morality. In this respect, the gendered nature of the 1937 Constitution, as contemporary feminists argued, bore the closest resemblance to Europe's more authoritarian constitutions.

[187] See Article 44.2.6: 'The property of any religious denomination or any educational institution shall not be diverted save for necessary works of public utility and on payment of compensation'.

[188] Ferriter, 2005, *The Transformation of Ireland*, pp. 406–7; Hogan, 2012, *The Origins of the Irish Constitution*, pp. 223–4.

## CONCLUSION

In 1930s Europe, economic depression coincided with liberal democratic collapse. The Irish Free State's social conflicts, in contrast, were not of a scale or nature to threaten its continued existence as an electoral-democracy. Fianna Fáil's nationalist and social reorientation of the state mobilised and incorporated heretofore marginalised groups into a cross-class, electoral and constitutional politics. Nevertheless, Ireland's state and civil society constitution-makers were faced with an uncertain future, a fact that heightened ideological volatility and class tensions. The ideologies, mobilisations, and constitutional designs of left- and right-wing actors were intimately bound up with the wider European context of growing authoritarianism or, in the case of Republican Spain, of emergent radical democracy. Ireland's militant organisations had been marginalised by the mid-1930s but the ideological differences associated with class conflict remained latent in the political culture. This owed partly to significant strike actions in transport and construction and partly to the anti-communist fervour mobilised by the Irish Christian Front and the Catholic hierarchy in response to Spanish anti-clericalism.

Constitution-makers' shared concern for Irish society's cohesion in the face of popular mobilisations and ideological conflict was the principal motivation both for including some gestures towards socio-economic rights as well as for excluding substantive, legally binding commitments. Catholic intellectuals sought to 'keep in check' domestic agitators through diverse forms of social legal thought. The Jesuit Committee, Edward Cahill, and Alfred O'Rahilly advanced cases for vocationalism, land redistribution, social credit, and limited welfare rights as palliative measures necessary for social harmony. Civil servants shared remarkably similar fears about agitators leading people 'astray' but arrived at different conclusions. MacElligott warned that concessions would only encourage agitators and prove politically dangerous to future governments. McQuaid's contributions were similarly conservative, preferring to emphasise 'private economic initiative' and to avoid 'noxious' words such as 'rights' in economic affairs. Weighing these diverse contributions, de Valera entrenched Catholic social thought more as rhetoric than as blueprint.

In Ireland, as in many peripheral, postcolonial countries, constitution-makers' forwarding of a distinctive or national family law accompanied their quieter acceptance of the pre-existing, liberal laws of the free market, reproducing peripheral-agrarian linkages with the UK and the state's comparatively low welfare effort. The 1937 Irish Constitution preserved inherited judicial and representative-democratic institutions. Its fundamental rights provisions safeguarded private property rights as well as the Irish Land Commission's limited work of redistribution. The Constitution protected the property rights of the church and of religious orders even more forcefully than that of ordinary citizens. Meanwhile, the Department of Finance achieved its preference for minimal state spending. Responsibility for welfare and education instead devolved to the family and the Catholic Church. The Constitution's 'Directive Principles' provided a mechanism for socio-economic rights' rhetorical inclusion only. This mechanism was subsequently replicated in the constitutions of India, Papua New Guinea, and Nigeria.[189]

The consequences were far-reaching. By the late 1950s, the state's deference to grazier-financier interests as well as the Catholic hierarchy ensured that Irish living standards and welfare service provision more closely approximated 1920s than contemporary standards in the UK or US.[190] The state's preservation of social harmony cohered with the institutionalisation and abuse of children, women, and the mentally ill, the censorship of publications and public discourse, and the strict policing of sexuality through health and education. Though Ireland retained representative democratic institutions, the country's social relations, welfare institutions, and cultural norms were often convincingly authoritarian in practice. Viewing the constitution-making process 'from below' anticipates subsequent experiences of exploitation and oppression, particularly insofar as a critical discourse analysis delineates drafters' strategies of ideological containment. In this respect, the Constitution's rhetorical qualities matter a great deal.

The Bunreacht's affirming of Irish national identity, most apparent in the Preamble and Articles 40–45, appealed to and helped reproduce ethnically narrow and patriarchal norms.[191] Constitutional recognition of the hetro-normative family as 'the fundamental unit of society' notably cohered within Irish society's gendered division of labour, premised on unwaged family labour and, in particular, on the unwaged labour of women. Similarly, the critical discourse analysis of the socio-economic provisions' drafting demonstrates constitution-makers'

[189] Steiner, Alston, and Goodman, 2008, *International Human Rights in Context*, p. 321.
[190] See Daly, 1981, *Social and Economic History of Ireland since 1800*.
[191] See Lentin, 1998, '"Irishness", the 1937 Constitution and Citizenship'.

deliberate choosing to frame class relations in terms of charity and state paternalism for 'the poor' and the 'weaker sections'. What matters here is not Catholic social thought per se, but rather drafters' very deliberate rearrangement of the terms of that discourse to bolster existing forms of power and domination. The success of political elites' strategy of ideological containment was not simply produced by dominant core-peripheral and social relations, nor did it depend solely on the state's coercive powers, redistributive capacities, or cultural resources. State constitution-makers' success also depended on the democratic or authoritarian nature and choices of oppositional groups and their ideological projects.

Groups explicitly advancing feminist and left-wing (or 'red republican') ideological projects met opposition in both state and civil society constitution-making. The IRA's strategy of ideological containment saw it rearrange the terms of Catholic social discourse in keeping with its organisational priorities and visions, thereby attempting to justify armed republicanism on national-spiritual grounds to bishops and labourers alike. By the 1930s, mirroring tendencies in the international Left as the entrenchment of party systems proceeded, left-wing and republican thinking in Ireland that had rejected militarism shifted to representative-democratic forms of politics, notably building small parties such as Clann na Talmhan (1939–65) or Clann na Poblachta (1946–65).[192] Among the governmental programmes for an Irish Republic in the 1930s there was no return to the syndicalist visions and agrarian-communal norms that had inspired popular militancy between 1917 and 1923. By the outbreak of World War II, just as state and market were to expand into ever more aspects of everyday life so too the mass party was to emerge as the primary locus of legitimate political activity, co-opting civil society energies and social movements into party-building and periodic electoral contests.

Nevertheless, the boycotts and strikes of the 1930s were not merely tactics to bypass established institutions or achieve temporary reforms. More basically, they were also exercises in collective self-determination, or sovereignty. Direct actions typically advance an alternative vision of selfhood, citizenship, and rights, one that assumes free individuals have the capacity to manage social affairs in a direct, ethical, and rational manner.[193] In a post-revolutionary culture of church-state control

[192] Clann na Poblachta (Irish: Family of the Republic).
[193] Bookchin, 2005, *The Ecology of Freedom*, p. 438.

and of intra-nationalist electoral politics, a sense of the importance of direct action remained. For the IWWU's Louie Bennett, while it was 'the mode of the moment to talk beautifully about woman in the home', groups of women helped dispel sexist prejudices directly by helping organise the strike in the building industry, their homes having been 'darkened by care and anxieties created by a system of working conditions which ought long ago to have been condemned as inhuman'.[194]

[194] Louie Bennett, 'Letter to the Editor' in *Irish Times*, 27 July 1937.

CHAPTER FOUR

# CONTESTING THE IRISH CONSTITUTION AND THE WORLD-SYSTEM: 1945–2008

*Our attempts in 'seeking to promote the common good' cannot be considered highly successful as long as large-scale emigration and unemployment are a permanent feature of our national life ... There is not much point in talking about the dignity of the individual to the unemployed man, to the man forced to emigrate [or] to the grossly overtaxed property owner and potential creator of wealth ...*

– 'Living up to the Bunreacht', *Irish Catholic*, 1959[1]

*I pose this issue for those who champion social and economic legal or constitutional rights ... If we were to create a society of enforceable rights, we create, by definition, a society based on enforceable duties. Flexibility, choice, dynamism, and 'freedom to' (as distinct from 'freedom from') are the qualities which provide the climate for change, growth, wealth creation, and social and cultural innovation. Could it be that a society based on an ever-increasing network of rights and duties would turn out to be as hidebound, as moribund, as economically unsuccessful and as intellectually unfree as the last great historical period of society based on rights and duties – the feudal period?*

– Michael McDowell, Minister for Justice, 2002[2]

Postwar, during the drafting of the Indian Constitution of 1950, the Indian Constituent Assembly looked to the Irish constitutional experience for a number of provisions, notably including a series of non-justiciable 'Directive Principles of State Policy'.[3] The Indian courts have subsequently re-interpreted the two categories of fundamental rights and directive principles integrally, according them equal status.[4]

1 Editorial, *Irish Catholic*, 8/1/1959. *De Valera Papers*, UCDA P150/2472.
2 Michael McDowell T. D., Minister for Justice, Equality, and Law Reform, 'Speech to the Annual Conference of the Irish Social Policy Association', 12 September, 2002. Available at: www.ispa.ie/documents/120902mmcdowell.doc.
3 See Lerner, 2011, *Making Constitutions in Deeply Divided Societies*, p. 49. This section develops ideas first explored in Thomas Murray, 2016, 'Contesting a World-Constitution? Antisystemic movements and constitutional forms in Ireland, 1848–2008' in *Journal of World-Systems Research*, 22 (1), pp. 77–107.
4 The landmark case, *Olga Tellis* v. *Bombay Municipal Corporation* (AIR 1986 Supreme Court 18) involved interpreting the right to life so as to include directive principles and acknowledge the right to livelihood. See Steiner, Alston, and Goodman, 2008, *International Human Rights in Context*, pp. 321–7.

In wider civil society, the Directive Principles of State Policy are constantly referred to in political debate, social agitation, and academic research.[5] In contrast, in Ireland, notwithstanding the close textual similarities of both sets of directive principles, Article 45 has not generated similar levels of political contestation, public identification, or judicial activism: its bearing on actual political, administrative, or legal practice remains slight.[6] In the Houses of the Oireachtas, the Directive Principles have been referred to on no more than fifty occasions since 1937.[7]

Ireland, like India, has also seen a greatly empowered judiciary emerge in the postwar era. By asserting a fundamental law on the basis of popular sovereignty, de Valera had provided for the emergence of an American-style Supreme Court with significant powers of judicial review.[8] The Irish courts, however, have generally not proved amenable to constitutionalising socio-economic rights. In recent years, public interest litigants and constitutional scholars have forwarded a variety of plausible justifications for reading social and economic rights into the Irish constitution, drawing partly on international jurisprudence but primarily on existing liberal democratic and communitarian constitutional norms, including those posited in Article 45. Contemporary scholars and practitioners accept, however, that such interpretations are extremely unlikely to succeed before the present bench, primarily in light of the history of actually existing constitutionalism in Ireland.[9]

5 John O'Dowd, 2011, 'Remembering the Constitution: The Easter Proclamation and Constitutionalism in Independent Ireland' , p. 9. See also Sudhir Krishnaswamy, 2009, *Democracy and Constitutionalism in India: A Study of the Basic Structure Doctrine*. New Delhi: Oxford University Press.

6 *Report of Constitution Review Group (1996)*; Tushnet, 2009, *Weak Courts, Strong Rights*, pp. 238–41.

7 O'Dowd, 2011, 'Remembering the Constitution', p. 7.

8 The 1937 Irish Constitution was not initially envisaged as a robust check on executive authority. Nevertheless, Ireland adopted the American model of concrete review whereby constitutional questions were dealt with through ordinary court proceedings, and a Supreme Court provided for uniformity of jurisdiction. This marked an important break with the United Kingdom. The Constitution also allowed for some borrowing from the European model by allowing for *a priori* review. Peter Mair, 'De Valera and Democracy' in T. Garvin, M. Manning, and R. Sinnott (eds.), 2004, *Dissecting Irish Politics: Essays in Honour of Brian Farrell*. Dublin: University College Dublin Press, p. 44; on the abandoned possibility of establishing a Constitutional Court, see Donal Coffey, 2012, 'The Need for a New Constitution: Irish Constitutional Change 1932–1935' in *Irish Jurist*, 48 (2), pp. 275–302.

9 Gerry Whyte, 'The Efficacy of Public Interest Litigation in Ireland' in Maluwa, Tiyanjana (ed.), 2014, *Law, Politics and Human Rights: Essays in Memory of Kader Asmal*. Leiden: Brill, pp. 252–86, p. 259.

Yet, we do not explain anything by appeal to tradition; rather we must ask why tradition persists.[10]

The politics of constitutionalising socio-economic rights in Ireland was simultaneously and inextricably a world-systemic politics. Though contested, Ireland's trajectory in the historical capitalist world-system continued to be semi-peripheral, 'national' forms of anti-systemic politics continued to take precedence over 'social' alternatives, and the population's welfare remained subordinate to the needs of stable, increasingly global capital flows. We might identify, however, two distinct periods in which this third tendency operated to lesser and greater effect. During the expansionary phase of the US-led cycle of accumulation, primarily between 1945 and 1968, the national appropriation of the social question in Ireland took the form of abandoning protectionism for free trade, prioritising economic development and, concomitantly, creating non-solidaristic welfare services. The second period, from 1968 to the economic crisis of 2008, came about following a signal crisis of the US-led accumulation cycle. During this period, the national appropriation of the social question in Ireland took an increasingly neoliberal form, prioritising global capital flows and economic growth ahead of domestic employment or living standards and, concomitantly, retrenching and privatising welfare and public services.

The politics of the Irish Constitution both registered and reproduced the politics of structural crisis in the world-system in particular ways. In Ireland, as elsewhere, the postwar courts acquired an increased political role with the development of judicial review. Social legal thought and institutions remained comparatively underdeveloped and underfunded however and judges robustly defended classic rights of property and contract from social demands. Following the neoliberal turn, the Irish (and then the European) courts continued to robustly defend classic rights of property and contract from social demands, while simultaneously eroding or liberalising the role of Catholic social constitutionalism in family law. What emerged was a much more American vision of Bunreacht na hÉireann as a constitution guaranteeing liberal individual rights.[11]

Within this broadly conservative trajectory of constitutional development pursued by Irish political and judicial actors, socio-economic rights were a subterranean discourse of sorts, occasionally emergent

[10] Mills, 1959, *The Sociological Imagination*, p. 154.

[11] Michael Böss, 2002, 'Constitutional and Legal Reform in Ireland, 1937–1998: The American Context' in *Nordic Irish Studies*, Vol. 1, pp. 121–45.

in the course of civil society protests but more usually limited to left-leaning, Catholic social proponents. From the 1990s onwards, however, Irish citizens, aided by an increasingly professionalised social justice and human rights advocacy sector, ensured that socio-economic rights featured prominently in Irish constitutional case-law and jurisprudence, as well as in contemporary political parties' agendas for constitutional reform. These developments, premised on the decline of traditional, collective forms of defence against capital and the rise of the 'new constitutionalism', are inseparable from the politics of the world-system. It is to the fuller elaboration of this politics and its implications for Irish constitutional development that we must first turn.

## THE WORLD-SYSTEMIC POLITICS OF WELFARE AND THE IRISH CONSTITUTION: 1945–1968

For some thirty years after World War II, the US-led 'free enterprise' cycle of accumulation introduced a new framework for global economic development. Growth would now centre on trade liberalisation, spearheaded by multinational corporations, regulated by global governance institutions and, notwithstanding the Cold War with the USSR, enforced by military supremacy.[12] Politically, the Old Left movements had achieved their historic goal of state power almost everywhere, at least on paper.[13] Communist parties ruled one-third of the world (the Eastern bloc) while social-democratic parties were in power, or at least alternating power, in most of another third, the pan-European world. (Moreover, welfare state expansion, the principal policy of the social-democratic parties, was accepted and practiced as well by their conservative opponents). Simultaneously, national liberation movements had come to power in most of the former colonial world.

In the core capitalist countries of North America and Europe, a class compromise between capital and labour underpinned a form of 'social liberalism', a belief that 'the state should focus on full employment, economic growth and the welfare of its citizens and that state power should be freely deployed, even substituting for market processes at times, to achieve those ends'.[14] Again, social-legal thought and institutions took

[12] The most important of these global governance institutions included the World Bank, the International Monetary Fund, and the Bank of International Settlements.

[13] Wallerstein, Hopkins, and Arrighi, 2011, *Anti-systemic Movements*.

[14] 'Fiscal and monetary policies, usually dubbed Keynesian, dampened business cycles and ensured reasonably full employment. A class compromise between capital and labour was generally

various specific forms and occasioned varieties of welfare state: 'liberal' in the US, social democratic in the UK, Christian democratic in Germany, and dirigiste in France. The combination occasioned unprecedented rates of economic growth in the core capitalist regions throughout the 1950s and 1960s.

In the decades after World War II, the world's constitutions and constitutional courts emerged as increasingly important national and international sites for the advancement and contestation of these transformations. New waves of constitution-making registered these dynamics. The US constitutional model determined the new, liberal democratic constitutions of Germany and Japan.[15] The USSR model, emphasising a much greater role for state involvement in national transformation, further influenced the wave of constitutions emergent in the Global South, as new nation-states, led by nationalist mass parties, replaced the former British and French Empires. The resulting constitutions varied between party-dominated socialism (Algeria, 1963) and more liberal democratic forms of Nehruvian state developmentalism (India, 1950). In the latter cases, much like the Irish experience, the new constitutions produced by nationalist parties organised executive authority in much the same manner as their former coloniser.[16]

Constitutional review had been introduced in a number of countries, including Czechoslovakia (1920), Liechtenstein (1925), Greece (1927), Egypt (1941), Spain (1931), and Ireland (1937). However, only federal states such as Australia, Canada, Switzerland, and the United States had active review in the immediate aftermath of World War II.[17] Constitutional courts increased in importance thereafter. Governing elites faced with conflicting pressures of tradition and of 'modernisation' in both market and family law acted strategically to displace ensuing disputes out of electoral politics and into non-majoritarian arenas, notably the judicial domain.[18] The trend was perhaps most notable in

advocated as the key guarantor of domestic peace and tranquillity. States actively intervened in industrial policy and moved to set standards for the social wage by constructing a variety of welfare systems (health care, education, and the like)' Harvey, 2005, *A Brief History of Neoliberalism*, p. 10. See also Judt, 2010, *Ill Fares the Land*, pp. 41–80.

15 Zachary Elkins, Tom Ginsburg, and James Melton, 2008, 'Baghdad, Tokyo, Kabul… Constitution-making in Occupied States' in *William and Mary Law Review*, 49 (4), pp. 1139–78; Elster, 1995, 'Forces and Mechanisms in the Constitution-Making Process'.

16 Thirty-eight out of 49 ex-British colonies adopted parliamentary systems while 18 out of 23 ex-French colonies adopted presidential systems. See Go, 2003, 'Views from the Postcolony'.

17 Alec Stone Sweet, 2011, 'Constitutions, Rights, and Judicial Power', pp. 162–80.

18 Hirschl, 2007, *Towards Juristocracy*, pp. 98–9.

the United States but soon came to be emulated elsewhere.[19] In Europe, the European Court of Justice (ECJ), a supra-national institution, provided the most striking example. In seminal decisions taken in the early 1960s, it ensured both the direct effect and supremacy of European law, 'pushing the project [of European integration] further and faster than the Member States had been prepared to go on their own'.[20]

In the Republic of Ireland, as this new free enterprise cycle of accumulation was emerging, successive governments adhered to the former semi-peripheral trajectory of protecting the dominant financier-grazier class, maintaining fiscal austerity and facilitating both agricultural exports to the UK and capital investment in the City of London. Thus, unlike the 'golden age' experienced in the US, Europe, and Japan in the 1950s, Ireland witnessed widespread unemployment and mass emigration.[21] By the decade's end, however, the state had abandoned residual protectionist policies and embarked on free trade and export-led industrialisation, some fifteen years after most Western states. The primary architects of Ireland's semi-peripheral transformation consisted of a cohort of 'modernisers' within successive Fianna Fáil governments (1957–73) and the state bureaucracy, notably the Department of Industry and Commerce. Planning for economic development, however, consistently occurred in consultation with the US as well as European and international governance institutions.[22]

The Republic re-incorporated into the new, US-led world-system by reproducing a recognisable semi-peripheral development trajectory. Unlike the European norm, Ireland's path to industrial expansion was not based on indigenous, state-led industry or manufacturing but rather centred primarily on government provision of tax breaks and financial incentives to attract foreign direct investment. In these circumstances, indigenous capital concentrated on providing services, including construction, banking, insurance, property, haulage, and legal, to foreign investors and multinational corporations.[23] Moreover, given the absence of robust returns from domestic industry, indigenous capital also sought returns from rents. A native 'middleman' class regularly directed capital towards property speculation, capturing the

[19] See David McKay, 2009, *American Politics and Society*. Oxford: Wiley-Blackwell, pp. 319–50.

[20] The ECJ ensured the direct effect of European law in *van Gend en Loos* (1963) and its supremacy in *Costa* v. *ENEL* (1964). See Alex Stone, 2010, 'The European Court of Justice and the judicialization of EU governance' in *Living Reviews in European Governance*, Vol. 5, (2), p. 5.

[21] Tom Garvin, 2004, *Preventing the Future: Why was Ireland so poor for so long?* Dublin: Gill and Macmillan.

[22] O'Hearn, 2001, *The Atlantic Economy*, p. 131.

[23] McCabe, 2011, *Sins of the Father*, p. 193.

'unearned increment' associated with the rising land values produced by foreign investment, population increases, and urbanisation.[24] Agricultural exports also remained important and in the countryside, agribusiness on larger, mechanised farms increasingly displaced small-scale and interdependent farming households.

The 1960s and 1970s were characterised by remarkable social and cultural transformation. Comparatively modest economic growth rates occasioned rising employment, improving living standards, a reversal of emigration, and the emergence of a suburban consumer society. Gender norms changed as the proportion of married women in the workforce rose from 5 per cent in 1961 to 15 per cent in the 1970s. New mass media, notably television, brought the 'American way of life' to people's homes and laid the basis for the eventual hegemony of liberalism.[25] The social thinking of the new, suburban, middle classes was not simply imported but rather owed much to the acquisitive society of peasant proprietorship they displaced.[26] An emergent consumer culture lessened habits of obedience and conformity and displaced traditional ideologies of nationalism and Catholicism. Politically, the pursuit of economic growth became the defining nation-building one.[27] The emergent welfare state further created a new public political culture where groups mobilised around new or reconstituted identities to redress diverse social and economic inequalities.[28]

The domestic balance of national and social relations adjusted in important ways. Within republicanism, left-leaning members moved into cultural criticism in the 1940s and 1950s as a more conservative IRA pursued two provocative bombing campaigns, in the United Kingdom during World War II, and along the Northern Ireland border in the late 1950s. Successive governments invoked 'emergency powers' to overrule the constitution and abridge civil liberties in its efforts to preserve state security. The most important constitutional cases of the 1940s and 1950s, taken by republicans such as Seán McBride, sought to challenge these measures.[29] Coercive legislation targeted at republicans had wider implications for class struggle: successive governments

[24] Fintan O'Toole, 2010, *Ship of Fools*. London: Faber and Faber, p. 31.
[25] O'Connor, 2011, *A Labour history of Ireland*, p. 218. [26] Ó'Faoláin, 1980, *The Irish*, p. 151.
[27] Fanning, 2008, *The Quest for Modern Ireland*.
[28] Smyth, 'Moving the Immovable', p. 114. See also Daniel Bell, 1976. *The Cultural Contradictions of Capitalism*. London: Heinemann.
[29] The state declared a state of emergency in World War II which remained in place until 1976 at which point, a new state of emergency was declared owing to the outbreak of conflict in Northern Ireland.

invoked emergency powers to repress striking workers and protests in the 1960s and 1970s. Returning to a political strategy over this period, the IRA coalesced with an increasingly left-leaning Sinn Féin.

In terms of capital-labour relations, economic growth from the 1960s onwards provided trade unions with an opportunity to recover the fall in real wages that had occurred during World War II; in the mid- to late 1960s, the Republic of Ireland almost topped the European strike league.[30] Trade union density rose from 25 per cent in the 1920s and 1930s to 45–50 per cent in the 1950s to a peak of 60 per cent in the 1980s.[31] Communists, socialists, and left-republicans initiated civil society campaigns, notably the Dublin Unemployed Association sit-down protests in pursuit of work and the nationwide Housing Action Committees' mass squatting campaign for social housing. Second-wave feminism successfully challenged the role of conservative, often specifically Catholic, norms, most notably through direct actions such as ignoring the ban on the importation of contraceptives. The social wage expanded dramatically. By the mid-1970s, the state provided free secondary education, community schools, regional technical colleges, and third-level education grants; it replaced free General Practitioner services for the poor with a general medical service; and it revived housing construction, although with a greater emphasis on private-sector provision.[32]

Compared to other European countries' welfare states, Ireland's was comparatively minimal and non-solidaristic, being based predominantly on cash transfers and means-testing rather than universal public service provision. The nature of Ireland's postwar class compromise was particularly significant in this regard. Elsewhere, trade unions formed the crucial support structure for advancing more solidaristic or universal systems of social security rights, notably through collective organisation and corporatist negotiating in Scandinavian and Bismarckian welfare states.[33] In Ireland, however, tripartite negotiations among government, employers' and unions' representatives were voluntary, centred on wage-bargaining and did not extend to the co-determination of public policy or social security rights. Postwar Irish-based unions,

30 O'Connor, 2011, *A Labour History of Ireland, 1824–2000*, p. 223.
31 O'Connor, 2011, *A Labour History of Ireland, 1824–2000*, p. 170.
32 Cousins, 2005, Explaining the Irish Welfare State, pp. 29–32.
33 See Tony Kerr, 1980, 'Trade Disputes, Economic Torts and the Constitution' in *Irish Jurist*, 16 (2), pp. 241–61, p. 242. See also Walter Korpi, 1990, *The Democratic Class Struggle*. London: Routledge.

hoping to formalise labour-state relations and to promote state-led employment, opted instead to influence public policy indirectly by supporting national economic development and its primary political agent, Fianna Fáil. This informal political bargain, industrial peace in return for dispute resolution mechanisms and government consultation, endured until the global crisis of 2008.

In the comparative absence of trade unions, private actors – notably, the Catholic Church, organised professional groups, and private companies – shaped social policy in Ireland to a more pronounced degree than the European norm. Perhaps most unusually, the Catholic Church retained tremendous influence over the public discussion of social policy as well as a central role in institutional provision. Notably, the hierarchy crushed by ukase the Inter-Party Government's Mother and Child Health Scheme in 1948–51 on the grounds that '[t]he right to provide for the health of children belongs to parents, not to the State'.[34] Opposition to universal or rights-based coverage shaped the parameters of subsequent legislation such as the Health Care Act (1953), the Voluntary Health Insurance Act (1957), and the Health Act (1970).[35] With particularly devastating consequences, the state continued to concede to religious orders the running and oversight of an 'Irish gulag' of Magdalene laundries for women, industrial schools for the young, asylums for the mentally ill, and homes for the destitute, elderly, or infirmed.[36]

Within the Irish party system, voters did not mobilise along a European-style left-right cleavage to contest these processes but rather continued along an intra-nationalist one, dividing between the two dominant nationalist and centrist parties, Fianna Fáil and Fine Gael.[37] National economic development allowed successive Fianna Fáil governments to create new opportunities for indigenous capital and, primarily through redistributive measures, to expand its mass appeal beyond its traditional base of small farmers, workers, and state-protected businesses to include the new suburban middle class. That

[34] Ó'Faoláin, 1980, *The Irish*, p. 162.

[35] See Lindsey Earner-Byrne, 2007, *Mother and Child: Maternity and Child Welfare in Ireland, 1920s–1960s*. Manchester: Manchester University Press.

[36] Mary Rafferty and Eoin O'Sullivan, 2000, *Suffer the Little Children: the inside story of Ireland's industrial schools*. Dublin: New Island Books. Frances Finnegan, 2004, *Do Penance or Perish: Magdalene Asylums in Ireland*. Oxford: Oxford University Press. Bruce Arnold, 2009, *Irish Gulag: How the State Betrayed its Innocent Children*. Dublin: Gill and MacMillan.

[37] Peter Mair, 1992, 'Explaining the absence of Class Politics in Ireland' in J. H. Goldthorpe and C. T. Whelan (eds.), *The development of Industrial Society in Ireland*. Oxford: Oxford University Press.

said, various social democratic parties, notably Labour, National Labour, and Clann na Poblachta, emerged in the changed political culture, managing to secure an aggregate vote of 17 per cent between 1948 and 1969.[38] A stronger left-right alignment of electoral politics floundered, however, on the national question. Following the British state's repression of the civil rights movement in Northern Ireland, the increased role of paramilitarism and state coercion on the island of Ireland split both nationalist and social tendencies.[39]

This shifting balance of core-peripheral and social relations crystallised in a series of changes to the 1937 Irish Constitution. Comparatively few constitutional amendments were proposed during this period of transition.[40] A cross-party Constitution Review Committee, created by Taoiseach Seán Lemass (Fianna Fáil), met in 1967 but its members were 'not aware of any public demand for a change in the basic structure of the Constitution'.[41] Thus, they did not consider the constitutional recognition of socio-economic rights but queried whether the articles on natural resources might obstruct the state's sale of such in the future. The group did, however, recommend removing certain Catholic confessional provisions, partly in response to changing social mores and partly with a view to furthering diplomatic relations with Terrence O'Neill's unionist administration in Northern Ireland. To this end, in 1972, the government proposed and a majority voted to remove the constitutional provision outlining the 'special position' of the Catholic Church in Irish society. Thereafter, the political parties' agenda for constitutional reform was increasingly shaped by the outbreak of civil conflict in Northern Ireland and by the growing number of people opposed to clericalist regulation of sexuality and the family.[42]

In Ireland, as elsewhere, constitutional change (and stability) owed, at least in part, to the emergence of an empowered judiciary. Chief Justice Cearbhall Ó'Dálaigh's court of the 1960s newly interpreted

38 O'Connor, 2011, *A Labour History of Ireland, 1824–2000*, p. 220. See also Mair, 1992, 'Explaining the absence of Class Politics in Ireland'.

39 O'Connor, 2011, *A Labour History of Ireland, 1824–2000*, p. 220.

40 On two occasions, Fianna Fáil proposed abandoning Proportional Representation (by means of Single Transferrable Vote) in favour of a majoritarian electoral system such as that in the UK. On both occasions, the proposed amendments to the 1937 Constitution were defeated. For a descriptive overview of the postwar period, see Brian McMahon, 'Developments in the Irish Legal System since 1945' in J. J. Lee (ed.), 1979, *Ireland: 1945–70*, pp. 83–95.

41 See *The Report of the Committee on the Constitution* (1967), Dublin: Stationary Office, p. 8. See also query relating to state ownership of resources.

42 Opposition to clericalism increasingly included Catholic clergy in the wake of the Second Vatican Council. Chubb, 1991, *The Politics of the Irish Constitution*, p. 85.

the constitution so as to acknowledge the existence of rights not explicitly listed in the constitution.[43] The Supreme Court proved particularly 'activist' regarding the preservation and enlargement of civil liberties, emphasising limits to police powers and rights of due process as well as expanding the private sphere, most notably with regard to the liberalisation of Catholic social or family law.[44] In the celebrated *McGee* case, the Supreme Court acknowledged an 'unenumerated' constitutional right to marital privacy and thereby struck down Catholic 'social' laws banning the importation of contraceptives.[45] In market law, however, the judges retained a classic liberal view of individual rights trumping collective rights or social justice concerns.

The Irish judiciary's celebrated 'discovery' of the constitution in the 1960s, although articulated in the idiom of a residual Catholic legal nationalism, owed its origins, more basically, to an emergent globalising culture of human rights and public law neoformalism. The US experience was particularly influential.[46] In both Ireland and the United States, the lack of a pronounced left-right party system, the presence of judicial review and legal support structures as well as the growth of rights consciousness in society provided the conditions both for citizens' use of the constitution to challenge government on socioeconomic issues and for elites' displacement of these issues to the judiciary. The outcome in both countries has been characterised as a 'rights revolution'.[47] Postwar US Supreme Courts, notably those under Chief Justices Warren and Burger, made landmark decisions regarding civil

43 *Ryan* v. *Attorney General* [1965] IR 294 In total, twenty-five such 'un-enumerated' rights have been identified in this manner. See Michael Gallagher, 2010, 'The Changing Constitution' in Coakley and Gallagher, 2010, *Politics in the Republic of Ireland*, pp. 72–108, pp. 84–94.

44 Gary Sturgess and Philip Chubb, 1988, *Judging the World: Law and politics in the world's leading courts*, London: Butterworths, p. 44.

45 Note the centrality of American precedent, notably *Griswold* v. *Connecticut*, 381 U.S. 479 (1965), in McGee v. *Attorney General* [1974] I.R. 284.

46 See Böss, 2002, 'Constitutional and Legal Reform in Ireland, 1937–1998: The American Context'.

47 'The new rights encompass, among other rights, freedom of speech and the press; free exercise of religion and prohibitions on official establishment of religion; prohibitions against invidious discrimination on the basis of race, sex, and a few other more or less immutable characteristics; the right of privacy; and the right to due process in law enforcement and administrative procedure'. Charles Epp, 1998, *The Rights Revolution: Lawyers, Activists and Supreme Courts in Comparative Perspective*. Chicago: University of Chicago Press, p. 7. Similarly, in Ireland, the courts oversaw 'nothing less than a revolution in constitutional jurisprudence, most particularly in the area of fundamental rights'. John Kelly, 1988, 'Fundamental Rights in the Constitution', p. 167.

liberties, due process, racial desegregation, and gender equality.[48] In Ireland, postwar political and judicial actors saw much to borrow. Lemass, an admirer of the US Constitution, privately encouraged liberal judicial appointees such as Brian Walsh to look to the judicial review practice of the activist US Supreme Court under Earl Warren.[49] In the wake of *McGee*, however, the spectre of liberalism, more exactly an Irish judge following American precedents on divorce or abortion, would mobilise a series of conservative Catholic lobby groups. Such reactions formed part of a global counteroffensive to the world-revolutionary moment of 1968.

## NEOLIBERALISM, CONSTITUTIONALISM, AND THE DETHRONEMENT OF POLITICS: 1968–2008

The world-system underwent a profound crisis in the 1970s, inaugurating the contemporary neoliberal era.[50] In the world-system's cores, industrial capital was compelled to respond to organised labour's relative success in defending higher wages and living conditions. Capital 'resolved' this barrier to profitable accumulation by introducing new technologies and communications as well as off-shoring domestic manufacturing from cores to peripheries. Concomitantly, peripheries 'no longer expected to follow the earlier Western path of industrial development but rather readjusted their developmental goals toward maximum participation in the world market'.[51] With the end of the Bretton Woods system of fixed exchange rates and the growth of a Eurodollar market (beyond the control of any single central bank), the mid-1980s saw the emergence of new financial markets. Speculative bubbles would increasingly overshadow the profitability of capital's returns from

[48] These landmark cases involved challenging racial segregation (*Brown* v. *Board of Education* (1954); *Alexander* v. *Holmes County Board of Education* [1969]), expanding criminal due process (*Mapp* v. *Ohio* (1961)), reforming the political process (*Baker* v. *Carr* (1962); *Wesberry* v. *Sanders* (1964); *Reynolds* v. *Sims* (1964); *United States* v. *Nixon* (1974)) and providing for abortion rights (*Roe* v. *Wade* (1973)). See McKay, 2009, *American Politics and Society*, pp. 319–50.

[49] As Judge Brian Walsh put it: 'When the Prime Minister offered me the appointment he said he would just like to mention one thing – that he would never again refer to it – but he said he would like the Supreme Court to become more like the United States Supreme Court [as it was under Warren]'. Cited in Sturgess and Chubb, 1988, *Judging the World*, p. 144. See also Tom Garvin, 2009, *Judging Lemass*. Dublin: Royal Irish Academy.

[50] Arrighi, 1994, *The Long Twentieth Century*, pp. 269–300; Harvey, 2007, *A Brief History of Neoliberalism*.

[51] O'Hearn, 2001, *The Atlantic Economy*, p. 169.

industrial production.[52] Amidst such confident booms, the end of the Soviet Union in 1989 appeared to mark not just the triumphant globalisation of liberal democratic capitalism but the elimination of any alternative form of social organisation.[53]

Throughout this period, the 'social compromise' between capital and labour was increasingly subject to retrenchment and to privatisation. Governments seeking to attract investment tended to adopt a monetarist consensus on subordinating labour's living standards to the needs of stable global capital flows. Typically, gaining the confidence of the markets involved the introduction of labour market 'flexibility', the deregulation of financial operations, and the privatisation of state assets and services. Moreover, as unemployment soared in the cores as a result of off-shoring and technological developments, tax revenues plunged, government borrowing increased, and various states underwent prolonged fiscal crises. Throughout the 1980s, power-brokers in both the core and periphery used such fiscal crises to introduce renewed rounds of social retrenchment and privatisation.[54]

The crisis of the US-led cycle of accumulation coincided with a pronounced transformation in the political-ideological norms of the world-system. The world revolution of 1968, marked by uprisings in the West (France, Italy, US), East (Czechoslovakia, China), and South (Mexico, Vietnam), ended the long reign of centrist liberalism as the dominant ideological position.[55] Both the radical left and the conservative right resumed their roles as autonomous ideological contestants in the world-system. Neoliberal politics, epitomised by Thatcher's Conservatives in the UK or Reagan's Republicans in the US, concentrated on restoring the power of economic elites by removing capital from the former constraints of social or centrist liberalism.[56] Its proponents, predominantly a cosmopolitan class of stockholders, financial operators, industrialists, finance officials, and conservative or social-democratic politicians, sought to destroy collective structures – the nation, the work group, unions, co-operatives, the family – that might impede the pure market logic.[57] Meanwhile, 1968 also signalled the decline of both the Old Left

[52] Dick Bryan and Mike Rafferty, 2006, *Capitalism with Derivatives: a political economy of financial derivatives, capital and class*, pp. 96–7, 103.

[53] Francis Fukuyama, 1992, *The End of History and the Last Man*. London: Free Press.

[54] On the parallels between contemporary debt crises post-2008 and earlier debt crises in New York City or the Global South, particularly in Latin America, see Harvey, 2007, *A Brief History of Neoliberalism*.

[55] Wallerstein, Hopkins, and Arrighi, 2011, *Anti-Systemic Movements*.

[56] Harvey, 2007, *A Brief History of Neoliberalism*, p. 11.

[57] Bourdieu, 1998, 'Utopia of Endless Exploitation: The Essence of Neoliberalism'.

party (whether social democratic or communist), and the national liberation party. The New Left elaborated a critique of both US and USSR hegemony, based in part on their repressing movements in the 'Third World'; it further criticised the Old Left strategy of seizing state power as a means of social transformation; and, finally, it emphasised issues of oppression on the bases of gender, race, ethnicity, and sexual orientation as well as issues of environmentalism, peace, and international solidarity.

Constitutionalism in the late twentieth and early twenty-first centuries reflected these new priorities. Neoliberal ideologues such as Milton Friedman emphasised the centrality of the rule of law to the proper functioning of a market order. Friedman further suggested that a constitutional structure could 'dethrone politics' by substituting general laws for discretionary government intervention in the market and its stultification of individual incentives, choices, and pursuits.[58] Presented with the opportunity to do so from the 1970s onwards, those political and economic actors with greatest access to treaties, constitutions, and judicial power attempted to manage popular resistance to neoliberal reforms by relocating such conflicts to the domain of legal expertise.[59] This process accompanied the ongoing 'hollowing out' of Western representative democracy, whereby 'citizens retreat into private life or more specialized and often ad hoc forms of representation, while party leaderships retreat into institutions, drawing their terms of reference ever more readily from their roles as governors or public-office holders'.[60]

By embedding neoliberal norms in non-majoritarian arenas, the regulatory framework for international trade (WTO) and for common markets (NAFTA, EU) has redefined the nature and purpose of ecological, social, and political commons in ever more privatised and commodified ways.[61] The post-1989 constitutions of semi-peripheral and peripheral regions, from Cape Verde (1992) to Iraq (2005), have combined

58 Even before the Second World War, the free market economist Frederick Hayek 'had envisaged a constitutional structure raised sufficiently high above the nations composing it to exclude the danger of any popular sovereignty below impinging on it . . . [O]nce heterogeneous populations were assembled in an inter-state federation, as he called it, they would not be able to re-create the united will that was prone to such ruinous [dirigiste and redistributive] interventions. Under an impartial authority, beyond the reach of political ignorance or envy, the spontaneous order of a market economy could finally unfold without interference'. Anderson, 2007, 'Depicting Europe', pp. 13–21.

59 Kennedy, 2006, 'Three Globalisations of Law and Legal Thought', p. 67.

60 Peter Mair, 2013, *Ruling the Void: the hollowing out of Western Democracy*. London: Verso, p. 33.

61 Gill, 1995, 'Globalisation, Market Civilisation and Disciplinary Neoliberalism'.

commitments to self-determination, democracy, and human rights with a valorisation of neoliberal economics.[62] To a more pronounced degree, the proposed supranational Constitution for Europe (2004) inscribed the imperatives of a 'highly competitive' market, 'free of distortions', as foundational principles of an enlarged Europe.[63] Importantly, social and economic rights are not incompatible with norms opposed to redistribution through collective, majoritarian politics. Hence, while the South African Constitution (1996) newly introduced social and economic rights provisions, it also contained both the strongest possible protection of individual property rights, including a bar on 'arbitrary or unreasonable' land redistribution, and the narrowest viable protection of workers' right to strike, unionise, and bargain collectively.[64]

Concomitantly, the trend towards increasingly powerful constitutional courts continued, notably in a number of peripheral and semi-peripheral nation-states. In Europe, this included post-dictatorship Portugal, Spain, and Greece in the 1970s and post-Soviet Central and Eastern Europe in the 1990s. Active judicial review was newly established in Sweden (1979), Egypt (1980), Mexico (1994), and Thailand (1997) as well as in Westminster-style systems of parliamentary sovereignty such as Canada, New Zealand, and Britain.[65] Judicial decision-making in these newly powerful arenas, Duncan Kennedy suggests, has been characterised by a transformed use of 'policy analysis' and by the emergence of 'public law neo-formalism'. In terms of the former, contemporary modes of policy analysis are based on 'conflicting

[62] Hence, the Constitution of Cape Verde (1992) replaced a former constitution's commitment to 'the building of an independent national economy' with articles emphasizing the importance of state support for 'the integration of Cape Verde into the world economic system' as well as for 'foreign investment which might contribute to the economic and social development of the Nation'. Constitution of Cape Verde 1975, Art. 10. Constitution of Cape Verde 1992, Art. 88, 89. Go, 2003, 'A Globalizing Constitutionalism? Views from the Postcolony'. See also Harvey, 2007, *A Brief History of Neoliberalism*, p. 66.

[63] Although defeated following popular rejection in referendums held in France and the Netherlands, the substance of the changes, shorn of constitutional symbolism, subsequently passed in the form of the Lisbon Treaty (2009). Walker, 2013, 'The Shifting Foundations of the European Union Constitution', p. 654; see also Anderson, 2007, 'Depicting Europe'.

[64] Kende, 2003, 'The South African Court's Embrace of Socio-Economic Rights: A Comparative Perspective'. In terms of the prioritisation of national over social politics in a semi-periphery, there are parallels between postcolonial Ireland and post-apartheid South Africa, notably in the African National Congress's ready embrace of neoliberalism. On the latter, see Adèle Kirsten and Tshepo Madlingozi, 2012, 2012, 100 Years of the ANC: From Liberation Movement to State Power in South Africa, *Black Agenda Report*, http://blackagendareport.com/print/content/100-years-anc-liberation-movement-state-power-south-africa.

[65] This occurred with the introduction of the Canadian Charter of Rights and Freedoms and judicial review (1982), New Zealand Bill of Rights Act (1990), and the Human Rights Act in Britain (1998), respectively. Ran Hirschl, 2004, 'The Political Origins of the New Constitutionalism' in *Indiana Journal of Global Legal Studies*, 11, pp. 71–108.

considerations' (or 'balancing' or 'proportionality'), resulting in the production of increasingly *ad hoc* compromises between 'individualist' and social desiderata. In a public law case, a judge may additionally bring to bear neoformalism, a disruptive mode of juridical activity aiming to change the status quo on the basis of 'supposedly transcendent but also positively enacted values in constitutions or treaties'.[66] Thus, in any given case, jurists can appeal either to 'classic' freedoms or to existing 'social' legislation.

The emergent culture of 'juristocracy' has facilitated the politics of neo-conservative reaction.[67] In the United States, from the 1980s onwards, the conservative right have dominated the Supreme Court and have mobilised constitutional rights in opposition to state intervention, redistribution, or regulation as well as to liberal abortion laws.[68] In Mexico, the Partido Revolucionario Institucional increased the power and autonomy of the Supreme Court in an attempt to 'lock in' and bind successor governments to policies of economic openness.[69] Similarly, the European Court of Justice has been neoformalist in its interpretation of the canonical 'freedoms' of goods and persons in a single market.[70] However, notwithstanding these political determinants, judges retain autonomy in their decision-making, an autonomy central to the legitimacy of the judiciary and to the wider success of the 'new constitutionalism' in civil society.[71]

In addition to neoliberalism's electoral success or the particular strategising of political, economic, and judicial actors in various states and transnationally, centrist liberal and social democratic parties as well as non-governmental organisations adopted the new discourse and associated practices as their own. In particular, remaining 'social' advocates,

66 Kennedy, 2006, 'Three Globalisations of Law and Legal Thought', p. 64.

67 See Hirschl, 2007, *Towards Juristocracy*. Harvey, 2007, *A Brief History of Neoliberalism*, p. 66.

68 McKay, 2009, *American Politics and Society*, pp. 343–50. Similarly, in the US experience of socio-economic rights, Nixon's appointees to the Supreme Court effectively signalled the death knell of federal jurisprudence leading towards their recognition. Sunstein, 2004, *The Second Bill of Rights*. From 1973 onwards, significant judicial interventions have instead occurred at state level, notably where courts have expanded the right to education with significant redistributive implications. Christopher Berry and Charles Wysong, 2012, 'Making Courts Matter: Politics and the Implementation of State Supreme Court Decisions' in *The University of Chicago Law Review* 79(1): pp. 1–29.

69 Pilar Domingo, 2000, 'Judicial Independence: The Politics of the Supreme Court in Mexico' in *Journal of Latin American Studies*, 32: 3, pp. 705–35.

70 Alex Sweet Stone, 2010, 'The European Court of Justice and the judicialization of EU governance' in *Living Reviews in European Governance*, Vol. 5, (2), p. 5. See Peebles, 1997, '"A Very Eden of the Innate Rights of Man"? A Marxist Look at the European Union Treaties and Case Law'.

71 Bourdieu, 1987, 'The Force of Law'.

faced with organised labour's retreat and the state's reconfiguration in international governance networks, looked to the same juristocratic domains to challenge social grievances. The rapid emergence of 'socio-economic rights' advocacy in Europe and North America, Mauro Capelletti suggested, owed primarily to civil society attempts to bypass the existing, blocked system of social democratic politics and trade union organising.[72] Circumventing electoral or majoritarian politics, both neoliberal and contemporary social advocates thus appealed directly either to 'natural' values or to rules positively embedded in domestic constitutions or international treaties and covenants.

Ideologically, an expansive range of societal conflicts have come to be thought of and fought primarily in terms of 'human rights', an amorphous concept covering all manner of minoritarian rights identities. In recent years, most notably in the 'Third World', social movements opposed to neoliberalism have critiqued the limitations of human rights, as well as the associated necessity of NGOs and judicial activism. Here too, judges' support of social and economic rights has not proved incompatible with developing opportunities for capital.[73] In India, for example, an increasingly active Supreme Court has interpreted the constitution both to discover social and economic rights and to facilitate state developmentalist projects such as dam construction, the latter notwithstanding mass community opposition to the projects' destruction of livelihoods, communities, and ecologies. In practice, the latter form of decision-making has impacted more decisively on Indian society than the former.[74]

## FAREWELL TO THE CATHOLIC SOCIAL CONSTITUTION

The world-systemic crisis of the 1970s also coincided with the outbreak of a thirty-year conflict in Northern Ireland (1968–98) in which the primary armed participants consisted of the Provisional IRA, the British army, the Royal Ulster Constabulary, and Loyalist paramilitaries. Some 3,400 people died and more than 50,000 were injured in the course

72 Cappelletti (ed.), 1981, *Access to Justice and the Welfare State*. See also G. McCormack, 1979, 'Review: Stevens's Cappelletti's Access to Justice' *in* Irish Jurist, 14 (1), pp. 195–8, p. 195.

73 Kennedy, 2006, 'Three Globalisations of Law and Legal Thought', pp. 69–70.

74 Rajagopol, 'Socio-Economic Rights and the Indian Supreme Court' in Steiner, Alston, and Goodman (eds.), 2008, *International Human Rights in Context*. pp. 326–7.

of the conflict. South of the border, successive governments, led by the nationalist parties, Fianna Fáil and Fine Gael, concurred on determined repression of the Provisional IRA, on censorship of its political wing, Sinn Féin, and, ultimately, on inter-state cooperation with Westminster to bring about an end to the fighting. The Good Friday Agreement (1998) functioned as a coordinating device to foster mutual commitment to peace, devolution of government to Northern Ireland, and power-sharing between nationalists and unionists. The conflict initially reanimated an irredentist nationalism. After three decades of paramilitary and state violence, however, more than 95 per cent of voters in the Republic endorsed the Good Friday Agreement, including the deletion of the 1937 Constitution's territorial claim to Northern Ireland.[75]

Nation-building increasingly focussed instead on national economic growth. Ireland acceded to the European Economic Community (EEC) in 1973, after which point the number of transnational companies' subsidiaries in the country increased dramatically.[76] Ireland's 'open door' strategy to multinationals, however, left it particularly vulnerable to international volatility. Changing course, towards more robust forms of state-led industrialisation for example, was unlikely. Breaching competition rules in Europe's common market threatened reduced structural funding at a time of deep recession. Subsequent fiscal crises thus entrenched peripheralisation while the Irish state became one of the most indebted in the world, heavily dependent on EEC fiscal transfers and farm subsidies.[77] Pronounced recession in the 1980s occasioned a return to mass unemployment and emigration. In crisis, Fianna Fáil, Fine Gael, and a newly emergent neoliberal party, the Progressive Democrats, converged on a 'competition state' strategy for development, supported in turn by both the Irish Business Employers Confederation and the National Economic and Social Council, a government-trade union consultative body.[78] Thereafter, the state would seek maximum participation in the global economy, primarily by identifying growth industries, attracting foreign investment, and subordinating labour's living standards and autonomy (via monetarism, austerity, and wage restraint) to the needs of stable capital flows.

[75] For contextualisation within the history of Irish constitutionalism, see Kissane, 2011, *New Beginnings*, pp. 124–9.

[76] O'Hearn, 2001, *The Atlantic Economy*, p. 168.

[77] Ó'Gráda, 1997, *A Rocky Road*, p. 31.

[78] O'Hearn, 2001, *The Atlantic Economy*, pp. 171, 191. See also Kieran Allen, 2009, *Ireland's Economic Crash: a radical agenda for change*. Dublin: Liffey Press, p. 32.

In the context of US economic growth and expansion into the European Union in the 1990s, Ireland functioned as a semi-peripheral site where 'US companies would shift their products into Europe, while accumulating profits in order to avoid taxation'.[79] Successive governments also advocated light-touch banking regulation to attract finance capital to the new Irish Financial Services Centre.[80] Opportunities for indigenous capital, however, remained concentrated in secondary or software development for multinationals, as well as the more traditional forms of service provision and rent-extraction.

Employment in the 'post-industrial' Irish economy rose dramatically and centred primarily on services.[81] Immigration diversified a comparatively homogenous society. Spectacular economic growth rates, full employment, and sustained rises in average incomes facilitated the emergence of a mass consumer society, characterised by increasing levels of private homeownership, and debt-fuelled consumption on an unprecedented scale. When US tech investment declined in the wake of the dotcom collapse of 2000–2, European Monetary Union, or 'euro' membership allowed Irish banks to access cheap credit from the banks of European cores, notably Germany and the UK. In these circumstances, a nexus of indigenous rentiéres, centred on a comparatively small circle of banking interests and property developers, reproduced a familiar boom-bust cycle of property speculation. Before the bust, however, improving living standards helped foster a broad acceptance of the new 'capitalist realism'.[82] Nevertheless, this emergent balance of social relations had occasioned disparities, polarisation, and social conflict.[83]

Initial adjustments met with escalations in unofficial trade union militancy and strike actions in the 1970s. In 1979, a tax revolt, organised primarily through the Dublin Trades Council and the Workers' Party,

79 O'Hearn, 2001, *The Atlantic Economy*, pp. 175–6.

80 See Patrick Honohan, 2010, *The Irish Banking Crisis: Regulatory and Financial Stability Policy, 2003–2008*. Dublin: Official Publications.

81 In 1966, industry accounted for a peak 35 per cent of employment, services for 34 per cent, and agriculture for 31 per cent. In 1992, the proportions were 28 per cent, 59 per cent, and 13 per cent, respectively. See Ó'Gráda, *A Rocky Road*, p. 170.

82 Fisher, 2009, *Capitalist Realism: Is there no alternative?*

83 Inequality in Ireland grew markedly as the country experienced economic growth from the 1990s onwards. From 1975 to the height of the boom in 2006, average gross incomes (adjusted for inflation and rounded to the nearest hundred) more than doubled (from €15,200 to €35,500). However, average incomes for the top 10 per cent more than tripled (from €43,500 to €134,400) while the top 1 per cent had almost five times as much income (from €90,500 to €444,100). See TASC, 2014, 'Income Inequality in Ireland'. Available at: www.tasc.ie/download/pdf/tasc_inequality_ireland_brief.pdf.

involved some 700,000 people in public demonstrations for tax justice, the largest in the history of the state. However, once again, the state's 'national' (or semi-peripheral) development strategy won over significant sections of the trade union movement. With the growth of non-union multinationals, union density declined from a peak of 60 per cent in the 1980s to less than 35 per cent in the 2010s, the majority of organised labour concentrating in the public sector. Wary of a Thatcher-like attack on their negotiating positions, unions opted to accept social corporatism and advocate labour restraint, this time not in return for wage increases but rather income tax reductions.[84] In 1990, a Fianna Fáil-Progressive Democrat coalition government replaced the Trades Disputes Act (1906) with the more restrictive Industrial Relations Act (1990). Practices and norms of collective solidarity atrophied as industrial unrest, official and unofficial, declined. The expansion of 'social partnership' to include NGOs further facilitated the depoliticisation of Irish civil society.

In terms of anti-systemic opposition, the 'new left' social movements grew in size and importance. Feminist and lesbian/gay/bisexual/transsexual (LGBT) groups succeeded in challenging and changing conservative norms and restrictive laws regarding divorce, homosexuality, and abortion. Environmental and community activists enjoyed a series of successes, notably preventing the introduction of nuclear power stations at Carnsore, Co. Wexford in the 1980s and delaying the construction of an experimental on-shore gas pipeline near Rossport, Co. Mayo in the 2000s. International solidarity movements, opposed to forms of state repression and apartheid in Latin America, Palestine, and South Africa, also scored significant victories in this period.[85] The anti-war movement, responding to the US 'war on terror' occasioned demonstrations of up to one million people; the Fianna Fáil-led government continued to facilitate the US military's use of Shannon airport, notwithstanding popular opposition and concerns over neutrality.

In electoral terms, contemporary political scientists anticipated a realignment of the Irish party system from intra-nationalist divisions towards a more conventional left-right divide.[86] This did not occur. Instead, opposition to republican paramilitaries combined with Fine Gael's (somewhat anomalous) left-ward turn reversed Labour's stance

[84] Terrence McDonough and Tony Dundon, 2010, 'Thatcherism Delayed? The Irish crisis and the paradox of social partnership' in *Industrial Relations Journal*, 41 (6), pp. 544–62.
[85] Allen, 2004, *No Global: the people of Ireland versus the multinationals*.
[86] Mair, 1992, 'Explaining the absence of Class Politics in Ireland'.

on entering coalition with the party. The tax revolt of 1979 was a watershed. Labour declined to identify with the protests before joining a Fine Gael-led government determined to reduce union influence on government policy.[87] From the late 1980s onwards, Labour joined with Fianna Fáil and Fine Gael consistently to support further European trade liberalisation and integration.[88] In the context of high economic growth rates, successive Fianna Fáil-led coalition governments (1997–2007) reduced personal taxation and engaged in strategically popular, short-termist expenditure to bolster electoral support. Over the same period, Sinn Féin, the Greens and various Trotskyist formations have filled the electoral space vacated by Labour and occasioned by the decline of the Workers Party.[89] In association with autonomous elements from broader social movements and community groups, these left-wing parties have generally led opposition to EU integration and to welfare-state retrenchment.

In the absence of European levels of public spending and taxation, a European social model of public services and supports remained unattainable. While total government expenditure increased over this period, it declined relative to levels of Gross Domestic Product/Gross National Product (GDP/GNP) growth and remained among the lowest in the Organisation of Economic Cooperation and Development (OECD).[90] Ireland's welfare state remained centred on targeted social expenditure, cash transfers, and means-testing, supplemented by voluntary networks of religious and familial care. Politically, such forms of redistribution are more vulnerable to retrenchment than cross-class or universal programmes; this proved to be the case in the course of

[87] O'Connor, 2011, *A Labour History of Ireland*, p. 220.

[88] Notably, the three parties have united on referenda concerning European integration, campaigning successfully for the public's endorsement of the Single European Act (1987) and subsequent EU treaties, including Maastricht (1992), Amsterdam (1998), Nice (2001/03), and Lisbon (2008/09). On the 'two and a half' party system's adaptation, see Seán McGraw, 'Adaptive Governance: The Art of Party Politics', in Niamh Hardiman (ed.), 2012, *Irish Governance in Crisis*, Manchester: Manchester University Press.

[89] Post-Good Friday Agreement, Sinn Féin has enjoyed the greatest electoral success among these parties, entering government in Northern Ireland and gaining seats in the Republic. Its priorities, however, remain more 'national' than 'social'. See Agnès Maillot, 2005, *New Sinn Féin: Irish republicanism in the twenty-first century*. London: Routledge, p. 103.

[90] Ireland's overall tax-take is peculiarly low in comparison to both the EU and the OECD averages and, indicative of wider OECD trends, no longer represents a commitment to progressive taxation. The primary factors involved in this 'low tax' regime are the very low level of social security contributions, the relatively low levels of local government revenue-raising, and the above-average levels of tax expenditures or tax breaks, the latter greatly undermining equity in the income tax system. TASC, 2014, *Budget 2014: Choosing an equitable route to recovery*. Dublin: TASC, p. 14.

austerity budgets in the 1980s and again following the 2008 crisis.[91] Additionally, the contemporary period of neoliberal hegemony has occasioned the opening up of the state's welfare effort to increased commodification and privatisation.[92]

This shifting balance of core-peripheral and social relations crystallised in a series of changes to the 1937 Irish Constitution. Six referendums on constitutional amendment occurred between 1937 and 1972; a further twenty-three took place between 1973 and 2008.[93] Within the predominantly 'national' party system and prevailing liberal and neoliberal norms, the dominant focus of successive governments has been the contested removal of capital from the constraints of 'social liberalism' and of society from the 'Catholic social' in family law. In terms of the former, seven referendums on EU treaties have occurred between 1972 and 2008. That the latter six referendums have been held stemmed from a Supreme Court decision in *Raymond Crotty* v. *An Taoiseach* that any EU treaty affecting competencies listed in the Irish Constitution required ratification by referendum.[94] Majority support for EU integration has declined steadily from a peak of 80 per cent approval for EEC membership in 1972. Remarkably, in the Nice (2001) and Lisbon (2008) referendums support fell below 50 per cent, pronouncedly so in working-class constituencies. On both occasions the treaties were rejected, modified, and approved at a second referendum.

The size of EU-critical opposition in Ireland is remarkable given that proponents of EU integration encompass the state's three largest political parties (Fianna Fáil, Fine Gael and, from the 1980s onwards, Labour) combined with the Irish Famers' Association, the Irish Business Employers' Confederation, the American Chamber of Commerce, and both state and private media. Multinational corporations intervened directly in the Lisbon (2009) referendum to advocate a 'yes' vote.[95] Conversely, both 'national' (Sinn Féin, the Irish Sovereignty

[91] See Walter Korpi and Joakim Palme, 1998, 'The Paradox of Redistribution and Strategies of Equality: Welfare State Institutions, Inequality, and Poverty in Western Countries' in *American Sociological Review*, 63 (5), pp. 661–87.

[92] This is perhaps most apparent in the government's subsidising a market for private health insurance through tax exemptions and free provision of public facilities. See Maev-Ann Wren, 2003, *Unhealthy State: Anatomy of a Sick Society*. Dublin: New Island.

[93] *Referendum Results, 1937–2008*. Dublin: Stationary Office.

[94] See *Crotty* v. *An Taoiseach* [1987] IR 713, a challenge to the constitutionality of the Single European Act, and Raymond Crotty's account of the experience. Crotty, 1988, *A Radical's Response*. Dublin: Poolbeg.

[95] John Kennedy, 'Why Lisbon Treaty vote has mobilised Ireland's tech multinational leaders' in *Irish Independent*, 27 August 2009.

Movement as well as Catholic conservatives) and 'social' (Trotskyite Parties and social movements) advocates have helped organise anti-systemic opposition. Social partnership inhibited this opposition's further growth. Notably, having remained neutral in 2008, SIPTU, the country's largest trade union, chose to support the 2009 Lisbon Treaty.[96]

In terms of family law, attempts to remove the Catholic social imprimatur on issues such as abortion, divorce, homosexuality, adoption, and illegitimacy acquired a further political resonance given the ongoing conflict in Northern Ireland, where religion functioned as an important signifier (rather than determining factor) of division. Attempting to win over unionist opinion, Fine Gael Taoiseach Garrett FitzGerald proclaimed a 'crusade' to remove sectarianism from the constitution, then bowed to Catholic pressure groups and held a referendum to prohibit abortion in 1983. The Fine Gael-Labour government failed to carry a referendum to legalise divorce in 1986. Public opinion, particularly in urban areas, swung towards the 'liberal agenda' in the 1990s. Referendums in 1992 constitutionalised a right to leave the state for and to obtain information on abortion while the constitutional ban on divorce was overturned in 1995.[97]

Within the prevailing party system and neoliberal norms, the agenda for constitutional reform did not extend to 'the future structure of society'.[98] Somewhat exceptionally, the Fine Gael-Labour coalition government of 1995–7 considered social and economic rights as part of a wider constitutional review process. Two members of the Constitutional Review Group argued that the constitution should have an article 'committing us to a democracy based on principles of social solidarity with the aim of eliminating poverty and promoting economic equality through a system of taxation based on principles of equality and progressiveness'.[99] The government concurred with the majority of the expert group, however, who opposed the constitutionalisation of socio-economic rights on the grounds that it would represent a 'distortion of democracy'. Parenthetically, the same experts did not consider it a 'distortion of democracy' to allow judicial supervisions of legislation in the allied field of property rights.[100]

96 O'Connor, 2011, *A Labour History of Ireland*, p. 262.
97 Ferriter, 2005, *The Transformation of Ireland*, pp. 717–9.
98 See Neumann, 1966, *Behemoth*, p. 17.
99 Alpha Connelly and Kathleen Lynch, 1996, 'Equality before the Law' in *Report of the Constitution Review Group*. Dublin: Stationary Office, pp. 586–91, p. 590.
100 Constitution Review Group Report, p. 235; Rory O'Connell and Andrew Butler, 1998, 'Ireland's Constitutional Review Group Report' in *Irish Jurist*, 33, pp. 237–65, p. 254.

In Ireland, as elsewhere, the courts continued to play an important role in constitutional development. Reflecting global developments, the sites where the constitution could be contested, however, evolved considerably in the course of Ireland's neoliberal turn. Integration into the European Union, in particular, occasioned the emergence of supranational court structures where EU statutes and case-law would take precedence over national law. Irish jurists increasingly came to consider and defer to the decisions of neoformalist courts such as the European Court of Justice (ECJ) and the European Court of Human Rights (ECHR). Within these overlapping jurisdictions, law projects seeking to remove capital from the constraints of 'social liberalism' have occurred alongside projects seeking to remove society from the 'Catholic social' in terms of family law. In the course of these socio-legal conflicts, the Constitution, the Irish Supreme Court, and the ECHR emerged as popularly recognised sites of human rights contestation.

Judicial activism in the 1960s and 1970s prompted successive Irish governments to make conservative (as opposed to liberal) appointments to the bench, primarily in order to maintain a tough line on IRA paramilitaries through the Special Criminal Court. There were further repercussions. During the 1980s, conservative judges tended to preserve the 'Catholic social' constitution, notably maintaining the criminalisation of homosexuality. From the mid-1990s onwards, possibly in response to the very public contestation of the X-case ruling in 1993, the Supreme Court no longer proved particularly 'activist' regarding constitutional interpretation.[101] Strict, literal interpretations of the constitution, not unlike the emergent 'originalist' legal culture in the US, gained greater support. Campaigns for choice regarding abortion and for the decriminalisation of homosexuality thus pursued legal actions to the ECHR.[102]

In the 1990s and 2000s, subsequent 'human rights' conflicts – fought by or on behalf of Travellers, asylum seekers, the disabled, and the transgendered – involved a similar combination of claiming rights in the courts and civil society activism, supported by an increasingly professionalised network of human rights organisations. This wider experience of constitutional rights contestation was a key factor in the emergence of both a series of high-profile constitutional challenges

[101] In the early 1990s, the Supreme Court acknowledged a constitutional right to abortion in certain, strictly limited circumstances (X v. *Attorney General* [1993]).

[102] See '*Case of Norris* v. *Ireland* (Application no. 10581/83)'. ECHR, 26.10.1988. A, B, and C v. Ireland (Application no. 25579/05) [2010] ECHR 2032, 16,12.2010.

concerning state provision for citizens with special needs as well as a much wider civil society engagement with socio-economic rights discourse. In the ensuing case-law and wider civil society debates, international human rights standards and jurisprudence, notably jurisprudence in India and South Africa, played an important role in arguments concerning the elaboration of social and economic rights in the Irish constitution. Politically, liberal-market advocates, most memorably Progressive Democrat and Minister for Justice Michael McDowell, rejected the arguments of 'the self-proclaimed human rights community' on the grounds that socio-economic rights might hinder economic growth.[103]

## CONCLUSION

Albeit a contested process, the Republic of Ireland reproduced its semi-peripheral position within the world-system: 'national' forms of anti-systemic politics continued to take precedence over 'social' alternatives, and the population's welfare remained subordinate to the needs of stable, increasingly global capital flows. The nation-building project, however, was reimagined. From the 1960s onwards, political actors ceased to appeal to de Valera's vision of a Gaelic-speaking, unpartitioned Ireland, instead reimagining national development in terms of economic growth rates. As during earlier phases of capitalism in Ireland, privileged interest groups, notably financiers, large landowners, rentiers, and middle-men service providers, secured the lion's share of growth. The costs were borne by society in terms of comparatively lower living standards and non-solidaristic forms of welfare provision, including ongoing state reliance on religious institutions for industrial schools, asylums, and care. The key mechanisms for preserving this political system were the export of surplus labour through mass emigration, the co-option of organised labour, and the shoring up of successive governments' support through a combination of increased borrowing and clientelistic politics. The political and institutional makeup of the Irish welfare state did not lend itself to constitutionalising social and economic rights so much as increasing reliance on voluntary forms of provision.[104]

Over this period of pronounced transformation, the Irish Constitution came to embody a more distinctly American vision of liberal individual rights, maintaining the priorities of a classic liberal market in

103 McDowell, 2002, 'Speech to the Annual Conference of the Irish Social Policy Association'.

104 On similar forms of reliance in the United States, see Mary Ann Glendon, 1992, 'Rights in Twentieth-Century Constitutions' in *University of Chicago Law Review*, Vol. 59, pp. 519–38.

property and contract while liberating the individual from Catholic social norms in family law. Constitutional changes happening in Ireland occurred in strictly analogous ways in other jurisdictions. These included the relocation of social conflicts between tradition and modernity, in market and family law, to the judicial domain, the increased role of judicial review, the growing use of supra-national courts, and the increasing prominence of neoliberal forms of constitutionalism. The development of social and economic rights discourse, in the courts and on the streets, complemented this process. It too came to be liberated from the parameters and proponents of Catholic social thought. New ways of thinking relied on the global diffusion of secular human rights norms as well as the local reinvention of advocacy practices and institutions.

Still, the emergent socio-economic rights discourses represented a politically determined, ideological containment of shared values. Globally, there remains a strong coherence between the emergence of neoliberalism and the globalisation of human rights discourse, between the decline of traditional, collective forms of resistance to capital and the rise of public interest litigation. In Ireland, moreover, there remains a strong continuity between the residual Catholic social and today's dominant forms of human rights or social liberal advocacy, principally in terms of the persistence of consensual understandings of social order and the associated dismissal of conflict-premised, subaltern, or revolutionary ones. This is not to reject such rights and public interest litigation as normatively objectionable but merely to point out their development as a somewhat contradictory one.[105]

The foregoing, condensed account of Irish socio-constitutional transformation in the world-system requires more detailed unpacking. This work falls into a series of linked, interconnected hypotheses, opening new windows on the social phenomenon of constitutional change and the development of socio-economic rights. The overarching goal is to demonstrate the inter-linkages between the general world-systemic account presented here and the more particular development of socio-economic rights decisions and discourses advocated in the courts and

[105] Contemporary political culture in Ireland is probably less emancipated from the preconceptions of Catholic Nationalist thought than is commonly supposed. Arguably, the population demolished the old value-consensus only to rebuild a new one with more up-to-date materials. For an analogous argument regarding the surprisingly medieval Age of Enlightenment, see Karl Becker, 1936, *The Heavenly City of the Eighteenth-Century Philosophers*. New Haven: Yale University Press, pp. 30–31.

on the streets. Doing so will involve a critical discourse analysis of property, trade union and family-welfare constitutional rights case-law and jurisprudence, as well as of forms of protest and advocacy that invoked socio-economic rights outside the courtroom over the same period. We must begin however with an analysis of the development of the Irish state's formal legal institutions through which some citizens attempted to mobilise their constitutional rights and from which some others were excluded.

**CHAPTER FIVE**

# THE POLARITIES OF JUSTICE AND LEGAL BUSINESS

> *From 1961 onwards the Constitution became very much part of life and its impact could be felt among the ordinary people, who suddenly became conscious of the fact that they had a constitution, that it could be implemented and that, in fact, many parts of it were self-executing and did not require any supporting legislation. The consciousness of this suddenly burst upon the public and it just happened to be that, in the years commencing around about 1960–61, the court, for a variety of reasons, became very active. The most important reason was that it got the cases. The court is not self-starting and depends on cases. So it was a happy coincidence of the right cases coming along at a time when the court was most receptive to new ideas.*
>
> – Judge Brian Walsh, 1988[1]

> *For a case to come to court there must be a dispute and there are rarely disputes involving an unfortunate child being committed to residential care. If the child has no parent or legal guardian, there is no one to dispute what the State does; if there are parents, they usually consent or, if they do not consent, they are not concerned or, if they are concerned, they are not aware of their and their children's constitutional rights or they cannot afford a lawyer who will help them to legally enforce such rights . . .*
>
> – Michael O'Mahony, solicitor, 1971[2]

The legal-political positions that judges, barristers, and commentators took on socio-economic rights had definite histories; they were not simply choices between abstract, equally valid 'principles'.[3] Socio-economic rights discourses and decisions cannot be understood independent of the particular working conditions in which they were generated or, more generally, the wider social conditions to which they referred. Ireland's changing court structure, the specific field within which socio-economic rights cases were contested, registered and reproduced the transformation and antagonisms of the historical

[1] Cited in Sturgess and Chubb, 1988, *Judging the World*, p. 420.
[2] O'Mahony, 1971, 'Legal Aspects of Residential Child Care' in the *Irish Jurist*, 6 (1) pp. 217–36, p. 220.
[3] Heydebrand, 1977, 'Organizational Contradictions in Public Bureaucracies', p. 97.

capitalist world-system. In particular, the litigation explosion occasioned by capitalist modernisation in the 1960s and neoliberalisation from the 1980s onwards had important implications for the rationalised reconfiguration of legal professional activity or 'business'.

Ongoing contradictions within the court structure, functioning simultaneously as a site of business and justice, had at least three important, inter-related implications. First, judges faced mounting pressures between traditional adjudicatory norms and the demands of increased administrative rationalisation. This necessitated or, at least, facilitated their adoption of the new constitutionalism, neoformalism, and proportionality doctrines. Second, legal professionals faced conflicting pressures between traditional, 'guild' privileges and neoliberal, market logics. Constituting one rent-extracting veto group among many in Irish political economy, the lawyers organised successfully to defend the former norms of 'legal business'. Third, in this context, the associated widening gap between legal business and justice produced latent tendencies towards conflict over 'access to justice', in particular, contestation over the politically determined distribution of capacities to raise legal and constitutional rights claims. In these circumstances, people unable to 'access justice' occasionally took the law into their own hands.

In Ireland, as elsewhere, the trajectory of constitutional development was a product (of the temporary resolutions) of these related antagonisms and conflicts. From the 1960s onwards, as outlined in the previous chapter, the Irish judiciary newly interpreted the Constitution so as to expand individual rights jurisprudence, notably in terms of invidious discrimination, Catholic social family law, and due process in law enforcement and administrative procedure. The presence of legal aid and support structures, however, partly determined the Irish rights revolution, particularly the kinds of property, trade union, and family-welfare rights cases to be heard in the courts as well as those excluded. Moreover, judicial discourses and decisions in these constitutional cases, as we will see in subsequent chapters, were influenced by the globalising 'new constitutional' norms of neoformalism and proportionality. Perhaps most pointedly, in the course of socio-economic rights conflicts in the 1990s and 2000s, judges' opposition to constitutionalising socio-economic rights was based, at least in part, on concerns that the Irish courts would be unable to process the potentially overwhelming increase in constitutional caseloads. Given its centrality to the development of constitutional norms and socio-economic rights discourses then, the political economy of the Irish Courts demands detailed examination.

## COURT PERSONNEL, STRUCTURE, AND ACTIVITY

Courts, in essence, are 'heteronomous, public professional bureaucracies' where both resources and jurisdiction or domain are externally controlled but where the central work functions are directed and carried out by a professionalised work force, the judicial service.[4] Courts are, moreover, highly labour-intensive service organisations where service (or production) takes the form of a series of decisions based on the skilled labour-power of judicial professionals and non-judicial service employees. Crucially, unlike most service organisations, courts are central to the structure of public authority, to the stability of political economy, and to the legitimation of social order. Primarily then, the legitimacy of the judiciary depends on its formal independence from executive, legislative, or private interference, and on the social reception of its judgments. The courts in Ireland have performed and continue to perform these evolving functions with varying degrees of success.

Historically, as discussed earlier, the Irish legal system formed as part of a complex colonial social process. The courts possessed a repressive function as part of the state apparatus and a valorisation function as the common law secured property rights and commercial transactions. Geographically, this occasioned a centralised court apparatus with legal practice centred on the Four Courts and the Bar Library in Dublin and, in the countryside, on the regional bars associated with each of the judicial 'circuits'.[5] The late nineteenth-century Victorian reorganisation of the courts further crystallised the emergence of a rationalised legal professional hierarchy.

In the Irish Free State, after repressing the popularly organised courts network, the government reestablished the old courts on almost identical lines.[6] Lord Justice O'Connor had urged that judges be highly paid and, furthermore, surrounded by great ceremony 'as the populace are impressed by pomp and show of power'.[7] The government,

[4] Heydebrand, 1977, 'Organisational Contradictions in Public Bureaucracies', p. 96.

[5] See Hogan, 1986, *The Legal Profession in Ireland*, p. 42.

[6] The Courts of Justice Act (1924). A right of appeal to the Privy Council was also provided for in the Constitution of the Irish Free State until its abolition in 1933.

[7] Cited in Kotsonouris, 1994, *Retreat from Revolution*, p. 111. See Kennedy Papers, UCDA P4/1092 for suggestions on the new legal system.

however, predominantly reflected commercial interests in maximising economy – judges' salaries were pegged at half their British counterparts – in increasing administrative efficiency, and in retaining a centralised, Dublin-based court system, close to the collective wisdom of the Law Library.[8] 'Irishing' the courts aided their legitimation. Nationalist jurists such as Hugh Kennedy and Timothy O'Sullivan now received senior judicial posts; black Irish poplin replaced the formal red gown of the English magistrate; the harp replaced the royal coat of arms above the court bench and, throughout the 1920s, court officials crowded into classrooms to meet new requirements that all public officials be fluent in the Irish language.[9] The 1937 Irish Constitution similarly provided for the courts' continuity.[10]

Governments in the Irish Free State continued traditional requirements that appointees to the Supreme Court, the High Court, and the Circuit Court be practising barristers of at least ten years' standing; District Court appointees were to have practised for ten years as barristers or solicitors. Thereafter, candidate selection was left to the executive, historically dominated by one of the two intra-nationalist political parties. Having secured appointment until retirement, judges cannot be removed by government save for a little-used mechanism: the calling of a Joint-Oireachtas Committee inquiry into alleged misbehaviour.[11] In these circumstances, governments have tended to appoint their own supporters to judicial office.[12] The introduction of an 'independent' agency, the Judicial Appointments Advisory Board (JAAB), in the mid-1990s 'made very little difference to the political patronage system'.[13] Irish governments, as elsewhere, have tended to appoint

[8] Captain Redmond, *Dáil Debates*, Vol. 5, Col. 361, 12.10.1923. Kotsonouris, 1994, *Retreat from Revolution*, p. 100. See also Keane, 1996, 'The Voice of the Gael', p. 217.

[9] Keane, 1996, 'The Voice of the Gael', p. 223. Some traditions endured. Senior barristers continued to be styled as 'King's Counsel', judges continued to be addressed as 'my lord', and the Four Courts, rebuilt by the government, officially reopened on 1 October 1931.

[10] Delaney, 1975, *The Administration of Justice in Ireland*, pp. 1–38.

[11] The president of each court also investigates complaints received.

[12] Ireland is unusual insofar as the more common practice is for judicial appointments to secure cross-party agreement. Instead, the traditional practice of giving the Attorney General (appointed by the Taoiseach) 'first refusal' on a High or Supreme Court vacancy was deliberately continued. Alternatively, the names of would-be judges tended to reach the government by 'a secret process involving the taking of soundings, with political connections playing an important role'. Delany, 1975, *The Administration of Justice in Ireland*, p. 69. Gallagher, 2010, 'The Changing Constitution', p. 89.

[13] Anonymous superior court judge cited in Jennifer Carroll, 2005, 'You be the Judge: Part II – The Politics and Processes of Judicial Appointments in Ireland' in *Bar Review*, 10, 182 ff, p. 186. The political patronage system was widely criticised following Fianna Fáil Taoiseach Albert Reynolds's appointment of Harry Whelehan as President of the High Court despite

judges capable of demonstrating 'safe, sound, middle-of-the-road opinions' characterised by 'moderation and attachment to regime norms'.[14] Irish judges, as elsewhere, have been predominantly white, male, and economically privileged.[15]

At a more basic level than the particular nature or orientations of the personnel manning the courts, the inherited and continued legal structure organised social conflicts hierarchically according to their complexity of subject-matter and monetary value. At the lowest tier of the court structure, Irish state territory was arranged into two groups of twenty-three District Court jurisdictions for criminal and civil law. The court's criminal jurisdiction included road traffic offences, assault, larceny, and crimes committed by children younger than sixteen.[16] Its civil jurisdiction included determining contract and tort actions, ejectments for non-payment of rent, and the recovery of small debts. District courts were also responsible for liquor and dance-hall licensing. In terms of family law, it enforced maintenance awards to 'illegitimate' children and to deserted wives. In the postwar legal structure, the amount at stake in these cases was typically set at a maximum of £250.[17]

Next in the judicial hierarchy, the Circuit Court was organised on the basis of a division of state territory into approximately eight circuits – Cork, Dublin, Eastern, Midland, Northern, South-East, South-West, and Western Circuits – with one judge attached to each. The Circuit Courts' criminal jurisdiction was unlimited with the exception of cases of murder, treason, and offences listed in emergency powers legislation, notably membership of the IRA.[18] Its civil jurisdiction involved securing valorisation in a range of economic disputes, including contract,

accusations that he, as Attorney General, had delayed proceedings against a priest accused of sexual offences. The Fianna Fáil-Labour coalition government collapsed in the aftermath of this crisis and the Judicial Appointments Advisory Board (JAAB) was established by the following government. The JAAB, however, has no role in the appointment of the Chief Justice, President of the High Court, Circuit Court, or District Court, or in any promotion from a lower court; and the government is not obliged to select from its list of seven nominees, merely to consider it. Tanya Ward, 2007, *Justice Matters: Independence, Accountability and the Irish Judiciary*, Dublin: ICCL, p. 52. See also Dermot Feenan, 'Judicial Appointments in Ireland in Comparative Perspective' in *Judicial Studies Institute Journal*, 2008, Vol. (1), pp. 37–66, p. 48.

14 Jacob, Herbert, 1996, 'Conclusion' in Herbert Jacob, Erhard Blankenburg, Herbert M. Kritzer, Doris Marie Provine, and Joseph Sanders, *Courts, Law and Politics in Comparative Perspective*. London: Yale University Press, pp. 389–400, pp. 390–1. See also Gallagher, 2010, 'The Changing Constitution', p. 92.

15 The relationship between the judiciary's sociological profile and their decisions and discourses on socio-economic rights cases will be examined in Chapter 9.

16 Delaney, 1975, *The Administration of Justice in Ireland*, pp. 46–8.

17 Bartholemew, 1971, *The Irish Judiciary*, p. 11. Delaney, 1975, *The Administration of Justice in Ireland*, pp. 69–70.

18 Delaney, 1975, *The Administration of Justice in Ireland*, pp. 48–9.

tort, and equity actions, contested titles to land, probate of wills, ejectment actions, lease applications, and club licensing. The Circuit Court also heard appeals from the District Court. In these cases, the amounts at stake did not exceed £2,000.[19]

'Superior' Court hearings usually took place in Dublin's Four Courts. The High Court possessed full civil and criminal jurisdiction.[20] Civil cases tended to involve claims in excess of the Circuit Court's upper limit. High Court judges had the capacity to issue 'prerogative writs' – *habeas corpus*, *certiorari*, *mandamus*, and prohibition – to overturn any improper exercise of court jurisdiction or to compel administrative, governmental, or other bodies to carry out a duty imposed by law.[21] At the apex of the judicial hierarchy, the Supreme Court consisted of the Chief Justice and four ordinary judges. Its appellate jurisdiction included all matters commenced in the High Court.[22] Sitting together for all cases, three judges constituted a quorum.[23] Judges based their decision-making on the record created in the trial court, their being free to reach any conclusion the trial judge might reasonably have arrived at. The judges possessed the capacity to reverse those cases deemed to be erroneously decided and, in doing so, to affect lower court procedure by creating a precedent for future decision-making.[24] The power of judicial review further enabled the Supreme Court to declare any law, any official action based on a law, or any other action by a public official, to be in conflict with the constitution and hence invalid.[25]

In the latter decades of the twentieth century, Fianna Fáil and Fine Gael-led governments introduced and adhered to two forms of 'extraordinary' court structures. The first emerged during the 1970s, primarily in response to the escalating conflict in Northern Ireland and increase in paramilitary actions. A Fianna Fáil majority government established a juryless 'Special Criminal Court' (SCC) to try non-scheduled ('terrorist') offences or crimes.[26] Notwithstanding the de-escalation of conflict in the 1990s, successive governments retained the SCC and extended

19 Delaney, 1975, *The Administration of Justice in Ireland*, p. 67.
20 Byrne and McCutcheon, 2002, *The Irish Legal System*, p. 112.
21 Bartholemew, 1971, *The Irish Judiciary*, p. 14.
22 Bartholemew, 1971, *The Irish Judiciary*, p. 16.
23 Byrne and McCutcheon, 2002, *The Irish Legal System*, p. 110.
24 Bartholemew, 1971, *The Irish Judiciary*, p. 11.
25 The constitutionality of a bill can be considered before it has become law by a presidential referral of the bill to the Supreme Court. The provision for concrete review, however, has proved to be the main method by which the constitution has developed. Gallagher, 2010, 'The Changing Constitution', p. 84.
26 Ferriter, 2005, *The Transformation of Ireland*, pp. 691, 729.

its jurisdiction to include drug trafficking charges. The Irish Council of Civil Liberties, Amnesty Ireland, and the UN Human Rights Commission have criticised the enduring SCC as obsolete, citing in particular the increased role it accedes to the opinion of the Garda Chief-Superintendent as well as notable miscarriages of justice.[27]

Additionally, from the 1990s onwards, following journalists' exposure of a range of illegal 'middleman' practices, successive governments established tribunals of inquiry into all manner of allegations of corruption, including payments to politicians, planning decisions, the beef industry, the award of telecommunications licenses, and tax evasion.[28] In those tribunals investigating public office holders, the procedures were intended to be inquisitorial (informal, speedy, and inexpensive in comparison to the overstretched and costly regular courts). Key superior court cases, however, ensured the tribunals became adversarial (more formal, prolonged, and costly). Significantly, the Supreme Court justified these decisions in neoformalist terms, elaborating from the constitution certain heretofore unrecognised rights such as those to 'cabinet confidentiality' and 'a good name'.[29] Thereafter, distinct advantages accrued to those actors who could afford a better legal team while the lack of prosecutions called into question the efficacy of such tribunals in ensuring accountability.

This structure for sorting social conflicts facilitated the law's uneven operation between classes, specifically in terms of creating a controlled site of legal service production with legal fees (the rents charged by collectively organised professionals with monopoly privileges) mediating 'access to justice'. Formally, any citizen affected by a law (and so generating *locus standi*) could challenge its constitutionality before the High Court, with the possibility of appeal to the Supreme Court. In practice, capacities to access the courts or to claim constitutional rights remained unevenly distributed. Successive governments' decisions to alter this structure or court practice and procedure approximated a process of

[27] Carol Coulter, 'Continuation of special court is justified, says majority' in *Irish Times*, 30 May 2002.

[28] Elaine Byrne, 2012, *Political Corruption in Ireland, 1922–2010: A Crooked Harp?* Manchester: Manchester University Press.

[29] In 1999, counsel for Liam Lawlor (Fianna Fáil TD) successfully challenged the Flood Tribunal's practice of summoning witnesses to give sworn evidence in private sessions prior to the public phase; this practice ensured that the constitutional 'right to good name' was not encroached upon and reduced the opportunity for lawyers to become involved. The full truth uncovered in the Beef Tribunal could not emerge because a Supreme Court ruling on cabinet confidentiality decided the interest of government confidentiality took precedence. Frank Barry and John O'Dowd, 2001, 'The Age of Tribunals' in *Studies*, Vol. 90 (1), pp. 58–69, p. 58.

rationalisation, more closely resembling a response to the staggering quantitative and qualitative extension of the courts' activity than to citizens' expressed needs or wishes. These initial observations, however, require further unpacking.

## 'LEGAL BUSINESS'

> I was called to the Bar of Ireland in 1971. When I commenced practising I felt a sense of stepping into a timeless institution which had existed for centuries. I was frequently the only woman barrister in a busy court – no women were judges of the superior courts, nor were any registrars, and jurors were usually men. The Court heard cases as they came before them as presented by counsel. The Circuits went out, in many ways unchanged from the Assizes of previous centuries. I was in a world evocative of the 19th Century, in an institution preserved in time. I believe that those of us in practice 40 years ago hold a folk memory of courts which reflects the centuries from 1701. However, over the last few decades there have been great changes. Indeed, most of the changes have come in the last 20 years.
>
> – Chief Justice Susan Denham, 2010[30]

Legal activity, caseloads, and specialisation co-evolved with Ireland's development trajectory in the historical capitalist world-system.[31] In the immediate postwar period, as for much of the nineteenth century, the fortunes of the legal profession remained closely knit to 'the prosperity enjoyed by the agricultural community'.[32] From the 1960s onwards, however, there occurred both a remarkable increase in the quantity of cases coming before the Irish courts as well as a transformation in the nature of those cases, with their becoming more complex, specialised, and time-intensive. Foreign investment and economic transformation

[30] Judge Susan Denham, 2010, 'The 21st Century Judge'. *Oration to the Australasian Institute of Judicial Administration*, pp. 1–45, p. 2. Available at: www.aija.org.au/Orations/Oration10.pdf.

[31] This section summarises the courts' 'business' (the word used in the administrative reports) during the period 1937 to 2008. The tables and analysis provided here are based on court records contained in the *Statistical Abstracts of Ireland* and, for the period from 2000 onwards, in the *Courts Service Annual Reports*. Invariably, administrators do not report numbers with a concern for future researchers. The mode of data presentation changes across decades in terms of what and how aspects of the legal field are analysed. For some years, only estimates can be provided. The changes in categorisation are themselves revealing, indicative not just of changes in the legal field but also in the priorities of the categorisers. The Courts Service reports include analysis of the Supreme Court's workload and categorise family law cases separately, indicating the increasing relative importance of both. They also foreground cases' 'turnover time', indicative of objective field pressures as well as the neoliberal 'consumer service' imaginary.

[32] Gerald Harris, 1939, 'The War' in *Irish Jurist* 5 (4), p. 53.

created a demand for new legal activities in areas such as taxation law or company organisation and similarly stimulated demands for increased specialisation.[33] The legal profession also tended to benefit from speculative urbanisation processes: the rising number of property transactions and steep increases in property values raised incomes associated with conveyancing.[34]

Surveying this period of transformation, the statistical data makes clear that constitutional rights cases very much constituted a tiny, unrepresentative courtroom experience. In recent years, the Irish courts have processed some 800,000 cases annually. Of this total caseload, District Court cases tend to account for approximately 86 per cent, Circuit Court cases 7.9 per cent, and High Court cases 6 per cent. Supreme Court appeals make up approximately 0.01 per cent only.[35] Historically, constitutional and public law cases were relatively rare but increased annually, particularly from the 1980s onwards. John Kelly's 1980 edition of the *Irish Constitution* could cite only 480 cases for constitutional and public law matters in the history of the state. In his updated 1984 version, there were 650.[36] During the 2000s, the annual volume of cases before the Supreme Court rose from 415 appeals in 2002 to 466 in 2010 and chiefly comprised of common law or personal injury appeals as well as judicial review cases.

Since the 1937 Irish Constitution came into effect, the caseload before the courts has increased exponentially. Quantitatively, the volume of cases before the District Court tended to average at some 250,000 cases per annum up to the 1960s at which point it rose dramatically to approximately 650,000 in the 2000s. Similarly, the number of the Circuit Court cases rose from approximately 15,000 in the immediate postwar period to more than 50,000 in the 1990s and 2000s (Table 5.1). Records on the precise nature of activity at the upper courts are more intermittent. The business of the High Court, as measured proximately, similarly increased over the same period (Table 5.2). The total number of summonses issued rose from 4–6,000 in the immediate postwar years to more than 15,000 throughout the 1990s and 2000s. Institutional reconfiguration, specifically the introduction of a Personal

[33] Delany, 1975, *The Administration of Justice in Ireland*, p. 78.

[34] P. R. Kaim-Caudle, 1970, 'Productivity, Income and Standards of Solicitors in the Irish Republic' in *Irish Jurist* 5 (1), pp. 40–9, p. 48.

[35] The Superior Courts' work is more specialised, labour-intensive, and consequential in terms of setting precedents.

[36] Ferriter, 2005, *The Transformation of Ireland*, p. 731.

TABLE 5.1 Number of entries for hearing/cases in the District and Circuit Courts

| Court | 1940 | 1962 | 1972 | 1985 | 2000 | 2010 |
|---|---|---|---|---|---|---|
| Circuit | 14,749 | 21,067 | 30,306 | 46,691 | 55,081 | 55,831 |
| District | 214,007 | 253,730 | 414,477 | 862,597 | 643,141 | 689,650 |

TABLE 5.2 Business of the High Court in each legal year ended 31 July

| Business | 1940 | 1962 | 1973 | 1985 | 2000 | 2005 |
|---|---|---|---|---|---|---|
| High Court | | | | | | |
| Summonses issued | 3,954 | 3,153 | 4,787 | 13,451 | 15,550 | 6,362 |

*Sources: Statistical Abstracts of Ireland. Courts Services Annual Reports*

TABLE 5.3 Number of judges working in the Irish courts: 1924, 1970, and 2010

| Court | 1924 | 1970 | 2010 |
|---|---|---|---|
| District | 33 | President + 34 | President + 63 |
| Circuit | 8 | President + 9 | President +37 |
| High | 6 | President + 6 | President + 36 |
| Supreme | 3 | CJ + 4 | CJ + 7 |
| | 49 | 57 | 147 |

*Source: Consolidated Courts and Court Officers Acts*

Injuries Assessment Board, accounts for subsequent recorded decreases. This increasing workload occasioned an analogous growth in the number of judges (Table 5.3).

Qualitatively, in recent years, the majority of District Court cases, approximately 70 per cent, have concerned 'criminal business' or summary-indictable offences, mainly road traffic and public order offences.[37] The remaining 30 per cent divides somewhat evenly

[37] Approximately 60 per cent of these concerned road traffic offences; some 20 per cent involved breach of bail, littering, street trading, and offences prosecuted by government agencies; the remainder concerned public order or assault (c. 12 per cent), theft (c. 6 per cent), illegal drugs

between licensing applications and civil proceedings, the latter concerning the securing of property rights as well as family law conflicts centred on maintenance, guardianship, custody, domestic violence, and childcare.[38] At the Circuit Court, the majority of cases, some 80 per cent, concerned civil or family business; criminal business accounted for the remainder. During the 1970s and 1980s, the Circuit Court's civil caseload consisted primarily of 'ordinary civil bills and transferred actions' (c. 60 per cent), 'equity' (c. 12.5 per cent), 'malicious injuries' (c. 20 per cent), and 'ejectments' (c. 5 per cent). During the 1990s and early 2000s, 'civil trials' and 'motions' accounted for the vast majority of civil proceedings (c. 84 per cent). Over the same period, following the legalisation of divorce, family law business, especially judicial separations and divorce, doubled (from 8 per cent to 17 per cent).

At the High Court, legal conflicts are sorted according to specialised court offices – Central, Wardship, Probate, and Examiner's – and a series of increasingly specialised court lists (Box 5.1). The majority of High Court summonses were plenary, the majority of these consisting of personal injury claims (some 70 per cent). Judicial review cases also featured prominently, more than half of which concerned asylum and immigration applications. The effective doubling of judicial review cases in the 2000s further owed to the High Court's increasingly being used to review decisions taken by the District Court as well as by new independent regulators. This latter phenomenon follows the increasing agencification of the Irish state bureaucracy which has tended to blur traditional lines of ministerial responsibility for public and welfare service provision.[39]

The increasing value of legal activity registered in the manner in which the courts' monetary jurisdiction augmented significantly. While the District Court's jurisdiction in civil actions ceased with claims in excess of £250 in the 1970s, this figure was €6,350 in the 2010s. Similarly, the Circuit Court's civil jurisdiction was limited to £2,000 in the 1970s; this limit stands at €38,000 in the 2010s. Again, there continued

(c. 2.5 per cent), and sexual offences (c. 0.2 per cent). Percentages are approximate and based on an analysis of the 2000, 2005, and 2010 Court Service reports.

38 The total number of such cases rose from 52,746 in 1972 to 127,596 in 1996, declining to 81,117 in 2005 before rising again to 112,048 in 2010. Family law cases typically involved maintenance, guardianship, custody, domestic violence, and childcare issues; in the 2000s, these approximated some 23,000 cases annually, a quarter of all civil proceedings.

39 Muiris MacCarthaigh, 'Politics, policy preferences and the evolution of Irish bureaucracy: A framework for analysis' in *Irish Political Studies* (2012), Vol. 27 (1), pp. 23–47. See also Owen Hughes, 2012, *Public Management and Administration*. London: Palgrave.

**Box 5.1 Specialist Lists in the High Court, 2010**

| | | |
|---|---|---|
| Admiralty | Examiner's Court List | Non Jury List |
| Asylum | Extradition | Nursing Council |
| Bail | Family Law | Personal Injuries (Dublin) |
| Bankruptcy | Garda Compensation | Personal Injuries (Provincial) |
| Chancery | Hague – Luxembourg Convention | Probate List |
| Chancery Summonses | Hepatitis C | Proceeds of Crime Act |
| Circuit Appeals (Dublin) | Judicial Review | Provincial – High Court Personal Injuries |
| Commercial | Jury List | Rulings |
| Common Law Motions | Land Registry | Section 150 Companies Act |
| Competition | Master's List | Solicitors Act |
| Dental Council | Medical Council | Taxing Master's List |
| European Arrest Warrants | | Wards of Court |

*Source: Courts Service Reports*[40]

TABLE 5.4 Business of the High Court in each legal year ended 31 July

| High Court | 1940 | 1952 | 1962 | 1973 | 1985 | 2000 | 2005 |
|---|---|---|---|---|---|---|---|
| Total amount recovered by verdicts £ 000 | 121 | 277 | 790 | 3,497 | –* | –* | –* |

* Not recorded.

to be no limit to how much money could be awarded by the High Court in compensation or damages and these awards increased exponentially. The total amount recovered by judges' verdicts escalated quickly in the 1960s and 1970s (Table 5.4). The escalating value of legal activity at the High Court may be gauged from the rising legal costs allowed by the Office of the Taxing Master (Table 5.5).[41] Moreover, since the

[40] See also Denham, 2010, 'The 21st Century Judge', p. 17.
[41] Legal costs incurred are a function of what barristers' deem a case to be worth to their client. Delany, 1975, *The Administration of Justice in Ireland*, p. 87.

TABLE 5.5 Business of the High Court in each legal year ended 31 July

| Taxing Office | 1940 | 1962 | 1973 | 1980* | 2000 | 2010 |
|---|---|---|---|---|---|---|
| Costs claimed £000 | 246 | 320 | 600 | 1,259 | 23,433<br>€29,753 | €66,675 |
| Costs allowed £000 | 222 | 260 | 468 | 998 | 19,010<br>€24,138 | €45,658 |

*Sources*: *Statistical Abstracts of Ireland*. *Courts Service Annual Reports*.
* Data not available for 1990s.

TABLE 5.6 Judicial salaries

| COURT | 1924 | 1962 | 1975 | 1990 | 2001 | 2011 |
|---|---|---|---|---|---|---|
| Supreme Court | £3,000 | £4,500 | £11,999 | £62,274 | £115,227<br>€146,320 | €270,000 |
| High Court | £2,500 | £4,000 | £10,419 | £57,498 | £106,107<br>€134,739 | €234,000 |
| Circuit Court | £1,700 | £3,250 | £ 8,652 | £45,825 | £83,500<br>€106,031 | €175,000 |
| District Court | £1,000 | £2,250 | £6,757 | £38,397 | £69,368<br>€88,086 | €120,000 |

*Sources*: Byrne and McCutcheon, *The Irish Legal System* (5th edition), 174. European Commission for the Efficiency of Justice (CEPEJ) report 2012.

inherited juridical structure presupposed that senior appointments would be made exclusively from the practising bar, payment levels to judges also tended to increase accordingly. Irish judicial salaries, as of 2011, were among the highest in the world (Table 5.6).

These developments had important implications. Within the established legal structure, the increasing volume, complexity, value, and cost of legal activities created significant tensions or points of conflict. The increasingly time-intensive nature of progressing legal cases through existing courts occasioned institutional reconfiguration and administrative rationalisation ('case management'). These processes of rationalisation have in turn compelled legal professional status groups to negotiate 'reforms' so as to defend traditional adjudicatory norms from administrative encroachment and to maintain traditional monopoly privileges in the provision of legal services. These tensions polarise the courts as sites of 'legal business' and of 'justice' in important ways. Market rationalisation and legal professional rentier practices constrained 'access to justice' and, with important implications for socio-economic rights contests, the range of possible interpretation in judicial constitution-making.

## THE CONTRADICTIONS OF JUSTICE AND LEGAL BUSINESS

The 'ever-rising tide of litigation which our increasingly complex society produces' occasioned the rationalisation of the legal structure.[42] In addition to the development of specialised court lists such as those outlined earlier, successive governments established specialised sub-units or agencies outside the regular courts system to process with greater efficiency employment appeals and personal injury cases. In this regard, the establishment of the Irish Courts Service (ICS) in 1999 was particularly significant. It was tasked with managing the courts, providing support services for judges, maintaining court buildings, providing facilities to court users, and providing information on the courts system to the public.

This independent corporation's deeper significance lay in its corporate managerial emphasis on achieving 'efficiencies', extending to the 'turnover time' of cases, and vision of serving 'consumers' of the courts' services. While the Minister for Justice hailed the ICS as 'the jewel in the crown of public administration' and Chief Justice John Murray praised it as the 'greatest revolution in the administration of justice in this country since independence',[43] Ken Murphy, the director-general of the Law Society, was nearer the mark in emphasising the benefits of a quicker turnover to clients and counsel: 'We just want the damn thing to work and move quickly – produce results – because as far as lawyers are concerned, we make money on the turnover of cases so we need to have the cases in the system moving, the lists moving, and access to justice'.[44]

[42] Ken Murphy, 'Secondment of judges to tribunals disrupts justice system, causes delay' in *Irish Times*, 15 February 2002.

[43] Denham, 2010, 'The 21st Century Judge', p. 29.

[44] Cristin Schmitz, 2009, 'Chief justices want to run their courts: Ireland cited as model for Canadian reform' in *The Lawyer's Weekly*, 4 September 2009 issue. Available at: www.lawyersweekly.ca/index.php?section=article&articleid=991.

The judge's role has been transformed in the process. In the traditional, *laissez-faire* approach, judges sat and heard counsel for the parties run their cases as they thought appropriate. Progressing cases in this manner, however, became increasingly time-intensive. From the mid-1990s onwards, the Irish judiciary introduced 'case management' techniques – e-filing, written (not oral) submission, and call-over lists – which aimed to reduce the expense and delay involved in litigation. The state has, in particular, developed very strict rules of case management for the Commercial Court, with the result that most cases are completed within eight weeks.[45] On occasions of public accolade such as appointment, retirement, or death, a High Court judge is now as likely to be praised for being a good administrator as for having the proverbial fine legal mind.

Judges would appear to have responded to the rapidly escalating tide of litigation before the Superior Courts by raising the bar for judicial intervention higher. In this regard, the judicial review of planning decisions has been criticised as overly deferential and based on fears that the courts would become a 'last-chance saloon' for objectors to planning decisions. Similarly, the judicial review of ministerial deportation orders prioritised the 'rather abstract objective of preserving the integrity of the asylum system' ahead of the unambiguously protected constitutional family rights enjoyed by Irish-born children of asylum-seekers.[46] There are grounds for thinking that the Irish courts did not recognise socio-economic rights, at least in part, for fear of creating insurmountable caseloads such that the existing legal system would be 'overwhelmed'.[47] Moreover, in conditions where institutional (in)capacity to process increasing caseloads remains subject to politically determined resource constraints, proportionality doctrine emerges in these cases as a suitable mode of justification for these judgments, a necessary legal-cultural 'fix' to reconcile the disjuncture between justice and legal business.

The second source of tension involved in rationalisation concerned the sheltering of legal professionals from 'market forces'. Traditionally, the profession was divided into two 'branches': solicitors and

45 Denham, 2010, 'The 21st Century Judge', p. 19.

46 On planning, see *O'Keefe* v. *An Bord Pleanála* [1993] 1 IR 39; *P&F Sharpe* v. *Dublin City and County Manager* [1989] IR 701. On asylum, see *Lobe and Osayende* v. *Minister for Justice* [2003] 1 IR 1. Niall Buckley, 2004, 'Merging Principles of Public Law: Towards Proportionality in an Irish Context', *Irish Jurist*, 39, pp. 161–214, pp. 199, 211–2.

47 Gerard Hogan, 2001, 'Directive Principles, Socio-Economic Rights and the Constitution' in *Irish Jurist*, 36 (2), pp. 293–320, p. 318.

barristers.[48] Solicitors performed less skilled legal work, held a state-guaranteed monopoly in the preparation of property deeds, and typically carried out clients' commercial matters in probate, in the making of wills and in preparing cases for litigation. Barristers' day-to-day business consisted of title work, such as the drafting of companies' memoranda and articles of association, and clients' litigation. Importantly, they possessed a monopoly right of audience in the higher courts and specialised in advocacy. Thus, while solicitors were busily engaged in interviewing clients and interacting with state and commercial bodies, barristers had 'time to engage in difficult legal problem solving'.[49]

Professional bodies such as the Incorporated Law Society and Bar Council regulated the quality and quantity of competent legal technicians and, by extension, the cost of legal services. Accompanying economic modernisation and the expansion of legal business, the number of solicitors rose from approximately 1,300 in the 1970s to some 7,500 in 2010;[50] the number of barristers rose from 200 in 1965 to some 2,300 in 2011.[51] While solicitors' costs tended to be regulated by statute, barristers' fees were not. As illustrated earlier, the level of barristers' costs claimed and allowed in the High Court rapidly escalated from the 1960s onwards, particularly during the boom years of the 1990s. Several institutionalised or traditional practices inhibited competition and generated 'above equilibrium' prices: clients had to approach barristers through solicitors, legal fees were frequently not agreed (or discussed) in advance, and fees were frequently set up by a professional body-government partnership. Or as one barrister said of the Cork Circuit in the 1990s: '[It is] hugely lucrative because it's so well sewn up'.[52]

However, the rising cost of legal services generated market-led opposition to traditional privileges. From the mid-1960s onwards successive Ministers for Justice raised the possibility of lowering the cost of legal services by fusing the two branches of the profession. As the Third Programme of Economic and Social Development (1969–72) observed,

48 Hogan, 1986, *The Legal Profession in Ireland*, p. 118.

49 Ronan Keane, 1965, 'The Future of the Irish Bar' in *Studies*, Vol. 54 (216), pp. 375–84.

50 Kaim-Caudle, 1970, 'Productivity, Income and Standards of Solicitors in the Irish Republic', p. 48. Carol Coulter, 'Law Society dismisses Competition Authority proposals' in *Irish Times*, 22 July 2005.

51 Keane, 1965, 'The Future of the Irish Bar', p. 384, n. 1. 2010 figure from www.lawlibrary.ie/viewdoc.asp?DocID=6.

52 Barry and O'Dowd, 2001, 'The Age of Tribunals', p. 62.

'[I]t would clearly be unfair to expose some sectors of our society to competitive market forces, while others [legal, auctioneering and architectural] retained positions of immunity or privilege'.[53] Government-commissioned reports by Indecon (2003) and the Competition Authority (2005) recommended the opening-up of the legal professions to competition. The formation of limited companies and allowing clients' direct access to barristers, they suggested, would increase efficiency and reduce legal fees.[54] Before the economic crisis of 2008, the Law Society and Bar Council, both well-connected lobby groups, countered such proposals successfully.

The third major tension was referenced by Judge Brian Walsh upon his retirement in the early 1990s. Commenting in the wake of the Concerned Parents against Drugs movement in Dublin, he claimed that rising legal fees was problematic because it placed 'access to justice' out of reach for families and communities, to the point that many might even 'take the law into their own hands'. Beyond the cost of legal fees, however, is the question of their necessity in the first instance. For the lay person to enter the legal field, she must be reduced to the status of client and abandon tacitly the direction of her conflict to a legal professional.[55] This monetary relationship introduces a recurring tension between the pursuit of justice and the pursuit of law as a private, business interest.

On the one hand, advantages in legal conflicts accrued to 'repeat players' (such as the state or insurance companies) over 'one-shotters' and, in particular, to those who could afford to spend more.[56] '[I]n general, the well-off have the best lawyers (as they do the best doctors, dentists, teachers and no doubt candle-stick makers)'.[57] In the course of the Laffoy tribunal into clerical abuse, for example, survivors could afford less legal representation than those religious orders accused of abuse.[58] On the other hand, innumerable cases were not taken to the Irish or European courts for lack of capacity to pay for legal advice and

[53] Chapter 10, paragraph 4; 1969, *Third Programme of Economic and Social Development* (1969–72). Dublin, State Papers Office.
[54] Carol Coulter, 'Report urges opening up of solicitor's profession' in *Irish Times*, 21 March 2003.
[55] Bourdieu, 1987, 'The Force of Law', pp. 828, 834.
[56] The classic study of this phenomenon is Marc Galanter, 1974, 'Why the "Haves" Come Out Ahead: Speculations on the Limits of Legal Change' in *Law and Society Review*, Vol. 9, No. 1, pp. 95–160.
[57] D. G. Morgan, 2002, 'Review: Whyte, Social Inclusion and the Legal System' in *Irish Jurist*, 37 (1), pp. 344–48, p. 346.
[58] Ferriter, 2005, *The Transformation of Ireland*, p. 739.

assistance.[59] Increasingly, from the 1970s onwards, this tension between justice and business manifested as a more explicit conflict between those seeking 'access to justice' and those in government responsible for the courts' funding. The course of that conflict shaped the nature of Ireland's 'rights revolution' generally and socio-economic rights jurisprudence in particular.

## ACCESS TO JUSTICE AND THE IRISH 'RIGHTS REVOLUTION'

Accounting for the presence or absence of 'rights revolutions' in the US, Canada, England, and India, the comparative political scientist Charles Epp has suggested that in conditions where the judicial process is costly, slow, and incremental, the key factor is the presence of 'support structures', organisations, lawyers, and money facilitating 'the process by which individuals make claims about their legal rights and pursue lawsuits to defend or develop those rights'.[60] Hence, in Canada, government funding for legal aid, including test-case litigation, facilitated rights advocacy organisations in expanding the range of individual rights, notably encompassing women's rights and criminal procedure. In England, lacking equivalent financial resources to their Canadian counterparts, advocacy organisations brought about a modest rights revolution in areas such as administrative procedure and sex discrimination but not criminal procedure. Conversely, in India, notwithstanding a sympathetic judiciary, women's advocacy organisations were poorly funded and unable to pursue a sustained litigation campaign: 'little happened' as a result.[61]

In Ireland, similarly, changing constitutional rights owed vitally both to citizens taking new rights claims to court and to supportive networks of barristers and civil society groups.[62] However, legal or constitutional 'support structures' have mirrored the state's wider welfare effort and centred on poorly financed, voluntary labour. Traditionally,

[59] Desmond Greer, 1969, 'Legal Services and the Poor in Ireland' in *Irish Jurist*, 4 (2), pp. 270–92, p. 271.

[60] Epp, 1998, *Rights Revolution*, p. 18.

[61] Epp, 1998, *Rights Revolution*, p. 71.

[62] See Sturgess and Chubb, 1988, *Judging the World*, p. 420. As barrister Patrick McEntee put it: '. . . we often tend to overlook and underestimate the passion for justice which people have. If the Oireachtas becomes blunt and will not legislate – and will not even debate imaginatively in committee – the passion for justice breaks out somewhere else. It is unavoidable. It is not a question of the courts having an appetite – it is forced upon them by the passion for justice of people'. Gerard Hogan, Donal Barrington, and Patrick McEntee, 1985, 'The Constitution, Law and Ideology' in *Crane Bag*, Vol. 9 (1), pp. 104–9, p. 107.

both branches of the legal profession recognised what came to be known as an 'access to justice' problem. While a nineteenth-century 'pauper's procedure' remained on the statute books, it was a dead letter and almost never invoked. Barristers and solicitors occasionally advised impecunious persons free of charge out of a shared professional sense of charity, duty, or propriety. Trade unions provided their members with free legal assistance in employment conflicts such as compensation claims for personal injuries or wrongful dismissal. In Dublin, the Catholic charity, St. Vincent de Paul, also provided free civil and criminal legal aid.[63]

The early 1970s occasioned a secular, NGO turn in voluntary legal provision and public interest litigation. Law students in Cork and Dublin established heavily oversubscribed Free Legal Aid Clinics (FLAC), whose work typically concerned employment rights, tenant rights, social welfare law, and family law.[64] FLAC established community law centres in Dublin's Coolock and Ballymun, and, by the 1990s, had further developed increasingly specialised law centres to meet the complex legal needs of asylum seekers, immigrants, and the disabled as well as Travellers.[65] FLAC along with organisations such as the Irish Council for Civil Liberties, the Immigrant Council of Ireland, Irish Refugee Council, Irish Traveller Movement Legal Unit, and Disability Legal Resource have been central to public interest litigation cases in both domestic and international courts.[66] These groups' funding for such actions or wider legal education remained 'insecure or inadequate'.[67]

Over the same period, in Ireland as elsewhere, a more explicitly political conflict arose between those seeking 'access to justice', notably led by FLAC, and those in successive Fianna Fáil- or Fine Gael-led governments responsible for the courts' funding. The Free Legal Aid movement combined public campaigning and demonstrations with public interest litigation. Victory at the European Court of Human Rights finally compelled the state to introduce a Legal Aid scheme in 1980.[68]

63 Greer, 1969, 'Legal Services and the Poor', p. 272.
64 Padraig O'Morain, 2003, *Access to Justice For All: The History of the Free Legal Advice Centres, 1969–1973*. Dublin: FLAC, p. 10.
65 O'Morain, 2003, *Access to Justice For All*, pp. 31, 33–5.
66 In terms of its public interest litigation, FLAC successfully challenged the Department of Social Welfare's retaining of fuel vouchers and welfare arrears. After the latter case at the ECHR, some 70,000 women received back payments totalling more than €350m. O'Morain, 2003, *Access to Justice For All*, p. 13.
67 FLAC, 2006, *Public Interest Law in Ireland*, p. 23.
68 See *Airey v. Ireland* (application No. 6289/73), 1979, ECHR.

Again, indicative of wider forms of welfare effort, the Irish state provided the minimum funding necessary to meet the critical ECHR judgment and further imposed a severe means test on applicants. Class actions and test cases were both excluded from the scheme. By the 2000s, the civil legal aid system continued to be confined almost exclusively to family law cases and strictly underresourced, prompting delays of up to a year throughout the 2000s. Generally, there is no legal aid to fund litigation through the international courts while in the exceptional case of the ECHR legal aid 'would just about pay for a train fare to Strasbourg'.[69]

The level of public interest litigation in Ireland is significantly lower than in neighbouring jurisdictions such as Northern Ireland or England and Wales where legal aid is available for such cases.[70] In 2003 and 2004, for example, only 33 written judgments from the High and Supreme Courts involved public interest litigation, just 3.5 per cent of the total. The casework included immigration law (14 cases), public health services (4), prisons (3), Traveller accommodation (3), and education (1) among others.[71] Such public interest litigation as has occurred in Ireland has tended to be effective in expanding criminal legal aid, removing bureaucratic anomalies and invidious discrimination, as well as protecting the procedural rights of welfare claimants. Public interest litigation, however, has not improved access to welfare income 'in any significant way'.[72]

In these conditions, the history of constitutional rights contestation is predominantly the history of those who could afford to take such cases, notably property-owners, private companies, and well-funded civil society organisations. There were notable, 'piecemeal, unplanned, even haphazard' exceptions to this rule. Many seminal elaborations of individual constitutional rights owed to the *pro bono* work of barristers such as Seán McBride, Tom Connolly, or Mary Robinson. These cases include *Doyle* v. *Minister for Education* (1953), *Ryan* v. *Attorney General* (1965), McGee v. *Attorney General* (1973), *Aireyv. Ireland* (1979), and

[69] Michael Farrell, 'Using Law and Litigation in the Public Interest' in FLAC, 2006, *Public Interest Law in Ireland*, pp. 131–4, p. 132.

[70] FLAC, 2006, *Public Interest Law in Ireland*, p. 21.

[71] FLAC, 2006, *Public Interest Law in Ireland*, pp. 42–3. Anti-discrimination legislation is particularly prominent in this regard. See Judy Walsh, 'Equality, the Legal System and Employment Law' in John Baker, Kathleen Lynch, Sara Cantillon, and Judy Walsh, 2009, *Equality: From Theory to Action*. London: Palgrave, pp. 118–39.

[72] Whyte, 2002, *Social Inclusion and the Legal System*, p. 176. See also pp. 210, 244, and 264.

*Norris* v. *Ireland* (1988) as well as more recent socio-economic rights cases, including those concerning Traveller accommodation as well as educational provision for the disabled.[73]

## CONCLUSION

The state's provision of legal services to working people, FLAC's Pádraig Ó'Moráin remarked, contrasted sharply with its paying the legal costs of parties represented at Tribunals of Inquiry, even those who were subsequently found guilty of lying and obstruction.[74] This cutting observation speaks to the profound inequalities that have characterised the Irish courts' and constitution's functioning in the years since the making of Bunreacht na hÉireann. At the root of such inequalities, the law's mediation by monetised social relationships underpinned the uneven distribution of capacities to raise legal claims and polarised the courts as sites of justice and legal business. The increasing volume, complexity, value, and cost of legal activities, associated with market liberalisation from the 1960s onwards and, in particular, with neoliberalisation from the late 1980s, generated significant tensions or friction with the inherited court structure.

Legal professional status groups such as the Bar Council and Law Society, however, maintained monopoly privileges in legal service provision throughout the 1937 Constitution's existence.[75] The increasingly time-intensive (and therefore costly) nature of progressing legal cases through existing courts occasioned the introduction of the Irish Courts Service, institutional reconfiguration as well as administrative rationalisation in decision-making ('case management'). Tensions also arose between traditional adjudicatory and executive-administrative

[73] Farrell, 'Using Law and Litigation in the Public Interest', p. 133.

[74] O'Morain, 2003, *Access to Justice For All*, p. 24. On Irish law's deference to white collar crime, see Joe McGrath, 2015, *Corporate and white-collar crime in Ireland*, Manchester: Manchester University Press.

[75] See Alan Shatter, 'Barristers' anti-competitive practices remain an issue' in *Irish Times*, 30 November 2015. Notably, the 'troika' (the European Commission, the European Central Bank, and the International Monetary Fund) included the reduction of Irish legal costs as a condition of Ireland's 2010 'bail-out' programme. Five years later, and twenty-five years after the Fair Trade Commission recommended an end to such privileges, the Bar Council and Law Society maintains self-regulation in key areas, preventing multidisciplinary law practices and lower legal fees. The Bar Council's motto, *Nolumnus Mutari* (We Shall Not Be Changed), remains as fitting as ever.

modes of decision, only to be resolved through a temporary cultural fix, the 'proportionality' doctrine that has featured centrally in the growth of the new constitutionalism. These reconfigurations are central to understanding judges' changing decision-making and discourses in the socio-economic rights cases examined in the following chapters.

**CHAPTER SIX**

# CONTESTING PROPERTY RIGHTS

*[T]he days of* laissez-faire *are at an end.*

– Judge Hanna, 1939[1]

*At the end of the day the Supreme Court will take the holy document of our Constitution and say that notwithstanding that clause which talks about the exigencies of the common good and all the lovely, flowery Articles that talk about the rights of people, notwithstanding that remarkable Preamble that proclaims us to be a Christian nation, when the chips are down, we have no choice because 'private property rights rule OK'.*

– Ruairí Quinn, Labour TD, 1982[2]

In 1983, Ronan Keane introduced his analysis of 'land use, compensation and the community' with the example of the property speculator who buys a farm of 100 acres close to a city, paying the prevailing price for agricultural land (£2,500 an acre) or £250,000. Subsequently, the planning authority alters the agricultural zoning of the farm to residential and extends water and sewerage services to the area, costing the public some £1.5 million. The speculator applies for and is granted planning permission before quickly selling the land to a building consortium for £5 million. When the revenue commissioners try to recover some of the profit (approximately £4.5 million) in capital gains tax, they find themselves 'defeated by a maze of interlocking overseas trusts and companies situated in various sunny tax havens' and left to recover some of the public's investment by attaching to the permission a condition requiring the developer to contribute to the cost of the services.[3] Sixty years after Clement France argued for a constitutional provision to capture it, the 'unearned increment' continued to prove elusive.

The development of property rights contestations in Ireland – those highly specific instances where participants in a conflict had recourse

[1] *Pigs Marketing Board* v. *Donnelly* [1939] IR pp. 413, 417–8.

[2] Ruairi Quinn, 'Housing (Private Rented Dwellings) Bill, 1982: Second Stage' in *Dáil Debates*, Vol. 333 No. 6, 1136. 31 March 1982.

[3] Ronan Keane, 1983, 'Land Use, Compensation and the Community' in *Irish Jurist*, 18 (1), pp. 23–33, p. 23.

to the 1937 Constitution's property provisions – cannot be understood in isolation from Ireland's semi-peripheral political economy. Systemic advantages, such as those France highlighted, accrued to propertied (specifically land-owning) and banking interests. The Irish Free State broadly reproduced classic, *laissez-faire* ground rules while successive governments intervened in the market for land and housing through the Irish Land Commission, the provision of social housing, as well as various taxation and rent restriction measures.[4] From the 1970s onwards, however, as urbanisation and neoliberalism gathered pace, government-sponsored privatisation of housing provision and expansion of the mortgage market occasioned periodic boom-bust cycles in property prices.[5] Land values in Ireland rose throughout the late twentieth century, from €2,000 per hectare in the early 1970s to €10,000 in the late 1990s, before escalating rapidly to some €58,000 per hectare prior to the 2007–8 crash.[6] Politically, the established class of landowners and financiers was now joined by a nouveau riche cohort of middlemen, primarily property speculators but also political office-holders responsible for housing policy and land rezoning.

While generally protected by successive Fianna Fáil- or Fine Gael-led governments, property-owners sometimes looked to the 1937 Constitution to contest the state's 'social' incursions on perceived 'classic' market rights of property and contract. In these circumstances, the history of the constitution's property rights provisions is primarily a history of actions taken by landlords, landowners, semi-state companies, and financial institutions against the state and its subordinate agencies. By invoking these provisions, actors typically sought to challenge the state's taxation policies as well as its regulation of markets for credit, housing, and land. In the process of translation that taking a constitutional case compelled, these conflicts all came to be directed towards changing specific legislation with the aim of securing remedies for *arbitrary* discrimination, towards rectifying purely formal inequalities

4 The credit system ensured small farmers lacked sufficient capital for adaptation. By the 1970s, land ownership was once again as concentrated as prior to the establishment of the Land Commission. See Dooley, 2004, *The Land for the People*.

5 Spectacular upsurges in commercial and residential property prices occurred on no less than five occasions from the 1970s onwards. McCabe, 2011, *Sins of the Father*, pp. 33–7, 50–1.

6 For rising land values see www.finfacts.ie/irishfinancenews/article_1015968.shtml. On office block booms, see Andrew MacLaran, Katia Attuyer, and Brendan Williams, 2010, 'Changing office location patterns and their importance in the peripheral expansion of the Dublin region 1960–2008' in *Journal of Irish Urban Studies*, Volumes 7–9, pp. 53–78, p. 55. See also Crotty, 1986, *Ireland in Crisis*.

**Box 6.1 Property Rights Cases**

*Pigs Marketing Board* v. *Donnelly* [1939] IR 413
*Fisher* v. *Irish Land Commission* [1948] IR 3
*Foley* v. *Irish Land Commission* [1952] IR 118
*Attorney General* v. *Southern Industrial Trust* [1960] 94 ILTR 161
*Central Dublin Development Association* v. *Attorney General* [1975] 109 ILTR 69
*Blake* v. *Attorney General* [1982] IR 117
*PMPS Ltd and Joseph Moore* v. *Attorney General* [1983] IR 339
*Jorg Dreher* v. *Irish Land Commission* [1984] ILRM 904
*Brennan* v. *Attorney General* [1984] ILRM 355
*Madigan* v. *Attorney General* [1986] ILRM 136
*Iarnród Éireann* v. *Ireland* [1996] 3 IR 321
Re: Article 26 and Part V of the Planning and Development Bill (1999)[2000] 2 IR 321

rather than substantive social inequalities. Rights claimants characteristically argued that the legislation affecting ownership was procedurally unfair and hence amounted to 'an unjust attack', emphasising the right to property of the human person (Article 40.3) over those which could be restricted on the basis of social justice or the common good (Article 43).

In the selection of seminal cases examined here (Box 6.1), judges generally deferred to parliamentary authority and denied the courts a 'policy-making' role. There were, however, some important exceptions. In the wider property rights jurisprudence examined here, jurists increasingly recognised the possibility of the property rights provisions being used to impede 'social' interventions in the market and, in particular, the market for land. The judges confirmed this possibility by striking down rent restrictions in *Blake* v. *Attorney General* [1982] and land taxation measures in *Brennan* v. *Attorney General* [1984]. Thereafter, legal commentators documented the role that the perceived constitutional protection of property rights played in securing the planning process for private interests.

The property rights discourses in these cases register a wider transformation in socio-legal thought, ranging from judicial acknowledgement of the end of *laissez-faire* in the 1930s to the judiciary's rediscovery of immutable or classic property rights in the 1980s. Linking these apparently discrete judgments to the globalisation of public law neoformalism, the justification for judicial action or inaction on property rights came to be described not in terms of 'parliamentary sovereignty' (the inherited common law doctrine) but in terms of proportionality (a more recent neoformal doctrine). Similarly, by the 1990s, judges could identify corporations as rights-bearers in neoformal ways, a form of justification unimaginable to an earlier generation of constitution-makers and judges oriented to theories of Catholic natural law. Moreover, beneath the shifting flotsam and jetsam of judges' property rights discourses over the twentieth century lay a fundamental, enduring consensus on the value of the value-consensus state, a normative orientation that continued to come without saying and therefore go without saying.

## ORIGINS

The leading property rights cases examined here typically involved individual property owners' challenges to 'social' or state constraints on perceived 'classic' market rights. This was precisely the kind of challenge at stake in *Pigs Marketing Board* v. *Donnelly* [1939]. The Pigs Marketing Board, which regulated the production, selling, and pricing of bacon in Ireland, sued the Donnelly group of bacon manufacturers for non-compliance with the protectionist Pigs and Bacon Acts (1935/7). In response, the Donnelly group challenged this social legislation's constitutionality. Similarly, the impact of customs legislation on property rights was at stake in *Attorney General* v. *Southern Industrial Trust and Simons* [1960]. David Simons had secured a car from Southern Industrial Trust, a hire-purchase company, which he then exported from Ireland. Since this was contrary to the Customs Act (1945), the Revenue Commissioners duly seized the car as forfeit. Southern Industrial Trust subsequently claimed the car as theirs and that the Customs Act, in this particular instance, was contrary to the constitution's property rights provisions.

Property owners similarly contested state intervention in the market for land. Notwithstanding de Valera's anticipation of such actions, landowners continued to challenge the Irish Land Commission (ILC) in the courts.[7] The case of *Fisher* v. *the Irish Land Commission* [1948] arose when Francis Fisher, a grazier tenant of a 392-acre farm near

[7] See Edgeworth, 2007, 'Rural Radicalism Restrained'.

Rahanna, Co. Louth, contested the Land Commission's order of resumption. When the ILC's Appeal Tribunal rejected his application, Fisher sought to declare the Land Acts (1933/9) unconstitutional. A second case, *Foley* v. *Irish Land Commission* [1952], originated in a dispute between Patrick Foley and the ILC, which assisted his purchase of 26 acres near Mohill, Co. Leitrim.[8] Foley, a farm labourer, had been made unemployed following the resumption of local farms and thereby made eligible for the receipt of land in 1937. Nine years later, however, the ILC's commissioners, having learned that he had not taken up permanent residence at his holding, notified Foley of their intention to take it back if he did not do so. When the commissioners subsequently instituted ejectment proceedings, Foley challenged both the validity of the ILC's notification and the Land Act (1946) prompting it.

A third case, *Dreher* v. *Irish Land Commission* [1984], illustrated how dramatically land prices rose during the economic upturn of the 1960s. Jorg Dreher purchased land in Co. Waterford for £9,450 in 1963, which the ILC attempted to purchase compulsorily for £24,000 only four years later. Dreher contested the order and the judicial land commissioner subsequently fixed a price of £30,000, payable in Land Bonds. Conflict arose, however, when, in 1971, the bonds stood at 0.98, giving a realisable value of £29,400. Dreher now realised he wanted to be paid in cash. When the ILC secured an order for possession, he used the property rights provisions to challenge its pricing procedure.

Moreover, as Ireland's cities grew rapidly from the 1960s onwards, property-owners and landlords used the constitution's property rights provisions to contest 'social' interventions in urbanisation processes. The Local Government (Planning and Development) Act (1963) empowered Dublin Corporation to acquire compulsorily and redevelop some 70 'obsolete' acres in Dublin city centre, bounded by O'Connell Street, Parnell Street, Capel Street, and Ormond Quay. The legislation provided that acquisition costs be split between the Corporation (£4m) and a private development company (£14m) but did not provide local businesses with any guarantee that they would be relocated in the area post-redevelopment. Faced with the termination of their businesses and the depreciation of their properties' land values over an indefinite period, local property owners formed the Central Dublin Development Association (CDDA) 'to promote and protect the

[8] Note that Foley received the typical ILC farm acreage which, as was pointed out, necessarily imposed upon small farmers an acute dependency upon the grazier production line. McCabe, 2011, *Sins of the Father*, pp. 78–9.

interests and property rights of people living or carrying on business in the area'. In *CDDA* v. *Attorney General* [1975], the group challenged the planning legislation's constitutionality.

The most prominent of property owners' challenges to 'social' intervention was *Blake* v. *Attorney General* [1982]. The British government had introduced rent restrictions as a temporary measure during World War I, placing a ceiling on the rents payable by tenants of dwelling-houses having rateable valuations which did not exceed specified sums. Restrictions also applied to landlords attempting to recover possession of those dwellings. Politically, this scheme proved difficult to remove and subsequent governments preserved it without limiting its duration. By the late 1970s, rent restrictions effectively froze rent for at least 45,000 'controlled' dwellings. In 1978, as inflation threatened to transform controlled rents into losses, a group of landladies, including Dorothy Blake, challenged the legislation's constitutionality.

Property owners also used the constitution to contest taxation measures associated with property values. In *Brennan* v. *Attorney General* [1984], the Irish Farmers' Association organised a group of five farmers from Co. Wexford to challenge the continuation of Griffith's Valuation Act (1852). This legislation provided for a valuation of agricultural land in accordance with agricultural prices obtaining in the 1850s. The recent introduction of agricultural machinery and modern fertilisers ensured that higher and drier agricultural land became more productive and valuable than alluvial soils but the ratings system continued to tax the latter more than the former. The five farmers on land of poor quality were liable for higher rates than their neighbours on better holdings and challenged the legislation.

Opposition to taxation measures in the countryside was matched in the cities. In *Madigan* v. *Attorney General* [1986], two homeowners challenged the Finance Act (1983) which introduced a residential property tax. Persons owning and occupying dwellings with an aggregate net market value exceeding £65,000 were to pay 1½ per cent per annum on the amount exceeding £65,000. Those whose aggregate household income fell below £20,000 were also exempt, meaning some 98 per cent of the total population were not liable. Patrick Madigan from Foxrock, Co. Dublin and Catherine Gallagher from Ranelagh, Co. Dublin owned properties that had escalated rapidly in value over the previous decade. (The Madigan's house had risen in value from £56,000 in 1975 to some £250,000 in the mid-1980s. Similarly, Catherine Gallagher's home, a property which her mother purchased for £2,300 in 1928, was now worth an estimated £95,000). Having ready access to legal expertise, both engaged in separate challenges to the legislation.[9]

The rapid rise of property prices observed in earlier cases owed in part to the government-sponsored privatisation of urban housing and expansion of the mortgage market, prompting something of a mini-boom in Irish banking.[10] One of the beneficiaries was the Private Motorists Provident Society (PMPS) which used its exemption from existing banking regulations to raise its loan portfolio from £200,000 in 1970 to £11,700,000 in 1979.[11] Responding primarily to pressures from the Irish banking cartel to regulate potential competitors out of the market, the government introduced the Industrial and Provident Societies (Amendment) Act (1978) which provided that, within five years, PMPS and others were no longer to accept or hold deposits. In *PMPS Ltd and Joseph Moore* v. *Attorney General* [1983], the society challenged the legislation's constitutionality.

The Irish property bubble of the 1990s and 2000s reproduced these familiar tendencies towards expanding credit for private homeownership. The Fianna Fáil-Progressive Democrat government introduced a range of tax reliefs for property developers, stimulating the property market to the point where house prices rose to eight times the average industrial wage.[12] To compensate for the decline in social housing construction, the Planning and Development Bill (1999) stipulated that a percentage of any land developed for residential use was to be reserved for 'affordable housing' for persons of different income levels and 'social backgrounds'. Earlier constitutional cases, however, raised fears that even these minimal restrictions might amount to an interference with developer-landowner property rights. Thus, when the legislation came before President Mary McAleese, she sought a decision from the Supreme Court as to its constitutionality.

The final property rights contestation examined here, *Iarnród Éireann* v. *Ireland* [1996], arose following an accident in September 1989 in which a train derailed outside Ballyhaunis, Co. Mayo. The crash occurred when cattle owned and driven by Patrick Diskin emerged

[9] Patrick Madigan was a solicitor and his wife had been recently called to the bar. Of Catherine Gallagher's five children who still lived at home and therefore liable to disclose their income under the legislation, three were solicitors and one was a barrister.

[10] McCabe, 2011, *Sins of the Father*, pp. 33–7.

[11] The existing regulations were contained in the Central Bank Act (1971).

[12] McCabe, 2011, *Sins of the Father*, pp. 50–1.

on to the rail tracks from land owned by Michael Diskin. By 1990, some 230 passengers had issued compensation claims for injuries sustained in the crash, the total liability amounting to some £3.9 million. Giovanni Gaspari, an injured passenger, took an action for damages against Iarnród Éireann (Irish: Irish Rail) and Patrick Diskin. He was awarded £16,000, 70 per cent of which was to be paid by Patrick Diskin and 30 per cent by Iarnród Éireann. Patrick Diskin, however, was unable to pay these damages with the result that, under the Civil Liability Act (1961), full compensation reverted to the other 'concurrent wrongdoer', Iarnród Éireann. The rail company subsequently challenged this 'social' legislation's constitutionality.

## TRANSLATION

At first, those challenging the constitutionality of 'social' interventions in the market attempted to assert an absolute or 'classic' right to property. The Donnelly bacon group's lawyers argued that the contested protectionist legislation offended the 1937 Constitution's social justice and private property provisions such that, in the words of the judge, 'any law passed by the State which interferes with the free operation of competition in trade or interferes with contractual or proprietorial rights of citizens, is unconstitutional'. Given the judiciary's rejection of this argument, subsequent challenges characteristically claimed that the legislation affecting ownership was arbitrary or procedurally unfair and hence amounted to 'an unjust attack'. This mode of argument typically emphasised the right to property of the human person (Article 40.3) over those which could be restricted on the basis of social justice or the common good (Article 43) (Box 6.2).

Lawyers typically highlighted perceived deficiencies in the procedures associated with state intervention in the market. In the Irish Land Commission cases, counsel for Francis Fisher argued that the ILC or 'the landlord' deprived their client of natural justice pre-resumption, specifically the right to the protection of a judicial decision from either a Judicial Commissioner or another lawfully appointed court. Counsel for the small farmer, Patrick Foley, similarly argued that the ILC had not adhered to fair procedure in not informing Foley of their inspection or allowing him to present his case before them. Similarly, counsel on behalf of the Central Dublin Development Association argued that the planning legislation resulted in an 'unjust attack' on business owners'

**Box 6.2 Property Rights Provisions**

**Article 40.3**
1° The State guarantees in its laws to respect, and, as far as practicable, by its laws to defend and vindicate the personal rights of the citizen.

2° The State shall, in particular, by its laws protect as best it may from unjust attack and, in the case of injustice done, vindicate the life, person, good name, and property rights of every citizen.

**Article 43**
1. 1° The State acknowledges that man, in virtue of his rational being, has the natural right, antecedent to positive law, to the private ownership of external goods.

   2° The State accordingly guarantees to pass no law attempting to abolish the right of private ownership or the general right to transfer, bequeath, and inherit property.

2. 1° The State recognises, however, that the exercise of the rights mentioned in the foregoing provisions of this Article ought, in civil society, to be regulated by the principles of social justice.

   2° The State, accordingly, may as occasion requires delimit by law the exercise of the said rights with a view to reconciling their exercise with the exigencies of the common good.

property rights because it did not provide a fair hearing.[13] Counsel for the Madigans and Gallaghers concentrated their attack on the property tax on the methods used for determining the market value of property, arguing that the criterion of 'net market value' was 'totally artificial'.[14]

Counsel also claimed that arbitrariness in procedure could accrue over time. In both *Blake* and *Brennan*, counsel for the landlords and farmers argued that the state's failure to amend the rent restrictions or valuation system on an ongoing basis ensured they were arbitrary

13 Moreover, since the legislation failed to define an 'obsolete area' and gave the Minister for Local Government extensive discretion to determine disputes, the CDDA's counsel argued that the envisaged restriction of property rights was not in accordance with the principles of social justice (and therefore repugnant to Article 43).

14 Specifically, the legislation ignored the fact that an owner might possess only a limited or, as in their case, a mortgage-encumbered interest in the property.

and thus constituted an 'unjust attack' on their clients' property rights. The absence or deficiency of compensation was also used to claim an 'unjust attack'. Counsel for Jorg Dreher argued that Articles 40 and 43 protected landowners from compulsory acquisition save at a 'just price' fixed by the ILC's commissioner. Payment in land bonds capable of fluctuating from this price, they argued, was unconstitutional. Again, counsel for the Central Dublin Development Association similarly argued that the planning legislation resulted in an 'unjust attack' on business owners' property rights because it did not provide reinstatement or compensation.

Responding to these claims, the state's legal team usually argued that the contested 'social' legislation or activity had been passed by parliament in accordance with the constitution; that the common good necessitated the contested delimitation of the property right (Article 43); and that the courts should not lightly interfere with government taxation and fiscal policy.[15] In *Blake*, for example, counsel for the state claimed that the rent restrictions were originally enacted for the common good and that inflation (which diminished landlords' returns on controlled rents) did not make unconstitutional legislation which was constitutional at the time of its enactment. In *Madigan*, counsel for the state defending the property tax urged the judge to distinguish between the constitution's consideration of citizens as human persons (Article 40.1) and the taxation system's consideration of citizens as homeowners.

By the 1990s, however, the property rights provisions came to be used differently. Legal counsel for property owners proposed that judges apply 'proportionality' doctrine. Counsel for Iarnród Éireann maintained that the disputed civil liability legislation unjustly attacked their client's property rights by making them liable for all compensation to injured parties, notwithstanding an earlier finding that the farmers whose cattle caused the train to derail were '70% responsible'. If the proportionality doctrine were applied, they argued, the legislation would be found to give rise to an excessive obligation in these circumstances. Similarly, counsel contesting the Planning and Development Bill (1999) underlined how compensation for compulsory transfers was neither based on the market value of the land nor based on the financial capacity of those benefitting or those adversely affected. Instead, one section of

[15] This separation of powers principle is contained in Article 15. See David Gwynn Morgan, 1996, *The Separation of Powers in the Irish Constitution*. Dublin: Round Hall Press.

the population, land developers, bore a disproportionate share of the costs of alleviating the socio-economic problems which the legislation claimed to address. This arbitrariness and absence of proportionality, they claimed, meant the bill unjustly attacked land developers' property rights.

Responding to these arguments, counsel for the state concentrated on their direct implications in practice. In *Iarnród Éireann*, they emphasised that the most seriously injured plaintiffs might find themselves deprived of 90 per cent of their damages because of the insolvency of a concurrent wrongdoer, a matter for which they had no responsibility. A 'manifest injustice' would thereby be created. Counsel arguing in favour of the Planning and Development Bill (1999) criticised the argument that every interference with property rights required compensating the owner for 'market value' as being wrong in principle and contrary to precedent. The legislation required would-be developers to contribute a relatively modest proportion of any enhanced value resulting from planning decisions taken for the benefit of the community. This restriction was not an 'unjust attack' but rather a permissible and reasonably proportionate measure.

## JUDGMENT

The judgments in these property rights contestations indicate judges' aversion to making 'public policy', which was understood as encroaching upon the legislature's prerogative of choosing between competing political, economic, social, or normative claims.[16] Judges generally claimed that the Oireachtas had duly passed the contested piece of 'social' legislation or that it had duly appointed state agencies such as the Irish Land Commission or the Planning Authority better qualified to perform the specific, 'expert' functions at issue. Thus, a 'heavy onus' rested with litigants to establish the unconstitutionality of the state's intervention. When a claim to an absolute, 'classic' property right was

[16] Judges were broadly willing to accept the legislature's lead except, however, insofar as they deemed it to impinge on the direction of their own competences. In *Buckley* v. *Attorney General [1950]* IR 67, 70, Judge Gavan Duffy rejected the government's attempt to prevent his hearing a politically sensitive property rights case, ruling that 'this court cannot, in deference to an Act of the Oireachtas, abdicate its proper jurisdiction to administer justice in a cause whereof it is duly seized'. Specifically, Gavan Duffy's rejection of the Attorney General's application included a rebuttal of his 'far-reaching proposition' that the legislature's decision on what constituted 'the exigencies of the common good' was absolute and incapable of review by the court. Judges in subsequent property rights cases would return to this precedent to justify their position.

at stake, the judges' position was straightforwardly justified on the basis of the constitutional text. In *Pigs Marketing Board*, Judge Hanna held that protectionist legislation did not infringe the Donnelly group's right because the constitution explicitly qualified that right and permitted the state to reconcile its exercise with the exigencies of the common good: 'the days of *laissez-faire*', he observed, 'are at an end'.[17]

Judges also tended to respond conservatively to counsels' subsequently more nuanced arguments against the manner or justice of the state's intervention or 'attack'. They justified this position by drawing a distinction between judicial ('natural justice') procedures and 'administrative' procedures. Judge Gavan Duffy rejected Francis Fisher's claims against the Land Commission on precisely this basis. He held that the ILC's powers were administrative in nature and that the 1937 Constitution had provided for their exercise.[18] Similarly, in the *Southern Industrial Trust* case, Judge Lavery dismissed the hire-purchase company's claim. He held that the regulation or taking away of ownership in the name of the common good (in this instance ensuring effective penalties for breaching customs legislation) was primarily a legislative matter whereas the court's role was strictly supervisory. The judge was simply to ensure that no accidental or deliberate breach of the constitution occurred and no more.[19] In dismissing the Central Dublin Development Association's claims, Judge Kenny held that the planning legislation was not repugnant to the constitution. The alleged 'quasi-judicial' powers granted to the Minister and Planning Authority were limited and, in any event, subject to appeal to the courts.[20]

Judges in these early cases further attempted to clarify the meaning of the property rights provisions. In *SIT*, Judge Davitt (High Court, H.C.) made a distinction between the property rights guaranteed in Articles 40.3 and 43 and thereby suggested their 'double protection'. On his interpretation, Article 40.3 provided an 'unlimited guarantee' of private property which Article 43 'cut down'. The latter provision, he further claimed, was a generally stated principle and 'never designed to apply to questions relating to acts of expropriation by the State'. Interpreting a 'classic' right into the constitution, Davitt suggested that

[17] *Pigs Marketing Board* v. *Donnelly* [1939] IR 413, 417–8.

[18] The court's emphasis on due process operated in favour of the small farmer, Patrick Foley. Judge O'Byrne ruled against the ILC for not providing Foley with an opportunity to state his case, thereby breaching the 'rules and dictates of natural justice'. *Foley* v. *Irish Land Commission* [1952] IR 118,156.

[19] *Attorney General* v. *Southern Industrial Trust* [1960] 94 ILTR 161, 176.

[20] *CDDA* v. *Attorney General* [1975] 109 ILTR 69, 86.

'to deprive a person of any part of his property is not a delimiting of the exercise of his rights but a denial of those rights altogether'.[21] Though contrary to the constitution-makers' intentions, Davitt's reading was nevertheless consonant with legal professional opinion which tended to ignore the 'social' legal thought at stake in the property rights provisions. Judge Lavery (S.C.) contradicted this line of jurisprudence directly but on different grounds, stating that the property rights guaranteed in Articles 40.3 and 43 were identical and that the court was not to engage in an evaluative or legislative function.[22] The proposed distinction would nevertheless prove significant.

Subsequent attempts to clarify the meaning of the property rights provisions accentuated their complexity. In *CDDA*, Judge Kenny elaborated seven conclusions concerning the constitution's property provisions.[23] The majority of these simply rearticulated the Catholic 'social' understanding of natural, personal property rights. However, Kenny, like Davitt, also read the provisions in a 'classic' mode. The natural right to private ownership of worldly wealth, he claimed, 'consists of a bundle of rights most of which are founded in contract'. While he acknowledged the possibility of 'social' interventions, Kenny further discovered an obligation on the state to provide compensation for abolishing or restricting ownership rights, only, however, 'if it is an *unjust* attack'. Various, presumably just, acts affected the legal rights of ownership while not providing for compensation: '. . . and nobody has ever suggested that the Rent Restrictions Acts . . . are made unconstitutional

[21] *Attorney General* v. *Southern Industrial Trust* [1960] 94 ILTR 161, 171. Davitt was, in part, citing a precedent for judicial intervention in overturning 'social' legislation set in the trade union case, *NUR* v. *Sullivan* [1947], examined in the next chapter.

[22] *Attorney General* v. *Southern Industrial Trust* [1960] 94 ILTR 161, 176. The regulation or taking away of ownership in the name of the common good was primarily a legislative matter. The court's role was simply to ensure no accidental or deliberate breach of a constitutional right.

[23] 'In my view, an analysis of the text of the Constitution and of the decisions on it leads to these conclusions: (1) the right of private property is a personal right. (2) In virtue of his rational being, man has a natural right to individual or private ownership of worldly wealth. (3) This Constitutional right consists of a bundle of rights most of which are founded in contract. (4) The State cannot pass any law which abolishes all the bundle of rights which we call ownership, or the general right to transfer, bequeath and inherit property. (5) The exercise of these rights ought to be regulated by the principles of social justice, and the State, accordingly, may by law restrict their exercise with a view to reconciling this with the demands of the common good. (6) The courts have jurisdiction to enquire whether the restriction is in accordance with the principles of social justice and whether the legislation is necessary to reconcile this exercise with the demands of the common good. (7) If any of the rights which together constitute our concept of ownership are abolished or restricted (as distinct from the abolition of all the rights) the absence of compensation for this restriction or abolition will make the Act which does this, invalid, if it is an unjust attack on property rights'. *CDDA* v. *Attorney General* [1975] 109 ILTR 69, 87.

by Article 43 or that the Constitution requires that owners should be compensated for the loss caused to them by the reduction in the amount of rents which they can get'.[24] The Supreme Court would, in fact, prove amenable to such suggestions.

The importance of these earlier interpretations became apparent in *Blake* when the Supreme Court struck down 'social' controls on rent and recovery of possession. In his justification, Chief Justice O'Higgins returned to Judge Davitt's suggestion of a 'double-but-separate protection' for property rights. Whereas Article 43 merely guaranteed, regulated, and delimited the general institution of private property, O'Higgins argued, the landladies affected by rent restrictions could claim a right in respect of particular items of property, a right that Article 40.3 guaranteed. Moreover, the basis for selecting properties for rent controls was deemed arbitrary and unrelated to tenants' needs, to landlords' resources or to 'any established social necessity'.[25] In response to this decision, the government introduced the Housing Bill (1981) in order to gradually phase out rent controls. The District Court was to determine a market rent for the controlled dwellings and tenants were to pay an increasing percentage of this gross rent over the course of five years until the benefits of the control were removed entirely. The president referred the bill to the Supreme Court to test its constitutionality. Once again, the court struck it down. The residual restrictions, O'Higgins declared, imposed 'different but no less unjust deprivations upon landlords'. With immediate effect, the gross rent was 'to be regarded as the just and proper rent'. These decisions resulted in dramatic rent increases for some 45,000 tenants.

A similar demonstration of the judges' preparedness to uproot 'social' restrictions on classic property rights occurred in *Brennan*. The Supreme Court accepted the Wexford farmers' case against the existing system of valuation and taxation. Chief Justice O'Higgins accepted Judge Barrington's (H.C.) earlier declaration that the 1852 valuation system was now 'shot through with unnecessary anomalies and inconsistencies'. The state's continued use of these valuations, with 'obvious' implication for a lack of uniformity, was arbitrary and constituted an 'unjust attack' (Article 40.3) on the farmers' property rights. These strident declarations of private property rights appeared to signal to jurists and policymakers that the courts would prioritise individual interests over the

[24] *CDDA* v. *Attorney General* [1975] 109 ILTR 69, 87.
[25] *Blake* v. *Attorney General* [1982] IR 117.

common good in interpreting the constitution. This perception would also have important implications.[26]

Such interventions, however, were exceptional. In the other property rights cases, the O'Higgins Court, like its predecessors, adopted conservative, non-interventionist positions. As Judge Walsh declared in *Dreher*, a state action authorised by Article 43 'cannot by definition be unjust for the purpose of Article 40.3.2'. The Supreme Court rejected Jorg Dreher's appeal on the grounds that the State's measures to compensate the landowner for expropriation had been 'reasonable'. Judge Carroll similarly dismissed PMPS's claims. Carroll claimed it was in the public interest that banking business be regulated according to 'the principles of sound banking'. In this regard, the Central Bank's criteria were also 'reasonable' and could not be described as expropriating business or unjustly attacking property rights. Again returning to an axiomatic acceptance of the constitutionality of legislation, Judge O'Hanlon (H.C) dismissed the Madigan-Gallagher action against the property tax. Due process and equal protection had been applied in the making of the tax law sufficient to ensure its constitutionality; the courts did not have to inquire into its effectiveness.

In the 1990s and 2000s, the Supreme Court's property rights judgments remained deferential to parliament, albeit a position justified in new, neoformalist language. Proportionality doctrine was increasingly used to justify judges' giving a greater 'margin of appreciation' to parliament and government. In *Iarnród Éireann*, Judge Keane (H.C.) dismissed the rail company's claim, declaring that the statute providing for concurrent wrongdoing was 'not disproportionate to the ends sought, arbitrary, unfair or irrational'. In the *Planning and Development Bill (1999) Reference*, the Supreme Court used the proportionality test to reject previously established and 'contradictory' jurisprudence providing for the 'double-but-separate' protection for a citizen's property rights. Chief Justice Keane declared that the legislation required developers 'to contribute a relatively modest proportion of the enhanced value resulting from planning decisions'. This 'permissible restriction' was 'reasonably proportionate to the end sought' and not repugnant to the constitution.[27]

[26] See Bryan McMahon, 1980, 'Review: J. M. Kelly, The Irish Constitution' in *Irish Jurist*, 16(1), pp. 190–203, p. 196.

[27] Keane declared that in cases where the state claims that legislation restricting property rights is required by the common good, an inquiry into whether, 'objectively viewed', it could be regarded as so required and into whether the delimitations were reasonably proportionate to

Judges nevertheless continued to be fascinated by the mysteries hidden in the property rights provisions. Significant in this respect was Judge Keane's declaration that corporate bodies and artificial legal entities – 'themselves capable in law of owning property' – could rely on the property guarantees contained in Article 40.3. In *Iarnród Éireann*, he declared that the companies' legislation was 'already a settled feature of the legal and commercial life of this country at the time of the enactment of the Constitution'. The word 'citizen' in Article 40.3 was not qualified by the addition of the words 'as human persons' such as occurred in Article 40.1. If the framers had wished to confine Article 40.3's comprehensive guarantee to 'human persons' only, he continued, 'there was nothing to prevent them including a similar qualification'. While this conclusion was not the outcome of 'a strict literal interpretation', it was nevertheless within 'the spirit of the provisions': 'It may be said of a constitution, more than of any other legal instrument, that "the letter killeth, but the spirit giveth life"'.[28]

## JURISPRUDENCE

Legal cultural dependency contributed to the process by which classic, *laissez-faire* ground rules came to be reproduced in the Irish Free State and, following the adoption of the 1937 Irish Constitution, had further implications for the interpretation of its property rights provisions.[29] Post-1937 Irish lawyers continued to use the inherited British law of property. Hence, while the former metropole was engaged in 'adventure and reform' – notably, the Birkenhead legislation provided for taxing aristocratic landowners' estates – Irish land-law, by contrast, was characterised by continuity and 'a rigid preservation of the old order'.[30] Similarly, the Irish bench adhered to the doctrine of parliamentary sovereignty and continued to follow British precedents closely.[31]

the ends was 'inevitable'; this test of proportionality was 'frequently adopted by the European Court of Human Rights'. *Re Article 26 and Part V of the Planning and Development Bill, 1999* [2000] 2 IR 321, 349–52.

[28] Chief Justice Keane, *Iarnród Éireann* v. *Ireland*, The Attorney General, Michael Diskin, Patrick Diskin, and Giovanni Gaspari, [1996] 3 IR 321, 346. He was citing Judge Henchy, *The People* v. *O'Shea* [1982] IR 384, citing 2 Corinthians 3.

[29] The conditions of legal cultural production are analysed in Chapter 9.

[30] Gerald Harris (ed.), 1948, 'Book Publications: Lectures on the Town and Country Planning Act by R. E. Megarry' in the *Irish Jurist*, 14 (4), p. 63.

[31] Gerald Harris (ed.), 1948, 'Books and Publications: Rent Restrictions Cases by Lionel Blundell of Gray's Inn' in *the* Irish Jurist, 14 (3).

During the 1940s and 1950s, contributors to the *Irish Jurist* recognised as particularly controversial two 'social' interventions in the classic market: town planning and rent controls. Occasioned by the Fianna Fáil-led house building programme in the 1930s, the Town (1934) and Regional (1939) planning acts were the first state interventions in planning and development.[32] Associated legal controversies concerned 'the control and restriction of development, the acquisition of development rights by the State, and the powers, procedure, and rights to compensation relating to compulsory acquisition'.[33] Contributions to the *Jurist* tended to specialise in legal minutiae, notably concerning challenges to restrictive covenants and compulsory acquisition, and practitioners strongly advocated legal representation for property-owners and citizens interacting with the Department of Local Government.[34]

Rent controls, according to Gerald Harris (1948), were subject to 'frequent and vehement, but not ill-deserved, abuse from the bench, bar, and solicitor's profession'.[35] Legal professionals regarded these controls as an aberration, a mere collection of statutory provisions and judicial decisions that had not 'evolved into anything like a body of principles' and was 'contemptuous of that sense of tradition which is usually so readily to be felt in the realm of property law'.[36] Successive Rent Restrictions legislation altered prior legislation 'though not the underlying principles or lack of principles' while the Irish bench's decisions in turn held 'numerous inconsistencies and contradictions'.[37] Barrister Michael Rynne (1964) bluntly dismissed rent controls as a 'protection racket'.[38]

[32] Gerald Harris (ed.), 1950, 'Books and Publications: Town and Regional Planning Law in Ireland' in *the* Irish Jurist, 16 (3), p. 37.

[33] Gerald Harris (ed.), 1948, 'Book Publications: Lectures on the Town and Country Planning Act, 1947 by R. E. Megarry' in the *Irish Jurist*, 14 (4), p. 63.

[34] VTH Delany (ed.), 1957, 'Restrictive Covenants' in the *Irish Jurist*, 23 (1), p. 1. The Planning and Development Act (1963), Gerald Clarke observed, was to be administered almost entirely through the Department for Local Government, making it unnecessary for parties to an appeal to be represented by a legal professional, a development to which the Incorporated Law Society Gazette had objected 'in the strongest possible terms'. Gerard Clarke, 1968, 'Planning and Development' in *The Irish Jurist*, 3 (1), pp. 107–11, p. 107.

[35] Gerald Harris (ed.), 1946, 'Book Review: On The Rent Acts by R. E. Megarry' in the *Irish Jurist*, 12 (3), p. 41.

[36] Gerald Harris (ed.), 1949, 'Books: The Law of Rent Restriction in Ireland by John Coghlan' in the *Irish Jurist*, 15 (3), p. 42.

[37] Gerald Harris (ed.), 1944, 'Book Review: The Law of Rent Restrictions in Eire by John Coghlan' in the *Irish Jurist*, 10 (4), p. 52.

[38] Michael Rynne, 1964, 'The Protection Racket: Observations on the Rent Restrictions Act, 1960' in the *Irish Jurist*, 30 (1), p. 13.

Throughout this period, the *Jurist* did not feature scholarship concerning the constitution's guarantee of the right of private property. Legal practitioners' attitudes to the property provisions possibly approximated the opinion expressed in John Kelly's (1967) *Fundamental Rights in the Irish Law and Constitution*, which regarded them primarily as a general statement of Catholic doctrine.[39] This impression can only have been strengthened by the vigour with which contributors to Catholic journals such as *Christus Rex* continued to claim that the Constitution's natural law provided a stronger defence of property rights and family values than alien forms of positivism and parliamentary sovereignty.[40] Kelly favoured these latter forms and warned that the Supreme Court might become 'a third house of the legislature' if it were to take an 'activist' or 'policy-oriented' approach to property rights.[41]

From the mid-1960s onwards, the Ó'Dálaigh Court's 'discovery' of the constitution prompted a number of jurists to reassess the significance of its property rights provisions for challenging the 'social'. Donal Barrington (1973) argued that while the minds of both bench and bar remained dominated by inherited ideas of parliamentary sovereignty, the 'philosophies underlying the Irish and British systems' were 'logically irreconcilable'. Thus, the state's granting of absolute powers to such administrative bodies as the Land Commission or Planning Authority was potentially inconsistent with constitutional guarantees of property as a natural right. These provisions were deemed latent with 'revolutionary implications' (for property owners). While Barrington argued that the 'governing criterion' qualifying the right to private property ought to be that of social justice, he admittedly thought it 'possible to imagine conditions of famine and economic disaster in which the State could, consistently with the principles of social justice, take from the rich to feed the poor'.[42] In a more directly neoliberal fashion, John Temple Lang (1971) observed how the constitution could be used to impede legislation attempting to control the price of goods

[39] John Kelly, 1967 (2nd edition), *Fundamental Rights in the Irish Law and Constitution*, p. 176.

[40] Grogan, Vincent, 1954, 'The Constitution and the Natural Law' in *Christus Rex*, Vol. 8 (3), pp. 201–18. Catholic conservatives such as E. J. Gray continued to present the constitution's natural law property rights as a bulwark against socialism into the 1970s. E. J. Gray, 'A Look at Capitalism: the Private Enterprise System' (1971), *Christus Rex*, Vol. 25, pp. 112, 113.

[41] Kelly, 1967, *Fundamental Rights in the Irish Law and Constitution*, p. 176.

[42] Donal Barrington, 1973, 'Private Property under the Irish Constitution' in *Irish Jurist*, 8 (1), pp. 1–17.

or the price of land for building purposes.[43] The same provisions, he argued, could be used to impede legislation designed to control salaries and wages.[44] Again, Mary Matthews (1972) claimed that 'private enterprise' was 'constitutionally enshrined' and that from Articles 43 and 45.3 'consumers' sovereignty, freedom of enterprise and initiative, and private ownership all flow'.[45]

Jurists considered, in particular, the protection that the property rights provisions appeared to afford landowners. By the early 1970s, as Dublin's urbanisation accelerated, the level of speculation in land values occasioned the government's establishment of a special committee, headed by Judge John Kenny, to inquire into the price of building land.[46] The *Kenny Report* (1973) found that land speculators' profits owed primarily to public investment in transforming agricultural land into building land and that price controls were necessary. Such controls were also permissible: the constitution did not give to each citizen 'the right to get the full market price for any of his property'.[47] The Kenny Report's recommendations were never implemented and land speculation continued unchecked. Jurists attributed this outcome to a persistent 'fear' among policy-makers that the courts would compel public authorities to pay full compensation for any land compulsorily acquired.[48] The Supreme Court's 'classic' interventions in *Blake* and *Brennan* cases seemed to confirm these apprehensions. Ronan Keane (1983) feared that legislation such as that proposed by the Kenny Report was 'more vulnerable than ever' and would not 'survive the somewhat uncertain perils of a voyage through the waters of Articles 40 and 43'.[49]

While James Casey (1986) claimed that the judiciary was not 'moving toward a *laissez-faire* approach in economic matters', jurists nevertheless identified instances of *laissez-faire* in practice.[50] Colin

43 John Temple Lang, 1971, 'Private Law Aspects of the Irish Constitution', in *The Irish Jurist*, 6, pp. 237–57.
44 Lang, 1971, 'Private Law Aspects of the Irish Constitution', p. 255.
45 Mary Mathews, 1972, 'Aspects of the Irish Law of Contract' in *Irish Jurist*, 7 (2), pp. 292–305, p. 293.
46 McCabe, *Sins of the Father*, pp. 102–4.
47 Committee on the Price of Building Land, 1974, *Report*, Dublin: Stationery Office.
48 Charles Lysaght, 2002, 'Review: Gwynn Morgan, A Judgment Too Far?' in *Irish Jurist*, 37, pp. 336–8, p. 337.
49 Keane, 1983, 'Land Use, Compensation and the Community', p. 32.
50 J. P. Casey, 1986, 'Constitutional Law under Chief Justice O'Higgins' in *Irish Jurist*, 21 (1), pp. 7–34, p. 28.

Stevenson's (1984) analysis of planning, development, and regulation practices concluded that the planning system operated to redistribute public finances from local authorities to homeowners in general and developers in particular. Planning authorities had, moreover, used private planning agreements, contracts, and covenants to dilute administrative controls on development.[51] The constitution's private property rights, Yvonne Scannell (1980) suggested, ensured the reproduction of this planning process, specifically the courts' tolerating the granting of compensation claims to landowners refused rezoning permission by the planning authority.[52] The threat of such claims provided landowners with leverage and 'often led to permission for development that was inappropriate'.[53] In contrast, the public's participation in the planning and development process was minimal. Planning, according to Scannell (1980), was characterised by: 'little official enthusiasm for public participation, haphazard (and largely ineffective) contributions by elected members of local authorities [and] no general public access to government documents'.[54]

Moreover, judicial review of planning decisions was criticised as ineffectual. An entire community could not initiate collective legal action to secure the general improvement of homes; litigation was instead piecemeal.[55] Judicial review, Gerard Hogan (1997) observed, functions such that 'the courts are required to focus on the operation of the law as it affects the individual plaintiff and do not, generally speaking, have the capacity to examine how such a law impacts on the public at large'.[56] This was particularly true of contemporary property rights where 'the entire thrust of the proportionality doctrine . . . is to focus on the rights of the individual'.[57] Jurists also observed an increasing primacy of administrative over adjudicatory modes of decision-making. During the 1990s and 2000s, as judicial reviews of planning decisions rose steadily, the superior courts attributed an ever wider 'margin of

[51] C. P. Stevenson, 1984, 'Negotiated Planning' in *Irish Jurist*, 19 (1), pp. 15–39, p. 16.

[52] Yvonne Scannell, 1980, 'Review: Alder, Development Control' in *Irish Jurist*, 15 (1), pp. 181–2, p. 181.

[53] Statutory development controls abolishing this practice were introduced in the Local Government (Planning and Development) Act (1990). Sara Dillon, 1999, 'Review: Scannell et al., The Habitats Directive' in *Irish Jurist*, 34, pp. 346–9, p. 348.

[54] Scannell, 1980, 'Review: Alder, Development Control', p. 181.

[55] D. J. Hughes, 1977, 'Review: David Hoath, *Council Housing*' in *Irish Jurist*, 12 (1), pp. 212–3, p. 213.

[56] Gerard Hogan, 1997, 'The Constitution, Property Rights and Proportionality' in *Irish Jurist*, 32, pp. 373–97, p. 396.

[57] Hogan, 1997, 'The Constitution, Property Rights and Proportionality', p. 396.

discretion' to public authorities, setting a higher bar on a wider body of administrative law and generally adopting what Niall Buckley (2004) described as an 'extremely hands-off approach'.[58]

## CONCLUSION

Ireland's political economy ensured that systemic advantages accrued to propertied interests. Constitutional jurisprudence, as demonstrated by the property rights contestations examined here, came to register and, in some instances, helped to reproduce those advantages. Property-owners used the constitution to challenge 'social' interventions in the market such as the powers of the Irish Land Commission or the public control or taxation of urbanisation processes. Their counsel highlighted perceived deficiencies in the procedures associated with state intervention in the market and cited the absence or deficiency of compensation as the basis of an 'unjust attack'. Judges did not always agree and, indeed, the property rights judgments examined here indicate judges' aversion to intervening in legislative policy-making. Formerly expressed as the doctrine of parliamentary sovereignty, in recent times judges have re-described and justified this position in terms of the neoformalist doctrine of proportionality.

Yet those instances where the judiciary did intervene – in *Brennan* and, in particular, *Blake* – had important ramifications beyond the loss of tax revenue or even the thousands of tenants affected by the removal of rent restrictions. Associated jurisprudence traced the manner in which the property rights provisions came to be viewed as an excuse for not implementing controls on rapidly rising land values. In these circumstances, these constitutional decisions formed part of a process whereby developers and landowners came to colonise the planning process, a process from which the vast majority of the population were absented. The established field of constitutional justice and legal business was one through which a landowner's 'unearned increment' could be more easily defended than challenged.

[58] Niall Buckley, 2004, 'Merging Principles of Public Law: Towards Proportionality in an Irish Context' in *Irish Jurist*, 39, pp. 161–214, pp. 195–6.

CHAPTER SEVEN

# CONTESTING TRADE UNION RIGHTS

*If a highwayman presents a pistol to my head and says, 'Your money or your life', he attempts to coerce me, though he gives me a choice of two courses. I may, indeed, adopt a heroic attitude and say, 'Shoot away', but if discretion or pusillanimity prevail and I disgorge my money, it seems to me idle to say that I have not been coerced into so doing.*

– Judge Kingsmill Moore on workers' strike action, 1961[1]

*The judiciary has not recognised that for workers freedom of expression is the picket placard; that freedom of assembly is picketing (and sometimes occupation) of premises; and that freedom to form association and unions means the ability to pursue potentially effective action through collective organisation . . . The effect of this has been to disadvantage workers as a class. The failure to recognise distinct labour interest is a denial by the judiciary of class difference in Irish society, despite the explicit recognition in Article 40.6.2 of the Constitution of the existence of such differences.*

– Brian Wilkinson, 'A Jurisprudence of Labour Liberty?' 1989[2]

The defeat of the Irish Transport and General Workers Union in the 1913 Dublin Lockout broadly indicated how the balance of class forces in the Irish Free State would reside with the employers, owing partly to the support of an emergent, native class of landowners and partly to the ideological dominance of Catholicism and nationalism. Internally, the labour movement remained divided between the British-based amalgamated unions who advocated continued sectionalist, wage-militant organisation and their less organised colleagues who wanted to formalise labour-state relations along industrial unionist lines in order to increase the unions' overall bargaining power. During World War II, the latter section of trade unions formed a partnership with Fianna Fáil to modernise industrial relations, a relationship that would endure into

1 *Educational Company* v. *Fitzpatrick* [1961] IR 339, 396.

2 Article 40.6.2° states: 'Laws regulating the manner in which the right of forming associations and unions and the right of free assembly may be exercised shall contain no political, religious or class discrimination'. Brian Wilkinson, 1989, 'Workers, Constitutions and the Irish Judiciary: A Jurisprudence of Labour Liberty?' in *Irish Jurist*, 24 (2), pp. 198–226, p. 221.

the twenty-first century.[3] Prior to the war, unions had to be combative in order to achieve gains. After it, they became 'part of the social furniture'.[4]

From the 1960s onwards, as Ireland industrialised, this cooperative relationship would translate into 'national' pay rounds or voluntary, tripartite wage-bargaining mechanisms. Nevertheless, common to wider European mobilisations, there were periods of heightened wage militancy, notably in the mid to late 1960s. In some cases, trade union demonstrations and strikes were matched or broken by governments' use of the Offences against the State Act (1939), notably deployed against farmers and workers picketing or demonstrating outside the Houses of the Oireachtas.[5] However, from the 1980s onwards, as the neoliberal transformation of Ireland gathered momentum, successive social partnership agreements introduced wage moderation in return for income tax cuts for workers. Increasingly bureaucratic and managerial, the trade union movement was effectively neutered as a combative, class force in Irish society. Trade union density declined, dramatically so outside the public sector. In the early 1990s, union activists feared that Irish workers would be left without the experience of solidarity in class struggle that had sustained earlier generations.

Comparatively then, the political and legal position of the trade union movement in Ireland was weaker than in most European countries. The Irish Free State, Eire, and the Republic of Ireland all retained the pluralist and voluntary framework of interest group articulation common to the United Kingdom and the United States, rather than the legally entrenched corporatist bargaining model of Germany or the Scandinavian countries. Unlike their European counterparts then, the trade unions in Ireland were structurally oriented towards the defence of their members' wages, terms, and conditions, and not a wider politics of social solidarity or welfare state development. Instead, the Irish Free State's continuation of the corpus of inherited trade union law closely paralleled its reproduction of the classic laws of market and property. Won by organised labour in the course of major struggles, the Trade Union Act (1871), the Conspiracy and Protection of Property Act

[3] O'Connor, 2011, *A Labour History of Ireland*, p. 293. Fianna Fáil outflanked the Labour party and successfully won union support, promising union recognition, modest welfare reforms, and greater industrialisation.

[4] O'Connor, 2011, *A Labour History of Ireland*, p. 170.

[5] See R. J. O'Hanlon, 1968, 'Notes: Criminal Justice Bill, 1967' in *The Irish Jurist*, 3 (1), pp. 102–7, p. 104.

(1875), and the Trade Disputes Act (1906) were common to both Great Britain and Ireland, providing immunities for unions to form 'closed shops' and to strike.

A labyrinthine, overlapping 'social' infrastructure for labour dispute resolution developed after World War II, underpinned by the Industrial Relations Act (1946). Earlier, during the making of the 1937 Constitution, John Charles McQuaid had responded to ongoing building and transport workers' strikes by advocating an arbitration board to 'neutralise the venom of communism'. In 1940, a Labour Court, closely matching his prescription, was established. Its decisions were not binding, however, and industrial-state relations remained organised in a voluntary system.[6] In the 1980s, however, the voluntarist system transformed. 'Growing pressure from both employers and unions, political concern at addressing the perceived inflationary result of free collective bargaining, and the increased intervention of the European Community' ensured Ireland's labour law became increasingly regulated, both at individual and collective levels.[7] Significantly, having witnessed the decimation of the trade unions in Thatcher's UK and Reagan's US, the Irish Congress of Trade Unions accepted the Industrial Relations Act (1990), which effectively immobilised unions' capacity for industrial action.[8]

A series of economic rights contestations – centring on the judiciary's interpretation of the 1937 Constitution's trade union or 'freedom of association' rights provisions – facilitated this outcome (Box 7.1). Similar to the property rights conflicts examined in the last chapter, these trade union rights contestations involved individuals' challenges to 'social' restrictions or state intervention on perceived 'classic' market or liberal rights. The courts held that picketing unprotected by the Trade Disputes Act (1906) was necessarily a nuisance ('without quite explaining why'[9]); that picketing to obtain compulsory union membership was illegal and, furthermore, that enforcing an employer-union agreement on compulsory union membership was

[6] J. P. Casey, 1972, 'Reform of Collective Bargaining Law: Some Constitutional Implications' in *Irish Jurist*, 7 (1), pp. 1–16.

[7] Ivana Bacik, 2002, 'Labour Law Profile: Ireland'. Available at: www.ilo.org/ifpdial/information-resources/national-labour-law-profiles/WCMS_158901/lang-en/index.htm.

[8] 'Social partnership in Ireland was rooted in the continuation of a tradition of a strong voluntarism with minimal employment rights. The labour rights that do exist were often begrudgingly legislated for only in response to European directives'. McDonagh and Dundon, 2010, 'Thatcherism Delayed? The Irish crisis and the paradox of social partnership', p. 544.

[9] Paul O'Higgins, 1966, 'English Law and the Irish Question' in the *Irish Jurist*, 1 (1) pp. 59–65, p. 64.

**Box 7.1 Trade Union Rights Cases**

*National Union of Railwaymen* v. *Sullivan* [1947] IR 77

*Educational Company of Ireland* v *Fitzpatrick* [1961] IR 345

*Meskell* v. *CIE* [1973] IR 121

invalid. Constitutional rights of association, as the judges elaborated in *NUR*, *Educational Company*, and *Meskell*, included 'rights of dissociation' that undermined closed shop agreements and, moreover, established that employers could obtain labour injunctions to restrain picketing and strike action.

Judges' decisions were recognisably neoformalist. They identified absolute rights in the newly discovered 'constitutional framework' that would disrupt and undermine not only contemporary 'social' legislation for industrial action but also pre-existing common law immunities. Labour jurists identified these tensions as problematic and judges' attempts at resolving them conservative, even comparatively odd. The courts appeared to prioritise individual over collective rights while the constitution's formal union guarantees did little to transform substantive material inequalities. Perhaps most importantly, the courts' free use of injunctions effectively robbed unions of the power to use the strike as a sanction in negotiations with employers. This, among other factors, featured in trade unions' subsequent willingness to accept the Industrial Relations Act (1990). Nevertheless, in some conflicts, striking and occupying workers understood justice differently and attempted to ignore such injunctions altogether through direct action.

## ORIGINS

One of the earliest efforts to modernise industrial relations, Fianna Fáil's Trade Union Act (1941) attempted to regulate union multiplicity. Acting in accordance with this legislation, the Irish Transport and General Workers' Union applied to a newly created tribunal for the exclusive right to organise workmen in the road passenger service of Córas Iompair Éireann (CIE), the state transport company. The British-based National Union of Railwaymen stood to lose some 350 members immediately and would have held long-term concerns for a further 5,000 members based in CIE's other transport divisions. In addition to the loss of members' dues, the NUR, being an English-registered union and affiliated with the Irish Labour Party, opposed its members' dues being seconded to the ITGWU-affiliated National Labour Party. In *National Union of Railwaymen* v. *Sullivan* [1947], the NUR challenged the wartime legislation in the High Court, claiming that it denied workers' constitutional rights to freedom of association.

Important state curbs on union activity remained in place throughout the contested modernising of industrial relations, a point suitably illustrated by the case of *Educational Company of Ireland* v. *Fitzpatrick* [1961]. The 'Educational Company' and 'Edward Healy and Company' manufactured, printed, and distributed school books from shared premises on Dublin's Talbot Street. (One of the former's publications is listed in the bibliography of the book you are currently reading.) In 1959, two employees, Tadhg Crowley and Thomas Byrne, began to organise coworkers, inviting them to join the Irish Union of Distributive Workers and Clerks (IUDWC) for better wages and working conditions. Thereafter, the organised workers followed a successful action to increase wages with further demands to introduce a 'closed shop', thereby making union membership compulsory on all workers.

When management refused attempts to form a closed shop, the IUDWC members called a strike and picketed the company's premises. The Educational Company then sought (and the courts swiftly provided) an injunction to restrain the picketing. The union responded by claiming that their actions were lawful and protected by the common law immunities of the Trade Disputes Act (1906). Transforming the conflict into a constitutional case, the employers counter-claimed that the 1906 Act, in authorising picketing to secure compulsory union membership, was repugnant to the rights of association of those workers not taking part in the picket.

A similar conflict between individual and collective rights of association resurfaced in *Meskellv. CIE* [1973]. Reflecting a wider norm of union multiplicity, CIE employed members of four trade unions: the ITGWU, the Workers' Union of Ireland (WUI), the Amalgamated Transport and General Workers Union (ATGWU) as well as the National Association of Transport Employees (NATE). Union leaders, seeking to boost membership and to reduce the number of members in arrears with their dues, requested that CIE withhold certain negotiated benefits from all but paid-up employees. The company refused but entered into an arrangement with the unions whereby it would terminate the contracts of its 3,000 workers but offer each immediate reemployment on existing terms, provided he or she agreed to be 'at all times' a member of one of the four existing unions.

However, John Meskell, a bus conductor for some fifteen years and a fully paid-up, active member of the WUI, objected to the collaborative process on principle. In particular, he was reluctant to bind himself to remain a member of one of the four unions whatever might happen in the following twenty or so years before his retirement. When CIE dismissed Meskell as per the union agreement, he was not reemployed as he refused to accept the special condition. Meskell then sued CIE, claiming the company had unlawfully interfered with his rights to freedom of association and to non-discrimination.

## TRANSLATION

When these trade union conflicts were 'put' before the court, counsel tended to claim an absolute right of freedom of association as trumps, understood as a right of individuals consistent with classic legal thought. Opposing counsel countered this by emphasising the priority of legislation duly passed by parliament. Arguing within these parameters, counsel for the National Union of Railwaymen claimed that the Trade Union Act (1941) allowed for giving 'an ultimate monopoly to a union which now represents only a minority of the workers in any particular industry'; moreover, they claimed, it provided for 'the conscription of labour' to the National Labour Party.[10] On both counts, they deemed the act repugnant to the constitution's guarantee of freedom of association (Article 40.6.1.iii) (Box 7.2). Similarly, counsel for the Educational Company contested the picketing workers' claims that the Trade Disputes Act (1906) applied to their actions, which they described as 'bogus' and simply for the purpose of union aggrandisement. If it did apply, they argued, the common law legislation was contrary to – and therefore struck down by – the constitution's guarantee of freedom of association.[11]

In both cases, counsel defending 'social' legislation on behalf of the ITGWU and the picketing IUDWC workers argued for the priority of the law as duly enacted by parliament. Counsel for the ITGWU claimed that the lawfully appointed Trade Union Tribunal had sole jurisdiction

[10] *NUR* v. *Sullivan* [1947] I.R. 77, 85, 93.
[11] *Educational Company of Ireland* v. *Fitzpatrick (No. 2)* [1961] IR 345, 352.

**Box 7.2 Freedom of Association and Union Provisions**

**Article 40**

6. 1° The State guarantees liberty for the exercise of the following rights, subject to public order and morality . . .

iii. The right of the citizens to form associations and unions. Laws, however, may be enacted for the regulation and control in the public interest of the exercise of the foregoing right.

for assessing the NUR's grievances. In the latter case, counsel for the IUDWC further claimed that workers' right to strike in furtherance of a trade dispute was 'an obvious personal right of all workers', a right, moreover, that the framers of the 1937 Constitution had never intended to prohibit.[12]

The *Meskell* case was argued on the basis of earlier judgments in *NUR* and *Educational Co.* that workers had a 'constitutional right to join a trade union or to abstain from joining one'. Furthermore, counsel for Meskell elaborated that he 'enjoyed a right of property' in being entitled to retain employment while free to remain inside or outside a trade union. CIE's insisting on continued union membership interfered with this property right.[13] Opposing counsel also invoked the right of private property but argued that CIE, as a corollary of that right, could employ whoever they might reasonably consider suitable for a given position. It followed that the state transport company was entitled to employ union members only. CIE had not broken any contract with Meskell, had not committed any tort, and could not reasonably have foreseen that he would suffer any damage.

## JUDGMENT

If counsel had argued these cases in terms broadly similar to the early property rights contestations, judges did not respond likewise and generally defer to parliamentary sovereignty. Instead, the Supreme Court justified the striking down of 'social' legislation on the basis of their

[12] *Educational Company v. Fitzpatrick* [1961] IR 345, 373.
[13] *Meskell v. CIE* [1973] I.R. 121, 127.

reading of the constitution. In *NUR*, Judge Murnaghan (S.C.) held that the contested Trade Union Act was 'not a control of the exercise of the right of association, but a denial of the right altogether'.[14] The constitution stated 'principles', he declared, which intended 'to limit the exercise by the legislature of its otherwise unlimited power of legislation' and which the judiciary had a duty to uphold.[15] Judges returned to this precedent in subsequent trade union cases.

In *Educational Co.*, Judge Teevan (H.C.) awarded the employers in the dispute an injunction to restrain their workers' picketing. The 'main consideration', he argued, was 'the balance of convenience and inconvenience which is likely to result to the parties from the granting or refusing of the order sought'. Judge Budd (H.C.) subsequently justified the protected 'right of dissociation' on the basis that if the Oireachtas could not infringe on constitutional rights of association through the Trade Union Act (1941) 'so much the less' could any 'unauthorised body of citizens'. The Supreme Court upheld his decision.[16] In *Meskell*, Judge Walsh (Supreme Court, S.C.) similarly interpreted the constitution to imply a right to abstain from joining unions. Finding that CIE had employed unlawful means to undermine that right, he awarded damages to John Meskell.

The *Educational Company* case illustrated precisely the tension between classic and social legal thought. Judge Budd literally reproduced an archetypal statement of the former, citing Sir John Earle's nineteenth-century treatise on Trade Unions:

> 'Every person has a right under the law as between himself and his fellow-subjects to full freedom in disposing of his own labour or his own capital according to his will. It follows that every other person is subject to the correlative duty arising therefrom, and is prohibited from any obstruction to the fullest exercise of this right which can be made compatible with the exercise of similar rights by others'.[17]

[14] *NUR* v. *Sullivan* [1947] I.R. 77, 102. [15] *NUR* v. *Sullivan* [1947] I.R. 77, 99.

[16] Judges Kingsmill Moore and O'Dálaigh held that Art. 40.6.1.iii carried an implicit guarantee that citizens should not be coerced to join associations against their will, or 'a right of dissociation'. Separately, Judge Haugh held that the nine workers in this particular case formed a combination for the purposes of staying out of the union which could not be interfered with without violating their freedom of association. *Educational Company* v. *Fitzpatrick* [1961] IR 345.

[17] *Educational Company* v. *Fitzpatrick* [1961] IR 339, 367. As discussed in Chapter 1, the wage-contract between labour and capital took on the appearance of a simple exchange between consenting parties. However, in practice, the contract concealed coercive social relations, namely

Although based on English case-law and an English treatise, Budd argued, these 'principles' were 'to a great extent enshrined in somewhat different language in the Constitution'.[18] In the same case, Kingsmill Moore spoke for the majority of the Supreme Court in articulating the classic doctrine of workers possessing a property right in their labour. For the worker, he suggested, the constitution's property provisions (Article 40.3.2) 'may perhaps include an undertaking to protect his right to dispose of his labour as he wills, and would include impliedly a right not to be forced against his will into a union or association which exacts from him a regular payment'.[19]

By no means were judges' interpretations of the 1937 Constitution obvious or unanimous. On the contrary, in *NUR*, Judge Gavan Duffy (H.C.) had initially agreed with the ITGWU's counsel and found that the regulation of union multiplicity was constitutional: a covering clause in the guarantee of freedom of association allowed for its 'regulation and control in the public interest'. Again, similar to the property rights judgments, Gavan Duffy refused to encroach upon policy-making and argued that the legislation had been passed by 'the appropriate organ of government, far better equipped than the judiciary to know the need'.[20] The Supreme Court, however, reversed this decision.

Similarly, in *Educational Co.*, the minority judgment of Chief Justice Maguire (S.C.) and Judge Lavery (S.C.) found in favour of the picketing workers. They interpreted Article 40.6.iii to include their exercising a right of association to choose their associates and to strengthen their union. The IUDWC workers were simply exercising the right of 'refusing to associate with workmen who are not members of their Union', a right necessary to bring in all those upon whose behalf they would be negotiating with employers.[21] Moreover, Chief Justice Maguire held that no constitutional provision prohibited 'such an obvious personal right of all workers' as the right to strike in furtherance of a trade dispute.[22] The workers' right to strike, however, remained unobvious to a majority of judges in the case.

capital's extraction of surplus-value from labour. See Marx's critique of Bentham on this point, Karl Marx, 2003 [1887], *Capital I: A Critique of Political Economy*, p. 172.

18 *Educational Company* v. *Fitzpatrick* [1961] IR 339, 367.

19 *Educational Company* v. *Fitzpatrick* [1961] IR 339, 395.

20 *NUR* v. *Sullivan* [1947] I.R. 77, 88.

21 *Educational Company* v. *Fitzpatrick* [1961] IR 339, 382–3.

22 *Educational Company* v. *Fitzpatrick* [1961] IR 339, 373, 379.

## JURISPRUDENCE

Industrial unrest sharpened jurists' attention to trade union rights, judicial decision-making and, in particular, the tension between old common law immunities for industrial action and the constitutional 'freedom of association' provisions recently discovered in *NUR* and *Educational Company*.[23] The Irish courts' approach to trade disputes, jurists concurred, was comparatively 'strict' and resulted in consistently narrowing the Trade Disputes Act (1906) protection for union organisation and strike action.[24] John Kelly (1967) criticised the judges' 'narrow construction' of the 1906 Act (which defined the term 'trade dispute') and their 'rigid' interpretation of Articles 40.6.1 (iii) and Article 40.6.2 (which outlined union rights to peaceable assembly). Judge Murnaghan's *NUR* judgment, in particular, displayed 'a lack of balance'.[25] The cumulative effect of the courts' decisions, James Casey (1972) observed, was to make the traditional strike weapon 'somewhat unreliable'.[26]

Irish judges, Mary Matthews (1973) outlined, had been 'more concerned to protect the individual's private rights to associate or dissociate as he wishes rather than the legal collective right of workers to combine'.[27] Similarly, according to Gerry Whyte (1981), the judiciary's 'not very cogent' reasoning failed to distinguish the individual right to join a union from the right to *form* a union, a collective right more greatly emphasised in the Irish text of the constitution.[28] The *NUR*, *Educational Company*, and *Meskell* decisions, in emphasising the individual 'right to dissociate', had important implications for the undermining of closed shop agreements and the persistence of union multiplicity. This created ongoing conditions for inter-union and 'unofficial' disputes.[29] Parenthetically, Whyte also observed that the

[23] Contributors included V. T. H. Delany, A. D. Hughes, E. P de Blaghd, J. B. McCartney, R. F. V. Heuston, John Kelly, James Casey, and Mary Matthews. See J. McCartney, 1964, 'Strike Law and the Constitution' in the *Irish Jurist*, 30 (4); R. F. V. Heuston, 1969, 'Trade unions and the Law' in *The Irish Jurist*, 4 (1), pp. 10–22, p. 11. James Casey, 1972, 'Reform of Collective Bargaining Law: Some Constitutional Implications', pp. 1–16, p. 1; Mary Matthews, 1973, 'The Tort of Conspiracy in Irish Labour Law' in the *Irish Jurist*, 8 (2), pp. 252–74, pp. 264–5, 266, 272–3; and Kelly, 1967, *Fundamental Rights and the Irish Law and Constitution*, p. 166.

[24] Max Abrahamson, 1961, 'Trade Disputes Act: Strict Interpretation in Ireland' in *Modern Law Review*, 24, pp. 596–603.

[25] Kelly, 1967, *Fundamental Rights and the Irish Law and Constitution*, p. 166.

[26] Casey, 1972, 'Reform of Collective Bargaining Law', p. 1.

[27] Matthews, 1973, 'The Tort of Conspiracy in Irish Labour Law', p. 268.

[28] Gerry Whyte, 1981, 'Industrial Relations and the Irish Constitution' in *Irish Jurist*, 16 (1), pp. 35–77, p. 55.

[29] Whyte, 1981, 'Industrial Relations and the Irish Constitution', p. 36.

European Court of Human Rights had recently affirmed this right in a similar case.[30]

The most important aspect of judges' constitutional decisions, however, was the ease with which employers could obtain injunctions to restrain picketing and strike action. As James Casey (1978) observed, Judge Kingsmill Moore's view that picketing was 'a murderous weapon' – by implication one to be withheld – seemed to prevail.[31] Specifically, Judge Teevan's 'novel' test – 'the balance of convenience and inconvenience' – and his decision granting an injunction to the employers in the case was subsequently taken to provide guidelines for the granting and refusing of labour injunctions. Newspaper reports suggested that it was only necessary to complain of picketing in an affidavit to obtain an injunction.[32] Injunctions were thus extremely popular with Irish employers: Ferdinand von Prondzynski (1980) conservatively estimated that judges issued some fifty annually.[33]

Judges typically viewed injunctions as a means of 'preventing the infliction of irreparable damage' and keeping matters in statu quo until the hearing. In reality, von Prondzynski claimed, full trials rarely if ever followed, the injunction stopped the union in its tracks while the employer resumed efforts to defeat the strike free from interferences.[34] Teevan's 'balance of convenience' test did not have regard to the loss of bargaining strength suffered by the union.[35] Effectively robbed of the power to use the strike as a sanction in negotiations with employers, unions called for the injunction's abolition. Exasperated by judicial interventions and injunctions, striking workers at the shipyards of New Ross, Co. Wexford and at the car assembly factory of Talbot Ireland in Tallaght, Co. Dublin simply refused to obey the court orders and persisted in their strikes, with varying degrees of success.[36]

30 See *Young, James and Webster* [1981] IRLR 408. Whyte, 1981, 'Industrial Relations and the Irish Constitution', p. 77.

31 *Educational Company* [1961] IR 345, 390. J. P. Casey, 1978, 'Review: McCarthy's Trade Unions in Ireland, 1894–1960' in *Irish Jurist*, 13 (2), pp. 396–99, p. 399.

32 Injunctions may be interlocutory or ex parte. An ex parte injunction may be obtained by a plaintiff (employer) from a High Court judge at any time or place (including the judge's home) without hearing the defendant. They last for a short period of one to two weeks. An interlocutory injunction is temporary, operative until the case comes to a full trial but is granted for an indefinite period. J. P. Casey, 1978, 'Review: McCarthy's Trade Unions in Ireland, 1894–1960', p. 399.

33 Ferdinand von Prondzynski, 1980, 'The Problem of the Labour Injunction' in *Irish Jurist*, 16 (2), pp. 228–40, p. 232.

34 Prondzynski, 1980, 'The Problem of the Labour Injunction', pp. 230–1.

35 Prondzynski, 1980, 'The Problem of the Labour Injunction', pp. 239–40.

36 See Chapter 10, 'Constitution-Making "from below"'.

From the 1980s onwards, contributors to the *Irish Jurist* registered the neoliberal transformation of capital-labour relations in Ireland. The complexities of modern industrial production, Tony Kerr (1980) argued, made the boundaries of industrial action increasingly unclear and the potential liabilities for unions increasingly open-ended.[37] '[I]ncreased capital mobility, Brian Wilkinson (1989) claimed, 'has dramatically altered the balance of power between capital and labour as employers threatened with a strike can shift production locations relatively easily'.[38] In these circumstances, trade unions seemed to be reverting to the 'friendly societies' role that Friedrich Hayek, the neoclassical economist, had envisaged for them.[39]

With the emergence of 'social partnership', economic growth, and industrial peace in the 1990s, state-labour relationships were newly regulated to register the new balance of class forces. The new Industrial Relations Act (1990), Tony Kerr (1990) observed, placed restrictions on an employer's ability to obtain injunctions – thereby removing a strong point of contention for unions. However, the legislation linked this to requirements that trade unions provide one week's notice to employers before taking strike action.[40] In practice, the balance of convenience test continued to ignore the loss of bargaining strength to the union. Instead, Wilkinson and Kerr both argued for a collective bargaining system such as that in Germany, based not on susceptible, common law immunities but on positive rights, including a constitutionally protected right to strike.[41]

Thereafter, as the 1990s and 2000s witnessed an ongoing decline in the percentage of the unionised workforce (from 60 per cent in the early 1980s to 30 per cent in 2010), a vacuum was left by the declining number of workers having their pay and conditions determined by social partnership agreements. EU employment law, Michelle O'Sullivan (2011) observed, has instead become pervasive, providing

[37] Tony Kerr, 1980, 'Trade Disputes, Economic Torts and the Constitution' in *Irish Jurist*, 16 (2), pp. 241–61, p. 242–3.

[38] Wilkinson, 1989, 'Workers, Constitutions and the Irish Judiciary', p. 199.

[39] Wilkinson, 1989, 'Workers, Constitutions and the Irish Judiciary', p. 224. See also Bob Simpson, 1985, 'Review: Kerr and Whyte, Irish Trade Union Law' in *Irish Jurist*, 20 (1), pp. 220–3, p. 220.

[40] Where a majority vote in favour of industrial action and one week's notice is given, the employer will not be entitled to apply to a court for an injunction unless notice is also give to the union; the court will not grant an injunction if the respondents establish a fair case for their acting in furtherance of a trade dispute. Tony Kerr, 1988, 'Review' in *Irish Jurist*, 23 (1), pp. 172–5, p. 174.

[41] Kerr, 1980, 'Trade Disputes, Economic Torts and the Constitution', pp. 242–3.

the substantive rules governing the terms and conditions of employment, including contracts and their termination, equality, leave, bullying, health and safety as well as industrial relations.[42] Analysing a specific set of EU regulations governing workers' rights in the course of business acquisitions or outsourcing, John McMullen (2001) criticised the extent to which employees remained exposed to 'the classic liberal contractual approach to the employment relation'.[43]

In this process of socio-legal transformation, the judiciary appeared to be neutral in applying constitutional rights. However, in Ireland as elsewhere, their approach was consistent with neoliberal economic prescriptions that emphasised formal equality and ignored the existence of substantive inequalities and material differences.[44] Notably, the courts' treatment of corporations – accepting that corporations can be protected from aspects of legislative control on the basis of the rights of the individuals – contrasted sharply with their restriction of unions' actions 'to the extent of being virtually meaningless'.[45] Any judge who recognised the need for workers to have collective protective rights *as workers* would undermine such formalist, neoliberal orthodoxies. Instead, she would necessarily have to recognise and elaborate a 'jurisprudence of labour liberty'.[46]

## CONCLUSION

The nature of the economic rights contestations at stake in *NUR*, *Educational Company*, and *Meskell* highlighted wider tendencies and issues within the evolving trade union movement in Ireland. *NUR* indicated the inter-union and inter-party rivalry that fragmented postwar labour organisation, primarily on the basis of inherited core-peripheral or national privileges, and facilitated a nationalist hegemony of the social question in subsequent decades. In these circumstances, unions' maintaining or increasing their membership and dues could be divisive. The strategy of doing so by collaborating with employers and by denying individual members a choice in what union to be a member

42 Michelle O'Sullivan, 2011, 'Review: Daly and Doherty, Principles of Irish Employment Law' in *Irish Jurist* 46(1), p. 235.

43 John McMullen, 2001, 'Transfer of Undertakings' in *Irish Jurist*, 36 (1), pp. 83–125, p. 125. See also Silvana Sciarra, 2001, *Labour law in the courts: national judges and the European Court of Justice*.

44 See Walsh, 2009, 'Equality, the Legal System and Employment Law'.

45 Wilkinson, 1989, 'Workers, Constitutions and the Irish Judiciary', p. 199.

46 Wilkinson, 1989, 'Workers, Constitutions and the Irish Judiciary', p. 226.

of, as was at stake in *Meskell*, was unimaginative, more characteristic of the instrumental reasoning of a bureaucratic organisation than the critical reasoning about means and ends typical of a more democratic, more egalitarian one.[47] Finally, and perhaps most importantly, the *Educational Company* case illustrated the key strength of Irish trade union organisation, the capacity to win gains in wages, terms, and conditions at the molecular level of the closed shop. This capacity, closely tied to workers' direct actions such as strikes, pickets, and boycotts, was to be undermined in the course of the neoliberal turn.

Judicial interventions in *NUR*, *Educational Company*, and *Meskell* played an important role in this process. The property rights contestations examined in the previous chapter similarly centred on individual property owners' challenges to 'social' restrictions or state intervention on perceived 'classic' market rights of property and contract. With the exception of the rent restrictions and land valuation cases, however, judges tended to defer to parliamentary sovereignty or, in the language of the new constitutionalism, to afford the executive a 'margin of appreciation'. The same cannot be said of the trade union or 'freedom of association' contestations. Here, a majority of judges drew on a neoformalist reading of constitutional 'principles' to identify an individual's 'right of dissociation'. Their judgments undermined closed shop agreements and, moreover, established a low threshold of court intervention in industrial disputes. In subsequent years, the associated proliferation of court injunctions prohibiting workers' collective, direct actions against employers was non-trivial and, in practice, tended to corral trade unions in costly, often unwinnable legal wrangles.

Throughout this period, similar to earlier property rights analyses, jurists identified the priority that the courts afforded to individual over collective claims and the associated limitations of purely formal guarantees in transforming substantive material inequalities. Contemporary jurists analysing these cases recognised the comparatively conservative – if not class-biased – nature of these judicial interventions. In more recent years, commentators further recorded the increasing displacement of the state's 'social' infrastructure, involving trade unions in voluntarist tripartite bargaining, with 'classic' contractual EU employment law. These criticisms provide a useful point of departure for understanding both the actions and socio-economic rights discourses

[47] On the distinction between instrumental and critical-emancipatory rationality, see Jurgen Habermas 1970. *Towards a Rational Society*. Boston: Beacon Press.

of striking Talbot workers who refused to obey court injunctions (an instance of constitutionalism 'from below' examined in Chapter 10) as well as the judicial decision-making and discourses evident in the family, education, and welfare rights contestations examined in the next chapter.

## CHAPTER EIGHT

# CONTESTING FAMILY, EDUCATION, AND WELFARE RIGHTS

> *. . . As a mother having him actually look at me and acknowledge that he knew I existed, you know, that recharges a mother. It enabled me to bring much more of myself to him. In practical ways within the family the fact that he was looking at brothers and sisters reinforced their interest in him. You know everything seemed to run better . . . every single thing he gained had huge practical consequences for us . . .*
>
> – Kathryn Sinnott, 2001[1]

> *[T]he rights to be found in the Constitution, anyway as elaborated by the judiciary, on the whole, protect the advantaged more than the disadvantaged. Examples are the rights to reputation, privacy and property and the right to do business (It is worth noticing that no one seems to have suggested that the last two are socio-economic rights and, hence, that they ought not to receive strong judicial protection). By contrast, the rights, which might help the disadvantaged – equality, free speech and socio-economic rights – have not been emphasised by the judiciary.*
>
> – David Gwynn Morgan, 2002[2]

Solicitor Michael O'Mahony responded critically to the publication of the Kennedy Report (1970) into industrial school reform. He argued that the statutory definition of an 'industrial school' ('a school for the industrial training of children in which children are lodged, clothed and fed as well as taught') was inaccurate: 'a place of detention would be closer to reality'.[3] At the Children's Court, children usually appeared without legal representation, the majority making 'involuntary confessions', or admitting guilt for fear of worse punishment. Insufficient numbers of social workers ensured that children were committed for want of time to investigate their respective situations.[4] Similarly, for want

[1] Cited by Judge Barr in *Sinnott* v. *Minister for Education* [2001] 2 IR 545, 568.

[2] D. G. Morgan, 2002, 'Review', p. 346.

[3] Michael O'Mahony, 1971, 'Legal Aspects of Residential Child Care' in the *Irish Jurist*, 6 (1) pp. 217–36, 226. On the practice of involuntary confessions (admitting guilt in response to the potential threat of worse punishment), see Peter Shanley, 1970, 'The Formal Cautioning of Juvenile Offenders' in *Irish Jurist*, 6 (1), pp. 262–79.

[4] F. J. Elliott (1972), a planning officer with the Eastern Health Board, supported O'Mahony's assessment. F. J. Elliott, 1972, 'Notes: Residential Child Care: Health Act Admissions' in the *Irish Jurist*, 7 (1), pp. 358–9.

of an interested party to act on the child's behalf, appeals were almost never taken. These practices, O'Mahony claimed, raised potential constitutional claims as to 'whether all citizens are in fact equal before the law . . .' Owing to the cost of legal services, however, such challenges were unlikely to arise.[5]

The development of family, education, and welfare rights contestations in Ireland, as O'Mahony's article indicates, cannot be understood in isolation from the semi-peripheral development of the Republic of Ireland and its welfare state. Evident in the 1922 and 1937 constitution-making processes, successive Irish governments prioritised securing stable capital flows for dominant class interests. The result was comparatively low living standards and levels of welfare effort combined with increased reliance on institutionalisation and on voluntary, highly gendered forms of care, notably provided by the Catholic Church and by the family.[6] The Irish state's institutions of welfare, care, and justice, subject to politically determined priorities, values, and resource constraints, intersected to reproduce instances of both domestic and institutional domination and abuse.[7]

In the course of social and economic transformation from the 1960s onwards, the Irish state significantly increased its welfare effort and service provision. However, decision-making power continued to concentrate in highly centralised bureaucracies while cash transfers rather than universal rights to welfare services remained the rule.[8] Such services as did exist were vulnerable to fiscal retrenchment and privatisation from the 1980s onwards. Socio-economic rights cases in the 1990s and 2000s revealed the limits of the state's transformation, its continued reliance on institutionalisation, and its continued refusal to countenance solidaristic or universal rights-based forms of welfare provisions as opposed to highly segmented, voluntarist ones (see Box 8.1). The conflicts examined in this chapter each share in common these more general conditions and social relations. Moreover, these socio-economic rights cases highlight the particularly severe implications of these conditions

[5] O'Mahony, 1971, 'Legal Aspects of Residential Child Care', pp. 226, 219.

[6] On the gendering of care relations, see John Baker, Kathleen Lynch, and Maureen Lyons (eds.), 2009, *Affective Equality: Love, Care and Injustice*. London: Palgrave. See also Silvia Federici, 2012, *Revolution at Point Zero: Housework, Reproduction, and Feminist Struggle*. Brooklyn: PM Press.

[7] Rafferty and O'Sullivan, 2000, *Suffer the Little Children*; Finnegan, 2004, *Do Penance or Perish: Magdalene Asylums in Ireland*; Bruce Arnold, 2009, *Irish Gulag*.

[8] See Mel Cousins, 2005, *Explaining the Irish Welfare State*. New York: Mellen Press.

**Box 8.1 Family, Education, and Welfare Rights Cases**

*Doyle* v. *Minister for Education* [1956] IR 217

*Ryan* v. *Attorney General* [1965] IR 294

McGee v. *Attorney General* [1974] I.R. 284

*Crowley* v. *Minister for Education* [1980] IR 102

*O'Reilly* v. *Limerick Corporation* [1989] ILRM 181

*Sinnott* v. *Minister for Education* [2001] 2 IR 545

*T.D.* v. *Minister for Education*, [2001] 4 IR 259

Re: Article 26 and the Health (Amendment) Bill 2004 [2005] 1 IR 105

for groups already experiencing discrimination, including women, children, Travellers, and the disabled.

Citizens in these constitutional cases found themselves in the contradictory position of having to invoke the constitution's Catholic social provisions to contest the implications of Catholic social legal design for the arrested development of the Irish state's welfare infrastructure. In the process of translating these social conflicts into legal cases, counsel claiming rights from the state characteristically invoked the constitutional rights provisions as absolute or as trumping ordinary statute legislation. From the late 1980s onwards, however, those claiming socio-economic rights against the state combined these earlier forms of appeal with newly globalising forms of human rights rhetoric, declaring civil-political and socio-economic rights to be 'universal, indivisible and interdependent and interrelated'.[9] Counsels' invocation of the doctrine of proportionality further registered and reproduced the globalisation of neoformalist modes of decision-making and discourse. Again, similar to the property and trade union rights cases examined earlier, counsel

[9] After the Cold War, the 1993 World Conference on Human Rights in Vienna formally reasserted the mutual importance of the International Covenant on Civil and Political Rights and the International Covenant on Economic, Social, and Cultural Rights. Steiner, Alston, and Goodman (eds.), 2008, *International Human Rights in Context*, p. 263.

for the state typically argued for the judiciary's non-interference with validly enacted legislation or a duly appointed administrative body.

The outcomes in these socio-economic rights cases were by no means easily predicted. Insofar as judges concurred with the liberalisation of Irish society and the elaboration of a right to privacy jurisprudence, they proved 'activist' and struck down Catholic 'social' legislation prohibiting the importation of contraceptives. The courts proved much slower, however, to impose additional economic costs on the state. Judges rejected such claims on the basis of a distinction between commutative and distributive forms of justice, and further invoked the separation of powers or a 'margin of appreciation' to justify the courts' non-intervention. Jurists debated the finer points of judges' reasoning in terms of conflicting principles and modes of interpretation. In some cases, they provided convincing counterarguments to judicial reasoning in the socio-economic rights judgments, at least sufficient to demonstrate the ambiguity of decision if not the element of political choice involved.[10] Others identified the courts system's apparent incapacity to cope with the possible volume of such cases as the pragmatic basis of Irish judges' opposition to constitutionalising socio-economic rights.

## ORIGINS

Illustrating the intersection of capital, church, and state in Irish welfare provision, *Doyle* v. *Minister for Education* [1956] arose after Desmond Doyle, a painter and decorator from Dublin's Fatima Mansions, was made unemployed during the recession of the 1950s. When Doyle and his wife separated, the National Society for the Prevention of Cruelty to Children (NSPCC) had their six children classified as 'found destitute' at the Children's Court, committing them to various industrial schools until the age of sixteen.[11] Doyle, understanding this to be a

[10] See Whyte, 2002, *Social Inclusion and the Legal System.*

[11] The Commission to Inquire into Child Abuse concluded that the NSPCC and its successor, the Irish Society for the Prevention of Cruelty to Children, played a key role in committing children to industrial schools, primarily on the grounds of poverty. Members were motivated by a need to regulate the lives of the poor and the working class, including the inculcation of Victorian values of 'responsibility'. Catholic Archbishop of Dublin John Charles McQuaid was an influential patron. Commission to Inquire into Child Abuse, Volume 5, Chapter 1. Available at: www.childabusecommission.com/rpt/05-01.php. See also Sarah-Anne Buckley, 2013, *The Cruelty Man: Child welfare, the NSPCC and the State in Ireland, 1889–1956*. Manchester: Manchester University Press.

temporary measure, gave his consent.[12] Seven months later, having secured a weekly wage (£8 7s 6d) and a new home with his father, Doyle employed a solicitor to apply to the Minister for Education for the discharge of his eight-year-old daughter Evelyn from St. Joseph's Industrial School. The Minister, Fine Gael's Richard Mulcahy, refused to intervene and cited Doyle's inability to furnish satisfactory evidence of either suitable accommodation or 'having procured suitable female assistance in his home'. (Doyle's new partner was Protestant and the minister was 'being got at' by the bishops).[13] He subsequently applied to the courts to compel the minister to release his daughter.

During the 1960s, as forms of state intervention and welfare provision gradually increased, the Dublin Health Authority's research on the high rate of tooth decay amongst Dublin's urban population prompted Fianna Fáil's Seán MacEntee to introduce the Health Act (1960). This legislation provided for the fluoridation of the piped water supply provided by Dublin Corporation. The Drumcondra home of Gladys Ryan, her husband, and five children was connected to this supply; no alternative water source was readily available. With political and legal support provided by Fine Gael TD Richie Ryan (no relation), Gladys Ryan opposed the fluoridation scheme on a number of grounds, including an ethical objection to mass medication, and began a legal challenge.[14]

Over the same period, liberal and feminist groups such as the Irish Family Planning Association and Irish Women's Liberation Movement increasingly challenged inherited Victorian and Catholic social legislation, including that which circumscribed women's bodily autonomy.[15] The Irish state's continued prohibition of the sale or importation of contraceptives under the Criminal Law Amendment Act (1935) provided an increasingly contested example of such legislation. Mary McGee was a 27-year-old woman, married with four children in Skerries, Co. Dublin. When she received medical advice that another pregnancy would put her life at risk, she and her husband decided to use a diaphragm and contraceptive jelly, the latter being manufactured in

[12] This impression was contributed to by advice from the District Justice 'not to leave the child in the school too long'. *Doyle* v. *The Minister for Education* [1956] IR 217, 218.

[13] Evelyn Doyle, 2002, *Evelyn: a true story*. London: Orion, p. 115.

[14] Adrienne Murphy, 'Judgement that permitted fluoridation of water may have been unsound' in *Hot Press*, 18 April 2013.

[15] Linda Connolly, 'The outcomes and consequences of second wave feminism in Ireland' in Linda Connolly and Niamh Hourigan (eds.), 2006, *Social Movements and Ireland*. Manchester: Manchester University Press. pp. 58–85.

England. The family's poor, cramped living conditions further influenced their decision. Upon the contraceptive's arrival by post, the customs authority duly seized and confiscated it. The case of *McGee* v. *the Attorney General* [1974] arose when McGee subsequently claimed a declaration from the High Court that the 1935 legislation was unconstitutional.

The Catholic 'social' also remained entrenched in education, notably in terms of controlling schools' 'ethos' and appointments. During the later 1970s, the Irish National Teachers' Organisation (INTO) disputed one such appointment at the National School in Drimoleague, Co. Cork. The local parish priest, Fr. John Crowley, had sent a list of applicants to the Department of Education accompanied by a letter stating the instructions of the Bishop of Cork and Ross, Cornelius Lucey. The Bishop's preference, Nicholas McCarthy, received the post, notwithstanding his having less than the five years' experience required by the existing rules of promotion. The INTO regarded the decision as a blatantly unfair attempt to give the post to an ineligible candidate at the expense of eligible union members, including one teacher and union member with twelve years' experience. In April 1976, following a unanimous ballot in favour of taking strike action, all teachers, except McCarthy, withdrew their services at Drimoleague, Castledonovan, and Cnoc Buí primary schools, directly affecting some two hundred children. In August, following an INTO instruction, teachers in neighbouring schools refused to enrol any Drimoleague pupils.

The Department of Education oversaw a makeshift arrangement to circumvent the strike. McCarthy continued teaching fourth, fifth, and sixth classes while parents paid unqualified teachers, mainly local girls who had just obtained their Leaving Certificate, to teach their children. In June 1977, the INTO withdrew its circular to neighbouring schools. Thereafter, a group of parents secured an order in the High Court for the provision of buses to bring children from the affected schools to other national schools in adjoining parishes. The case of *Crowley* v. *Ireland* [1980] arose when Patricia Crowley and other parents contested these arrangements, bringing a constitutional challenge for the provision of free primary education and, as directed against the INTO, damages for a conspiracy to deprive their children of their constitutional rights.

During the 1980s, the privatisation of social housing supplies that occurred alongside government austerity measures had particular and severe implications for Travellers. Some 1,149 Traveller families were living on the roadside in unofficial sites throughout the state.[16] In Limerick City, where conditions were not atypical, existing halting sites lacked toilet facilities, running water, refuse collection, or hard surfaces for caravans. In the mid-1980s, a group comprised of Travellers, the Saint Vincent de Paul, and the Limerick Council of Trade Unions made proposals to Limerick City Council for creating new sites, which, though approved 'in principle', came to nothing. Accordingly, for some eight years, John O'Reilly's family along with four others had been living in caravans 'illegally and as trespassers' on a site owned by Limerick Corporation on the Childers Road. When road works necessitated the caravans' removal, O'Reilly's solicitor threatened injunction proceedings unless the Corporation provided an alternative site. Negotiations fell through, however, 'mainly as a result of successful picketing by residents living in the vicinity of the proposed new site'.[17] Some 150 children were directly affected. In *O'Reilly* v. *Limerick Corporation* [1989], the O'Reilly family and others sought the provision of appropriate halting site facilities and compensation for damages.

The number of social and economic rights cases appearing before the Irish Courts increased significantly in the 1990s, many of which followed the *O'Reilly* example of combining public interest litigation with wider civil society campaigns. The most high profile of these constitutional challenges centred on the Irish state's low welfare effort and continued reliance on informal, voluntary provision of care, treatment, and education to autistic children. In the experience of Jamie Sinnott, a 23-year-old autistic adult, and Kathyrn Sinnott, his mother and primary caregiver, Southern Health Board officials had relied on discredited practices for treating autism and were unaware of well-documented alternatives. Following budget cuts, the Education and Development Centre at Lota, Co. Cork where Jamie had received some two years of education, was restructured such that the class was ultimately discontinued. Up to the hearing of the Sinnotts' court action in 1999, the State had provided Jamie with no more than two years of primary education. By that time, hundreds of similar claims were outstanding against the state. Kathryn Sinnott's attempts to secure treatment and educational facilities for Jamie had evolved into a broader campaign on behalf of

16 Travelling People Review Body, 1980, *Report of the Travelling People Review Body*. Dublin: Stationary Office.
17 *O'Reilly* v. *Limerick Corporation* [1989] ILRM 181, 183.

autistic children, notably featuring the Irish Autism Alliance of which Sinnott, a Catholic social activist, was patron.[18]

Over the same period, a series of constitutional cases were also taken seeking to direct the state to make adequate provision in relation to both the accommodation and educational needs of children with behavioural problems. On a number of occasions, the Departments of Health and Education assured the High Court that such children would be provided with 'high support units'.[19] Notwithstanding the courts' issuing of several declaratory orders to this effect, the state did not implement the policy in a timely manner. While sixty units were required by the early 2000s, only eighteen were available. As a result, applicants for institutional care were being placed in detention centres intended for children convicted of criminal charges. The case of *TD* v. *Minister for Education* [2001] arose in these circumstances. Responding favourably to the application of TD, a minor, along with eight other teenagers and young adults, Judge Peter Kelly granted a mandatory injunction requiring the Minister for Education to complete the development of suitable accommodation within a specified time scale.[20] The Departments of Health and Education subsequently appealed this decision to the Supreme Court.

The final socio-economic rights case examined here again illustrated recent Irish governments' neoliberal approach towards residential care for the elderly and, in particular, the potential implications of the state's centralised administration of welfare provision. Following the Health

[18] See Anna Kingston, 2007, *Mothering Special Needs*. London: Kingsley Publishers. p. 38.

[19] *FN* v. *Minister for Education* [1995] involved a twelve-year-old orphan for whom the Eastern Health Board, under the Children's Act (1908), failed to provide accommodation. Judge Geoghegan ruled that the State had a constitutional obligation to establish 'suitable arrangements of containment with treatment' and, once assured that the provision of high support units was forthcoming, adjourned the case. Two years later, however, in *D.B.* v. *Minister for Justice* [1999], Judge Peter Kelly discovered these arrangements had been 'substantially departed from without that fact ever having been made known to the court'. He described as a 'scandal' the government's frequent policy changes and interdepartmental wrangles which delayed the needed legislation and claimed jurisdiction for the court 'to intervene in what has been called policy' in certain, urgent circumstances.

[20] *TD* v. *Minister for Education*, [2001] 4 IR 259. TD was born in 1983, raised in Inchicore, Co. Dublin, and enrolled in a series of schools for pupils with 'emotional disturbance'. In 1996, the District Court, acting under the Children's Act (1908), issued an order so as to place the thirteen year old in St. Laurence's industrial school, Finglas, Co. Dublin. The eight other applicants attached to the TD case were teenagers or young adults who had come into contact with either the Dublin Metropolitan Children's Court or the Eastern Health Board and had come to be accommodated in centres such as Trinity House, Newtown House, St. Michael's Remand and Assessment Centre, Oberstown Centres, Churchtown, St. Augustine's Special School in Blackrock, St. Laurence's, Killinarden House, An Grianán, Whitehall, or St. Peter's Special School.

Act (1970), the Health Board was obligated to maintain certain categories of patients, mainly elderly persons of limited means, in a hospital or home free of charge. Notwithstanding the law, however, these patients had incurred charges, allegedly through administrative error. In response, the Fianna Fáil-Progressive Democrat coalition government introduced the Health (Amendment) Bill (2004) which aimed to validate these illegal charges retrospectively. The case of *Re: Article 26 and the Health (Amendment) Bill 2004* [2005] arose on foot of President McAleese's subsequent referral of this legislation to the Supreme Court.

## TRANSLATION

Similar to the property and trade union rights cases, counsel claiming rights from the state characteristically invoked the 'social' rights provisions as absolute or as trumping ordinary statute legislation (see Box 8.2). Conversely, counsel for the state usually argued for the judiciary's non-interference in a duly appointed body or constitutionally valid legislation (or argued on the basis of an 'exceptions' clause in the constitution itself). Remarkably, as illustrated in the *Doyle* case, those who contested the implications of the Catholic social for their everyday lives often found themselves arguing their claim in a constitutional rights discourse favoured by clericalists.

At the High Court, counsel for Desmond Doyle argued that his rights as a father were superior to the Children's Act (1908), including rights to enjoy Evelyn's company (Article 41) and to direct her education (Article 42). Conversely, counsel for the Minister for Education raised a technical objection to Doyle's application for the release of his daughter: since the law required the consent of 'the parents' (plural), the application, which lacked his wife's signature, was deemed invalid. Similarly, Article 41 referred to 'the family' and did not confer on either parent individually an absolute right to their children's custody. Counsel for the state further argued that the particular facts of the case brought it within the 'exceptional cases' allotted to parliamentary oversight (Article 42.5).

In the water fluoridation case, counsel for Gladys Ryan claimed that the Health Act violated the authority of the family (Article 41) and the family's right to educate their children (Article 42), provided that the word 'education' was given 'a wide meaning so that it

**Box 8.2 Personal, Family, and Education Rights Provisions**

**Personal Rights, Article 40**

3. 1° The State guarantees in its laws to respect, and, as far as practicable, by its laws to defend and vindicate the personal rights of the citizen. 2° The State shall, in particular, by its laws protect as best it may from unjust attack and, in the case of injustice done, vindicate the life, person, good name, and property rights of every citizen.

**The Family, Article 41**

1. 1° The State recognises the Family as the natural primary and fundamental unit group of Society, and as a moral institution possessing inalienable and imprescriptible rights, antecedent and superior to all positive law. 2° The State, therefore, guarantees to protect the Family in its constitution and authority, as the necessary basis of social order and as indispensable to the welfare of the Nation and the State.
2. 1° In particular, the State recognises that by her life within the home, woman gives to the State a support without which the common good cannot be achieved. 2° The State shall, therefore, endeavour to ensure that mothers shall not be obliged by economic necessity to engage in labour to the neglect of their duties in the home.

**Education, Article 42**

1. The State acknowledges that the primary and natural educator of the child is the Family and guarantees to respect the inalienable right and duty of parents to provide, according to their means, for the religious and moral, intellectual, physical and social education of their children. . . .
4. The State shall provide for free primary education and shall endeavour to supplement and give reasonable aid to private and corporate educational initiative, and, when the public good requires it, provide other educational facilities or institutions with due regard, however, for the rights of parents, especially in the matter of religious and moral formation.

5. In exceptional cases, where the parents for physical or moral reasons fail in their duty towards their children, the State as guardian of the common good, by appropriate means shall endeavour to supply the place of the parents, but always with due regard for the natural and imprescriptible rights of the child.

would include rearing and nurturing'.[21] Her counsel also argued that the scheme violated her right to 'bodily integrity', a right which, though not explicitly mentioned in the constitution, could be inferred from a heretofore novel reading of Article 40.3.1–2. (In essence, they argued that while Article 40.3.1 outlined the state's guarantee of the 'personal rights of the citizen, the phrase 'in particular' in Article 40.3.2 suggested the existence of rights other than those particularly stated in that article). Counsel for the state did not contest this interpretation or the existence of an 'unenumerated' right to bodily integrity. They denied, however, that any 'natural right' to water existed independent of a legal contract with the local authority. Both sides drew on international expert testimony as to whether water fluoridation did in fact infringe upon citizens' bodily integrity.

Similarly, in the contraceptives case, counsel for Mary McGee claimed that Article 40.3 included an unenumerated right to marital privacy. In support of this claim, they cited a number of US precedents, notably *Griswold* v. *Connecticut*, in which the US Supreme Court held that the constitution's right to privacy necessitated overturning legislation outlawing the use of contraceptives.[22] Conversely, counsel for the state raised a technical objection to the use of these precedents. Irish law did not ban the use of contraceptives, merely their importation and sale; hence, American jurisprudence was inappropriate to the particular facts of the case. Moreover, the prohibition on the importation of contraceptives was enacted in order to implement 'the social policy of the legislature'. Mary McGee's action thus amounted to 'an attempt to secure judicial interference in a matter which is within the exclusive domain of the legislature'.[23]

In the Drimoleague school conflict, counsel for Eilish Crowley and associated parents raised two claims. First, they challenged the INTO and, in particular, its use of a circular to union members directing them

[21] *Ryan* v. *Attorney General*, [1965] 1 I.R., 294, 309.
[22] *Griswold* v. *Connecticut* (1965) 381 U.S. 479. McGee v. *Attorney General* [1974] I.R. 284, 292.
[23] McGee v. *Attorney General* [1974] I.R. 284, 297.

against registering Drimoleague children in neighbouring schools. This was, they claimed, an unlawful interference with the children's constitutional rights to free primary education (Article 42.4); the means adopted by the INTO to achieve their aims were therefore unconstitutional. Conversely, counsel for the INTO argued that the teachers had a constitutional right to withdraw their labour and that the circular was a step taken lawfully to protect their material interests. Any injury to the children's constitutional right was merely incidental to the INTO members' exercise of their constitutional rights.

Secondly, Eilish Crowley challenged the state for allegedly defaulting on a constitutional obligation to provide for free primary education (Article 42.4). Counsel claimed that this was not a conflict exclusively between teachers and school managers but rather involved a failure by the Minister for Education to make effective provision for the Drimoleague children's education; he could not 'simply do nothing'.[24] Counsel for the state responded by accepting that the children were entitled to sue the state if such a failure had occurred. However, according to the text of Article 42.4, this duty was to 'provide for' not to 'provide'. This distinction, they argued, recognised that primary education was state aided but based on 'local' (that is to say, religious) management. The period during the strike when buses to alternative schools were not available (from March 1976 to December 1977) amounted to a temporary breakdown in the primary education system but, having regard to the nature of that system, did not constitute a denial of the children's right to such education. The 'impossibility of the Minister taking any action', counsel further contended, was 'obvious and clear to all'. He 'was entitled to refrain from taking sides, lest action by him lead to a broadening of the strike and, perhaps, to a general strike of national school teachers throughout the country'.[25]

In the cases from the late 1980s onwards, those claiming socio-economic rights against the state combined an appeal to reinterpret the constitution's family-welfare provisions with a globalising, post-Cold War rhetoric that declared all human rights to be universal, interdependent, indivisible, and interrelated. Hence, in presenting the legal case for Traveller accommodation in Limerick, John O'Reilly's counsel claimed that each individual in society required a certain minimum standard of living to protect his or her dignity and freedom as

[24] *Crowley* v. *Minister for Education* [1980] IR 102, 111.
[25] *Crowley* v. *Minister for Education* [1980] IR 102, 123.

a human person. O'Reilly's right to be provided with these conditions, they further claimed, was both an unenumerated personal right (Article 40.3.2) and a correlative of the State's duty to protect 'the constitution and authority' of the family (Article 41.2). On the basis of a breach of these constitutional rights, they argued for the provision of both an adequately serviced halting site and compensation for past suffering.

Appeals to international human rights norms and the constitution's family-education provisions similarly featured in *Sinnott*, *TD*, and *Health Amendments Bill Reference*. Counsel for the Sinnotts argued that the state had failed in its constitutional duty to provide primary education to Jamie Sinnott (Article 42.4) and, consequently, by imposing inordinate burdens on Kathryn Sinnott, had failed to respect her rights as mother (Article 41). Similarly, in the *Health Amendment Bill* (2004) reference, counsel acting on behalf of elderly patients asserted a series of unenumerated rights to life, bodily integrity, and human dignity (Article 40.3.1). Citing comparable South African precedents to support these claims, they argued that the state had a duty to assist people who could not fend for themselves: '. . . we say that constitutional socio-economic rights must be protected by the court'.[26]

In *TD*, the case concerning the provision of high support units to 'disturbed' young people, counsel requested that the court apply a proportionality test. If such a test were applied, they argued, Judge Kelly's (HC) earlier decision to impose a mandatory order on the state to make high support units available could not be said to have failed to balance the interest of the parties in a proportionate manner. The juveniles' suffering through the absence of these units was substantial and, given that the Departments themselves had in earlier cases framed the programme of implementation, it could not be said that the judge had imposed a disproportionate burden on them. The judiciary, they further claimed, had a duty to supervise the government's exercise of its powers and to intervene insofar as it acted unconstitutionally.

Counsel for the state in these cases characteristically responded by diminishing or narrowing rights claims, by drawing attention to the separation of powers or by emphasising practical objections to the courts' involvement in 'policy-making'. In *Sinnott*, counsel for the Minister for Education argued that appropriate facilities were in fact available because Jamie Sinnott was not autistic but rather suffered from a

[26] Re: Article 26 and the Health (Amendment) Bill 2004 [2005] 1 IR 105, 113.

profound mental and physical handicap with some autistic features. The state's obligation to educate, they argued, ceased when a child reached eighteen. In addition, since the tort at stake did not exist until established in an earlier case, Jamie Sinnott was not entitled to maintain a retrospective claim prior to that date.[27]

Counsel for the state in both *TD* and the *Health Amendment Bill* reference sought to apply a proportionality test. In the former, counsel for the state argued that Judge Kelly had concerned himself with policy matters 'of general application' and had attempted to direct the administration of the national budget. The courts had not established how to distinguish culpable from non-culpable delays and, moreover, could not be involved in policy-making on an ongoing basis. In the latter case, counsel for the state argued that if the 'conscientious legislator' was unable to legalise charging elderly patients retrospectively then the government would be faced with a choice between transferring resources to the descendants of those who paid the charges and allocating money to those currently sick. This would be a 'disproportionate' outcome, not in accordance with the 'common good'. Responding to arguments in favour of socio-economic rights, counsel for the state further claimed that the alleged rights were indistinct, difficult to satisfy, and dissonant with the constitution's text and the framers' intentions.

## JUDGMENT

Judges' decision-making in these cases alternated between declaring rights as trumps and adhering to the doctrine of parliamentary sovereignty, newly described as a 'margin of appreciation'. Under the separation of powers doctrine, only where a 'clear disregard' of the executive's constitutional powers and duties existed would the courts intervene to protect the rights of those affected. Traditionally, the Irish Courts adopted a high threshold of intervention. In *Doyle*, High Court judges Haugh and Murnaghan agreed with counsel for the Minister for Education that Desmond Doyle's application, lacking his wife's signature, was never properly before the minister. Judge McLoughlin supported this position, 'however unreasonable' it happened to be.[28] The Supreme Court, however, overturned this decision. Chief Justice Maguire interpreted the constitution's 'family' guarantee to include a

[27] The earlier case was *O'Donoghue* v. *Minister for Health* [1996] 2 IR 20 (27 May 1993).
[28] *Doyle* v. *Minister for Education* [1956] IR 217, 224.

husband whose wife had deserted him, asserted its superiority to statute law and granted an order for Evelyn's discharge.

In *Ryan*, Judge Kenny (H.C.) rejected claims that water fluoridation threatened familial authority or parental control of children's education.[29] However, he held that the court's jurisdiction extended to the consideration of whether the legislature respected and, 'as far as practicable', defended and vindicated the personal rights of the citizen. This general guarantee included rights not specifically mentioned in Article 40, which 'have to be formulated and defined by the High Court' and 'include all those rights which result from the Christian and democratic nature of the State'.[30] What Judge Kenny meant by 'Christian and democratic' was left open to interpretation, but strong evidence of a particular bias may be adduced from his citing the papal encyclical 'Pacem in Terris' (1963) to support his conclusion that 'a right to bodily integrity' existed. Kenny accepted the scientific evidence in favour of water fluoridation presented by the state and rejected that presented by counsel for Gladys Ryan, dismissing the plaintiff's action on these grounds. The Supreme Court reaffirmed this decision and dismissed the subsequent appeal.

The *Ryan* doctrine of interpretation opened the possibility of activist judges interpreting all manner of unenumerated rights into the 1937 Constitution, including socio-economic ones.[31] In practice, liberal counsel and judges now used this doctrine to challenge Catholic 'social' restrictions in family law. In the contraceptives case, Judge O'Keefe (H.C.) denied that Article 40.3.1 conferred an unenumerated right to privacy and dismissed Mary McGee's claims.[32] At the Supreme Court, Chief Justice Fitzgerald agreed with the state's counsel that the contested legislation did not prohibit the use of contraceptives, merely their

[29] Kenny similarly denied that 'education' included 'rearing and nurturing' at the time of the constitution's becoming law, relying on the 1933 Oxford English Dictionary for proof. *Ryan* v. *Attorney General* [1965] IR 294, 309.

[30] *Ryan* v. *Attorney General* [1965] IR 294, 314.

[31] *Pacem en Terris*, the encyclical cited by Judge Kenny in *Ryan*, for example, further outlined a number of socio-economic rights: 'Man has the right to live, the right to bodily integrity and to the means necessary for the proper development of life, particularly food, clothing, shelter, medical care, rest, and, finally, the necessary social services. In consequence, he has the right to be looked after in the event of ill health; disability stemming from his work; widowhood; old age; enforced unemployment; or whenever through no fault of his own he is deprived of the means of livelihood'. On Catholic communitarian ideology and interpreting socio-economic rights into the 1937 Constitution, see Irish Commission for Justice and Peace (ICJP), 1998, *Re-righting the Constitution: the case for new social and economic rights*. Dublin: Irish Commission for Justice and Peace.

[32] *McGee* v. *Attorney General* [1974] IR 284, 290–1.

importation or sale. He further denied that Article 40.3.1 conferred an unenumerated right to marital privacy: to strike down the legislation, he declared, would amount to an invalid usurpation of legislative authority.[33] The majority verdict, however, upheld Mary McGee's appeal. Judges Walsh, Budd, Henchy, and Griffin looked to the practical consequences of the 1935 legislation and claimed that the effective restriction on the availability of contraceptives was unreasonable. As such, the legislation constituted an unjustified invasion of the privacy of the plaintiff and was, accordingly, struck down.

If *McGee* signalled the emergence of a liberalising judiciary, judgment in the Drimoleague schools conflict underlined the courts' traditional reluctance to impose economic costs on the state. The Supreme Court agreed with counsel for the state and held that the plaintiffs had failed to establish any breach of a constitutional duty.[34] Judge Kenny declared that this duty was not 'to provide' but 'to provide for' education. Hence, the state was under no obligation to educate. Kenny attributed this distinction to the Catholic Church's role in the formation of the education system in the nineteenth century, and to 'how tenaciously the people resisted the idea of State schools'.[35] In his partially dissenting judgment, Chief Justice O'Higgins suggested that the Minister for Education had an obligation to assist in financing the limited teaching that parents had independently provided. The majority declared, however, that the payment of salaries to unqualified teachers would have been a misapplication of public monies and 'would have run the risk of provoking a countrywide strike'.[36]

Parenthetically, the *Crowley* decision further demonstrated how constitutional rights could be used against trade unions. Judge McMahon (H.C.) declared that the teachers:

> '. . . did not act primarily for the purpose of exercising a right to work or not to work, or to choose the conditions under which they would work. In my view their purpose was to deprive the Drimoleague children of primary education in order to exert pressure on Fr. Crowley; what was done amounted to the use of unlawful means to deprive the Drimoleague children of their constitutional right'.[37]

[33] *McGee* v. *Attorney General* [1974] IR 284, 303.
[34] Judges Kenny, Griffin, and Henchy provided the judgment; Chief Justice O'Higgins and Judge Parke dissented.
[35] *Crowley* v. *Minister for Education* [1980] IR 102, 126.
[36] *Crowley* v. *Minister for Education* [1980] IR 102, 130.
[37] *Crowley* v. *Minister for Education* [1980] IR 102, 110.

Since constitutional rights, as interpreted by the courts, were superior to the common-law right to strike, McMahon held that there was 'no answer' to the children's claim. The Supreme Court agreed. The purpose for which the constitutional right to withdraw labour was allegedly being exercised, O'Higgins declared, was 'not the purpose for which it existed' – rather 'it was being exercised for the purpose of infringing the constitutional rights of the plaintiffs to obtain free primary education' and was, for this reason, 'an abuse of a constitutional right'.[38]

Throughout the 1990s and 2000s, the Irish judiciary broadly rejected socio-economic rights claims on the basis of a distinction between commutative and distributive justice. In the legal case to secure Traveller accommodation, Judge Costello (H.C.) declared the 'question' to be the 'constitutional propriety' of whether the courts could adjudicate on the fairness of the manner in which the State had administered 'the nation's wealth'.[39] He denied that any such power existed in the Constitution. Thus, Costello granted John O'Reilly a declaration obliging Limerick Corporation to review its building programme but refused to grant an order directing the corporation to provide serviced sites. Costello distinguished between a claim against the state's wrongful interference in some activity and 'an entirely different kind of claim' that a citizen has a right to be provided with certain physical resources and services. O'Reilly's claims, he argued, were to be advanced in the parliament at Leinster House rather than the Four Courts.[40]

Judgments in both the *Sinnott* and *TD* cases relied on this distinction between commutative and distributive justice to justify the courts' non-intervention and to allow the state's appeal against socio-economic rights claims. In the *Sinnott* case, Judge Barr (H.C.) found that, while the applicant was over eighteen, he was still entitled to free primary education appropriate to his needs for as long as he was capable of benefitting from such education. The High Court granted damages as well as a mandatory injunction enforcing this entitlement. On appeal, however, the Supreme Court reversed important aspects of this decision, deciding that the State's duty to provide primary education did not extend to adults.[41] The Supreme Court also took a more restrictive view

38 *Crowley* v. *Minister for Education* [1980] IR 102, 120.
39 *O'Reilly* v. *Limerick Corporation* [1989] ILRM 181, 193.
40 *O'Reilly* v. *Limerick Corporation* [1989] ILRM 181, 195.
41 Chief Justice Keane dissented to declare that Jamie Sinnott was entitled to education as long as he was capable of benefitting from it; Judge Murphy also dissented but held that the state's obligation to educate ceased at twelve years.

of the role of the courts in the enforcement of the right to education, and in particular in relation to the types of relief the courts are entitled to grant.[42]

The Supreme Court majority produced a variety of justifications in *Sinnott* to deny that the state had a duty to provide for free primary education to adults. Judge Denham claimed that the education provision's 'constitutional setting' meant it referred to children within the family unit, not to adults' relationship to the state.[43] Judge Geoghegan underlined the importance of their restrictive interpretation. Illustrating the state's meagre welcome for migrants, he further declared that 'still less [than a child at a time of schooling or in later life] would some adult immigrant be entitled to invoke the Article, an idea which was mooted at the hearing'.[44] Chief Justice Keane suggested that the Minister for Education's objections to Jamie Sinnott's claim arose because of 'the more far-reaching implications of adults, as distinct from children, being entitled to free primary education'.[45] A different Supreme Court majority similarly allowed the state's appeal against Kathryn Sinnott.[46]

In *TD* v. *Minister for Education*, a majority distinguished between civil and political rights and those of 'the economic sphere' and further opposed identifying any more unenumerated rights in general and 'socio-economic rights' in particular.[47] The Supreme Court reversed Judge Kelly's decision and indicated that, in accordance with the separation of powers doctrine, mandatory injunctions can only be obtained in the rarest of circumstances.[48] The Court defined such circumstances as being restricted to where an organ of the State had shown a 'clear disregard' for its constitutional obligations, described by Judge Murray as 'a conscious and deliberate decision by the State to act in breach of its constitutional obligations to other parties accompanied by bad faith or

42 *Sinnott* v. *Minister for Education* [2001] 2 IR 545. See also IHRC (2005), *Making ESCR Effective*, p. 101.

43 *Sinnott* v. *Minister for Education* [2001] 2 IR 545, 664.

44 *Sinnott* v. *Minister for Education* [2001] 2 IR 545, 720.

45 *Sinnott* v. *Minister for Education* [2001] 2 IR 545, 633. Some 25 per cent of Irish adults have literacy difficulties. See National Adult Literacy Agency Survey, www.nala.ie/literacy/literacy-in-ireland.

46 Judge Denham dissented and held that the State's failure to provide education amounted to 'invidious discrimination' and an undermining of the institution of the family.

47 Keane criticised the Ryan doctrine of interpretation and called for judicial restraint in identifying unenumerated rights. *TD* v. *Minister for Education* [2001] 4 IR 259, 281.

48 *TD* v. *Minister for Education* [2001] 4 IR 259.

recklessness'. The European Court of Human Rights has since offered a sharply contrasting opinion on the Irish State's provision for detained minors, finding it to be in breach of obligations under the European Convention on Human Rights.[49]

The Supreme Court produced a variety of principled and pragmatic justifications to support this decision. Judge Murphy concluded that there were no express provisions in the constitution cognisable by the courts to 'impose an express obligation on the State to provide accommodation, medical treatment, welfare or any other form of socio-economic benefit for any of its citizens, however needy or deserving'.[50] The absence of an express reference – and the failure to correct that absence by referendum since then – suggested 'a conscious decision' to withhold these rights. Moreover, the courts, Judge Hardiman claimed, could not 'fill the vacuum' in policy-making because it would transfer power to 'an unelected judiciary at the expense of the politically accountable branches of government'.[51] Furthermore, the courts' mandatory procedures ('whereby the courts give judgment only on legal evidence . . . and legal submissions') did not remotely equip them to make policy. Hardiman appealed to the consequences of judicial policy-making and further argued that the courts would become equally available in cases without popular approval. They 'would certainly be appealed to again and again'.[52]

Similarly, in the *Health Bill (2004)* reference, Judge Geoghegan rejected socio-economic rights claims, declaring the unlikelihood of an alleged constitutional right if it involved huge expense. Somewhat unusually, Chief Justice John Murray acknowledged that in a discrete case, in exceptional circumstances, a constitutional obligation to

[49] D. G. v. *Eastern Health Board* [1997], 3 IR 511; *D.G.* v. *Ireland* (2002) 35 E.H.R.R. 1153. D. G., a homeless teenager, was considered to have a personality disorder and to be a danger to himself and others. In the absence of a high-support therapeutic unit, the High Court ruled that D. G. be detained in St. Patrick's Institution, a prison, even though he was not facing any criminal charges. D. G. filed a complaint to the European Court of Human Rights. The Court found the State to be in breach of the European Convention on Human Rights because of its failure to make provision for the education of the teenager during his temporary detention. Gerry Whyte, 2014, 'The Efficacy of Public Interest Litigation in Ireland', p. 261.

[50] *TD* v. *Minister for Education* [2001], 4 IR 259, 316.

[51] *TD* v. *Minister for Education* [2001], 4 IR 259, 339. In a dissenting opinion, Judge Denham claimed that the checks and balances between these branches were as important as the institutions' separation and independence. TD's claims, Denham continued, were 'exceptional' (see Article 42.5) and thus generated the courts' duty to intervene as 'the guardians of the Constitution'. *TD* v. *Minister for Education* [2001], 4 IR 259, 301.

[52] *TD* v. *Minister for Education* [2001], 4 IR 259, 339.

provide shelter and maintenance might constrain parliamentary discretion in public expenditure. But the 'core issues' of the case, Murray declared, were, in fact, the patients' property rights claims and the state's justifications for delimiting them. He stated that there was never 'a substantive constitutional right to receive in-patient services free of charge'; rather, at most, there was a statutory right to receive a 'benefit'.[53] In reality, the object of the legislation was to absent the state from compensation claims by extinguishing a property right. Without compensation or satisfactory justification, the Health Bill's retrospective elements were, therefore, unconstitutional.

## JURISPRUDENCE

Family, education, and welfare law in the Irish Free State approximated a continuation of classic patriarchal and property norms under the veneer of the Catholic 'social'. Hence, while the 1937 Constitution contained provisions suggesting that a woman's place was in the home (Article 41.2), of greater practical significance was the quieter continuation of the doctrine of the legal unity of man and wife. As contributors to the *Irish Jurist* observed, this prohibited either party from suing the other for personal torts such as slander or assault and battery.[54] The continuation of classic norms also applied to children, viewed in a legal sense as the property of their father. This 'paternal power', Vincent Delany (1952) observed of custody cases, 'had the great merit of certainty'.[55] Regarding the legal infrastructure for institutionalisation, Gerald Harris (1940) advocated adopting the recommendations of the 1925 Commission of Inquiry into the public case of 'mentally defective persons'.[56] For the most part, however, *Irish Jurist* contributors rarely engaged with the law as it applied to families and children during the 1940s and 1950s. Articles on 'juvenile delinquency' at St. Patrick's Industrial School as well as on the efficacy of institutionalisation more generally began to appear in the late 1960s.[57]

[53] *Re: Article 26 and the Health (Amendment) Bill 2004* [2005], 1 IR 105, 195.

[54] Gerald Harris (ed.), 1951, 'Editorial' in the *Irish Jurist*, 17 (3), p. 38.

[55] V. T. H. Delaney, 1952, 'The Custody and Education of Children: A Changing Legal Concept in Eire' in the *Irish Jurist*, 18 (2), p. 23.

[56] Gerald Harris (ed.), 1940, 'The Need for Legal Reform' in the *Irish Jurist*, 6 (2), pp. 17–18, p. 17.

[57] Anne Flynn, Nuala McDonald, and E. F. O'Doherty, 1967, 'A Survey of Boys in St. Patrick's Institution: Project on Juvenile Delinquency' in *The Irish Jurist*, 2 (2), pp. 222–32. Mary O'Flynn, 1971, 'Prison After-Care in the Irish Republic' in the *Irish Jurist*, 6 (1), pp. 1–17.

From the mid-1960s onwards, the feminist movement secured legislative changes to guarantee formal equality in familial relationships, including provisions to enable married women to sue their husbands and to be held as equal guardians of their children. Formal equality, however, often did not translate into better living conditions. Nial Osborough (1969) recognised that the principle of equal pay for equal work still remained 'underdeveloped'.[58] By focussing on the constitutionality of marriage and the banning of divorce, William Duncan (1972) claimed, lawyers and politicians ignored the extent to which matrimonial breakdown was occurring in Ireland. Moreover, owing to legal fees, separation proceedings were expensive, almost exclusively middle-class events. Thus, the absence of state intervention produced 'impossible' situations of desertion and cruelty into which wives were forced by their economic dependence on their husbands.[59]

During the 1980s, to the extent that contributors to the *Irish Jurist* considered equality and welfare rights, they tended to concentrate on access to justice and education rights; analysis of alternative socio-economic rights featured intermittently. Drawing on American 'social' jurisprudence, Michael Forde (1982) examined whether the Irish constitution's equality guarantee (Article 40.1) and 'how our courts have given meaning to the concept' required that wealth be redistributed or that the state inaugurate an advanced welfare programme.[60] He questioned whether a welfare state was envisaged by the electorate who supported the constitution in 1937 and, moreover, declared the courts ill-equipped to stipulate social policies or expenditure.[61] Similarly, Imelda Maher (1989) examined judicial decision-making in *O'Reilly* [1989] to assess whether a constitutional right to shelter could be recognised as an unenumerated right.[62] She concluded that the Irish courts were slow to impose 'a positive economic responsibility' on the state: 'The financial cost of the right claimed is an important consideration in determining the practicability of the right sought'.[63] Again, Gerry Whyte (1990) outlined the judiciary's reluctance to impose positive economic

[58] Nial Osborough, 1969, 'Notes: Commission on the Status of Women' in *Irish Jurist*, 4 (2), pp. 327–9, p. 328.

[59] William Duncan, 1972, 'Desertion and Cruelty in Irish Matrimonial Law' in *Irish Jurist*, 7 (1) pp. 213–40, 222.

[60] M. Forde, 1982, 'Equality and the Constitution' in *Irish Jurist*, 17 (2), pp. 295–339.

[61] Forde, 1982, 'Equality and the Constitution', p. 308.

[62] Imelda Maher, 1989, 'Grafting the Homeless on to the Housing Code' in *Irish Jurist*, 24 (2), pp. 182–97, p. 182.

[63] Maher, 1989, 'Grafting the Homeless on to the Housing Code', p. 182.

responsibilities, citing the Drimoleague school conflict (*Crowley* v. *Ireland* [1980]) as evidence of an extremely minimalist view of the state's role in education.[64]

A much more explicit debate on the merits of constitutionalising social and economic rights recurred throughout the *Irish Jurist* in the 1990s and 2000s, primarily in response to their substantive rejection by the judiciary and by the Constitution Review Group. Jurists' arguments notably drew on international human rights law as well as Irish case-law. Chief Justice Ronan Keane (2001), responding to the prospect of the EU Charter of Fundamental Rights, claimed that were the Council of Ministers to include socio-economic rights, it would cause 'concern in many quarters': 'the national courts and ultimately the courts in Luxembourg would be determining policy in social and economic areas which would hitherto have been regarded as the exclusive preserve of the elected parliament of the individual member states'.[65] Conversely, Rory O'Connell and Andrew Butler (1998) argued for the indivisibility of rights and accused the Constitution Review Group of invoking double standards when assessing property and socio-economic rights.[66] Similarly, Mark de Blacam (2002) criticised the Supreme Court's reasoning in the *Sinnott* case. Not one member of the majority, he argued, explained why one mode of interpreting the constitution was to be preferred over the other. Instead, adopting a lawyer's response or 'result-oriented' jurisprudence, 'they reached for the rules of constitutional interpretation and applied them as they saw fit'.[67]

Concentrating on how socio-economic rights might function in practice, Hogan (2001) queried whether the protection of such rights would be feasible in circumstances ('not too long ago') where the state

64 Gerry Whyte, 1990–2, 'Review' in *Irish Jurist*, 25–7 (1), pp. 69–82, p. 71. According to Nial Osborough (1978), the primacy accorded to the 'family' in education was a piece of constitutional fiction. Parents rarely exercised rights to educate their children, assigning responsibility instead to schools controlled by religious orders and subject to a centralised state authority. Nial Osborough, 1978, 'Education in the Irish Law and Constitution' in *Irish Jurist*, 13 (1), pp. 145–80, p. 149.

65 Ronan Keane, 2001, 'Brave New World' in *Irish Jurist*, 36, pp. 1–16, p. 13.

66 'It seems to us incompatible to assert that socio-economic rights should not be constitutionalised because they raise issues of policy and practicality which should remain in the hands of the government and parliament "elected to represent the people and do their will" unlike the "unelected judiciary", yet to maintain that it is no "distortion of democracy" to allow judicial supervisions of the decisions of those same representatives in the allied fields of property rights'. Andrew Butler and Rory O'Connell, 1998, 'Ireland's Constitutional Review Group Report' in *Irish Jurist*, 33 (1), pp. 237–65, p. 254.

67 Mark de Blacam, 2002, 'Children, Constitutional Rights and the Separation of Powers' in *Irish Jurist*, 37 (1), pp. 113–42.

could plead a lack of resources.[68] Judicial prudence, he concluded, dictates that the role of the courts in protecting newly emerging socio-economic rights (ranging from education to healthcare) must be a strictly limited one, confined to the most exceptional of cases and circumstances.[69] Similarly, Paul Anthony McDermott (2000) claimed that the courts were 'correct not to intervene in how the Government chooses to distribute tax-payers' money' but that this principle should not be extended to cases of prisoners or juveniles in need of high support units or psychiatric care.[70] The merits of public interest litigation and judicial review on behalf of the 'socially excluded' also featured prominently in this debate. Gerry Whyte (2002) accepted a limited role for legal action aiming at judicial review in the interests of the marginalised and 'disadvantaged', though he emphasised the deficiencies of 'representative action' and the consequent need for a class action system on US lines.[71] Conversely, Gwynn Morgan (2002) argued that judicial activism was more likely to help the 'advantaged' because firstly, the constitution protected their rights more than the 'disadvantaged' and, secondly, 'in the nature of things', the well-off have the best (or the most time-rich) lawyers to argue their claims.[72]

## CONCLUSION

The socio-economic rights cases examined here demonstrate the contested reproduction and legacy of the Catholic 'social' in the 1937 Irish Constitution, understood as a politically determined affinity between *laissez-faire* economic orthodoxies, minimal state intervention in market interactions, and Catholic Church control of family law and of welfare provision. The act and necessity of people having to take socio-economic rights claims to the Irish Courts highlighted the ongoing underdevelopment of the state's welfare infrastructure, evident in its continued reliance on voluntary networks of care as well as on cost-effective forms of institutionalisation. While the Irish state's welfare infrastructure owed to more widely shared social conditions and class relations, it was most immediately the responsibility of a majoritarian political arena.

[68] Hogan, 2001, 'Directive Principles, Socio-Economic Rights and the Constitution', p. 190.
[69] Hogan, 2001, 'Directive Principles, Socio-Economic Rights and the Constitution', p. 198.
[70] P. A. McDermott, 2000, 'The Separation of Powers' in *Irish Jurist*, 35 (1), pp. 280–304, p. 282.
[71] Whyte, 2002, *Social Inclusion and the Legal System: Public Interest Law in Ireland*.
[72] Morgan, 2002, 'Review', p. 346.

Socio-economic rights cases were thus taken by members or representatives of minoritarian groups severely affected by these conditions, notably Travellers, children, and the severely autistic or mentally ill, and unlikely to challenge or improve these conditions in the short term through majoritarian forms of politics, such as elections or trade union mobilising. Concomitantly, the structure for contesting the 1937 Constitution in the courts on a case-by-case or individual basis did not allow for a group of people to contest these conditions as a 'class action'. Moreover, owing to politically determined resource constraints, innumerable potential cases were never heard at all. However, in some of the partially successful socio-economic rights cases examined here, notably in *Sinnott*, individuals and associated NGOs combined public interest litigation with wider civil society campaigning and awareness raising, ultimately directed at lobbying and influencing government policy in the majoritarian arena.

In conventional analyses of the Irish Courts' decision-making, commentators have broadly identified the judiciary's handling of the 1937 Constitution as progressive and inspired by nationalist or increasingly liberal orientations.[73] John Kelly's endorsement of the courts' handling of constitutional issues as, on the whole, 'beneficial, rational, progressive and fair' amounted to a conventional wisdom.[74] Of less acknowledged significance, perhaps, is the role of US precedents in seminal cases such as *Ryan* and *McGee*. Similarly, counsels' and judges' invocation of the doctrine of proportionality in later cases indicate the extent to which the Irish experience was typical of a wider globalisation of neoformalist modes of constitutional decision-making. Counsels' and judges' invocation of the doctrine of proportionality in the 1990s similarly registered and reproduced the globalisation of neoformalist modes of decision-making and discourse.

The Supreme Court's celebrated discovery of the Constitution in the 1960s made plausible the possibility of a future judiciary interpreting unenumerated social and economic rights into the Constitution. However, while the judges challenged Catholic social constitutionalism in family law in some of the cases examined here, its presence in the field of welfare provision remained broadly unthreatened. With partial exceptions at lower levels of the court, the judicial decisions examined here

[73] See Gerard Hogan, 1986, 'Irish Nationalism as a Legal Ideology' in *Studies*, 75:4, 528 ff; Farrell, 1988, *De Valera's Constitution and Ours*, Dublin: Gill and Macmillan.

[74] '[T]hose concerned with property rights, homosexuality, and abortion may have dissented from [Kelly's] view'. Diarmaid Ferriter, 2004, *The Transformation of Ireland*, p. 731.

demonstrate a remarkable continuity in prioritising classic market laws of contract and property, in asserting individual over collective rights or the common good and, above all, in denying judicial capacity to intervene in state expenditure, even in defence of a potential constitutional right. While judges ostensibly invoked the separation of powers or a margin of appreciation to justify the courts' non-intervention, a pragmatic rejection of constitutionalising socio-economic rights on the basis of institutional incapacity is also strongly suggested in the judgments and associated jurisprudence.

Notwithstanding these continuities in decision-making, counsels' and judges' discourse on socio-economic rights has nevertheless evolved over the twentieth and early twenty-first century. Rights claimants challenging the lived experience of the Catholic 'social' initially found themselves compelled to argue their claim before the state in the discourse of the Catholic social. In more recent socio-economic rights cases, however, those claiming socio-economic rights against the state have combined these earlier forms of appeal to natural law or family rights principles with newly globalising forms of human rights rhetoric. This transformation, again symptomatic of the broader globalisation of neoformal and neoliberal legal thought, indicates underlying social changes, notably growing secularism and liberalism in a context of increasingly rapid globalisation. Politically, these discursive changes further indicate the emergence of NGO-led support structures capable of ensuring at least some rights claimants can contest the 1937 Constitution in the courts.

In sum, the previous three chapters have mapped evolving property, trade union, and family-welfare rights jurisprudence alongside the globalisation of public law neoformalism, the shifting priority judges attached to particular modes of interpretation, as well as the consequences of their decisions. The significance of this socio-economic rights jurisprudence however does not entirely reside in its immediate implications for rights claimants or in jurists' explicit disagreements over decisions or modes of interpretation. Beneath the flotsam and jetsam of surface disagreements amongst judges, jurists, and rights claimants lay a rather more basic consensus, premised on the law's objectification of social relations and promulgation of value-consensus norms. The following chapter concentrates on these more fundamental structures of thought that framed judges' interpretive choices and resultant disagreements. Deeply embedded orthodoxies tended towards the prioritisation of the transcendent and the immutable over the transitory and the contingent, of 'principles' ahead of politics or people's everyday lived experience. Jurists' imagined value-consensus community arose out of shared social structures and performed an ideological function insofar as the particular interests of landlords and corporations came to be portrayed as universal ones.

**CHAPTER NINE**

# REPRODUCING THE VALUE-CONSENSUS STATE

*The Constitution is a constitution of the people expressing principles for its society. It sets the norms for the community. It is a document for the people of Ireland, not an economy or a commercial company.*

– Judge Susan Denham, 2001[1]

*No distinction has ever been made between living and dead property owners.*

– Judge Adrian Hardiman, 2005[2]

Socio-economic rights judgments, according to the professional ideology of the judiciary, were based primarily 'on the facts' of the case. From counsels' presentation of these facts, the judges discerned central questions or issues to be resolved authoritatively and then looked to 'apply the law' as established in the 1937 Constitution, in statute or in precedent. Few judges or lawyers would regard this ordered progression from conflict to truth as mechanical. Judges had to choose between the competing precedents, principles, and 'tests' offered by counsel. They also had to decide how much and what kind of 'context' was necessary to constitute the 'facts' of the case or to substantiate their judgment. A range of interpretive choices had to be made, including interpreting the 'letter' and 'spirit' of the 1937 Constitution.[3] Jurists similarly engaged with these judgments by identifying a weak line of reasoning or an ignored mode of interpretation and then proceeded to argue that an alternative principle or precedent may have produced a different,

1 *Sinnott* v. *Minister for Education* [2001] 2 IR 545, 664.

2 *Re: Article 26 and the Health (Amendment) Bill (2004)* [2005], 1 IR 105, 131.

3 John Kelly identified several recurring judicial approaches to interpreting the Irish Constitution. These included literal interpretation ('reading from within the four corners of the text'); harmonious interpretation (reading within the context of the overall Constitution); broad, purposive interpretation (construing provisions or legislation in light of their aims or their framers' intentions); the historical approach (assessing the original meaning of the 1937 Constitution at the time of its creation) and the natural law approach (appealing to universal norms and values determined by nature). (Hogan and Whyte, eds.), 2003, *J. M. Kelly: The Irish Constitution*, pp. 3–38.

more favourable outcome.[4] Jurisprudential positions on socio-economic rights, however, remained within certain parameters.

The critical analysis of judicial discourse in the preceding socio-economic rights cases demonstrates the prioritisation of principles over politics, of the immutable over the transient, of an imagined 'value-consensus' community over social forms of exploitation, oppression, and conflict. Value-consensus discourse may be described as an expression of a deeply embedded belief in the rule of law, as abstract and transcendent, objective and just, placing beyond question the question of judicial legitimacy in a coercive social order.[5] This form of discourse represented the state as a consensual, value-neutral framework through which competing interests could be resolved. Conversely, oppositional understandings of the state represent it as being controlled by (or predominantly defending the interests of) the dominant power group in society.[6] Irish judges (re)produced this discourse when promoting as transcendent, objective, and just the 1937 Irish Constitution (which, as we earlier established, registered a set of particular economic interests and power relations). In this manner, socially made practices came to be portrayed as natural, unchangeable ones, the particular, private interests of landlords and corporations conveyed as universal ones.

Value-consensus modes of thinking share an important affinity with the division of juridical labour. Irish governments, as discussed earlier, have tended to appoint judges capable of demonstrating 'safe, sound, middle-of-the-road opinions' characterised by 'moderation and attachment to regime norms'.[7] The absence of potentially oppositional understandings of the state, however, owes more basically to the

[4] Scholars have emphasised that the 1937 Irish Constitution's synthesis of liberal democratic and Catholic communitarian principles provides a plausible basis for the interpretation into the constitution of social and economic rights. See Whyte, 2002, *Social Inclusion and the Legal System*.

[5] Importantly, the analysis of embedded orthodoxies will not reveal the literal thinking of any one judge or even an ideal type so much as a spectrum of characteristic tendencies, present in judges' reasoning and aligned closely with their positions in the legal field. Pierre Bourdieu uses the term 'habitus' to denote groups' tendencies to inculcate and reinforce dispositions that render unthinkable practices beyond the 'common' or 'practical' sense produced by collective euphemisation. The complicities of habitus organise agents' visions of the world in a way that is resistant to articulation, critical reflection, or conscious manipulation. Bourdieu, 1994, 'Structures, Habitus, Power: Basis for a Theory of Symbolic Power'.

[6] See Introduction. See also Hillyard, 1972, 'Public Attitudes towards the Police in a medium-sized town in Northern Ireland'.

[7] Jacob, 1996, 'Conclusion', pp. 390–1. See also Gallagher, 2010, 'The Changing Constitution', p. 92.

absence of 'the people' as active subjects or collective agents in the client-professional relationships of formal constitutional practice and to the nature of professional-institutional positions locating barristers and judges at a necessary distance from the fray. Notably, the social trajectory followed by judges of the Supreme Court, from class privilege through education and training to appointment, facilitated the acquisition and prevalence of these value-consensus orthodoxies. The conditions of legal cultural production in twentieth-century Ireland reinforced these dispositions, partly through focussing predominantly on practitioners' techniques and partly through further absenting 'the people' via the absence of sociological critique. The second half of this chapter aims to demonstrate the characteristic attitudes and dispositions acquired in Ireland's typical course of offices and legal professional culture. First, however, it is necessary to demonstrate the salience of value-consensus discourse to the preceding economic and social rights contestations.

## SOCIO-ECONOMIC RIGHTS DISCOURSE AND THE VALUE-CONSENSUS STATE

A distancing effect accompanied participants' movement of a social conflict into the highly regulated social space of the courtroom. Judicial discourse registered and reproduced the manner in which law both objectifies social relations (reification) and simultaneously envisages living relations between things (fetishisation). Hence, Chief Justice O'Higgins could declare that the conflict at stake in the *Brennan* case did not concern the state's treatment of the Wexford farmers' 'as human persons' but rather the manner in which 'as occupiers and owners of land' their property was rated and taxed.[8] Only in this one-sided consideration of social relations is it possible to comprehend Judge Hardiman's otherwise curious statement: 'No distinction has ever been made between living and dead property owners'.[9] Conversely, judges tended to attribute living characteristics to things. The constitution was repeatedly declared a 'living' document. Similarly, the three 'organs' or 'branches' of government were said to owe one another 'respect'; Judge Gavan Duffy even attributed to the Four Courts a

[8] *Brennan v. Attorney General* [1984] ILRM 355, 365.
[9] *Re: Article 26 and the Health (Amendment) Bill (2004)* [2005], 1 IR 105, 131.

special 'legal atmosphere'.[10] At a distance then, judges reproduced value-consensus understandings of the state, of political economy, and of society.

The state emerges in judges' discourse as the guarantor of 'the rule of law', of 'government for the common good', and of 'a free and democratic society'. Reification further involved the representation of human relationships as formal relations between 'rights' bearers within the state. The courts were thus understood as the 'proper place' for conflicting parties to an economic dispute to have their rights vindicated. Before the law, workers and employers, graziers and labourers found themselves 'equal'. These reified forms of social relationship were purely formal. Hence, in the rent restrictions case, by considering the landlord-tenant relationship as a matter of conflicting rights only, judges subsumed a social relation based on unequal power relations into one of equal citizenship and applied the same considerations to each. Judge McWilliam's claim that the landlords were 'a group of citizens arbitrarily selected' obfuscated the more zero-sum landlord-tenant relationship to which the initial 'social' legislation was addressed; the landlords were arbitrarily selected from among landlords not from among 'citizens'. Again, in the *Iarnród Éireann* case, the property rights of personhood were extended to corporations.[11] Otherwise, as Judge Keane concluded, there would be a 'spectacular deficiency in the guarantee to *every* citizen that his or her property rights will be protected against unjust attack'.[12]

Judges' discourse concerning political economy and the state's relationship to it similarly registered and reproduced the individualist and harmonious axioms of value-consensus discourse. Judges usually described government budgeting or resource allocation in terms of its being for the 'common weal' or of 'national importance'. Hence, Judge Costello asserted both the existence of 'common goods and common burdens' in the 'political community' and that government should prioritise the idea of 'the common good' in deciding their allocation.[13] Similarly, Gavan Duffy could lament 'the dreadful plight of small holders struggling with uneconomic farms' while praising the Irish Land Commission for its aim of creating a 'peasant proprietorship of a

[10] *Fisher* v. *Irish Land Commission* [1948] IR 3, 10.
[11] *Iarnród Éireann* v. *Ireland* [1996] 3 IR 321, 345.
[12] *Iarnród Éireann* v. *Ireland* [1996] 3 IR 321, 345.
[13] *O'Reilly* v. *Limerick Corporation* [1989] ILRM 181, 194.

certain standard'.[14] Again, in the *Planning Bill Reference* [2004], land development was perceived to benefit all in society: increased demand for 'affordable housing' simply necessitated an 'adequate supply' of housing.[15]

Within the discourse of the value-consensus state, communal or class or social relations were disaggregated and expressed in terms of individual rights-bearers or minoritarian rights-bearing 'sectors'. Hence, for Judge Barr, the bureaucracy had to show 'real awareness and appreciation of the constitutional obligations of the State to all sectors of the community'.[16] Similarly, Judge Keane accepted as given the legislative categorisation of persons 'of different social background'. (On this principle of vision and division, the homeless and Travellers are implicitly distinguished from 'first time buyers').[17] More pointedly, the economy came to be discussed in terms more appropriate to a natural rather than political phenomenon, with judges naturalising as 'a fact of life' the socially constructed, politically determined practices of taxation and austerity.[18] (Almost inevitably, low taxation was understood in these terms as a 'happy' circumstance.)[19] Similarly, Judge Murphy could speak of 'the sick, the poor and the underprivileged in our society' and how to enable them 'to make the best use of the limited resources nature may have bestowed on them'.[20]

Within the parameters of judges' value-consensus discourse, people's experiences of exploitation or oppression (re)appeared as unfortunate, if at all. From Desmond Doyle's attempts to have his daughter released from an industrial school through TD's attempts to be provided with an appropriate 'high support unit' to Kathyrn Sinnott's attempts to have her son provided with appropriate educational care, sympathetic Irish judges presented such experiences not in terms of power or inequality, but rather in terms of their representing, as Judge Haugh put it, 'a tragic

[14] *Fisher* v. *Irish Land Commission* [1948] IR 3, 10.

[15] The 'inadequate supply of housing . . . was probably the most important feature in contributing to the present difficulties'. *Re: Article 26 and Part V of the Planning and Development Bill (1999)* [2000] 2 IR 321, 338–9.

[16] *Sinnott* v. *Minister for Education* [2001] 2 IR 545, 568.

[17] *Re: Article 26 and Part V of the Planning and Development Bill (1999)* [2000] 2 IR 321, 327; Judge Keane, 342–3.

[18] Judge Barr: 'It is, of course, a fact of life that in times of economic difficulty the State may be obliged to rein back severely on expenditure', *Sinnott* v. *Minister for Education* [2001] 2 IR 545, 555 and 568.

[19] Judge Barr stated that meeting minimal constitutional obligations might entail the raising of new tax revenue, 'happily a situation which has not pertained for several years'. *Sinnott* v. *Minister for Education* [2001] 2 IR 545, 568.

[20] *TD* v. *Minister for Education* [2001] 4 IR 259, 321.

case'.[21] Again, in *Crowley*, while Chief Justice O'Higgins declared the particular form of Church-State collaboration in sanctioning a teacher's appointment to have been 'strange' and the absence of any explanation as to why he was appointed 'stranger still', Judge Kenny merely declared the church appointee lack of experience to have been 'unfortunate'.[22]

Alternatively, unsympathetic judges could glean experiential narratives from the relevant facts of the case, while still absenting wider social relations or inequalities. Hence, when Mary McGee forwarded her family's living conditions in support of her right to access contraceptives, citing the difficulties associated with four children living in 'a cabin' on her husband's weekly earnings of £20, Chief Justice Fitzgerald could claim these facts irrelevant simply by remarking that the 'economic situation of her husband and herself is no different to thousands of other couples'.[23] Again, in *Blake*, Judge McWilliam (H.C.) could dismiss commission reports on rent restrictions as irrelevant: 'I am confined to a consideration of the direct effects of the Act and its compliance or non-compliance with the provisions of the Constitution'.[24] Similarly, when considering whether the court's striking down of rent restrictions would amount to 'an unjust attack upon the property rights of the tenant', Chief Justice O'Higgins presumed that since 'any such hardship will be provided for adequately by the State' it was 'unnecessary to consider this matter further'.[25]

Having been absented from judges' discourse as active subjects, 'the people' re-appeared as the imagined bearers of shared values, moral qualities, histories, and national identities.[26] In *Crowley*, for example, Judge Kenny's account of how tenaciously 'the Irish people' resisted state schools rested on an imagined shared history.[27] Similarly, Judge Denham declared the right to free primary education to be 'a promise

[21] *Doyle* v. *Minister for Education* [1956] IR 217, 223. Whereas Judge Barr's High Court judgment in favour of the Sinnotts and of socio-economic rights featured extensive reference to Kathryn Sinnott's testimony as to the labour of care involved in Jamie's upbringing, the Supreme Court judges who accepted the Irish state's appeal against the elaboration of socio-economic rights focussed their justification on parsing the constitution's text and elucidating the separation of powers doctrine. Similarly concentrating on unfortunate or tragic circumstances, they described the *Sinnott* case in terms of 'a depressing saga' or 'an arduous odyssey pursued with remarkable perseverance and fortitude by his mother'. *Sinnott* v. *Minister for Education* [2001] 2 IR 545, 609 and 676. Judge Murphy described the cases of *TD* and *Sinnott* as 'equally tragic', *TD* v. *Minister for Education* [2001] 4 IR 259, 321.

[22] *Crowley* v. *Minister for Education* [1980] IR 102, 127.

[23] McGee v. *Attorney General* [1974] IR 284; 301 and 322.

[24] *Blake* v. *Attorney General* [1982] IR 117.

[25] *Blake* v. *Attorney General* [1982] IR 117.

[26] Benedict Anderson. 1991, *Imagined Communities*. London: Verso. Hogan, 1986, 'Irish Nationalism as a Legal Ideology'.

[27] *Crowley* v. *Minister for Education* [1980] IR 102, 126.

to the people', 'reflective of community values', and 'reflective of the approach of the people of Ireland to education'.[28] To justify their declaring these state/community norms, judges looked to the 1937 Irish Constitution itself. On this highly questionable basis of ascertaining society's opinion then, 'the family remains the core unit of our society' and owning property remains integrally related to the dignity of the individual.[29]

Judges justifying faith in the value-consensus state further appealed to knowledge of extra-nationalist traditions, ranging from religious creeds to classic works in law and philosophy. Jurists' religious, sometimes specifically Catholic, discourse underpinned their claims that 'principles' were 'enshrined' in the 1937 Irish Constitution.[30] As Judge Murphy declared in *Sinnott*, the preamble asserts the Trinity 'as our final end' and 'that destiny . . . provides the logical basis for the constitutionally recognised rights of the individual'.[31] Similarly, in *O'Reilly*, Judge Costello accepted as axiomatic 'the traditional academic distinction' between commutative and distributive justice, that is to say, the classical and religious authority of Aristotle and Thomas Aquinas.[32]

Secular or positivist forms of value-consensus discourses, invoking the words of the 'founding fathers' of modern democracy, produced a homologous effect. In *TD*, for example, Judge Murray paraphrased the eighteenth-century conservative philosopher Edmund Burke to downplay claims of exceptional circumstances justifying recognition of socio-economic rights. Circumstances were 'infinite . . . variable and transient', he claimed, while 'one cannot lose sight of the fundamental principles according to which the power of judicial review is exercised'.[33] Similarly, his treatment of the 'Federalist Papers' of eighteenth-century America aimed at conveying 'a constant in the evolution of the modern democratic state'.[34] Whether nationalist, religious, or secular, judges were fundamentally scholastic and tended to prioritise transcendent 'principles' over politics, experience, or social practice.[35]

[28] *Sinnott* v. *Minister for Education* [2001] 2 IR 545, 653.
[29] *Sinnott* v. *Minister for Education* [2001] 2 IR 545, 664.
[30] *TD* v. *Minister for Education* [2001] 4 IR 259, 278.
[31] *Sinnott* v. *Minister for Education* [2001] 2 IR 545, 672–3.
[32] *O'Reilly* v. *Limerick Corporation* [1989] ILRM 181, 194.
[33] *TD* v. *Minister for Education* [2001] 4 IR 259, 333.
[34] *TD* v. *Minister for Education* [2001] 4 IR 259, 322.
[35] See Pierre Bourdieu, 1990, 'The Scholastic Point of View' in *Cultural Anthropology*, 5 (4), pp. 380–91.

The assertion of a value-consensus state and the downplaying of social relations applied with particular vigour in situations where socio-economic rights conflicts were articulated by working-class organisations. Hence, Judge Gavan Duffy held that the state's regulation of trade unions was in 'the public interest':

> 'I shall not attempt to define that elusive conception, which in its application to industrial relations may vary from time to time. But I suppose *everyone* must agree that it includes *satisfactory relations between masters and men* and that the welfare of an important third party, *the general public*, has a claim to consideration under the same head, so that the maintenance of industrial peace, or its restoration, if disturbed, must be a prominent feature of the public interest'.[36]

Here we see the taking of social divisions – between 'masters and men' as well as between industrial relations and the 'general public' – as given. Moreover, characteristic of the ideological quality of the value-consensus state, particular interests, namely those pertaining to 'industrial peace', are projected as universals.

The apparently natural order of things being upset by industrial action, to diminish or condemn the strike was to reduce the cognitive dissonance associated with challenges to various forms of authority, whether that of the state or capital or the Catholic Church. Hence, Judge Kingsmill Moore considered strike action as a 'murderous weapon' and agreed that the Educational Company's workers were engaged in a form of 'coercion', reasoning by analogy that their actions amounted to a form of highway robbery.[37] Similarly, analysing the direct effect of the INTO's action rather than the circumstances that characterised it, O'Higgins could declare that one 'could only speculate' at the INTO's motives in issuing the directive and attributed 'anger or resentment' to the teacher's union (notwithstanding its having gone to a ballot). 'Whatever these motives may have been, they cannot have been worthy of a responsible organisation concerned for and with the education of young children'. (Note the implicit assumption here that the Church and State are responsible forms of organisation.) The possibility of a countrywide strike was thus considered 'a greater evil than the continuance of the dispute in Drimoleague'.[38]

36 *NUR* v. *Sullivan* [1947] IR 77, 88.
37 *Educational Company* v. *Fitzpatrick* [1961] IR 339, 396.
38 *Crowley* v. *Minister for Education* [1980] IR 102, 130.

## THE SOCIAL ORIGINS OF VALUE-CONSENSUS DISCOURSE

> The person who is a judge in Ireland is most likely to have been born in urban surroundings, in fact to have lived in Dublin at the time of appointment, to have had one or more lawyers in his family relationship . . . to be from the strata [sic] of society known as the upper middle class, to have had no judicial experience before appointment . . . Further, the typical Irish judge had a father who was a lawyer or in business, he himself is almost certainly a Catholic, he is pure Irish in ancestry, he is almost certainly also to have been a politically active member of the Fianna Fáil party at the time of his appointment . . . His first self-supporting job was in law as a barrister or a solicitor, he regards himself as a liberal in ideology, and thinks he was named to his judicial post because of his professional status.
>
> – Paul Bartholemew, 1971[39]

Judges' value-consensus representations of the social world did not fall from the sky or occur outside of particular social conditions. The process by which legal professionals acquired these symbolic forms demands our attention, in particular the process of education and training through which they acquired the capacity to speak authoritatively and to adjudicate in court. The development of the judiciary's 'common' or 'practical' sense owes partly to professional training and practice and partly to the imposed logic of a class-based society, whereby, most basically, access to the cultural capital necessary to engage in legal practice was mediated by economic conditions. The emergence of a 'value-consensus' ideology, communicated implicitly and explicitly in the conservative schooling process, formed an integral part of a judge's biographical movement from privilege to socially legitimated coercive authority.

Typically, at the time of their appointment to the Supreme Court, judges tend to be in their sixties. The current incumbents, for example, were born in the late 1940s or early 1950s. Necessarily imposed by the structural requirements of educational attainment and professional experience, this collective age profile diverges significantly from the population's median age (mid-thirties in 2016) and has important, normally conservative implications.[40] Analysis of the Supreme

[39] Bartholemew, 1971, *The Irish Judiciary*, p. 42.

[40] For a literary meditation on intergenerational change opposed by conservative stasis on the Irish bench, see Colm Tóibín, 1992, *The Heather Blazing*. London: Picador.

Court judges' biographical details must therefore be grounded in an understanding of class, educational, and professional dynamics operative much earlier than the time of their appointments.[41]

During the nineteenth century, judges tended to be the sons of landlords, lawyers, or businessmen.[42] Following the establishment of the Irish Free State, a privileged class background continued to constitute one of the legal profession's characteristic attributes (see Table 9.1). Of the seven appointees to the first Irish Supreme and High Courts during this period, four came from legal households, two from professional, and one from a farming family. Senior judges such as O'Sullivan, Fitzgibbon, and O'Connor could trace their ancestry back several generations of judges.[43] Paul Bartholemew's *The Irish Judiciary* (1971) demonstrated that class background continued to inform court composition in subsequent decades.

None of the judges in Bartholemew's survey self-identified as being of 'humble' family origin: almost two-thirds came from what they subjectively perceived to be the 'upper middle class', the remainder from the 'middle class'. This 'middle to upper' class status equated with professional or managerial paternal occupations. A number of judges considered themselves to have been 'born to the law' insofar as more came from families where the father had been a lawyer than where the father had any other occupation. After law, the chief paternal occupation was in the professions (civil service, teaching, medicine, engineering, and journalism), business at a managerial level, and politics.[44] Similar research carried out in 2004, although of Supreme Court judges only, attested to the continued salience of Bartholemew's initial observations.[45]

Economic capital facilitated success in securing access to the cultural and social capital necessary to enter professional legal practice. The Supreme Court judges appointed between 1973 and the present day would have received a secondary education between 1930 and 1960. They constituted a privileged group. For the vast majority of children, prior to the introduction of free secondary education in 1966, formal

41 Accordingly, paternal occupation can be taken as indicating class status throughout this period.
42 McBride, 1991, *The Greening of Dublin Castle*, p. 31. F. E. Ball, 1921, *The Judges in Ireland*, pp. 331–87.
43 Ferguson, 2005, *King's Inns Barristers*, p. 40.
44 Bartholemew, 1971, *The Irish Judiciary*, pp. 32, 42.
45 Carroll, 2005, 'You be the Judge: Part I', p. 153.

TABLE 9.1 High and Supreme Court judges: 1924–63

| Paternal occupation | | University attended | |
|---|---|---|---|
| Clergyman | 3 | UCD | 10 |
| Dr. or professor | 2 | Trinity | 10 |
| Dr. of medicine | 3 | NI | 2 |
| Lawyer | 6 | Abroad | 2 |
| Solicitor | 5 | No Reply | 7 |
| Bank, merchant, civil servant | 4 | | |
| Farmer, builder | 3 | | |
| Journalist, statesman | 3 | | |
| No information | 2 | | |

*Source*: Stein Ugelvik Larsen, 1965, *Law and Politics in Ireland*, p. 21.

learning continued to finish at primary school.[46] In the 1930s, only some 38,000 students (or 6 per cent of the potential school-going population) attended second level; by the late 1950s, of those aged 14–19, only 50,000 (36 per cent of the total age-group) attended secondary or technical schools. Progression toward legal appointment was simultaneously gendered. In 1963, of those who sat the leaving certificate, 43 per cent of boys but only 19 per cent of girls went on to university. Gender balance in the student body at university law courses occurred in the mid-1980s but gender imbalances persist in terms of career progression and subsequent court appointments.[47]

Access to education was significantly class-determined. In 1961, 46.5 per cent of children of professional people aged 15–19 were in full-time education but less than 10 per cent of children of semi-skilled and unskilled workers.[48] Landed, commercial, and professional interests consistently sent their sons to Dublin's private preparatory schools – Clongowes, Belvedere, and Blackrock in the case of boys, Alexandra College in the case of girls.[49] Of the thirty-six judges appointed to the

[46] The following statistics are taken from Ferriter, 2005, *The Transformation of Ireland*, pp. 88, 596–7.

[47] Ivana Bacik, Cathryn Costello, and Eileen Drew, 2003, *Gender inJustice: feminising the legal professions*. Dublin: Trinity College, Dublin Law School.

[48] Ferriter, 2005, *The Transformation of Ireland*, p. 597.

[49] Peter Costello, 1989, *Clongowes Wood: the history of Clongowes Wood College*, p. 64. Bartholemew's survey demonstrated the longevity of this practice into the 1960s. Bartholemew, 1971, *The Irish Judiciary*, p. 41.

TABLE 9.2 Supreme Court judges: 1973–2012

| Paternal occupation | | School attended | | University attended | |
|---|---|---|---|---|---|
| Judge/lawyer | 6 | Clongowes | 5 | UCD | 25 |
| Professional | 4 | Belvedere | 4 | Trinity | 5 |
| Business | 3 | Blackrock/Rockwell | 3 | UCC | 1 |
| Civil servant | 3 | Alexandra | 2 | Night | 1 |
| Politician | 3 | St. Mary's | 2 | Other | 2 |
| Clergyman | 1 | Catholic Uni. School | 2 | | |
| Builder | 1 | Other (Dublin) | 4 | | |
| | | Glenstal Abbey | 4 | | |
| | | Other | 6 | | |
| No information | 13 | No information | 3 | | |

*Source: Irish Times. Dictionary of Irish Biography.*

Supreme Court between 1973 and 2012, only ten did not receive secondary schooling in Dublin; of these, Glenstal Abbey, Co. Limerick, schooled four (Table 9.2). An effect of value-consensus mystification, when recalling their education, judges tended not to recognise themselves as privileged. Countering an allegation of judicial exclusivity, Donal Barrington said he was 'a little bit taken aback' by suggestions that judges came from a privileged class.[50]

Two universities – Trinity College Dublin and, increasingly post-1922, University College Dublin – supplied those graduates that would go on to occupy the most senior positions in the juridical field. University College Dublin supplied the overwhelming majority of graduates (25) to the Supreme Court (1973–2012). Here too, would-be judges constituted a privileged cohort. Although third-level education expanded gradually at this time, rising from the hundreds in the 1930s to more than 12,000 in the mid-1960s, this latter figure represented no more than 5 per cent of all students.[51] Furthermore, the high fees payable for courses in the King's Inns and Law Society, owing to the professional societies' monopoly on full-time legal training, and the fact that barristers had to undertake a year's unpaid apprenticeship

[50] Barrington cited the altogether singular example of Hamilton who had paid for his legal education while working as a clerk. Ronan McGreevy, 'Judges still an elite group – report' in *Irish Times*, 18 July 2007.

[51] Ferriter, 2005, *The Transformation of Ireland*, p. 532.

combined to make training at the bar difficult for people on low income.[52]

The legal curriculum featured such canonical subjects as Jurisprudence, Roman Law, and Constitutional Law. Professor Daniel Binchy's argument, that these provided avenues into the classics, 'the most valuable of all the intellectual disciplines', was a significant admission.[53] Historically, the Greco-Roman classics, whatever their intrinsic worth, have tended to supply the higher strata of the ruling class with a system of references for the forms of their own idealised behaviour, in particular, their privileging mental over manual labour and providing a system of etiquette for the supposedly dignified exercise of power.[54] Specifically in terms of constitutional law, the older generation of judges (sitting on the Kennedy, Sullivan, and Maguire courts) would have been taught in the old, British tradition, emphasising the common law, judicial precedent, and parliamentary sovereignty.[55] Those educated in the 1950s, including Donal Barrington and Ronan Keane, could recall the influence of Patrick McGilligan, UCD's Professor of Constitutional Law, in pointing out a role for normative (natural law) interpretation and judicial activism.[56]

The curriculum was shaped primarily by the changing demands of the market for legal services and by funding constraints on Irish universities. Such conditions ensured a preeminent focus on professional practice in legal education. The canon came to be increasingly displaced by more professionally oriented or 'practical' subjects of 'Contracts, Torts, Real and Personal Property and Evidence'.[57] Irish universities, however, did not engage in conveying practical legal advocacy skills. Instead, the debating societies of both universities, 'the Hist' and 'the L&H', respectively, functioned not only as networking sites for subsequent legal appointments but also as training grounds for the acquisition of those rhetorical devices necessary to legal practice.[58] The young Irish

[52] Irish Council of Civil Liberties, 2007, Annual Report.

[53] Daniel A. Binchy, 1949, 'The Law and the Universities' in *Studies*, Vol. 38, No. 151, pp. 257–74, pp. 258–9.

[54] John Berger, 2008 [1972], *Ways of Seeing*, Penguin, London, 95.

[55] Keane, 2001, 'Brave New World', p. 6.

[56] Donal Barrington, 1987, 'The Constitution in the Courts', in Litton, Frank (ed.), *The Constitution of Ireland: 1937–1987*, pp. 110–27, p. 110. Ronan Keane, 2000, 'The Sinn Féin Funds Case' in O'Dell, Eoin, 2000, *Leading Cases of the Twentieth Century*, p. 188.

[57] Binchy, 1949, 'The Law and the Universities', p. 260; Michael Tierney, 1949, 'The Law and the Universities: Response' in *Studies*, Vol. 38, No. 151, pp. 257–74, p. 268.

[58] Ferguson, 2005, *King's Inns Barristers*, p. 70. Hugh Kennedy used his inaugural address as L&H auditor to argue for the Catholic Church's role in higher education. *Kennedy Papers*, UCDA

law graduate, according to Gerald Harris, thus combined an 'almost unfailing lack of scholarship' with 'a mantle of practical ignorance'.[59] This 'nutshell' legal education, James Brady later observed, 'sustained the widely held view that the best university training for the aspirant barrister or solicitor was a course in Arts'.[60]

For the most part, legal education did not take place in the university. Law was learned by apprenticeship through practice.[61] For solicitors, apprenticeships were based on a period of five years training and compulsory examinations provided by the Incorporated Law Society. For barristers (and would-be judges), candidates were required to become students of and to pass examinations at the King's Inns. Throughout this process, expanding social connections was crucial: the importance of the personal loyalties established at the Inns could not be overemphasised in the career pattern of a judge.[62] A junior counsel, forbidden by etiquette from actively soliciting work, benefitted from professional family members acting on his behalf. These connections were particularly important for a practice known as 'devilling', whereby newly qualified barristers would spend some six months as a pupil of a practising member of the bar in order to acquire practical and technical expertise. Whilst some of the judges of this period engaged in teaching, journalism, public administration, and business, well over half were in law from their careers' beginning.[63]

In the course of progressing towards office, would-be judges and legal practitioners were keenly aware of the salience of connections to political parties, engendering particular forms of political behaviour.[64] Of the judges Bartholemew interviewed about 16 per cent had been affiliated

P4/114. A generation later, Cearbhall Ó'Dálaigh was 'a stout defender of the Irish language and an exponent of the philosophy of Saint Thomas' in 1930s' debating circles. P. F. Donovan , 'New Beginnings (1923–1930)' in James Meenan, 2005, *Centenary History of the Literary and Historical Society of University College Dublin, 1855–1955*, p. 165.

59 Harris, 1948, 'Book Publications', pp. 62–3.

60 James C. Brady, 1975, 'Review: Wylie's *Irish Land Law*' in *Irish Jurist*, 10 (2), pp. 358–60, p. 358.

61 V. T. H. Delany, 1975, *The Administration of Justice in Ireland*, pp. 77, 81.

62 Bartholemew, 1971, *The Irish Judiciary*, p. 41.

63 Bartholemew, 1971, *The Irish Judiciary*, p. 42.

64 Gerald Harris examined the fortunes of the legal team employed by Fianna Fáil during the Economic War to negotiate the end of land annuities payments to Britain: 'Of the counsel consulted seven agreed with the view of the party that the sums in question were not payable; of these seven, one, for personal reasons, did not wish to accept a government post; each of the remaining six later received a judicial appointment'. Gerald Harris, 1950, 'The Recruitment of the Judiciary' in *The Irish Jurist*, 16 (3), pp. 35–7, p. 36.

with the government in some capacity before appointment and 75 per cent had been active in party politics, delivering campaign speeches or assisting in other ways.[65] Some judges did indeed recognise that their work as counsel in 'state cases' or personal contacts with politicians may have helped their career advancement. Collectively, however, judges denied that party loyalties had any influence on their decision-making, effectively reasserting the juridical orthodoxy that the realm of the law was a 'politics-free' zone.[66]

The ideological structures of the judiciary further developed in affinity with everyday activity and work. The division of labour in the field of law – implying distinctions between client and legal professional, between solicitor, barrister, and judge and between levels of competency in the court hierarchy – gave rise to a necessarily limited awareness of the field's overall operation. In this regard, the sheer volume of cases handled by solicitors and barristers, combined with the specific effects of having to manage offices as a site for the sale of legal services, tended towards routine if not quite mechanical efficiency in decision-making.[67] In these circumstances, as *Irish Jurist* editor Gerald Harris observed, the practitioner 'seldom permits himself to think of the law as anything more than the source of his means of livelihood'.[68]

## THE CONDITIONS OF LEGAL CULTURAL PRODUCTION

> If the well-being of the Republic's legal community could be measured by the state of its literature, then one would have to conclude that that community has been semi-moribund since the inception of the state in 1921, during which time there has been an almost total lack of indigenous legal literature. The importance of a national literature was not something to which the legal fraternity in Ireland addressed its mind and the inevitable consequence of a 'nutshell' trained and oriented profession, and one would include both branches thereof, is a form of legal philistinism which is occasionally writ large in our Law Reports and which undergirds a curious antipathy to legal scholarship which this reviewer has encountered at all levels of the profession here.
>
> – James Brady, 1975[69]

65 Bartholemew, 1971, *The Irish Judiciary*, p. 35.
66 Bartholemew, 1971, *The Irish Judiciary*, pp. 33–4.
67 Keane, 1965, *The Future of the Bar*, p. 377.
68 Gerald Harris, 'The Lawyer and his Profession' in *The Irish Jurist*, 4:2: 1938, p. 22.
69 Brady, 1975, 'Review: Wylie's *Irish Land Law*', p. 358.

Knowledge of the Irish legal field was produced predominantly by professors and practitioners necessarily drawn from the same milieu as those inhabiting the field's formal decision-making centres and positions of authority. During the period under survey, the prevailing material conditions of legal practice and publication did not favour scholarship. The market for works on Irish law was limited, indicated by the fact that three incarnations of the *Irish Jurist* collapsed over the late nineteenth and early twentieth centuries. The 'prohibitive' cost of book production also tended to deter potential authors.[70] Legal scholarship in Ireland thus remained predominantly oriented around English centres of production. Even by the late 1960s, Nial Osborough could still claim that '[t]he law in force in Ireland is Irish law but the only worthwhile books, with a few exceptions, are devoted to English law'.[71]

Throughout the 1940s and 1950s, the *Jurist* was under barristers' editorial supervision and tended to concentrate on 'lawyer's law', or topics of immediate and practical concern to barristers and solicitors. Hence, the most recurring lead editorials concerned property law, particularly landlord-tenant relations, rent restrictions, and conveyancing, as well as employers' and professionals' liability.[72] Tellingly, the *Jurist*'s book reviews concentrated on the cost of legal publications as well as their functionality for practice or exam preparation. Contributors consistently wrote of Irish lawyers suffering from an absence if not an outright suspicion of 'abstract learning'. As the attorney general, Andreas O'Keefe, chided: 'Too rarely do we find in any Irish legal journal an analysis of decisions of our Courts in a scholarly way, to see how they can be reconciled with sound legal principles'.[73] Lawyers' hostility to theory, Vincent Delany observed, was 'traditional': '"law is law", they will say, "and that's all about it"'.[74] Low fees and arduous working conditions,

[70] See Vincent Delany (ed.), 1951, 'Book Review' in *The Irish Jurist*, 17 (3), p. 42.

[71] Nial Osborough, 1969, 'Review: The Practical Police Surgeon' in *The Irish Jurist*, 4 (1), p. 203.

[72] See Gerald Harris (ed.), 1939, 'Recent Cases Under Deasy's Act: The Fundamental Position of Landlord and Tenant' in *The Irish Jurist*, 5 (2); 1945, 'The Landlord and Tenant (Amendment) Act, 1943' in *The Irish Jurist*, 11 (2); 1946, 'The Rent Restrictions Act, 1946' in *The Irish Jurist*, 12 (1); 1947, 'Compulsory Acquisition of Land and Buildings for Housing of the Working Classes' in *The Irish Jurist*, 13 (2); 1948, 'A Tenant's Liabilities for Repairs; Deasy's Act' in *The Irish Jurist*, 14 (1); 1948, 'Assignments and Sub-Lettings by a Lessee in breach of agreement' in *The Irish Jurist*, 14 (2); 1948, 'Stamp Duties on Conveyances of Land Control' in *The Irish Jurist*, 14 (3); 1950, 'Compensation for damage to property' in *The Irish Jurist*, 16 (2). See Vincent Delany (ed.), 1957, 'Restrictive Covenants' in *The Irish Jurist*, 23 (1); and 1959, 'A Landlord's Implied Obligation to Repair' in *The Irish Jurist*, 25 (1–2).

[73] Andreas O'Cuiv, 1960, '*The Irish Jurist*: A Retrospective' in *The Irish Jurist*, 26 (1), p. 4.

[74] V. T. H. Delaney (ed.), 1953–4, 'Books: Criminal Law by Glanville Williams' in *The Irish Jurist*, 19–20 (2), 20.

Gerald Harris suggested, prompted the average lawyer to concentrate on private practice and 'periodical endeavours to obtain for himself and his fellows some concession or other from the Government'; seldom was it possible to take an 'impersonal interest in the profession'.[75]

In these circumstances, the 1937 Constitution was rarely considered in the *Jurist's* pages. Instead, Catholic academic journals, notably *Studies* and *Christus Rex*, published articles from proponents of a 'native' jurisprudence, arguing for a shift in legal education from practice towards classical philosophy. Barristers such as William Binchy, Richard O'Sullivan, Vincent Grogan, and Declan Costello further advocated a 'Christian jurisprudence', replacing positivism with natural law theory in constitutional jurisprudence.[76] Gerald Harris compared contemporary natural law theorists basing the validity of legal institutions on assumed first principles to early nineteenth-century French theocrats for whom 'it was necessary to remind man that the only omnipotent Reason in the universe was the Supreme Reason of God'. He suggested that the law be better understood as requiring adjustment to existing conditions, 'aiming at the delimitation of the various interests within the community'.[77]

The 1960s occasioned a significant transformation in the conditions of legal cultural production. Economic 'modernisation', burgeoning transnational communications, and the gradually increasing accessibility of higher education further stimulated both demand and potential for Irish legal scholarship. Significantly, the purchase by John Maurice Kelly, Professor of Roman Law and Jurisprudence at UCD, of the Irish Jurist Publishing Company newly established the *Jurist* as a scholarly journal devoted to modern and historical jurisprudence.[78] From the outset, newly emergent branches of legal activity prompted demands for increasingly specialised scholarship, typified by the regular contributions by Alexis Fitzgerald on corporate taxation laws or John Temple Lang's analysis of the embryonic European Common Market.

The dominant form of legal writing produced in the *Irish Jurist* was that associated with professional training and consisted

[75] Harris, 1938, 'The Lawyer and his Profession', p. 22.

[76] See Grogan, 1954, 'The Constitution and the Natural Law', p. 207. See also Declan Costello, 1956, 'The Natural Law and the Irish Constitution' in *Studies*, Vol. 45, No. 180, pp. 403–14, p. 405. Richard O'Sullivan, 1949, 'The Law and the Universities: Response' in *Studies*, Vol. 38, 151, pp. 257–74, p. 274.

[77] Gerald Harris, 1951, 'Book Review: University of Notre Dame Law Institute Proceedings: Volume V' in *The Irish Jurist*, 17 (4), pp. 61–2, p. 62.

[78] 'History of the Irish Jurist'; available at: www.irishjurist.com/history.htm.

primarily of 'an intricate analysis of... statutory provisions discussed in conjunction with concordant and conflicting *ratios* and *obiter dicta* drawn from appropriate cases',[79] an 'over-familiar, if practitioner-friendly, formula'.[80] Irish legal research was overwhelmingly directed 'at the content of the law itself and the application of lawyer's reasoning (mostly, formal logic) to it'.[81] Justifying this form as opposed to 'policy-oriented' analyses, R. V. F. Heuston claimed that 'the lawyer can only obtain and retain the confidence of all parties if he emphasises his traditional skills and virtues, especially those of impartiality and rationality'.[82]

In terms of constitutional scholarship, the Irish judiciary's 'discovery' of the 1937 Constitution in the 1960s reconfigured constitutional law as a subject demanding specialised attention. Here too, John Kelly was influential, being 'almost the first person to identify and analyse the main problems'.[83] Contemporaries recognised the publication of his 'Fundamental Rights in the Irish Law and Constitution' as 'a notable event in Irish legal writing', one associated with 'an ever-growing public awareness of the Constitution'.[84] John Kelly's (1981) *The Irish Constitution* was generally acknowledged to be the subject's leading text.[85] Significantly, his commentary consisted of the traditional, practitioner-friendly elaboration of statute, cases, and *ratios*.

While new schools of jurisprudence insisted on 'putting the study of law into its social context', established intellectual limitations proved enduring.[86] Paul Bartholemew's survey of the judiciary found that a majority still considered Irish law reviews 'insufficiently critical'.[87] The law schools' continued focus on legal practice occasioned a range of corresponding absences in legal scholarship. Nial Osborough, then editor of the *Irish Jurist*, readily acknowledged the neglect of 'theoretical, historical and philosophical training'.[88] The neglect of normative

79 Stevenson, 1984, 'Negotiated Planning', p. 156.
80 Rossa Fanning, 2006, 'Review: O'Neill, *The Constitutional Rights of Companies*' *in* Irish Jurist 41(1), pp. 144–6.
81 D. G. Morgan, 1985, 'Review' in *Irish Jurist*, 20 (2), pp. 445–50, p. 446.
82 Heuston later defines 'rationality' as 'close adherence to legal reasoning'. Heuston, 1969, 'Trade unions and the Law', p. 12.
83 R. V. F. Heuston, 'Foreword' in Hogan and Whyte, 2003, *J. M. Kelly's The Irish Constitution*, v.
84 B. B., 1968, 'Review: J. M. Kelly, Fundamental Rights in the Irish Law and Constitution (2nd edition)' in *The Irish Jurist*, 3 (1), pp. 196–9, p. 196.
85 R. F. V. Heuston, 1990–2, 'John Kelly' in *Irish Jurist*, 25–7 (1), pp. 1–3, p. 1.
86 Cedric Jones, 1964, 'Review: "Power Politics, Georg Schwarzenberger"' in *Irish Jurist*, 30 (2), p. 26.
87 Bartholemew, 1971, *The Irish Judiciary*, p. 135.
88 Nial Osborough, 1976, 'Irish Legal Scholarship' in *Irish Jurist*, 11 (1), pp. 1–2, p. 1.

jurisprudence, Attracta Ingram argued, 'provided the ideological vacuum filled by the Catholic Church with respect to the 1937 Constitution and subsequent natural law interpretations, these latter often little more than derivatives of the personal moral beliefs of judges'.[89] Moreover, the need for primary research on so many aspects of Irish law compounded the practitioner's traditional suspicion of academic criticism.

The absence of sociological research, in particular, was widely recognised. Sociology, according to Osborough had 'almost totally been ignored' in both legal education and research.[90] Jurists recorded a whole series of associated deficiencies. These included a lack of elementary data on the workings of the criminal justice system;[91] on the social, legal, and economic effects of the absence of divorce or the removal of rent control;[92] and on the socio-legal consequences of the European Community in Ireland.[93] A detailed sociology of the Irish legal profession, including biographical surveys, and an evaluation of the profession's performance was also needed.[94] The most striking absence, according to Ferdinand Von Prondzynski and Tony Kerr, was the neglect of labour law by university law schools and legal professionals; even the law reports failed to record the courts' use of labour injunctions to undermine strikes.[95] Similarly, notwithstanding *in camera* rules, the extent to which court decisions on children's legislation or committal procedures went unreported was 'disquieting'.[96] In general, legal research in Ireland consistently overlooked law-as-process by failing to examine either 'the policy which underlies, or is claimed to underlie, the particular bloc of law under consideration' or 'the "delivery" of the law, i.e. the impact which it actually makes on the individuals affected and the wider society'.[97]

[89] Attracta Ingram, 1987, 'Review: Clarke, *Church and State*' in *Irish Jurist*, 22 (1), pp. 142–4, p. 144.
[90] Osborough, 1976, 'Irish Legal Scholarship', p. 2.
[91] Osborough, 1976, 'Irish Legal Scholarship', p. 2.
[92] Morgan, 1985, 'Review', p. 446.
[93] Imelda Maher, 1989, 'Review' in *Irish Jurist*, 24 (2), pp. 309–12, p. 312.
[94] Morgan, 1985, 'Review', p. 446.
[95] von Prondzynski, 1981, 'The Problem of the Labour Injunction', p. 228. Kerr, 1981, 'Trade Disputes, Economic Torts and the Constitution', p. 241.
[96] O'Mahony, 1971, 'Legal Aspects of Residential Child, p. 227.
[97] Morgan, 1985, 'Review', p. 446. The practitioner's neglect of the structure and functioning of government, Morgan claimed, created a 'communication barrier' between administrators and lawyers. D. G. Morgan, 1986, 'Review: Casey's *Constitutional Law in Ireland*' in *Irish Jurist*, 21 (1), pp. 146–53, p. 147.

## CONCLUSION

The critical analysis of judicial discourse in the preceding cases demonstrates that jurisprudential positions on socio-economic rights remained within certain parameters. Accompanying the relocation of a social conflict to the highly regulated world of the courtroom, judicial discourse registered and reproduced the manner in which law both objectifies social relations and simultaneously envisages living relations between things. Judges thereby subsumed unequal social relations, such as those between landlords and tenants, employers and workers, or corporations and wider society, into purely formal relationships of equal, rights-bearing citizens. Upon these molecular, linguistic instances of objectification and reification hinged more elaborate ideological edifices. Thus, while judicial position-taking on classic or social legal thought, on positivism or natural law, and on socio-economic rights shifted over time, a more fundamental, 'axiomatic', or 'taken-as-given' framework for thinking – namely, the mental walls of the value-consensus state – structured jurists' interpretive choices and resultant disagreements.

Irish judges (re)produced this value-consensus discourse when promoting as transcendent, objective, and just the 1937 Irish Constitution (which, as we earlier established, registered a particular, contested balance of core-peripheral and social relations). Value-consensus discourse involved the prioritisation of principles over politics, of the immutable over the transient, of an imagined community over social forms of exploitation, oppression and conflict. Within the discourse of the value-consensus state, communal or class or social relations are disaggregated and expressed in terms of individual rights-bearers or minoritarian rights-bearing 'sectors'. The state and the law thus appear as a consensual, value-neutral framework through which competing interests can be resolved. In this manner, the particular, private interests of landlords, employers, religious organisations, and corporations appear as universal ones while socially made and contested practices, notably those associated with political economy and government budgeting, come to be portrayed as natural, unchangeable 'facts of life'.

Concomitantly, the voices of the discontented and dispossessed, their experiences of exploitation and oppression are absented in this discourse, or rather misrecognised in terms more appropriate to fatalistic world-views (misfortune, or tragedy) than to a recognition of politically determined inequalities or social agency. Having been absented from judges' discourse as active subjects, 'the people' reappeared as the imagined bearers of shared values, moral qualities, histories, and national identities. To justify faith in this value-consensus state, judges looked to the 1937 Irish Constitution itself and further appealed to knowledge of extra-nationalist traditions, ranging from religious creeds through classic works in law and philosophy to the words of the 'founding fathers' of liberal democracy. The scholastic assertion of a value-consensus state and the downplaying of social relations applied most pointedly in situations where rights conflicts were pursued along class lines by working class organisations, notably by trade unions challenging employers or Church-State control of education.

Jurists' reproducing a value-consensus understanding of the state necessarily owed to the absenting of the voices of the dispossessed in legal practice, education, and scholarship. In addition to the implications of the intra-nationalist political parties' immediate control over judicial appointment in Ireland, the absence of potentially oppositional understandings of the state further owed to the absence of 'the people' as active subjects or collective agents in the client-professional relationships of formal constitutional practice and to the nature of professional-institutional positions locating barristers and judges at a necessary distance from the fray. The division of juridical labour, in which the practitioner primarily viewed the law as 'the source of his means of livelihood', encouraged a socially legitimated thoughtlessness as to the lived reality of exploitation, oppression, and conflict in society, an acceptance of orthodoxy placing beyond question the question of the state's legitimacy.

The social trajectory followed by judges of the Supreme Court from class privilege through education and training to appointment facilitated the acquisition and prevalence of these value-consensus orthodoxies. The conservative schooling process provided the basis for the misrecognition of class, gender, and political privilege, as well as for the acquisition of a system of references for ruling class behaviour. These references included those classical, legal, and philosophical distinctions utilised in various socio-economic rights judgments in defence of the state or as a surrogate for 'the people'. Concomitantly, the conditions of legal cultural production in twentieth-century Ireland reinforced these dispositions, partly through focussing predominantly on practitioners' techniques and partly through further absenting 'the people' via the absence of sociological critique, overlooking the social origins or impact of law.

In sum, the strict parameters of judges' value-consensus discourse suggests that underpinning the formal battles over constitutionalising socio-economic rights, a deeper, less obvious form of politics is at stake here. Judges decided constitutional rights cases in binary terms: either to defer towards parliamentary sovereignty ('the representatives of the people') or towards popular sovereignty ('the rights of the people'). While presenting the appearance of a conflict between two positions, both tacitly grant faith in the legitimacy of the state and the conservative judicial process; both make 'the people' speak. These are inherently political positions. The preceding analysis thus suggests that rights discourse is a potentially flawed, limited, or perhaps contradictory form of political expression. With this critique in mind, it is time to analyse the actual experience of those people claiming socio-economic rights while breaking from the formal constitutional field's social and ideological structures.

**CHAPTER TEN**

# CONSTITUTION 'FROM BELOW' IN IRELAND: 1945–2008

Judge Butler: You see, there must be some social order. People cannot take the law into their own hands and what I am here for is to see that does not happen. It is distasteful for me . . . to have to make decisions like this but I have no option.

Denis Dennehy (Dublin Housing Action Committee): There appears to be a contradiction between the Constitution and what this injunction is asking me to do. The State has a duty to protect the family, according to the Constitution, and this injunction means the family is going to be broken up . . . I think the family is more important than the rights of private property.

– Courtroom exchange, 1970[1]

Distinguished by a strong focus on the state and a curious neglect of society, Irish constitutional studies have not yet attempted to see Bunreacht na hÉireann from the perspective of those constitutionalised. This omission is surprising, not least because people in Ireland, on occasion, have taken the law into their own hands. Seeing a constitution 'from below' denotes tracing this twofold social phenomenon whereby participants in a conflict both challenge received interpretations of a constitution and create new forms of justice.[2] Minimally, this might involve people lobbying government and contacting media to draw attention to the gap between a constitution's expressed ideals and existing state practices. Maximally, people can take direct action to realise their aims themselves, including boycotting, striking, or squatting vacant property.[3] Such activities forward a different vision of selfhood, citizenship, and rights, one that assumes free individuals have

[1] 'Judge orders family to leave house' in *Irish Times*, 26 November 1968.

[2] This theoretical understanding draws on scholarship critically incorporating the role of global-local social movements in the contestation and development of law. See Rajagopal, 2003, *International Law from Below*; de Sousa Santos and Rodriguez, 2005, *Law and Globalisation from Below*. See also Antonio Negri, 2003, *Time for Revolution*; John Holloway, 2010, *Crack Capitalism*.

[3] David Graeber, 2009, *Direct Action: An Enthnography*. Edinburgh: AK Press.

the capacity to manage their affairs together in a direct, ethical, and rational manner.[4] In the Irish context, people have interpreted all manner of socio-economic rights and demands into the 1937 Irish Constitution, challenging the highly regulated space of the courtroom and the law's ideological prerequisites, and, in some cases, forming or constituting entirely new spaces, senses, and practices of justice.

The present chapter incorporates heretofore neglected civil society and social movement voices into a more complex account of constitutional and socio-economic rights development in Ireland. It is not intended to be a complete survey of every popular invocation of the 1937 Irish Constitution. Instead, by analysing some key examples of how civil society groups contested socio-economic rights, I aim to open up a broader terrain of debate about their development. The five moments of conflict or civil society struggle examined here include the Dublin Unemployment Association protests (1953–4), the Housing Action Committee's squatting campaigns (1968–71), the 'Proclamation of Children's Rights' by the Campaign for the Care of Deprived Children (1976), the Talbot workers' factory occupation and boycott (1981), as well as the Threshold/ALONE campaign for fair property valuations following the state's removal of rent restrictions post-*Blake* (1983). Viewed together, these rights conflicts point towards the necessity of a much broader understanding of the 1937 Irish Constitution's role in social life than formal legal ideology might suggest.

Civil society struggles over social and economic rights matter.[5] First, they illustrate how the Irish constitutional framework for property, union, family, welfare, and care relationships worked in practice. All of the mobilisations examined here emerge from collective rejections of the atomisation, humiliation, and violence inflicted in the course of the state's everyday functioning in capitalist society, ranging from mass unemployment and poverty through child abuse within state institutions to elderly suicides in the wake of spiralling rent increases.[6] Second, these groups' declarations provide insight into

[4] Bookchin, 2005, *The Ecology of Freedom*, p. 438.

[5] As noted earlier, civil society is understood critically here to mean those contested, changing spaces of human interaction, association, and community formation in which competing norms and organisations emerge, develop, and reshape society. Civil society is distinct from and presents an implicit challenge to both state and capital, suggesting a potentiality for the greater diffusion of power in society. See Ginsborg, 2005, *The Politics of Everyday Life*..

[6] See Hannah Arendt, 1969, *On Violence*. Orlando: Houghton, Mifflin, Harcourt; David Graeber, 2015, *The Utopia of Rules: on technology, stupidity, and the secret joys of bureaucracy*. London: Melville House.

comparatively subaltern understandings and usages of the 1937 Irish Constitution and further indicate the changing nature, strength, and limits of socio-economic rights discourse in Irish society. Third, their collective actions illustrate the forms not just of ideological consensus but also of state coercion and conciliation underpinning the constitutional framework. Working class organisations, in particular those explicitly advocating direct action, very quickly met with police violence and court injunctions. Situating these experiences in historical perspective provides an important means of understanding the origins, role, and limits of contemporary forms of advocacy for social and economic rights.

Ireland's civil society contestations both shaped and were shaped by changing circumstances. The country's contested trajectory in the world-system, outlined in earlier chapters, was broadly semi-peripheral: 'national' forms of anti-systemic politics continued to take precedence over 'social' alternatives, the state's welfare effort developed along non-solidaristic lines and the population's welfare remained subordinate to the needs of stable, increasingly global capital flows. Within these broad parameters, a number of particular factors distinguish the field of voluntary organisation and community mobilisation in Ireland.[7] These include a comparative lack of cohesion or formal policy environment, the lack of funding sources, the strong though dissipating presence of the Catholic Church, and the role of rural social action.[8] The state began informal corporatist negotiations with trade unions from the 1960s onwards, and further included voluntary and community sectors from the 2000s onwards. There has been a strong coherence between the emergence of neoliberalism and the globalisation of human rights discourse in Ireland, between the decline of traditional, collective forms of resistance to capital and the rise of public interest litigation.

The new socio-economic rights discourses of the 1990s and 2000s thus represented a politically determined, ideological containment of more widely shared, community-based norms and values concerning democracy and justice.[9] There remained a strong continuity between

[7] Brian Harvey, 'Ireland and Civil Society: reaching the limits of dissent' in Deiric Ó Broin and Peadar Kirby (eds), 2009, *Power, dissent and democracy: civil society and the state in Ireland*. Dublin: A&A Farmar, pp. 25–33.

[8] Nicholas Acheson, 2004, *Two Paths, One Purpose: Voluntary Action in Ireland, North and South*. Dublin: IPA.

[9] This is not to reject socio-economic rights and public interest litigation as normatively objectionable but merely to point out their development as ideologically and politically limited in significant ways.

residual Catholic social and emergent liberal forms of human rights advocacy, principally in terms of the persistence of consensual understandings of the state and the associated dismissal of conflict-premised ones. The distinction remains an important one. Each mobilisation examined here varied along a spectrum demarcated by the degree to which participants were prepared to accept the legitimacy of the 1937 Irish Constitution and associated ideologies of the value-consensus state.[10] In the emergent neoliberal era, in circumstances where professional or voluntary organisations spoke on behalf of children, elderly tenants, or workers, NGOs articulated a contradiction between constitutional theory and state practice, questioning whether, in reality, the state prioritised the family, workers, or social justice ahead of children's institutionalisation or the rights of landlords and multinational companies. Associated political action included publicity marches, parliamentary lobbying, and directing socio-economic rights claims towards government.

Conversely, earlier groups such as the Dublin Unemployed Association (DUA) and the Dublin Housing Action Committee (DHAC) shared an oppositional, specifically class-based, understanding of the state. They not only attacked the constitution's value system for upholding property and capital to the detriment of families, workers, and communities, but insisted that people change their loyalty to a different value system and start acting for it. Beyond offering alternative, critical interpretations of the 1937 Irish Constitution, both groups created alternative spaces of justice by choosing to locate their sit-down protests, marches, and direct actions in the heart of Dublin city at O'Connell Bridge, College Green, the G.P.O., and Mountjoy Jail. When challenged through the legal system, these groups subverted its legitimacy by transforming court appearances into causes for celebration and wider publicity. Challenging the complicity of the legal profession in jailing squatters, the DHAC even occupied the Four

[10] The key question here is to what extent proponents and critics of socio-economic rights are ideologically driven, defining the terms of their contestation in such a way as to dissimulate relations of power. Constitution-makers, privileged political actors, and judges usually adopt a 'value-consensus' discourse, tending to absent social processes, power relations, and conflict and to present the state as a consensual, value-neutral framework in which competing interests can be resolved. Conversely, political actors attempting to articulate and to mobilise for socio-economic rights from below have often relied on a more oppositional understanding of the state, considering it in terms of unequal power relations and depicting it as being controlled by (or representing the interests of) society's dominant group or class. On the value-consensus state, see Hillyard, 1972, 'Public Attitudes towards the Police in a medium-sized town in Northern Ireland', p. 71. See also Bourdieu, 1987, 'The Force of Law', p. 814.

Courts. Workers' and community activists' organisation of participatory networks of trust and solidarity amongst the discontented and the dispossessed produced new social visions and considerable redistributive victories.

## OPPOSING THE CONSTITUTION: 1945–73

During the golden era of capitalism, as Ireland was reincorporated into an expansionary, US-led cycle of accumulation, social forms of anti-systemic resistance, most notably the trade union movement, tended to be subsumed within nationalist priorities, primarily those of the newly 'developmentalist' Fianna Fáil party.[11] Catholic social action dominated wider civil society activity. The Catholic Church and associated religious orders, primarily at the instigation of Archbishop John Charles McQuaid and through his Catholic Social Service Bureau, occupied a hegemonic position within the field of community and voluntary labour.[12] Communists, left-republicans, trade unionists, and community associations nevertheless initiated popular campaigns over this period in opposition to mass unemployment and to the state's low welfare effort. The most prominent included the Dublin Unemployed Association sit-down protests (1953–4) and the nationwide occupations led by various Housing Action Committees (1968–71). Both organisations responded to police violence and court injunctions by questioning the constitution and challenging the judiciary through mass assemblies and direct action. In doing so, their members appealed to sharply oppositional understandings of justice and alternative socio-economic rights discourses.

## THE DUBLIN UNEMPLOYED ASSOCIATION (1953–4)

During the 1950s, while the rest of Europe enjoyed a period of prolonged economic growth, the reassertion of financier/grazier-led dependency in Ireland occasioned economic stagnation and renewed government austerity.[13] Trade unions indicted successive Fianna Fáil or Fine

[11] Harvey, 2009, 'Ireland and Civil Society: reaching the limits of dissent', pp. 25–33. On the general phenomenon of anti-systemic resistance, see Arrighi, Hopkins, and Wallerstein, 2011, *Anti-Systemic Movements*.

[12] Acheson, 2004, *Two Paths, One Purpose*, p. 84.

[13] O'Hearn, 2001, *The Atlantic Economy: Britain, the US and Ireland*. pp. 108–40; Garvin, 2004, *Preventing the Future: Why was Ireland so poor for so long?* Mjoset, 1992, *The Irish Economy in Comparative Institutional Perspective*.

Gael-led governments for allowing the banks to restrict credit and for failing to launch any serious programme for industrial development as manufacturing and construction went into a sharp decline. Unemployment and emigration reached record levels. Living standards for the unemployed were dire, particularly so in urban centres where the provision of local authority housing had ceased. Unemployment benefit, at 50 shillings per family regardless of size, was meagre, obliging dole recipients to live on a diet of bread, margarine, milk, and tea. Many pensioners were unable to afford fuel.[14] In these circumstances, in January 1953, a small number of unemployed men at the Werburgh Street Labour Exchange formed the Dublin Unemployed Association, electing Thomas Pearle as Chairman and William McGuiness as Secretary of the group. The Irish Workers League, a Communist organisation, played a key role in the Association's development.[15]

The Dublin Unemployed Association's basic demands were for the right to work and, failing that, to relief work at union rates; abolition of the three-day waiting period for unemployment assistance; payment of benefits for each child; the reintroduction of food subsidies; and the introduction of health benefits. To secure these aims, the DUA organised regular public meetings, rallies, and marches. Taking to the streets en masse not only demonstrated and validated popular grievances over unemployment and degrading welfare assistance but further showed that the unemployed could self-organise.[16] This was significant. Not unlike Abelard's Paris, Dublin in the 1950s was a city physically colonised by religious orders, including the Franciscans at Merchants Quay, the Augustinians of Thomas Street, the Dominicans of Dominick Street, the Jesuits of Gardiner Street, the Carmelites of Clarendon Street, as well as numerous churches.[17] Catholicism was part of the pattern of everyday life of working people, many of whom experienced poverty as shameful while continuing to accept Victorian ideas of the deserving and undeserving poor. Moreover, as during the 1930s, the Catholic right at the height of the Cold War used the 'red scare' to undermine the legitimacy of protest groups.[18] Conversely, the

[14] Kilmurray,1988, *Fight, Starve or Emigrate*, p. 8. See also Ferriter, 2005, *The Transformation of Ireland*, p. 491.
[15] Matt Treacy, 2012, *The Communist Party of Ireland: 1921–2011*. Dublin: Brocaire Books. p. 252.
[16] Kilmurray, 1988, *Fight, Starve or Emigrate*, p. 18.
[17] Ulick O'Connor, 2001, *The Ulick O'Connor Diaries: 1970–81*, London: John Murray, p. 91.
[18] O'Connor, 2011, *A Labour History of Ireland*, p. 174.

DUA appealed to local traditions of labour solidarity. The unemployed marched with the Starry Plough flag of the Irish Citizen Army, formed during the 1913 Dublin Lock-Out, at their head.[19]

The DUA's impact was electrifying. Social welfare grievances of labourers, widows, and the urban poor began to flood into DUA members who, in turn, began to negotiate on a collective basis with the state's Relieving Officers on their behalf. In addition to publicising meetings and marches, the DUA's monthly journal, *The Torch*, began to educate politicians, trade unionists, and the inhabitants of the city on the extent of these cases of deprivation. In doing so, the DUA managed to broaden its support beyond left-leaning members and the marches became progressively bigger. The first official march of the DUA, held on 3 June, 1953, attracted sixty members and proceeded to parliament buildings at Leinster House, the first time such a protest was held at its gates. On 25 June, the DUA blocked traffic to hold a public meeting at Christchurch. By 7 July, some 1,000 members of the DUA demonstrated in the city's main streets, prompting the Gardaí to draw batons to prevent the gates of Leinster House being stormed. By now, the DUA was in a position to stage regular sit-ins of hundreds of people on O'Connell Bridge, blocking both sides of the city centre roadway at peak traffic hours. Their placards proclaimed 'We demand work', 'Is this justice?', and 'Get off your knees – March with us'.[20]

The inevitable sequel to these protests was court summonses. After the demonstrations, sixteen DUA members appeared in the Dublin District Court charged with obstruction. The 1937 Irish Constitution and its Directive Principles of Social Policy featured prominently in their defence. Solicitor Con Lehane asked Inspector McCabe: 'Isn't there a direction in the Constitution that the State shall direct their policy so that every man shall have the opportunity of earning his livelihood?' To which the Inspector replied, 'I am not conversant with that'. Summing up, Lehane further argued that the sixteen accused men 'realised that the Constitution contained a directive that the State should so order its policy that everyone would have the opportunity of employment in support of their families'.[21] Judge T. G. O'Sullivan nevertheless fined the

[19] For newsreel footage, see 'Dublin Workless March In Protest, 1953'. Available at: www.britishpathe.com/video/dublin-workless-march-in-protest. See also http://comeheretome.com/2010/05/07/dublin-workless-march-in-protest-1953/.

[20] 'Dublin Workless March In Protest, 1953'. Available at: www.britishpathe.com/video/dublin-workless-march-in-protest.

[21] 'Sixteen Unemployed Men Fined for Causing Obstruction' in *Irish Times*, 29 July 1953.

men sums ranging from 10 to 40 shillings. (The average weekly assistance benefit was 50s). Eleven were 'bound to the peace' for 12 months on surety of 5 pounds or, in default, three months' imprisonment.

The Dublin Unemployed Association subverted notions of criminality usually attached to an unfavourable court judgment. Its members marched together to the District Court at Morgan place and cheered the defendants as they came out, thereby appealing to an alternative moral force or value system through continued civil disobedience. Thomas Pearle spoke at a meeting in Foster place, held immediately after the case. He claimed that the men would not pay the fines and if brought to jail, they would demand to be treated as political prisoners and go on hunger strike.[22] Pearle, McGuinness, and Kearney were subsequently charged under the Road Traffic Act. Refusing to be bound to the peace, they were imprisoned in Mountjoy for three months. Upon their release, a large meeting was held at College Green at which representatives of the Dublin Trades' Union Council spoke as well as the veteran left-republican activist, Peadar O'Donnell.

By that point, however, a combination of conservative forces had undermined the Dublin Unemployed Association. The Industrial Relations Act (1946) had dissipated the militancy of the Irish labour movement: the Congress of Irish Unions refused to support the DUA during the 1953 protests.[23] The Fianna Fáil government invoked emergency powers legislation to violently repress further DUA sit-down protests. The numbers of arrests and summonses grew.[24] By August, police intimidation had begun to take its toll on attendance and DUA leaders had to sign declarations that they would be of good behaviour on any proposed march. Concomitantly, the Catholic *Standard* exposed the involvement of communists in the DUA, calling for new leaders and even advocating another unemployed pressure group, *Deo Duce*. Pearle responded angrily that 'if it is Communism to protest for three meals a day, then all of you are Reds'.[25]

The Dublin Unemployed Association could not regain its earlier momentum and had all but vanished by the spring of 1954. The group had ultimately compelled Dublin Corporation to introduce a relief works scheme, albeit a minor one employing a few hundred men only. The protests succeeded more generally, however, in challenging the

22 'Sixteen Unemployed Men Fined for Causing Obstruction' in *Irish Times*, 29 July 1953.
23 Ferriter, 2005, *The Transformation of Ireland*, p. 492.
24 Kilmurray, 1988, *Fight, Starve or Emigrate*, p. 24.
25 Kilmurray, 1988, *Fight, Starve or Emigrate*, p. 19.

conception, popular among the working class, that unemployment was the sole responsibility of the unemployed and in emphasising that government had a moral duty to help unemployed citizens.[26] A successor organisation, the Unemployed Protest Committee (1957), succeeded in having its candidate, Jack Murphy, elected to the Dáil. Shortly afterwards, however, Archbishop McQuaid persuaded Murphy, a republican, to ask all communists to leave the organisation, a move ultimately precipitating its collapse. Fianna Fáil reclaimed the seat at the subsequent election. Arguably, these groups' mobilisations for better treatment of the unemployed and domestic economic transformation played a part in prompting Fianna Fáil to abandon protectionism in favour of free trade, developmentalism, and full employment.[27] At the very least, as Con Lehane observed, the DUA's demonstrations over two months succeeded in forcing de Valera's government to acknowledge the unemployment crisis, something that the opposition parties of Dáil Éireann had failed to do over the past two years.[28]

## THE DUBLIN HOUSING ACTION COMMITTEE (1968–71)

Historically, the political economy of Dublin's housing combined a minimal welfare effort with state-assisted slum landlordism, resulting in poor housing conditions for working-class families for much of the twentieth century. In the 1960s, however, a number of factors combined to make the chronic acute. Austerity cutbacks on housing provision in the 1950s combined with population increases in the 1960s to pressure the state's available housing resources. Some 10,000 applicants waited on Dublin Corporation's 'approved' housing list; an equivalent number waited off it. At the same time, the collapse of inner-city tenements resulted in four fatalities, including two children.[29] The Fianna Fáil government's immediate response was to condemn the buildings and to compel several hundred families to be rehoused in suburbs without social amenities or public transportation. This fitted a broader urbanisation process whereby Dublin's working class were to be suburbanised and the city centre adapted for offices, services, and

[26] Kilmurray, 1988, *Fight, Starve or Emigrate*, p. 35.
[27] Acheson, 2004, *Two Paths, One Purpose*, p. 84.
[28] 'Sixteen Unemployed Men Fined for Causing Obstruction' in *Irish Times*, 29 July 1953.
[29] See Erika Hanna, 2013, *Modern Dublin: Urban Change and the Irish Past, 1957–1973*. Oxford: Oxford University Press, p. 124.

car-parking spaces.[30] This urbanisation process in turn would centre on private homeownership with the state reducing and privatising its stock of social housing, thereby generating payoffs for property speculators as well as political actors responsible for planning and rezoning.[31]

An active, broad-based campaign, however, mobilised in the wake of the state's attempts to clear tenement residents. In May 1967, left-leaning members of Sinn Féin established the Dublin Housing Action Committee. Although individual IRA members were also involved, the DHAC was not, as the Department of Justice suspected, merely an 'IRA offshoot'.[32] The Committee maintained an ostensibly independent structure and soon expanded to include a diverse range of left-wing parties, trade unions, and community organisations. These included the Irish Communist Organisation, Connolly Youth, various Labour party branches, the Worker's Party, as well as the Dublin Trades Council and local housing groups such as the Ballymun Tenants' Association and the Dublin Flat-dwellers' Association. Members pledged to fight for '(1) Adequate housing for the citizens of Dublin, (2) Fair rents for proper homes, (3) Protection from eviction by unscrupulous landlords, (4) An end to the scandal of empty homes, and (5) Protection for squatting families'.[33] Several left-leaning priests also supported the campaign's emphasis on families, including Fr. Michael Sweetman of St. Francis Xavier's in Gardiner Street who notably proposed that church land be sold for low-income accommodation.[34]

The Dublin Housing Action Committee combined building voluntary networks of the homeless with holding prominent, public demonstrations aimed at publicising collective demands for social housing. Initially, the DHAC picketed Dublin Corporation meetings to call for more housing. By September 1968, however, the Committee had moved to direct action, organising homeless families to squat vacant property. Throughout 1968 and 1969 the Committee contested office block developments such as those in Mount Street, disseminated

[30] McCabe, 2011, *Sins of the Father*, pp. 31–2.

[31] Developers accumulated large land-banks at the outskirts of urban areas that they then released slowly so as to maintain high prices. Associated private interests systematically bribed numerous Fianna Fáil and Fine Gael councillors to ensure rezoning and development. O'Toole, *Ship of Fools*, pp. 31, 42.

[32] Brendan O Cathaoir, 'Government urged to encourage split in IRA' in *Irish Times*, 3 January 2000.

[33] Dublin Housing Action Committee, 1969, 'Crisis Bulletin: Aims and Objectives'. Available at: https://irishelectionliterature.wordpress.com/tag/dublin-housing-action-committee/.

[34] Archbishop McQuaid took a characteristically dim view of expressions of Christian socialism of this sort. See Hanna, 2013, *Modern Dublin*, p. 128.

information on suitable locations for squatting and helped people to resist evictions.[35] Housing Action Committees in Derry, Cork, and Limerick adopted similar organising models.[36] The DHAC, like the Dublin Unemployed Association before them, appealed to a combination of civil disobedience and moral force. When the legal system served injunctions against the Committee, activists responded by challenging the existing sites and values of state justice. Alternative interpretations of the 1937 Constitution, notably prioritising the rights of the family over the rights of private property, featured prominently in their legal and public defence.

The most prominent squatter to be taken to court was Dennis Dennehy, Secretary of the DHAC and member of the Irish Communist Organisation. During the summer of 1968, Dennehy squatted with his wife, Máire, and children at No. 20, Mountjoy Square. Before squatting, the Dennehys had been living in a leaking caravan, their children 'shivering at the side of the road'.[37] Ivor Underwood, landlord and owner of the property, had a portfolio of Dublin properties, including some seventy Georgian houses.[38] Residents at Mountjoy Square had previously signed a petition demanding that the square be rebuilt as working-class housing (not as offices or gentrified, single-family dwellings), and marched to the Custom House to raise awareness of the city's housing shortages. When Underwood sold a number of houses on Mountjoy Square to a development company, slogans denouncing the sale were painted on the walls of his Dalkey residence and his car was damaged by a homemade pipe bomb.[39] The Dennehys offered to pay rent but the landlord refused. He subsequently sought an injunction to restrain them from occupying the premises.

Subsequent High Court hearings suggested a tension between law and justice. Dennehy, representing himself in court, explained to the judge that he could see two crimes: 'the crime of empty houses and the crime of people homeless'. He thought it was the lesser crime to occupy empty houses. Besides, Dennehy claimed, he had nowhere else to go. If Dublin Corporation provided a place for his family, however, he would be in a position to leave.

35 See Dublin Housing Action Committee, 1969, *The Squatter*. Available at: http://cedarlounge.files.wordpress.com/2008/06/dhac-1969.pdf.

36 'Gardai hurt in street row in Cork' in *Irish Times*, 17 February 1969.

37 'Judge orders family to leave house' in *Irish Times*, 26 November 1968.

38 Underwood left an estate of some €69m on his death in the 2000s. 'Ireland's Rich List: No. 176' in *Irish Independent*, 31 March 2010.

39 'Explosion damages car outside home' in *Irish Times*, 09 October 1968.

Judge Butler: Did you get in touch with the Relieving Officer of the Dublin Corporation and tell him there was an order of this court, that you were to leave the house?

Dennehy: The official told me – and I quote his words – he said: 'High Court judges know as much about Corporation houses as the birds in the sky'.[40]

The judge replied that he had sworn to uphold the Constitution, had no choice but to do so, and held that squatters had no right to be on the premises. In response, Dennehy appealed to an alternative understanding of the 1937 Constitution:

Judge Butler: You see, there must be some social order. People cannot take the law into their own hands and what I am here for is to see that does not happen. It is distasteful for me and I am sure it is distasteful for Mr. Mackey [Underwood's counsel] to have to make decisions like this but I have no option.

Dennehy: Can I ask for your advice on one thing before I reply? There appears to be a contradiction between the Constitution and what this injunction is asking me to do. The State has a duty to protect the family, according to the Constitution, and this injunction means the family is going to be broken up.[41]

Judge Butler replied that the Constitution also required people to respect private property and that this was being flouted, as was the authority of the court. Dennehy responded, 'I think the family is more important than the rights of private property'.[42] By January, after a number of hearings, it was clear that the Dennehys had no intention of leaving No. 20. Rex Mackey insisted on the Dennehys being involved in a 'criminal conspiracy' against Ivor Underwood, against 'your lordship' and against 'the Constitution which this gentleman has had the temerity to invoke'.[43] Judge Butler professed his sympathies for Dennehy while issuing an order for his committal to Mountjoy Prison.

By foregrounding the concept of 'the family', the Dublin Housing Action Committee not only revealed the contradiction between constitutional theory and state practice but further presented social democratic housing demands in a discourse of traditional, Catholic nationalist values.[44] The DHAC returned to this interpretation of the

40 'Judge orders family to leave house' in *Irish Times*, 26 November 1968.
41 'Judge orders family to leave house' in *Irish Times*, 26 November 1968; 'Landlord seeks to restrain occupiers' in *Irish Times*, 23 November 1968.
42 'Family who occupied room in Dublin house must go' in *Irish Times*, 17 December 1968.
43 'Room Squatter to be Imprisoned' in *Irish Times*, 4 January 1969.
44 See Hanna, 2013, *Modern Dublin*, p. 127.

1937 Constitution in subsequent legal challenges to injunctions against their squatting, as well as at public demonstrations in support of jailed squatters.[45] Bernard Brown, the Committee's newly appointed chairman, cited Article 41 in defence of three men jailed for refusing to obey a High Court order to vacate their squat at the Carlton Hotel, Harcourt Street: 'The State recognises the Family as the natural primary and fundamental unit group of society, and as a moral institution, possessing inalienable and imprescriptible right, antecedent and superior, to all positive law'; yet, despite this, he said, 'three men who wanted nothing more than accommodation for their families had been sent to jail'.[46]

Con Lehane, a solicitor for the DHAC, also pointed to the Constitution's Directive Principles of Social Policy:

> The Minister is hardly having regard to the principles of social justice when he asks the Dáil to enact legislation providing for up to three years imprisonment for a father who 'squats' his wife and children, so that the developers and builders of offices and luxury flats can make bigger profits quicker. The Minister chose to talk of democracy in his introductory speech to the second reading. I wonder what kind of democracy he had in mind. Is it the 'democratic' right of the speculators who make big contributions to the party funds to have the use of the Garda Síochána as a private crowbar brigade? . . . The people who have introduced this Bill, and the people who have *procured* its introduction; the people loudest in their condemnation of the squatters and of those who have sought to help them; the people who talk about alien ideologies and make a political parade of their professed Christianity, forget that there was a Child born to squatter parents in a stable in Bethlehem because there was no room for them at the Inn.[47]

The state, Lehane concluded, considered 'the rights and profits of the property speculators and developers . . . more important than the misery of the homeless parents who seek the shelter of the empty houses of the speculators'.[48]

The imprisonment of DHAC members focussed media attention on the state's housing policy and ignited popular discontent at housing shortages. When Denis Dennehy went on hunger strike, a wave of protests erupted across Dublin. Public meetings took place outside the

[45] 'Another Court Order to Squatters' in *Irish Times*, 14 August 1969.
[46] 'Protest March over Jailed Squatters' *Irish Times*, 24 September 1969.
[47] Con Lehane, 'Letter to the Editor' in *Irish Times*, 29 January 1971.
[48] Con Lehane, 'Letter to the Editor' in *Irish Times*, 29 January 1971.

General Post Office where nightly marches would set off for Mountjoy Prison to show solidarity with imprisoned squatters. Hundreds also took part in regular sit-down protests at O'Connell Bridge. Joseph Clarke, a disabled veteran of the 1916 Battle of Mount Street Bridge, interrupted state celebrations in the Mansion House commemorating the fiftieth anniversary of the First Dáil to protest Dennehy's treatment. Leaning on his crutches, Clarke heckled President de Valera, exclaiming, 'The programme of the old Dáil has never been implemented. This is a mockery. There are people on hunger strike in Mountjoy'.[49] As security guards carried Clarke outside, students greeted them with banners proclaiming 'Evictions: English landlords, 1868; Irish landlords, 1968–69'.[50] People's Democracy, en route from Belfast to the GPO as part of the campaign for civil rights in Northern Ireland, held a meeting of 800 people outside Dennis Dennehy's squat at No. 20 Mountjoy Square to protest about the housing situation on both sides of the border. The Dublin Trades Council passed a resolution calling for street demonstrations by trade unionists. Dennehy was eventually released and found housing. Undeterred, he supported a more extensive campaign of squatting.

Subsequent protests aimed at foregrounding the judiciary's complicity with the property-owning class. In September 1969, three women and two men from the DHAC occupied the Four Courts in Dublin.[51] The group arrived at 11am and announced that they had an appointment to see a senior counsel. When they found the Master's Court vacant, they barricaded the door with furniture and then painted a sign on a window blind overlooking Inn's Quay proclaiming: 'DHAC. We are occupying the Four Courts to demand the release of jailed homeless'. The five activists aimed to highlight the imprisonment of Patrick Brady and Patrick Geraghty for refusing to vacate a squat at the Carlton Hotel, Harcourt Street. Seán Dunne, vice-chairman of the DHAC, claimed that Brady and Geraghty were being treated as criminals and that their food had been cut off when they complained about the prison's 'atrocious conditions'. At 1pm a force of twenty gardaí arrived, cleared photographers and reporters from the corridors and broke down the barricade. According to activists Eric Fleming and Isolda Byrne, the Gardaí ignored claims that their protest was peaceful, compelled

[49] Brian Murphy, 2014, 'Angry protests greet de Valera's last address to the Oireachtas' in *History Ireland*. Vol. 22 (1).
[50] Hanna, 2013, *Modern Dublin*, p. 139.
[51] 'Protestors forced from Four Courts' in *Irish Times*, 26 September 1969.

them to sit on the floor and kicked them in the head and mouth.[52] The *Irish Times* reporter noted that Byrne had 'a deep bleeding gash on her upper lip, a black mark under one of her eyes and other bruises on her face'.[53]

State violence was not infrequently directed against the Dublin Housing Action Committee. Dublin Corporation's 'crowbar brigades' were known to eject squatters without recourse to the law. Several occupations and marches ended in barricades and 'running battles' with the police.[54] Hilary Boyle, a 70-year-old social justice campaigner, described how the Gardaí charged at one peaceful demonstration on O'Connell Street 'like mad bulls . . . They hit out with their batons, they kicked and punched and generally acted as agents provocateurs'.[55] For its part, the Dublin Housing Action Committee insisted it was not 'anti-police', citing as proof their helping a Garda widow threatened with eviction from her home of thirty-five years.[56] In response to growing street protests in 1968 and to the escalating conflict in Northern Ireland, the government introduced a Criminal Justice Act to give Gardaí greater power to prohibit demonstrations and to arrest people for 'conduct likely to lead to a breach of the peace'.[57] The Prohibition of Forcible Entry and Occupation Act (1971) made the forcible possession of squatted property a criminal offence and, furthermore, made its public endorsement illegal.[58]

The Dublin Housing Action Committee met with considerable success. In a large number of cases, the organisation had succeeded in negotiating on behalf of tenants with Dublin Corporation and private landlords, many of whom, unwilling to be publically shamed by protests, accepted squatters as legal tenants.[59] These victories came, however,

52 'Housing Group seeks inquiry into police attitude at Four Courts' in the *Irish Times*, 27 September 1969.

53 'Protestors forced from Four Courts' *Irish Times* (Dublin, 26 September 1969).

54 Tensions were heightened by the outbreak of conflict in Northern Ireland and by attempts to reinvigorate the IRA throughout the island. Brian Hanley and Scott Millar, 2010, *The Lost Revolution: The Story of the Official IRA and the Workers' Party*. Dublin: Penguin, pp. 97, 108–9.

55 O Cathaoir, 'Government urged to encourage split in IRA' in *Irish Times*, 03 January 2000.

56 'Housing Group seeks inquiry into police attitude at Four Courts' in the *Irish Times*, 27 September 1969.

57 Hanley and Millar, 2009, *The Lost Revolution*, p. 106.

58 A diverse coalition unsuccessfully attempted to oppose the legislation as unjust and unconstitutional, including Citizens for Civil Liberties, the National Association of Tenant Organisations, the Union of Students of Ireland, Labour party branches, and the Irish Congress of Trade Unions. 'Demand for Axing Anti-Squat Bill' in *Irish Times*, 2 March 1971.

59 Mary Maher, 'The Making of a Revolutionary' in *Irish Times*, 19 January 1970.

as the DHAC fractured under the pressures of its own internal politics, largely centring on how members interpreted and responded to the escalation of paramilitarism and state coercion on the island of Ireland.[60] Members of the DHAC identified their primary achievement as one of a deeper politicisation of social life. Speaking of the thirty or so families she had personally encouraged to occupy empty houses, the feminist organiser Máirín de Búrca observed: 'They won't ever lie down again and accept whatever the law says if they think the law is unjust'.[61]

## CONTRADICTIONS IN THE CONSTITUTION? 1973-PRESENT

With the onset of capitalism's neoliberal era throughout Europe, inherited nationalist and social forms of anti-systemic resistance, notably the parties of National Liberation and of the Old Left (Communist and Social Democratic), gradually declined.[62] In Ireland, the old national project, consisting of ending partition, reviving the Irish language, and economic autarky, was abandoned. In its place, national development was now premised on achieving growth on the basis of semi-peripheral reincorporation into the European Economic Community and a 'globalised', US-led cycle of accumulation. In terms of social mobilisations, the state incorporated Ireland's trade union movement into enduring neo-corporatist wage-bargaining and policy-making negotiations. Advocacy and care networks, formerly the preserve of religious orders, increasingly took the form of professionalised NGO activity and lobbying. While collective organisation against capital may have become less visible, less popular, and less effective, demands for the 'recognition of difference' became increasingly prominent with groups mounting challenges to oppression on the bases of gender, race, ethnicity, sexual orientation, and multiple 'other' identities.[63] Such apparently 'minoritarian' conflicts were increasingly thought of and fought over in terms of 'human rights'.[64]

60 See Hanley and Millar, 2010, *The Lost Revolution*.

61 Mary Maher, 'The Making of a Revolutionary' in *Irish Times*, 19 January 1970.

62 Immanuel Wallerstein, 2010, 'Structural Crises' in *New Left Review*, 62, March/April, pp. 133–42, pp. 135–6.

63 Nancy Fraser, 1997. *Justice Interruptus: Critical reflections on the 'postsocialist' condition*. London: Routledge. p. 11

64 Kennedy, 2006, 'Three Globalisations of Law and Legal Thought: 1850–2000', pp. 65–6.

The three mobilisations examined in this section illustrate the growing contestation of the Catholic social compact in both family and market law during Ireland's neoliberal transformation. The first case centres on NGOs' creation of a 'Proclamation of Children's Rights' (1976). The socio-economic rights discourse here featured concerns about public services' treatment of vulnerable children, and coincided with a broader challenging of Catholic social legal thought and institutions. The second case, the Talbot car workers' factory occupation (1981), indicates workers' capacity to overcome constitutional restrictions on industrial action as well as the state's capacity to defuse such forms of militancy through clientelism. The final case examines an NGO-led campaign (1986) to contest decontrolled rents in the wake of the *Blake* case. It suggests the structural constraints facing those lobby groups who would attempt to recall the state to its alleged constitutional or moral duties.

## THE 'PROCLAMATION OF CHILDREN'S RIGHTS' CAMPAIGN (1976)

From the 1970s onwards, the contestation of Catholic social norms in Irish family law gathered pace. In June 1976, the Supreme Court reasserted those norms in a decision to have a six-year-old adopted boy be returned to his 'natural' parents.[65] A range of childcare groups and NGOs claimed that the courts had failed to take into account the best interests of the child. Responding to the decision, CARE (Campaign for the Care of Deprived Children), Children First, and the Irish Association of Social Workers organised a demonstration to the Four Courts 'to protest the fact that the needs and rights of children are not being met in the laws of the State or in their interpretation'.[66] Two weeks after their initial protest, a group of 2,000 people marched from the Four Courts to Leinster House where they handed 'A Proclamation of Children's Rights' to a Garda officer and asked that it be given to the Taoiseach. The Proclamation called on the state to respect and protect the best interests of the child and for a comprehensive reform of childcare provision, incorporating changes to adoption, fostering, and residential care.[67] Significantly, the Proclamation envisaged increased

[65] M v. An *Bord Uchtala*. [1977] IR 287.
[66] '2,000 protest at child care laws' in *Irish Times*, 14 June 1976.
[67] '2,000 protest at child care laws' in *Irish Times*, 14 June 1976.

financial assistance for single parents. The children's rights lobby also called on the state to informalise court proceedings involving children in order to make them less intimidating.[68]

The children's rights lobby drew both media and public attention to a number of specific issues regarding the state's interaction with minors and, in particular, the constitutional framework facilitating it. They highlighted the state's continued neglect of childcare provision and, in particular, its continued dependence on institutions such as religious orders and industrial schools for welfare provision. The state's failure to adopt reforms, CARE claimed, owed primarily to social expenditure cutbacks. Moreover, owing to specifically Catholic social predispositions, successive governments were also reluctant to support alternative childcare practices such as adoption or fostering or to support one-parent families. The absence of appropriate funding or facilities for children led to cases of child homelessness and prostitution.[69] CARE highlighted further consequences: 'There are newspaper reports on two youngsters in Ireland who died in circumstance in which child care agencies were involved. Who knows their names? There were no public enquiries and no subsequent Ministerial initiatives'.[70]

The children's rights groups also drew attention to the role of the courts in infringing children's rights. The state continued to incarcerate young children, disproportionately drawn from working-class or Traveller backgrounds, on the basis of the Children's Act (1908).[71] Among other things, this legislation maintained the age of criminal responsibility in Ireland was seven and necessitated formal, intimidating hearings at the Children's Court. The sentencing of a ten-year-old child for six years in an industrial school, Phyllis Huet of the Joint Committee of Women's Societies and Social Workers claimed, had become the rule and not the exception.[72] Children appearing before the courts were also subject to racial discrimination. The *Irish Times* journalist Christina Murphy investigating a court case involving a Traveller child in Kilkenny, demonstrated the prejudice of the District Justice against

[68] Christina Murphy, 'Children have no independent rights under Constitution', in *Irish Times*, 9 June 1976.

[69] Christina Murphy, 'Children have no independent rights under Constitution', in *Irish Times*, 9 June 1976.

[70] CARE Council, 'Why Care? Letters to the Editor' in *Irish Times*, 17 September 1974.

[71] The recent Kennedy Report (1970) had also provided detailed criticism of the industrial school system.

[72] Phyllis Huet, 'Letter to the Editor' in *Irish Times*, 4 April 1974.

**Box 10.1 Remarks Attributed to District Justice McCay[73]**

> 'If you want to keep your larcenous paws on other people's property you will pay dearly for it'. (To a 16-year-old youth in Waterford Children's Court).
>
> – *Waterford News and Star*, 1971
>
> '. . . The district justice described the youths as 'degenerates' and told the father of one of them that his only chance of keeping him out of trouble was to lock him up like a dog and spancel him to the wall . . .'
>
> – *Irish Times*, August, 1971
>
> '. . . Justice McCay said that the defendant did not have the morals of a dog or a cat . . . He would be behind bars for the rest of his life. He would wait for him to come of age and then, the moment he became available for prison, he would be put in'. (To a 14-year-old youth in Waterford's Children's Court, charged with theft to the value of £504).
>
> – *Waterford News and Star*, July, 1973
>
> 'You and your breed put me in bad humour'. (To a Traveller).
>
> – *Waterford News and Star*, May, 1973

Travellers in previous cases as well as the unwillingness of the Minister for Justice to censure his actions (see Box 10.1).[74]

The various children's groups' public statements critiqued the 1937 Irish Constitution for facilitating the state's actions, inactions, and institutions. The groups articulated contradictions between constitutional theory and state practice, both in terms of the actual commitment of the state to provide for families' material needs and whether, in fact, the prioritisation of family rights was in the best interests of the child. For Phyllis Huet, the state's unwillingness to fund appropriate welfare programmes made the former contradiction clear: 'Does our Constitution recommend family life or life in institutions?'[75] Other demonstrators, such as Brian Gallagher of CARE, argued that the

[73] Christina Murphy, 'Mother-and-Child Issue with a Difference' in *Irish Times*, 3 August 1974.
[74] Christina Murphy, 'Mother-and-Child Issue with a Difference' in *Irish Times*, 3 September 1974.
[75] Phyllis Huet, 'Mother-and-Child: Letters to the Editor' in *Irish Times*, 3 September 1974.

Constitution appeared to give inalienable rights to the natural parents: 'In our legal system children are very much the property of their parents'.[76] 'Children', as one contemporary newspaper headline put it, 'have no independent rights under the Constitution'.[77] Similarly, Seamus Ó'Cinnéide challenged the extent to which the rights of the family might contravene the best interests of the child, and further questioned 'whether the family existed for the individual, or the individual for the family'.[78]

In the short term, the NGOs did not achieve the goals stated in the Proclamation of Children's Rights. The mobilisation, however, formed part of a broader strengthening of those elements in civil society seeking to liberalise Catholic social influence in family law and to improve state expenditure and provision. Social workers and women activists played prominent roles as organisers and spokespersons in the children's rights campaign, indicating both the gradual expansion of secular welfare provision and of a nascent feminist movement, often at the expense of the institutional control of religious orders.[79] Change occurred slowly. Only in the 1990s, following a series of public revelations of child abuse by family members, by clergy, and by others in positions of trust and authority, did the Irish state introduce the called-for reforms of childcare laws. Successive government reports recommended the explicit recognition of children's rights in the Constitution.[80] Most recently, in 2012, a 'Children's Rights' constitutional amendment to Article 42 was put to and approved by referendum. The amendment introduced child protection measures, including an obligation for the state to consider 'the best interests of the child' as the 'paramount consideration' in child welfare and adoption cases.[81]

[76] Christina Murphy, 'Children have no independent rights under Constitution', in *Irish Times*, 9 June 1976.
[77] Christina Murphy, 'Children have no independent rights under Constitution', in *Irish Times*, 9 June 1976.
[78] Seamus Ó'Cinnéide quoted in Paul Murray, 'Child care groups mount adoption decision attack' in *Irish Times*, 5 June 1976.
[79] Acheson, 2004, *Two Paths, One Purpose*, p. 138.
[80] According to the Report on the Kilkenny Incest case (1993), the high emphasis on the rights of the family in the Constitution may have been interpreted as giving higher value to the rights of parents than to the rights of children. The Constitution Review Group (1996) subsequently recommended including an express obligation to treat the child's best interests as being of paramount importance.
[81] Liam Thornton, 2012, 'The Children's Rights Referendum Result' in *Human Rights in Ireland*. Blog. Available at: http://humanrights.ie/children-and-the-law/the-childrens-referendum-the-result/.

The children's rights groups of the 1970s, however, had also campaigned for redistributive measures. While state expenditure increased over the intervening period, it remained easier for the state to concede rights of recognition than rights of redistribution. The socio-economic rights cases of the 1990s and 2000s vividly illustrated the state's continued reliance on low-cost institutionalisation, as well as on both religious orders and family care networks for welfare provision. Similarly, in the aftermath of those cases, the Oireachtas Committee charged with drafting the children's rights amendment considered but ruled out explicitly including children's socio-economic rights or other international human rights obligations.[82] Primarily important for enabling the adoption of children in long-term foster care, the Children's Rights amendment ultimately contained little to protect services for children from post-crisis austerity measures.[83] In Ireland's constitutional field, from 1937 to the present, children's rights requiring state expenditure have been more honoured in the breach than the observance.

## THE TALBOT WORKERS' OCCUPATION AND BOYCOTT (1981)

Throughout the neoliberal era, the inherited constitutional framework for trade unions, specifically the judiciary's use of constitutional rights to undermine old common law immunities for industrial action, had enduring implications for industrial relations. During the 1970s and early 1980s, as unemployment skyrocketed, industrial unrest mounted to protect jobs and redundancy packages. Many of these disputes, particularly in manufacturing, were rear-guard actions against the inexorable job losses resulting from Ireland's recent membership of the European Economic Community.[84] Car industry workers were to the fore in these struggles and, in the case of those workers who occupied the Talbot plant in 1981, quickly compelled to defend their actions in the

[82] This included the UN Convention on the Rights of the Child. See Aoife Nolan, 2010, 'The Proposed Constitutional Amendment on the Child' in *Human Rights in Ireland*. Blog. Available at: http://humanrights.ie/children-and-the-law/the-constitutional-amendment-on-the-child-an-initial-analysis-from-a-crc-perspective/.

[83] Gareth Noble, 2012, 'The Children's Referendum: Little to Write Home About' in *Human Rights in Ireland*. Blog. Available at: http://humanrights.ie/children-and-the-law/the-childrens-referendum-childrens-rights-in-practice/.

[84] Fear of job losses in traditional industries caused the Irish Congress of Trade Unions to campaign against entry in 1973. By 1980, one in four jobs had been lost. See David Begg, 2014, 'The trade union experience of European integration' in *Administration*, 62 (2), pp. 131–9, p. 132.

courts. Like the Children's Rights campaign, the incident demonstrated how the constitutional framework operated in practice, as well as the possibility of challenging that framework from below. However, similar to the more oppositional unemployed marches and housing action campaigns, the Talbot workers' dispute involved a conflict between state-sanctioned and collectively created sites and practices of justice, with the latter's potential ultimately and effectively contained.

The Talbot workers' dispute owed to the company's breaching of an agreement among government, car manufacturers, and unions. After an eight-month strike, during which time workers had 'blacked every spare part, every imported car, the length and breadth of this country', all parties had agreed to a special protocol to EEC entry protecting car workers' jobs until 1984, and, in the interim, obliging their employers to develop alternative employment opportunities.[85] By 1980, however, owing to the extension of labour-saving technologies, the Talbot/Citroen/Peugot group sought to scale down its Irish operations. In 1980, in spite of protests that the redundancies violated the existing protocol, the plant's workforce was reduced from 500 to 122 employees. Acquiescing in the company's decision, Des O'Malley, the Minister for Industry in a Fianna Fáil government, claimed a deal had been reached. In return for the government's granting a license to Talbot to import premanufactured cars, the group's UK plant would place a £6m tyre-order with Dunlops of Cork, thereby maintaining at least ninety jobs.[86] On foot of this deal, in the spring of 1981, Talbot announced a further eighty-six layoffs.

Thereafter, in order to protect their jobs and redundancy packages, some ninety workers occupied the Talbot plant at Shanowen Road, Santry, Co. Dublin. They barricaded themselves in, locking the entrances and chaining up the gates with padlocks. Placards (with 'abusive legends' according to one *Irish Times* reporter) were placed in the windows.[87] The employee's union, the Amalgamated Transport and General Workers Union, announced an embargo, calling on all union members not to handle or facilitate the import of Talbot's manufacturing components by road, rail, sea, or air. On 27 March, the executive council of the Irish Congress of Trade Unions endorsed the

85 Michael O'Reilly, 2000, 'Matt Merrigan: A marvellous legacy' in *RedBanner* (8), pp. 4–10. Available at: www.redbannermagazine.com/Merrigan.pdf.

86 This order never materialised; instead, Dunlop began the run-down of their Cork plant which closed in 1983. Matt Merrigan, 1989, *Eagle or Cuckoo? The Story of the ATGWU in Ireland*. Dublin: Matmer, p. 266.

87 'Talbot strikers ordered to end occupation of car plant' in *Irish Times*, 26 March 1981.

embargo, claiming that Talbot had known since 1965 that they were going to be unable to continue assembling cars in Ireland and, consequently, like every other company, should have been helping to provide alternative arrangements for their employees.[88] For Talbot, the embargo resulted in the non-delivery of post, oil, and petrol, the non-collection of refuse, and a failure to have machinery and equipment repaired or maintained. More generally, the embargo produced a rapid shutdown of the car assembly and components supply industry, involving some 10,000 workers.

Talbot's directors looked to the existing constitutional framework and sought a High Court injunction to remove the occupying workers. Ben Kearney of the Dublin Council of Trade Unions highlighted the discrepancy in the law's treatment of employers and workers: 'These companies have lawyers immediately available but it takes workers a lot of time to sort out how they will answer a case. By the time they do it could be a week and they are already on the road to Mountjoy'.[89] When Judge Costello granted an injunction to restrain the workers' sit-in, picketing commenced. The judge then granted a further court order limiting the number of picketers to four at each of the factory's five gates. When people attempting to enter the factory were allegedly abused and intimidated, Judge Barrington granted yet another interim order prohibiting picketing. This special sitting of the High Court took place at the judge's home. Eleven workers defied the order and were committed to Mountjoy prison. They were released several days later but only after having purged their contempt by giving an undertaking to abide by the court order.[90]

Having ended the factory occupation and restrained effective picketing, Talbot's directors next applied for an interlocutory injunction restraining the ATGWU's general secretary Matt Merrigan and the Irish Congress of Trade Unions from imposing the embargo. The judges displayed a remarkable creativity in their judgment. On 10 April, the High Court granted the injunction, declaring that the embargo fell outside the scope of the Trade Disputes Act (1906), and that it 'further infringed the Constitutional property rights of third parties'.[91]

[88] Andrew Hamilton, 'Total Talbot withdrawal threatened' in *Irish Times*, 7 April 1981.

[89] Quoted in Donal Byrne, 'Why more industrial rows end in Mountjoy' in *Irish Times*, 16 May 1984.

[90] On 23 April the employees purged their contempt by giving an undertaking to abide by Judge Costello's original order. Kerr, 1980, 'Trade Disputes, Economic Torts and the Constitution', pp. 243–5.

[91] Kerr, 1980, 'Trade Disputes, Economic Torts and the Constitution', pp. 243–5.

Merrigan, however, refused to observe the injunction and continued to support the boycott. Moreover, the ATGWU's Shop Stewards mobilised in his defence. The particularly well-organised Electricity Supply Board group of shop stewards announced that they were prepared to 'pull the plug on the system' if Merrigan was jailed.[92] On 23 April, Judge Barrington committed Merrigan to prison for contempt of court.

On appeal, the Supreme Court upheld the High Court injunction on the embargo.[93] Judge Kenny similarly held that the Trade Disputes Act did not apply, distinguishing the breach of a contract of employment from the breach of commercial contracts. In any event, Judge Henchy argued, whether a 'trade dispute' existed or not, unions had to operate 'within the constitutional framework and the constitutional guarantees in Article 40'. Judge Henchy claimed the embargo amounted to a breach of contract between the company and those with whom it did business, including dealers and customers: '[I]t would have to be borne in mind that innocent persons could not be damnified and when I speak of 'innocent persons' I am not referring to the union or the company but to persons, such as dealers, who had no dispute with anybody or the owners of vehicles who had no dispute with anybody, but who, because of this embargo, could not get their vehicles serviced, a service they were entitled to under their contract'.[94] The Supreme Court had identified an unenumerated right for 'innocent' third parties to a conflict between capital and labour, and thereby permitted the injunction against Merrigan and the ICTU executive to stand. The judges' extraordinarily creative jurisprudence was not officially recorded and, only for news reporters who happened to be in the court, would not have been available for public attention.

Trade unionists and workers criticised the judiciary as 'class-prejudiced'.[95] At ICTU's Annual Meeting, John Hall of the Association of Scientific, Technical, and Management Staffs moved an emergency motion on the Talbot dispute:

> 'Conference believes that the law is totally useless as a means to resolve industrial conflict and the use of injunctions is deliberately designed to destroy trade union objectives and trade union solidarity. Conference

92 Merrigan, 1989, *Eagle or Cuckoo?*, p. 266.
93 Kerr, 1980, 'Trade Disputes, Economic Torts and the Constitution', pp. 244–5.
94 Kerr, 1980, 'Trade Disputes, Economic Torts and the Constitution', pp. 251.
95 Merrigan, 1989, *Eagle or Cuckoo?*, p. 268.

> therefore having regard to the judgement of the Supreme Court which has extended the concept of inducement of breach of contract resolves to support the Executive Council by whatever means are necessary and its endeavours to have this interlocutory decision overturned'.[96]

'One thing emerged quite clearly from the dispute', Merrigan similarly observed, 'and this was the Judiciary solidarising with business':

> '... The Constitution was dredged to ground the Judgement on the Property Covenant of damage to third parties by reason of the embargo. There is no strike where third parties are not affected or contracts not breached between second and third parties in some way. Given this Judgment the 1906 [Trade Disputes] Act is out with the Property Covenant in the Constitution where third parties have these rights violated by a strike in conformity with the provisions of the 1906 Act. Perhaps it is for that reason that the Judgement was never committed to paper by Judge McWilliams?'[97]

Nevertheless, on foot of the Supreme Court decision, the Irish Congress of Trade Unions' executive advised unions to call off the embargo for fear of damages claims arising from its continued operation.

Although now empowered to do so, the Talbot company did not execute the committal order against Merrigan. The Fianna Fáil government intervened instead. Facing a general election in June, the party feared the dispute escalating into a wider industrial conflict. If Merrigan was imprisoned, as the ATGWU put it, 'all hell would break loose'. There were additional considerations. Somewhat exceptionally among trade union leaders, Merrigan played an active role in the 'Anti H-Block' campaign in support of Irish republican hunger strikers and their demands for political prisoner status.[98] The hunger strikers stood twelve candidates for election in the Republic of Ireland, including the Dublin North-Central constituency of Taoiseach Charles Haughey in which the Talbot factory was located. Haughey instructed his staff to enter negotiations with the unions and the Industrial Development Authority to seek a replacement industry. He then arranged a special grant from the Department of the Taoiseach and AnCO, the state's unemployed assistance agency, to be paid through the ATGWU to keep the ninety Talbot workers in full pay.[99]

96 Merrigan, 1989, *Eagle or Cuckoo?*, p. 268.
97 Merrigan, 1989, *Eagle or Cuckoo?*, p. 267.
98 See Ferriter, 2004, *The Transformation of Ireland*, pp. 639–40.
99 O'Connor, 2011, *A Labour History of Ireland*, p. 236.

By June, when the promised replacement industry had failed to materialise, a smaller group of twenty-five car-workers resumed their occupation in protest. The sit-in took place without official union backing and the shop stewards had not been informed. Spokesman Brendan Dalton claimed they were fully prepared for the consequences of their action, including jail: 'We hope to highlight the situation of the multinationals who are intransigent and not concerned about the workforce, some of whom worked here for 30 years'.[100] Unwilling to lose trade union support in an election year, Haughey defused the crisis by undertaking to find jobs in the public service for the ninety workers and to provide severance pay on foot of any drop in earnings. In this instance, the state's apparent largesse was a function both of workers' determined organisation and of government's unwillingness to provoke wider industrial action or nationalist opprobrium in an election year. It was, as Matt Merrigan put it, 'a unique agreement'.[101]

The Talbot factory occupation and embargo illustrated a number of key socio-legal dynamics at play in Irish industrial relations. First, in terms of state coercion, the inherited constitutional framework, notably providing employers' ready access to injunctions to restrain industrial action, tilted the balance of power in industrial disputes against workers. Uniquely in Europe, the number of injunctions issued to Irish employers against workers engaged in industrial action rose steadily in subsequent years.[102] The Industrial Relations Act (1990) thereafter widened the grounds on which an injunction could be obtained and further restricted industrial actions such as sympathetic strikes or pickets. Second, the Talbot dispute illustrated the state's complicity with multinational corporations in circumventing the rights of unionised workers. It further showed the manner in which governments would resolve adjustments to Ireland's neoliberal transformation more through clientelism and consultation than a legally entrenched corporatism.[103]

Third and most important, the Talbot dispute illustrated how the wider trade union movement and the ICTU executive broadly accepted this position, notably conceding the substantive point of defending the

[100] Renagh Holohan, 'Talbot plant occupied in redundancy pay protest' in *Irish Times*, 4 June 1981.

[101] Merrigan, 1989, *Eagle or Cuckoo?*, p. 267.

[102] Quoted in Donal Byrne, 'Why more industrial rows end in Mountjoy' in *Irish Times*, 16 May 1984.

[103] Ireland's voluntarist or Anglo-American system of interest group articulation notably absented collective bargaining rights for unions.

right to mount industrial action in support of workers in other industries. Writing several years later, Matt Merrigan situated the outcome of the Talbot conflict amidst the onset of a 'virulent modern laissez-faire' and the state's withdrawal from processes of wealth redistribution. The decline in Irish trade unions' politicisation would have harmful consequences for civil society more generally: 'Hundreds of thousands of Irish people will never experience in the future the very basic lessons of a collectivist ethos derived from membership of a Trade Union, that gave the Movement in the past the old certitudes of organisational solidity and continuity as a major force in society'.[104] It was a prescient forecast.

## THRESHOLD AND ALONE CAMPAIGN FOR RENT TRIBUNALS (1983)

After containing various cities' housing action campaigns in the early 1970s, the Irish state increasingly withdrew from providing social housing, and assisted families with mortgages and private homeownership instead, at least initially.[105] In this context, the Supreme Court's decision in *Blake* (1982) to strike down rent restrictions had important consequences. Rent increases for some 45,000 tenants were dramatic. New rents fixed in the District Court yielded many multiples of landlords' original investments. In determining the value of newly decontrolled tenements, individual District Court judges did not look to the actually existing market for accommodation but rather to the properties' 'commercial possibilities'.[106] Lilberne Ltd., for example, secured increases for five properties in Kimmage, raising total annual rents 900 per cent, from £976 to £8,398.[107] This entirely hypothetical determination also assumed that both landlord and tenant had met their obligations to keep the house in good repair. In reality, many houses were 'about to fall down'.[108] Moreover, since landlords often delayed registering their properties in order to avoid tax, the Department of Social Welfare's processing of rent allowances and government subsidies to newly

[104] Merrigan, 1989, *Eagle or Cuckoo?*, p. 270. More than twenty years of voluntarist social partnership meant that existing union structures were poorly positioned to resist the assault on labour that followed the 2008 global financial crisis. McDonagh and Dundon, 2010, 'Thatcherism Delayed? The Irish crisis and the paradox of social partnership', p. 559.

[105] Conor McCabe, 2011, Sins of the Father, p. 32.

[106] Maurice Walsh, 'Landlords prosper as rent curbs end' in *Irish Times*, 2 March 1983.

[107] Maurice Walsh, 'Landlords prosper as rent curbs end' in *Irish Times*, 2 March 1983.

[108] Donal Dorcey, 'Starving in order to pay the rent' in *Irish Times*, 8 June 1983.

decontrolled tenants was slow. In the first six months of 1983, while some 500 rent valuations had been set, only 35 allowances had been granted. NGOs subsequently reported cases of elderly tenants starving themselves slowly rather than falling behind with the rent. At least two ended their lives by suicide.[109]

Landlords and tenants held opposing views as to the justice offered by the courts in these rent valuation cases. The rent escalations occasioned a broader civil society questioning of the 1937 Constitution's property rights provisions. Deirdre Kelly of the Living City Group highlighted the gap between constitutional theory and practice:

> 'Why, in a constitution which is supposed to treat all the people of the nation equally, does the owning or buying of a property as an investment give one person the right to remove the home from another person, who never had, and possibly never will have, the opportunity to own a home? This is not equality; this is treating a human being in the same way as an investment in a mine, or cattle or pigs. It must stop'.[110]

In a critique of the *Blake* judgment, she argued that the 'controlled' landlords had not been arbitrarily 'selected'. On the contrary, they bought a house 'of their own free will, with full legal advice, as an investment' and in full knowledge of its limitations. Two NGOs, Threshold, the national housing advice charity, and ALONE (A Little Offering Never Ends), a charity for the care of isolated, elderly people, attempted to articulate decontrolled tenants' immediate concerns and voiced opposition to rent increases.

Landlords, conversely, were 'agreeably surprised by the leniency of the District Court in fixing new rents'.[111] William Martin, Chairman of the National Private Rental Law Reform Group, criticised a recent NGO advertisement condemning the rents being set by the Rent Courts:

> ALONE fails to point out to your readers that the owners of this property were (a) Refused the right to increase their rents over a period of seventy years. (b) The average basic rent was ten pence a room per week. (c) Ninety per cent of the sitting tenants were extremely well-to-do. Many owned other property and a great many could afford to house themselves. (d) The State made no provision to house these tenants. Neither did the local authority. (e) There was no investigation of the means of the

[109] Donal Dorcey, 'Starving in order to pay the rent' in *Irish Times*, 8 June 1983.
[110] Deirdre Kelly, 'Rent Revision Case' in *Irish Times*, 2 July 1983.
[111] Maurice Walsh, 'Landlords prosper as rent curbs end' in *Irish Times*, 2 March 1983.

> tenant to establish the need for subsidisation of the rent or his ability to pay a proper rent. (f) Most of the accommodation affected by the Rent Restriction Act were large flats or whole houses. As for the tenants being 'poor' and 'old', property owners found this type of tenant most argumentative and demanding.[112]

Similarly, Patrick Madigan, the solicitor who brought the action against the rent restrictions, observed: 'The courts have worked very well so far. They have been very realistic and have set very reasonable rents from the landlord's point of view'.[113]

Threshold and ALONE, not unlike the Children's Rights NGOs, lobbied government to introduce a more informal tribunal to decide rent valuations, staffed by the county registrar, a social worker, and a valuer. Applicants would retain a right of appeal to the courts. Fr. Donal O'Mahony and Willie Birmingham (of Threshold and ALONE, respectively) claimed that the existing process made tenants feel criminalised and intimidated:

> 'The fear of some tenants going into court was absolutely amazing. They were being cross-examined by barristers for the landlord. One lady collapsed after the court case'.[114]

> 'To them a court is a place for those who have broken the law. Added to this fear, they are questioned (on oath) about their income, their age, their savings, all very personal questions, which must be humiliating and awkward, particularly for people reared in an age when such things were not discussed openly. How many landlords are asked their age in court, or to state their savings or their incomes?'[115]

Landlords, however, were 'implacably opposed' to change.[116] Patrick Madigan explained: 'Judges are more *au fait* with money and dealing with money . . . [A] rent tribunal would be totally biased towards the tenant'.[117]

Threshold and ALONE achieved a partial success. In August 1983, the Fine Gael-Labour coalition government introduced a Rent Tribunal, thereby changing the legal setting of rent valuations.[118] The

112 William Martin, 'Rent Revision Case' in *Irish Times*, 2 July 1983.
113 Maurice Walsh, 'Landlords prosper as rent curbs end' in *Irish Times*, 2 March 1983.
114 Maurice Walsh, 'Landlords prosper as rent curbs end' in *Irish Times*, 2 March 1983.
115 Donal Dorcey, 'Starving in order to pay the rent' in *Irish Times*, 8 June 1983.
116 Maurice Walsh, 'Landlords prosper as rent curbs end' in *Irish Times*, 2 March 1983.
117 Maurice Walsh, 'Landlords prosper as rent curbs end' in *Irish Times*, 2 March 1983.
118 Rent Tribunal (Date of Establishment) Order, 1983.

incident was illustrative of NGOs' representational function and mode of action. Both spoke on behalf of newly 'decontrolled' tenants and concentrated on representative actions through media and government lobbying, appealing to the state for justice. Contemporary newspaper reports also highlighted the tendency of Catholic social activists to downplay class conflict. Threshold's Father O'Mahony, we are told, 'has sympathy for the landlords too'.[119] Ultimately, however, the Threshold and ALONE campaign highlighted the state's commitment to withdrawing from housing provision in favour of merely regulating a housing market. Writing in response to the campaign, Seamus Rattigan, Chairman of the Democratic Socialist Party, described how tenants would be increasingly exposed to 'the full blast of brutal "market forces", . . . one more form of exploitation ruthlessly pursued by a privileged minority for their own selfish interests'.[120] Successive governments' commodification of housing escalated rapidly in subsequent years.[121]

## CONCLUSION

Opposition to oppression has been a constant of the modern world-system.[122] The civil society struggles over social and economic rights examined in this chapter all present particular ways in which people organised to contest a fundamentally violent process of capitalist development in Ireland. The subordination of the population's welfare to the needs of stable capital flows underpinned the poverty and hunger experienced by the unemployed in the 1950s, the deaths caused by building collapses in the 1960s, the elderly suicides provoked by spiralling rent increases in the 1980s, and the sexual abuse of successive generations of children in state institutions over the twentieth century. This slow, bureaucratic, and structural violence was less obvious but no less real than the court injunctions and police rapidly deployed against the Dublin Unemployed Association, the Housing Action Committees, and the Talbot factory workers who sought to resist capital.

A number of collective associations were particularly important to mobilising civil society in these contestations, including the Dublin Council of Trade Unions, community and tenant organisations, religious orders or parish networks, as well as numerous Left- and

[119] Donal Dorcey, 'Starving in order to pay the rent' in *Irish Times*, 8 June 1983.
[120] Seamus Rattigan, Letter to the Editor' in *Irish Times*, 23 January 1984.
[121] Conor McCabe, 2011, *Sins of the Father*. pp. 32–60.
[122] Arrighi, Hopkins, and Wallerstein, 2011, *Anti-Systemic Movements*, pp. 29–30.

Left-Republican political parties or groupings. In more recent decades, however, as many of these collective organisations have fallen into decline, civil society mobilisations have comprised of increasingly secular, often philanthropic or state-funded NGOs.[123] The prevailing pressure on such organisations today is to prioritise service-provision over social transformation.[124] In short, the development of contemporary human rights discourse and advocacy in Ireland emerged from the long-standing 'globalisation' of human rights norms and the local, secular reinvention of Catholic social advocacy practices and organisations.[125]

Changing civil society mobilisations co-evolved with changing socio-economic rights discourses and alternative mobilising strategies. The Dublin Unemployed Association and Housing Action Committees both appealed to the heroic nationalist and socialist traditions of Ireland's revolutionary period, carrying the Starry Plough of the Irish Citizen Army, rallying at the General Post Office, and invoking the Democratic Programme of the First Dáil.[126] Both groups reinvented the 1937 Irish Constitution's Catholic social ideology, notably its Directive Principles and Family provisions, to advance their fundamentally redistributive demands for work and housing. Sharing a more oppositional, class-oriented understanding of the role of the state, the Dublin Unemployed Association, the Dublin Housing Action Committee, and the Talbot workers went further in challenging the legitimacy of the state. Conversely, NGOs such as CARE, Threshold, and ALONE acted and spoke on behalf of minoritarian groups such as children and elderly or disadvantaged tenants in the course of publicity marches, media campaigns, and government lobbying. The NGOs articulated a contradiction between constitutional ideology and state practice, questioning whether the state really prioritised the family and social justice ahead of children's institutionalisation or the rights of speculators and landlords. While successful in compelling public and state recognition of these groups' conditions, lobbying, at least in these cases, proved notably unsuccessful in ensuring more substantive rights to redistribution.

123 Harvey, 2009, 'Ireland and Civil Society: reaching the limits of dissent', pp. 25–33.

124 The chilling effect of the 'non-profit industrial complex' on social justice movements has been well documented. See INCITE! Women of Color against Violence, 2009, *The Revolution Will Not Be Funded*. Cambridge, MA: South End Press.

125 See Kennedy, 2006, 'Three Globalisations of Law and Legal Thought: 1850–2000'.

126 On affirming the heroic tradition in Irish nationalism, see Brown, 2004, *Ireland: A Social and Cultural History*, p. 69.

The prevailing form of socio-economic rights discourse in Irish civil society today more closely resembles the latter groups' orientation towards the state. From the 1990s onwards, public interest litigation to secure resources for special needs adults, young offenders, children, and carers was accompanied by civil society campaigning for the judicial recognition of socio-economic rights, notably featuring the Irish Autism Alliance of which Kathy Sinnott, a Catholic social activist, was patron.[127] Thus, while the Supreme Court broadly rejected the constitutional argument for recognition of socio-economic rights in the *Sinnott* case, the litigants' dual approach yielded immediate concessions. On the day of the verdict, the Minister for Education stated that he had a 'virtually open cheque book' to ensure 'full and appropriate provision' for both the education and care of people with disabilities.[128] New, remedial legislation followed soon after.[129] Success, however, proved short-lived. Since the onset of the global financial crisis of 2007–8, disability service users, service providers, and statutory bodies have reported a cumulative 14 per cent cut to their core organisational funding between 2009 and 2012.[130] Moreover, elements of legislation specifying commitments to inclusion were quickly postponed or suspended due to austerity.[131] Rights to redistribution remain politically elusive.

In sum, civil society contestations of the 1937 Irish Constitution varied along a spectrum demarcated by the degree to which participants were prepared to break with the legitimacy of the 1937 Irish Constitution and associated ideologies of the value-consensus state. NGOs' and public interest litigants' raising the Constitution's family and social justice provisions to recall the state to its apparent duties registered and reproduced orthodox understanding of the value-consensus state. So

[127] Kingston, 2007, *Mothering Special Needs*, p. 38.

[128] Whyte, 2002, *Social Inclusion and the Legal System*, p. 357.

[129] Within the following months, the Irish government announced the creation of a National Council for Special Education to improve services for adults with autism and to provide adequate special needs education for children. Government commitments to inclusion also followed, underpinned by legislation such as the Disability Act (2005), the Education of Persons with Special Education Needs Act (2004), and the Equal Status Acts (2000, 2004).

[130] Trish McKeogh, 2012, 'Assessing the impact of European governments' austerity plans on the rights of people with disabilities: Ireland'. European Foundation Centre, p. 27. Available at: www.efc.be/programmes_services/resources/Documents/Ireland%20Country%20Report_FINAL.pdf.

[131] Sections conferring statutory rights to assessment, education plans, and appeals processes have been deferred. Significantly, since the state was unwilling to include a role for the legal system in the Disability Act 2005, such postponements cannot be contested in the courts. See McKeogh, 2012, 'Assessing the impact of European governments' austerity plans on the rights of people with disabilities: Ireland', pp. 16, 20.

too did their attempts to reconfigure the judicial space so as to alleviate the intimidation of Travellers, children, and the disadvantaged. Conversely, the pervasiveness of the value-consensus state as ideology was most fully challenged in situations where working-class groups began to exercise autonomy and solidarity against capital and, in doing so, to deny the legitimacy of the state. Members went about contesting the constitution-in-practice by claiming public and private spaces – including roads, state buildings, speculators' properties, and multinational workplaces – and transforming them into generative sites of participation where grievances and demands came to be aired. When challenged through the legal system, these groups subverted its legitimacy by transforming court appearances into causes for celebration, and wider publicity. In the present moment of crisis, it is precisely these experiences of constitution from below that raise the most challenging questions and the most exciting possibilities.

# CONCLUSION: CONTESTING ECONOMIC AND SOCIAL RIGHTS TODAY

*In the middle-run (that is, the next 20–40 years), the debate is fundamental and total. There is no compromise. One side or the other will win. I call this the battle between the spirit of Davos and the spirit of Porto Alegre. The spirit of Davos calls for a new non-capitalist system that retains its worst features – hierarchy, exploitation, and polarization. They could well install a world-system that is worse than our present one. The spirit of Porto Alegre seeks a system that is relatively democratic and relatively egalitarian . . . [T]he chances of tilting the bifurcation in our direction depends on us. The odds are fifty-fifty. It follows that our efforts as activists are not merely useful; they are the essential element in our struggle for a better world.*

– Immanuel Wallerstein[1]

*We are also going to go about raising a struggle in order to demand that we make a new Constitution, new laws which take into account the demands of the Mexican people, which are: housing, land, work, food, health, education, information, culture, independence, democracy, justice, liberty and peace. A new Constitution which recognizes the rights and liberties of the people, and which defends the weak in the face of the powerful.*

– Zapatista Army of National Liberation[2]

The contemporary moment of crisis, austerity, and struggle illustrates how diverse groups across the political spectrum can use the discourse of universal human rights ideologically, which is to say in a manner that promotes particular forms of politics in order to advance particular interests and values. In the Republic of Ireland, the state considers its commitment to socio-economic rights to be compatible with continuing austerity policies in pursuit of economic growth. In June 2015, the government's submission to the United Nations Committee for Economic, Social, and Cultural Rights effectively reaffirmed this position. Conversely, trade unions and NGOs continue to demand that socio-economic rights be realised more immediately through state intervention and constitutional entrenchment. Throughout 2015, the

[1] Wallerstein, 2014, 'Anti-Systemic Movements, Yesterday and Today', pp. 171–2.

[2] EZLN, 2005, 'Sixth Declaration of the Selva Lacandona'. Available at: http://enlacezapatista.ezln.org.mx/sdsl-en/.

Right2Water campaign helped mobilise tens of thousands of people in support of the constitutional recognition of rights to water and to housing, as well as rights to jobs and decent work, to health, to debt justice, to education, and to democratic reform. The campaign sought a 'Progressive Irish Government' to implement these aims.[3]

In the wider and ongoing battle over crisis-resolution in Ireland, the 1937 Irish Constitution has featured prominently as have calls for constitutionally entrenching socio-economic rights.[4] Notably, in February 2014, following concerted NGO interventions, the government-appointed Convention on the Irish Constitution voted by a majority of 85 per cent to insert constitutional rights to health, housing, and adequate living standards, as well as those rights contained in the International Covenant for Economic and Social Rights.[5] A majority also favoured including a provision in the Constitution stipulating 'that the State shall progressively realise ESC rights, subject to maximum available resources and that this duty is cognisable by the Courts'. Here too, however, the Fine Gael-Labour coalition government (2011–16) exercised a veto over putting this proposal to a referendum.[6] NGOs have nevertheless used the Convention process to demonstrate wider civil society's support for socio-economic rights. Recent polls suggest that more than 70 per cent of the Irish public believe that the Irish Constitution should be amended to protect additional human rights like the right to health and social security.[7]

Contemporary anti-austerity struggles, however, have ruptured this traditional left-right debate on the role of the state in protecting

[3] Right2Water, 2015, 'Policy Principles for a Progressive Irish Government'.

[4] Calls for a 'Second', 'New' or 'Renewed' Republic post-2008 frequently contrasted the 'acquiescent' 1937 Constitution unfavourably with the more 'militant' 1916 Proclamation and the 1919 Democratic Programme. See Kissane, 2011, *New Beginnings*, pp. 136–40; Gallagher, 2010, 'The Changing Constitution', pp. 97–101.

[5] Eighty per cent voted in favour of giving constitutional protection to the full range of rights within the International Covenant on Economic Social and Cultural Rights. As mentioned earlier, Ireland signed the ICESCR in 1989, and further signed up to introducing a complaints mechanism in 2012. However, in the absence of sufficient political will, the state has yet to give domestic legal effect to the range of rights committed to under international law, or to fund effective complaints and monitoring systems. See Noeline Blackwell, 'Government only paying lip service to economic right to housing' in *Irish Times*, 10 December 2015.

[6] During the 2015 UN Committee examination of the state's compliance with the ICESCR, the Attorney General's office claimed there would be 'resource implications' if socio-economic rights were to be made justiciable in Irish courts, and that state parties were committed 'to do the best they can within the resources available in the context'. Kitty Holland, 'UN Committee examines State's social rights record' in *Irish Times*, 9 June 2015.

[7] Amnesty International Ireland, 2014, *Bringing ESC Rights Home*. Dublin: Amnesty Publications, p. 7.

socio-economic rights. In recent years, many of Ireland's water and housing protestors have taken the law into their own hands, taking direct action to prevent the installation of water meters or to squat vacant buildings in support of claimed human rights. Direct actions, as the preceding analysis suggests, are not simply tactics to bolster electoral support or to attract publicity. These exercises in collective self-determination advance an alternative vision of selfhood, citizenship, and rights, one that assumes free individuals have the capacity to manage social affairs in a direct, ethical, and rational manner.[8] The actions of water protestors and squatters in recent years make explicit the disjuncture between direct democratic forms of popular self-organisation and representative democratic forms such as the party and constituent assembly. Contemporary anti-capitalist movements, from the Zapatistas to Occupy Wall Street and beyond, have (re)posed precisely this historically contested disjuncture as the vital question of transformative praxis today.

Far from a new occurrence, this disjuncture has been at the heart of successive attempts to articulate and to constitutionalise economic and social rights from the popular, democratic revolts of 1848 through to the present day. Since our intellectual and political commitments are, to a limited though important degree, a function of how we understand our history, the politics at stake in the success or failure of such attempts demands critical analysis. Throughout this book, I have attempted to reconstruct the genesis of those socio-economic rights ultimately constitutionalised, to detail the conflicts of the 1937 Irish Constitution's early beginnings and to document the discarded possibles that accompanied its development to the present day. Importantly, the politics of socio-economic rights in Ireland were not *sui generis* but rather may and, indeed, should be understood as a world-systemic politics. In particular, insofar as the 1937 Irish Constitution contained socio-economic rights provisions, these expressed as legal form a shifting balance of contested core-periphery and social relations in the historical capitalist world-system.

In this conclusion, I summarise this book's key findings regarding the Irish experience of contesting the constitutionalisation of socio-economic rights, tracing how this politics unfolded and varied according to locally contested transformations within the world-system, from 'classic liberalism' (1850–1930) through 'social liberalism'

[8] Bookchin, 2005, *The Ecology of Freedom*, p. 438; see also Graeber, 2009, *Direct Action*.

(1900–c. 1970) to contemporary 'neoliberalism' (c. 1970 onwards). Of primary and enduring importance here is how conservative and nationalist constitutional projects dominated social and radical ones, albeit a form of domination that was contested at critical junctures by civil society and by the organised left. The purpose of this summary is threefold: first, to delineate clearly the obstacles and opportunities that contemporary projects to realise socio-economic rights in Ireland face; second, to outline a critical appreciation of the issues posed by the advocacy of social and economic rights in the current crisis of capitalism; and third, to highlight key insights for future scholarship on the politics of constitutions and socio-economic rights.

In the current crisis of capitalism, the advocacy and discourse of socio-economic rights is ambiguous, and compatible with a variety of political projects, from the technocratic, conservative policies of Davos to the more democratic, more egalitarian politics of Porto Alegre.[9] Particular forms of socio-economic rights advocacy will vary according to the specific circumstances of each locale. In Ireland, the welfare state is characterised by a comparatively low tax-take and welfare effort, as well as by highly segmented and targeted provision, with its limitations offset by a network of family and voluntary networks of care.[10] The constellation of political forces shaping its development (as well as the development of the 1937 Irish Constitution) has ensured that socio-economic rights are more often conceived in terms of cash transfers and managerial performance targets rather than expressing universal or solidaristic norms of democracy and social equality.[11]

The present analysis of the Irish case, however, also makes clear the politics or power relations at stake in constitutionalising projects generally. This research problematises the goal of constitutionalising socio-economic rights by questioning the means used to achieve it. This questioning is not simply about reproducing the Marxist critique of bourgeois rights consciousness. Rather, by taking seriously the voices and discourses at stake in forms of constitution from below, the critical historical memory presented here affirms socio-economic rights activism as a necessarily majoritarian practice. Moreover, when moving against and beyond ideologies of the value-consensus state, collective political practice is at its most vibrant and generative. At stake here is an

[9] See Wallerstein, 'Anti-Systemic Movements, Yesterday and Today', p. 171.
[10] Cousins, 2005, *Explaining the Irish Welfare State.*
[11] See Irish Human Rights Commission, 2005, *Making Economic, Social and Cultural Rights Effective*. Dublin: IHRC Publications.

invitation to think and act against and beyond a state or constitutional politics towards a social politics of constitution, of creating new forms of community in our resistance to capital.[12]

## THE WORLD-SYSTEMIC POLITICS OF SOCIO-ECONOMIC RIGHTS IN IRELAND

Ireland, the world's 'second most globalised nation', is dominated by the world-systemic core economically and by international governance networks politically, as existing forms of collective solidarity (political parties, unions, communities) fall into decline as independent, self-organised entities.[13] The impact of the global economic crisis beginning in 2007–8 has been pronounced, and greatly exacerbated because of past policies that facilitated major credit and property market bubbles. In the course of a major financial crisis and a severe contraction in economic output, successive centre-right coalition governments have prioritised financial interests, including those most directly responsible for the latest crisis, ahead of society's living standards or democratic capabilities. In 2010, the Irish state, faced with bankruptcy, appealed for an €85 billion 'bailout' from the European Union Commission, European Central Bank, and International Monetary Fund and agreed to continue and extend its existing austerity programme, facilitating an ongoing neoliberal project to dis-embed 'social' measures such as state industry, labour protections, and comparatively minimal welfare services. The National Assets Management Agency and the Irish Bank Resolution Corporation sold off public assets in fire sales. Assorted elites and the higher punditry justify this seemingly inexorable process in terms of altogether magical hopes of a newly competitive Ireland's export-led recovery.[14]

[12] On how new social relations can emerge in the course of resisting capital and creating commons, see Holloway, 2010, *Crack Capitalism*, pp. 29–32.

[13] Ernst & Young's 2011 annual Globalisation Index has five measurements to assess a country's individual global ranking including: openness to global trade, global capital movements, global exchange of technology, global labour movements, and cultural integration. See www.ey.com/IE/en/Newsroom/News-releases/Press-release-2011–Ireland-overtakes-Singapore-to-become-the-worlds-second-most-globalised-nation.

[14] Financial administration, exercising an influence over national economic policy entirely disproportionate to the sector's size and employment levels, is central to the state's 'recovery' mantras. This form of growth relies on Ireland's functioning, for all intents and purposes, as a tax haven for multinational corporations. McCabe, 2011, *Sins of the Father*, pp. 240–1. On the inter-state dynamics also operative, see John Weeks on German mercantilism in the Eurozone. 'Ireland: Star Pupil of the Euro Fiasco' available at: www.social-europe.eu/2013/02/

International financial institutions do not incorporate human rights impact assessments when negotiating structural adjustment lending programmes. The social costs of nationalising banking debts have been predictable and, for some, catastrophic. High rates of unemployment and emigration emerged from 2009 onwards.[15] Risk of poverty has increased from 23.1 per cent in 2007 to 29.4 per cent in 2011, compared to EU-27 averages of 24.4 and 24.2 per cent, respectively.[16] In 2012, some 1,230,000 people, more than one in four of all people in the state, suffered two or more deprivation experiences. At 26.9 per cent in 2012, the level of enforced deprivation has more than doubled since 2007, when it was 11.8 per cent.[17] Some 10 per cent of the Irish population is now in food poverty.[18] In 2008, 6.8 per cent of Irish children were living in consistent poverty; by 2013 that proportion had almost doubled to 11.7 per cent, or some 138,000 children.[19] By the summer of 2015, more than 620 families, including more than 1,300 children, were homeless.[20] Inequality remains pronounced: in 2011, 10 per cent of the Irish population received almost 14 times more disposable income than the poorest 10 per cent.[21] Austerity budgets have impacted disproportionately on women and minorities, most egregiously in the case

ireland-the-star-pupil-of-the-euro-fiasco/#comments; Heiner Flassbeck and Costas Lapavitsas, 2015, *Against the Troika: Crisis and Austerity in the Eurozone*. London: Verso.

15 Ireland entered recession in 2009, with its unemployment rate rising to 14.8 per cent. A total of 46,500 Irish people, predominantly young, emigrated in the year to April 2012, a rise of 16 per cent on the previous 12 months. TASC, 2014, *Budget 2014: Choosing an equitable route to recovery*, Dublin: TASC. p. 6.

16 TASC, 2014, *Budget 2014: Choosing an equitable route to recovery*, p. 6.

17 The Central Statistics Office sets out eleven enforced deprivation experiences: (a) Without heating at some stage in the last year, (b) Unable to afford a morning, afternoon, or evening out in the last fortnight, (c) Unable to afford two pairs of strong shoes, (d) Unable to afford a roast once a week, (e) Unable to afford a meal with meat, chicken, or fish every second day, (f) Unable to afford new (not second-hand) clothes, (g) Unable to afford a warm waterproof coat, (h) Unable to afford to keep the home adequately warm, (i) Unable to afford to replace any worn-out furniture, (j) Unable to afford to have family or friends for a drink or meal once a month, (k) Unable to afford to buy presents for family or friends at least once a year. Those who suffer two or more of these experiences are officially categorised as deprived. See CSO (2012) *Survey on Income and Living Conditions*. Dublin: CSO.

18 Caroline Carney and Bertrand Maître, (2012), 'Constructing a Food Poverty Indicator for Ireland using the Survey on Income and Living Conditions', Social Inclusion Technical Paper No. 3, Dublin: Department of Social Protection.

19 Fintan O'Toole, 'Poverty, in our republic of equals, is written on children's bodies' in *Irish Times*, 26 May 2015. UNICEF ranked Ireland in 37th place in a league table measuring relative changes in child poverty in 41 developed countries. UNICEF Office of Research (2014). 'Children of the Recession: The impact of the economic crisis on child well-being in rich countries', Innocenti Report Card 12, UNICEF Office of Research, Florence.

20 Olivia Kelly, 'Dublin city social housing list tops 20,000' in *Irish Times*, 25 May 2015; Sr. Stanislaus Kennedy, 'We should hold referendum on the right to a home' in *Irish Times*, 24 July 2015.

21 TASC, 2010, *The Solidarity Factor: Public Responses to Economic Inequality in Ireland*. Available at: www.tascnet.ie/upload/file/Solidarity%20Factor_upload.pdf.

of Travellers, whose projects and services underwent budget reductions in excess of 80 per cent.[22]

In these circumstances, the question of whether constitutionalising social and economic rights may be useful in defending what remains of the European and Irish social model is timely. A critical historical memory is vital to such assessments. Today, the Irish state conceives of socio-economic rights primarily in terms of benefits or cash payments rather than social services, emphasising managerial 'performance' targets to the detriment of responding to the concerns of those who work in or depend on the state's welfare infrastructure. Welfare provision on these lines has proven highly susceptible to retrenchment in times of crisis.[23] The relationship between Ireland's constitution, economy, and welfare state was not inevitable but rather owed to a contested process of semi-peripheral development within the historical capitalist world-system. Constitution-makers' consistent privileging of classic nationalist constitutionalism over more social democratic alternatives in the 1920s and 1930s was strictly conditioned by the Irish Free State's semi-peripheral trajectory and, in particular, by the manner in which this trajectory, culturally and structurally, favoured popular, anti-systemic mobilisation along 'national' rather than 'social' lines.

That 'economic rights' featured so prominently in the making of both the 1922 Irish Free State Constitution and the 1937 Irish Constitution owed in no small part to the mass mobilisations that preceded their drafting. In the 1913 Lock-Out, the Constitution of the Irish Citizen Army reasserted the idea that 'the ownership of Ireland, moral and material, is vested of right in the people of Ireland'. During the 1917–23 period of popular militancy in Ireland, a dense network of self-governing communities, agrarian agitators, arbitration courts, trade union strike committees, and workers' soviets made this principle a living reality. Again, in the course of the Great Depression of the 1930s, as social polarisation generated campaigns and strikes for greater democracy and equality, the constitutions of feminists, red republican, and

[22] Ursula Barry and Pauline Conroy, 2012, Untold Story of the Crisis: Gender, Equality and Inequalities. Available at: www.nwci.ie/download/pdf/barryconroy2012.pdf; Brian Harvey, 2013, Travelling with Austerity: Impacts of Cuts on Travellers, Traveller Projects and Services. Available at: www.paveepoint.ie/wp-content/uploads/2013/10/Travelling-with-Austerity_Pavee-Point-2013.pdf. Budgetary priorities have serious consequences. In October 2015, ten Travellers, including a five-month-old baby, died in a fire at a 'temporary' halting site in Carrickmines, Co. Dublin. See Kitty Holland, 'Councils must do more for Travellers after fire' in *Irish Times*, 12 October 2015.

[23] Amnesty International Ireland, 2014, *Bringing ESC Rights Home*, p. 7.

communist groups competed with those created by fascist, nationalist, and labour groups.

Throughout the 1920s and 1930s, 'social' constitutionalism emerged primarily as an elite response to these anti-systemic threats to the existing social order. To varying degrees, social legal thought ostensibly appeared as a middle way between right- and left-wing alternatives to classic constitutionalism and liberal democracy. In the making of the 1922 Irish Free State Constitution, the American social jurist Clement France argued for the state's challenging of financier-grazier interests through the constitution's regulation of property rights and control of the 'unearned increment' arising from land speculation. Labour's T. J. O'Connell proposed children's rights provisions, including redistributive welfare measures. In the making of the 1937 Irish Constitution, similar proposals to regulate land redistribution and the credit system or to advance redistributive welfare policies also featured prominently. Nationalist decision-makers such as Éamon de Valera and clericalist contributors such as Edward Cahill or John Charles McQuaid, however, disagreed with conservative civil servants such as J. J. MacElligott on the tactical necessity of including provisions as a means of forestalling class conflict. The Catholic social form of fundamental rights and directive principles ultimately adopted in Articles 40–45 belied the conservative entrenchment of existing state institutions and welfare norms in practice.

The Irish experience of deliberating socio-economic rights in successive constitution-making experiments presents something of a hybrid case, one that is readily comparable to contemporary constitutional projects. Created in the same wave of constitutions emanating from the tumultuous, world-revolutionary moment of 1917, constitution-making in semi-peripheral Dublin in 1922 featured socio-economic rights discourses similar to those advanced both for land reform in peripheral Querétaro in 1917 and for a social welfare state in core Weimar in 1919. Again, in 1937, the form of social constitutionalism proposed, particularly by clericalists, more closely resembled the highly selective Catholic corporatism advanced by Europe's Catholic authoritarian regimes than other forms of social constitutionalism, perhaps most notably in its defence of patriarchy. The balance of contending core-peripheral and social relations in Ireland, however, produced a greater acceptance of existing liberal democratic institutions than the regimes emergent elsewhere. Nevertheless, the preservation of class privilege, the institutionalisation of children, women, and the mentally ill, the censorship of publications and public discourse, the religious regulation of sexuality all formed part of the 'ordered tranquillity' subsequently enforced by the Irish state.

The Irish state's constitutional projects were instead predominantly classic articulations of national sovereignty, envisaging the silent reproduction of market law and the strident defence of an Irish nationalist, often specifically Catholic, culture, one that was most clearly expressed in family law and resulted in a remarkably enduring defence of patriarchal relations. The form of social and economic rights adopted in the 1922 and 1937 constitutions thus protected the rights of those who benefitted from the reproduction of financier/grazier-led dependency and further guaranteed the blessing of the Catholic Church's hierarchy by outsourcing the state's comparatively minimal welfare effort to the clergy. Meanwhile, universalising discourses of 'Irish Ireland' and of the 'Catholic social', both premised on the ideology of the value-consensus state, operated to reproduce those particular relations of power and exploitation which they helped to conceal. This outcome owed directly to the manner in which the Sinn Féin nationalist party substituted itself for a much wider anticolonial movement and associated 'social' or class concerns in the early 1920s and how successor parties, notably Fianna Fáil, managed to reproduce the conditions necessary for nationalist hegemony in the 1930s and beyond.[24]

The subsequent politics of constitutional change in Ireland was simultaneously a world-systemic politics. Post–World War II, in the course of the world-system's transformation from a 'social liberal' form of development to a 'neoliberal' one, the Republic of Ireland reproduced its semi-peripheral position within it. Albeit a contested process, 'national' forms of anti-systemic politics continued to take precedence over 'social' alternatives. Notably co-opted into the orbit of Fianna Fáil, organised labour was not in a position in Ireland, as elsewhere in Europe, to generate a cross-class coalition of support for universal forms of welfare provision. In these circumstances, privileged interest groups, notably financiers, large landowners, rentiers, and middle-men service providers, captured the national growth agenda while Ireland's working class endured comparatively lower living standards and lower, non-solidaristic forms of welfare provision, including ongoing state reliance on religious institutions for industrial schools, asylums, and care.

[24] See Fanon, 2001, *The Wretched of the Earth*. Rajagopal, 2003, *International Law from Below*.

Constitutional changes happening in Ireland occurred in strictly analogous ways in other jurisdictions in the world-system. The political and institutional makeup of the Irish state, as with the hegemonic core country of the United States, did not lend itself to constitutionalising social and economic rights.[25] To date, no Irish government has decided to offer a referendum on the constitutional recognition of socio-economic rights. While a Constitution Review Group meeting in 1968 did not envisage a demand for socio-economic rights, a later review group in 1995 explicitly rejected their constitutionalisation. Instead, political actors in Ireland, as elsewhere, faced conflicting pressures between tradition and transformation in both market and family law and relied on constitutional rights and judicial review to shift resulting disputes out of the realm of majoritarian politics towards insulated domains of judicial expertise. Concomitantly, the rapid emergence of public interest litigation owed primarily to civil society attempts to bypass existing, blocked systems of representative politics and trade union organising. For both sets of actors, given the highly centralised, party-dominated nature of Irish government and administration, the 1937 Irish Constitution appears as a robust constraint on executive power. Accentuating these tendencies, the increased prominence of both supra-national courts and neoliberal constitutional forms in Ireland suggest a more widely experienced dethronement of politics.

In these circumstances, changing forms of constitutional rights owed vitally to citizens taking new rights claims to court and, furthermore, to supportive networks of barristers and civil society groups. Particularly from the 1970s onwards, all manner of high-profile constitutional cases have sought to defend 'minoritarian' rights for women, children, prisoners, homosexuals, Travellers, the disabled, the transgendered, and asylum seekers. However, Irish 'support structures' mirrored the state's wider welfare effort and centred on poorly financed, voluntary labour. The polarisation of the courts as sites of justice and of legal business curtailed the nature of Ireland's 'rights revolution' by ensuring the predominance of those privileged with capacities to fund cases and the absenting of the innumerable potential rights cases of those without.

Meanwhile, the empowered Irish Supreme Court retained a narrow conception of rights, emphasising liberal individualism, anti-statism,

[25] See Glendon, 1992, 'Rights in Twentieth-Century Constitutions'.

and 'negative liberties' at the expense of 'positive' rights to welfare or the interests of the 'common good'. These positions are by no means atypical and owe to a combination of factors, including the strong defence of individual and property rights in the common law, the sociological conditions shaping judges' formation and ideological preferences as well as the centre-right, party-dominated judicial appointments process. From the 1960s onwards, the judiciary proved particularly 'activist' regarding the preservation and enlargement of civil liberties, emphasising limits to police powers and rights of due process as well as expanding the private sphere. The Irish Constitution thus came to embody a more distinctly US constitutional vision, maintaining a continuing commitment to 'classic', individual rights of property and contract while gradually disembedding Catholic social norms in family law.

The trajectory of socio-economic rights cases in the Irish courts registered and reproduced these institutional and jurisprudential dynamics. The Supreme Court, ostensibly distinguishing between 'distributive' and 'commutative' justice as well as claiming a commitment to the principle of the separation of powers, has characteristically refrained from challenging duly enacted legislation or issuing compulsory injunctions to the government in the realm of social expenditure. Seminal cases concerning court-ordered public expenditure, notably the introduction of free legal aid and the payment of welfare arrears, have been fought and won at the European Court of Human Rights instead.

In a number of instances, however, the Irish Court has struck down social legislation in defence of negative liberties or property rights. Special interest groups, including employers, landlords, and farming associations, have successfully used the constitution to challenge state regulation of the market place. These cases included successful constitutional challenges to rent restrictions, land taxation measures as well as trade union protections for industrial action.[26] Beyond the very real implications for those immediately affected by the loss of rent

[26] The judiciary's resuscitation of classic legal norms continues. According to John Hendy QC, a trilogy of recent cases – *Ryanair* v. *the Labour court* [2007] IESC 6, John Grace Fried Chicken Ltd & others *v*. The Catering Joint Labour Committee & others [2011] IEHC 277, and *McGowan & others* v. *The Labour Court*, Ireland & another [2013] IESC 21 – 'all but destroyed the Irish system of industrial relations'. The courts 'achieved in Ireland precisely the strategy applied by the Troika elsewhere in Europe'. John Hendy QC, 2014, 'McGowan and Collective Bargaining in Ireland'. Lecture at Trinity College, Dublin, pp. 1–51, pp. 1–2. Available at www.ictu.ie/download/pdf/collective_bargaining_ireland_jan_30.pdf. The subsequent Industrial Relations (Amendment) Act 2015 provided a statutory definition of collective bargaining and clarified when a trade dispute can be referred to the Labour Court for a legally binding order. However,

restrictions or of immunities for industrial actions or of special needs education, these decisions had wider, possibly unintended, ramifications for society. Though not the sole factor, these decisions formed part of a process whereby a political economy centred on Clement France's 'unearned increment' or dependent on atomised, insecure labour or characterised by Church-State welfare provision could be more easily defended than challenged.

Irish judges' shifting socio-economic rights discourses registered and reproduced the globalising forms of classic, social, and neoformalist legal thought in the world-system. Underpinning the shifting nature of these discourses lay a fundamental, enduring, and professional consensus on the value of the value-consensus state, a deeply embedded belief in the rule of law, as abstract and transcendent, objective and just, representing the state as a consensual, value-neutral framework through which competing interests could be resolved and placing beyond question the question of judicial legitimacy in a coercive social order. Irish judges (re)produced this value-consensus discourse in their decision-making. They promoted as transcendent, objective, and just the 1937 Irish Constitution which, as we earlier established, registered a particular balance of contending core-peripheral and social relations. In this manner, the particular, private interests of landlords, employers, religious organisations, and corporations appear as universal ones while socially contested practices, notably those associated with political economy and government budgeting, come to be portrayed as natural, unchangeable 'facts of life'.[27]

The scholastic assertion of a value-consensus state and the downplaying of social relations applied most pointedly in situations where socio-economic rights conflicts were pursued along class lines by working-class organisations, notably by trade unions challenging employers or Church-State control of education. The strict parameters of judges'

there is still no legal obligation for Irish employers to recognise trade unions and, excepting some specific collective consultation scenarios, there is still no legal requirement for Irish employers to bargain collectively.

27 The South African Supreme Court has similarly exhibited reluctance to probe the underlying conditions that give rise to economic deprivations, taking existing resource distributions for granted. In the *Soobramoney* case, for example, the injustice that money can purchase needed treatment in the private health sector was portrayed as a 'hard and unpalatable fact'. *Soobramoney* v. Minister of Health, KwaZulu-Natal 1997(12) BCLR 1696 (CC), pp. 24–9. As Sandra Liebenberg has argued, while the Court's restraint may be understandable from the perspective of institutional relations, it nonetheless serves to naturalise systemic socio-economic inequalities. Sandra Liebenberg, 2006, 'Needs, Rights and Transformation: Adjudicating Social Rights' in *Stellenbosch Law Review*, 17:1, pp. 5–36.

value-consensus discourse suggest that underpinning the formal battles over constitutionalising socio-economic rights, a deeper, less obvious form of politics is at stake here. This discourse, centred on making 'the people' speak, tacitly grants faith in the legitimacy of the state and the conservative judicial process; both are inherently political positions. This shared orthodoxy was one developed in the course of judges' professional trajectory from class privilege to professional authority, one that came without saying and therefore went without saying. The judges, however, were not alone.

To varying degrees, value consensus understandings of the state also, almost necessarily, appear in the discourse and practices of public interest litigants and civil society actors pursuing diverse socio-economic rights projects. The ideological limits of this discourse stand out most firmly in those instances where groups such as the Dublin Unemployed Association, the Dublin Housing Action Committee, or the Talbot workers adopted a more oppositional understanding of the state, rejected assumptions of its legitimacy and created alternative spaces and practices of justice. More clearly recognising the ideological nature of value-consensus discourse is essential to recognising the opportunities and limitations at stake in contemporary projects to both constitutionalise and make effective in practice social and economic rights.

## THE FUTURE OF ECONOMIC AND SOCIAL RIGHTS IN IRELAND

Contemporary projects to constitutionalise socio-economic rights, in Ireland as elsewhere, occur in historically specific circumstances. The inherited field for contesting the 1937 Irish Constitution conditions the substance and likely success of such projects. In parliament, the intra-nationalist party system continues to prioritise national integration into the world economy, its two largest parties either championing neoliberal reforms or accepting 'capitalist realism' and the necessity of 'tough' decision-making, albeit to varying degrees. In these circumstances, a majority of those political representatives with formal decision-making authority over the amendment of the 1937 Irish Constitution remains opposed or, at best, non-committed to constitutionalising socio-economic rights. Responding to successful disability rights campaigns in the 1990s and 2000s, the Fianna Fáil-Progressive Democrat coalition government ensured subsequent legislation curtailed opportunities for public interest litigation around disability provision.[28] Over the same period, Fine Gael and Labour members of parliament voted in favour of a motion to recognise economic, social, and cultural rights in the Constitution.[29] In government from 2011 to 2016, however, Fine Gael and Labour vetoed putting the Constitutional Convention's proposals on socio-economic rights to popular referendum.

Registering and reproducing long-standing patterns of semi-peripheral politics, the social articulation of alternatives to the current constellation of neoliberal forces has thus far taken a predominantly populist, nationalist form, with contemporary Sinn Féin occupying a role not altogether dissimilar to late 1920s Fianna Fáil (against the banks and for national sovereignty).[30] Independent (non-party) candidates as well as the Socialist and Socialist Workers' parties have also gained greater electoral representation in national and local government. While left of Labour political parties are also used to claiming socio-economic rights in opposition – witness Sinn Féin's 'Demand Your Right to Health' rallies or the Socialist Workers' Party 'Right to Work' and 'Right to Housing' campaigns – their capacity to form an alternative government remains limited. Regardless, in the absence of a broader counterpower to capital, Ireland's neoliberal-led underdevelopment appears likely to continue.

In these circumstances, NGOs and civil society actors have concentrated on appealing to the Supreme Court to interpret the Constitution anew so as to read socio-economic rights into it. Most scholars and practitioners accept that such interpretations are unlikely to succeed before the bench in the near future, particularly in the wake of the *Sinnott* and *TD* precedents. On the contrary, the history of actually existing constitutionalism on socio-economic rights charted here demonstrates a somewhat countervailing tendency to preserve classic,

[28] The Disability Rights Act (2005), for example, prohibits access to an independent arbiter until internal review procedures are exhausted. Trish McKeogh, 2012, 'Assessing the impact of European governments' austerity plans on the rights of people with disabilities: Ireland', p. 20. See also Jurgen de Wispelaere and Judy Walsh, 2007, 'Disability Rights in Ireland: Chronicle of a Missed Opportunity' in *Irish Political Studies*, 22.4, pp. 517–43.

[29] In 1999, the Labour Party proposed a Bill, the Twenty-First Amendment of the Constitution (No. 3) Bill, which sought to recognise economic, social, and cultural rights in the Constitution. Both Labour and Fine Gael members of the current Cabinet voted in favour of this bill. See Louise Glennon, 'A call for the examination of economic, social and cultural rights in Ireland'. www.constitution.ie/AttachmentDownload.ashx?aid=1b3a5054-b9e3-e211-a5a0-005056a32ee4.

[30] Social challenges to the state-finance nexus typically take a populist hue. Harvey, 2010, *The Enigma of Capital*, pp. 55–6.

liberal, and individual rights, including those of property. These dispositions would remain operative even if socio-economic rights were explicitly constitutionalised at some point in the future. It seems likely that the judiciary in Ireland, as elsewhere in the world's neoformalist courts, will produce a series of *ad hoc* compromises on socio-economic rights rather than their clear-cut development or neoliberal rollback.[31]

A further, insufficiently acknowledged influence on judges' conservatism is institutional capacity to process caseloads, a capacity subject to politically determined resource constraints. Judges would appear to have responded to the rapidly escalating tide of litigation before the Superior Courts by raising the bar for judicial intervention higher.[32] There are grounds for thinking that the Irish courts did not recognise socio-economic rights, at least in part, for fear of creating insurmountable caseloads that might overwhelm the existing legal system.[33] Following a recent amendment to the Constitution, a new Court of Appeal will take over the appellate functions of the Supreme Court. The government's express aim was to remove the four-year, 500-plus case backlog at the Supreme Court.[34] The new Court thus continues the pattern of administrative rationalisation outlined earlier and will still be bound by the time-intensive, costly norms and rules guiding the conduct of litigation.[35]

Insofar as the courts remain polarised as sites of justice and legal business then, the uneven distribution of capacities to access the court remains operative. 'Support structures' for litigants attempting to contest constitutional rights are limited. The Irish state's free legal aid scheme continues to impose a strict means-test on applicants and remains severely underresourced. Moreover, post-2008, the Irish

31 Kennedy, 2006, 'Three Globalisations of Law and Legal Thought', pp. 69–71. Recall also that socio-economic rights, as Cass Sunstein has pointed out, are minimally compatible with neoliberal marketisation. Sunstein, 2005, 'Why does the American Constitution lack Social and Economic Guarantees?'

32 Buckley, 2004, 'Merging Principles of Public Law: Towards Proportionality in an Irish Context', pp. 199, 211–2.

33 Judge Adrian Hardiman explicitly stated that if the courts acknowledged socio-economic rights they 'would certainly be appealed to again and again . . . ' and cited media coverage of the 'hundreds of cases' recently taken by parents of children with special needs. *TD v. Minister for Education* [2001] 4 IR 259. Beyond the courts, legal practitioners similarly suggested that the 'huge increase in litigation in this area' demonstrated how recognising socio-economic rights would result in the courts being 'overwhelmed'. Hogan, 2001, 'Directive Principles, Socio-Economic Rights and the Constitution'.

34 Report of Working Group on a Court of Appeal, 2009.

35 Michael Williams, 2013, *Serving the People? The need for reform in the Irish legal system*. Dublin: Four Courts Press.

state has drastically shrunk key human rights monitoring organisations, merging the Equality Authority and the Irish Human Rights Commission and reducing their budgets. The bill for the new 'Irish Human Rights and Equality Commission' has attracted criticism that the director will not be independent of government and, moreover, that the body's mandate with respect to socio-economic rights will be weakened.[36] State and philanthropic support for non-governmental organisations has also declined significantly, while those sources of funding that remain are often tied to NGOs' remaining uncritical of either government or pro-market policies and impose significant constraints on these organisations' internal democracy.[37]

Finally, even if social and economic rights were constitutionalised and successful cases taken, victories on an individual, case-by-case basis in other jurisdictions suggest their capacity to advance progressive notions of social solidarity or distributive justice is strictly limited.[38] This might be particularly true of Ireland given the highly segmented nature of its social security provision, the unavailability of a class action system on US lines, and the correspondingly narrow focus of representative action. Judicial review, as Gerard Hogan puts it, functions such that 'the courts are required to focus on the operation of the law as it affects the individual plaintiff and do not, generally speaking, have the capacity to examine how such a law impacts on the public at large'.[39] The combination of these prohibiting factors in the Irish case enjoins us to pay attention to Ran Hirschl's comparative analysis of socio-economic rights constitutionalisation in Canada, Israel, South Africa, and New Zealand and his conclusion that the capacity of socio-economic rights to advance distributive justice concerns, even when constitutionalised, is strictly limited.[40]

Civil society proponents of economic, social, and cultural rights, however, increasingly express a critical awareness that better protecting such rights in the Irish Constitution will not solve all

[36] Amnesty International Ireland, 2014, *Bringing ESC Rights Home*, p. 92. See also 'Alan Shatter defends plan to appoint Human Rights and Equality Commission director', 9 July 2012. Available at: www.rte.ie/news/2012/0709/328456-alan-shatter-human-rights-equality-commission.

[37] See Mary Murphy, 2011, 'Civil society in the shadow of the Irish state' in *Irish Journal of Sociology*, 19 (2), pp. 170–87.

[38] Hirschl, 2007, *Towards Juristocracy*, p. 148; O'Connell, 2011, 'The Death of Socio-Economic Rights', pp. 551–2.

[39] Hogan, 1997, 'The Constitution, Property Rights and Proportionality', p. 396.

[40] Hirschl, 2007, *Towards Juristocracy*, p. 148; Hirschl and Rosevear, 'Constitutional Law Meets Comparative Politics: Socio-economic Rights and Political Realities', pp. 217–8.

problems.[41] Proponents instead draw on international experience, primarily in India and South Africa, to show that minimally socio-economic rights entrenchment would require government to provide more detailed justification for its decisions and to promote more meaningful engagement amongst state authorities, service providers, and citizens, thereby facilitating better planning processes and outcomes, as well as greater accountability and transparency. This dialogic role for the courts may be particularly necessary in contemporary situations where the state's welfare and public service functions are increasingly disaggregated into agencies or privatised. While customers of privatised water or health services may have access to the law of contract or tort for restitution, citizens without a relationship to the private entity delivering state services currently have limited to no recourse to domestic constitutional remedies. Socio-economic rights may address this deficit.[42]

NGOs and public interest litigants also accept that there remains a political struggle over ensuring forms of redistributive justice, particularly regarding attempts to use socio-economic rights in a maximal sense so as to compel state expenditure to ensure the state meets a certain 'core' duty or obligation. For these forms of advocacy, constitutional rights litigation, when combined with accompanying civil society mobilisation and advocacy, can function as a corrective for minoritarian groups, requiring the political system to address issues of social exclusion that might otherwise be ignored.[43] Ireland's socio-economic rights cases tentatively support recent empirical studies suggesting that litigation strategies can have a redistributive effect, not necessarily owing to the direct benefits of litigation but in the broad, indirect effects of the social rights mobilisation accompanying a courtroom strategy.[44] Without disability rights activists pursuing such a dual-track campaign in the 1990s and 2000s, for instance, it is

41 See Amnesty International Ireland, 2014, *Bringing ESC Rights Home*, p. 5.

42 Des Hogan (IHRC), 2013, 'Human Rights and Austerity in Ireland: Address to the European Group of National Human Rights Institutions Berlin/ Brussels'. Available at www.ihrc.ie/download/pdf/address_by_des_hogan_at_nhri_austerity_seminar13_june_2013_brussels.pdf.

43 Whyte, 2002, *Social Inclusion and the Legal System*, pp. 176, 210, 244.

44 See Daniel M. Brinks and Varun Gauri, 2014, 'The Law's Majestic Equality? The Distributive Impact of Judicializing Social and Economic Rights' in *American Political Science Association*, 12 (2), pp. 375–93; César Rodríguez-Garavito, 2011,' Beyond the Courtroom: The Impact of Judicial Activism on Socioeconomic Rights in Latin America' in *Texas University Law Review*, 89, pp. 1669–98; Martin Heywood, 2009, 'South Africa's Treatment Action Campaign: Combining Law and Social Mobilization to Realize the Right to Health' in *Journal of Human Rights Practice*, 1 (1), pp. 14–36, p. 14.

unlikely that the state would have introduced legislation and increased expenditure for disabled children and adults.

The verdict on litigation strategies to advance socio-economic rights, however, remains a mixed one, always dependent on the contextual prerequisites that will either facilitate or frustrate participants' freedom of action. Fragile and temporary as some of them have been, victories for minoritarian groups in the courts cannot be ignored. This is particularly true in situations where majoritarian forms of politics, such as parliamentary elections or trade union mobilising, appear incapable of improving the conditions of minoritarian groups directly or in the short term.[45] Nevertheless, the somewhat optimistic literature on litigation has yet to acknowledge sufficiently the opportunity costs of social movements' pursuit of litigation strategies over other forms of collective action.[46] There are grounds, then, for simultaneously conceiving of socio-economic rights advocacy in majoritarian terms.[47] This is particularly the case when we wish to move beyond the mere declaration of rights towards the institutions and collective practices necessary to make rights effective.[48]

Historically, trade unions have been the crucial means of advancing more solidaristic or universal systems of social rights, notably through corporatist negotiating in Scandinavian and Bismarckian welfare states in Europe.[49] This majoritarian form of politics centres on using universal social and economic rights as a means to de-commodify nature, labour and social reproduction to an ever greater degree. In Ireland's pluralist model of interest group articulation, trade unions have traditionally played a weaker consultative role in tripartite decision-making with government and employers.[50] Today, the present division of labour in Irish society, particularly the extent to which substantially non-unionised parts of the labour force such as multinational employees as

[45] On the unequal terrain of policy-making and lobbying in Ireland, see Deiric Ó Broin and Peadar Kirby (eds), 2009, *Power, dissent and democracy: civil society and the state in Ireland*. Dublin: A&A Farmer.

[46] See Hirschl and Rosevear, 'Constitutional Law Meets Comparative Politics: Socio-economic Rights and Political Realities', pp. 207–28.

[47] Newly emerging socio-economic and ecological rights discourses have been linked to imaginative proposals for participatory budgeting or popular constitution-making assemblies. Peadar Kirby and Mary Murphy, 'Vital Role for the People in Rewriting the Constitution' in *Irish Times*, 24 January 2012.

[48] See Polanyi, 1944, *The Great Transformation*, p. 76.

[49] Korpi, 1983, *The Democratic Class Struggle*.

[50] Rory O'Donnell, 2008, 'The partnership state: building the ship at sea', in Maura Adshead, Peadar Kirby, and Michelle Millar (eds.), *Contesting the State: Lessons from the Irish Case*. Manchester: Manchester University Press, pp. 73–99.

well as highly unionised public-sector employees are covered by private and occupational welfare, hinders the formation of cross-class coalitions in favour of welfare state expansion.[51] Though far from easy in contemporary circumstances, constructing a coalitional politics across this division would appear to be the most effective vector of realising solidaristic forms of social and economic rights in practice.[52] This would involve re-imagining the organising role and democratic purpose of the trade union.[53]

The analysis presented here, however, further provides considerable support for thinking about and pursuing the development of socio-economic rights in Ireland in terms of a more militant politics of 'class abatement'.[54] Historically, from France (1848) through Mexico (1917) to Germany (1918), established political elites have proposed economic and social rights to forestall more threatening revolutionary projects. This was the case with Jesuit proponents of Catholic social discourses in response to widespread labour militancy during the 1913 Lock-Out. Again, the socio-economic rights discourses forwarded by nationalist elites in the course of the making of the 1922 and 1937 constitutions owed predominantly to a desire to placate civil society campaigns and direct actions, including boycotts, strikes, soviets, and land redistribution organised alongside committed feminists, republicans, syndicalists, and communists. The subsequent history of constitution from below, from the Dublin Unemployed Association of the 1950s through the Housing Action Committees of the early 1970s to the Talbot strike and boycott of the 1980s, further suggests the immediate gains to be won through direct action as well as the wider significance of breaking silences on domination, exploitation, and suffering.

51 Public-sector employees and multinational private-sector employees receive relatively high benefits through public occupational pensions and private occupational benefits, respectively; the largest group, indigenous private-sector employees are covered only by flat-rate public welfare benefits. Cousins, 2005, *Explaining the Irish Welfare State*, p. 330.

52 On the need for coalitional politics and the resuscitation of a 'second bill' of social and economic rights, see Harvey, 2007, *A Brief History of Neoliberalism*; 2010, *The Enigma of Capital*. Insofar as this politics might affect the 1937 Irish Constitution, it might further mean constitutionalising a formal role for trade unions in corporatist negotiations and, concomitantly, abolishing existing restrictions on industrial action.

53 '[T]he old Larkinites, if you talked to them, never called a union official an official, but called him [*sic*] a delegate. They used that language on the basis that he's someone you can recall and someone you can control'. See O'Reilly, 2000, 'Matt Merrigan: A marvellous legacy', p. 10.

54 Marshall, 1950, *Citizenship and Social Class*, pp. 32–3. Analysing the global wave of 'horizontal' social movements emerging in 2011 and 2012, Paul Mason more colourfully characterises the dynamic as 'reform by riot'. 2013, *Why It's Still Kicking Off Everywhere*. London: Verso.

Ideologically, this latter form of majoritarian politics involves a new mode of thinking, against and beyond the ideology of the value-consensus state. Subaltern forms of socio-economic rights advocacy involved, to varying degrees, an oppositional sense of the state as reflecting the interests of a dominant group or class as well as a patient development of voluntary networks of trust and organisation. This involves a rejection of the ideological notion that the Constitution and the courts are somehow 'above politics'. There is nothing more political than the need for law. The resulting political dynamic is not one of petitioning the state for support so much as acting to make a right a reality by acting and living as if it already existed. Simultaneously, this politics of solidarity in opposition is a rejection of the majoritarian/minoritarian dichotomy involved in conventional rights struggles, and a revitalisation of the old syndicalist slogan of Irish labour, 'an injury to one is an injury to all'. The constraints and tensions, hopes, and possibilities at stake in socio-economic rights advocacy outlined here are not, of course, unique to Ireland but rather draw sustenance from a much wider, contemporary moment of world-systemic crisis.

## SOCIO-ECONOMIC RIGHTS AND THE CRISIS OF CAPITALISM

> 'The working class did not expect any miracle from the Commune. The workers do not have any utopia ready to implement *par décret du peuple*. They know that in order to achieve their own emancipation, and with it a superior form of life . . . they will have to go through lengthy struggles and through a whole series of historical processes. They do not have to fulfil any ideals, only to give free reign to the elements of a new society . . .'
>
> – Karl Marx[55]

We return then to the present crisis of capitalism, and to what Immanuel Wallerstein has described as the battle between 'the spirit of Davos' and 'the spirit of Porto Alegre'. The former, currently in the ascendant, is a function of the tremendous concentration of wealth and power in the historical capitalist world-system. A transnational class, comprised of cosmopolitan investors, shareholders, corporate managers,

[55] Cited in Gustavo Esteva, 1997, 'The Meaning and Scope of the Struggle for Autonomy'. Presentation to the Latin American Studies Association, Guadalajara, Mexico, 18 April 1997. For a more prolix translation, see Karl Marx, 'The Civil War in France' in Carver, 1996, *Marx's Later Political Writings*. Cambridge: Cambridge University Press, p. 188.

as well as politicians and administrators of both left and right, would pursue a greater enclosure of existing social, environmental, and intellectual commons and a greater undermining of democratic norms. The international treaties that form the putative constitution of the global economy will feature prominently in the formation and legitimation of these new, violent regimes of accumulation.[56] From *Laval* in the European Court of Justice through *Citizens United* in the US Supreme Court and beyond, examples of judicial activism in the service of corporate power will likely proliferate.[57]

Social and economic rights could feature in these emergent national or supranational constitutional forms but primarily as a mere formal guarantee of equal access to ever diminishing forms of state provision, or of accountability in a reduced, disaggregated, and privatised form of welfare state. In the courts, there may even be successful legal victories for socio-economic rights advocates but the wider institutional, cultural, and political resources necessary for their effective and substantive realisation would remain undermined. In these circumstances, it is not difficult to imagine a situation where an institutional innovation such as the 'constitutional dialogue' model advanced in South Africa today could be interpreted in isolation from its historical and sociological embeddedness and reduced to a few abstract traits composing a governance model to be applied elsewhere by expert knowledge. Socio-economic rights would be adopted by the World Bank only to be 'ground, pasteurised and converted into new appendages of conditionality'.[58]

Conversely, proponents of the spirit of Porto Alegre want to make the world more democratic, more egalitarian. It is no coincidence that this horizon of possibility for direct democratic practices emerged in

[56] The negotiation of the Trade in Services Agreement and the Transatlantic Trade and Investment Partnership are the latest examples of a flourishing 'Eden of the innate rights of man', instituted by governments prioritising the permanent plebiscite of global markets to the plebiscite of the ballot box. See Slavoj Žižek, 'How capital captured politics' in *The Guardian*, 13 July 2014.

[57] On the world's potential return to the classic jurisprudence of the Lochner-era US Supreme Court, see E. D. Ewing, 'Economic Rights' in Michel Rosenfeld and Andras Sajó (eds.), 2012, *The Oxford Handbook of Comparative Constitutional Law*. Oxford: Oxford University Press, pp. 1036–56. *Laval Un Partneri Ltd* v. *Svenska Byggnadsarbetareförbundet* [2008] IRLR 160; *Citizens United* v. *Federal Election Commission*, 558 U.S. (2010); see also Editorial, 'How Corporate Money Will Reshape Politics' in *New York Times*, 21 January 2010.

[58] Boaventura de Sousa Santos outlines this dilemma of 'the rare bird of realistic utopia' in a discussion on the future of participatory budgeting. See de Sousa Santo, 1998, 'Participatory Budgeting in Porto Alegre' in *Politics and Society*, 26 (4), pp. 461–510, p. 507.

peripheral or semi-peripheral regions of the Global South as organised labour and left-wing parties sought to challenge the long-standing hegemony of neoliberal economics and international governance networks.[59] Following the mass mobilisations of farmers, organised labour, and indigenous groups in Bolivia and Ecuador in the early 2000s, constitutions drafted by popular assemblies featured as a means of concretising demands for social and economic rights and decentralised decision-making, as well as recognising indigenous autonomy and new ideals of 'buen vivir' and ecological well-being.[60] Following the global economic crisis of 2008, oppositional movements animating the world's city squares and centres of financial power, from Tahrir Square to the Plaza del Puerta del Sol, from Zuccotti Park to Gezi Park, have locally reinterpreted remarkably similar principles. In Iceland, a popular constitution-making process in 2011 directly advanced proposals for 'public participation in the democratic process', environmental protections, and public ownership of natural resources.[61]

In this vision of society, claims for social and economic rights may represent a revitalised social legal thought, positioning the state to intervene in the market so as to preserve increasingly eroding forms of social equality.[62] For those opposed to the narrative of 'necessary sacrifices' that legitimises austerity and neoliberal reforms, human rights discourse, by recognising the intrinsic worth or dignity of every human being, offers a possible counternarrative.[63] For the old revolutionary left, claiming such rights is no longer necessarily 'reformist' but rather a means of mobilising popular support for 'non-reformist reforms'

59 Raúl Zibechi, 2012, *Territories in Resistance: A cartography of Latin American Social Movements*. Edinburgh: AK Press.

60 See King, 2013, 'Neo-Bolivarian Constitutional Design'.

61 Unsurprisingly, opponents to the popularly approved amendments successfully obstructed constitutional change through litigation at the Icelandic Supreme Court. The Icelandic experiment, however, was not in vain. 'Never again', as one contributor to the process observed, 'can the world be told by the custodians of the old that the people cannot be relied upon to write the contract between citizens and government, and write it well'. Richard Bater cited in Anne Meuwese, 2013, 'Popular Constitution-Making in Iceland', p. 469.

62 The emerging literature on using socio-economic rights standards in budgetary analysis and creation is impressive in this respect. See Aoife Nolan, Rory O'Connell and Colin Harvey (eds.), 2013, *Human Rights and Public Finance: Budgets and the Promotion of Economic and Social Rights*. Oxford: Hart Publishers.

63 Nina Tzouvala, 2015, 'Human Rights and Social Movements: the Right2Water case'. Available at http://humanrights.i/economic-rights/human-rights-and-social-movements-the-right2water-case/. On the use of 'dignity' to preserve hierarchy, see Samuel Moyn, 2015, 'A Powerless Companion: Human Rights in the Age of Neoliberalism', *Law and Contemporary Problems* 77 (4), pp. 147–69.

and a more radical, anti-capitalist politics.[64] In the latter instance, proponents recognise that 'rights talk', while consistently supported by a self-interested legal intelligentsia, is only conjuncturally and contingently useful to social movements.[65] Specifically, in neoliberal capitalist democracies, if a demand on the state to provide greater subsidies to working-class people impinges on capital's prerogatives, we can expect capital 'to pot-hole the road' to socio-economic rights.[66] Hence, with varying degrees of scepticism, proponents recognise that judicial review can work both for and against reprivatisation or the erosion of participatory democracy and that social movements might therefore pursue litigation strategies not as a panacea but as a means of attracting support, a tool to be used strategically and sparingly.[67]

The recent wave of social movements in 2011 and 2012, however, has suggested an alternative to this alternative.[68] We might term this alternative 'the spirit of Chiapas', delineating the radical political imagination and feminist or horizontal decision-making practices demonstrated by the Zapatista movement in the course of their uprising in southern Mexico in the mid-1990s.[69] Similarly, by occupying

[64] See Harvey, 2007, *A Brief History of Neoliberalism*; Al Campbell, 'Reformist and Revolutionary Demands in the US "Great Recession"', Presentation to the 6th Forum of the World Association for Political Economy, Amherst MA, 27 May 2011. See also Sandra Liebenberg, 2006, 'Needs, Rights and Transformation: Adjudicating Social Rights' in *Stellenbosch Law Review*, 17:1, pp. 5–36.

[65] Kennedy, 1997, A Critique of Adjudication; on the importance of conducive historical contexts and political developments, see Karl Klare, 1998, 'Legal Culture and Transformative Constitutionalism' in *South African Journal of Human Rights*, 14:1, pp. 146–88. For similar evaluations of social movement experiences of socio-economic rights litigation in India and South Africa, see Rajagopol (2008, 'Socio-Economic Rights and the Indian Supreme Court') and Madlingozi, (2013, 'Post-Apartheid Social Movements and Legal Mobilisation'), respectively.

[66] Patrick Bond, 2010, 'South Africa's Bubble Meets Boiling Urban Social Protest' in *Monthly Review*, 62 (2), pp. 17–28.

[67] On the South African experience of judges acting for and against reprivatisation and participatory democracy, see Danie Brand, 2005, 'The "Politics of Need Interpretation". On social movement strategy in such circumstances, see the comparative analysis of Colombian and South African social movements forwarded by Katharine Young and Julieta Lemaitre, 2013, 'The Comparative Fortunes of the Right to Health: Two Tales of Justiciability in Colombia and South Africa' in *Harvard Human Rights Journal*, Jan., pp. 179–216.

[68] The uprising of the Ejército Zapatista de Libéración Nacional (EZLN) in January 1994 was the beginning of a world Left counteroffensive against the relatively short-lived successes of the world right between the 1970s and 1994. The EZLN paved the way for successful alterglobalisation protests at Seattle in 1999, for the formation of the World Social Forum in Porto Alegre in 2001, and for the emergence of what is now known as the Global Justice Movement. See Immanuel Wallerstein, 2014, 'The Neo-Zapatistas: Twenty Years After'. Available at: http://iwallerstein.com/neozapatistas-twenty-years/.

[69] The horizontal practices that movements evolved in Mexico or in postfinancial crisis Argentina in the 2000s are a vital reference point for contemporary waves of resistance. See Marina Sitrin, 'Occupy: Making Democracy a Question' in Federico Campagna and Emanuele

public squares and centres of financial power, the Occupy and Indignados movements, the Tahrir square occupation in Egypt, the Quebec red square movement, the Gezi Park occupation in Turkey as well as Nuit debout in France have challenged accepting the state as a useful mechanism of social transformation and have suggested an alternative trajectory of mass, direct democracy.[70] On an unprecedented scale, in 'occupied' squares and cities around the world, people rediscovered and reinvented old habits of self-organisation and collective action. The critique here is that seizing state power, the typical strategy pursued by anti-systemic movements, too readily subordinates popular energies, creativity, and capacities for democracy and thereby too readily subsumes these activities within established demands of valorising capital.

Politically, what is at stake is a questioning of the necessity of using state power and an affirmation of collective political agency, 'a revolution at the level of common sense'.[71] Occupy and similar movements remind us that we need not resign ourselves to having our politics acted upon us, striking a blow against the prevailing cynicism, a necessary function of neoliberalism's 'relentless campaign against the human imagination' and a powerful force for reinforcing individual isolation in workplaces and communities.[72] Instead, the new wave of movements in the world's city squares 'give new meanings to freedom, our relation to the common, and a series of central political arrangements, which far exceed the bounds of the current republican constitutions . . . They are foundational principles that we already take to be inalienable rights, like those that were heralded in the course of the eighteenth-century revolutions'.[73] The immediate task at hand for those transcending nation-state borders was 'constitution': how they, having declared their independence in Tahrir Square and Zucotti Park, could make or rather 'constitute' a new and sustainable society.[74] In terms of resolving social and economic inequality then, the

Campiglio, 2012, *What We Are Fighting For: a radical collective manifesto*. London: Pluto, pp. 85–95.

70 Mason, 2013, *Why It's Still Kicking Off Everywhere*; see also Stéphane Hessel, 2011, *Time for Outrage: Indignez-vous!* New York: Hachette.

71 See David Graeber, 2013, *The Democracy Project*.

72 See David Graeber, 2013, *The Democracy Project*.

73 Hardt and Negri, 2012, 'Take Up the Baton'.

74 Hardt and Negri, 2012, 'Take Up the Baton'. On the commons, see Elinor Ostrom, 1990. Governing the commons. New York: Cambridge University Press; Silvia Federici, 2012, *Revolution at Point Zero: Housework, Reproduction, and Feminist Struggle*. Brooklyn: PM Press; Peter Linebaugh, 2014, *Stop, Thief! The Commons, Enclosures, and Resistance*. Oakland CA: PM Press.

spirit of Chiapas is less one of claiming rights from the state than that of creating 'commons' directly and of developing practices of mutual aid.[75] For those seeking to go against and beyond the rule of money, there is no right answer, party, or state to build towards, just millions of experiments in self-determination, taking place right here, right now.[76]

In this moment of crisis and transformation, the struggle between these contending perspectives and strategies provides us with an opportunity to challenge our mode of thinking and, in the present instance, to reassess the future of scholarship on social and economic rights. The analysis presented here has tried to reconfigure the coordinates of the dominant debate on socio-economic rights, that of the legitimacy of their constitutional entrenchment or judicial recognition, towards a clear-sighted, critical analysis of the broader ethico-political processes and relations out of which these decisions arise and to which they refer. In an initial sense, this mode of inquiry rejects the surface analysis of the symptoms of social problems (unequal distribution) rather than their source (the process by which unequal distributions are produced). It also rejects proponents of any political project that would dissimulate power relations, thereby reproducing existing structures of authority and domination or replacing them with new ones. Instead, if we wish to look beyond the fetish of the final constitutional form, inquiry into the politics of constitutionalising 'socio-economic rights' must begin with the labour process involved in constitution-making and development.

In this dialectical mode of inquiry, constitutions and socio-economic rights are accorded neither primacy nor epiphenomenality; their development is accounted for in neither formalist nor instrumentalist terms. Constitutions and human rights cannot be reduced to abstract norms or to an economic base but rather form part of and provide a terrain of contestation within 'a rich totality of many determinations and relations'.[77] Constitutional transformation is understood as a subjective movement,

[75] John Holloway has described this process as changing the world without seizing state power. 2005. *Change the World Without Taking Power: the meaning of revolution today*. London: Pluto. For detailed criticism and development of this thesis, see International Institute for Research and Education (ed.), 2005, 'Change the World without taking power?... or ... Take Power to change the world? A Debate on Strategies on how to build another world'. Available at: http://archive.iire.org/pamphlet_nsf_2006.pdf; on the historical recurrence of these debates, see Wallerstein, 2014, 'Anti-systemic Movements, yesterday and today'.

[76] Holloway, 2010, *Crack Capitalism*, p. 256.

[77] Marx, [1857]. '"Introduction" to the Grundrisse' in Carver, 1996, *Marx's Later Political Writings*, p. 146.

or 'sensible human activity, practice' as a young Marx put it, in which material conditions (natural and social) are constraints that delimit a range of possibilities for human action.[78] Any particular, historically achieved matrix of law and rights thus registers a crystallisation of the balance of power, coercive and consensual, between contending social forces. Methodologically, the critical discourse analysis of texts generated in the course of constitution-making and development brings back into view all the conflicts and discarded possibles of a constitution's early beginnings, of those relatively fluid moments of formulation prior to the crystallisation of a particular constitutional form. In doing so, this approach can demonstrate the ethico-political structures – institutional and interest-based as well as normative and discursive – that support the acceptance or rejection of socio-economic rights.

This form of inquiry coheres within a world-systems analysis but further highlights the danger that an analysis of the 'globalisation' of constitutional forms in the abstract risks speaking past concrete practices and subaltern cultures of contestation and resistance. Paralleling the critical world-systemic analysis of changing forms of socio-economic rights in Ireland's constitution then is an attempt to engage with the lived experience of those constitutionalised. In the present instance, this latter form of inquiry is inevitably incomplete. A number of important issues suggest themselves for future research on the Irish case. These issues include but are not limited to the role of the courts in the state-religious abuse complex; the relationship between gendered, patriarchal norms and legal activity; court relations to ethnic minorities, including Travellers, and asylum-seekers; as well as the role of the constitution in providing for a particular socio-ecological regime.[79] The present work at least provides a fresh impetus to reintegrate analysis of the 1937 Constitution's contested development over time with those class, race, and gender dynamics that remain operative in Ireland today.

78 Karl Marx, 1992, *The German Ideology, including Theses on Feuerbach*. New York: Prometheus Books. See also Peter Osborne, 2005, *How to Read Marx*. London: Granta Books, pp. 27, 43.

79 On the interaction of class, race, and gender dynamics with the 1937 Irish Constitution, see Ronit Lentin, 1998, '"Irishness", the 1937 Constitution and Citizenship: a Gender and Ethnicity View'; Bacik, Costello, and Drew, 2003, *Gender injustice*; Kieran Allen, 2004, *Citizenship and Racism: the case against McDowell's referendum*. Dublin: Bookmarks; Graham Finlay and JoAnne Mancini, 2016, '"Her life within the home": The construction of gender and female international migrant workers in the Republic of Ireland' in Zahra Meghani (eds.), *Women migrant workers: Ethical, political and legal problems*. Routledge: New York; on ecological crisis and constitutional reform, see Mark Garavan, 2004, 'A Democracy for an Ecological Age' in *Feasta Review* (2), pp. 155–61.

More generally, when evaluating a constitution, it is necessary to take seriously the difficult task of assessing whether it has actually contributed to the substantive well-being of those 'constitutionalised', and whether any perceived societal-constitutional harmony is genuine or merely indicative of constellations of power capable of blocking calls for change. Constitutional studies instead conclude prematurely with a number of jarring assertions concerning what the constitution is or what its creators achieved.[80] Scholars' focus on legal norms, political elites, and institutional transformation prohibits this wider consideration of the demos and its relationship to the constitution. In its absence, evaluative claims about the constitution, socio-economic rights, and democracy seem premature, partial, and incomplete. We might well conclude that the constitution has achieved a successful form of socio-economic rights entrenchment, but for whom?

In constructing a critical assessment, the recuperation of lived experiences of rights contestation and social movement struggle challenges the extent to which established critical and Marxian socio-legal analysis may privilege theory over the popular experience of history as life. This tendency is perhaps particularly true of left-wing projects of social transformation which, as John Holloway argues, tend to accentuate categorisations of domination to the detriment of new ways of talking about liberation.[81] With decidedly ethico-political implications, starting from lived experiences of rights contestation provides an approach to inquiry more sympathetic to including and understanding the diverse voices of gender, race, postcoloniality, and sexual orientation amongst all kinds of 'others'. Attempts to genuinely recuperate lived experiences and discourse pose a challenge for those who, confusing the things of logic for the logic of things, inevitably threaten to impose their favoured categorisation of the social world too readily upon the people living through it.[82]

A transformative politics, a social counterpower to capitalism, must involve listening to people's experience non-instrumentally while

[80] Brian Farrell's celebratory appraisal upon the 1937 Irish Constitution's fiftieth anniversary ranks highly in this regard. 'One man's document' had apparently 'become a political community's common charter – a living and effective guarantee of broadly based and expanding liberties'. Farrell, 1988, 'Preface' in Brian Farrell (ed.), *De Valera's Constitution and Ours*. Dublin: Gill and Macmillan, pp. vii–ix, p. viii. See also Thomas Murray, 2012, 'Where we are in *Dublin Review of Books*. Available at: www.drb.ie/essays/where-we-are.

[81] See Holloway, 2010, *Crack Capitalism*, pp. 10–17.

[82] Pierre Bourdieu frequently advanced this citation of Marx's *German Ideology* to critique the scholastic point of view and to appeal for a reflexive, self-aware form of social inquiry. 1990, *In Other Words: Essays toward a Reflective Sociology*, Stanford: Stanford University Press, p. 191.

proposing the dialectical relation and understanding of such experiences with shared social conditions.[83] Neoliberal hegemony involves, for example, the discursive extension of the market's categorisation of the social world into all areas of social life. For those who would challenge this process, it is not enough to advocate an alternative categorisation in the abstract. Certainly, socio-economic rights discourse, by recognising the intrinsic worth of every human being, can help justify opposition to the doctrine of 'necessary sacrifices' currently legitimising austerity in the EU and beyond. Nevertheless, the cultural domination at play in characterising, say, a hospital closure as *either* a human rights infringement or an incident in class struggle exists in tension with and threatens to undermine people's own attempts at describing, communicating, and therefore consciously realising a collective condition. Listening matters because, imprecisely, in the very possibility of our recognising and naming a collective condition together emerges the possibility of our collective response.

Questioning new and old forms of constitution along these lines emerges as more important than ever given the ongoing incapacitation of existing or former tools of collective defence against capital and the state, including left-wing and social democratic political parties as well as trade unions. What was recently suggested and performed in the world's squares as a 'possible' – an alternative constitution of social relations based on direct democracy and the collective promotion of the commons – is far from obviously true, not because it is necessarily false but rather because it has not yet been realised. The force of this 'not yet', in true dialectical fashion, is not apparent *a priori* but in our working it out in practice.[84] In Ireland, the history of those who challenged established structures of justice is similarly rich in the imagination of alternatives. For those determined to be free, it is these protean acts of constitution that will provide most inspiration.

[83] This emphasis on 'horiztonalidad' (or leaderless organising) coheres within the wider and renewed debates occurring, particularly in the aftermath of the 2011–12 movements, on the intersection of class and exploitation, the traditional focus of conflict for the Left, with various forms of identity and experiences of oppression, notably those of race, gender, trans, and queer identities. See Zillah Eisenstein, 'Renewing Intersectionality' in Campagna and Campiglio, 2012, *What We Are Fighting For*, pp. 123–30; Graeber, 2013, *The Democracy Project*; Bookchin, 2015, *The Next Revolution*.

[84] See Ernst Bloch, 1995, *The Principle of Hope*. London: MIT Press.

# BIBLIOGRAPHY


**Library and archives**

National Archives of Ireland
*Department of the Taoiseach Papers*
National Library of Ireland
*Thomas Johnson Papers*
New York Public Library
University College Dublin Library and Archives
*Dáil Éireann Debates*
*Alfred O'Rahilly Papers*
*Cearbhall Ó'Dálaigh Papers*
*Coyle O'Donnell Papers*
*Eamon de Valera Papers*
*George Gavan Duffy Papers*
*Hugh Kennedy Papers*

**Journals and newspapers**

*An Phoblacht*
*Hot Press*
*Irish Jurist*
*Irish Press*
*Irish Times*
*Irish Independent*

**Reports**

*Statistical Abstracts of Ireland (various years)*
*Courts Service Annual Reports (various years)*
*Cussen Report (1936)*
*Report of the Constitution Review Group (1967)*
*Kennedy Report (1970)*
*Report of the Committee on the Price of Building Land (1974)*
*Report of the Travelling People Review Body (1980)*
*Report of the Constitution Review Group (1995)*
*Indecon Report on Legal Services Reform (2003)*
*Competition Authority Report on Legal Services (2005)*
*Report of the Irish Council of Civil Liberties (2007)*

*Report of the Commission to Inquire into Child Abuse (2009)*
*Report of Working Group on a Court of Appeal (2009)*
*Central Statistics Office, Survey on Income and Living Conditions (2012)*
*European Commission for the Efficiency of Justice (CEPEJ) report (2012)*
*Report on the Recognition of Traveller Ethnicity (2014)*

**Articles**

Abrahamson, Max, 1961, 'Trade Disputes Act: Strict Interpretation in Ireland' in *Modern Law Review*, 24, pp. 596–603.

Akenson, D. H. and J. F. Fallin, 1970, 'The Irish Civil War and the Drafting of the Free State Constitution' in *Eire Ireland* (5), pp. 42–93.

Alston, Philip, 'Foreword' in Langford (ed.), 2012, *Social Rights Jurisprudence*, Cambridge: Cambridge University Press, pp. ix–xiv.

Amnesty International Ireland, 2014, *Bringing ESC Rights Home*. Dublin: Amnesty Publications.

Anderson, Perry, 2007, 'Depicting Europe' in *the London Review of Books*, Vol. 29 (18), pp. 13–21.

Barnard, T. C., 1993, 'Lawyers and the Law in Later Seventeenth-Century Ireland' in *Irish Historical Studies*, 28 (111), pp. 256–82.

Barrington, Donal, 1987, 'The Constitution in the Courts', in Frank Litton (ed.), *The Constitution of Ireland: 1937–1987*, Dublin: Institute of Public Administration, pp. 110–27.

Barrington, Donal, 1973, 'Private Property under the Irish Constitution' in *Irish Jurist*, 8 (1), pp. 1–17.

Barry, Frank and John O'Dowd, 2001, 'The Age of Tribunals' in *Studies*, Vol. 90 (1), pp. 58–69.

B. B., 1968, 'Review: JM Kelly, Fundamental Rights in the Irish Law and Constitution (2nd edition)' in *The Irish Jurist*, 3 (1), pp. 196–9.

Bellamy, Richard, 1994, 'Dethroning politics: Liberalism, constitutionalism, and democracy in the thought of F. A. Hayek' in *British Journal of Political Science*, 24 (3), pp. 419–32.

Ben-Bassat, Avi and Momi Dahan, 'Social Rights in the Constitution and in Practice' in *Journal of Comparative Economics*. 36 (1), March 2008, pp. 103–19.

Berry, Christopher and Charles Wysong, 2012, 'Making Courts Matter: Politics and the Implementation of State Supreme Court Decisions' in *The University of Chicago Law Review* 79(1), pp. 1–29.

Binchy, Daniel A., 1949, 'The Law and the Universities' in *Studies*, 38 (151), pp. 257–74.

Bond, Pat, 2010, 'South Africa's Bubble Meets Boiling Urban Social Protest', *Monthly Review*, 62 (2), pp. 17–28.

Böss, Michael, 2002, 'Constitutional and Legal Reform in Ireland, 1937–1998: The American Context' in *Nordic Irish Studies*, 1, pp. 121–45.

Bourdieu, Pierre, 'The Cunning of Imperialist Reason' in Wacquant, Loic, 2005, *Pierre Bourdieu and Democratic Politics*, Cambridge: Polity Press.

Bourdieu, Pierre, 'Structures, Habitus, Power: Basis for a Theory of Symbolic Power' in Dirks, N. B., Eley, G., and Ortner, S. B. (eds.), 1994, *Culture/Power/History: a reader in contemporary social theory*, Princeton: Princeton University Press.

Bourdieu, Pierre, 1994, 'Rethinking the State: Genesis and Structure of the Bureaucratic Field' in *Sociological Theory*, 12 (1), pp. 1–18.

Bourdieu, Pierre, 1990, 'The Scholastic Point of View' in *Cultural Anthropology*, 5 (4), pp. 380–91.

Bourdieu, Pierre, 1987, 'The Force of Law: Toward a Sociology of the Juridical Field' in *Hastings Law Journal*, Vol. 38, pp. 805–53.

Braconier, Henrik, Giuseppe Nicoletti, and Ben Westmore, 2014, 'Policy Challenges for the Next 50 Years', *OECD Economic Policy Papers*, No. 9, Paris: OECD Publishing.

Brady, James, 1975, 'Review: Wylie's *Irish Land Law*' in *Irish Jurist*, 10 (2), pp. 358–60.

Brand, Danie, 'The "Politics of Need Interpretation" and the Adjudication of Socio-Economic Rights Claims in South Africa' in A. J. van der Walt (ed.), 2005, *Theories of Social and Economic Justice*. Stellenbosch: Sun Press.

Brand, Danie, 'Introduction' in Danie Brand and Christof Heyns (eds.), 2005, *Socio-Economic Rights in South Africa*. Pretoria: Pretoria University Law Press, pp. 1–56.

Brinks, Daniel, and Varun Gauri, 2014, 'The Law's Majestic Equality? The Distributive Impact of Judicializing Social and Economic Rights' in *American Political Science Association*, 12 (2), pp. 375–93.

Buckley, Niall, 2004, 'Merging Principles of Public Law: Towards Proportionality in an Irish Context' in *Irish Jurist*, 39, pp. 161–214.

Butler, Andrew and Rory O'Connell, 1998, 'Ireland's Constitutional Review Group Report' in *Irish Jurist*, 33, pp. 237–65.

Carney, Claire, 1979, 'The Growth of Legal Aid in the Republic of Ireland' in *Irish Jurist*, 14 (1), pp. 61–82, p. 66, 72.

Carney, Caroline, and Bertrand Maître, (2012), 'Constructing a Food Poverty Indicator for Ireland using the Survey on Income and Living Conditions', *Social Inclusion Technical Paper No. 3*, Dublin: Department of Social Protection.

Carozza, Paulo W., 2003, 'From Conquest to Constitutions: Retrieving a Latin American Tradition of the Idea of Human Rights' in *Human Rights Quarterly*, 25 (2), pp. 281–314.

Carroll, Jennifer, 2005, 'You be the Judge: Part I – A Study of the Backgrounds of Superior Judges in Ireland in 2004' in *Bar Review*, 10, p. 153 ff.

Carroll, Jennifer, 2005, 'You be the Judge: Part II – The Politics and Processes of Judicial Appointments in Ireland' in *Bar Review*, 10, p. 182 ff.

Casey, James, 1986, 'Constitutional Law under Chief Justice O'Higgins' in *Irish Jurist*, 21 (1), pp. 7–34.

Casey, James, 1978, 'Review: McCarthy's Trade Unions in Ireland, 1894–1960' in *Irish Jurist*, 13 (2), pp. 396–99.

Casey, James, 1972, 'Reform of Collective Bargaining Law: Some Constitutional Implications' in *Irish Jurist*, 7 (1), pp. 1–16.

Casey, James, 1970, 'Republican Courts in Ireland 1919–1922' in *Irish Jurist*, 5 (2) pp. 321–42, p. 342.

Clarke, Gerard, 1968, 'Planning and Development' in *The Irish Jurist*, 3 (1), pp. 107–11.

Coakley, John, 'Society and Political Culture' in John Coakley and Michael Gallagher (eds.), 2010, *Politics in the Republic of Ireland*, London: PSAI Press/Routledge, pp. 37–71.

Coakley, John, 2009, '"Irish Republic", "Eire" or "Ireland"? The Contested Name of John Bull's Other Island' in *Political Quarterly*,80 (1), pp. 49–58.

Coffey, Donal, 2012, 'The Need for a New Constitution: Irish Constitutional Change 1932–1935' in *The Irish Jurist*, 48 (2), pp. 275–302.

Congost, Rosa, 2003, 'Property Rights and Historical Analysis' in *Past and Present*, 181 (Nov.), pp. 73–106.

Connolly, Linda, 'The outcomes and consequences of second-wave feminism in Ireland' in Linda Connolly and Niamh Hourigan (eds.), 2006, *Social Movements and Ireland*. Manchester: Manchester University Press. pp. 58–85.

Costello, Declan, 1956, 'The Natural Law and the Irish Constitution' in *Studies*, 45 (180), pp. 403–14.

Coughlan, A., 1988, 'The Constitution and Social Policy' in Litton, F. (ed.), *The Constitution of Ireland 1937–1987*, Dublin: Institute of Public Administration.

Cross, F. B., 2001, 'The Error of Positive Rights' in *UCLA Law Review*, 48 (4), pp. 857–924.

Crossman, Virginia, 1991, 'Emergency Legislation and Agrarian Disorder in Ireland, 1821–1841' in *Irish Historical Studies*, 27 (108), pp. 309–23.

Dahl, Robert, 1957, 'Decision-making in a Democracy: Supreme Court as national policy-maker' in *Journal of Public Law*, 6 (2), pp. 279–95.

Davis, D. M., 2006, 'Adjudicating the socio-economic rights in the South African constitution: towards "deference lite"?' in *South African Journal on Human Rights*, 22, pp. 301–27.

de Blacam, Mark, 2002, 'Children, Constitutional Rights, and the Separation of Powers' in *Irish Jurist*, 37, pp. 113–42.

de Mille, Anna George, 1944, 'Henry George: The Fight for Irish Freedom,' in *The American Journal of Economics and Sociology*, 3 (2), pp. 251–72.

de Sousa Santos, Boaventura, 1998, 'Participatory Budgeting in Porto Alegre' in *Politics and Society*, 26 (4), pp. 461–510.

de Wispelaere, Jurgen and Judy Walsh, 2007, 'Disability Rights in Ireland: Chronicle of a Missed Opportunity' in *Irish Political Studies*, 22.(4), pp. 517–43.

Delany (ed.), VTH, 1957, 'Restrictive Covenants' in the *Irish Jurist*, 23 (1), p. 1.

Delany (ed.), VTH, 1953–4, 'Books: Criminal Law by Glanville Williams' in *The Irish Jurist*, 19–20 (2), p. 20.

Delaney, VTH, 1952, 'The Custody and Education of Children: A Changing Legal Concept in Eire' in the *Irish Jurist*, 18 (2), p. 23.

Delany (ed.), Vincent, 1951, 'Book Review' in *The Irish Jurist*, 17 (3), p. 42.

Dillon, Sara, 1999, 'Review: Scannell et al., The Habitats Directive' in *Irish Jurist*, 34, pp. 346–9.

Dixon, Rosalind, 2007, 'Creating dialogue about socio-economic rights' in *International Journal of Constitutional Law*, 5 (3), pp. 391–418.

Domingo, Pilar, 2000, 'Judicial Independence: The Politics of the Supreme Court in Mexico' in *Journal of Latin American Studies*, 32 (3), pp. 705–35.

Donovan, P. F., 'New Beginnings (1923–1930)' in Meenan, James (ed.), 2005, *Centenary History of the Literary and Historical Society of University College Dublin, 1855–1955*, Dublin: AA and Farmer.

Duncan, William, 1972, 'Desertion and Cruelty in Irish Matrimonial Law' in *Irish Jurist*, 7 (1), pp. 213–40.

Edgeworth, Brendan, 2007, 'Rural Radicalism Restrained: The Irish Land Commission and the Courts (1933–1939)' in *Irish Jurist*, 42 (1), pp. 1–28.

Elkins, Zachary, Tom Ginsburg, and James Melton, 2008, 'Baghdad, Tokyo, Kabul . . . Constitution-making in Occupied States' in *William and Mary Law Review*, 49 (4), pp. 1139–78.

Elliott, F. J., 1972, 'Notes: Residential Child Care: Health Act Admissions' in the *Irish Jurist*, 7 (1), pp. 358–9.

Elster, Jon, 1995, 'Forces and Mechanisms in the Constitution-Making Process' in *Duke Law Journal*, 45, (2), pp. 364–96.

Ewing, E. D., 'Economic Rights' in Michel Rosenfeld and Andras Sajó (eds.), 2012, *The Oxford Handbook of Comparative Constitutional Law*. Oxford: Oxford University Press, pp. 1036–56.

Fahey, Tony, 2002, 'Catholicism and Industrial Society in Ireland' in J. H. Goldthorpe and C. T. Whelan (eds.) *The development of Industrial Society in Ireland* Oxford: Oxford University Press, pp. 241–63.

Fanning, Ronan, 1988, 'Mr. de Valera drafts a constitution' in Farrell, B., *De Valera's Constitution and Ours*, Dublin: Gill and Macmillan.

Fanning, Rossa, 2006, 'Review: O'Neill, *The Constitutional Rights of Companies*' in *Irish Jurist* 41(1), pp. 144–6.

Farrell, Brian, 1970–1, 'The Drafting of the Irish Free State Constitution: I, II, III and IV' in *Irish Jurist*, 5/6, pp. 115, 343, 111, and 345.

Farrell, Michael, 2006, 'Using Law and Litigation in the Public Interest' in FLAC, *Public Interest Law in Ireland: The Reality and the Potential*. FLAC: Dublin, pp. 131–4.

Feenan, Dermot, 2008, 'Judicial Appointments in Ireland in Comparative Perspective' in *Judicial Studies Institute Journal*, (1), pp. 37–66.

Finlay, Graham, and JoAnne Mancini, 2016, '"Her life within the home": The construction of gender and female international migrant workers in the Republic of in Meghani, Z. (ed.) *Women migrant workers: Ethical, political, and legal problems*. New York: Routledge.

FLAC, 2006, *Public Interest Law in Ireland: The Reality and the Potential*. FLAC: Dublin.

Fletcher, Ruth, 2001, 'Post-Colonial Fragments: Representations of Abortion in Irish Law and Politics' in *Journal of Law and Society*, 28 (4), pp. 568–89.

Flood, Andrew, 2010, How not to make a revolution: Young Ireland, the Chartists, and 1848'. Available at: www.anarchism.pageabode.com/andrewnflood/revolution-young-ireland-1848.

Flynn, Anne, Nuala McDonald, and E. F. O'Doherty, 1967, 'A Survey of Boys in St. Patrick's Institution: Project on Juvenile Delinquency' in *The Irish Jurist*, 2 (2), pp. 222–32.

Forbarth, William with Joseph Fishkin, 2014, 'The Anti-Oligarchy Constitution' in Boston University Law Review, 94, ff. 669.

Forbath, William, 2012, 'Workers' Rights and the Distributive Constitution' in *Dissent*, Spring, pp. 58–65.

Forde, M., 1982, 'Equality and the Constitution' in *Irish Jurist*, 17 (2), pp. 295–339.

France, Clement, 1923, 'Comments on the Foregoing Article' in *Studies*, 12 (47), pp. 356–60.

Galanter, Marc, 1974, 'Why the "Haves" Come Out Ahead: Speculations on the Limits of Legal Change' in *Law and Society Review*, 9 (1), pp. 95–160.

Gallie, W. B., 1955–6, 'Essentially Contested Concepts' in *Proceedings of the Aristotelian Society, New Series*, Vol. 56, pp. 167–98.

Garvin, Tom, 2008, 'An Irish Republican Tradition?' in Iseult Honohan (ed.), *Republicanism in Ireland: Confronting Theories and Traditions*. Manchester: Manchester University Press, pp. 23–30.

Garvin, Tom, 1986, 'The Anatomy of a Nationalist Revolution: Ireland, 1858–1928' in *Comparative Studies in Society and History*, 28 (3), pp. 468–501, p. 479.

Gill, Stephen, 1995, 'Globalization, Market Civilization, and Disciplinary Neoliberalism' in *Millennium*, 24, pp. 399–412.

Glendon, Mary Ann, 1992, 'Rights in Twentieth-Century Constitutions' in *University of Chicago Law Review*, Vol. 59, pp. 519–38.
Go, Julian, 2003, 'A Globalizing Constitutionalism? Views from the Postcolony, 1945–2000' in *International Sociology*, 18 (1), pp. 71–95.
Graham, R. J. and Susan Hood, 1994, 'Town Tenant Protest in late nineteenth and early twentieth century Ireland' in *Irish Economic and Social History*, Vol. 21, pp. 39–58.
Greer, Desmond, 1969, 'Legal Services and the Poor in Ireland' in *Irish Jurist*, 4 (2), pp. 270–92.
Guinnane, Timothy and Ronald Miller, 1997, 'The Limits to Land Reform: The Land Acts in Ireland, 1870–1909' in *Economic Development and Cultural Change*, 45 (3), pp. 591–612.
Hardt, Michael and Antonio Negri, 2012, 'Take Up the Baton' in *Jacobin Magazine*, 5. Available at: www.jacobinmag.com/2012/05/take-up-the-baton/.
Harris, Gerald, 1951, 'Book Review: University of Notre Dame Law Institute Proceedings: Volume V' in *The Irish Jurist*, 17 (4), pp. 61–2.
Harris, Gerald, 1951, 'Editorial' in the *Irish Jurist*, 17 (3), p. 38.
Harris, Gerald, 1950, 'The Recruitment of the Judiciary' in *The Irish Jurist*, 16 (3), pp. 35–7.
Harris, Gerald, 1950, 'Books and Publications: Town and Regional Planning Law in Ireland' in the *Irish Jurist*, 16 (3), p. 37.
Harris, Gerald, 1949, 'Books: The Law of Rent Restriction in Ireland by John Coghlan' in the *Irish Jurist*, 15 (3), p. 42.
Harris, Gerald, 1948, 'Book Publications: Lectures on the Town and Country Planning Act by R. E. Megarry' in the *Irish Jurist*, 14 (4), p. 63.
Harris, Gerald, 1948, 'Books and Publications: Rent Restrictions Cases by Lionel Blundell of Gray's Inn' in the *Irish Jurist*, 14 (3), p. 61.
Harris, Gerald, 1946, 'Book Review: On The Rent Acts by R. E. Megarry' in the *Irish Jurist*, 12 (3), p. 41.
Harris, Gerald, 1944, 'Book Review: The Law of Rent Restrictions in Eire by John Coghlan' in the *Irish Jurist*, 10 (4), p. 52.
Harris, Gerald, 1940, 'The Need for Legal Reform' in the *Irish Jurist*, 6 (2), pp. 17–18.
Harris, Gerald, 1939, 'The War' in *Irish Jurist*, 5 (4), pp. 53–4.
Harris, Gerald, 1938, 'The Lawyer and his Profession' in *The Irish Jurist*, 4 (2), p. 22.
Hearne, Rory, 2015, 'The Irish water war, austerity and the "Risen people": An analysis of participant opinions, social and political impacts and transformative potential of the Irish anti water-charges movement', pp. 2, 15; Available at: www.maynoothuniversity.ie/sites/default/files/assets/document/TheIrishWaterwar_0.pdf.
Heuston, R. F. V., 1990–2, 'John Kelly' in *Irish Jurist*, 25–7 (1), pp. 1–3.

Heuston, R. F. V., 1969, 'Trade unions and the Law' in *The Irish Jurist*, 4 (1), pp. 10–22.

Heydebrand, Wolf, 1977, 'Organizational Contradictions in Public Bureaucracies: Toward a Marxian Theory of Organizations' in *The Sociological Quarterly*, 18 (1), pp. 83–107.

Hillyard, Patrick, 1972, 'Public Attitudes towards the Police in a medium-sized town in Northern Ireland', in the *Irish Jurist*, 7 (1), pp. 62–76.

Hirschl, Ran and Evan Rosevear, 'Constitutional Law Meets Comparative Politics: Socio-economic Rights and Political Realities' in Tom Campbell, K. D. Ewing, and Adam Tomkins (eds.), 2011, *The Legal Protection of Human Rights: Sceptical Essays*. Oxford: Oxford University Press, pp. 207–28.

Hirschl, Ran, 2011, 'The Continued Renaissance of Comparative Constitutional Law' in *Tulsa Law Review*, 45, pp. 771–80.

Hirschl, Ran, 2004, 'The Political Origins of the New Constitutionalism' in *Indiana Journal of Global Legal Studies*, 11, pp. 71–108.

Hogan, Gerard, 2005, 'De Valera, the Constitution and the Historians' in *Irish Jurist*, 40 (2), pp. 293–320.

Hogan, Gerard, 2001, 'Directive Principles, Socio-Economic Rights and the Constitution' in *Irish Jurist*, 36 (2), pp. 293–320.

Hogan, G., 1997, 'The Constitution Review Committee of 1934' in Fionán Ó Muircheartaigh (ed.), *Ireland in the Coming Times: Essays to Celebrate T. K. Whitaker's 80 Years*, Dublin: Institute of Public Administration, pp. 342–69.

Hogan, Gerard, 1997, 'The Constitution, Property Rights and Proportionality' in *Irish Jurist*, 32 (2), pp. 373–97.

Hogan, Gerard, 1987, 'The Supreme Court and the Single European Act' in *Irish Jurist*, 22 (1), pp. 55–70, p. 70.

Hogan, Gerard, 1986, 'Irish Nationalism as a Legal Ideology' in *Studies*, 75 (4), 528 ff.

Hogan, Gerard, Donal Barrington, and Patrick McEntee, 1985, 'The Constitution, Law and Ideology' in *Crane Bag*, 9 (1), pp. 104–9.

Howson, Richard, 'From ethico-political hegemony to Post-Marxism' in Marcus E. Green (ed.), 2011, *Rethinking Gramsci*. London: Routledge, pp. 167–76.

Hughes, D. J., 1977, 'Review: David Hoath, *Council Housing*' in *Irish Jurist*, 12 (1), pp. 212–3.

Ingram, Attracta, 1987, 'Review: Clarke, *Church and State*' in *Irish Jurist*, 22 (1), pp. 142–4.

Jones, Cedric, 1964, 'Review: "Power Politics, Georg Schwarzenberger"' in *Irish Jurist*, 30 (2), p. 26.

Jung, Courtney and Evan Rosevear, 2011, *Economic and Social Rights in Developing Country Constitutions: preliminary report on the TIESR data set*. Toronto Initiative on Economic and Social Rights.

Kaim-Caudle, P. R., 1970, 'Productivity, Income and Standards of Solicitors in the Irish Republic' in *Irish Jurist* 5 (1), pp. 40–9, p. 48.
Keane, Ronan, 2001, 'Brave New World' in *Irish Jurist*, 36, pp. 1–16.
Keane, Ronan, 2000, 'The Sinn Féin Funds Case' in O'Dell, Eoin (ed.), 2000, *Leading Cases of the Twentieth Century*, p. 188.
Keane, Ronan, 1996, '"The Voice of the Gael": Chief Justice Kennedy and the emergence of the new Irish court system, 1921–36' in *Irish Jurist*, 31 (2), pp. 205–25.
Keane, Ronan, 1983, 'Land Use, Compensation and the Community' in *Irish Jurist*, 18 (1), pp. 23–33.
Keane, Ronan, 1965, 'The Future of the Irish Bar' in *Studies*, Vol. 54 (216), pp. 375–84.
Kelly, J. M., 1988 b., 'The Constitution: Law and Manifesto' in Litton, F (ed.), 1988, *The Constitution of Ireland 1937–1987*, Dublin: Institute of Public Administration.
Kende, Mark, 2003, 'The South African Court's Embrace of Socio-Economic Rights: A Comparative Perspective' in *Chapman Law Review*, Vol. 6 (Spring), pp. 137–60.
Kennedy, Duncan, 'Three Globalisations of Law and Legal Thought: 1850–2000' in Trubek, David and Alvaro Santos (eds.), 2006, *The New Law and Economic Development: a Critical Appraisal.*
Kennedy, Duncan, 1982, 'Legal Education as Training for Hierarchy' in *Journal of Legal Education*, 32, pp. 591–615.
Kennedy, Duncan, 1982, 'Antonio Gramsci and the Legal System', *ALSA Forum*, VI (1), 1979, p. 36.
Kenny, Colum, 1987, 'The exclusion of catholics from the legal profession in Ireland, 1537–1829' in *Irish Historical Studies*, 25 (100), pp. 337–57.
Keogh, D., 1988 b., 'The Constitutional Revolution: An Analysis of the Making of the Constitution' in Litton, F. (ed.), *The Constitution of Ireland 1937–1987*, Dublin: Institute of Public Administration.
Kerr, Tony, 1988, 'Review' in *Irish Jurist*, 23 (1), pp. 172–5.
Kerr, Tony, 1980, 'Trade Disputes, Economic Torts and the Constitution' in *Irish Jurist*, 16 (2), pp. 241–61.
Kiberd, Declan, 'Patrick Pearse: Irish Modernist' in Róisín Higgins and Regina Ní Chollatáin (eds.), 2009, *The Life and After-Life of Patrick Pearse*, Dublin: Irish Academic Press, pp. 65–80.
King, Phoebe, 'Neo-Bolivarian Constitutional Design' in Denis Galligan and Mila Versteeg, 2013, *Social and Political Foundations of Constitutions*. Cambridge: Cambridge University Press, pp. 366–97.
Kirby, Peadar and Mary Murphy, 2011, 'Globalisation and models of state: debates and evidence from Ireland' in *New Political Economy*, 16 (1), pp. 9–30.

Kirsten, Adèle and Tshepo Madlingozi, 2012, '100 Years of the ANC: From Liberation Movement to State Power' in South Africa Black Agenda Report, available at: http://blackagendareport.com/print/content/100-years-anc-liberation-movement-state-power-south-africa.

Kissane, Bill, 2004, 'Defending Democracy? The Legislative Response to Political Extremism in the Irish Free State, 1922–39' in *Irish Historical Studies*, 34 (134), pp. 156–74.

Klare, Karl, 1998, 'Legal Culture and Transformative Constitutionalism' in *South African Journal of Human Rights*, 14 (1), pp. 146–88.

Korpi, Walter and Joakim Palme, 1998, 'The Paradox of Redistribution and Strategies of Equality: Welfare State Institutions, Inequality, and Poverty in Western Countries' in *American Sociological Review*, 63 (5), pp. 661–87.

Lang, John Temple, 1971, 'Private Law Aspects of the Irish Constitution', in *Irish Jurist*, 6 (2), pp. 237–57.

Langford, Malcolm, 'The Justiciability of Social Rights: From Practice to Theory' in Malcolm Langford (ed.), 2008, *Social Rights Jurisprudence: emerging trends in international and comparative law*. Cambridge: Cambridge University Press, pp. 3–45.

Langford, Malcolm and Jeff A. King, 'Committee on Economic, Social and Cultural Rights: Past, Present and Future' in Malcolm Langford (ed.), 2008, *Social Rights Jurisprudence: emerging trends in international and comparative law*. Cambridge: Cambridge University Press, pp. 477–516.

Larsen, Stein and Oliver Snoddy, 1973, '1916 – A Workingmen's Revolution? An analysis of those who made the 1916 revolution in Ireland' in *Social Studies*, 2 (4), pp. 377–98.

Lentin, Ronit, 1998, '"Irishness", the 1937 Constitution and Citizenship: a Gender and Ethnicity View' in *Irish Journal of Sociology*, 8 (1), pp. 5–24.

Liebenberg, Sandra, 2006, 'Needs, Rights and Transformation: Adjudicating Social Rights' in *Stellenbosch Law Review*, 17 (1), pp. 5–36.

Luddy, Maria, 2005, 'A "Sinister and Retrogressive" Proposal: Irish women's opposition to the 1937 draft constitution' in *Transactions of the Royal Historical Society*, 15, pp. 175–95.

Lysaght, Charles, 2002, 'Review: Gwynn Morgan, A Judgment Too Far?' in *Irish Jurist*, 37 (2), pp. 336–8.

MacCarthaigh, Muiris, 2012, 'Politics, policy preferences and the evolution of Irish bureaucracy: A framework for analysis' in *Irish Political Studies*, 27 (1), pp. 23–47.

MacKinnon, Catharine A., 1982, 'Feminism, Marxism, Method, and the State: An Agenda for Theory' in *Signs*, 7 (3), pp. 515–44.

MacLaran, Andrew, Katia Attuyer, and Brendan Williams, 2010, 'Changing office location patterns and their importance in the peripheral expansion of the Dublin region 1960–2008' in *Journal of Irish Urban Studies*, Volumes 7–9, pp. 53–78.

MacMenamin, John, 2008, 'Review: Foxton, *Revolutionary Lawyers*' in *Irish Jurist* 43(1), pp. 137–9.

McAleavey, Richard, 2014, 'Whatever happened to the Irish democracy?' In: *Cunning Hired Knaves*. Available at: https://hiredknaves.wordpress.com/2014/03/21/whatever-happened-to-the-irish-democracy.

McAuliffe, Mary, 2011, 'The Irish Woman Worker and the Conditions of Employment Act, 1936: Responses from the Irish Free State Women Senators', *Saothar*, Vol. 36, pp. 37–46.

McCartney, J., 1964, 'Strike Law and the Constitution' in the *Irish Jurist*, 30 (4), pp. 65–70.

McDermott, P. A., 2000, 'The Separation of Powers' in *Irish Jurist*, 35, pp. 280–304.

McDonagh, Enda, 1987, 'Philosophical-Theological Reflections on the Constitution' in Litton, Frank (ed.), *The Constitution of Ireland 1937–1987*. Dublin: Institute of Public Administration, pp. 192–205.

McDonough, Terrence, and Tony Dundon, 2010, 'Thatcherism Delayed? The Irish crisis and the paradox of social partnership' in *Industrial Relations Journal*, 41 (6), pp. 544–62.

McDowell, R. B., 1957, 'The Irish Courts of Law, 1801–1914' in *Irish Historical Studies*, 10 (40), pp. 363–91, p. 363.

McEldowney, John, 2004, 'Challenges in Legal Bibliography' in *Irish Jurist*, 39 (1), pp. 215–42.

McGraw, Seán, 'Adaptive Governance: The Art of Party Politics', in Niamh Hardiman (ed.), 2012, *Irish Governance in Crisis*, Manchester: Manchester University Press.

McMahon, Bryan, 1980, 'Review: J. M. Kelly, The Irish Constitution' in *Irish Jurist*, 16 (1), pp. 190–203.

McMahon, Bryan, 1979, 'Developments in the Irish Legal System since 1945' in J. J. Lee (ed.), *Ireland: 1945–70*, pp. 83–95.

McMullen, John, 2001, 'Transfer of Undertakings' in *Irish Jurist*, 36 (1), pp. 83–125.

Macias, Anna, 1980, 'Women and the Mexican Revolution, 1910–1920' in *The Americas*, 37 (1), pp. 53–82.

Madlingozi, Tshepo, 2013, 'Post-Apartheid Social Movements and Legal Mobilisation' in M. Langford, B. Cousins, J. Dugard, and T. Madlingozi (eds.), *Socio-economic Rights in South Africa: Symbol or Substance?* Cambridge: Cambridge University Press.

Maher, Imelda, 1989, 'Review' in *Irish Jurist*, 24 (2), pp. 309–12.

Maher, Imelda, 1989, 'Grafting the Homeless on to the Housing Code' in *Irish Jurist*, 24 (2), pp. 182–97.

Mair, Peter, 2004, 'De Valera and Democracy' in T. Garvin, M. Manning, and R. Sinnott (eds.), 2004, *Dissecting Irish Politics: Essays in Honour of Brian Farrell*. Dublin: University College Dublin Press.

Mair, Peter, 1992, 'Explaining the absence of Class Politics in Ireland' in J. H. Goldthorpe and C. T. Whelan (eds.), *The development of Industrial Society in Ireland* Oxford: Oxford University Press.
Mathews, Mary, 1973, 'The Tort of Conspiracy in Irish Labour Law' in the *Irish Jurist*, 8 (2), pp. 252–74.
Mathews, Mary, 1972, 'Aspects of the Irish Law of Contract' in *Irish Jurist*, 7 (2), pp. 292–305.
Meenan, F. O. C., 1969, 'The Georgian Squares of Dublin and the Professions' in *Studies*, 58 (232), pp. 405–14.
Meuwese, Anne, 2013, 'Popular Constitution-Making in Iceland' in Denis Galligan and Mila Versteeg (eds.), *Social and Political Foundations of Constitutions*. Cambridge: Cambridge University Press, pp. 469–96.
Mohr, Thomas, 2008, 'The Rights of Women under the Constitution of the Irish Free State' in *Irish Jurist*, 41 (1), pp. 20–59.
Mohr, Thomas, 2008, 'British Involvement in the Creation of the Constitution of the Irish Free State' in *Dublin University Law Journal*, 30 (1), pp. 166–86.
Molony, T., 1931, 'Legal Aid for Poor Persons' in *Journal of the Statistical and Social Inquiry Society of Ireland*, 17, (1) p. 16.
Morgan, David Gwynn, 2006, 'Review: Sampford, Retrospectivity and the Rule of Law' in *Irish Jurist* 41 (1), pp. 137–9.
Morgan, D. G., 2002, 'Review: Whyte, Social Inclusion and the Legal System' in *Irish Jurist*, 37 (1), pp. 344–48.
Morgan, D. G., 1986, 'Review: Casey's *Constitutional Law in Ireland*' in *Irish Jurist*, 21 (1), pp. 146–53.
Morgan, D. G., 1985, 'Review' in *Irish Jurist*, 20 (2), pp. 445–50.
Moyn, Samuel, 2015, 'A Powerless Companion: Human Rights in the Age of Neoliberalism', Law and Contemporary Problems, 77 (4), pp. 147–69.
Murphy, Mary, 2011, 'Civil society in the shadow of the Irish state' in *Irish Journal of Sociology*, 19 (2), pp. 170–87.
Murray, Thomas, 2016, 'Contesting a World-Constitution? Anti-systemic movements and constitutional forms in Ireland, 1848–2008' in *Journal of World-Systems Research*, 22 (1), pp. 77–107.
Murray, Thomas, 2015, 'Socio-economic Rights versus Social Revolution? Constitution Making in Germany, Mexico, and Ireland, 1917–23' in *Social and Legal Studies*, 24 (4), pp. 487–508.
Murray, Thomas, 2015, 'Socio-Economic Rights and the Making of the 1937 Irish Constitution' in *Irish Political Studies*. Available at: http://dx.doi.org/10.1080/07907184.2015.1095738.
Murray, Thomas, 2012, 'Where we are: Review of Bill Kissane's New Beginnings' in *Dublin Review of Books*. Available at: www.drb.ie/essays/where-we-are.

Nolan, Aoife, 2012, 'Ireland' in Malcolm Langford (ed.), *Social Rights Jurisprudence: emerging trends in international and comparative law*. Cambridge: Cambridge University Press, pp. 295–322.

Norris, Michelle, and Tony Fahey, 2011, 'From Asset Based Welfare to Welfare Housing? The Changing Function of Social Housing in Ireland' in *Housing Studies*, 26 (03), pp. 459–69.

O'Connell, Paul, 2011, 'The Death of Socio-Economic Rights' in *Modern Law Review*, 74 (4), pp. 532–54.

O'Cuiv, Andreas, 1960, 'The Irish Jurist: A Retrospective' in *The Irish Jurist*, 26 (1), p. 4.

O'Dowd, John, 2011, 'Remembering the Constitution: The Easter Proclamation and Constitutionalism in Independent Ireland', *IBIS Working Paper Series*, 104, pp. 1–18. Available at: www.ucd.ie/ibis/filestore/wp2011/104_odowd.pdf.

O'Dricoll, Finín, 2000, 'Social Catholicism in Independent Ireland: The Challenge to the Fiscal System' in Mike Cronin and John Regan (eds.), *Ireland: The Politics of Independence, 1922–49*. Dublin: Macmillan.

Ó Drisceoil, Donal, 2009, 'When Dev defaulted: the land annuities dispute, 1926–38' in *History Ireland*.

O'Flynn, Mary, 1971, 'Prison After-Care in the Irish Republic' in the *Irish Jurist*, 6 (1), pp. 1–17

O'Hanlon, R. J., 1968, 'Notes: Criminal Justice Bill, 1967' in *The Irish Jurist*, 3 (1), pp. 102–7.

O'Higgins, Paul, 1966, 'English Law and the Irish Question' in the *Irish Jurist*, 1 (1), pp. 59–65.

O'Keefe, Denis, 1941, 'Catholic Political Theory' in *Studies*, Vol. 30 (120), pp. 481–88.

O'Mahony, Michael, 1971, 'Legal Aspects of Residential Child Care' in the *Irish Jurist*, 6 (1), pp. 217–36.

O'Neill, Thomas, 1955, 'The Irish Land Question, 1830–1850' in *Studies*, 44 (175), pp. 325–36, p. 330.

O'Rahilly, A., 1914, 'The Gospel of Superman' in *Studies*, Vol. III (12), pp. 381–403.

O'Rahilly, A., 1918, 'Suarez and Democracy' in *Studies*, Vol. VII (25), pp. 1–22.

O'Rahilly, A., 1919, 'The Catholic Origin of Democracy' in *Studies*, Vol. VIII (29), pp. 1–18.

O'Rahilly, A., 1919, 'The Sources of English and American Democracy' in *Studies*, Vol. VIII (31), pp. 189–209.

O'Rahilly, A., 1921, 'The Sovereignty of the People' in *Studies*, Vol. X (37), pp. 39–56.

O'Shaughnessy, Mark, 1872, 'On Legal Education in Ireland' in *Journal of the Statistical and Social Inquiry Society of Ireland*, Vol. VI, Part XLII, pp. 124–66.

O'Sullivan, Michelle, 2011, 'Review: Daly and Doherty, Principles of Irish Employment Law' in *Irish Jurist* 46 (1), p. 235.

O'Sullivan, Richard, 1949, 'The Law and the Universities: Response' in *Studies*, 38 (151), pp. 257–74.

Ollmann, Bertell, 2000, 'What Is Political Science? What Should It Be?' in *New Political Science*, 22 (4), pp. 553–62.

Orridge, Andrew, 1983, 'The Blueshirts and the "Economic War"' in *Political Studies*, 31 (3), pp. 351–69.

Osborough, Nial, 1996, 'Letters to Ireland' in *Irish Jurist*, 31 (1), pp. 226–54, p. 252.

Osborough, Nial, 1978, 'Education in the Irish Law and Constitution' in *Irish Jurist*, 13 (1), pp. 145–80.

Osborough, Nial, 1976, 'Irish Legal Scholarship' in *Irish Jurist*, 11 (1), pp. 1–2.

Osborough, Nial, 1969, 'Review: The Practical Police Surgeon' in *The Irish Jurist*, 4 (1), p. 203.

Osborough, Nial, 1969, 'Notes: Commission on the Status of Women' in *Irish Jurist*, 4 (2), pp. 327–9.

Pole, Adam, 2005, 'Sheriffs' Sales during the Land War, 1879–82' in *Irish Historical Studies*, 34 (136), pp. 386–402.

Peebles, Gustav, 1997, '"A Very Eden of the Innate Rights of Man"? A Marxist Look at the European Union Treaties and Case Law' in *Law & Social Inquiry*, 22 (3), pp. 581–618.

Pieterse, Marius, 2007, 'Eating Socioeconomic Rights: The Usefulness of Rights Talk in Alleviating Social Hardship Revisited' in *Human Rights Quarterly*, 29 (3), pp. 796–822.

Pyne, Peter, 1970, 'The Third Sinn Féin party, 1923–1926,' in *Economic and Social Review*, 1 (1), pp. 29–50, 229–57.

Rajagopal, Balakrishnan, 2003, 'International Law and Social Movements: challenges of theorising resistance' in *Colombia Journal of Transnational Law*, 41 (2), pp. 397–433.

Ramos, F. Y., 1967, 'The Social Rights Enshrined in the Mexican Constitution of 1917' in *International Labour Review*, 96 (6), pp. 590–9.

Right2Water, 2015, Policy Principles for a Progressive Irish Government. Available at: www.mandate.ie/Documents/111930_12796_R2W-Unions_Policies_A5.pdf.

Ryan, Louise, 2006, 'An analysis of the Irish suffrage movement using new social movement theory' in Linda Connolly and Niamh Hourigan (eds.), *Social Movements and Ireland*. Manchester: Manchester University Press, pp. 40–57.

Rynne, Michael, 1964, 'The Protection Racket: Observations on the Rent Restrictions Act, 1960' in the *Irish Jurist*, 30 (1), p. 13.

Scannell, Yvonne, 1980, 'Review: Alder, Development Control' in *Irish Jurist*, 15 (1), pp. 181–2.

Schneiderman, David, 2000, 'Investment Rules and the New Constitutionalism' in *Law and Social Inquiry*, 25 (3), pp. 757–87.

Shanley, Peter, 1970, 'The Formal Cautioning of Juvenile Offenders' in *Irish Jurist*, 6 (1), pp. 262–79.

Shotwell, J. T., 1933, 'The International Labor Organisation as an Alternative to Violent Revolution' in *The Annals of the American Academy of Political and Social Science*, 166, pp. 18–25.

Simpson, Bob, 1985, 'Review: Kerr and Whyte, Irish Trade Union Law' in *Irish Jurist*, 20 (1), pp. 220–3.

Slater, Eamonn and Terrence McDonough, 2008, 'Marx on 19th-Century Colonial Ireland: Analysing Colonialism beyond Dependency Theory', *NIRSA Working Paper Series*, 36, pp. 1–35.

Smyth, Jim, 2006, 'Moving the Immovable: the civil rights movement in Northern Ireland' in Linda Connolly and Niamh Hourigan (eds.), *Social Movements and Ireland*. Manchester: Manchester University Press, pp. 106–23.

Stannard, John, 2010, 'Review: Lesaffer, *European Legal History*' in *Irish Jurist* 45 (1), pp. 254–5.

Stevenson, Colin, 1985, 'Review' in *Irish Jurist*, 20 (1), pp. 228–33.

Stevenson, Colin, 1984, 'Negotiated Planning' in *Irish Jurist*, 19 (1), pp. 15–39.

Stirk, P., 2002, 'Hugo Preuss, German political thought and the Weimar constitution' in *History of Political Thought*, 23 (3), pp. 497–516.

Stone, Alex, 2010, 'The European Court of Justice and the judicialization of EU governance' in *Living Reviews in European Governance*, 5 (2), p. 5.

Stradling, R. A., 1996, 'Battleground of Reputations: Ireland and the Spanish Civil War' in Paul Preston and Ann MacKenzie (eds.), *The Republic Besieged: Civil War in Spain 1936–39*, Edinburgh: Edinburgh University Press, pp. 107–34.

Sunstein, Cass, 2005, 'Why does the American Constitution lack Social and Economic Guarantees?' in *Syracuse Law Review*, 56 (1), pp. 1–25.

Sunstein, Cass, 1993, 'Against Positive Rights' in *East European Constitutional Review*, 2 (1), ff. 35.

Tierney, Michael, 1949, 'The Law and the Universities: Response' in *Studies*, 38 (151), pp. 257–74.

Tzouvala, Nina, 2015, 'Human Rights and Social Movements: the Right2Water case'. Available at: http://humanrights.ie/economic-rights/human-rights-and-social-movements-the-right2water-case/.

Unger, Roberto, 1996, 'Legal Analysis as Institutional Imagination' in *Modern Law Review*, 59 (1), pp. 1–23.

von Beyme, Klaus, 2003, 'Constitutional Engineering in Central and Eastern Europe' in Stephen Whyte, Judy Batt, and Paul Lewis (eds.), *Developments in Central and East European Politics*. Durham: Duke University Press.

von Prondzynski, Ferdinand, 1980, 'The Problem of the Labour Injunction' in *Irish Jurist*, 16 (2), pp. 228–40.

Wallerstein, Immanuel, 2015, 'The Neo-Zapatistas: Twenty Years After'. Available at: http://iwallerstein.com/neozapatistas-twenty-years/.

Wallerstein, Immanuel, 2014, 'Anti-systemic Movements, yesterday and today' in *Journal of World-Systems Research*, 20 (2), pp. 158–72, p. 159.

Wallerstein, Immanuel, 2011, 'Structural Crisis in the World-System: Where Do We Go from Here?' in *Monthly Review*, 62 (10), pp. 1–7.

Wallerstein, Immanuel, 2010, 'Structural Crises' in *New Left Review*, 62 (2), pp. 133–42.

Wallerstein, Immanuel, 1989, 'The French Revolution as a World-Historical Event' in *Social Research*, 56 (1), pp. 33–52.

Walker, Neil, 'The Shifting Foundations of the European Union Constitution' 2013, in Denis Galligan and Mila Versteeg (eds.), *Social and Political Foundations of Constitutions*. Cambridge: Cambridge University Press, pp. 637–60.

Walsh, Judy, 2009, 'Equality, the Legal System and Employment Law' in John Baker, Kathleen Lynch, Sara Cantillon and Judy Walsh, *Equality: From Theory to Action*. London: Palgrave, pp. 118–39.

White, Laurence, 2005, 'Peadar O'Donnell, 'Real Republicanism' and the Bell' in *Culture in the Republic*, Dublin: Ireland Institute, pp. 80–99.

Whyte, 2014, 'The Efficacy of Public Interest Litigation in Ireland' in Maluwa, Tiyanjana (ed.), *Law, Politics and Human Rights: Essays in Memory of Kader Asmal*. Leiden: Brill, pp. 252–86.

Whyte, Gerry, 1990–2, 'Review' in *Irish Jurist*, 25–7 (1), pp. 69–82.

Whyte, Gerry, 1981, 'Industrial Relations and the Irish Constitution' in *Irish Jurist*, 16 (1), pp. 35–77.

Wilkinson, Brian, 1989, 'Workers, Constitutions and the Irish Judiciary: A Jurisprudence of Labour Liberty?' in *Irish Jurist*, 24 (2), pp. 198–226.

Young, Katharine and Julieta Lemaitre, 2013, 'The Comparative Fortunes of the Right to Health: Two Tales of Justiciability in Colombia and South Africa' in *Harvard Human Rights Journal*, Jan., pp. 179–216.

**Books**

Allen, Kieran, 2009, *Ireland's Economic Crash: A Radical Agenda for Change*. Dublin: Liffey Press.

Allen, Kieran, 1997, *Fianna Fáil and Irish Labour: 1926 to the Present*. London: Pluto Press.

Allen, Robert, 2004, *No Global: The People of Ireland Versus the Multinationals*. London: Pluto Press.

Anderson, Benedict, 1991, *Imagined Communities*. London: Verso.

Arnold, Bruce, 2009, *Irish Gulag: How the State Betrayed its Innocent Children*. Dublin: Gill and MacMillan.

Arrighi, Giovanni, 1994, *The Long Twentieth Century*. London: Verso.
Bacik, Ivana, Cathryn Costello, and Eileen Drew, 2003, *Gender inJustice: Feminising the Legal Professions*. Dublin: TCD Law School.
Baker, John, Kathleen Lynch, Sara Cantillon, and Judy Walsh, 2009, *Equality: From Theory to Action*. London: Palgrave.
Baker, John, Kathleen Lynch, and Maureen Lyons, 2009, *Affective Equality: Love, Care and Injustice*. London: Palgrave.
Ball, F. E., 1921, *The Judges in Ireland, 1221–1921, Vol. 2*, London: John Murray.
Bell, Daniel. 1976. *The Cultural Contradictions of Capitalism*. London: Heinemann.
Barrington, Ruth, 1987, *Health, Medicine, and Politics in Ireland 1900–1970*. Dublin: Institute of Public Administration.
Bartholomew, Paul, 1971, *The Irish Judiciary*. Dublin: The Institute of Public Affairs.
Beard, Charles, 1921 [1913], *An Economic Interpretation of the Constitution of the United States*. New York: Macmillan.
Becker, Karl, 1936, *The Heavenly City of the Eighteenth-Century Philosophers*. New Haven: Yale University Press.
Bellamy, Richard, 2007, *Political Constitutionalism: A Republican Defence of the Constitutionality of Democracy*. Cambridge: Cambridge University Press.
Berger, John, 2008 [1972], *Ways of Seeing*. London: Penguin.
Berger, Peter, 1969, *The Sacred Canopy: Elements of a Sociological Theory of Religion*. London: Doubleday.
Berlin, Isaiah, 1958, *Two Concepts of Liberty*. Oxford: Clarendon Press.
Blaug, Ricardo and David Schwarzmantel (eds.), 2004, *Democracy: A Reader*. New York: Columbia University Press.
Bookchin, Murray, 2015, *The Next Revolution*. London: Verso.
Bookchin, Murray, 2005, *The Ecology of Freedom*. Edinburgh: AK Press.
Bookchin, Murray, 2005, *The Third Revolution: Popular Movements in the Revolutionary Era*. New York: Continuum.
Bookchin, Murray, 1997, *The Spanish Anarchists: The Heroic Years, 1868–1936*. New York: Free Life Editions.
Bourdieu, Pierre, 1990, *In Other Words: Essays toward a Reflective Sociology*. Stanford: Stanford University Press.
Brown, Terence, 2004, *Ireland: A Social and Cultural History, 1922–2002*. London: Harper Perennial, 2004.
Bryan, Dick and Mike Rafferty, 2006, *Capitalism with Derivatives: A Political Economy of Financial Derivatives, Capital, and Class*. Basingstoke: Palgrave.
Buckley, Sarah-Anne, 2013, *The Cruelty Man: Child Welfare, the NSPCC and the State in Ireland, 1889–1956*. Manchester: Manchester University Press.
Bush, Barbara, 2014, *Imperialism and Postcolonialism*. New York: Routledge.
Byrne, Elaine, 2012, *Political Corruption in Ireland, 1922–2010: A Crooked Harp?* Manchester: Manchester University Press.

Byrne, Raymond and J. Paul McCutcheon, 2002, *The Irish Legal System*. Dublin: Butterworth.

Cahill, Edward, 1932, *The Framework of a Christian State*. Dublin: Gill and Son.

Caramani, Daniele (ed.), 2011, *Comparative Politics*. Oxford: Oxford University Press.

Carver, Terrell (ed.), 1996, *Marx's Later Political Writings*. Cambridge: Cambridge University Press.

Campagna, Federico and Emanuele Campiglio, 2012, *What We Are Fighting For: A Radical Collective Manifesto*. London: Pluto.

Campbell, Colm, 1994, *Emergency Law in Ireland, 1918–1925*. Oxford: Clarendon Press.

Campbell, Tom, K. D. Ewing, and Adam Tomkins (eds.), 2011, *The Legal Protection of Human Rights: Sceptical Essays*. Oxford: Oxford University Press.

Campbell, Tom, 2006, *Rights: A Critical Introduction*. London: Routledge.

Campbell, Tom, 1983, *The Left and Rights: A Conceptual Analysis of the Idea of Socialist Rights*. London: Routledge and Kegan Paul.

Casanova, Julián, 2010, *The Spanish Republic and Civil War*. Cambridge: Cambridge University Press.

Chatterjee, Partha, 1994, *The Nation and its Fragments: Colonial and Postcolonial Histories*. Princeton: Princeton University Press.

Chubb, B., 1991, *The Politics of the Irish Constitution*. Dublin: Institute of Public Administration.

Chubb, B., 1978, *The Constitution and Constitutional Change in Ireland*. Dublin: Institute of Public Administration.

Clarke, Matthew, 2008, *Language Teacher Identities: Co-constructing Discourse and Community*. Toronto: *Multilingual Matters*.

Coakley, John and Michael Gallagher, 2010, *Politics in the Republic of Ireland*. London: PSAI Press/Routledge.

Constitution Review Group, 1996, *Report of the Constitution Review Group*. Dublin: Official Publications.

Coogan, Tim Pat, 2002, *The IRA*. Palgrave: New York.

Cooney, John, 2003, *John Charles McQuaid: Ruler of Catholic Ireland*. Dublin: O'Brien Press.

Costello, Peter, 1989, *Clongowes Wood: The History of Clongowes Wood College*. Dublin: Gill and Macmillan.

Cousins, Mel, 2005, *Explaining the Irish Welfare State: An Historical, Comparative, and Political Analysis*. New York: Edwin Mellen Press.

Cousins, M., 2003, *The Birth of Social Welfare in Ireland, 1922–1952*. Dublin: Four Courts Press.

Cronin, Mike, 1997, *The Blueshirts and Irish Politics*. Dublin: Four Courts Press.

Crotty, Raymond, 1988, *A Radical's Response*. Dublin: Poolbeg.

Crotty, Raymond, 1986, *Ireland in Crisis: A study in capitalist colonial underdevelopment*. Dingle: Brandon Press.

Cullen, L. M., 1987, *An Economic History of Ireland since 1660*. London: Batsford.

Curtin, Nancy, 1994, *The United Irishmen: Popular Politics in Ulster and Dublin, 1791–1798*. Oxford: Oxford University Press.

Dahl, Robert, 1956, *Preface to Democratic Theory*. Chicago: University of Chicago Press.

Daly, Mary E., 1997, *The Buffer State: The Historical Roots of the Department of the Environment*. Dublin: Institute of Public Administration.

Daly, Mary E., 1992, *Industrial Development and Irish National Identity, 1922–1939*. New York: Syracuse University Press.

Daly, Mary E., 1981, *Social and Economic History of Ireland since 1800*. Dublin: Educational Company.

Davis, Mike, 2000, *Late Victorian Holocausts: El Nino Famines and the Making of the Third World*. London: Verso.

de Blacam, Aodh, 1921, *What Sinn Féin Stands For*. Dublin: Sinn Féin.

de Sousa Santos, Boaventura and César A. Rodríguez-Garavito, 2005, *Law and Globalization from Below: Towards a Cosmopolitan Legality*. Cambridge: Cambridge Studies in Law and Society.

Delany, V. T. H., 1975, *The Administration of Justice in Ireland*. Dublin: Institute of Public Administration.

Dicey, Alfred Venn, 2005 [1885], *An Introduction to the Study of the Law of the Constitution*. London: Elibron.

Dirlik, Arif, 1993, *Anarchism in the Chinese Revolution*. Berkeley: University of California Press.

Dixon, R. (ed.), 1972, *Ireland and the Irish Question: A Collection of Writings by Karl Marx and Frederick Engels*. New York: International.

Doolan, Brian, 1988, *Constitutional Law and Constitutional Rights in Ireland*. Dublin: Gill and MacMillan.

Dooley, Terence, 2004, *The Land for the People: The Land Question in Independent Ireland*. Dublin: University College Dublin Press.

Douglas, James, (J. A. Gaughan, ed.), 1998, *Memoirs of Senator James G. Douglas (1887–1954)*. Dublin: University College Dublin Press.

Doyle, Evelyn, 2002, *Evelyn: A True Story*. London: Orion.

Duchacek, I., 1973, *Power Maps: The Comparative Politics of Constitutions*. California: University of California Press.

Dubois, Louis, 1908, *L'Irlande Contemporaine*. Dublin: Maunsel.

Duffy, Peter, 2007, *The Killing of Major Denis Mahon*. London: Harper.

Duménil, Gérard and Dominque Lévy, 2010, *The Crisis of Neoliberalism*. Cambridge: Harvard University Press.

Dunphy, Richard, 1995, *The Making of Fianna Fáil Power in Ireland: 1923–1948*. Oxford: Clarendon Press.

Earner-Byrne, Lindsey, 2007, *Mother and Child: Maternity and Child Welfare in Ireland, 1920s–1960s*. Manchester: Manchester University Press.

Eide, Asborn, 2001, *Economic, Social, and Cultural rights: A Textbook*. London: M. Nijhoff.

Elkins, Zachary, Tom Ginsburg, and James Melton, 2009, *The Endurance of National Constitutions*. Cambridge: Cambridge University Press.

Epp, Charles, 1998, *The Rights Revolution: Lawyers, Activists, and Supreme Courts in Comparative Perspective*. Chicago: University of Chicago Press.

Fabre, Cecil, 2000, *Social Rights under the Constitution: government and the decent life*. Oxford: Oxford University Press.

Fanon, Franz, 2001, *The Wretched of the Earth*. London: Penguin.

Farrell, Brian (ed.), 1988, *De Valera's Constitution and Ours*. Dublin: Gill and Macmillan.

Fairclough, Norman, 2003, *Analysing Discourse: Textual Analysis for Social Research*. London: Routledge.

Ferguson, Kenneth, 2005, *King's Inns Barristers, 1868–2004*. Dublin: Honorable Society of King's Inns in association with the Irish Legal History Society.

Fanning, Bryan, 2008, *The Quest for Modern Ireland: The Battle of Ideas, 1912–86*. Dublin: Irish Academic Press.

Fanning, Ronan, 1978, *The Irish Department of Finance, 1922–58*. Dublin: Institute of Public Administration.

Ferriter, Diarmaid, 2005, *The Transformation of Ireland: 1900–2000*. London: Profile Books.

Fine, Robert, 1985, *Democracy and the Rule of Law*. London: Pluto.

Finnegan, Frances, 2004, *Do Penance or Perish: Magdalene Asylums in Ireland*. Oxford: Oxford University Press.

Fisher, Mark, 2009, *Capitalist Realism: Is There no Alternative?* London: Zero Books.

Flassbeck, Heiner, and Costas Lapavitsas, 2015, *Against the Troika: Crisis and Austerity in the Eurozone*. London: Verso.

Foster, Roy, 1988, *Modern Ireland: 1600–1972*. London: Penguin.

France, Royal Wilbur, 1957, *My Native Grounds*, New York: Cameron.

Fredman, Sandra, 2008, *Human Rights Transformed? Positive Rights and Positive Duties*. Oxford: Oxford University Press.

Freeland, Chrystia, 2013, *Plutocrats: The Rise of the New Global Super-rich*. London: Penguin.

Frevert, Ute, 1989, *Women in German History: From Bourgeois Emancipation to Sexual Liberation*. New York: St. Martin's Press.

Fukuyama, Francis, 1992, *The End of History and the Last Man*. London: Free Press.

Galeano, Eduardo, 1997, *Open Veins of Latin America*. New York: Monthly Review Press.

Galligan, Denis and Mila Versteeg, 2013, *Social and Political Foundations of Constitutions*. Cambridge: Cambridge University Press.

Garvin, Tom, 2009, *Judging Lemass*. Dublin: Royal Irish Academy.
Garvin, Tom, 2004, *Preventing the Future: Why Was Ireland so Poor for so Long?* Dublin: Gill and Macmillan.
Garvin, Tom, 1996, *1922: The Birth of Irish Democracy*. Dublin: Gill and Macmillan.
Gauri, Varun and Daniel Brinks (eds.), 2010, *Courting Social Justice: Judicial Enforcement of Social and Economic Rights in the Developing World*. Cambridge: Cambridge University Press.
Gellner, Ernest, 1983, *Nations and Nationalism*. Ithaca: Cornell University Press.
George, Henry, 2009 [1881], *Progress and Poverty*. Cambridge: Cambridge University Press.
Ghandhi, P. R., 2000, *Blackstone's International Human Rights Documents*. London: Blackstone.
Ginsborg, Paul G., 2005, *The Politics of Everyday Life: Making Choices, Changing Lives*. Cambridge: Yale University Press.
Ginsburg, Tom (ed.), 2012, *Comparative Constitutional Design*. Cambridge: Cambridge University Press.
Ginsburg, Tom, 2003, *Judicial Review in New Democracies: Constitutional Courts in Asian Cases*. Cambridge: Cambridge University Press.
Girvin, Brian, 2002, *From Union to Union: Nationalism, Democracy and Religion in Ireland*. Dublin: Gill and Macmillan.
Graeber, David, 2013, *The Democracy Project: A History, a Crisis, a Movement*. London: Allen Lane.
Gramsci, Antonio [Quentin Hoare and Geoffrey Smith (eds.)], 1971, *Selections from the Prison Notebooks of Antonio Gramsci*. London: Lawrence and Wishart.
Habermas, Jurgen, 1970. *Towards a Rational Society*. Boston: Beacon Press.
Hall, F. G., 1949, *History of the Bank of Ireland*. Dublin: Hodges Figgis.
Hancock, W. N., 1850, *Impediments to the Prosperity of Ireland*. London: Simms and McIntyre.
Hanley, Brian, and Scott Millar, 2010, *The Lost Revolution: The Story of the Official IRA and the Workers' Party*. Dublin: Penguin.
Hart. H. L. A., 1997, *The Concept of Law*. Oxford: Oxford University Press.
Harkness, D. W., 1969, *The Restless Dominion: The Irish Free State and the British Commonwealth of Nations, 1921–1931*. London: Macmillan.
Harvey, David, 2012, *Rebel Cities*. London: Verso.
Harvey, David, 2010, *The Enigma of Capital*. London: Profile.
Harvey, David, 2007, *A Brief History of Neoliberalism*. Oxford: Oxford University Press.
Harvey, David, 1989, *The Conditions of Postmodernity*. Oxford: Blackwell.
Haywood, William Dudley, 1929, *The Autobiography of Big Bill Haywood*. New York: International Publishers.

Headlam-Morley, Agnes, 1929, *The New Democratic Constitutions of Europe*. London: Oxford University Press.

Healy, Maurice, 1939, *The Old Munster Circuit*. London: M. Joseph Ltd.

Held, David (ed.), 1991, *Political Theory Today*. Stanford: Stanford University Press.

Hessel, Stéphane, 2011, *Time for Outrage: Indignez-vous!* New York: Hachette.

Hickey, D. J. and J. E. Doherty, 2003, *A New Dictionary of Irish History*. Dublin: Gill and MacMillan.

Hickey, Éanna, 1999, *Irish Law and Lawyers in Modern Folk Tradition*. Dublin: Four Courts.

Hirschl, Ran, 2007, *Towards Juristocracy: The Origins and Consequences of the New Constitutionalism*. Cambridge: Harvard University Press.

Hobsbaum, Eric, 2011, *How to Change the World: Reflections on Marx and Marxism*. London: Brown.

Hobsbawm, Eric, 1994, *Age of Extremes: The Short Twentieth Century, 1914–1991*. London: Michael Joseph.

Hobsbawm, Eric, 1992, *Nations and Nationalism since 1780: Programme, Myth, Reality*. Cambridge: Cambridge University Press.

Hogan, Daire, 1986, *The Legal Profession in Ireland: 1789–1922*. Dublin: Law Society.

Hogan, Gerard, 2012, *The Origins of the Irish Constitution: 1928–41*. Dublin: RIA.

Holloway, John, 2010, *Crack Capitalism*. London: Pluto.

Hughes, Owen, 2012, *Public Management and Administration*. London: Palgrave.

Hunt, Lynn, 2007, *Inventing Human Rights: A History*. London: Norton.

INCITE! Women of Colour against Violence, 2009, *The Revolution Will Not Be Funded*. Cambridge, MA: South End Press.

Inglis, Tom, 1998, *Moral monopoly: The Rise and Fall of the Catholic Church in Modern Ireland*. Dublin: University College Dublin Press.

Irish Commission for Justice and Peace (ICJP), 1998, *Re-righting the Constitution: The Case for New Social and Economic Rights*. Dublin: Irish Commission for Justice and Peace.

Irish Human Rights Commission (IHRC), 2005, *Discussion Document on Social and Economic Rights*. Dublin: IHRC.

Jacob, Herbert, Erhard Blankenburg, Herbert M. Kritzer, Doris Marie Provine, and Joseph Sanders, 1996, *Courts, Law and Politics in Comparative Perspective*. London: Yale University Press.

Jameson, Fredric, 1981, *The Political Unconscious: Narrative as a Socially Symbolic Act*. Ithaca: Cornell University Press.

Jordan, Don and Michael Walsh, 2008, *White Cargo: The Forgotten History of Britain's White Slaves in America*. New York: NYU Press.

Joyce, Paul, 2003, *An End Based on Means*. Dublin: FLAC.

Judt, Tony, 2011, *Ill Fares the Land: A Treatise on our Present Discontents*. London: Allen Lane.

Kelly, John, 2003 (4th edition), Gerard Hogan and Gerry Whyte (eds.), *J. M. Kelly: The Irish Constitution*. Dublin: LexisNexis Butterworths.

Kelly, John, 1967 (2nd edition), *Fundamental Rights in the Irish Law and Constitution*. Dublin: Allen Figgis and Co.

Keogh, Dermot and Andrew McCarthy, 2009, *The Making of the Irish Constitution 1937*. Cork: Mercier Press.

Kelsen, Hans, 1967, *Pure Theory of Law*. Berkeley: University of California Press.

Kennedy, Duncan, 1998, *A Critique of Adjudication: fin de síecle*. Harvard: Havard University Press.

Kickham, Charles, 1988 [1870], *Knocknagow: Or the Homes of Tipperary*. Dublin: Anna Livia Press.

Kilmurray, Evanne, 1988, *Fight, Starve or Emigrate: A History of the Unemployed Associations in the 1950s*. Dublin: Larkin Unemployed Centre.

Kingston, Anna, 2007, *Mothering Special Needs*. London: Kingsley Publishers.

Kissane, Bill, 2011, *New Beginnings: Constitutionalism and Democracy in Modern Ireland*. Dublin: University College Dublin Press.

Kohn, Leo, 1932, *The Constitution of the Irish Free State*. London: G. Allen and Unwin Ltd.

Korpi, Walter, 1992, *Welfare State Development in Europe since 1930: Ireland in Comparative Perspective*. Dublin: Economic and Social Research Institute.

Korpi, Walter, 1990, *The Democratic Class Struggle*. London: Routledge.

Kostick, Conor, 2009, *Revolution in Ireland: Popular Militancy, 1917–1923*. Cork: Cork University Press.

Kotsonouris, Mary, 1994, *Retreat from Revolution: The Dáil Courts, 1920–24*, Dublin: Irish Academic Press.

Krishnaswamy, Sudhir, 2009, *Democracy and Constitutionalism in India: A Study of the Basic Structure Doctrine*. New Delhi: Oxford University Press.

Laffan, Michael, 1999, *The Resurrection of Ireland: the Sinn Féin party, 1916–1923*. Cambridge: Cambridge University Press.

Laird, Heather, 2005, *Subversive Law in Ireland, 1879–1920: From 'unwritten law' to the Dáil courts*. Dublin: Four Courts Press.

Langford, M., B. Cousins, J. Dugard, and T. Madlingozi (eds.), 2013, *Socio-economic Rights in South Africa: Symbol or Substance?* Cambridge: Cambridge University Press.

Langford, Malcolm, 2009, *Social Rights Jurisprudence: Emerging Trends in International and Comparative Law*. Cambridge: Cambridge University Press.

Lassalle, Ferdinand, 1976 [1862]. *What Is a Constitution?* Barcelona: Editorial Ariel.

Lee, J. J., 1989, *Ireland 1912–1985: Politics and Society*. Cambridge: Cambridge University Press.

Lerner, Hanna, 2011, *Making Constitutions in Deeply Divided Societies*. Cambridge: Cambridge University Press.
Lipset, Seymour Martin, 1960, *Political Man*. London: Heinemann.
Luebbert, Gregory, 1991, *Liberalism, Fascism, or Social Democracy*. Oxford: Oxford University Press.
Lukes, Stephen, 1974, *Power: A Radical View*. London: Macmillan.
Lyons, F. S. L., 1973, *Ireland since the Famine*. Collins: Glasgow.
MacPherson, Stewart and James Midgley, 1987, *Comparative Social Policy and the Third World*. Brighton: Wheatsheaf.
McBride, Lawrence, 1991, *The Greening of Dublin Castle*. Washington, DC: Catholic University of America Press.
McCabe, Conor, 2011, *Sins of the Father: Tracing the decisions that shaped the Irish economy*. Dublin: History Press.
McDonough, Terrence (ed.), 2005, *Was Ireland a Colony? Economics, Politics and Culture in Nineteenth-Century Ireland*. Dublin: Irish Academic Press.
McGee, Owen, 2005, *The IRB: The Irish Republican Brotherhood from The Land League to Sinn Féin*. Dublin: Four Courts Press.
McGowan, Padraig, 1990, *Money and Banking in Ireland*. Dublin: Institute of Public Administration.
McGrath, Joe, 2015, *Corporate and White-Collar Crime in Ireland*. Manchester: Manchester University Press.
McGuire, J., and Quinn. J., 2009, *The Dictionary of Irish Biography*. Cambridge: Cambridge University Press.
McKay, David, 2009, *American Politics and Society*. Oxford: Wiley-Blackwell.
Maillot, Agnès, 2005, *New Sinn Féin: Irish Republicanism in the Twenty-first Century*. London: Routledge.
Mair, Peter, 2013, *Ruling the Void: The Hollowing of Western Democracy*. London: Verso.
Mannion, Padraig (ed.), 2013, *Lock-Out Centenary*. Dublin: Dun Laoghaire Commemorative Committee.
Marshall, Thomas, 1950, *Citizenship and Social Class*. Cambridge: Cambridge University Press.
Marx, Karl, 2003 [1887], *Capital I: A Critique of Political Economy*, London: Lawrence and Wishart.
Marx, Karl, 1992, *The German Ideology, including Theses on Feuerbach*. New York: Prometheus Books.
Mason, Paul, 2015, *Postcapitalism*. London: Allen Lane.
Mason, Paul, 2013, *Why It's Still Kicking Off Everywhere*. London: Verso.
Merrigan, Matt, 1989, *Eagle or Cuckoo? The Story of the ATGWU in Ireland*. Dublin: Matmer.
Miller, Robert, Jacinta Ruru, Larissa Behrendt, and Tracey Lindberg, 2010, *Discovering Indigenous Lands: The Doctrine of Discovery in the English Colonies*. Oxford: Oxford University Press.

Mills, C. Wright, 1959, *The Sociological Imagination*. New York: Oxford University Press.

Moloney, John, 1991, *The Worker Question: A New Historical Perspective on 'Rerum Novarum'*. Dublin: Gill and MacMillan.

Morgan, David, 1996, *The Separation of Powers in the Irish Constitution*. Dublin: Round Hall Press.

Murray, Patrick, 2000, *Oracles of God: the Roman Catholic Church and Irish politics, 1922–37*. Dublin: University College Dublin Press.

Negri, Antonio, 2003, *Time for Revolution*. London: Continuum.

Nevin, Donal (ed.), 2011, *Writings of James Connolly: Collected Works*. Dublin: SIPTU.

Neumann, Franz, 1966 [1942], *Behemoth: The Structure and practice of national socialism*. New York: Oxford University Press.

Ó Broin, Deiric and Peadar Kirby (eds.), 2009, *Power, Dissent and Democracy: Civil Society and the State in Ireland*. Dublin: A&A Farmer.

O'Casey, Seán, 1919, *The Story of the Irish Citizen Army: 1913–16*. Dublin: Maunsel.

Ó Comhraí, Cormac, 2013, *Revolution in Connacht*. Cork: Mercier Press.

O'Connor, Emmet, 2011, *A Labour History of Ireland, 1824–2000*. Dublin: University College Dublin Press.

O'Connor, Frank, 1953, *The Stories of Frank O'Connor*. London: Hamish.

O'Connor, Ulick, 2001, *The Ulick O'Connor Diaries: 1970–81*. London: John Murray.

O'Day, Alan, 1998, *Irish Home Rule, 1867–1921*. Manchester: Manchester University Press.

O'Dell, Eoin, 2000, *Leading Cases of the Twentieth Century*. Dublin: Round Hall Sweet & Maxwell.

O'Donnell, Peadar, 2001 [1963], *There Will Be Another Day*. Cork: Cork University Press.

Ó Gráda, Cormac, 1997, *A Rocky Road: The Irish Economy Since the 1920s*. Manchester: Manchester University Press.

O'Halpin, Eunan, 1999, *Defending Ireland: The Irish State and Its Enemies Since 1922*. Oxford: Oxford University Press.

O'Hearn, Denis, 2001, *The Atlantic Economy: Britain, the US and Ireland*. Manchester: Manchester University Press.

O'Malley, Ernie, 2008 [1936], *On Another Man's Wound*. Dublin: Anvil Books.

O'Malley, Joseph (ed.), 1994, *Marx's Early Political Writings*. Cambridge: Cambridge University Press.

O'Morain, Padraig, 2003, *Access to Justice For All: The History of the Free Legal Advice Centres, 1969–1973*. Dublin: FLAC/Printwell.

O'Rahilly, Alfred, 1937, *Thoughts on the Constitution*. Dublin: Browne and Nolan.

O'Sullivan, Eoin, and Ian O'Donnell, 2012, *Coercive Confinement in Ireland: Patients, Prisoners and Penitents*. Manchester: Manchester University Press.

O'Toole, Fintan, 2010, *Ship of Fools: How Stupidity and Corruption Sank the Celtic Tiger*. London: Faber and Faber.

Oakeshott, Michael, 1950, *The Social and Political Doctrines of Contemporary Europe*. New York: Cambridge University Press.

Ollman, Bertell, 2003, *Dance of the Dialectic: Steps in Marx's Method*. Champaign, IL: University of Illinois Press.

Osborne, Peter, 2005, *How to Read* Marx. London: Granta Books.

Pawlisch, Hans S., 1985, *Sir John Davies and the Conquest of Ireland: A Study in Legal Imperialism*. Cambridge: Cambridge University Press.

Pomfret, John, 1969, *The Struggle for Land in Ireland, 1800–1923*. New York: Russell & Russell.

Prager, Jeffrey, 1986, *Building Democracy in Ireland*. Cambridge: Cambridge University Press.

Puirseíl, Niamh, 2007, *The Irish Labour Party, 1922–73*. Dublin: University College Dublin Press.

Rafferty, Mary and Eoin O'Sullivan, 2000, *Suffer the Little Children: The Inside Story of Ireland's Industrial Schools*. Dublin: New Island Books.

Rajagopal, Balakrishnan, 2003, *International Law from Below: Development, Social Movements and Third World Resistance*. Cambridge: Cambridge University Press.

Robertson, Priscilla, 1952, *Revolutions of 1848*. Princeton: Princeton University Press.

Rumpf, Erhard and A. C. Hepburn, 1977, *Nationalism and Socialism in Twentieth-Century Ireland*. New York: Barnes and Noble.

Sartori, Giovanni, 1994, *Comparative Constitutional Engineering: An Inquiry into Structures, Incentives and Outcomes*. Basingstoke: Macmillan.

Seaman, L. C. B., 1964, *From Vienna to Versailles*. London: Routledge.

Sen, Amartya, 1999, *Development as Freedom*. New York: Random House.

Sciarra, Silvana, 2001, *Labour Law in the Courts: National Judges and the European Court of Justice*. Oxford: Hart.

Shue, Henry, 1996, *Basic Rights: Subsistence, Affluence, and US Foreign Policy*. Princeton: Princeton University Press.

Steiner, Henry, Philip Alston, and Ryan Goodman (eds.), 2008, *International Human Rights in Context*. Oxford: Oxford University Press.

Stoneybatter and Smithfield People's History Project (SSPHP), 2014, *The Irish Citizen Army in Stoneybatter, Smithfield and the Markets*. Dublin: SSPHP.

Sturgess, Garry and Philip Chubb, 1988, *Judging the World: Law and Politics in the World's Leading Courts*. London: Butterworths.

Sunstein, Cass, 2004, *The Second Bill of Rights*. New York: Basic.

Synge, John M., 1979 [1907], *The Aran Islands*. London: Penguin.

TASC, 2014, *Budget 2014: Choosing an Equitable Route to Recovery*. Dublin: TASC.

TASC, 2010, *The Solidarity Factor: Public Responses to Economic Inequality in Ireland*. Dublin: TASC.

Thompson, E. P., 1981, *Whigs and Hunters: The Origin of the Black Act*. London: Breviary.

Thornhill, Chris, 2013, *A Sociology of Constitutions*. Cambridge: Cambridge University Press.

Tóibín, Colm, 1992, *The Heather Blazing*. London: Picador.

Trotsky, Leon, 1937, *The Revolution Betrayed*, New York: Doubleday & Doren Company.

Turner, Rachel, 2008, *Neo-Liberal Ideology: History, Concepts and Policies*. Edinburgh: Edinburgh University Press.

Tushnet, Mark, 2009, *Weak Courts, Strong Rights: Judicial Review and Social Welfare Rights in Comparative Constitutional Law*, Princeton: Princeton University Press.

Wacquant, Loïc, 2005, *Pierre Bourdieu and Democratic Politics*. Cambridge: Polity.

Wallerstein, Immanuel, 2004, *World-Systems Analysis: An Introduction*. Durham, NC: Duke University Press.

Ward, Tanya, 2007, *Justice Matters: Independence, Accountability and the Irish Judiciary*. Dublin: Irish Council for Civil Liberties.

Williams, Michael, 2013, *Serving the People? The Need for Reform in the Irish Legal System*. Dublin: Fourt Courts Press.

Williams, Raymond, 1977, *Marxism and Literature*. London: Oxford University Press.

Whelehan, Niall, 2012, *The Dynamiters: Irish Nationalism and Political Violence in the Wider World*. Cambridge: Cambridge University Press.

Whyte, Gerry, 2002, *Social Inclusion and the Legal System: Public Interest Law in Ireland*. Dublin: Institute of Public Administration.

Wolf, Eric, 2010, *Europe and the People Without History*. Berkeley: University of California Press.

Young, Katharine, 2012, *Constituting Economic and Social Rights*. Oxford: Oxford University Press.

Zibechi, Raúl, 2012, *Territories in Resistance: A Cartography of Latin American Social Movements*. Edinburgh: AK Press.

# INDEX


abortion, 121, 151, 171, 175, 179, 182, 183
Age of Revolutions, 25
agrarian Bolshevism, 73, 108
*Airey* v. *Ireland* (1979), 206
*Alexander* v. *Holmes County Board of Education* (1969), 170–1
Alexandra College, 281
Algeria, 164
Amalgamated Transport and General Workers Union, 234, 314, 315–16, 317
American Committee for Relief in Ireland, 72, 85
American Federation of Labour, 84
Amnesty Ireland, 193
*An Phoblacht* (newspaper), 124
Anglo-Irish Economic War (1932–8), 117, 119–20, 150
Anglo-Irish Treaty (1921), 80, 87, 93, 116
Anti H-Block campaign, 317
apartheid, 179
*Aran Islands, The* (Synge), 67
Arbitration Board, 139–40, 232
arbitration courts, 49, 66 *See also* courts
  in 1880s, 77–8
  creation of, 73
  replacement with Dáil Courts, 79–80
  restructuring of, 106–7
  in West of Ireland, 106–7
Archdale, Betty, 142
Argentina, 153
Army Comrades Association, 114, 127–8
Arrighi, G., 27
Artisan Dwelling Company, 79
Association of Scientific, Technical, and Management Staffs, 316–17
Astor family, 96–7
Athlone Manifesto, 125
*Attorney General* v. *Southern Industrial Trust and Simons* (1960), 212, 220–1
Australia, 164
Austria, 68, 113, 154
authoritarianism, 113

bailiffs, 67
balance of convenience test, 240
Ballinrobe, Co., 78
Ballymun Tenants' Association, 302
banking cartel, Irish, 52, 96, 116, 117, 118, 122, 126
Bar Council, 61, 202, 203, 207
Bar Library, 189
Bar of Ireland, 194
Barrington, Donal, 226, 283, 315
barristers, 59, 201–2
Bartholomew, Paul, 279, 280, 288
Bartley, Patrick, 131
Barton, Robert, 80
Beard, C., 17
Belton, Paddy, 129
Bennett, Louie, 147
Binchy, Daniel, 283
Binchy, William, 287
Birmingham, Willie, 321
Blacam, M. de, 266
*Blake* v. *Attorney General* (1982), 211, 214, 217–18, 222, 227, 276, 319, 320
Blueshirt Constitution, 114
Blueshirts, 127
Blythe, Ernest, 103
Bolivia, 11, 347
Bolshevik Revolution, 30, 68
boom-bust cycle of property speculation, 178
Bourdieu, P., 1–47
Boyle, Hilary, 307
Brady, James, 284, 285
Brady, Patrick, 306
Brazil, 52, 153
*Brennan* v. *Attorney General* (1984), 211, 214, 222–3, 227, 273
Bretton Woods system, end of, 171
British Empire, 28
British Free Trade, 29
Brown, Bernard, 305
*Brown* v. *Board of Education* (1954), 170–1
Browne, Michael, 120
Bunreacht na hÉireann (1937). *See* Irish Constitution (1937)
Burke, Edmund, 277
Butler, A., 266
Byrne, Isolda, 306

Byrne, Thomas, 234
Byrne, William, 128

Cahill, Edward, 112, 121, 131, 133, 136, 140, 333
Campaign for the Care of Deprived Children (CARE), 294, 309, 310
Canada
  constitutional review in, 164
  Imperial decline in, 116
  legal aid in, 204
  socio-economic rights constitutionalisation in, 341
  Westminster parliamentary sovereignty in, 174
Canavan, Joseph, 131
Cape Verde, 173
Capeletti, Mauro, 176
capitalism. *See also* cycle of accumulation
  end of Soviet Union and globalisation of, 172
  golden era of, 31, 297
  neoliberal, 5, 308
  Occupy movements and, 7
  socio-economic rights and crisis of, 345–53
  urban-industrial, 85
  world-system of. *See* world-system of historical capitalism
capitalist world-system. *See* historical capitalist world-system
capitalists. *See also* financier-grazier class
  in early 1900s, 53
  rights as free owners of private property, 22
capital-labour relations, 17, 68, 90–1, 107–8, 113, 118, 167–8, 178, 241, 333–4
Cardenas, Lazaro, 153
Carlton Hotel, 305
*Carta del Lavoro* (1927), 127, 152
Casey, James, 227, 240
Catholic Church
  charitable relief to strikers' children, 69
  condemnation of communists and republicans in 1930s, 128
  constitution-making and, 333–4
  Dublin Unemployed Association's protests and, 298
  feminist movement and, 108
  influence on Ireland's postwar social policy, 168
  Irish Constitution (1937) and, 35, 133–4, 150–1
  Irish Free State and, 120–1
  legitimation of Provisional Government and, 90–1
  opposing the Constitution in 1945–73, 297
  policing population's sexuality, 57
  private property rights and, 126–7
  right to education and, 135
  role in Irish popular culture, 37
  Spanish Civil War and, 129
  Spanish Constitution and, 154
  special position in Irish society, 169
  support for Anglo-Irish Treaty, 89
  welfare institutions and, 56–7, 100
  welfare provision and, 81, 122, 123
Catholic Emancipation movement, 37
Catholic Social Service Bureau, 297
Catholics
  IRA and, 126
  non-involvement with communists and republicans, 128
  petite bourgeoisie, 62
  Spanish Civil War and, 128
Catholic-social constitutionalism. *See also* social constitutionalism
  constitution-making and, 333–4
  doctrinal and institutional limits to, 97
  drafting Irish Constitution and, 148
  end of, 176–84
  family-welfare rights and, 247–8
*caudillos*, 153
*CDDA* v. *Attorney General* (1975), 214, 221–2
Central Dublin Development Association, 213, 216, 218, 220
Central Europe, 174
Central Office of the High Court, 197
Chamberlain, Austen, 101
Chiapas, 348, 350
Childers, Erskine, 73
Children First, 309
Children's Act (1908), 253, 310
Children's Court, 245, 248, 310
children's rights, 309–13, 333 *See also* human rights
China, 52, 172
Christian/farming calendar, 60
*Christus Rex*, 226, 287
Chubb, B., 38, 39
Circuit Court. *See also* courts
  jurisdictions of, 191–2
  limit in civil jurisdiction, 197
  salaries in, 199*t*
  structure of, 191–2
  types of cases in, 197
  volume of cases, 195, 196*t*
*Citizens United* v. *Federal Election Commission* (2010), 346
Civil Liability Act (1961), 216
civil society, 293–325, 341–2 *See also* social movements
  Catholic Emancipation movement, 37
  components of, 12

Dublin Housing Action Committee, 301–8
Dublin Unemployed Association, 297–301
opposing the Constitution in 1945–73, 297
overview, 293–7
Proclamation of Children's Rights' campaign (1976), 309–13
socio-economic provisions and, 142–51
Talbot workers' factory occupation and boycott, 313
Threshold/ALONE campaign for rent tribunals, 319–22
civil war (1922–3), 87–8
Clann na Poblachta, 169
Clann na Talmhan, 151
Clarke, Joseph, 306
classic constitutionalism, 27*t*, 26–7, 30, 132, 133 *See also* constitutionalism
classic liberalism, 328
closed shop agreements, 239–40
Coercion Acts, 66–7
Collins, Michael, 80, 88
Commercial Court, 201
Commission of Inquiry (1925), 264
Commission on Banking, Currency, and Credit (1934–8), 122
Commonwealth of Nations, 80
communism
anti-communism, 127–8
de Valera's opposition to, 148–9
Fianna Fáil and, 120
neutralising, 140, 232
Spanish Civil War and, 129
Communist Party of Ireland, 125, 126, 308
Competition Authority (2005), 203
Concerned Parents against Drugs movement in Dublin, 203
Congested Districts Board, 56
Congress of Irish Unions, 300
Connolly, James, 68, 76, 125
Connolly Youth, 302
Conspiracy and Protection of Property Act (1875), 231
Constitution and Governmental Programme for the Republic of Ireland (1933), 114, 126
Constitution for Europe (2004), 174
Constitution of Ireland (1937). *See* Irish Constitution (1937)
Constitution of Ireland Bill (1937), enactment of, 131
Constitution of Saor Éire (1931), 114, 125
Constitution of the Army Comrades Association (1932), 127–8
Constitution of the Irish Citizen Army, 48, 50
ownership of Ireland in, 74, 106
socio-economic rights in, 332
Constitution of the Irish Free State (Saorstát Éireann) Act 1922, 91
Constitution of the Society of United Irishmen (1797), 54
Constitution Review Group, 266, 335
Constitutional Convention, 2
constitutional courts, 164, 174–5
constitutional laws, 15–16
constitutional nationalists, 55–6
constitutional review, 164
constitutionalism, 25
classic, 27*t*, 26–7, 30, 132, 133
free market and, 32
in Irish Free State, 87–91
nation-state building and, 29
neoformal, 27*t*, 26–7, 31
neoliberal, 27*t*, 32, 173
social, 30, 95–7
social antagonism and, 28
social origins of, 87–91, 115–24
state, 25–7
constitution-making
Catholic corporatism in, 333–4
Irish Constitution (1937), 132*t*, 112–59
Irish Free State Constitution, 92*t*, 84–111
Mexican Constitution, 106
seven waves of, 25–7
constitutions. *See also* Irish Constitution (1937); Irish Free State Constitution (1922)
earliest written, 25
'from below', 48–67, 83
in historical capitalist world system, 25–33
modern, 25–7
proletarian, 24
socio-economic rights and, 25–33
contraception, 121
Convention on the Irish Constitution, 327
coolie class of labourers, 56
Córas Iompair Éireann (CIE), 233, 236
Cosgrave, W. T., 103, 145
Costello, Declan, 287, 315
Council for Civil Liberties, 205
Court of Appeal, 340
courts, 187–208
access to justice, 204–7
appointees, requirements for, 190–1
arbitration, 49, 66
in 1880s, 77–8
creation of, 73
replacement with Dáil Courts, 79–80
restructuring of, 106–7
case management, 201
constitutional rights cases, 195
costs of legal services and, 202–3
Dáil Courts, 79–80
illegal middleman practices, 193

courts (*cont.*)
Irish 'rights revolution' and, 204–7
judicial review, 201
as legal business, 194–200
number of judges in, 196*t*
party, 76
personnel, structure, and activity, 189–94
popular, 76
'repeat players' and 'one-shotters', 203
role in constitutional development, 183
as sites of business and justice, 187–208
contradictions, 200–4
implications of, 188
Courts of Justice Act (1924), 81
Coyne, Edward, 131
Criminal Justice Act, 307
Criminal Law Amendment Act (1935), 249
critical discourse analysis, 41–7, 86
crowbar brigades, 307
Crowley, John, 250
Crowley, Patricia, 250–1
Crowley, Tadhg, 234
*Crowley* v. *Ireland* (1980), 250, 255–6, 260–1, 265–6, 276–7
cultural contextualists, 16
Cumann na mBan, 69, 71, 77, 108
Cumann na nGaedheal
Blueshirts' support for, 127
insertion of Article 2A into Irish Free State constitution, 129
parity between sterling and Saorstát punt, 116, 117
support from elites, 118
custody cases, 264
Customs Act (1945), 212
cycle of accumulation. *See also* capitalism
British Empire and, 51–2
British Free Trade, 29
crisis in 1970s, 31
in Ireland, 165
United States as leader of, 28, 163–4
after World War II, 163–4
Czechoslovakia, 164, 172

Dáil Constitution and Democratic Programme (1919), 50
Dáil Courts, 79–80
Dáil Éireann, 87, 131, 301–8
Dalton, Brendan, 318
Daly, Mark, 130
dance-hall licensing, 191
dangerous associations, 71
Davos, 6, 11, 329, 345
De Valera, Eamon
drafting of Irish Constitution and, 88
establishment of Irish Republic and, 71
radio broadcast in support of new constitution, 148–9
on socio-economic rights provisions, 115, 130–41
Deasy's Act (1860), 64
debt-defaulters, 67
Defenders, 53
Delany, Vincent, 287
Democratic Programme of the First Dáil (1919), 76, 98, 102, 107
Denham, Susan, 194, 271, 276–7
Denmark, 12
Dennehy, Denis, 293, 303–4
*Deo Duce*, 300
Department of Education, 250
Department of Industry and Commerce, 165
Derrig, Thomas, 132, 133, 139
Dicey, A. V., 25, 63
*Dictionary of Irish Biography*, 41
directive principles
in constitutions of India, Papua New Guinea, and Nigeria, 157
in Indian Constitution, 33, 157, 160–1
in Irish Constitution (1937), 140–1, 144–5, 299, 305
Disability Legal Resource, 205
discourse, definition of, 45
Diskin, Patrick, 216
District Court. *See also* courts
appointees, requirements for, 190
civil jurisdictions, 191
constitutional rights cases, 195
criminal jurisdictions, 191
family law and, 191
limit in civil jurisdiction, 197
salaries in, 199*t*
types of cases in, 196
volume of cases, 195, 196*t*
divorce, 121, 171, 179, 182, 265
dotcom collapse of 2000–2, 178
Douglas, James, 92
Doyle, Desmond, 248–9, 259, 275
*Doyle* v. *Minister for Education* (1953), 206
*Doyle* v. *Minister for Education* (1956), 248–9, 253, 258–9, 276
Dreher, Jorg, 213, 218, 223
*Dreher* v. *Irish Land Commission* (1984), 213, 223
Dublin
housing conditions in 1939, 123–4
housing conditions in 1960s, 301
Spanish Civil War and, 129
Dublin Castle
antagonism towards, in 1919, 77–81
capitalist class and, 53
cessation of public services in 1917, 72
coercion acts, 67

Deasy's Act and, 64
Dublin Tramways strike and, 69
introduction of paid resident magistrates, 60
landlords and, 53
proclamation of dangerous associations, 71
Dublin Corporation, 213, 249, 300, 301, 302, 307
Dublin Council of Trade Unions, 315
Dublin Employers' Federation, 68
Dublin Flat-Dwellers Association, 302
Dublin Health Authority, 249
Dublin Housing Action Committee, 294, 301–8, 338
establishment of, 302
imprisonment of members, 305
objectives of, 302
opposition to 1937 Irish constitution, 296
Dublin Lock-Out (1913–14), 68–9, 332
Dublin Metropolitan Force, 69
Dublin Tenants' Association, 302
Dublin Trades Council, 178, 302, 306
Dublin Trades' Union Council, 300
Dublin Tramways, 129
Dublin Unemployed Association, 294, 297–301, 338
basic demands of, 298–9
fines on, 300
impact of, 299
marches, 299
opposition to 1937 Irish constitution, 296
sit-down protests, 167
successor to, 301
Duffy, Gavan, 220, 273, 274, 278
Duffy, George, 80
Duggan, Eamon, 80
Duncan, W., 265

Earle, John, 237
Easter Rising of 1916, 70, 71
Eastern bloc, 163
Eastern Europe, 174
Economic Co-operation and Development (OECD), 180
'Economic Life' articles, 135–6
economic rights. *See* socio-economic rights
Ecuador, 11, 347
education, 254
Catholic social and, 250
educational provisions in Irish Constitution (1937), 131–2, 135, 137
annotations to, 138
educational provisions in Irish Free State Constitution, 99
in Irish Free State, 123
of judges, 281*t*, 282*t*, 280–4
legal
curriculum, 283
sociology in, 289
universities, 282
right to, 14, 131–2, 137, 138, 256
Education and Development Centre, 251
*Educational Company of Ireland* v. *Fitzpatrick* (961), 233, 234, 236, 237, 238, 239
Edwards, Frank, 128
Egypt, 164, 174
Ejército Zapatista de Libéración Nacional (EZLN), uprising of, 7
Electricity Supply Board, 316
Elster, J., 25–7
embedded liberalism, 31, 32
emigration, 52–3, 72, 118, 165, 298
employment, 178
Enforcement of Law (Occasional Powers) Act, 90
England, public interest litigation in, 206
Epp, Charles, 204
Equality Authority, 341
Ethiopia, 52
Eucharist Congress (1932), 121
Eurodollar market, growth of, 171
European Central Bank, 330
European Common Market, 287
European Convention on Human Rights (ECHR), 206
European Court of Human Rights, 183, 239–40
European Court of Justice, 31, 165, 175, 182, 183, 346
European Economic Community, 177, 308, 313
European Monetary Union, 178
European Revolutions of 1848, 28, 54
European Union Charter of Fundamental Rights, 266
European Union Commission, 330
European Union (EU), 32, 173
eviction. *See also* landlord–tenant relationships
evictions
anti-eviction activities, 67
Deasy's Act and, 64
forced, 11
'land wars' and, 55
liberalisation of property rights and, 66
protection from, 302
secret societies' role in stopping, 53
Examiner of the High Court, 197

family, 122, 136–7, 254, 305
family law, 63, 191
family-welfare rights, 245–70 *See also* welfare state
cases for analysis, 247
Catholic social provisions and, 247–8

family-welfare rights (*cont.*)
development of, 246
discarding, 8
judgments, 258–64
jurisprudence, 264–7
origins of, 248–53
translation, 253–8
Fanon, Franz, 48, 49
Farmer's Party, 88, 89
Farwell, B., 38
fascism, 127, 148–9
feminist movement, 63, 108, 147, 179, 249, 265
Fenians. *See* Irish Republican Brotherhood (IRB)
Ferguson, William, 64
Fianna Fáil, 149, 297, 339
abandonment of protectionism, 301
competition state strategy for development, 177
disability rights and, 338
Good Friday Agreement and, 177
housing and Land Commission programmes, 134–5
indigenous capital, 168
national self-sufficiency and, 119
national-popular base of, 118–19
overturning of Anglo-Irish Treaty settlement, 116
partnership with trade unions, 230
pro-treaty opponents and, 128
republicanism and, 116
Sinn Féin's entry in government as, 113
social reorientation of Irish Free State, 120, 122–3
support for European trade liberalisation and integration, 180
Figgis, Darrell, 92, 99
Finance Act (1983), 214–15
financier-grazier class, 53, 96–7, 98, 100, 108–9, 118, 165, 298, 333
Fine Gael, 168, 339
coalition with Labour Party, 179
competition state strategy for development, 177
criticism of draft Irish Constitution, 143
formation of, 127
Good Friday Agreement and, 177
questioning the powers of Land Commission, 131
Finland, 12
First Dáil, Democratic Programme of, 76
Fisher, Francis, 212–13, 216, 220
*Fisher* v. *Irish Land Commission* (1948), 212–13, 275
Fitzgerald, Alexis, 287
FitzGerald, Garrett, 182
FitzGerald, William, 276
Fleming, Eric, 306
flu pandemic of 1918, 72
fluoridation, 249, 253–5, 259
Foley, Patrick, 213, 216
*Foley* v. *Irish Land Commission* (1952), 213
Forde, M., 265
Four Courts, 77, 88, 189, 192, 309
France, 28
Matignon Agreements, 112, 153
uprising in, 172
France, Clement, 84, 92, 94, 95–6, 107, 155, 209, 333, 336–7, 344
Franco, General Francisco, 129
Free Legal Aid Clinics (FLAC), 205, 340–1
free market, 32
free trade, 51–2
freedom of association provisions, 236, 239
Freikorps, 105
French Constituent Assembly of 1848, 29
French Revolution, 54
Friedman, Milton, 32, 173
Friedrich, Carl, 25
*Fundamental Rights in the Irish Law and Constitution* (Kelly), 226

Gallagher, Brian, 311
Gallagher, Catherine, 214–15
Gardaí, 307
Gaspari, Giovanni, 216
George, Henry, 96
George, Lloyd, 81
Geraghty, Patrick, 306
Germany
corporate social management in, 113
Great Powers' interstate-system and, 28
Nazi Law for the Organisation of Labour (1934), 152
socio-economic rights in, 344
Weimar Constitution, 105
worker uprisings in, 68
Gezi Park occupation in Turkey, 349
Ghana, 18
Gilmore, George, 124
global economic crisis of 2007–8, 6, 330, 347
Global Justice Movement, 7
Global North, 6, 14
Global South, 14, 164, 346
Good Friday Agreement, 177
Gostello, John, 143
Government of Ireland Bill (1886), 63
grazier class, 73, 96–7, 116
Great Depression of 1930s, 30, 112, 113, 151, 332
Great Hunger (1845–52), 52–3
Great Powers, 28
Great War (1914–18), 104–5

Greece, 164, 174
Greek Orthodox Church, 151
Green Party, 180
Griffith, Arthur, 78, 80
Griffith's Valuation Act (1852), 214
*Griswold* v. *Connecticut* (1965), 255
Grogan, Vincent, 287

Hall, John, 316–17
Hancock, William, 64
Hardiman, Adrian, 271
Harris, Gerald, 225, 264, 284, 287
Haughey, Charles, 317
Hayek, Friedrich, 32, 241
Health (Amendment) Bill (2004), 253
Health Act (1960), 249, 253–5
Health Act (1970), 168, 253
*Health Amendment Bill*, 258
*Health Bill (2004)*, 263–4
Health Board, 253
Health Care Act (1953), 168
health care, right to, 14
Hearts of Oak, 53
hegemony, 23
Henchy, Seamus, 316
Heron, Denis Caulfield, 58
Heydebrand, W., 22
High Court, 192 *See also* courts
  amounts recovered by verdicts, 198*t*, 198–9
  appointees, paternal occupation of, 281*t*
  business in each legal year, 196*t*
  costs claimed and allowed, 199*t*, 198–9
  salaries in, 199*t*
  specialised court offices, 197, 198
  volume of cases, 195–6
Hirschl, Ran, 341
historical capitalist world-system, 4, 27
  constitutional waves in, 27*t*, 25–7
  effects of, 52–3
  Irish Constitution (1937) and, 151–5, 160–86
    in 1945–68, 163–71
    in 1968–, 171–6
  Irish constitutionalism and, 33–41
  Irish Free State Constitution and, 104–9
  revolution and rights in Ireland and, 51–8
  socio-economic rights in Ireland and, 25–33, 330–8
  transformation in political-ideological norms of, 172–3
Hogan, G., 38, 228, 341
Hogan, Patrick, 90
Hohenzollern monarchy, end of, 105
Holloway, John, 352
Home Rule bill, 69
homelessness, 331
homosexuality, 179, 183
Hopkins, T., 27
Horgan, John, 122
House of Commons, 62
Houses of the Oireachtas, 161, 219, 231
housing, affordable, 275
Housing Action Committee, 344
Housing Bill (1981), 222
Huet, Phyllis, 310, 311
human dignity, right to, 14
human rights
  children's rights, 309–13
  conflicts in 1990s and 2000s, 183
  contestation of, 183
  interdependence and indivisibility of, 9, 256–7
  lending programmes and, 331
  monitoring organisations, 341
  neoliberal economics and, 173
  neoliberalism and, 176
  socio-economic rights and, 2–3, 9, 10, 12–13, 266
Hungary, 68, 113, 120

*Iarnród Éireann* v. *Ireland* (1996), 215–16, 219, 223–4, 274
Iceland, 11–12
ideology, 44–5
Immigrant Council of Ireland, 205
Incorporated Law Society, 202
Indecon (2003), 203
India
  famine, 52
  legal aid in, 204
  socio-economic rights in, 12, 342
  state developmentalism in, 164
  Supreme Court, 33, 176
Indian Constitution of 1950, 160
  directive principles in, 33, 157, 160–1
Indignados movement, 7, 349
Industrial and Provident Societies (Amendment) Act (1978), 215
Industrial Finance Corporation, 96
Industrial Relations Act (1946), 232
Industrial Relations Act (1990), 179, 232, 233, 241, 300, 318
Industrial Workers' Co-operative, 125
Industrial Workers of the World, 84
Ingram, Attracta, 289
International Covenant for Economic, Social, and Cultural Rights (ICESCR), 2, 327
International Covenant on Economic, Social, and Cultural Rights (ICESCR), 2–3
International Monetary Fund, 330
involuntary confessions, 245

Iraq, 173
Ireland
  capital-labour relations in 1960s and 1970s, 167–8
  Catholic identity, 37
  civil war (1922–3), 87–8
  constitution 'from below', 1848–1922, 48–83
  constitutionalism in, 33–41
  decline in population, 1800–1900, 52
  economic conditions in 2008 onwards, 331
  economic development in, 36
  free enterprise cycle of accumulation in, 165
  free trade in 1800s, 51–2
  historical capitalist world-system and, 51–8
  land, law, and justice in, 58–67
  legal professions, 59–64
  militancy in, 49
  open door strategy to multinationals, 177
  politics of constitutional change in, 334–5
  reincorporation into world-system, 165–6
  revolution and rights in, 51–8
  as semi-peripheral site for US companies, 178
  social and cultural transformations in 1960s and 1970s, 166
  social origins of constitutionalism in 1930s, 115–24
  social policy, 168
  social stability in, 36
Irish Association of Social Workers, 309
Irish Banks' Standing Committee, 122, 123
Irish Business Employers Confederation, 177
*Irish Catholic*, 160
Irish Christian Front, 129
*Irish Citizen*, 63
Irish Citizen Army
  constitution of, 74
  declaration as dangerous association, 71
  protection of Dublin Tramways strikers, 69
  support for workers' republic, 125
Irish Communist Organisation, 302, 303
Irish Congress of Trade Unions, 232, 314, 315, 317
Irish Constitution (1937), 37–8, 112–59, 338
  analysis of, 35
  annotations to draft provisions, 137–8
  Article 34.5, 135–6
  Article 38.1, 135
  Article 40, 216, 220–1, 223, 238, 239, 253–5, 256–7, 259, 265
  Article 41, 253–5, 256–7, 264
  Article 42, 253, 254, 256, 312
  Article 43, 144, 216, 220–1, 223
  Article 45, 140–1, 144–5, 161
  Article 46, 145
  Catholic pressure groups and, 182
  Catholic social provisions in, 133–4, 143–4
  Catholic-social constitutionalism and, 148, 176–84
  children's rights and, 311–12
  class system and, 114
  contradictions in, 308–9
  Directive Principles of Social Policy, 140–1, 144–5, 299, 305
  dominant social group's shaping of, 117
  draft property provisions, 142
  educational provisions, 131–2, 135, 137
    annotations to, 138
  emergence as conservative and electro-democratic instrument, 155
  emergence of social state and, 115
  family rights provision in, 134, 136–7
  family-welfare rights provisions, 254
  freedom of association rights provision, 232–3, 236
  gendering of, 136–7
  MacElligott's commentary on, 138–9
  neoliberalism and, 171–6
  plebiscite on, 131, 150
  poverty, charity, and state paternalism discourse on, 145
  preamble, initial versions of, 132, 133
  private property rights provision in, 144
  property rights contestations and, 210–11
  property rights provisions in, 217
  proposed amendments, 169
  pursuit of ordered society in, 135–6
  referendums, 181
  social origins of constitutionalism and, 115–24
  socio-economic rights provisions in, 130–42, 327
    civil society's reception, 142–51
    parliamentary debates on, 142–51
  timeline of constitution-making process, 132*t*
  women's rights in, 147
  in world-system, 151
    in 1945–68, 163–71
    in 1945–2008, 160–86
    in 1968–, 171–6
*Irish Constitution* (Kelly), 42, 195, 288
Irish Council of Civil Liberties, 193
Irish Courts Service, 200, 207
*Irish Democrat* (newspaper), 147
Irish Family Planning Association, 249
Irish Farmers' Union, 73
Irish Financial Services Centre, 178
Irish Folklore Commission, 65
Irish Free State, 81
  agrarian economy in, 117
  Commonwealth of Nations and, 80
  courts in, 189–90

economic peripheralisation of, 86
exports, 122
legal system, 77
living standards in, 123–4
peripheral agrarian class structure, 117, 153
semi-peripheral status of, 332
social conflicts in, 113
state support for financier-grazier interests, 118
welfare state development in, 35–6
Irish Free State Constitution (1922), 37, 84–111
Article 10, 103, 104
Article 11, 103, 104
Article 2A, 129
Article 40.3 and, 220–1
Article 43, 220–1
Catholic political theory and, 95
drafting committee, 92–3
drafting of, 91–8
economic sovereignty provision, 98, 100
education provision, 99
enactment of, 91
fundamental rights in, 85–6
programmatic declarations, 103
property rights in, 333
removal of oath of fidelity from, 116
review in 1934, 130–1
social constitutional discourses, 95–7
social origins of constitutionalism of, 87–91
socio-economic rights in, 86, 332–3
socio-economic rights provisions, 98–104
sovereignty provision, 101
timeline of constitution-making process, 92*t*
world-system perspectives, 104–9
Irish Free State Constitution Act 1922, 91
Irish Human Rights Commission, 341
*Irish Independent* (newspaper), 150
Irish Ireland policy, 94
*Irish Judiciary, The* (Bartholomew), 280
*Irish Jurist*, 42, 225, 241, 264, 265, 266, 286–8
Irish Labour Party, 88, 101–2, 103, 120, 131, 143–4, 180, 339
Irish Land Commission (ILC), 56, 60, 108, 118, 119, 131, 134–5, 140, 143, 149, 210, 212–13, 216, 219
Irish Land League, 64–5, 67
*Irish Law Times*, 60
Irish National Land League, 55
Irish National Teachers' Organisation, 250, 278
*Irish News* (newspaper), 150
Irish Parliamentary Party, 56, 62, 64–5, 69, 70
Irish pound, 117
*Irish Press* (newspaper), 150
Irish Refugee Council, 205
Irish Republic, proclamation of, 70–1
Irish Republican Army (IRA)
Anglo-Irish Treaty and, 87
bombing campaigns, 166
Constitution and Governmental Programme for the Republic of Ireland (1933), 126
courts and, 77, 78–9
end of presence in South or Munster Republic, 88
formation of, 70
labour/agrarian militancy and, 72
Irish Republican Brotherhood (IRB), 54–5, 58
Irish Revolution (1913–23), 48
*Irish Statistical Abstracts or Courts Service Reports*, 42
*Irish Times* (newspaper), 41, 150
Irish Transport and General Workers Union (ITGWU), 68, 72, 74, 230, 233, 234, 235–6
Irish Travel Movement Legal Unit, 205
Irish Union of Distributive Workers and Clerks (IUDWC), 234, 235–6, 238
Irish Volunteers, 69, 70, 71, 77
Irish Water, protests against, 1
Irish White Cross, 72, 85, 95
Irish Women Worker's Union, 124
Irish Women's Franchise League, 108
Irish Women's Liberation Movement, 249
Irish Women's Workers' Union, 108
Irish Workers League, 298
Israel, 341
Italy, 68, 113, 120, 172

Jesuit Order, 121, 133, 154, 344
Johnson, Thomas, 75, 76, 102
Joint Committee of Women's Societies and Social Workers, 147
Joint-Oireachtas Committee, 190
judges
ages, 279–80
apprenticeship, 284, 285–9
class background, 280
court structure contradictions and, 188
education, 281*t*, 282*t*, 280–4
in Irish courts, in years 1924, 1870, and 2010, 196*t*
paternal occupation, 282*t*
requirements for, 190
salaries, 199*t*
school attended, 282*t*
transformation of roles of, 201
university attended, 281*t*, 282*t*
judicial activism, in 1960s and 1970s, 183
Judicial Appointments Advisory Board, 190
judicial review, 228
juristocracy, 175

Justices of the Peace, 59
juvenile delinquency, 264

Keane, Ronan, 209, 227, 266, 283
Kearney, Ben, 315
Kelly, Deirdre, 320
Kelly, John, 38, 42, 195, 226, 239, 287, 288
Kelly, Seán T., 139
Kennedy, Duncan, 26–7, 85, 174
Kennedy, Hugh, 80, 84, 86, 92, 94, 101, 190, 276–7
*Kennedy Report*, 245
Kenny, John, 316
*Kenny Report*, 227
Kenya, 18
Kerr, Tony, 241, 289
Kickham, Charles, 58
Kinane, Jeremiah, 126
King's Inns, 61, 62, 284, 285–9
Kissane, B., 38
*Knocknagow* (Kickham), 58
Kohn, L., 71, 85–6
Korea, 52

labour
  rights of free labourers, 22
  wage-contract between capital and, 22
Labour Court, 232
*laissez-faire*, 85, 99, 107–8, 123, 131, 138–9, 151, 153, 210, 220, 227
Lalor, James Fintan, 48, 65, 74
land
  market value of, 217–18
  private ownership in, 96–7
Land Act (1933), 119, 213
Land Act (1946), 213
Land Acts, 60
Land Commission, 226
Land Courts, 77
land reform, 66, 72
land taxation, 211
land values, rise in, 210
landlordism, 53, 61, 66, 123, 124, 128
landlords, 303
  in legal professions, 61
  liberalisation of property rights of, 66
landlord-tenant relationships, 274, 303–4
  arbitration of disputes, 66
  coercion acts, 66–7
  evictions, 11, 53, 55, 64, 66, 67, 302
  feudal tenure agreements and, 64
  irremovable tenants and, 64–5
  peasant proprietorships and, 65
  rent valuations and, 319
Lang, John Temple, 226, 287
Larkin, Jim, 69
Lasalle, Ferdinand, 1
Latin America
  decolonisation of, 35–6
  repression in, 179
  socio-economic rights in, 15, 16, 17
  welfare reforms in, 153
*Laval Un Partneri Ltd* v. *Svenska Byggnadsarbetareförbundet* (2008), 346
Law Society of Ireland, 61, 63, 203, 207
League of Nations, collapse of, 112
legal aid, 205, 340–1
legal business, 188, 194–200
legal education
  curriculum, 283
  sociology in, 289
  universities, 282
legal professions
  apprenticeship, 284, 285–9
  barristers, 201–2
  books of authority in, 63
  branches of, 201–2
  court structure contradictions and, 188
  fees, 202–3
  feminist movement and, 63
  in Ireland, 59–64
  organisations, 61
  pauper's procedure and, 205
  solicitors, 201–2
legal year, 60
Lehane, Con, 299, 301, 305
Leinster House, 309
Lemass, Seán, 169
Leo XIII, Pope, 57, 120, 126
LGBT advocates, 179
liberalism. *See also* neoliberalism
  classic, 328
  embedded, 31, 32
  social, 163–4, 183, 328
liberal-social constitutionalism, 95–7
Lilberne Ltd., 319
Limerick Corporation, 251, 261
Limerick Council of Trade Unions, 251
Limerick Workers' Housing Association, 78
liquor licensing, 191
Living City Group, 320
living standards, in Irish Free State, 123–4
Local Government (Planning and Development) Act (1963), 213
Lucey, Cornelius, 120, 121, 250
Luxembourg, 266

MacElligott, James, 115, 131, 138–9, 140, 333
MacEntee, Seán, 143, 249
Mackey, Rex, 304
MacSwiney, Mary, 126
Madigan, Patrick, 214–15, 321
*Madigan* v. *Attorney General* (1986), 214–15, 218

Maher, I., 265
*Mapp* v. *Ohio* (1961), 170–1
market law, 64
Marshall, T., 8, 18
martial law, declaration of, 71
Martin, William, 320–1
Marx, Karl, 12, 19, 21, 22, 345, 351
Marxist theory, 19
material contextualists, 16
Matheson, Arthur, 141
Matignon Agreements, 112, 153
Matthews, Mary, 227, 239
McAleese, Mary, 215
McBride, Seán, 166, 206
McCarthy, Nicholas, 250
McCay, Justice, 311
McDermott, P. A., 267
McDowell, Michael, 160
McDunphy, Michael, 130
McErlean, John, 131
McGee, Mary, 249–50, 255, 259–60, 276
*McGee* v. *Attorney General* (1974), 170, 171, 206, 249–50, 255, 259–60, 276
McGuiness, William, 298
McMullen, John, 241–2
McNeill, James, 92
McQuaid, Archbishop John Charles, 112, 115, 131, 136, 139–40, 141, 144, 232, 297, 301, 333
Mellows, Liam, 89
mentally defective persons, 264
Merrigan, Matt, 315–16, 317, 319
Meskell, John, 235, 237
*Meskell* v. *CIE* (1973), 233, 234–5, 237
Mexican Constitution, social liberalism of, 106
Mexico
  constitution, 14, 16, 30
  judicial review in, 174
  social constitution-making in, 106
  socio-economic rights in, 30, 85, 344
  uprising in, 172
  welfare reforms in, 153
middle class, creation of, 133
militias, creation of, 73
minimal living standards, state's protection of, 9
Moore, Kingsmill, 230, 238, 240, 278
Morgan, David Gwynn, 245, 267
Mother and Child Health Scheme, 168
Moynihan, Maurice, 131
Mulcahy, Richard, 249
Munster Republic, 88
Murnaghan, James, 92, 239
Murphy, Christina, 310
Murphy, Jack, 301
Murphy, Ken, 200
Murphy, William, 68
Murray, John, 200, 263–4
Mussolini, Benito, 127, 152

National Association of Transport Employees, 234
National Economic and Social Council, 177
National Guard, 127
National Labour Party, 169, 235
National Land Bank, 78
National Private Rental Law Group, 320–1
National Society for the Prevention of Cruelty to Children, 248
National Union of Railwaymen, 233, 235
*National Union of Railwaymen* v. *Sullivan* (1947), 233, 234, 236, 237, 238, 239, 278
Natividad, Jose, 106
Nazi Law for the Organisation of Labour (1934), 152
Nazi propaganda, 152
negative liberties, 336–7
negative rights, 9
Negri, Antonio, 24
neoformal constitutionalism, 27*t*, 26–7, 31
neoliberal capitalism, 5
neoliberal constitutionalism, 27*t*, 32
neoliberalism, 31, 171–6, 328, 353
  constitutionalism and, 173
  limitations of humans rights and, 176
  socio-economic rights and, 11–12
net market value, 217–18
Neumann, F., 14, 39
New Caledonia, 52
New Deal, 37, 112
New Left, 173
new left social movements, 179
New Zealand, 174, 341
Nigeria, 18, 157
non-governmental organisations (NGOs), 3, 308, 327, 339–40, 342–3
*Norris* v. *Ireland* (1988), 206
North American Free Trade Agreement (NAFTA), 32, 173
Northern Ireland
  conflict in, 176–7
  public interest litigation in, 206
Norton, William, 143–4

O'Brien, Kate, 150
O'Brien, William, 75, 98–100
O'Byrne, John, 92
Occupy movements, 7, 24, 349
Ó'Cinnéide, Seamus, 312
O'Connell, Rory, 266
O'Connell, T. J., 102, 107, 333
O'Connell. Daniel, 55

O'Connor, Lord Justice, 189
Ó'Dálaigh, Cearbhall, 169
O'Donnell, Peadar, 124, 147, 300
O'Donoghue, Philip, 130, 143, 147
O'Duffy, Eoin, 124, 127
Offences against the State Act (1939), 231
Office of the Taxing Master, 198
O'Higgins, Kevin, 103
O'Higgins, Tom, 273, 276, 278
Oireachtas, 161, 219, 231, 313
O'Keefe, Andreas, 286
O'Kelly, J. J., 126
O'Kelly, Sean T., 76, 120
Old Left, 172, 308
O'Mahony, Donal, 321, 322
O'Mahony, Michael, 187, 245, 246
O'Malley, Des, 314
O'Malley, Ernie, 58, 78
Ó'Moráin, Pádraig, 207
O'Neill, Terence, 169
open door strategy, 177
O'Rahilly, Alfred, 75, 92, 97, 107, 133, 142, 143–4, 148, 155, 277
*O'Reilly* v. *Limerick Corporation* (1989), 251, 256–7, 265, 274, 277
Osborough, N., 265, 286, 288, 289
O'Shiel, Kevin, 73
O'Sullivan, Michelle, 241–2
O'Sullivan, Richard, 287
O'Sullivan, T.G., 299
O'Sullivan, Timothy, 190
Outcomes, 124

*Pacem in Terris* (1963), 259
Paine, Tom, 54, 121–2
Palestine, 179
Papua New Guinea, 157
Parnell, Charles Stewart, 56
Partido Revolucionario Institucional, 175
party courts, 76
paternal power, 264
Paul-Dubois, Louis, 62
pauper's procedure, 205
Pearle, Thomas, 298, 300
Pearse, Patrick, 70, 76, 125
Pearse statement, 98
People's Democracy protest, 306
Peron, Juan, 153
Personal Injuries Assessment Board, 195–6
personal rights, 140–1, 254
Philippines, 52
picketing, 240
Pigs and Bacon Acts (1935/7), 212
*Pigs Marketing Board* v. *Donnelly* (1939), 212, 220
Piludski, Josef, 154
Pius XI, Pope, 120
Plan of Ayala, 106
*Planning and Development Bill (1999) Reference*, 223
Planning Authority, 219, 226
*Planning Bill Reference* (2004), 275
Planning Development Bill (1999), 215, 218, 219
*PMPS Ltd and Joseph Moore* v. *Attorney General* (1983), 215
Poland, 113, 154
Polanyi, Karl, 13
Poor Law, 56
popular courts, 76
popular militancy in Ireland, 49, 72–3, 75
Porto Alegre, 7, 11, 329, 345, 346
Portugal, 17, 113, 120, 154, 174
positive rights, 9, 336
poverty, 95, 145, 331
prerogative writs, 192
Preuss, Hugo, 105
Priestly-McCracken, Elizabeth, 63
primary education, right to, 256
private enterprise, 227
Private Motorists Provident Society, 215
privatisation, 172
Privy Council of the House of Lords, 101, 116
Probate Office, 197
Proclamation of Children's Rights' campaign (1976), 309–13
Proclamation of the Irish Republic (1867), 55
Proclamation of the Irish Republic (1916), 50, 70–1, 98
production, decentralised worker control of, 13
Programme of the Republican Congress (1934), 114
Progressive Democrats, 177, 338
Prohibition of Forcible Entry and Occupation Act (1971), 307
proletarian constitution, 24
property bubble, 215
Property Defence Association, 64
property prices
  boom-bust cycles in, 210
  rise in, 215
property rights, 64, 217
  Article 40.3 and, 220–1
  Article 43 and, 220–1
  contestations, 209–29
    cases, 211
    development of, 209–10
    Irish Constitution (1937) and, 210–11
    judgments, 219–24
    jurisprudence, 224–9
    origins of, 212–16
    translation, 216–19
  feudal tenure agreements and, 64

private property rights, 99, 126–7, 133–4, 136, 148
proportionality doctrine and, 218–19
property speculation, 178, 209, 227
property tax, 214–15, 217–18
proportionality doctrine, 218–19
Protestants, 151
Catholics as counterweight to, 95
in legal professions, 61
as minority rulers of Ireland, 51
protests, 327–8
in 2011–12, 348–50
of Dublin Unemployed Association, 298
against Irish Water, 1
People's Democracy protest, 306
Seattle protests in 1999, 7
Provisional Government
Anglo-Irish Treaty and, 88
authority over IRA, 88
civil war (1922–3) and, 89
classic *laissez-faire* norms and, 107–8
draft constitutions, 98
land distribution by, 89
preference for classic constitution, 99
prioritisation of state power and economic necessity, 102
special powers and public safety resolutions, 90
public law neoformalism, 31
public spending, 180–1

*Quadrageissmo Anno* (1931), 120, 121
Quakers, 72
Quarter Sessions, 59
Querétaro Constitutional Congress of 1917, 106
Quinn, Ruairí, 209

Rattigan, Seamus, 322
*Raymond Crotty* v. *An Taoiseach*, 181
*Re: Article 26 and the Health (Amendment) Bill 2004* (2005), 253
Reagan, Ronald, 11, 172
Redmond, John, 56, 69
referendums, 181
Reichswehr-Freikorps, 86
rent controls, 211, 214, 225, 274
Rent Courts, 320–1
Rent Restriction Acts, 221, 321
rent tribunals, 319–22
Republican Congress (1934), 124, 125, 148
*Rerum Novarum* (1870), 57
residential property tax, 214–15
retrenchment, 172
Ribbonmen, 53
right of dissociation, 233, 237
right to life, 14
Right2Water campaign, 2, 327
*Rights of Men, The* (Paine), 54, 121–2
Road Traffic Act, 300
Robinson, Mary, 206
Roche, Stephen, 130
Roosevelt, Franklin, 153
Ross, Co. Wexford, 240
Royal Irish Constabulary, 70, 71
Russia
Five-Year Plans, 113
Stalin's Constitution, 151–2
Russian Revolution (1917), 18, 49, 126
Russian-Internationalist Revolution (1917–23), 104–5
Ryan, Frank, 124, 147
Ryan, Richie, 249
*Ryan* v. *Attorney General* (1965), 206, 253–5
Rynne, Michael, 225

Saint Vincent de Paul, 205, 251
Salazar, António, 121, 154
Saor Éire (1931), 124
Saorstát punt, 117
Scannell, Yvonne, 228
Seattle, Washington, 84
Seattle protests in 1999, 7
Second Bill of Rights, 11, 16, 37
secret societies, 53–5, 66–7
Seventeen-Article Constitution (seventh-century Japan), 25
Shinto, 151
Shotoku, Prince, 25
Sinn Féin
acceptance of Anglo-Irish Treaty, 87
arbitration courts and, 77
authority over courts, 78
by-election victories, 74–5
Courts, 79–80
declaration as dangerous association, 71
Dublin Housing Action Committee and, 302
election manifesto in 1918, 75
emerging as Fianna Fáil after civil war, 113
Good Friday Agreement and, 177
neoliberalism and, 339
opposition to EU integration and welfare state, 180
popular militancy and, 108–9
Proclamation of the Irish Republic (1916) and, 71
restrain of agrarian agitation and class conflict, 48–9
support from elites, 89
Sinn Féin Manifesto (1918), 50
Sinnott, Jamie, 251, 257
Sinnott, Kathryn, 245, 251, 257, 275

*Sinnott* v. *Minister for Education* (2001), 257–8, 261–2, 266, 277, 339
Sinzheimer, Hugo, 105
Skeffington, Hannah, 147, 148
slum landlordism, 123, 124, 128
social antagonism, 28–9
social constitutionalism
  Catholic-social constitutionalism, 97, 148, 176–84, 247–8, 333–4
  as elite response to anti-systemic threats, 333
  emergence of, 30
  historical capitalist world-system and, 27*t*, 26–7
  liberal-social, 95–7
  of the right and left, 124–30
social credit, 134, 140
Social Democrats, 308
Social Democrats (Germany), 105
Social Europe, 6
social justice, 60
social liberalism, 163–4, 183, 328
social movements, 34 *See also* civil society
  in 2011–12, 348–50
  analysis of, 39
  decolonisation and, 35–6
  Dublin Housing Action Committee, 301–8
  Dublin Unemployed Association, 297–301
  growth after 1848, 57
  'new left', 179
  opposition to neoliberalism, 176
  Proclamation of Children's Rights' campaign (1976), 309–13
  Sinn Féin's by-election victories and, 74–5
  Talbot workers' factory occupation and boycott, 313
  Threshold/ALONE campaign for rent tribunals, 319–22
social partnership, 241
social rights. *See* socio-economic rights
socialism, 151, 164
Socialist Workers' Party, 339
socio-economic rights, 1–47, 210
  ambiguities in theory and practice of, 12–13
  co-constitutive transformation of, 20–5
  constitutional laws and, 15–16
  constitutionalising, 8
  constitutions and, 25–33
  contesting, 326–53
  in crisis, 5–13
  crisis of capitalism and, 345–53
  discourses of, 11, 13
  functionalist accounts of, 16–17
  future of, 338–45
  as historical phenomena, 8
  human rights and, 2–3, 9, 10, 12–13, 266
  improving living standards with, 9
  interest-based accounts of, 17–18
  interpretation of, 7–8
  in Irish Constitution (1937), 129–30
  in Irish Free State Constitution, 84–104, 111
  judicial review of, 10–11
  justiciability of, 10
  'new right' or neoliberal rhetorics and, 11–12
  politics of, 8
  politics of constitutionalising, 4–5, 13–20
  value-consensus state and, 273–8
  world revolution of 1917 and, 68–76
  world-systemic politics of, 330–8
sociology, in legal education, 289
Solemn League and Covenant, 69
solicitors, 59, 201–2, 284, 285–9
South Africa
  apartheid in, 179
  Constitution (1996), 33, 174
  Constitutional Court, 9
  constitutional dialogue model in, 346
  Imperial decline in, 116
  socio-economic rights in, 12, 14, 341, 342
*Southern*, 220
Southern Industrial Trust, 212, 220
Southern Ireland, small-scale industry in, 52
Soviet Constitution, 14
Soviet Union
  collapse of, 14, 172
  Russian Revolution in 1917, 18, 49, 126
Spain
  Catholic Church and, 120
  Constitution of the Second Republic, 154–5
  constitutional court in, 174
  constitutional review in, 164
  socio-economic rights in, 17
  worker uprisings in, 68
Spanish Civil War, 28, 114, 129
Spartacists, 105, 106–7
Special Criminal Court, 183, 192
Special Infantry Corps, 90
specialised court offices, 197, 198
squatting, 303–4
Stalin, Joseph, 113
Stalin's Constitution, 151–2
starvation, 52–3
state
  constitutionalism, 25–7
  role of, 22
Statute of Westminster (1931), 116
sterling, 116, 117
Stevenson, Colin, 227
strikes
  in 1918–23, 72–3
  in 1935–7, 129–30

on Dublin Tramways, 69
injunction to restrain, 240
as potent form of social agitation, 139–40
*Studies*, 287
Superior Courts, 201, 340
Supreme Court
appellate jurisdiction, 192
appointees
ages, 279–80
class background, 280
education, 281*t*, 282*t*, 280–4
paternal occupation, 282*t*
requirements for, 190
school attended, 282*t*
university attended, 281*t*, 282*t*
backlog of cases in, 340
Catholic social laws and, 170
constitutional rights cases, 195
narrow conception of rights in, 335–6
salaries in, 199*t*
structure of, 192
volume of cases, 195
Supreme Court of Judicature (Ireland) Act 1877, 60
Sweden, 12, 174
Sweetman, Michael, 302
Switzerland, 99, 164
Synge, John Millington, 67

Taioseach, 121
Talbot workers' factory occupation and boycott, 294, 313–19
Tallaght, Co. Dublin, 240
Taparelli, Luigi, 60
*TD* v. *Minister for Education* (2001), 252, 257, 258, 262–3, 275, 277, 339
Teevan, Thomas, balance of convenience test, 240
*Telegraph* (newspaper), 150
Thailand, 174
Thatcher, Margaret, 11, 172
Third Dáil, 88
Third Programme of Economic and Social Development (1969–72), 202
Third World, 176
Thrashers, 53
Threshold/ALONE campaign, 294, 319–22
Tierney, Michael, 122
town planning, 225
Trade Disputes Act (1906), 231, 232–3, 234, 235, 239, 315
Trade Union Act (1871), 231
Trade Union Act (1941), 233, 235, 237
Trade Union Congress, 88, 120
trade union rights contestation, 230–44
cases for analysis, 233
judgments, 236–8
jurisprudence, 239–42
origins of, 233–5
translation, 235–6
Trade Union Tribunal, 235–6
trade unions, 3, 167–8, 205
decline from 1980s to 2010s, 178–9
labour dispute resolution, 232
militancy in 1935–7, 129–30
partnership with Fianna Fáil, 230
wage bargaining with, 231
welfare state and, 343–4
Trades Disputes Act (1906), 179
Travellers (ethnic minority), 205, 251, 310
Trinity College, 61, 282
Trotskyists, 180
Twomey, Moss, 126

UH Human Rights Commission, 193
ulema, 151
Ulster Volunteer Force, 69
Underwood, Ivor, 303, 304
Unemployed Protest Committee (1957), 301
unemployment, 13, 52–3, 165, 298, 331
United Kingdom
Age of Revolution in, 25
Commonwealth of Nations, 80
incorporation of Ireland into regional economy of, 51
United Nations Committee on Economic, Social, and Cultural Rights, 2–3, 9, 326
United States
Age of Revolution in, 25
as leading capitalist core after World War II, 28
second bill of rights in, 11, 16, 37
United States Constitutions, 17
United States Supreme Court, 31, 170–1, 175
Universal Declaration of Human Rights (1948), 14
University College Dublin, 282

value-consensus discourse, 45, 271–92
government budgeting/resource allocation and, 274–5
juridical labour and, 272
legal cultural production and, 281
overview, 272
secular or positivist forms of, 277
social origins of, 279–85
socio-economic rights and, 273–8, 337–8
state and, 274
Vance, Andrew, 64
Vargas, Getúlio, 153
Vietnam, 52
uprising in, 172
Vignoles, Paul, 79

*Volkstaart*, 105
Voluntary Health Insurance Act (1957), 168
Von Prondzynski, F., 240, 289

wage-contract, 21
Wales, public interest litigation in, 206
Wall Street Crash of 1929, 30, 116
Wallerstein, Immanuel, 5, 27, 326, 345
Walsh, Brian, 171, 187, 203
Ward, A., 38
Wards of Court, 197
water, right to. *See also* human rights
  fluoridation of water supply, 249, 253–5, 259
  opposition to Irish Water, 1
  protestors, 327–8
  Right2Water campaign, 2, 327
  Travellers (ethnic minority) and, 251
Waters, B. B., 148
wealth, concentration of, 6
Weber, Max, 105
Weberian theory, 19
Weimar Constitution, 30, 105
Weimar Germany, 14, 17, 85, 86
welfare rights. *See* family-welfare rights
welfare state, 180, 332 *See also* family-welfare rights
  characteristics of, 329
  Christian democratic, 163–4
  dirigiste, 163–4
  electorates and, 265
  expansion of, 153, 163
  family and church responsibilities, 121–2
  family-welfare rights contestations and, 246
  forms of, 163–4
  in Irish Free State, 35–6
  liberal, 163–4
  Poor Law system and, 56
  social expenditure, cash transfers and means-testing in, 180
  trade unions and, 343–4
  World War I and, 68
welfare structures, collapse of, 72
West of Ireland, 106–7
Westminster parliamentary sovereignty model, 93–4, 99, 153
White Army, 72, 73
Whiteboys, 53
Whitehall model of administration, 93–4, 117
Whyte, G., 239–40, 265–6, 267
Wilkinson, Brian, 230, 241
Williams, R., 45
*Wohlfahrtsstaat* principles, in German Constitution, 30, 105
Women's Graduates' Association, 147
women's liberation, 63, 108, 249, 265
women's rights, 136, 147
Workers' and Soldiers' Councils (Germany), uprising of, 105
Workers' Party, 178, 180, 302
Worker's Republic (1936), 114, 120
Workers' Union of Ireland, 234
World Bank, 346
World Social Forums, 7
World Trade Organization (WTO), 32, 173
World War I, 17, 28, 68, 105
World War II, 28, 163–4
world-system of historical capitalism
  constitutional waves in, 27*t*
  effects of, 52–3
  Irish Constitution (1937) and, 151, 160–86
    in 1945–68, 163–71
    in 1968–, 171–6
  Irish Constitution (1937) in, 151–5
  Irish constitutionalism and, 33–41
  Irish Free State Constitution and, 104–9
  socio-economic rights and, 25–33
  socio-economic rights in Ireland and, 330–8
  transformation in political-ideological norms of, 172–3
world-systems analysis, 4
wren-boys, 67
Wright-Carozza, P., 16

*X v. Attorney General* (1993), 183

Young Ireland, 64–5

Zapata, Emiliano, 106
Zapatistas, 326, 348

Lightning Source UK Ltd.
Milton Keynes UK
UKOW05n2250271016
286324UK00002B/56/P

9 781107 155350